Lecture Notes in Computer Science 13098

More information about this series at https://link.springer.com/bookseries/558

Ricardo Chaves · Dora B. Heras ·
Aleksandar Ilic · Didem Unat et al. (Eds.)

Euro-Par 2021: Parallel Processing Workshops

Euro-Par 2021 International Workshops
Lisbon, Portugal, August 30–31, 2021
Revised Selected Papers

 Springer

Editors
Ricardo Chaves (iD)
University of Lisbon
Lisbon, Portugal

Aleksandar Ilic (iD)
University of Lisbon
Lisbon, Portugal

Dora B. Heras (iD)
Department of Computer Engineering
CiTIUS, University of Santiago de
Compostela
Santiago de Compostela, La Coruña, Spain

Didem Unat (iD)
Koç University
Istanbul, Turkey

Additional Editors *see next page*

ISSN 0302-9743   ISSN 1611-3349   (electronic)
Lecture Notes in Computer Science
ISBN 978-3-031-06155-4   ISBN 978-3-031-06156-1   (eBook)
https://doi.org/10.1007/978-3-031-06156-1

This Springer imprint is published by the registered company Springer Nature Switzerland AG
The registered company address is: Gewerbestrasse 11, 6330 Cham, Switzerland

Workshop Editors

Rosa M. Badia
Barcelona Supercomputing Center
Barcelona, Spain

Patrick Diehl
Louisiana State University
Baton Rouge, USA

Oh Sangyoon
Ajou University
Suwon, Korea (Republic of)

Laura Ricci
University of Pisa
Pisa, Italy

Andrea Bracciali
University of Stirling
Stirling, UK

Anshu Dubey
Mathematics and Computer Science
Argonne National Laboratory
Lemont, IL, USA

Stephen L. Scott
Tennessee Technological University
Cookeville, TN, USA

Preface

The International European Conference on Parallel and Distributed Computing (Euro-Par) is an annual, international conference in Europe, which covers all aspects of parallel and distributed processing. These range from theory to practice, from small to the largest parallel and distributed systems and infrastructures, from fundamental computational problems to full-fledged applications. It also covers architecture, compiler, language, and interface design and implementation, as well as tools, support infrastructures, and application performance aspects.

The Euro-Par conference is complemented by a workshop program, where workshops dedicated to more specialized themes, to cross-cutting issues, and to upcoming trends and paradigms can be easily and conveniently organized. In addition to workshops, the first edition of the Euro-Par PhD Symposium was also organized at the Euro-Par 2021 conference, with the aim at gathering PhD students in broadly defined areas related to parallel and distributed processing.

The 27th Euro-Par Workshops and PhD Symposium were held in Portugal during August 30–31, 2021, following the well-established format of its predecessors. The events were organized with the support of INESC-ID and Instituto Superior Técnico (Técnico Lisboa) – the Faculty of Engineering of the University of Lisbon. Although Euro-Par 2021 had been planned to take place in Lisbon, Portugal, it was organized as a virtual conference, as a result of the COVID-19 pandemic.

Overall, eleven workshop proposals were submitted. The following seven workshops were co-located with the Euro-Par 2021 edition, namely:

1. Workshop on Data Locality (COLOC)
2. Workshop on Algorithms, Models and Tools for Parallel Computing on Heterogeneous Platforms (HeteroPar)
3. Workshop on Future Perspectives of Decentralized Applications (FPDAPP)
4. Workshop on Resiliency in High Performance Computing in Clouds, Grids, and Clusters (Resilience)
5. Workshop on Parallel Programming Models in High-Performance Cloud (ParaMo)
6. Workshop on Large Scale Distributed Virtual Environments (LSDVE 2021)
7. Workshop on Asynchronous Many-Task systems for Exascale (AMTE)

After a careful revision process, and from a total of 67 submitted workshop papers, 39 papers were accepted, resulting on an acceptance rate of 58%. Each workshop had an independent program committee, which was responsible for selecting the papers. The workshop papers received more than three reviews per paper on average.

The Euro-Par PhD Symposium received 12 submissions from 10 countries, with each submission reviewed by at least three technical program committee members of the Euro-Par PhD Symposium. After the thorough peer-reviewing process, 10 submissions were accepted for presentation at the Euro-Par 2021 PhD Symposium, which are also included as extended abstracts in these proceedings.

In addition to the technical program, we had the pleasure of hosting two keynotes held by:

- Chuck Yoo, Korea University, South Korea
- Attila Kertesz, University of Szeged, Hungary

This volume contains the papers and extended abstracts presented at Euro-Par 2021 Workshops and PhD Symposium, divided into 8 track sections (corresponding to each of the workshops and PhD Symposium).

The success of the Euro-Par Workshops and PhD Symposium depends on the work of many individuals and organizations. We therefore thank all the organizers and reviewers for the time and effort that they invested. We would also like to express our gratitude to the members of the Euro-Par 2021 Organizing Committee and the local staff. Lastly, we thank all participants, panelists, and keynote speakers of the Euro-Par Workshops and PhD Symposium for their contribution to a productive meeting. It was a pleasure to organize and host the Euro-Par Workshops and PhD Symposium 2021 in Lisbon.

August 2021   Ricardo Chaves
                                                        Dora B. Heras
                                                        Aleksandar Ilic
                                                        Didem Unat

Organization

The Euro-Par Steering Committee

Full Members

Luc Bougé (Chair)	ENS Rennes, France
Fernando Silva (Vice-chair)	University of Porto, Portugal
Dora B. Heras (Workshops Chair)	CiTIUS, University of Santiago de Compostela, Spain
Marco Aldinucci	University of Turin, Italy
Emmanuel Jeannot	Inria, France
Christos Kaklamanis	Computer Technology Institute, Greece
Paul Kelly	Imperial College, UK
Thomas Ludwig	University of Hamburg, Germany
Tomàs Margalef	University Autonoma of Barcelona, Spain
Wolfgang Nagel	Dresden University of Technology, Germany
Francisco Fernández Rivera	CiTIUS, University of Santiago de Compostela, Spain
Krzysztof Rzadca	University of Warsaw, Poland
Rizos Sakellariou	University of Manchester, UK
Henk Sips (Finance Chair)	Delft University of Technology, The Netherlands
Leonel Sousa	Universidade de Lisboa, Portugal
Domenico Talia	University of Calabria, Italy
Massimo Torquati (Artifacts Chair)	University of Pisa, Italy
Phil Trinder	University of Glasgow, UK
Denis Trystram	Grenoble Institute of Technology, France
Felix Wolf	Technical University of Darmstadt, Germany
Ramin Yahyapour	GWDG, Germany

Honorary Members

Christian Lengauer	University of Passau, Germany
Ron Perrott	Oxford e-Research Centre, UK
Karl Dieter Reinartz	University of Erlangen-Nuremberg, Germany

General Chair

Leonel Sousa	INESC-ID, IST, Universidade de Lisboa, Portugal

Workshop Chairs

Ricardo Chaves	INESC-ID, IST, Universidade de Lisboa, Portugal
Dora B. Heras	CiTIUS, University of Santiago de Compostela, Spain

PhD Symposium Chairs

Aleksandar Ilic	INESC-ID, IST, Universidade de Lisboa, Portugal
Didem Unat	Koç University, Turkey

Submissions Chair

Nuno Roma	INESC-ID, IST, Universidade de Lisboa, Portugal

Publicity Chairs

Gabriel Falcão	IT, Universidade de Coimbra, Portugal
Maurício Breternitz	ISCTE, Instituto Universitário de Lisboa, Portugal

Web Chairs

Pedro Tomás	INESC-ID, IST, Universidade de Lisboa, Portugal
Helena Aidos	LASIGE, FCUL, Universidade de Lisboa, Portugal

Local Chairs

Tiago Dias	INESC-ID, ISEL, Instituto Politécnico de Lisboa, Portugal
Ricardo Nobre	INESC-ID, Portugal

Artifact Evaluation Committee

Nuno Neves	INESC-ID, Universidade de Lisboa, Portugal
Massimo Torquati	University of Pisa, Italy

Additional Reviewers

Aktulga, Metin H.
Aliaga, Ignacio José
Amini, Parsa
Augonnet, Cédric
Biddiscombe, John
Brandt, Steven
Castelló, Adrián
Cuomo, Salvatore

Daiss, Gregor
Dazzi, Patrizio
Demeshko, Irina
Di Napoli, Claudia
Dimakopoulos
  Vassilios V.
Ezzatti, Pablo
Faloci, Francesco

Grubel, Patricia
Gupta, Nikunj
Guzzi, Hiram Pietro
Hammond, Jeff
Heller, Thomas
Huck, Kevin
Igual, Francisco D.
Kaiser, Hartmut
Kale, Laxmikant
Khatami, Zahra
Koniges, Alice
Lakymchuk, Roman
Larkin, Jeff
Laure, Erwin
Lelbach, Adelstein
  Bryce
Lemoine, Adrian
Lepore, Cristian
Lercher, Alexander
Limet, Sébastien
Lisi, Andrea

Lumsdaine, Andrew
McCormick, Pat
Mehran, Narges
Nikolskiy, Vsevolod
Oden, Lena
Pleiter, Dirk
Richardson, Brad
Ristov, Sasko
Samani, Najafabadi
  Zahra
Santander-Jiménez
Sergio
Shipman, Galen
Shirzad, Shahrzad
Simberg, Mikael
Talia, Domenico
Tonellotto, Nicola
Treichler, Sean
Unat, Didem
Valverde, Carlos Jose
Wu, Nanmia

Contents

**FPDAPP – International Workshop on Future Perspectives
of Decentralized Applications**

Resilience – Fourteenth Workshop on Resiliency in High Performance Computing in Clouds, Grids, and Clusters

ParaMo – Workshop on Parallel Programming Models in High-Performance Cloud

COLOC – 5th Workshop on Data Locality

5th Workshop on Data Locality (COLOC)

Workshop Description

With increasing heterogeneity in both computational devices and memory organization in high performance computing platforms, movement of data between devices and layers of memory have become a critical challenge for science and engineering users of these platforms. Imminent arrival of exascale platforms has brought these concerns to the forefront. The objective of this workshop was to understand the impact of abstractions and tools that have been around for some time and have seen some adoption.

The different areas or research interest include, but are not limited to:

- Modeling node topology
- Modeling network and communication
- Performance analysis of application to understand affinity
- Affinity metrics
- Runtime support for extracting affinity from application
- Code analysis in order to understand communication pattern
- Algorithm to improve locality
- Language, abstraction and compiler support for data locality
- Data structure and library support to better manage memory access
- Runtime-system and dynamic locality management
- System-scale locality optimization
- Validating locality optimization at thread or process level
- Memory management
- Locality management in large-scale application
- Impact of Locality to scientific applications

We have received 5 submissions and we have accepted 4. All 4 of them are published in these proceedings. The workshop also featured two invited talks: Data-Centric Python – Productivity, portability and all with high performance! by Torsten Hoefler of ETH Switzerland, and ECP: Data Analytics and Optimization Applications On Accelerator-Based Systems by William E. Hart of Sandia National Laboratory and a Leader of the Exascale Computing Project, U.S.A.

The workshop also featured a panel at the end with an open floor discussion format.

Organization

Steering Committee

Emmanuel Jeannot   Inria, France

Program Chair

Anshu Dubey   Argonne National Laboratory, USA

Program Committee

George Bosilca	UTK, USA
Florina Ciorba	University of Basel, Switzerland
Didem Unat	Koç University, Turkey
Matthias Diener	University of Illinois at Urbana-Champaign, USA
Karl Fuerlinger	Ludwig-Maximilians-University, München, Germany
Aleksandar Ilic	INESC-ID/IST, Universidade de Lisboa, Portugal
Vitus Leung	Sandia National Laboratories, USA
Hatem Ltaief	KAUST, Saudi Arabia
Allen Malony	Institution: University of Oregon, USA
Hartmut Mix	Technische Universität Dresden, Germany
Marc Perache	CEA, France
Mohamed Wahib	AIST, Japan
Rajeev Thakur	Argonne National Laboratory, USA
Jack Deslippe	Lawrence Berkeley National Laboratory, USA

Locality-Aware Scheduling of Independent Tasks for Runtime Systems

Maxime Gonthier[1](✉), Loris Marchal[1](✉), and Samuel Thibault[2](✉)

[1] LIP, CNRS, ENS de Lyon, Inria & Université Claude-Bernard Lyon 1, Lyon, France
{maxime.gonthier,loris.marchal}@ens-lyon.fr
[2] LaBRI, University of Bordeaux, CNRS, Inria Bordeaux - Sud-Ouest,
Talence, France
samuel.thibault@u-bordeaux.fr

Abstract. A now-classical way of meeting the increasing demand for computing speed by HPC applications is the use of GPUs and/or other accelerators. Such accelerators have their own memory, which is usually quite limited, and are connected to the main memory through a bus with bounded bandwidth. Thus, particular care should be devoted to data locality in order to avoid unnecessary data movements. Task-based runtime schedulers have emerged as a convenient and efficient way to use such heterogeneous platforms. When processing an application, the scheduler has the knowledge of all tasks available for processing on a GPU, as well as their input data dependencies. Hence, it is able to order tasks and prefetch their input data in the GPU memory (after possibly evicting some previously-loaded data), while aiming at minimizing data movements, so as to reduce the total processing time. In this paper, we focus on how to schedule tasks that share some of their input data (but are otherwise independent) on a GPU. We provide a formal model of the problem, exhibit an optimal eviction strategy, and show that ordering tasks to minimize data movement is NP-complete. We review and adapt existing ordering strategies to this problem, and propose a new one based on task aggregation. These strategies have been implemented in the STARPU runtime system. We present their performance on tasks from tiled 2D and 3D matrix products. We present their performance on tasks from tiled 2D, 3D matrix products. Our experiments demonstrate that using our new strategy together with the optimal eviction policy reduces the amount of data movement as well as the total processing time.

Keywords: Memory-aware scheduling · Eviction policy · Tasks sharing data · Runtime systems

1 Introduction

High-performance computing applications, such as physical simulations, molecular modeling or weather and climate forecasting, have an increasing demand in

R. Chaves et al. (Eds.): Euro-Par 2021, LNCS 13098, pp. 5–16, 2022.
https://doi.org/10.1007/978-3-031-06156-1_1

computer power to reach better accuracy. Recently, this demand has been met by extensively using GPUs, as they provide large additional performance for a relatively low energy budget. Programming the resulting heterogeneous architecture which merges regular CPUs with GPUs is a very complex task, as one needs to handle load balancing together with data movements and task affinity (tasks have strongly different speedups on GPUs). A deep trend which has emerged to cope with this new complexity is using task-based programming models and task-based runtimes such as PaRSEC [4] or STARPU [2]. These runtimes aim at scheduling scientific applications, expressed as directed acyclic graphs (DAGs) of tasks, onto distributed heterogeneous platforms, made of several nodes containing different computing cores.

Data movement is an important problem to consider when scheduling tasks on GPUs, as those have a limited memory as well as a limited bandwidth to read/write data from/to the main memory of the system. Thus, it is crucial to carefully order the tasks that have to be processed on GPUs so as to increase data reuse and minimize the amount of data that needs to be transferred. It is also important to schedule the transfers soon enough (prefetch) so that data transfers can be overlapped with computations and all tasks can start without delay. We focus in this paper on the problem of **scheduling a set of tasks on one GPU with limited memory, where tasks share some of their input data but are otherwise independent**. More precisely, we want to determine the order in which tasks must be processed to optimize for locality, as well as when their input must be loaded/evicted into/from memory. Our objective is to minimize the total amount of data transferred to the GPUs for the processing of all tasks with a constraint on the memory size. We start focusing on independent tasks sharing input data because when using usual dynamic runtime schedulers, the scheduler is exposed at a given time to a fairly large subset of tasks which are independent of each others. This is in particular the case with linear algebra workflows, such as the matrix multiplication or Cholesky decomposition: except possibly at the very beginning or very end of the computation, a large set of tasks is available for scheduling. Thus, solving the optimization problem for the currently available tasks can lead to a large reduction in data transfers and hence a performance increase.

Because of space limitation, the complete review of related work is devoted to the extended version of the paper [8]. In this paper, we make the following contributions:

- We provide a formal model of the optimization problem, and prove the problem to be NP-complete. We derive an optimal eviction policy by adapting Belady's rule for cache management (Sect. 2).
- We review and adapt three heuristic algorithms from the literature for this problem, and propose a new one based on gathering tasks with similar data patterns into packages (Sect. 3).
- We implement all four heuristics into the STARPU runtime and study the performance (amount of data transfers and total processing time) obtained on both 2D and 3D blocked matrix multiplications (Sect. 4). Overall, our evaluation shows that our heuristic generally surpasses previous strategies, in particular in the most constrained situations.

Note that while we focus our experimental validation on GPUs, the optimization problem studied in this paper is not specific to the use of such accelerators: it appears as soon as tasks sharing data must be processed on a system with limited memory and bandwidth. For example, it is also relevant for a computer made of several CPUs with restricted shared memory, and limited bandwidth for the communication between memory and disk.

2 Problem Modeling and Complexity

We consider the problem of scheduling independent tasks on one GPU with memory size M. As proposed in previous work [9], tasks sharing their input data can be modeled as a bipartite graph $G = (\mathbb{T} \cup \mathbb{D}, E)$. The vertices of this graph are on one side the tasks $\mathbb{T} = \{T_1, \ldots, T_m\}$ and on the other side the data $\mathbb{D} = \{D_1, \ldots, D_n\}$. An edge connects a task T_i and a data D_j if task T_i requires D_j as input data. For the sake of simplicity, we denote by $\mathcal{D}(T_i) = \{D_j \text{ s.t. } (T_i, D_j) \in E\}$ the set of input data for task T_i. We here consider that all data have the same size. The GPU is equipped with a memory of limited size, which may contain at most M data simultaneously. During the processing of a task T_i, all its inputs $\mathcal{D}(T_i)$ must be in memory.

For the sake of simplicity, we here do not consider the data output of tasks. In the case of linear algebra for instance, the output data is most often much smaller than the input data and can be transferred concurrently with data input. Data output is then not the driving constraint for efficient execution. Our model could however easily be extended to integrate task output.

All m tasks must be processed. Our goal is to determine in **which order** to process them, and **when each data must be loaded or evicted**, in order to **minimize the amount of data movement**. More formally, we denote by σ the order in which tasks are processed, and by $\mathcal{V}(t)$ the set of data to be evicted from the memory before the processing of task $T_{\sigma(t)}$. A schedule is made of m steps, each step being composed of the following three stages (in this order):

1. All data in $\mathcal{V}(t)$ are evicted (unloaded) from the memory;
2. The input data in $\mathcal{D}(T_{\sigma(t)})$ that are not yet in memory are loaded;
3. Task $T_{\sigma(t)}$ is processed.

An example is shown in Fig. 1. This example illustrates that input data are loaded in memory as late as possible: loading them earlier would be pointless and possibly trigger more data movements. In real computing systems, a pre-fetch is usually designed to load data a bit earlier so as to avoid waiting for unavailable data, however, for the sake of simplicity, we do not consider this in our model: if needed, we may simply book part of our memory for the pre-fetch mechanism.

Using the previous definition, we define the *live data* $L(t)$ as the data in memory during the computation of $T_{\sigma(t)}$, which can be defined recursively:

$$L(t) = \begin{cases} \mathcal{D}(T_{\sigma(1)}) & \text{if } t = 1 \\ L(t) = (L(t-1) \backslash \mathcal{V}(t)) \cup \mathcal{D}(T_{\sigma(t)}) & \text{otherwise} \end{cases}$$

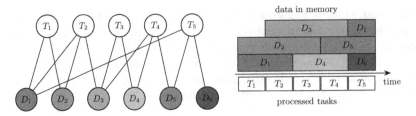

Fig. 1. Example with 5 tasks and 6 data, with a memory holding at most $M = 3$ data. The graph of input data dependencies is shown on the left. The schedule on the right corresponds to processing the tasks in the natural order with the following eviction policy: $\mathcal{V}(1) = \mathcal{V}(2) = \emptyset$, $\mathcal{V}(3) = \{1\}$, $\mathcal{V}(4) = \{2\}$, $\mathcal{V}(5) = \{3,4\}$. This results in 7 loads (only D_1 is loaded twice).

Our memory limitation can then be expressed as $|L(t)| \leq M$ for each step $t = 1, \ldots, m$. Our objective is to minimize the amount of data movement, i.e., to minimize the number of *load* operations: we consider that data are not modified so no *store* operation occurs when evicting a data from the memory. Assuming that no input data used at step t is evicted right before the processing ($\mathcal{V}(t) \cap \mathcal{D}(T_{\sigma(t)}) = \emptyset$), the number of loads can be computed as follows:

$$\#Loads(\sigma, \mathcal{V}) = \sum_t \left| \mathcal{D}\left(T_{\sigma(t)}\right) \backslash L(t) \right|$$

There is no reason for a scheduling policy to evict some data from memory if there is still room for new input data. We call *thrifty scheduler* such a strategy, formalized by the following constraints: if $\mathcal{V}(t) \neq \emptyset$, then $|L(t)| = M$. For this class of schedulers, the number of loads can be computed more easily: as soon as the memory is full, the number of loads is equal to the number of evictions. That is, for the regular case when not all data fit in memory ($n > M$), we have:

$$\#Loads(\sigma, \mathcal{V}) = M + \sum_t |\mathcal{V}(t)|$$

Our optimization problem is stated below:

Definition 1 (MinLoadsForTasksSharingData). *For a given set of tasks* $\mathbb{T}$ *sharing data in* $\mathbb{D}$ *according to* $\mathcal{D}$, *what is the task order* σ *and the eviction policy* $\mathcal{V}$ *that minimizes the number of loads* $\#Loads$?

A solution to this optimization problem consists in two parts: the order σ of the tasks and the eviction policy $\mathcal{V}$. Note that when each task requests a single data, finding an efficient eviction policy corresponds to the classical cache management policy problem. When the full sequence of data requests is known, the optimal policy consists in evicting the data whose next use is the furthest in the future. This is the well-known Belady MIN replacement policy [3]. We prove in the following theorem that this rule can be extended to our problem, with tasks requiring multiple data (see proof in the extended version of the paper [8]).

Theorem 1. *We consider a task schedule σ for a* MINLOADSFORTASKS-
SHARINGDATA *problem. We denote by MIN the thrifty eviction policy that
always evicts a data whose next use in σ is the latest (breaking ties arbitrar-
ily). MIN reaches an optimal performance, i.e., for any eviction policy $\mathcal{V}$,*

$$\#Loads(\sigma, MIN) \leq \#Loads(\sigma, \mathcal{V}).$$

For cache management, Belady's rule has little practical impact, as the
stream of future requests is generally unknown; simple online policies such as
LRU (Least Recently Used [7]) are generally used. However in our case, the full
set of tasks is available at the beginning. Hence, we can take advantage of this
optimal offline eviction policy. Thanks to the previous result, we can restrict our
problem to finding the optimal task order σ. Unfortunately, this problem is NP-
complete. The proof, available in [8], consists in a reduction from the cutwidth
minimization problem on graphs.

Theorem 2. *Given a set of tasks $\mathbb{T}$ sharing data in $\mathbb{D}$ according to $\mathcal{D}$ and an
integer B, finding a task order σ such that $\#Loads(\sigma, MIN) \leq B$ is NP-complete.*

3   Algorithms

We present here several heuristics to solve the MINLOADSFORTASKSSHARING-
DATA optimization problem. Two of them are adapted from the literature
(Reverse-Cuthill-McKee and Maximum Spanning Tree), one of them is the actual
dynamic strategy from the STARPU runtime (Deque Model Data Aware Ready)
and we finally propose a new strategy: Hierarchical Fair Packing.

Reverse-Cuthill-McKee (RCM). We have seen above that our problem is close to
the cutwidth minimization problem, known to be NP-complete. This motivates
the use of the Cuthill-McKee algorithm, which concentrates on a close metric:
the bandwidth of a graph. It permutes a sparse matrix into a band matrix so
that all elements are close to the diagonal [6]. If the resulting bandwidth is k,
it means that vertices sharing an edge are not more than k edges away. We
apply this algorithm on the graph of tasks $G^T = (\mathbb{T}, E^T, w^T)$ where there is
an edge (T_i, T_j) if tasks T_i and T_j share some data, and where $w^T(T_i, T_j)$ is
the number of such shared data. If the bandwidth of the graph is not larger
than k, this means in our problem that any task T_i processed at time t has all
its "neighbours" tasks (tasks sharing some data with T_i) processed in the time
interval $[t - k; t + k]$. Hence, if k is low, this leads to a very good data locality.
Reversing the obtained order is known to improve the performance of the Cuthill-
McKee algorithm, which we also notice in our experiments. The straightforward
adaptation of the Reverse-Cuthill-McKee algorithm to our model is available in
the extended version [8].

Maximum Spanning Tree (MST). Yoo et al. [10] proposed another heuristic to
order tasks sharing data to improve data locality. They first build a Maximum
Spanning Tree in the graph G^T using Prim's algorithm and then order the

---

Algorithm 1. Hierarchical Fair Packing heuristic

1: Let $P_i \leftarrow [T_i]$ for $i = 1 \ldots m$ and $\mathbb{P} = \{P_1, \ldots, P_m\}$
2: *SizeLimit* $\leftarrow$ *true*, *MaxSizeReached* $\leftarrow$ *false*,
3: **while** $|\mathbb{P}| > 1$ **do**
4:     **while** (*MaxSizeReached* = *false* or *SizeLimit* = *false*) and $|\mathbb{P}| > 1$ **do**
5:         *MaxSizeReached* $\leftarrow$ *true*
6:         **for** all packages P_i with the smallest number of tasks **do**
7:             Find a package P_j such that $|\mathcal{D}(P_i) \cap \mathcal{D}(P_j)|$ is maximal
8:             **if** $weight(P_i \cup P_j) \leq M$ or *SizeLimit* = *false* **then**
9:                 Merge P_i and P_j (append P_j at then end of P_i and remove P_j from $\mathbb{P}$)
10:                *MaxSizeReached* $\leftarrow$ *false*
11:            **end if**
12:        **end for**
13:    **end while**
14:    *SizeLimit* $\leftarrow$ *false*
15: **end while**
16: Return the only package in $\mathbb{P}$

---

vertices according to their order of inclusion in the spanning tree. By selecting the incident edge with largest weight, they increase the data reuse between the current scheduled tasks and the next one to process. The direct adaption of the Maximum Spanning Tree to our model algorithm is described in the extended version [8].

Deque Model Data Aware Ready (DMDAR). DMDA or "Deque Model Data Aware" is a dynamic scheduling heuristic designed to schedule tasks on heterogeneous processing units in the STARPU runtime. It takes data transfer time into account and schedules tasks where their completion times is expected to be minimal [1] (also called tmdp). We focus here on a variant, DMDAR, which additionally uses a *ready* strategy at runtime, to favor tasks whose data has already been loaded into memory. If at some point the next task T_i planned for execution requires some data which is not yet loaded in the GPU memory, then it looks further in the list of scheduled tasks. If it finds a task T_j that needs to load strictly less data than task T_i, it will first opportunistically compute that task T_j (see the extended version for details [8]). In our context with a single processing unit, DMDAR is reduced to selecting the next task with this strategy. DMDAR is a dynamic scheduler that relies on the actual state of the memory, it thus depends on the eviction policy, which is the LRU policy.

Hierarchical Fair Packing (HFP). HFP builds packages (denoted $P_1, P_2, \ldots$) of tasks, which are stored as lists of tasks, forming a partition of $\mathbb{T}$. To do so, it gathers tasks that share the most input data. By extension, we denote by $\mathcal{D}(P_k)$ the set of inputs of all tasks in P_k. We aim at building the smallest number of packages so that the inputs of all tasks in each package fit in memory: $\mathcal{D}(P_k) \leq M$. The intuition is that once the data $\mathcal{D}(P_k)$ are loaded, all tasks in the package can be processed without any additional data movement. We have

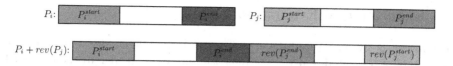

Fig. 2. Flipping packages to improve HFP. Here we assume that the pair of sub-packages (P_i^{end}, P_j^{end}) is the one with the most shared input data, so that only P_j is reversed before merging packages.

proven that building the minimum number of packages is NP-complete [8], hence we rely on a greedy heuristic to build them, described in Algorithm 1. We start with packages containing a single task. Then we consider all packages with fewest tasks and try to merge each of them with another package with whom it shares the most input data. When it is not possible to merge packages without exceeding the M bound any more, we perform a second step where we gather packages in the same way but ignore the M bound on the input size. The intuition is to create meta-packages that express the data affinity between packages already built. Note that we do not modify the order of tasks within packages when merging them, hence keeping the good data locality inside packages. Eventually, the last remaining package after all merges is the list of tasks for the schedule.

We note $\Delta = \max_i |\mathcal{D}(T_i)|$ the maximal number of data for any task. For linear algebra applications, it is most often a very small constant number. The worst-case complexity of HFP (detailed in the extended version [8]) is $O(m^3 \Delta^2)$.

Improving HFP with Package Flipping. A concern appears in the second step of HFP (when we merge packages without taking care of the M bound): if P_i is merged with P_j, the merged package contains the tasks of P_i followed by the ones of P_j. However, the last tasks of P_i might have very little shared data with the first tasks of P_j, leading to poor data reuse when starting P_j. Hence, for each package P_i, we consider two sub-packages P_i^{start} and P_i^{end} containing the first and last tasks so that the weight of their input data is smaller than M but their cardinal is maximal, as illustrated on Fig. 2. Then, we count the common input data of each pair: $(P_i^{start}, P_j^{start})$, (P_i^{start}, P_j^{end}), (P_i^{end}, P_j^{start}), (P_i^{end}, P_j^{end}). We identify the pair with most common input data and selectively reverse the packages so that tasks in this pair of sub-packages are scheduled consecutively in the resulting package.

Optimal Eviction Policy. Lastly, we make another improvement to HFP: it is equipped with the optimal eviction policy adapted from Belady's rule (see Lemma 1). To make it compatible with dynamic runtimes, such as the StarPU runtime used in our experiments, we use a dynamic version of the eviction policy: whenever the runtime needs to evict some data, we choose the one whose next usage is the latest.

HFP's packing and package flipping allows it to be applicable and have good performance with other classes of problem such as the Cholesky factorization or random tasks graphs.

4   Experimental Evaluation

We present below a subset of the experimental evaluation conducted to compare the strategy presented above.[1] We refer the interested reader to the extended version of the paper [8] for a more thorough discussion of these results, as well as experiments on other datasets (Cholesky and randomized 2D multiplication tasks sets). We used cuBLAS 10.2 GPU kernels with single precision.

4.1   Settings

All strategies mentioned above have been implemented in the STARPU runtime system [2]. This allows us to test them on a variety of applications expressed as sets of tasks. We performed both real experiments on a tesla V100 GPU as well as simulations using the ability to run STARPU code over the SimGrid simulator [5] to test our strategies in various experimental conditions. The use of simulation is motivated both by the fidelity of the simulated results as well as the saving of energy consumption. Even on the actual GPU, we have divided the original 12000 MB/s PCI bandwidth by two (by generating traffic between the CPU memory and another GPU) to represent the bandwidth share typically available for a given GPU in a multi-GPU platform. We have limited the GPU memory to 500 MB in order to better distinguish the performance of different strategies even on small datasets. The scheduling algorithms receive the whole set of tasks of the application in a natural order (row by row for a matrix multiplication for instance), then output this same set of tasks in a new order, which is used in STARPU to process tasks on the GPU. We measure the obtained performance (in GFlop/s) as well as the total volume of data transferred between CPU and GPU. When measuring GFlop/s, the cost of computing the MST, RCM, and HFP heuristics is not considered, to only observe their benefit as a first approach.

We use two sets of tasks for these experiments (see [8] for more datasets).

Square 2D Matrix Multiplication. To compute $C = A \times B$ in parallel, each task corresponds to the multiplication of one block-row of A per one block-column of B. Input data are thus the rows of A and columns of B.

Square 3D Matrix Multiplication. All matrices (A, B, C) are tiled, and the computation of each tile of C is decomposed into multiple tasks, each of which requires one tile of A and one tile of B. Each tile of C is also used as input for all tasks on this tile but the first one.

We use the four scheduling heuristics presented above, together with Eager, a scheduler that processes tasks in the natural order (i.e. row major for matrix multiplications) as a baseline. Unless specified otherwise, for HFP we enable all of the *Ready* dynamic task reordering of DMDAR (see Sect. 3), the package flipping (called flip on the plots), and Belady's optimal eviction policy (called Belady on the plots). We also show results when enabling only one of them.

---

[1] The code used to reproducibly obtain the results of this paper is available at https://gitlab.inria.fr/starpu/locality-aware-scheduling/-/tree/coloc2021.

4.2   Results on the 2D Matrix Multiplication

On Fig. 3, we plot the performance of each scheduling heuristic when varying either the size of the problem, or conversely the size of the available memory. On these graphs, the dotted horizontal black line represents the maximum GFlop/s (12557) that the GPU can achieve when processing elementary matrix product (without I/Os) and is our asymptotic goal. The red dotted vertical line denotes the situation when the GPU memory can fit exactly only one of the two input matrices, and the orange line denotes the situation when it can accommodate both input matrices.

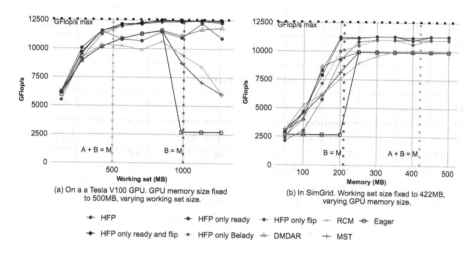

(a) On a a Tesla V100 GPU. GPU memory size fixed to 500MB, varying working set size.

(b) In SimGrid. Working set size fixed to 422MB, varying GPU memory size.

- HFP
- HFP only ready
- HFP only ready and flip
- HFP only flip
- HFP only Belady
- RCM
- DMDAR
- Eager
- MST

Fig. 3. Performance on the 2D matrix multiplication.

The Eager, MST and RCM heuristics switch to pathological behavior at the red line. Indeed, they tend to process tasks along the rows of C. This allows us to reuse the same block-row of matrix A for tasks that compute tiles of the same row of C, but requires reloading the whole matrix B for each new block-row of A, which is a well-known pathological case of the LRU eviction policy.

DMDAR does not suffer from this pathological case because its *Ready* strategy allows it to rather process tasks that need the block-column of B already in memory instead of reloading the whole matrix.

The HFP heuristic gets performance very close to ideal. Indeed, it tends to gather tasks that compute a square part of C that require parts of A and B, that can fit in memory size M. This allows us to execute a lot of tasks with very few data to load. On Fig. 3a which shows native execution measurements, we notice that, with larger working sets, the cost of our implementation of the Belady rule brings significant overhead. On other figures which show simulated execution, this overhead is not included, which allows to observe its benefit. Here are the percentage of improvement of HFP with only *Ready* and *flip* over the other heuristics, averaged on the nine points:

Reference	Eager	MST	RCM	DMDAR	HFP only flip	HFP only ready
Improvement	51.5%	25.6%	26.0%	8.3%	1.9%	−0.2%

Figure 3b shows the dual view of Fig. 3a: the working set is now set to 422MB and we simulate varying amounts of available GPU memory. The measurements at 500 MB on Fig. 3b are the same as the measurements at 422 MB on Fig. 3a. We can observe the same results as on Fig. 3a but reversed: when the available memory is smaller than the working set, heuristics get pathological behavior. Since we strongly reduce the amount of available memory, we get a more restrictive situation, and the *Ready* task selection provides a large improvement here. The Belady rule or package flipping alone do not provide the same amount of improvement.

4.3   Results on the 3D Matrix Multiplication

On Fig. 4, we plot the performance and amount of data transfers for all heuristics on the 3D matrix multiplication. On this set of tasks, matrix C now plays a role in affinities, which is why we added a vertical green dotted line to denote the situation when all A, B, and C matrices fit in memory. On Fig. 4b, the black dotted line represents the maximum number of transfers that can be done during the minimum time for computation (given by the bound on the GFlop/s), thus the hard limitation induced by the PCI bus bandwidth: a heuristic exceeding this amount necessarily requires more than the optimal time for computation.

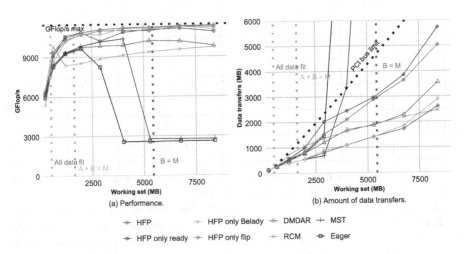

(a) Performance.   (b) Amount of data transfers.

Fig. 4. Results on 3D matrix multiplication on SimGrid: GPU memory size fixed to 500 MB, varying working set size.

MST keeps ordering tasks along the rows of C, and thus still gets pathological performance when memory can not fit matrix B. This is confirmed on Fig. 4b: the number of loads gets dramatically high. RCM and DMDAR, however, do not have the same problem. RCM (resp. DMDAR) computes tasks along columns (resp. rows) of C but alternates between tasks of a few consecutive columns (resp. rows). This allows them to improve data reuse: Fig. 4b shows that they exhibit a limited number of transfers, even with a large working set.

HFP keeps gathering tasks forming a square part of C, which provides better locality. Here are the percentages of average improvement of HFP over the other heuristics:

Reference algorithm	Eager	MST	RCM	DMDAR	HFP only flip	HFP only ready	HFP only Belady
Improvement	79.4%	48.1%	16.2%	11.0%	2.0%	1.9%	2.7%

As the 3D matrix multiplication already exhibits a better data locality than the 2D multiplication, the differences in performance between heuristics is less pronounced than on Fig. 3a, but HFP is still better on average. It is worth noticing that HFP without the Belady rule gets higher performance than RCM and DMDAR, even if it triggers a larger number of transfers. The latter heuristics indeed tend to periodically require a sudden burst of data loads, while HFP tends to require loads that are nicely distributed over time, and thus well overlapped with computation. We however notice that HFP without *Ready* gets a number of transfers very close to the PCI bus limit in the 3014 MB working set case, which translates into lower performance. We can also see on Fig. 4b that the Belady rule significantly reduces the quantity of data transfers.

5 Conclusion and Future Work

To take the best performance out of GPUs, it is crucial to avoid moving data as much as possible. We provided in this paper a formalization of the problem of ordering independent tasks sharing input data in order to minimize the amount of data transfers, and showed that this problem is NP-complete. We also exhibited an optimal eviction scheme, based on Belady's rule. We adapted three heuristics for the ordering problem, based on the state of the art, and compared them with a new algorithm gathering tasks with similar input data into packages of increasing size, called HFP. We also present an improvement of HFP based on package flipping. All four ordering strategies have been implemented in the STARPU runtime and tested on various sets of tasks. In all cases, the proposed HFP heuristic provides significant speedups. For instance, it allows on average a 8.3% (resp. 11%) improvement over the most advanced StarPU scheduler for 2D (resp. 3D) matrix multiplication. HFP is very relevant and obtains important speedups particularly in the case when the memory is very constrained compared to the size of the total working set. The Belady rule reduces drastically the number of data transfers. Without this rule, HFP may entail much more data transfers than other heuristics, but achieves better performance, which shows that HFP is also good at distributing data transfer over time to increase transfer/computation overlap. Studying this final problem (minimizing computation time with overlap) is one of our future directions. We also plan to focus on the very beginning of the execution, where it is crucial to first schedule tasks with few input data. Optimizing the implementation of Belady's rule and adapting it to the *Ready* dynamic task reordering will allow to integrate it in native executions. On a longer term, we want to tackle the general case with tasks not only sharing input data, but also with inter-task dependencies, as well as targeting multi-GPU platforms, for which our approach with packages seems particularly well suited.

Acknowledgement. This work was supported by the SOLHARIS project (ANR-19-CE46-0009) which is operated by the French National Research Agency (ANR).

Experiments presented in this paper were carried out using the Grid'5000 testbed, supported by a scientific interest group hosted by Inria and including CNRS, RENATER and several Universities as well as other organizations (see https://www.grid5000.fr).

References

1. Augonnet, C., Clet-Ortega, J., Thibault, S., Namyst, R.: Data-aware task scheduling on multi-accelerator based platforms. In: 16th International Conference on Parallel and Distributed Systems, Shangai, China, December 2010
2. Augonnet, C., Thibault, S., Namyst, R., Wacrenier, P.A.: StarPU: a unified platform for task scheduling on heterogeneous multicore architectures. Concurr. Comput.: Pract. Exp. Special Issue: Euro-Par 2009 **23** (2011). https://doi.org/10.1002/cpe.1631
3. Belady, L.A.: A study of replacement algorithms for a virtual-storage computer. IBM Syst. J. **5**(2) (1966). https://doi.org/10.1147/sj.52.0078
4. Bosilca, G., Bouteiller, A., Danalis, A., Faverge, M., Hérault, T., Dongarra, J.: PaRSEC: a programming paradigm exploiting heterogeneity for enhancing scalability. Comput. Sci. Eng. **15**(6), 36–45 (2013). https://doi.org/10.1109/MCSE.2013.98
5. Casanova, H., Giersch, A., Legrand, A., Quinson, M., Suter, F.: Versatile, scalable, and accurate simulation of distributed applications and platforms. J. Parallel Distrib. Comput. **74**(10), 2899–2917 (2014)
6. Cuthill, E., McKee, J.: Reducing the bandwidth of sparse symmetric matrices. In: Proceedings of the 1969 24th National Conference. ACM (1969). https://doi.org/10.1145/800195.805928
7. Denning, P.J.: The working set model for program behavior. Commun. ACM **11**(5), 323–333 (1968)
8. Gonthier, M., Marchal, L., Thibault, S.: Locality-aware scheduling of independant tasks for runtime systems. Research report, Inria (2021). https://hal.inria.fr/hal-03144290
9. Kaya, K., Uçar, B., Aykanat, C.: Heuristics for scheduling file-sharing tasks on heterogeneous systems with distributed repositories. J. Parallel Distributed Comput. **67**(3) (2007). https://doi.org/10.1016/j.jpdc.2006.11.004
10. Yoo, R.M., Hughes, C.J., Kim, C., Chen, Y.K., Kozyrakis, C.: Locality-aware task management for unstructured parallelism: a quantitative limit study. In: ACM Symposium on Parallelism in Algorithms and Architectures (SPAA) (2013). https://doi.org/10.1145/2486159.2486175

High Performance Computing with Java Streams

Rui Silva (ID) and João L. Sobral[(✉)] (ID)

Centro Algoritmi, Universidade do Minho, Braga, Portugal
{ruisilva,jls}@di.uminho.pt

Abstract. Java streams enable an easy-to-use functional-like programming style that transparently supports parallel execution. This paper presents an approach that improves the performance of stream-based Java applications. The approach enables the effective usage of Java for HPC applications, due to data locality improvements (i.e., support for efficient data layouts), without losing the object-oriented view of data in the code. The approach extends the Java collections API to hide additional details concerning the data layout, enabling the transparent use of more memory-friendly data layouts. The enhanced Java Collection API enables an easy adaptation of existing Java codes making those Java codes suitable for HPC. Performance results show that improving the data locality can provide a two-fold performance gain in sequential stream applications, which translated into a similar gain over parallel stream implementations. Moreover, the performance is comparable to similar C implementations using OpenMP.

Keywords: Java parallel streams · Data layout · Data locality

1 Introduction

The development of high-performance applications requires the exploitation of parallelism and efficient data access. Programming languages should now support the exploitation of parallelism and efficient data storage, promoting data locality to deliver high performance. Data storage is also essential to exploit all the potential of modern processing units (e.g., vector processing). Traditionally, to improve performance, the developer introduces the optimisations in the domain code, making the code less abstract and dependent on the execution platform.

The Java language brings the *write once run anywhere* philosophy: the same program can run on any system that supports a Java Virtual Machine. Java 8 introduced the Stream API [1], which enables easy-to-use parallelism over Java collections (e.g., data-parallel processing). Unfortunately, the Java object model compromises the suitability of the Java stream-based processing for High Performance Computing (HPC). The main limitation is the lack of data locality in Java collections (including arrays of objects). Java collections are implemented with pointers to objects (e.g., an ArrayList is stored as an Array of Pointers (AoP) to objects). This is a consequence of using type erasure [2] to implement

© Springer Nature Switzerland AG 2022
R. Chaves et al. (Eds.): Euro-Par 2021, LNCS 13098, pp. 17–28, 2022.
https://doi.org/10.1007/978-3-031-06156-1_2

generic collections in order to avoid code bloat. With type erasure, a single collection implementation can be used for all concrete types, since the collection only needs to store pointers to [generic] objects. The AoP-based storage is also convenient to implement many object-oriented features, like polymorphism.

The AoP-based implementation of Java collections has negative consequences for HPC, namely: 1) additional memory references are required to access object fields; 2) entities in collections might not be stored in contiguous memory (no spatial locality); 3) object headers and memory alignment waste space in memory (object headers are required for JVM runtime checks). These result in a higher number of instructions (memory accesses) and lower data locality, which decreases the performance due to stronger impact of the memory bottleneck.

The data locality can be improved by using a layout with higher data locality, by storing object collections as a Structure of Arrays (SoA). However, in this case, the programmer must "give up" of the Java object-oriented view of data (e.g., using raw arrays of data). Moreover the programmer might be forced to drop the usage of the Java collections API (and consequently, the Stream API). Additionally, it is not feasible to use SoA layouts on the wide base of existing Java code, since a huge code refactoring effort would be necessary.

The research challenge addressed in this paper is how to improve the data locality of Java collections in order to make the Java stream API more suitable for HPC, without dropping the object-oriented view of data collections (i.e., preserving compatibility with the stream API and with the Java object model). Specifically, how to transparently support more efficient data layouts (e.g., SoA layouts) in Java stream-based parallel processing.

2 Java Stream API

The *Stream* interface (left of Fig. 1) provides methods to process a data stream, namely: 1) *forEach*: performs an operation on each element of the data stream; 2) *filter*: generates a new stream with a subset of the original stream and 3) reductions, such as *count*, that returns the number of elements in a stream. The *Collection* interface is the root of all Java collections and was enriched in Java 8 with the *stream* default method that returns a stream view of a collection. Thus, conceptually, stream-based processing is supported over all Java collections.

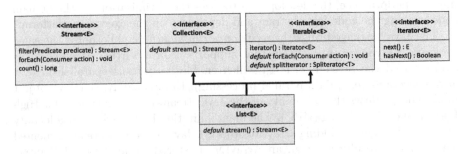

Fig. 1. Java collections and stream API

A parallel stream enables parallel processing over the objects in a collection. Thus, the introduction of the stream API enabled the specification of explicit data-parallel processing over the wide range of Java collections. In particular, the *List* interface (bottom of Fig. 1) extends the *Collection* interface, providing a set of default methods for stream-based parallel processing over index-based collections (e.g., the *ArrayList* implements *List* interface).

The stream API relies on well-defined collection interfaces, making it possible to provide new collection implementations that comply to the stream API, avoiding the need to reimplement a parallel computing infrastructure. This is the key point in the context of the presented work, since user-provided collection implementations can use the Java stream API and fully exploit the parallel processing stream infrastructure.

Java collections rely on the *Iterable* and *Iterator* interfaces (see right side of Fig. 1) to hide the implementation details of collections. The classes implementing the *Collection* interface must also implement the *Iterable* interface, which provides a method to return an *Iterator*. User-provided collections must implement a collection interface and the *Iterable/Iterator* interfaces to take advantage of the Java stream API.

The most commonly used data structure in Java, according to the study in [7], is the *ArrayList*, whose implementation is based on the AoP data layout. Figure 2 illustrates the data layout of an *ArrayList* of objects of a class *Particle*. The array of pointers itself requires a header (at least 16 bytes) and there is also a header on each object (at least 12 bytes). This layout has three main problems: i) there is a pointer de-refencing to access each object, which introduces an additional memory access per element; ii) object headers and object alignment introduce a significative memory space for small objects, which might saturate the faster levels of cache on modern processing units (e.g., the small L1 cache); iii) objects referenced by those pointers might not be in consecutive memory addresses (i.e., weak locality of reference). The locality of references can be improved by sorting objects in memory (e.g., a modified JVM implementation was presented in [9] that performs object sorting during garbage collecting), but the problems i) and ii) still remain. The AoP layout is not well-suited for HPC due to its pointer-based nature and is not compatible with vectorisation, but it can abstract from the details about the object pointed-to making it well-suited to implement object models. For instance, it supports inheritance (e.g., a collection can hold pointers

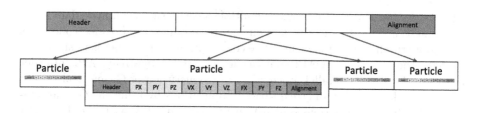

Fig. 2. Java collections data layout example

to objects from different classes that implement same [sub]type), pointers to generic objects can be used in method calls, etc.

One alternative is the use of an Array of Structures (AoS) layout where data entities are stored on consecutive memory addresses. Wimmer et al. [12] modified a JVM implementation for this purpose, which automatically inlines object fields by placing the parent and children in consecutive memory places and by replacing memory accesses by address arithmetic. They concluded that an automatic AoP to AoS transformation at JVM level requires a global data flow analysis, since Java byte-codes for accessing array elements have no static type information (i.e., they suffer from type erasure due to its AoP nature). The AoS layout is more memory-friendly than AoP making it more suitable for HPC but it is still not effective for vectorisation [3] (requires scatter and gather operations). Moreover, the Java object model is more difficult to support in the AoS layout (e.g., inheritance) and it requires low-level workarounds since Java has no support for pointers and, consequently, has limited support for this layout. Therefore, the AoS layout is not an attractive solution for HPC in Java.

The most effective layout for HPC is a Structure of Arrays (SoA), since it is also essential to enable efficient vectorisation. In this layout a collection is backed by multiple arrays, one for each data field. However, this layout drops the object-oriented view of the data, presenting several challenges to support the Java object model, namely, how to support objects and method calls on these objects, inheritance, etc. The main advantage of this work is to support the Java object model when using the more memory-friendly SoA layout.

There are some Java-based approaches that avoid the AoP layout problem for arrays of primitive types [4,5], but they do not support collections of structured data types (e.g., a transparent SoA layout for generic object collections). Moreover, these are not drop-in replacements for Java collections, since the generic Java interfaces (e.g., the *List* interface) are not supported. As a consequence they are not compatible with the stream infra-structure. The work presented in this paper supports the SoA layout for collections of complex data types and provides a drop-in replacement for Java collections, supporting the stream interface. Thus, the Java stream parallel processing infra-structure becomes available for HPC programmers.

3   Gaspar Stream-Based API and Implementation

The Gaspar framework [10] provides multiple mechanisms to improve data locality, namely, it encapsulates the data entities into framework provided collections that support efficient data layouts. The contribution of this paper is to show how to make the Gaspar data API compatible with the Java stream API, in order to: i) use the stream parallel processing infra-structure over Gaspar collections; ii) improve data locality of stream-based applications by using the Gaspar supported locality optimisations and iii) ensure compatibility with the Java API (including the object model).

3.1   Stream-Based Gaspar API

The Java collections API (i.e., Fig. 1) can hide details of the collection representation (e.g., the internal usage of an array or linked-list). However, it can expose
details of the object layout, so it cannot hide a change in a collection layout from
an AoP to a SoA. The Gaspar data API can hide additional details concerning
the data representation, including the concrete data layout. The key difference
to the Java API is that data entities should be represented using interfaces with
getter and setter methods for each data property.

The left side of Fig. 3 presents an example of a *Particle* interface with PX,
PY and PZ properties. The code on the right illustrates the Gaspar API usage
to get the position (x, y, and z) of a particle. The key difference to the Java API
is the usage of getter methods in lines 5–7.

The Gaspar API was extended to provide compatibility with Java collections
and streams, by extending the framework collections the implement the Java
List interface. This opens the door to the usage of Gaspar collections in Java
applications that rely that interface: only an update to the usage of getter and
setter methods is required, something that well-designed code probably already
includes. The Gaspar collections now also implement the Java *Iterable/Iterator*
interfaces, which were already used in the example of Fig. 3.

Parallel processing can now be transparently explored using parallel streams.
This enables the usage of the stream parallel processing infra-structure, instead
of the built-in Gaspar parallel maps. Figure 4 illustrates the usage of the *forEach*
method on a collection of *Particles* to call the *move* method on each particle
in parallel. This uses a lambda function define the operation to apply to each
stream element.

3.2   Design and Implementation

The Gaspar API was designed for HPC and to support most features of the
Java object model, some of which are difficult to support when using SoA or
AoS layouts as a backend of object collections. This is a consequence of using
an object model relying on AoP data layouts. For instance, in the Java model,
objects are always passed by reference.

```
interface Particle {        1  // col is a List<Particle>
  double getPX();           2  Iterator<Particle> it = col.iterator();
  double getPY();           3  while (it.hasNext()) {
  double getPZ();           4    Particle p = it.next();
}                           5    x = p.getPX();
                            6    y = p.getPY();
                            7    z = p.getPZ();
                            8    (...)
                            9  }
```

Fig. 3. Gaspar API usage example (*Particle* example). The code on the left defines the
particle interface and the code on the right in an example of the Gaspar API usage

```
col.parallelStream().forEach( p -> p.move(); );
```

Fig. 4. Example of parallel streams: *col* is a Gaspar collection (*gCollection<Particle>*) that implements the interface *List<Particle>*. The method *move* of class particle can be called, in parallel, on all particles in the stream

```
// Gaspar API              // AoP layout (JGF MD)      // SoA layout
force(Particle p){         force(Particle p){          force(Particles p,
  dx=this.getX()-p.getX();   dx = this.x - p.x;             int p1, int p2){
  ...                        ...                         dx = p.x[p1]-p.x[p2];
}                          }                               ...
                                                       }
```

Fig. 5. Particle force computation example in Gaspar API, Java AoP and SoA

Figure 5 illustrates the code of several data layouts for a collection of *Particles* using a code snippet from the MD case study. The Gaspar API (left of the figure) is used for all layouts, but plain Java requires different codes for AoP and SoA layouts (e.g., the AoP layout is from the JGF MD benchmark [11]). This example illustrates the complexity of using the efficient SoA layout in Java streams:

1. *Entities and methods.* The *force* method computes the force between two particles. In the AoP layout, the class *Particle* represents an entity from the domain and that entity defines a method *force*. In a SoA implementation there is no particle entity in the code (only array of properties, such as the x array), so the force method must be declared outside of the *Particle* class. This has a huge impact when using Java streams since there is no object *Particle* (e.g., it is not possible write the example of Fig. 4, which calls the *move* method on each particle of a collection).

2. *Object references.* The method *force* receives another *Particle* as an argument. In the AoP layout this is implemented by simply passing a pointer to another object. In the SoA layout the integer index of each particle should be used instead. Moreover, if the force is an external method that receives two particles, it will also require access to the *Particles* data. An alternative would be to "construct" a particle from the SoA data, when required, but it could lead to additional overhead and cannot be used in cases where the original particle is updated, since in the Java model objects are always passed by reference. This layout also makes the support for Java iterators complex since the next method should return a reference to an object in the collection (which might be updated). Providing support for Java iterators is fundamental to use the Stream API.

3. *Compositions of objects.* In object-oriented applications it is common to define objects as being composed of other objects (e.g., a particle might be composed by three objects: position, velocity and force). This is trivially supported in AoP layouts by using pointers to other objects. In the SoA layout these compositions can be manually implemented by using a single structure of arrays for all object fields.

Implementation Overview. The Gaspar API relies on the *gCollection* and *gIterator* interfaces, which now also support the Stream API (e.g., *List* and *Iterator*), implementing the necessary methods as *default methods*. As a consequence, *gCollections* can now be used in the Java stream processing infra-structure.

The development of an application in the Gaspar framework starts with a specification of a diagram similar to an UML domain model (e.g., yellow box in Fig. 6), where programmers specify the properties of each domain entity (i.e., their getter and setter methods and other relevant properties) as well as the relationship among them (aggregations). The Gaspar framework provides a visual tool (eclipse plug-in) to support this step.

A second tool generates the concrete implementations for the AoP and SoA layouts, based on the provided domain model. Figure 6 includes the generated classes for the SoA layout. The class *gCollectionParticleSoA* implements the interface *gCollection<Particle>* (note that the *gCollection* interface extends the *List* interface) with the SoA layout and the class *gIteratorParticleSoA* implements both *Particle* and *gIterator<Particle>* interfaces. In this implementation strategy the *gIterator* acts as a proxy to the actual *Particle* implementation, enabling the *gIterator* to also behave as a *Particle*, and to be used where an object of type *Particle* is expected. This allows the use of *Particle* entities in the base program, which could also include methods (e.g., *Particle move* method of Fig. 4) and the use of object references (a *gIterator* can be used as method parameter, copied, etc.). One feature of the developed tool is the ability "to flatten" aggregations defined in the domain model when generating the SoA representation. This enables the efficient support of composite objects in the stream API.

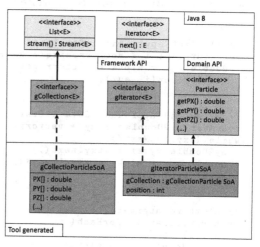

Fig. 6. Gaspar API and implementation overview

4   Evaluation

The benchmarks presented in this section were collected on a Linux machine with 24-cores (two Xeon E5-2695v2 processors) running Cent OS 6.3. The presented performance results are the median of 5 executions, after one warmup execution. The Java results use the OpenJDK 13.0.2 and C results use the GNU g++ 8.2.0.

4.1   Low Level Evaluation: DAXPY

The widely used DAXPY function adds two vectors: $Y \mathrel{+}= alfa * X$. This case study evaluates the overhead of accessing the elements of a collection, as well as the feasibility of the automatic JVM vectorisation. The DAXPY is an easy-to-vectorise case study, however, it requires two iterators, one for each vector, which might degrade the performance and disable the automatic vectorisation.

Figure 7 shows the pseudo-code of three coding alternatives: 1) a traditional index-based approach to access each vector; 2) Java iterators and a single collection to store both X and Y vectors (the *my2Double* object stores both x and y elements[1]) and 3) stream-based interface with a lambda function.

```
// 1) first approach: index based (two collections)
for (int i=0; i < vectorx.size() && i < vectory.size(); i++) {
   double aux = alpha * vectorx.get(i) + vectory.get(i);
   vectory.set(i, aux);
}

// 2) second approach: Java iterator (single collection)
Iterator<my2Double> itxy = vectorxy.iterator();
while(itxy.hasNext()){
   my2Double xyval = itxy.next();
   double aux = alpha * xyval.getX()+ xyval.getY();
   xyval.setY(aux);
}

// 3) third approach: stream based (single collection)
vectorxy.stream().forEach(
   (xyval) -> {
         double aux = alpha * xyval.getX() + xyval.getY();
         xyval.setY(aux);
   } );
```

Fig. 7. DAXPY implementation alternatives

Table 1 compares the JVM effectiveness to optimise alternatives in Fig. 7:

- The table rows are the three ways of accessing elements of the collection: i) index-based (first approach in Fig. 7); ii) external-iterator based (second approach); and iii) internal-iterator based (stream-based, third approach).
- The table columns are four alternatives to store X and Y vectors: i) using one or two collections (first and second columns); ii) using an AoP or a SoA layout; and iii) using the Gaspar Stream-compatible collections and iterators.
- The value in each cell is the number of instructions to compute each element of Y. The cells in bold are the cases where the JVM successfully vectorised the code[2], resulting in a lower number of instructions. The table also indicates the unrolling degree of the generated code (number in parenthesis).

---

[1] The use of a single collection for both x and y elements is mandatory, since streams require a single iterator for accessing all the elements (i.e., for internal iteration).

[2] Vectorisation was confirmed by inspection of the assembly generated.

Table 1. Instructions/element and vectorisation results on the DAXPY case study

	Java AoP (2 col)	Java AoP (1 col)	Gaspar AoP (1 col)	Gaspar SoA (1 col)
Index-based	20.0 (1×)	12.5 (4×)	8.3 (4×)	**1.3** (4×)
Iterators (external)	44.0 (1×)	14.5 (4×)	10.1 (4×)	**1.3** (4×)
Streams (internal)	N/A	12.3 (4×)	9.8 (4×)	**1.3** (4×)

Using two different collections (1st column) introduces high overhead, especially when using iterators. A single collection reduces the instruction count and makes it possible to use the Java stream API. The Gaspar AoP layout (3nd column) provides additional reductions on the number of instructions due to more efficient collection management (the compiler removes the type-checking of the elements in the collections, because those elements are created all at once). The Gaspar SoA implementations enable the vectorisation in all cases, including the implementation that uses the stream API. On the other hand, versions using AoP layouts are never vectorised, as expected, due to the usage of pointers.

The Fig. 8 shows the relative performance for vectors with 25M elements. Using two collections delivers the worst performance, due to less data locality (X and Y elements are different objects), resulting in more memory loads, misses, etc. The stream interface has a small performance penalty relative to index/iterator versions. Gaspar implementations provide a gain of around 2.5× when using the SoA layout: the Java compiler was able to optimise the stream-based code to the level of index-based/iterators. The graph on the right of Fig. 8 presents the relative performance of parallel streams and the most efficient C+OpenMP implementation (a parallel loop over raw arrays of X and Y elements, that is also automatically vectorised). The Java parallel streams implementation provides a 2× speed-up, a low gain for a 24-core machine. The Gaspar AoP implementation is slightly better (3× improvement), but the Gaspar SoA parallel stream provides a speed-up of 6× (note that part of this gain is due to better data locality), which is pretty close to the efficient C+OpenMP implementation (6.5× gain).

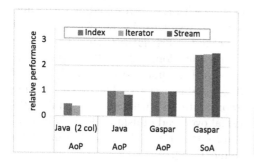
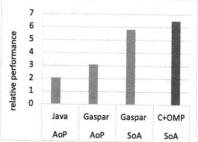

Fig. 8. DAXPY performance: sequential execution at the left and parallel at right. Performance results are relative to the base Java AoP layout with a single collection

4.2   Evaluation of Java Code: JECoLi

The Java Evolutionary Computation Library (JECoLi) [6,8], is a highly configurable Java framework, with a large number of classes that implement algorithms and data representation alternatives used in that domain. The JECoLi framework comes with a large set of case studies that were all updated to use Gaspar collections (e.g., using *gCollections* where a *List* is expected). This case study illustrates how the Gaspar framework avoided a huge refactoring work in order to take advantage of the SoA Layout in the large JECoLi code base.

```
int countOnes(ILinearRepresentation< gBoolean > genomeRep) {
  int countOneValues = 0;
  for(int i = 0;i < genomeRep.getNumberOfElements();i++)
    if ((genomeRep.getElementAt(i)) .getValue() ) countOneValues++;
  return countOneValues;
}
```

Fig. 9. Changes made to the CountOnes case study: Java Boolean was replaced by the Gaspar gBoolean interface and the introduction of the getValue getter method

The results presented in this section are for the CountOnesEATest problem that is the case study with the largest data size (and most time-consuming). The CountOnes optimisation example creates 10 random solutions, each one with 10000 gnomes that can be true (1) or false (0). The optimal solution is the one with all gnomes set to true.

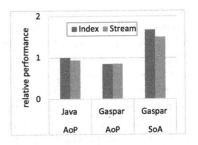

Fig. 10. JECoLi performance

The Fig. 9 illustrates the small impact of the changes required in the CountOnesEATest. The original ILinearRepresentation<Boolean> interface was internally implemented as an ArrayList, implying the usage of an inefficient AoP representation. To overcome that bottleneck the internal ArrayList<Boolean> was replaced by a gCollection<gBoolean> (gBoolean is the framework Boolean interface with the corresponding setter and getter methods). The code in Fig. 9 show the result of this change: the use of the gBoolean interface and the getter method. This quick change to use the Gaspar API allows generating a SoA representation. Figure 10 compares the performance of various implementations (the base line is the original JECoLi implementation, i.e., Java AoP with index-based iterations). The execution time slightly increases when using the framework data API with an AoP representation. This can be explained by an additional overhead of using gBoolean instead of the built-in Java Boolean, but it enables the usage of a SoA layout which improves the performance (a gain of around 1.7×).

4.3   High-Level Evaluation: MD

The third case study is a molecular dynamics simulation, based on the code from the MD benchmark from the JGF Suite [11], which performs a simulation of the behavior of Argon atoms (i.e., Argon particles). The JGF code uses an AoP of particle objects, where each particle has nine properties: position, velocity and a force in 3D space (see Fig. 2). The original benchmark was refactored to use stream-based processing, but the third newton law optimisation (symmetry of forces) was removed from the code to use a simple map parallelism pattern. This case study shows how the proposed approach can provide huge improvements delivering a highly scalable parallel application. A sketch of the code of this case study was already presented (i.e., Fig. 3 and 5). The domain model of this case study was developed using the Gaspar API, which enables the framework to generate the collection representation, making it easier to assess the performance implications of several implementation decisions. Figure 11 summarises the performance results for a problem size of 500000 particles.

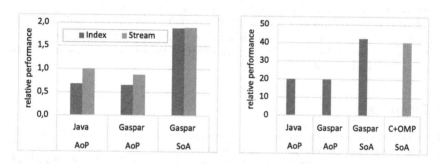

Fig. 11. MD performance: left: sequential execution time; right: parallel versions

In this case study, the stream AoP implementation is used as the baseline for performance comparison, instead of the original JGF AoP index-based implementation, since it is the fastest sequential version (it is faster due to additional virtual machine optimisations). The Gaspar AoP stream implementation introduces a slight overhead, but the Gaspar SoA implementation provides a speedup of 1.8× over the base stream AoP implementation. The Java parallel stream execution provides a speedup of 20× and the Gaspar SoA parallel stream implementation provides a self-speed-up of 22×. This speed-up is closer to the ideal since the SoA version has better data locality. Overall, the Gaspar SoA implementation gets a performance gain of 42× over the base reference (stream AoP), which is ever faster than C+OpenMP (the C version uses the SoA layout and a parallel loop to compute the forces among particles). The slight advantage of Java is due to the NUMA-aware allocation which is used by default. A fine-tuned C implementation, using the thread binding feature of OpenMP 4.0 was able to get a speed-up of 43.2×, slightly faster than Java, but this fine-tuning does not introduce performance gains in other case studies.

5 Conclusion and Future Work

The Gaspar framework improves the performance of stream-based Java applications by transparently using SoA layouts for object collections. The framework supports the Java object model making it possible to use the more efficient SoA layout almost transparently, in way similar to the built-in AoP Java layout. This enables a more high-level, object-oriented, view of the data. The alternative would be to drop the high-level view and use arrays of object properties. Moreover, the Gaspar framework provides a cost-effective way of improving the data locality of existing Java applications, making those applications better suited for HPC. Performance results show that SoA layouts improve performance by using a better memory footprint and enables automatic vectorisation on modern JVM. Future work includes support for more advanced features of Java, such as polymorphism and support for irregular data structures (e.g., graphs).

Acknowledgements. This work has been supported by FCT - Fundação para a Ciência e Tecnologia within the R&D Units Project Scope: UIDB/00319/2020. The evaluation used the computing infra-structure of the project Search-ON2: Revitalization of HPC infrastructure of UMinho, (NORTE-07-0162-FEDER-000086), co-funded by the North Portugal Regional Operational Programme (ON.2-O Novo Norte), under the National Strategic Reference Framework (NSRF), through the European Regional Development Fund (ERDF).

References

1. https://docs.oracle.com/javase/8/docs/api/java/util/stream/Stream.html
2. https://docs.oracle.com/javase/tutorial/java/generics/erasure.html
3. https://www.intel.com/content/dam/develop/external/us/en/documents/31848-compilerautovectorizationguide-703156.pdf
4. https://bitbucket.org/trove4j/trove/src/master/
5. https://labs.carrotsearch.com/hppc.html
6. https://github.com/jecoli
7. Costa, D., Andrzejak, A., Seboek, J., Lo, D.: Empirical study of usage and performance of Java collections. In: International Conference on Performance Engineering, ICPE 2017, pp. 389–400 (2017). https://doi.org/10.1145/3030207.3030221
8. Evangelista, P., Maia, P., Rocha, M.: Implementing metaheuristic optimization algorithms with JECoLi. In: International Conference on Intelligent Systems Design and Applications, pp. 505–510 (2009). https://doi.org/10.1109/ISDA.2009.161
9. Hirzel, M.: Data layouts for object-oriented programs. In: International Conference on Measurement and Modeling of Computer Systems, SIGMETRICS 2007, pp. 265–276 (2007). https://doi.org/10.1145/1254882.1254915
10. Silva, R., Sobral, J.L.: Gaspar data-centric framework. In: Dutra, I., Camacho, R., Barbosa, J., Marques, O. (eds.) VECPAR 2016. LNCS, vol. 10150, pp. 234–247. Springer, Cham (2017). https://doi.org/10.1007/978-3-319-61982-8_21
11. Smith, L.A., Bull, J.M., Obdržálek, J.: A parallel Java Grande benchmark suite. In: Supercomputing, SC 2001 (2001). https://doi.org/10.1145/582034.582042
12. Wimmer, C., Mössenböck, H.: Automatic array inlining in Java virtual machines. In: International Symposium on Code Generation and Optimization, CGO 2008, pp. 14–23 (2008). https://doi.org/10.1145/1356058.1356061

Exploring Strategies to Improve Locality Across Many-Core Affinities

Neil Butcher[(✉)] and Peter Kogge[(✉)]

University of Notre Dame, Notre Dame, IN, USA
{nbutcher,kogge}@nd.edu

Abstract. Several recent rank one systems in the Top500 include many-core chips with complex memory systems, including intermediate levels of memory, multiple memory channels, and explicit affinity of specific memory channels to specific sub-blocks of cores. Creating codes to utilize these features efficiently is thus a significant challenge. This paper uses Intel's Knights Landing (KNL) processor as a testbed, as it includes both intermediate memory and multiple architectural knobs to adjust affinity. This paper also uses a 2D Fast Fourier Transform (FFT) as a test case to explore what combination of architectural and algorithmic techniques are of most benefit. Several codes are used, including state-of-the-art FFT codes FFTW and MKL, along with two additional simple parallel 2D FFT codes exploring explicit options. The conclusions are that intermediate memory does provide a significant boost, that there are architectural modes in the memory subsystem that are better suited to FFT than others.

Keywords: Multilevel memory · FFT · Cache-oblivious · Buffering · Affinity

1 Introduction

Processor chips are trending towards increased numbers of cores to increase the achievable flops/s. For many applications, increasing the number of cores creates a higher demand for memory bandwidth. Modern chips increase bandwidth by adding more channels to conventional memory and, in many cases, by adding a new class of memory that may lie in between main memory and the highest cache level. Today, this **Intermediate Memory (IM)** is frequently in the form of 3D stacks of DRAM chips, each with multiple channels to the processor chip.

Creating a cache coherent memory system that scales to a number of cores and memory channels is a challenging task. When a core initiates a memory access, the processor has to determine if the data is resident in another cache. If so, the processor routes the value from the core currently holding the data to the core requesting the data. When accessing data not already in a cache, the processor has to determine which memory channel contains the data and

R. Chaves et al. (Eds.): Euro-Par 2021, LNCS 13098, pp. 29–40, 2022.
https://doi.org/10.1007/978-3-031-06156-1_3

then routes the data to the requesting core. Researchers have studied ways to maintain cache coherence in manycore systems [1,7,8].

The standard cache coherency protocols are a snoopy protocol and directory protocol. Snoopy protocols operate communicate a cache modifying value to all cores. The cores then snoop to see if the change is relevant to their data. Directory protocols rely on a "directory" structure. A directory keeps track of which cache currently has the data. There can be multiple directories or "home agents," each one responsible for maintaining coherence for a different portion of memory.

In many applications, the key to effective use of the memory hierarchy is efficient *memory affinity*: the mapping of data to memory controllers. Linux decides the affinity of memory using a *first-touch* policy, meaning Linux places pages on memory channels based on the first core to access it. A first-touch policy thus enforces an affinity of cores to memory channels. A typical memory affinity groups cores and memory channels based on proximity. Creating groups of cores and assigning them to memory channels that limit the distance accesses need go, given they are on the group's designated memory controller. These groups are referred to as Non-Uniform Memory Access (*NUMA*) domains. Application designers often create codes that minimize accesses across NUMA domains.

There are at least two types of affinity: logical memory affinity and physical memory affinity. *Logical affinity* is the relationship between home agents and the logical address spaces - the mapping between cache directory and logical memory. *Physical affinity* is the relationship between cache directories and the physical address spaces - the mapping between home agents and memory controllers. The KNL makes an interesting test-bed because users can adjust both affinities via setting "clustering modes."

This work explores how the memory affinities in the KNL affect the performance of Fast Fourier Transform (FFT). We run four different FFT codes: one written to be architecture-agnostic but self-tuning (FFTW), one designed explicitly for the KNL architecture (MKL), one that performs thread-buffering, and one designed to be "cache-oblivious". **Cache-oblivious** means it is agnostic to the cache parameters but still has an asymptotic optimal number of cache misses. We adapt the last two to use IM.

The goal of this paper is thus three-fold: first, demonstrate how functional is IM to a real problem (FFT), second, understand how codes can utilize IM efficiently without introducing architecture-specific optimizations, and finally give insight into which of the cluster modes offered by the KNL are of most value. We also analyze the impact that size and shape have on FFT strategies' effectiveness to utilize IM. Together such information should be helpful in architecting future systems that can use IM effectively with relatively simple codes.

The organization of this paper is as follows. Section 2 discusses the baseline architecture we assumed and some details of the implementation. Section 3 reviews the nature of an FFT, and two popular FFT codes used as reference points. Section 4 describes what a cache oblivious algorithm is and our implementation of a cache oblivious algorithm. Section 5 describes our thread buffering algorithm. Section 6 discusses the experimental setup. Section 7 describes the results. Section 8 discusses related work. Section 9 concludes.

2   Architectural Background

Many-core machines are beginning to include IM layers to the memory hierarchy to match the increasing bandwidth demand. Often high-bandwidth IMs have limited capacity, resulting in them being implemented alongside a larger main memory.

Implementing an IM is most beneficial when the problem size is larger then the IM. If the problem fits entirely in the IM, the main memory is obsolete and all data can be stored on IM. IM acting as a cache allows programs to utilize IM without redesigning the code. It also requires data evictions and replacements to be communicated between the memory banks. However, on the KNL there are many cases where configuring IM as a cache actually lowers performance.

Architechtures with IM are still emerging, and the most effective memory structure is uncertain. Memory systems have used various strategies to map different sections of logical address space to a processor's physical memory ports and how to distribute directory information about such mappings among the cores. Comparing these strategies is complex, especially across chips.

Our baseline system for testing uses Intel's PHI 7250 (a.k.a. "Knight's Landing" (KNL)) as its processor. This chip has 34 "tiles" each of which contains two physical cores, a 1 MB shared L2, and a "Caching Home Agent" (CHA) that serves as a directory for coherency traffic in some part of the address space [13]. Each of the physical cores is capable of supporting four hyperthreads. A 2D mesh connects the 68 cores, with a subdivision of tiles into four "quadrants." The cores can also be divided into two hemispheres. There are two memory controllers and six conventional DDR4 ports (three per controller) to provide roughly 96 GB of storage with 90 GB/s of bandwidth.

The KNL also has a configurable IM called MCDRAM implemented with eight 3D stacks of DRAM chips, each with 2 GB capacity and a separate port into the processor chip. Two such ports are physically close to each quadrant of the chip. The behavior of the MCDRAM is adjusted in the BIOS at boot time and can act as an extension to the main memory ("flat mode"), a large L3 cache ("cache mode"), or a hybrid. The aggregate MCDRAM has roughly 16 GB of storage and provides approximately 400 GB/s bandwidth.

Given a large number of cores and memory ports, how does a load/store that misses all on-chip caches make its way to the appropriate physical memory port while also performing cache coherency checks? First, the KNL allows at boot time several different "clustering modes" for defining how CHAs are associated with physical MCDRAM ports. Coupled with this are options as to how to associate different logical memory pages to a particular CHA.

Figure 1 demonstrates the available clustering modes on the KNL. Figure 2 illustrates how the clustering mode affects how logical memory maps to memory controllers, as well as CHAs to memory controllers. In Fig. 2, CHAs and core groups with the same color mean the core group sends requests directly to those CHAs. Memory controllers and portions of the logical address space that are the same color mean that the memory controller is responsible for that portion of the logical address space. In all modes, the CHAs communicate to ensure cache

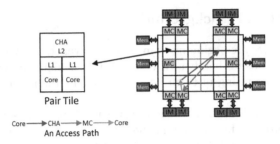

Fig. 1. KNL access modes.

coherency. There is a potential for collision when CHAs are passing messages. A CHA can only pass so many messages in a single cycle, creating the possibility of network congestion.

The simplest mode is "all-to-all" (A2A), where the physical CHAs mapping different partitions have no relationship to the nearest physical IM port connected to the associated physical memory. It appears that in this mode, the relationship between logical pages and controlling CHAs is one-to-one but unconstrained. Thus a reference to two sequential pages of IM may end up going to two different CHAs almost anywhere on the chip. In this case, an L2 cache miss, tag directory probe, and data access could be on opposite sides of the chip. This option has the downside of memory requests having to traverse many CHAs before reaching the memory controller. The advantage is that it reduces the probability of collisions when many cores are accessing memory simultaneously.

In contrast, "Quadrant mode" ensures data is in the same quadrant as the CHA managing it. Sequential pages in logical memory are striped across the quadrants, increasing the memory controllers' utilization. Each page is stored inside a quadrant, with the following pages being stored in a different quadrant. The downside is a strided access pattern could have all accesses go to the same memory controller, resulting in contention.

The "Hemisphere mode" is similar but divides the memory ports in half rather than quarters. However, it appears that two sequential pages in logical space may still be in two different quadrants/hemispheres of the chip.

"Subnuma Clustering Four (SNC-4)" is similar to Quadrant mode in that a CHA only handles requests to memory controllers in its quadrant. The distinction from Quadrant mode is that in SNC-4 mode each quadrant acts as a separate NUMA node. SNC-4 aggregates logical memory in each quadrant to act as a contiguous partition of the address space. Thus if all cores in a quadrant work on the same data, no memory reference to the shared partition will cross a quadrant boundary. For example, this would allow four MPI ranks to run essentially independent of each other, at least in memory access traffic. In SNC-4, the memory controllers in each quadrant operate on a contiguous block of memory. Localized memory operations are more efficient, but accesses across the quadrants are expensive. For example, streaming a large block of data in

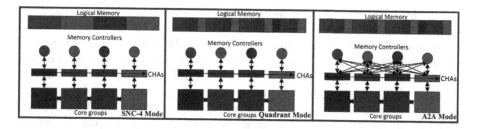

Fig. 2. Examples of directory and logical memory layout in three clustering modes

another quadrant creates a high amount of traffic and increases the chance for accesses to interfere with each other. SNC-4 is effective if the programmer is aware of memory affinity in the program and localizes data accesses.

"Subnuma Clustering Two (SNC-2)" is similar but where the CHAs controls half the logical memory space in the physical half closest to the memory ports holding the associated physical memory [16].

Two other many-core chips used in TOP500 systems with similar properties are the A64FX and SW26010. Both have the equivalent of 4 quadrants. The A64FX has 12 cores and eight channels to a separate HBM per quadrant. Each quadrant in the A64FX has a local memory channel but maintains cache coherency. A64FX has not adjustable clustering mode and most closely resembles the KNL in SNC-4 mode. The SW26010 has a scratchpad IM for each of its 256 compute cores and a DDR3 channel for each quadrant of 64.

3 Fast Fourier Transforms

Fast Fourier Transforms (FFT) have a non-unit stride access pattern inherent in the algorithm [15]. The access pattern of FFT computations are challenging for cache prefetchers to predict. Thus the memory system plays an important role of FFT-based codes. Our work focuses on 2D FFTs, which take an N×M complex matrix as the input and produces an N×M complex matrix as the output. A typical algorithm uses a *pencil decomposition* i.e., it computes a series of 1D FFTs or "pencils." We first compute a 1D FFTs of each column, and then 1D FFTs of each row, i.e., M pencils of size N, then N pencils of size M. The matrices are stored in row-major order and we transpose the input matrix to keep pencils contiguous when necessary.

A 1D FFT of size N has a complexity of $O(Nlog_2(N))$. Likewise, the complexity of a 2D FFT is $O(NMlog_2(NM))$. Note that NM is the size of the matrix in complex points, i.e., the problem size. For this work, we put the dimensions in terms of a ratio r such that M=N*r making the computational complexity $O(N^2r\ log_2(N^2r))$. By keeping the problem size constant, the number of flops is unchanged, but by changing r we see a change in the overall performance, which we attribute to the memory access patterns. We examine ratios ranging from $r = 1/512$ (tall/skinny) to $r = 512$ (short/fat).

For the KNL, we use as a baseline two respected multi-dimensional FFT codes, MKL and FFTW. The FFTW3 library adapts to the hardware on which it is running [11]. During a preliminary phase, FFTW looks at the problem size, vector capabilities, and the number of available threads. Using this information FFTW measures the performance of a variety of FFT algorithms before choosing the most efficient strategy represented by what they refer to as "plans." Plans can be precomputed and saved for reuse, or calculated at run-time. FFTW plans are hardware agnostic but can make use of vector units if compiled correctly. The planning phase is often time-consuming, but can provide speedup if multiple FFTs of the same size reuse the same plan. Using IM is not an option the planner explores. Experiments with FFTW on the KNL have to either treat MCDRAM as main memory (with the matrix preloaded into it and the result going back to it), or another layer of cache.

The FFTW library is memory affinity unaware, meaning when invoking the planner with a first-touch policy, it does not attempt different memory affinities. The planner uses as input a specified memory allocation, allowing the user to provide a memory affinity before invoking the planner. We have seen no information suggesting FFTW is NUMA-aware.

In contrast Intel developed the MKL library to specifically target Intel processors and utilize all available features. The MKL FFT routines support the same interface as FFTW, allowing FFT applications to be easily ported to MKL. Options exist in the MKL library to leverage MCDRAM but based on the performance we have observed, we do not believe MKL manages the IM at runtime.

4   Cache Oblivious Programming

For the third of our codes, we use the established technique of cache-oblivious algorithms. Frigo et al. introduced such algorithms [12] and others have implemented cache-oblivious algorithms on real systems [6,17]. Cache-oblivious algorithms often use a divide-and-conquer strategy. Most cache-oblivious algorithms have recursive calls breaking the problem into parts and solve in a depth-first manner. The base case is typically a problem so small that solving it is trivial. The recursion ensures effective use of cache because two trivial solutions are produced at the bottom level and then reused in subsequent recombination steps. As computation gets higher in the recursion tree, the size of the working set grows. The lower levels of recursion make efficient use of the cache without awareness of the cache size. Once the recursion reaches a point where the problem no longer fits in the cache, the cache is no longer used efficiently.

To prove the algorithms are optimal a **ideal cache model** is used which assumes the cache will make optimal decisions on replacement choices. The ideal cache is assumed to be tall (large capacity with short cache lines) and fully associative with an optimal offline replacement strategy that always makes an optimal choice, i.e., the data accessed furthest in the future is chosen to be replaced. A typical L1 cache found in a processor will often approximate "ideal" behavior in many applications.

Researchers have updated the cache-oblivious model to more closely resemble modern architectures. They extended the sequential cache-oblivious work with multicore cache-oblivious algorithms [6,9]. Cache oblivious research was later extended to include dynamically sized caches in **cache adaptive algorithms** [2–5]. The multithreaded CO work assumes caches are non-interfering, or more precisely, data accesses from one processor does not force data to be evicted from another cache. When threads operate independently on separate regions of memory, this assumption is realistic. When moving to manycore machines, coherency and data sharing has to be considered to represent performance accurately. Manycore processors with a large shared IM cache results in each core having a dynamically sized local cache. Using IM as a cache leads to contention among threads, permitting the amount of cache available to each thread dynamic. In our work, creating cache-adaptive algorithms benefits performance because cache size will naturally vary.

The original cache-oblivious FFT code was introduced by Frigo in [12]. The algorithm computed a 1D FFT of size n by viewing the 1D input into a matrix of size n_1 and n_2 such that $n_1 * n_2 = n$. Frigo's strategy chooses $n_1 = 2^{\lceil log_2(n) \rceil}$ and $n_2 = 2^{\lfloor log_2(n) \rfloor}$. The 1D input is transposed into a $n_2 * n_1$ matrix. Then n_2 FFTs of size n_1, are computed, and each element is multiplied by a twiddle factor. The matrix is transposed again, then we compute n_1 FFTs of size n_2. The FFT is solved through recursion until the subproblem is just a single element. Finally the matrix is transposed again to put the output in correct order.

In our work, we focus on solving 2D FFTs. We solve pencils of the columns, then rows. We perform transposes to make the pencil contiguous in memory. We use a similar approach to Frigo's cache-oblivious algorithm to solve the 1D FFT; with the slight modification, we choose $n_1 = 64$ and solve the subproblems invoking MKL. By choosing n_1 to be small, we avoid a great deal of the overhead of recursion and still increase cache locality.

5   Thread-Level Buffering

Thread buffering assumes two memories, a large, slower "main memory" and smaller IM memory that provides a bandwidth improvement. The idea is based on conventional buffering techniques where the input is broken into chunks approximately the size of the fast memory. A single chunk is moved into fast memory at a time. The subproblem in fast memory is computed and then moved back to main memory. Once all the chunks have been computed, the chunked solutions are merged to produce a final result. A similar strategy has been implemented successful on multicore processors in the work of Popovici et al. [14]. Popovici achieves speedup of 1.2–3× speedup over FFTW and MKL by utilizing some of the threads to perform 'soft DMA' operations.

Our fourth FFT code is specially written to use explicit thread level buffering to compute a FFT. To do this we divide threads into compute threads and copy threads. Each compute thread is given three buffers that are the size of the largest dimension of the 2D FFT. There are three buffers per thread to overlap computation with data movement. While one buffer is being computed on, one of the others is copied out, and the other has data copied in. Each copy thread is assigned to specific compute threads. The copy threads are placed in the same tile as the compute thread they manage, but on a separate physical core. In this work we chose a one-to-one ratio of copy threads to compute threads. The copy threads perform non-temporal accesses so they do not interfere with the compute threads. While a compute thread is operating on a block, the copy thread is able to move out the last block and bring in the next block. If the copy threads do not transport data quickly enough the compute thread idles, waiting for the copy to finish. We chose a one-to-one ratio because one thread the copy operations could be completed before the computation.

We use both implicit and explicit copying of data into IM. Implicit copying refers to putting IM in cache mode and having copy threads act as soft DMA devices by accessing the data they want to move into IM. In explicit copying, the copy threads directly move data into IM. The disadvantage of explicit copying is that it requires two memory accesses to perform the copy (a load and a store for each data element). Implicit copying requires loading a single address of memory and relies on the hardware/OS to efficiently move data into IM, but performs poorly if the accessed data set is too large, resulting in thrashing in the cache.

6   Methodology

Our experiments compare four codes: MKL, FFTW, Cache Oblivious (CO), and thread buffering (TB). We run all codes with 64 threads, except the thread-buffering code, which has 128 threads. We run in 5 cluster modes (SNC-2, SNC-4, A2A, Quad, Hemi) with the MCDRAM in flat and cache mode. The CO, MKL, and FFTW codes do not use the MCDRAM in flat mode, so those options are not run. We run 5 ratios (1/512, 1/8, 1, 8, 512) with 4 problem sizes for each ratio. All problems use dimensions that are a power of two, and for each ratio we ran problem sizes with (6.71E7, 2.68E8, 1.07E9, 4.29E9) complex numbers, except the ratio 1 which used (3.35E7, 1.34E8, 5.37E8, 2.15E9). The $1\times$ ratio used different problem sizes due to the limitations of powers of two.

We run the thread buffering code in three forms, flat mode with buffers in IM, flat mode with buffer in main memory, and cache mode with the buffers also in memory. The TB code runs with the KMP_AFFINITY variable set to balanced with 64 compute and 64 copy threads. Copy threads are placed on the same core as the compute threads they manage. We run MKL version 2020.0.166 using the FFTW interface. We create plans using the FFTW-ESTIMATE flag. We do not include the planning time in our measurement of the run time analysis.

7   Results

We compare the execution time of the different FFT algorithms in quadrant mode in Fig. 3. To keep the chart readable, we only include the largest problem sizes we ran at each ratio. The "thread-buffering IM" strategy runs in flat mode

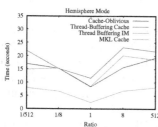

Fig. 3. Cache Quadrant mode

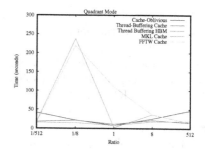

Fig. 4. Cache Hemisphere mode

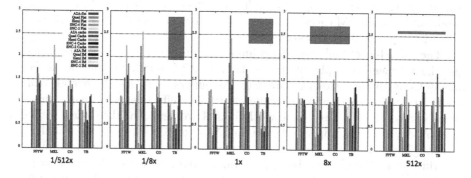

Fig. 5. Speedup of FFT codes relative to A2A flat. Each chart represents a separate ratio. The rectangle in the top left approximates the shape of the input matrix

with the buffers allocated to MCDRAM. The rest of the lines are runs with MCDRAM in cache mode. MKL performs best in quadrant mode on square problems, with a relative speedup of roughly 4× over the cache-oblivious algorithm. These speedups vary in magnitude with smaller problem sizes of the same ratio, but the general trend shows the CO algorithm performs at its best at large problem sizes. The cache-oblivious strategy appears to perform slightly better than the thread buffering, with a performance difference of 1–1.5×.

We show a similar chart for FFT in hemisphere mode in Fig. 4. Performance in this mode is more consistent than for quadrant mode, but quadrant mode has better performance in many cases. MKL computes a square problem in hemisphere mode up to four times faster than the cache-oblivious algorithm. MKL is roughly 2× faster than cache-oblivious FFT code for the 512 ratio cache mode. The square ratio has a smaller problem size, hence the lower execution time.

Figure 5 shows the speedup of each code relative to A2A flat mode at five different ratios. The figure shows the variance of the codes across different clustering modes and ratios. The biggest performance gain MCDRAM gives our FFT computations is quadrant mode ran on a square problem. Quadrant mode exhibit generally the best performance of all the clustering modes. In a few cases and algorithms, the hemisphere algorithm performs the best.

For square FFTs, MKL gains roughly 2.5× speedup from utilizing the IM in quadrant mode and 2.3× in hemisphere mode. At nonsquare ratios, IM is consistently beneficial in hemisphere mode, with MKL having speedups of from 1.3×–2.5×. MKL in SNC-4 cache and SNC-2 cache has improved performance square ratios with a steady decrease in performance at larger ratios, particularly SNC-4 cache.

The cache-oblivious algorithm benefits from MCDRAM acting as a cache in almost all of the clustering modes. MCDRAM does not improve the performance of the CO FFT on the 512 and 1/512 ratios in quadrant mode and square ratio in SNC-2. The cache-oblivious does not vary widely between clustering modes, suggesting the code is portable to other architectures with IM. In hemisphere mode, utilizing the IM cache improved the performance of the CO algorithm by 1.4×–1.6× across all the ratios.

The thread-level buffering algorithm consistently gains performance managing the IM memory explicitly, particularly in A2A, quadrant, and hemisphere mode. Copy threads moving data into IM buffers increases the overall bandwidth utilization and improves performance. The effectiveness of copy threads demonstrates that FFT is a bandwidth-limited problem. The thread-level buffering strategy does not appear effective in SNC-2 or SNC-4 mode, even with the buffers allocated to IM. We ensure the buffers are in the same quadrant as the threads utilizing them, but the incoming data copied could reside in any quadrant. The thread-level buffering algorithm in hemisphere mode gains performance of roughly 1.2×–1.4×. Since most of the increased bandwidth utilization comes from the copy threads, thread-level buffering does not exhibit the same performance gains the other strategies do.

8   Related Work

Popovici et al. [14] improves 2D and 3D FFTs by repurposing cores/threads as soft direct memory access (DMA) engines, with an improvement of up to 1.3× over MKL and FFTW. They utilize a highly efficient 1D algorithm to perform the 'pencil' computations, and focus on improving performance on FFTs on nodes with significant main memories. They note that for the processors they tested, FFTW/MKL achieved at most 47% of the peak FLOPs. In comparison, the highest performance we have seen from the KNL is roughly 13% of peak.

The Locality Aware Roofline Model [10] builds a roofline model that applies to NUMA machines, especially the KNL. They identify three main bottlenecks in memory accesses in a NUMA memory system: congestion, contention, and remote access. Congestion is when many data requests simultaneously go through a single CHA, delaying the data requests. Congestion occurs when many cores are accessing a single memory bank. The memory bank can only process a certain number of requests simultaneously, resulting in delayed responses. Each of the bottlenecks delays the overall memory requests of a system. They also discuss a method to create additional roofs based on the KNL hardware and the memory access patterns of the problem. They use a series of simple kernels to explore the variations in performance on the KNL. Often in manycore memory hierarchies, the available bandwidth fluctuates with problem size and algorithm. We relate this to our work because varying the problem size and ratio of an FFT naturally leads to these bottlenecks. It is often difficult to tell if/which of these bottlenecks is happening without carefully observing performance.

Cache adaptive algorithms are not aware of the size of the cache just like cache oblivious algorithms, with the distinction they remain optimal even if the cache size changes dynamically. This distinction comes up in a variety of situations, but in our work it occurs when multiple threads are contesting a shared cache. Shared caches have to be considered very differently than private caches, and being cache oblivious is not sufficient to state an algorithm is cache adaptive [5].

9 Conclusion

We provided a detailed explanation of the different clustering modes available to the KNL. We demonstrate how the clustering mode impacts the performance of a 2D FFT using many different sizes, shapes, and algorithms. All of the algorithms gain performance when utilizing IM in one mode or another. Whether or not an algorithm effectively utilizes the IM varies with the clustering mode. Many of the algorithms we ran have excellent speedup with the IM in quadrant mode on square ratios but perform poorly on non-square ratios. Hemisphere consistently benefits from the IM configured as a cache across all ratios.

The exact reason hemisphere mostly outperforms quadrant mode is unclear, although we have some ideas. Often FFTs have powers-of-two strided memory accesses, which causes makes accessing memory problematic. One typical example is every access mapping to the same cache set, reducing the effective cache size. We suspect a large enough stride will result in subsequent accesses to map to the same CHA. Note that the KNL has 34 CHAs, so two quadrants will have eight CHAs, the other two will have nine. The quadrants with eight CHAs may have implications for strides that are a power of two. In future work, we plan to do a more investigative analysis of how striding affects CHAs.

We implemented thread-level buffering and cache-oblivious FFT codes that have competitive performance with highly optimized codes. Both our FFT codes contain no architecture-specific optimizations. Both of these algorithms benefit from the IM across all the ratios. Our results show the most effective clustering mode to compute a square FFTs is quadrant, and hemisphere for non-square problems. When computing both square and non-square FFTs, the best strategy is to run in the hemisphere as the quadrant tends to be more erratic in performance. Our thread buffering algorithm is an effective strategy to use the IM in flat mode, which no other existing FFT codes does, to our knowledge.

References

1. Al-Hothali, S.: Snoopy and directory based cache coherence protocols: a critical analysis. J. Inf. Commun. Technol. (JICT) **4**(1), 11 (2010)
2. Barve, R.D., Vitter, J.S.: A theoretical framework for memory-adaptive algorithms. In: 40th Symposium on Foundations of Computer Science (Cat. No. 99CB37039), pp. 273–284. IEEE (1999)
3. Bender, M.A., Chowdhury, R.A., Das, R., et al.: Closing the gap between cache-oblivious and cache-adaptive analysis. In: Proceedings of the 32nd ACM Symposium on Parallelism in Algorithms and Architectures, pp. 63–73 (2020)
4. Bender, M.A., Demaine, E.D., Ebrahimi, R., et al.: Cache-adaptive analysis. In: Proceedings of the 28th ACM Symposium on Parallelism in Algorithms and Architectures, pp. 135–144 (2016)
5. Bender, M.A., Ebrahimi, R., Fineman, J.T., Ghasemiesfeh, G., Johnson, R., McCauley, S.: Cache-adaptive algorithms. In: Proceedings of the Twenty-Fifth Annual ACM-SIAM Symposium on Discrete Algorithms, pp. 958–971. SIAM (2014)
6. Blelloch, G.E., Gibbons, P.B., Simhadri, H.V.: Low depth cache-oblivious algorithms. In: Proceedings of the 22nd ACM Symposium on Parallelism in Algorithms and Architectures, pp. 189–199 (2010)
7. Caheny, P., Casas, M., Moretó, M., et al.: Reducing cache coherence traffic with hierarchical directory cache and numa-aware runtime scheduling. In: 2016 International Conference on Parallel Architecture and Compilation Techniques (PACT), pp. 275–286. IEEE (2016)
8. Chaiken, D., Fields, C., Kurihara, K., Agarwal, A.: Directory-based cache coherence in large-scale multiprocessors. Computer **23**(6), 49–58 (1990)
9. Chowdhury, R.A., Ramachandran, V., Silvestri, F., Blakeley, B.: Oblivious algorithms for multicores and networks of processors. J. Parallel Distrib. Comput. **73**(7), 911–925 (2013)
10. Denoyelle, N., Goglin, B., Ilic, A., Jeannot, E., Sousa, L.: Modeling large compute nodes with heterogeneous memories with cache-aware roofline model. In: Jarvis, S., Wright, S., Hammond, S. (eds.) PMBS 2017. LNCS, vol. 10724, pp. 91–113. Springer, Cham (2018). https://doi.org/10.1007/978-3-319-72971-8_5
11. Frigo, M., Johnson, S.G.: The design and implementation of FFTW3. Proc. IEEE **93**(2), 216–231 (2005)
12. Frigo, M., Leiserson, C.E., Prokop, H., Ramachandran, S.: Cache-oblivious algorithms. In: Proceedings of the 40th Annual Symposium on Foundations of Computer Science, p. 285 (1999)
13. León, E.A., Hautreux, M.: Achieving transparency mapping parallel applications: a memory hierarchy affair. In: Proceedings International Symposium on Memory Systems, pp. 185–189 (2018)
14. Popovici, D.T., Low, T.M., Franchetti, F.: Large bandwidth-efficient FFTs on multicore and multi-socket systems. In: 2018 IEEE International Parallel and Distributed Processing Symposium (IPDPS), pp. 379–388. IEEE (2018)
15. Rockmore, D.N.: The FFT: an algorithm the whole family can use. Comput. Sci. Eng. **2**(1), 60–64 (2000)
16. Weinberg, V.: PRACE Autumn School 2016-Intel Xeon Phi Programming (2016)
17. Yotov, K., Roeder, T., Pingali, K., et al.: An experimental comparison of cache-oblivious and cache-conscious programs. In: Proceedings of the 19th ACM Symposium on Parallel Algorithms and Architectures, pp. 93–104 (2007)

Monitoring Collective Communication Among GPUs

Muhammet Abdullah Soytürk$^{(\boxtimes)}$, Palwisha Akhtar , Erhan Tezcan ,
and Didem Unat

Department of Computer Science and Engineering, Koç University, Istanbul, Turkey
{msoyturk20,pakhtar19,etezcan19,dunat}@ku.edu.tr

Abstract. Communication among devices in multi-GPU systems plays
an important role in terms of performance and scalability. In order to
optimize an application, programmers need to know the type and amount
of the communication happening among GPUs. Although there are prior
works to gather this information in MPI applications on distributed systems and multi-threaded applications on shared memory systems, there
is no tool that identifies communication among GPUs. Our prior work,
COMSCRIBE, presents a point-to-point (P2P) communication detection
tool for GPUs sharing a common host. In this work, we extend COM-
SCRIBE to identify communication among GPUs for collective and P2P
communication primitives in NVIDIA's NCCL library. In addition to
P2P communications, collective communications are commonly used in
HPC and AI workloads thus it is important to monitor the induced
data movement due to collectives. Our tool extracts the size and the
frequency of data transfers in an application and visualizes them as a
communication matrix. To demonstrate the tool in action, we present
communication matrices and some statistics for two applications coming
from machine translation and image classification domains.

Keywords: Inter-GPU communication · Multi-GPUs · Profiling

1 Introduction

Nowadays, multi-GPU systems are commonly employed for parallel applications
either to reduce execution time or to enable processing a large amount of data.
In a multi-GPU application, there are many alternative ways for devices to
communicate, thus choosing the right communication type can become a critical
performance contributor. In convolutional neural networks (CNNs), for instance,
while data and spatial parallelism based implementations may perform gradient
exchange at the end of each iteration, filter and channel parallelism based implementations may require multiple collective communication calls at each layer
[11], resulting different performance behaviour and scalability. Hence, identifying
the type and size of the communication among GPUs can guide the programmer
in many aspects for performance optimization.

© Springer Nature Switzerland AG 2022
R. Chaves et al. (Eds.): Euro-Par 2021, LNCS 13098, pp. 41–52, 2022.
https://doi.org/10.1007/978-3-031-06156-1_4

Broadly speaking, communication on a multi-processor system can be categorized into two types: P2P communication between two processors (e.g., GPUs) or collective communication among multiple processors. For P2P communication, CUDA API offers various data transfer schemes to the programmer by utilizing Unified Virtual Addressing (UVA), Zero-copy Memory and Unified Memory paradigms. For collective communication, NVIDIA offers NCCL [21] library which provides efficient and topology-aware collectives. Collective primitives are used in various parallel algorithms that require collective work done by a group of processors. For example, many deep learning applications require data to be distributed in many processors and share the gradients among themselves, typically with an All-Reduce collective. Hence, deep learning frameworks such as PyTorch, Tensorflow and MxNet have already integrated NCCL into their frameworks to perform collective calls [21].

Communication monitoring among GPUs can help reason about scalability issues and performance divergence between different implementations of the same application, and guide the programmer to utilize the interconnects for better performance. For instance, if a single GPU application is scaled up to multiple GPUs, it may follow a master-slave communication pattern, which would underutilize the GPU interconnects. Because of the aforementioned reasons, identifying the volume of communication for different communication patterns offer avenues to improve performance and tune software for scalability.

To the best of our knowledge, there is no communication monitoring tool for NCCL collective communication primitives in multi-GPU systems. Previous work on communication monitoring includes identification of MPI collectives on distributed systems such as EZTrace [28]. EZTrace can identify explicit P2P communication functions that CUDA offers such as cudaMemcpy but it cannot identify Unified Memory, Zero-Copy memory and NCCL collective communication primitives. Similarly, NVIDIA's profiler *nvprof* [18] cannot provide any information about data transfers in NCCL primitives because data movement in NCCL is not based on *cudaMemcpy* API. *Nsight Systems* [19], a system-wide performance analysis tool by NVIDIA, visualizes the timeline of collective calls together with other kernel information but does not present overall picture of the data movement. Moreover, it does not provide any visual or machine readable data on the amount of data movement between GPU pairs.

This work extends COMSCRIBE [1], a tool that can monitor, identify, and quantify different types of communication among GPU devices, to support collective communication primitives. COMSCRIBE can extract communication-related activities in an application and generate a communication matrix that shows the amount of data movement between GPU-GPU or GPU-CPU pairs. It leverages the NVIDIA's profiling tool *nvprof* to monitor P2P communication. However, a significantly different approach is required to monitor collective communications because *nvprof* is not capable of providing any information about NCCL collectives. Our extension to the COMSCRIBE tool overcomes this limitation and works in three steps: First, we preload the NCCL library with extra functionality for logging the data transfers. Second, we collect GPU-GPU memory transfer information during the execution. Finally, we perform post-processing to quantify communication among GPUs and generate the communication matrices. Our contributions are summarized below:

- We extend COMSCRIBE to provide a more complete coverage of the communication types and monitor data transfers between GPUs during the execution of collective communication primitives.
- We present communication statistics and communication matrices for a machine translation and an image classification applications to demonstrate how COMSCRIBE can be used for explaining different implementations of data parallelism.
- The extensions are incorporated in COMSCRIBE, which is available at https://github.com/ParCoreLab/ComScribe.

The rest of the paper is organized as follows. In Sect. 2, we discuss the previous work on P2P communication monitoring with COMSCRIBE and introduce NVIDIA Collective Communication Library (NCCL). It also explains all NCCL collective communication primitives. In Sect. 3, we discuss the design and implementation of collective communication monitoring. Section 4 shows the results on selected applications. Section 5 describes the related work. Section 6 presents our conclusions.

2   Background

In this section, we first introduce the previous work on point-to-point communication monitoring with COMSCRIBE. Then, we discuss the collective communication primitives supported by the NCCL.

2.1   Point-to-Point Communication Monitoring with ComScribe

COMSCRIBE was originally developed to identify P2P communication of host-device and device-device pairs for various data transfer types offered by CUDA APIs. It supports the monitoring of explicit data transfers such as cudaMemcpy as well as implicit data transfers such as Zero-Copy Memory and Unified Memory. It is implemented on top of NVIDIA's profiling tool *nvprof*, which can generate intra-node P2P communication information together with computation-related information in a machine readable format. Once the necessary profiling data is generated, COMSCRIBE extracts the relevant information and generates communication matrices.

Host-Device Communication. In CUDA programming, a memory transfer between a host and a device can be realized in two ways: explicit transfer and implicit transfer. An explicit transfer refers to the cudaMemcpy or cudaMemcpyAsync function in CUDA Runtime API where the programmer can explicitly specify the kind (Host-to-Device, Device-to-Host, or cudaMemcpyDe-fault) of the memory transfer. Implicit transfer types are Zero-Copy memory and Unified Memory. Zero-Copy memory paradigm allows a GPU to directly access host memory over PCIe or NVLink interconnect by pinning a memory region in host memory and mapping it to the GPU. A memory region allocated with Unified Memory via `cudaMallocManaged` is accessible from any processor (CPU or GPU) in the system. Page faults are handled by the page migration engine automatically.

Device-Device Communication. As in host-device communication, there are two types of a data transfer: explicit transfers and implicit trans-fers. In an explicit transfer, the programmer can use either `cudaMemcpy` or `cudaMemcpyPeer`. If peer access is disabled, the data will be copied to the host and then transferred to the destination device. In P2P communication, implicit transfer types are also Zero-Copy memory or Unified Memory. In Zero-Copy memory, devices with peer access capability can read and write to each oth-ers' memory through the data pointer. In Unified Memory, any memory region allocated with `cudaMallocManaged` can be accessed by the peer GPUs.

2.2 NCCL for GPU-Based Collective Communication

NCCL is NVIDIA's Collective Communications Library that provides efficient and topology-aware inter-GPU communication. It implements both collective and point-to-point communication primitives for intra-node and inter-node com-munication. NCCL has the ability to detect and utilize various interconnects such as PCIe, NVLINK, InfiniBand Verbs, and IP sockets. This feature elimi-nates the burden of optimizing applications for systems with different topology or interconnects.

Collective communication involves a data transfer between more than one GPU, unlike P2P communication where there is only one sender and receiver. In order to use a collective primitive on a group of GPUs (i.e. in a communicator), each GPU within the communicator is assigned a zero-based rank and each rank involved in a collective communication must call the same communication primitive function with compatible arguments. For example, they must be in the same communicator.

The need for efficient implementation of collective communication primitives comes from the fact that many parallel algorithms share data among a group of processors (i.e., communicator). Especially, the need for abundance of data in deep learning models require data to be distributed in many processors and share the gradients among processors, typically with an All-Reduce collective. Hence, deep learning frameworks such as PyTorch, Tensorflow and MxNet have already integrated NCCL into their frameworks to perform collective calls.

Before the advent of NCCL, collective primitives would be implemented through a combination of CUDA memory copy operations and CUDA kernels for local reductions. In NCCL, each collective is implemented in a single kernel that handles both communication and computation operations in order to speed up the synchronization and minimize the resources needed to reach peak bandwidth.

Collective Communication Primitives. NCCL provides five collective communication primitives: Broadcast, Reduce, ReduceScatter, AllGather, and AllReduce. Especially, AllReduce is frequently used in deep learning applications to share the local gradients among processors. NCCL's collective communication primitives are similar to MPI's collective communication primitives. The functionality of each collective primitive is described below:

- Broadcast: The Broadcast collective copies data buffer that resides in the root rank's memory to the all other ranks.
- Reduce: The Reduce collective performs a reduction operation on data (e.g. sum, max) aggregated from all ranks in a communicator and writes the result in the specified rank.
- ReduceScatter: The ReduceScatter collective performs the same operation as the Reduce operation, except the result is scattered in equal blocks among ranks, each rank getting a chunk of data based on its rank index.
- AllGather: In AllGather, each rank in the communicator aggregates N values from every rank into an output buffer. The output is ordered by rank index.
- AllReduce: The AllReduce collective is similar to the Reduce collective. The only functional difference is that the result of the reduction is written into each rank's receive buffer in the communicator instead of one rank. AllReduce is a rank agnostic operation, i.e. reordering of ranks does not affect the outcome since all ranks will have identical data at the end. This operation is functionally equivalent to a Reduce followed by a Broadcast.

Point-to-Point Primitives. P2P primitives (ncclSend, ncclRecv) were added to NCCL 2.7. These primitives allow users to express primitives that are not directly implemented in NCCL such as one-to-all (scatter), all-to-one (gather), and all-to-all communication operations.

3 Collective Communication Monitoring

In COMSCRIBE, design of collective communication monitoring is significantly different than P2P communication monitoring. COMSCRIBE leverages *nvprof* to capture P2P communication information to construct the communication matrices. However, this approach is not applicable to collective communication monitoring because *nvprof* does not provide any memory transfer information about NCCL collective primitives. NVIDIA's new profiling tool Nsight Systems could serve as an alternative approach for NCCL profiling but even though it can visualize the execution timeline of NCCL kernels, it does not provide any information on data transfers in a machine readable format. Moreover, the information provided by Nsight Systems is convoluted with the compute kernel information required for the collective primitives, which makes it hard for the programmer to distill the communication related activities.

Figure 1 illustrates the collective communication monitoring workflow added to COMSCRIBE. COMSCRIBE employs LD_PRELOAD utility to intercept NCCL

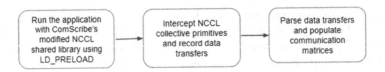

Fig. 1. Workflow diagram of COMSCRIBE

calls and records the data transfers of collective primitives. The main benefit of this approach is that it eliminates the need to change the source code of the binary being investigated by the user.

In order to use NCCL, the initialization step is to create a communicator and allocate a send buffer and a receive buffer for each device. Creation of the communicator involves generating a unique id for the communicator and assigning zero-based rank to each device in the communicator. After the initialization, the programmer can make multiple collective calls on the communicator. The same collective call must be performed by each rank in the communicator.

Internally, NCCL computes the data transfer channels and decides on which algorithm to be used based on the estimation of how long each algorithm would take for each collective call and enqueues the work to a queue. COMSCRIBE retrieves this data before the execution of the collective call on the devices. At the end of the execution, COMSCRIBE generates a single output file that contains the data transfers of each device in the communicator. Then, it parses these output files and generates communication matrices and other communication related statistics.

AllReduce. While NCCL implements Broadcast, Reduce, AllGather and ReduceScatter operations with only ring algorithm, it provides three algorithms for AllReduce: ring, tree and collnet. The algorithm used for is important for profiling because it affects the amount of communication among ranks. Table 1 shows the data movement induced by each algorithm.

Table 1. Number of bytes sent and received by a rank in the communicator for AllReduce operation. S is the size of the data, N is the number of ranks

Algorithm types	Intranode	Internode
Ring	$2 \times (N-1) \times S/N$	$2 \times (N-1) \times S/N$
Tree	root: S, others: $2 \times S$	root: S, others: $2 \times S$
Collnet	$2 \times S$	S

Ring is a high latency, bandwidth optimal algorithm, where each rank in the communicator sends data to the next rank and receives data from the previous rank. It offers maximum bandwidth by partitioning data into small chunks and pipelines them along the ring. For AllReduce, this setup leads to $2 \times (N-1)$

sends and receives with size S/N, where S is the size of the data to be reduced and N is the number of ranks in the communicator.

The tree algorithm was introduced in NCCL 2.4 to improve the scalability. It is a logarithmic latency algorithm which has a good performance on small and medium size operations [25]. It uses a double binary tree approach which pipelines a Reduce and a Broadcast to implement an AllReduce operation. Each rank in AllReduce primitive with tree algorithm sends and receives $2 \times S$ except the root, which is just S.

The collnet algorithm allows GPUs on multiple nodes to do in-network reductions by using SHARP plugin [17] for Mellanox switches. In-network reductions improve performance by eliminating the need to send data multiple times between endpoints.

4   Evaluation

We evaluate the results of our tool on two applications: a machine translation application, which uses Google's Neural Machine Translation model [29] and an image classification application, which employs a 18 layer Residual Neural Network (ResNet-18) model [9]. A DGX-2 system with 16 NVIDIA Tesla V100 GPUs is used for evaluation. CUDA 10.1 and NCCL 2.7.8 are used for the experiments. The overhead of COMSCRIBE for collective communication profiling is 1.4x on average. Since the prior work [1] already shows the P2P capabilities of COMSCRIBE, we mainly focus on collective communications in our evaluation.

4.1   Machine Translation Model

To demonstrate the capabilities of COMSCRIBE, we profile a data parallel Google's Neural Machine Translation (GNMT) model with an improved attention mechanism [20] on WMT16 English-German dataset [13]. Figure 2 shows the communication matrix of GNMT model for both P2P and collective communication combined in log scale. The communication matrix generated with COMSCRIBE is a $(d + 1) * (d + 1)$ matrix where d is the number of GPUs. X- and Y-axis indicate the GPU ids. (0,0) entry is reserved for the host. Other entries in the matrix show the number of bytes transferred between a CPU-GPU or GPU-GPU pairs.

Table 2 shows the number of calls made to each communication type and the amount of data movement for each type. An interesting observation from the table is that the implementation of the GNMT model performs explicit transfers more than any other transfer types. Since explicit data transfer time is composed of a fixed latency and a component that is proportional to the transfer size, small sized transfers are dominated by the fixed latency. An optimization could be to bundle these fine-grained messages into more coarse-grained transfers.

To better understand the usage of collective communication primitives, our tool can also produce matrices for each collective and P2P operation separately. The implementation of GNMT uses three collective primitives during the training of the machine translation model: AllReduce, Broadcast and AllGather.

Figure 3 shows that AllReduce operation is responsible for most of the collective communications. Hence, the time spent on optimizing AllReduce operation might have a good return on investment.

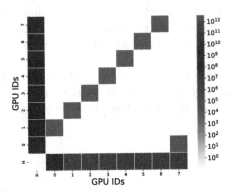

Fig. 2. Communication matrix of GNMT on 8 GPUs that shows the number of bytes transferred between CPU-GPU and GPU-GPU pairs for both P2P and collective communication. (0,0) is reserved for host.

Table 2. Communication primitive usage analysis of GNMT application.

Communication type	Number of calls	Total size (in Mbytes)
AllReduce	30739	3, 661, 704
Broadcast	5	612
AllGather	3	3
Explicit transfers	778694	15, 711
Unified memory	0	0
Zero copy memory	0	0

4.2 Image Classification Model

Convolutional Neural Networks (CNNs) are widely used to classify images as they are capable of extracting various features from the given set of training images and infer the class of unseen images. We use a distributed data-parallel PyTorch implementation of ResNet-18 model with NCCL backend [24] to classify images on a subset of ImageNet [6] dataset, which consists of 120000 images, where the size of each image is 64×64.

In a data-parallel training, the data is first distributed across GPUs in the system and each GPU runs the same model on mini-batches from its own local data. Once each GPU completes its forward and backward passes independently in an iteration, a gradient exchange among GPUs occur to aggregate the gradients of the weights. However, there are various optimizations [10, 16, 23] that can

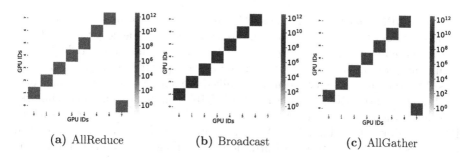

(a) AllReduce   (b) Broadcast   (c) AllGather

Fig. 3. Communication matrix for each collective that is used during the training of GNMT model. Number of bytes transferred with AllReduce on the left, Broadcast in the middle, and AllGather on the right in logarithmic scale

be implemented by library developers or the users of the libraries to complete the second step, which changes the collective communication frequency. For example, instead of launching AllReduce in every iteration to update gradients, the application can conduct a number of local training iterations before synchronizing gradients globally. Another optimization example that PyTorch implements is gradient bucketing [16], which increases throughput and decreases latency. Gradient bucketing method buckets multiple gradients into one `ncclAllReduce` call instead of sending each tensor separately.

COMSCRIBE can help users to understand the effect of gradient bucketing on data movement. Table 3 shows the number of calls to each NCCL primitive used during the training and the total size of the communication detected by COMSCRIBE. A naive implementation of the gradient exchange step would be calling AllReduce operation for each parameter as soon as the gradient is ready for that parameter. In this naive approach, the number of AllReduce calls in an epoch would be equal to DxN, where D is the number of parameters and N is the number of iterations, yet since PyTorch implements gradient bucketing, the number of calls to the AllReduce operation is less than the naive approach.

Table 3. Number of execution of each primitive, total size used in ResNet-18 trained on a subset of ImageNet dataset for one epoch

Collective operation	Number of calls	Total size (Bytes)
ncclAllReduce	1174	3.2×10^{10}
ncclBroadcast	789	6.1×10^{7}

5   Related Work

There are several tools that can trace memory transfers of host-device and device-device pairs with LD_PRELOAD utility (EZTrace [28], Extrae [4], and Score-P [12]). These tools can generate execution traces for various programming models including MPI, OpenMP, CUDA, and PThread. However, the profiling support for CUDA memory transfer functions is limited with explicit memory transfer types (i.e. *cudaMalloc* and *cudaMemcpy*) and NCCL tracing is not supported by any of them. Our tool can detect collective communication primitives of NCCL and various P2P communication types such as Unified Memory and Zero-Copy memory.

Tartan, multi-GPU benchmark suite [14,15], consists of micro-benchmarks and applications to evaluate the performance of modern interconnects such as PCIe, NVLink 1.0, NVLink 2.0, NV-SLI, NVSwitch and Infiniband systems with GPUDirect RDMA in scale-up (intra-node) and scale-out (inter-node) scenarios. Even though Tartan assesses interconnect performance in terms of latency, bandwidth, and efficiency on message size for P2P and collective communications, it is not a tool that can be used to monitor and detect communications of an application.

Nsight Systems is NVIDIA's visualization tool that aims to help users to identify potential optimizations for their applications. It can provide a timeline of the executed functions and data transfer information for CUDA memory operations. With 2020.5 and 2021.2 releases, NCCL support was added for timeline visualization but currently it does not show the underlying communication among GPUs. Our tool can log communication among GPUs for collective NCCL calls in a machine readable format whereas to our knowledge Nsight Systems command line interface can only show the time it takes to run a single collective call at the moment.

Scope [22] is a benchmark framework which consists of various benchmark suites such as Comm|Scope, NCCL|Scope and many others. Comm|Scope is a NUMA-Aware multi-CPU multi-GPU benchmark suite that measures point-to-point transfer latency and bandwidth within a single node for different data transfer scenarios with CUDA P2P communication types such as Unified Memory and Zero-copy Memory. NCCL|Scope consists of micro-benchmarks to measure the bandwidth of all five NCCL primitives with *cudaEvent*. Even though our work and Scope have features in common such as the categorization of communication types, our work supports the recording of communication for any application.

There are number of tools to generate communication patterns for multi-core applications. ComDetective [26] detects inter-thread data transfers by using debug registers and Performance Monitoring Units for multi-threaded applications. Similar to ComDetective, Azimi et al. [2] and Tam et al. [27] use kernel support to access PMUs and the kernel generates the communication pattern for the applications. Simulator-based approaches to collect memory access traces for generating communication patterns include Barrow-Williams et al. [3] and Cruz et al. [5]. Numalize [7,8] uses binary instrumentation to intercept memory accesses and captures communication between threads accessing the same address in memory. None of the aforementioned tools, however, have support for multi-GPU communication.

6   Conclusion

The communication among GPUs is a critical performance and scalability contributor in multi-GPU systems. COMSCRIBE, our prior work, identifies and analyzes implicit and explicit P2P communication types. This work extends COMSCRIBE to support collective communication profiling for GPUs sharing a common host. To implement the collective communication support in COMSCRIBE we take advantage of LD_PRELOAD utility to identify and extract the communication among GPUs in a communicator. We evaluated our tool against two deep learning applications. Our tool can provide insights to study the communication patterns of collective operations.

Acknowledgement. The work is supported by the Scientific and Technological Research Council of Turkey (TUBITAK), Grant no. 120E492. Dr. Didem Unat is supported by the Royal Society-Newton Advanced Fellowship.

References

1. Akhtar, P., Tezcan, E., Qararyah, F.M., Unat, D.: ComScribe: identifying intranode GPU communication. In: Wolf, F., Gao, W. (eds.) Bench 2020. LNCS, vol. 12614, pp. 157–174. Springer, Cham (2021). https://doi.org/10.1007/978-3-030-71058-3_10
2. Azimi, R., Tam, D.K., Soares, L., Stumm, M.: Enhancing operating system support for multicore processors by using hardware performance monitoring. ACM SIGOPS Oper. Syst. Rev. **43**(2), 56–65 (2009)
3. Barrow-Williams, N., Fensch, C., Moore, S.: A communication characterisation of splash-2 and parsec. In: 2009 IEEE International Symposium on Workload Characterization (IISWC), pp. 86–97. IEEE (2009)
4. BSC-Performance-Tools: Extrae. https://tools.bsc.es/extrae. Accessed 19 Sept 2021
5. da Cruz, E.H.M., Alves, M.A.Z., Carissimi, A., Navaux, P.O.A., Ribeiro, C.P., Méhaut, J.F.: Using memory access traces to map threads and data on hierarchical multi-core platforms. In: 2011 IEEE International Symposium on Parallel and Distributed Processing Workshops and Ph.D. Forum, pp. 551–558. IEEE (2011)
6. Deng, J., Dong, W., Socher, R., Li, L.J., Li, K., Fei-Fei, L.: ImageNet: a large-scale hierarchical image database. In: 2009 IEEE Conference on Computer Vision and Pattern Recognition, pp. 248–255 (2009)
7. Diener, M., Cruz, E.H., Alves, M.A., Navaux, P.O.: Communication in shared memory: concepts, definitions, and efficient detection. In: 2016 24th Euromicro International Conference on Parallel, Distributed, and Network-Based Processing (PDP), pp. 151–158. IEEE (2016)
8. Diener, M., Cruz, E.H., Pilla, L.L., Dupros, F., Navaux, P.O.: Characterizing communication and page usage of parallel applications for thread and data mapping. Perform. Eval. **88**, 18–36 (2015)
9. He, K., Zhang, X., Ren, S., Sun, J.: Deep residual learning for image recognition. In: 2016 IEEE Conference on Computer Vision and Pattern Recognition (CVPR), pp. 770–778 (2016). https://doi.org/10.1109/CVPR.2016.90
10. Hermans, J., Spanakis, G., Moeckel, R.: Accumulated gradient normalization. arXiv abs/1710.02368 (2017)
11. Kahira, A.N., Nguyen, T.T., Bautista-Gomez, L., Takano, R., Badia, R.M., Wahib, M.: An oracle for guiding large-scale model/hybrid parallel training of convolutional neural networks. CoRR (2021)

12. Knüpfer, A., et al.: Score-P: a joint performance measurement run-time infrastructure for Periscope, Scalasca, TAU, and Vampir. In: Brunst, H., Müller, M., Nagel, W., Resch, M. (eds.) Tools for High Performance Computing 2011, pp. 79–91. Springer, Heidelberg (2012). https://doi.org/10.1007/978-3-642-31476-6_7

13. Koehn, P.: Europarl: a parallel corpus for statistical machine translation. In: MT Summit, vol. 5, pp. 79–86. Citeseer (2005)

14. Li, A., et al.: Evaluating modern GPU interconnect: PCIe, NVLink, NV-SLI, NVSwitch and GPUDirect. IEEE Trans. Parallel Distrib. Syst. **31**(1), 94–110 (2020)

15. Li, A., Song, S.L., Chen, J., Liu, X., Tallent, N., Barker, K.: Tartan: evaluating modern GPU interconnect via a multi-GPU benchmark suite. In: 2018 IEEE International Symposium on Workload Characterization (IISWC), pp. 191–202 (2018)

16. Li, S., et al.: Pytorch distributed: experiences on accelerating data parallel training (2020)

17. Mellanox: Nvidia® mellanox® scalable hierarchical aggregation and reduction protocol (sharp) (2020). https://docs.mellanox.com/display/sharpv214. Accessed 19 May 2021

18. NVIDIA: CUDA profiler user's guide, July 2020. https://docs.nvidia.com/cuda/pdf/CUDA_Profiler_Users_Guide.pdf. Accessed 18 May 2021

19. NVIDIA: Nvidia nsight systems documentation (2020). https://docs.nvidia.com/nsight-systems/index.html. Accessed 18 May 2021

20. NVIDIA: Deep learning examples (2021). https://github.com/NVIDIA/DeepLearningExamples. Accessed 18 May 2021

21. NVIDIA: Nvidia collective communication library, May 2021. https://developer.nvidia.com/nccl. Accessed 17 May 2021

22. Pearson, C., et al.: Evaluating characteristics of CUDA communication primitives on high-bandwidth interconnects. In: Proceedings of the 2019 ACM/SPEC International Conference on Performance Engineering, pp. 209–218 (2019)

23. PyTorch: Distributed data parallel. https://pytorch.org/docs/stable/notes/ddp.html. Accessed 25 May 2021

24. PyTorch: Examples. https://github.com/PyTorch/examples. Accessed 19 May 2021

25. Sanders, P., Speck, J., Träff, J.L.: Two-tree algorithms for full bandwidth broadcast, reduction and scan. Parallel Comput. **35**(12), 581–594 (2009)

26. Sasongko, M.A., Chabbi, M., Akhtar, P., Unat, D.: ComDetective: a lightweight communication detection tool for threads. In: Proceedings of the International Conference for High Performance Computing, Networking, Storage and Analysis, pp. 1–21 (2019)

27. Tam, D., Azimi, R., Stumm, M.: Thread clustering: sharing-aware scheduling on SMP-CMP-SMT multiprocessors. ACM SIGOPS Oper. Syst. Rev. **41**(3), 47–58 (2007)

28. Trahay, F., Rue, F., Faverge, M., Ishikawa, Y., Namyst, R., Dongarra, J.: EZTrace: a generic framework for performance analysis. In: 11th IEEE/ACM International Symposium on Cluster, Cloud and Grid Computing, pp. 618–619. IEEE (2011)

29. Wu, Y., et al.: Google's neural machine translation system: bridging the gap between human and machine translation. CoRR abs/1609.08144 (2016). http://arxiv.org/abs/1609.08144

HeteroPar – Workshop on Algorithms, Models and Tools for Parallel Computing on Heterogeneous Platforms

Workshop on Algorithms, Models and Tools for Parallel Computing on Heterogeneous Platforms (HeteroPar)

Workshop Description

HeteroPar is a forum for researchers working on algorithms, programming languages, tools, and theoretical models for efficiently solving complex problems on heterogeneous parallel platforms. Heterogeneity is emerging as one of the most profound and challenging characteristics of today's parallel environments. From the macro level, where heterogeneous networks interconnect distributed computers of diverse architectures, to the micro level, whereever deeper memory hierarchies and specialized accelerator architectures are increasingly common, the impact of heterogeneity on parallel processing is rapidly increasing. Traditional parallel algorithms, programming environments and tools designed for legacy homogeneous multiprocessors will at best achieve a small fraction of the efficiency and the performance expected from tomorrow's highly diverse parallel computing architectures. Therefore, efficiently using these new and multifarious parallel architectures require innovative ideas, new models, novel algorithms, and other specialized or unified programming environments and tools.

The 19th International Workshop on Algorithms, Models and Tools for Parallel Computing on Heterogeneous Platforms (HeteroPar 2021) took place (virtually in Lisbon, Portugal, organized for the 13th time in conjunction with the Euro-Par annual international conference. The format of the workshop included one keynote and 12 technical presentations. The workshop received good attendance of around 25 people on average throughout the day. This year, the workshop received 22 paper submissions from 14 countries. After a thorough peer-reviewing process that included discussion and agreement among reviewers whenever necessary, the program chair selected 12 papers for presentation at the workshop. The review process focused on the quality of the papers, their innovation, and applicability to heterogeneous architectures. The quality and the relevance of the selected papers is high.

The accepted papers represent an interesting mix of topics, addressing the implementation of algorithms and kernels for heterogeneous computing, programming models, data management, runtime and resource management, energy efficiency, cloud computing, and artificial intelligence-based methods oriented towards heterogeneous platforms, as the basis for the next generation exascale computers. The program chair thanks all authors, the Program Committee, and the Steering Committee for their support in making the workshop a successful event. Special thanks are due to the Euro-Par organizers for hosting the HeteroPar community, and especially to the workshop chairs Dora Blanco Heras and Ricardo Chaves for their help and support.

Organization

Steering Committee

Alexey Kalinov   Cadence Design Systems, Russia
Alexey Lastovetsky   University College Dublin, Ireland
Yves Robert   Ecole Normale Supérieure de Lyon, France
Leonel Sousa   INESC-ID/IST, Technical University of Lisbon, Portugal
Denis Trystram   University Grenoble-Alpes, France

Program Chair

Rosa M. Badia   Barcelona Supercomputing Center, Spain

Program Committee

Hartwig Anzt   Karlsruhe Institute of Technology (KIT), Germany
Michael Bader   TU München, Germany
Jorge Barbosa   Faculdade de Engenharia do Porto, Portugal
George Bosilca   University of Tennesse, USA
Sunita Chandrasekaran   University of Delaware, USA
Jorge Ejarque   Barcelona Supercomputing Center, Spain
Toshio Endo   Tokyo Institute of Technology, Japan
Edgar Gabriel   University of Houston, USA
Aleksandar Ilic   University of Lisbon, Portugal
Emmanuel Jeannot   Inria, France
Helen Karatza   Aristotle University of Thessaloniki, Greece
Joanna Kolodziej   NASK, Warsaw, Poland
Hatem Ltaief   KAUST, Saudi Arabia
Maciej Malawski   AGH University of the Science and Technology, Poland
Ravi Reddy Manumachu   University College Dublin, Ireland
Xavier Martorell   Universitat Politècnica de Catalunya and Barcelona Supercomputing Center, Spain
Hiroki Matsutani   Keio University, Japan
Rafael Mayo   Universidad Jaume I, Spain

Porting Sparse Linear Algebra to Intel GPUs

Yuhsiang M. Tsai[1]([envelope]) [iD], Terry Cojean[1] [iD], and Hartwig Anzt[1,2] [iD]

[1] Karlsruhe Institute of Technology, 76131 Karlsruhe, Germany
{yu-hsiang.tsai,terry.cojean,hartwig.anzt}@kit.edu
[2] University of Tennessee, Knoxville, TN 37996, USA

Abstract. With discrete Intel GPUs entering the high performance computing landscape, there is an urgent need for production-ready software stacks for these platforms. In this paper, we report how we prepare the Ginkgo math library for Intel GPUs by developing a kernel backed based on the DPC++ programming environment. We discuss conceptual differences to the CUDA and HIP programming models and describe workflows for simplified code conversion. We benchmark advanced sparse linear algebra routines utilizing the converted kernels to assess the efficiency of the DPC++ backend in the hardware-specific performance bounds. We compare the performance of basic building blocks against routines providing the same functionality that ship with Intel's oneMKL vendor library.

Keywords: oneAPI · Intel GPUs · Ginkgo · Math library · SpMV

1 Introduction

In the past, Intel GPUs were primarily available as an integrated component of Intel consumer-grade CPU architectures. With the announcement that the Aurora Supercomputer will be composed of general purpose Intel CPUs complemented by discrete Intel GPUs, it becomes clear that Intel has committed to enter the arena of discrete high performance GPUs. Compared to integrated GPUs, discrete GPUs are usually not exclusively intended to accelerate graphics, but they are designed to also deliver computational power that can be used, e.g., for scientific computations. To enable the programmers to use Intel GPUs, Intel has teamed up with partners from academia and industry to create the oneAPI ecosystem, a platform for C++ developers to develop code in the DPC++ language, based on the SYCL language, that can be executed on any Intel device, including CPUs, GPUs, and FPGAs. As application scientists are in need of high performance math functionality for Intel GPUs, we develop a DPC++ backend for the GINKGO open source math library that enables to run both basic linear algebra building blocks and complex algorithms like iterative Krylov solvers on Intel's GPUs. Up to our knowledge, we are the first to present the functionality and performance of an open source math library on Intel discrete GPUs.

© Springer Nature Switzerland AG 2022
R. Chaves et al. (Eds.): Euro-Par 2021, LNCS 13098, pp. 57–68, 2022.
https://doi.org/10.1007/978-3-031-06156-1_5

In this paper, we describe the process of preparing Ginkgo for Intel's GPUs by first providing an overview of the Ginkgo library design in Sect. 2 and introducing the oneAPI ecosystem and the DPC++ programming model in Sect. 3. The core of the paper is Sect. 4, where we discuss some differences between the CUDA/HIP programming environment and the oneAPI environment, detail how we reflect these particularities in the development of the DPC++ backend, and report how we developed a small framework for converting CUDA kernel code to DPC++ equivalents. In Sect. 5, we evaluate the performance of GINKGO on different Intel GPU generations: we initially benchmark both the Intel generation 9 and 12 GPUs in terms of feasible bandwidth and peak performance to derive a roofline model, then evaluate the performance of GINKGO's SpMV kernels (also in comparison to Intel's oneMKL library), and finally assess the performance of GINKGO's Krylov solvers. We conclude with a summary of the porting effort and performance evaluation in Sect. 6.

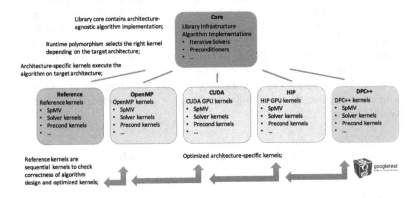

Fig. 1. The GINKGO library design overview.

2 Ginkgo Design

GINKGO [1] is a GPU-focused cross-platform math library focusing on sparse linear algebra. The library design is guided by combining ecosystem extensibility with heavy, architecture-specific kernel optimization using the platform-native languages CUDA (NVIDIA GPUs), HIP (AMD GPUs), or OpenMP (Intel/AMD/ARM multicore) [2]. The software development cycle ensures production-quality code by featuring unit testing, automated configuration and installation, Doxygen code documentation, as well as continuous integration and continuous benchmarking framework. GINKGO provides a comprehensive set of sparse BLAS operations, iterative solvers including many Krylov methods, standard and advanced preconditioning techniques, and cutting-edge mixed precision methods.

A high-level overview of GINKGO's software architecture is visualized in Fig. 1. The library design collects all classes and generic algorithm skeletons in the "core" library which, however, is useless without the driver kernels available in the "omp", "cuda", "hip", and "reference" backends. We note that "reference" contains sequential CPU kernels used to validate the correctness of the algorithms and as the reference implementation for the unit tests realized using the googletest framework. We note that the "cuda" and "hip" backends are very similar in kernel design, so we have "shared" kernels that are identical for the NVIDIA and AMD GPUs up to kernel configuration parameters [6]. Extending GINKGO's scope to support Intel GPUs via the DPC++ language, we add the "dpcpp" backend containing corresponding kernels in DPC++.

3   The oneAPI Programming Ecosystem

oneAPI[1] is an open and free programming ecosystem that aims at providing portability across a wide range of hardware platforms from different architecture generations and vendors. The oneAPI software stack is structured with the new DPC++ programming language at its core, accompanied by several libraries to ease parallel application programming.

DPC++ is a community-driven (open-source) language based on the ISO C++ and Khronos' SYCL standards. The concept of DPC++ is to enhance the SYCL [4] ecosystem with several additions that aim at improving the performance on modern hardware, improving usability, and simplifying the porting of classical CUDA code to the DPC++ language. Two relevant features originally introduced by the DPC++ ecosystem now also integrated into the SYCL standard are[2]: 1) a new subgroup concept that can be used inside kernels. This concept is equivalent to CUDA warps (or SIMD on CPUs) and allows optimized routines such as subgroup-based shuffles. In the GINKGO library, we make extensive use of this capability to boost performance. 2) a new Unified Shared Memory (USM) model which provides new `malloc_host` and `malloc_device` operations to allocate memory which can either be accessed both by host or device or respectively accessed by a device only. Additionally, the new SYCL `queue` extensions facilitates the porting of CUDA code as well as memory control. Indeed, in pure SYCL, memory copies are entirely asynchronous and hidden from the user, since the SYCL programming model is based on tasking with automatic discovery of task dependencies.

Another important aspect of oneAPI and DPC++ is that they adopt platform portability as the central design concept. Already the fact that DPC++ is based on SYCL (which leverages the OpenCL's runtime and SPIRV's intermediate kernel representation) provides portability to a variety of hardware. On top of this, DPC++ develops a plugin API that allows to develop new backends and switch dynamically between them[3]. Currently, DPC++ supports the standard OpenCL backend, a new Level Zero backend which is the backend of

---

[1] https://spec.oneApi.com/versions/latest/index.html.

[2] These extensions are now part of the SYCL 2020 Specification: https://www.khronos.org/news/press/khronos-releases-sycl-2020-final-specification.

[3] https://intel.github.io/llvm-docs/PluginInterface.html.

choice for Intel hardware[4], and an experimental CUDA backend for targeting CUDA-enabled GPUs. As our goal is to provide high performance sparse linear algebra functionality on Intel GPUs, we focus on the Intel Level Zero backend of DPC++.

4 Porting to the DPC++ Ecosystem

Though porting GINKGO to a new hardware ecosystem requires acknowledging the hardware-specific characteristics, the GINKGO design exposed in Sect. 2 induces a general porting workflow: 1) As a first step, core library infrastructure needs to be ported manually. This includes the GINKGO Executor which allows transparent and automatic memory management as well as the execution of kernels on different devices. Another example of manual porting in this preparatory step is the cooperative group and other shared kernel helper interfaces used for writing portable kernels and simplify advanced operations. 2) A set of scripts can be used to generate non-working definitions of all kernels for the new backend. The completion of this step creates a compilable backend for the new hardware ecosystem. 3) For an initial kernel implementation, we rely whenever possible on existing tools to facilitate the automatic porting of kernel implementations from one language to the target language, doing only manual fixes when appropriate. The successful completion of this step provides a working backend. 4) Finally, we analyze and validate the observed performance for the ported kernels. Often, simple kernels already provide competitive performance, but advanced kernels require either manual tuning or algorithmic adaptation to reach the hardware limits.

In this section, we concentrate on step 3) of this workflow and parts of step 1). These steps which we detail now are the more library agnostic aspect of the porting workflow and our lessons learned can be of practical use to other libraries. In addition, step 4) is a more complex effort and some portions of the library have been tuned, such as the GINKGO SpMV kernels, and their performance will be showcased in Sect. 5. To facilitate the porting in step 3), we can rely on the Intel "DPC++ Compatibility Tool" (DPCT), which converts CUDA code into compilable DPC++ code. DPCT is not expected to automatically generate a DPC++ "production-ready" executable code, but "ready-to-compilation" and it requires the developer's attention and effort in fixing conversion issues and tuning it to reach performance goals. However, with oneAPI still being in its early stages, DPCT still has some flaws and failures, and we develop a customized porting workflow using the DPC++ Compatibility Tool at its core, but embedding it into a framework that weakens some DPCT prerequisites and prevents incorrect code conversion. In general, DPCT requires not only knowledge of the functionality of a to-be-converted kernel, but also knowledge of the complete library and its design. This requirement is hard to fulfill in practice, as for complex libraries, the dependency analysis may exceed the DPCT capabilities. Additionally, many libraries do not aim at converting all code to DPC++, but

---

[4] https://spec.oneApi.com/level-zero/latest/core/INTRO.html.

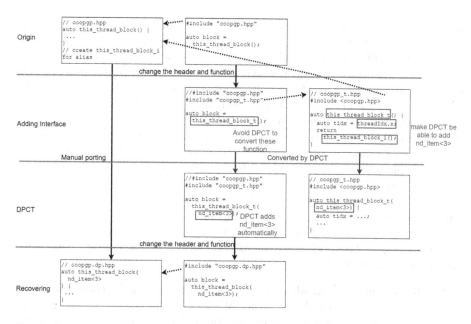

Fig. 2. Summary of the workflow used to port the cooperative groups functionality and isolating effort such that we get the correct converted DPC++ codes.

only a subset to enable the dedicated execution of specific kernels on DPC++-enabled accelerators. Thus, we employ a strategy where we first isolate kernels we want to convert and then re-integrate them into the library.

Isolated Kernel Modification. DPCT converts all files related to the target file containing any CUDA code that are in the target (sub)folders. To prevent DPCT from converting files that we do not want to be converted, we have to artificially restrict the conversion to the target files. We achieve this by copying the target files into a temporary folder and considering the rest of the GINKGO software as a system library. After the successful conversion of the target file, we copy the file back to the correct destination in the new DPC++ submodule. By isolating the target files, we indeed avoid additional changes and unexpected errors, but we also lose the DPCT ability to transform CUDA kernel indexing into the DPC++ nd_item<3> equivalent. As a workaround, we copy simple headers to the working directory containing the thread_id computation helper functions of the CUDA code such that DPCT can recognize them and transform them into the DPC++ equivalent. For those complicated kernels, DPCT fails in the kernel conversion, and we need a fake interface that enables DPCT to apply the code conversion for nd_item<3>.

Fake Interface - Workaround for Cooperative Groups. While DPC++ provides a subgroup interface featuring shuffle operations, this interface is different from CUDA's cooperative group design as it requires the subgroup size as a function attribute and does not allow for different subgroup sizes in the same global group. As GINKGO implementations aim at executing close to the hardware-induced limits, we make heavy use of cooperative group operations. Based on the DPC++ subgroup interface, we implement our own DPC++ cooperative group interface. Specifically, to remove the need for an additional function attribute, we add the `item_ct1` function argument into the group constructor. As the remaining function arguments are identical to the CUDA cooperative group function arguments, we therewith achieve a high level of interface similarity. This workflow resolves the porting not only for the cooperative group functionality but also other custom kernels replacing the automated DPCPP conversion.

A notable difference to CUDA is that DPC++ does not support subgroup vote functions like "ballot", or other group mask operations yet. To emulate this functionality, we need to use a subgroup reduction provided by oneAPI to emulate these vote functions in a subgroup setting. This lack of native support may affect the performance of kernels relying on these subgroup operations. We visualize in Fig. 2 the workflow we use to port code making use of the cooperative group functionality via four steps:

1. Origin: We prepare an alias to the cooperative group function such that DPCT does not catch the keyword. We create this alias in a fake cooperative group header we only use during the porting process.
2. Adding Interface: As explained previously, we isolate the files to prevent DPCT from changing other files. We also add the simple interface including `threadIdx.x` and make use of the alias function. For the conversion to succeed, it is required to return the same type as the original CUDA type, which we need to extract from the CUDA cooperative group function `this_thread_block`.
3. DPCT: Apply DPCT on the previously prepared files. Adding `threadIdx.x` indexing to the function allows DPCT to generate the `nd_item<3>` indexing.
4. Recovering: During this step, we change the related cooperative group functions and headers to the actual DPC++ equivalent. We implement a complete header file that ports all the cooperative group functionality to DPC++.

In Fig. 3, the final result of the porting workflow on a toy example with cooperative groups. For the small example code in Fig. 3a, if we do not isolate the code, DPCT will throw an error like Fig. 3b once encountering the cooperative group keyword. A manual implementation of the cooperative group equivalent kernel is shown in Fig. 3c. Our porting workflow generates the code shown in Fig. 3d, which is almost identical to the original CUDA code Fig. 3a.

Pushing for Backend Similarity. To simplify the maintenance of the platform-portable GINKGO library, our customized porting workflow uses some abstraction to make the DPC++ code in this first version look more similar to CUDA/HIP code. We note that this design choice is reflecting that GINKGO was originally designed as a GPU-centric sparse linear algebra library using the CUDA programming language and CUDA design patterns for implementing GPU kernels and that the developers of GINKGO are currently used to designing GPU kernels in CUDA. However, this may not be preferred by developers

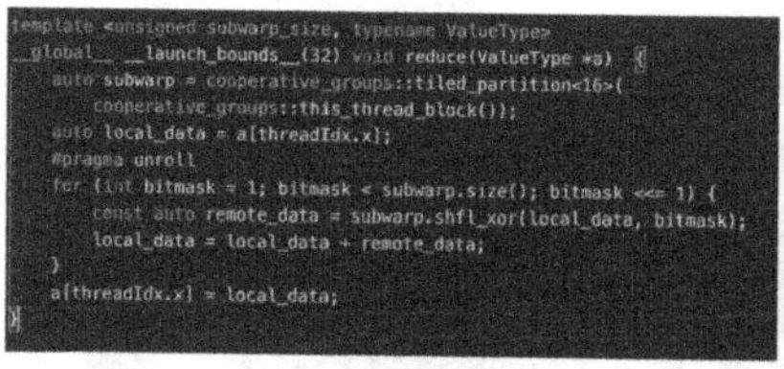

(a) CUDA cooperative group example

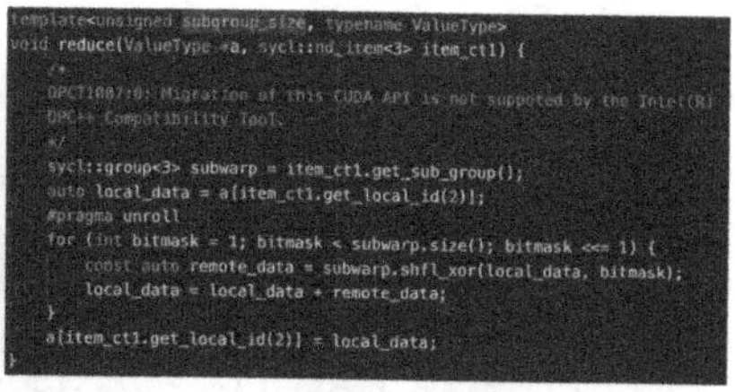

(b) DPCT conversion reports an error

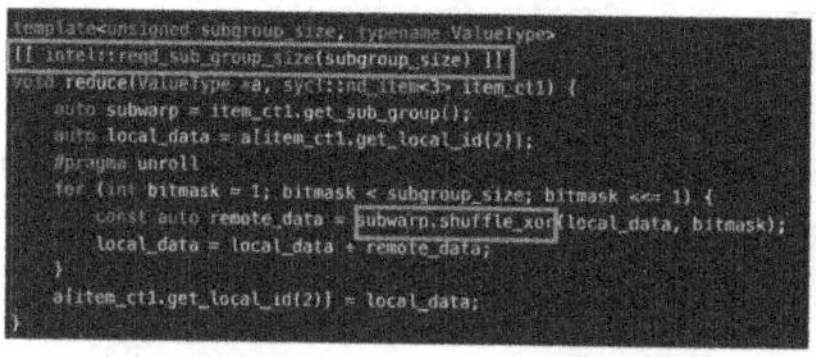

(c) Manual DPC++ subgroup implementation. The main difference from CUDA are in orange

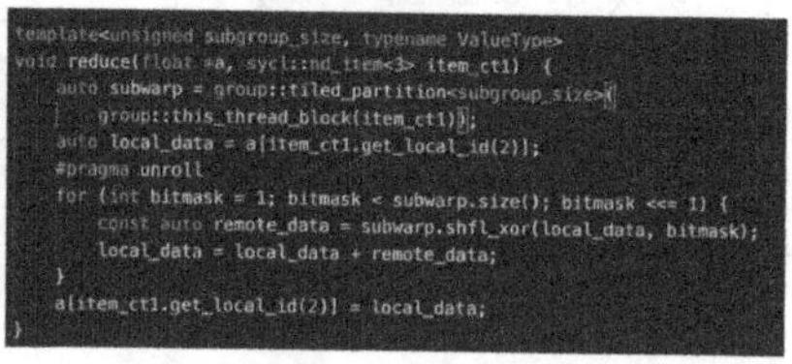

(d) The result converted by our porting script

Fig. 3. The cooperative group example

used to programming in task-based languages, and it may also narrow down the tasking power of the SYCL language. We may thus decide at a later point to move closer to the SYCL programming style, which is possible given GINKGO'S strict decoupling between algorithms and hardware backends. For now, we aim for a high level of code similarity by not only adding the customized cooperative group interface previously discussed, but also adding a dim3 implementation layer for DPC++ kernel launches that uses the same parameters and parameter order as CUDA and HIP. We simply reverse the dim3 in the interface layer.

One fundamental difference remaining between the CUDA or HIP ecosystems and DPC++ is that the latter handles the static and dynamic memory allocation in the main component. CUDA and HIP handle the allocation of static shared memory inside the kernel and the allocation of dynamic shared memory in the kernel launch parameters. Another difference is the kernel invocation syntax since DPC++ relies on a hierarchy of calls first to a queue, then a parallel instantiation. For consistency, we add another layer that abstracts the combination of DPC++ memory allocation and DPC++ kernel invocation away from the user. This enables a similar interface for CUDA, HIP, and DPC++ kernels for the main component, and shared memory allocations can be perceived as a kernel feature, see Fig. 4. In Fig. 4, the right purple block (additional_layer_call) has the same structure as the left gray block (cuda_kernel_call). The enhanced porting script not only handles the kernel conversion but also the addition of the intermediate layer.

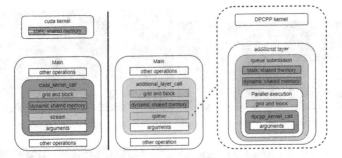

Fig. 4. Hierarchical view of usual CUDA (left) and DPC++ (right) kernel call and parameters. Wrapping the hardware-specific kernels into an intermediate layer enables consistency in the kernel invocation across all backends.

5   Performance Assessment of Ginkgo's DPC++ Backend

Experiment Setup. In this paper, we consider two Intel GPUs: the generation 9 (GEN9) integrated GPU UHD Graphics P630 with a theoretical bandwidth of 41.6 GB/s and the generation 12 Intel® Iris® Xe Max discrete GPU (GEN12)[5] which features 96 execution units and a theoretical bandwidth of 68 GB/s. To better assess the performance of either GPUs, we include in our analysis the performance we can achieve in bandwidth tests, performance tests, and sparse linear algebra kernels. We note that the GEN12 architecture lacks native support for IEEE 754 double precision arithmetic, and can only emulate double precision arithmetic with significantly lower performance. Given that native support for double precision arithmetic is expected for future Intel GPUs and using the double precision emulation would artificially degrade the performance results while not providing insight whether GINKGO'S algorithms are suitable for Intel GPUs, we use single precision arithmetic in all performance evaluation on the GEN12 architecture[6]. The DPC++ version we use in all experiments is Intel oneAPI DPC++ Compiler 2021.1 (2020.10.0.1113). All experiments were conducted on hardware that is part of the Intel DevCloud.

Bandwidth Tests and Experimental Performance Roofline. Initially, we evaluate the two GPUs in terms of architecture-specific performance bounds. For that purpose, we use the BabelStream [3] benchmark to evaluate the peak bandwidth, and the mixbench [5] benchmark to evaluate the arithmetic performance. In the upper part of Fig. 5, we visualize the bandwidth we achieve for different memory-intense operations. On both architectures, the DOT kernel requiring a global synchronization achieves lower bandwidth than the other kernels. We furthermore note that the GEN12 architecture achieves for large array

---

[5] https://ark.intel.com/content/www/us/en/ark/products/211013/intel-iris-xe-max-graphics-96-eu.html.

[6] GINKGO is designed to compile for IEEE 754 double precision, single precision, double precision complex, and single precision complex arithmetic.

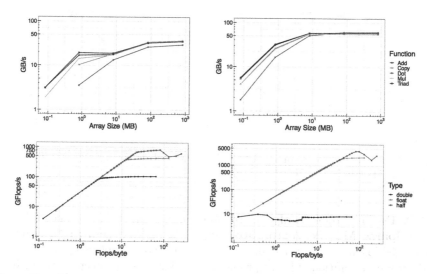

Fig. 5. Top: Bandwidth analysis on the Intel GEN9 (left) and the GEN12 (right) GPUs using double and single precision values, respectively. Bottom: Experimental performance roofline for the GEN9 (left) and GEN12 (right) GPUs.

sizes about 58 GB/s and the GEN9 achieves 37 GB/s. The experimental roofline visualized in the lower part of Fig. 5 reveals that the GEN9 architecture achieves about 105 GFLOP/s, 430 GFLOP/s, and 810 GFLOP/s for IEEE double precision, single precision, and half precision arithmetic, respectively. The GEN12 architecture does not provide native support for IEEE double precision, and the double precision emulation achieves only 8 GFLOP/s. On the other hand, the GEN12 architecture achieves 2.2 TFLOP/s and 4.0 TFLOP/s for single precision and half precision floating point operations.

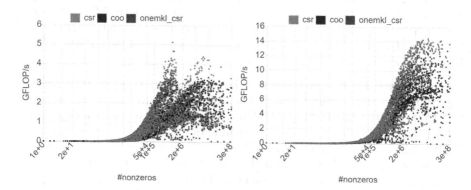

Fig. 6. SPMV kernel performance for GINKGO and Intel's oneMKL library on GEN9 (left) and GEN12 (right) using double and single precision, respectively.

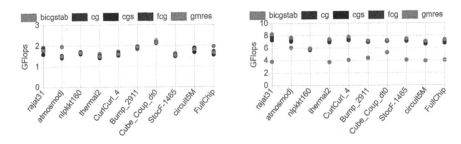

Fig. 7. Performance evaluation of GINKGO'S Krylov solvers on Intel's GEN9 (left) and GEN12 (right) GPUs.

SpMV Performance Analysis. An important routine in sparse linear algebra is the **Sparse Matrix Vector product** (SPMV). This kernel reflects how a discretized linear operator acts on a vector, and therewith plays the central role in the iterative solution of linear problems and eigenvalue problems. We consider two sparse matrix formats: 1) the "COOrdinate format" (COO) that stores all nonzero entries of the matrix along with their column- and row-indices, and the "Compressed Sparse Row" (CSR) format that further reduces the memory footprint of the COO format by replacing the row-indices with pointers to the first element in each row of a row-sorted COO matrix. We focus on these popular matrix formats not only because of their widespread use, but also because Intel's oneMKL library provides an optimized CSR-SPMV routine for Intel GPUs.

In Fig. 6, we visualize the performance of the CSR and COO SPMV kernels of the GINKGO library along with the performance of the CSR SPMV kernel from the oneAPI library. Each dot represents the performance achieved for one of the test matrices of the Suite Sparse Matrix Collection. GINKGO'S CSR reaches up to 4 GFlop/s for several problems using double precision arithmetic, oneMKL CSR up to 3 GFlop/s similarly to GINKGO'S COO format. For GEN12, GINKGO'S CSR reaches up to 14 GFlop/s, oneMKL 13 GFlop/s and GINKGO'S COO 10 GFlop/s. These results highlight that GINKGO'S formats CSR and COO are at least competitive with the oneMKL CSR on both GEN9 and GEN12[7]. The achieved performance in terms of percentage of peak bandwidth are exposed in Fig. 8.

Krylov Solver Performance Analysis. We now turn to advanced numerical algorithms typical to scientific simulation codes. The Krylov solvers we consider – CG, BiCGSTAB, CGS, FCG, and GMRES – are all iterative methods popular for solving large sparse linear systems. They all have the SPMV kernel as the central building block, and we use GINKGO'S COO SPMV kernel and test matrices from the Suite Sparse Matrix Collection that are orthogonal in their characteristics and origin. We run the solver experiment for 1,000 solver iterations after a warm-up phase. In Fig. 7, we visualize the performance of the Krylov solvers on the

---

[7] At the point of writing, oneMKL does not provide a COO implementation and CSR can only operate on shared memory on the GEN12 architecture.

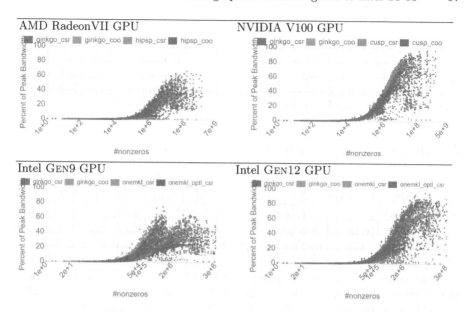

Fig. 8. SpMV performance relative to the hardware bounds on various GPUs.

GEN9 architecture (left) and GEN12 architecture (right). On the GEN9, the performance varies between 1.5 GFLOP/s and 2.5 GFLOP/s. We notice that the performance differences in-between the solvers are quite small compared to the performance differences for the distinct problems. Running GINKGO's Krylov solvers in single precision on the GEN12 architecture, we achieve between 5 GFLOP/s and 9 GFLOP/s for the distinct systems. We note that all Krylov solvers based on short recurrences (BiCGSTAB, CG, CGS, FCG) are very similar in terms of performance, while GMRES usually achieves lower performance. This highlights that the kernels of GMRES require specific tuning.

Platform Portability. Finally, we evaluate the hardware efficiency of the GINKGO DPC++ backend compared to the other backends. For that, we focus on the relative performance the functionality achieves on GPUs from AMD, NVIDIA, and Intel, taking the theoretical performance limits reported in the GPU specifications as the baseline. This approach reflects the aspect that the GPUs differ significantly in their performance characteristics, and that Intel's oneAPI ecosystem and GPU architectures are still under active development and have not yet reached the maturity level of other GPU computing ecosystems. At the same time, reporting the performance relative to the theoretical limits allows us to both quantify the suitability of GINKGO's algorithms and to estimate the performance we can expect for GINKGO's functionality when scaling up the GPU performance. In Fig. 8 we report the relative performance of different SpMV kernels on AMD Radeon VII ("hip" backend), NVIDIA V100 ("cuda" backend), and Intel GEN9 and GEN12 GPUs (both "dpcpp" backend). As expected, the achieved bandwidth heavily depends on the SpMV kernel and the characteristics of the test matrix. Overall, the performance figures indicate that the SPMV kernels achieve about 90% of peak bandwidth on V100 and GEN12, and about 60–70% of peak bandwidth on RadeonVII and GEN9. On all hardware, GINKGO's SPMV kernels are competitive to the vendor libraries, indicating the validity of the library design and demonstrating good performance portability.

6   Summary and Outlook

We have prepared the GINKGO open source math library for Intel GPUs by developing a DPC++ backend. We presented strategies that are practical to accommodate the design differences between CUDA/HIP and the oneAPI ecosystem. We also evaluated the efficiency of GINKGO's functionality in terms of translating hardware performance into algorithm performance and comparing basic building blocks against equivalent kernels shipping with Intel's oneMKL library. In this performance evaluation, we demonstrated that GINKGO's kernels are competitive to Intel's oneMKL library, and that GINKGO's advanced math functionality is readily available to run on Intel GPUs. While the oneAPI ecosystem itself aims for providing portability to GPUs from other vendors, we have acknowledge that this is currently not possible, and we thus have to postpone the evaluation of Ginkgo's DPC++ backend on AMD and NVIDIA platforms.

References

1. Anzt, H., et al.: Ginkgo: a high performance numerical linear algebra library. J. Open Source Softw. **5**(52), 2260 (2020). https://doi.org/10.21105/joss.02260
2. Cojean, T., Tsai, Y.H.M., Anzt, H.: Ginkgo - a math library designed for platform portability (2020). https://www.sciencedirect.com/science/article/abs/pii/S0167819122000096
3. Deakin, T., Price, J., Martineau, M., McIntosh-Smith, S.: Evaluating attainable memory bandwidth of parallel programming models via babelstream. Int. J. Comput. Sci. Eng. **17**, 247–262 (2017)
4. Keryell, R., Reyes, R., Howes, L.: Khronos SYCL for OpenCL: a tutorial. In: Proceedings of the 3rd International Workshop on OpenCL, IWOCL 2015. Association for Computing Machinery, New York (2015). https://doi.org/10.1145/2791321.2791345
5. Konstantinidis, E., Cotronis, Y.: A quantitative roofline model for GPU kernel performance estimation using micro-benchmarks and hardware metric profiling. J. Parallel Distrib. Comput. **107**, 37–56 (2017). https://doi.org/10.1016/j.jpdc.2017.04.002
6. Tsai, Y.M., Cojean, T., Ribizel, T., Anzt, H.: Preparing Ginkgo for AMD GPUs – a testimonial on porting CUDA code to HIP. In: Balis, B., et al. (eds.) Euro-Par 2020. LNCS, vol. 12480, pp. 109–121. Springer, Cham (2021). https://doi.org/10.1007/978-3-030-71593-9_9

Continuous Self-adaptation of Control Policies in Automatic Cloud Management

Włodzimierz Funika[1]([✉]) [iD], Paweł Koperek[1] [iD], and Jacek Kitowski[1,2] [iD]

[1] AGH-UST, Faculty of Computer Science, Electronics and Telecommunication,
Institute of Computer Science, al. Mickiewicza 30, 30-059 Kraków, Poland
{funika,kito}@agh.edu.pl
[2] AGH, ACC Cyfronet AGH, ul. Nawojki 11, 30-950 Kraków, Poland

Abstract. Deep Reinforcement Learning has been recently a very active field of research. The policies generated with use of that class of training algorithms are flexible and thus have many practical applications. In this paper we present the results of our attempt to use the recent advancements in Reinforcement Learning to automate the management of resources in a compute cloud environment. We describe a new approach to self-adaptation of autonomous management, which uses a digital clone of the managed infrastructure to continuously update the control policy. We present the architecture of our system and discuss the results of evaluation which includes autonomous management of a sample application deployed to Amazon Web Services cloud. We also provide the details of training of the management policy using the Proximal Policy Optimization algorithm. Finally, we discuss the feasibility to extend the presented approach to further scenarios.

Keywords: Computing clouds · Autonomous control · Digital twin · Deep Reinforcement Learning

1 Introduction

In the last few years, computing clouds have gained wide-spread adoption. Almost every newly created software utilizes resources which are available through a cloud-like interface. On the one hand this approach allowed to greatly improve the development time, on the other hand it also posed a number of challenges. One of the more prominent ones is the optimization of costs, especially when working with Infrastructure-as-a-Service (*IaaS*) environments. Since the resources (Virtual Machines - VMs) are charged usually based on how long they are being used, in order to limit the costs one needs to reduce the usage time. Unfortunately, this is a non-trivial task, especially given that there might be special constraints imposed by Service Level Agreements (*SLAs*).

In the recent years we could also observe a lot of progress being made in the field of Reinforcement Learning (*RL*) [19]. Initially, the algorithms which are part of that domain, were only perceived as applicable to relatively simple

© Springer Nature Switzerland AG 2022
R. Chaves et al. (Eds.): Euro-Par 2021, LNCS 13098, pp. 69–80, 2022.
https://doi.org/10.1007/978-3-031-06156-1_6

problems. It was assumed that the controlled environment could be observed with the use of only a few metrics and there could not be too many actions to execute. Fortunately, combining RL with the Deep Learning techniques allowed to mitigate those limitations and reach new state-of-the-art results [14,15,18]. The main advantage of the mentioned methods is the ability to learn through observing and interacting with an environment which is similar to or the same as the one the agent is going to operate in. Using such an approach allowed to achieve results surpassing the performance of humans.

There are also first attempts to utilize Deep Reinforcement Learning (*DRL*) in the context of autonomous cloud management. These systems share one common flaw: their policies are able to make good decisions only in situations, which they were exposed to in the prior training. Without external intervention there is no way to update the policy after deployment. One might argue that an obvious solution to this problem would be to continuously train the policy while it is in control of the cloud environment, in other words: use an *online* policy training algorithm. Unfortunately, there is one significant disadvantage to this approach. Due to the nature of the training process, the new versions of the policy might not make decisions as good as the current policy. Making constant changes introduces a risk that the update might trigger applying potentially disastrous changes into the managed environment. To avoid such a situation, the performance of a new version of the policy needs to be verified prior to its deployment. One way of doing this is to compare the reward achieved by the old and new policies within a tightly controlled environment. A good example is a simulation, where the conditions: time flow, workload, available resources are provided equally and the decisions coming from the policies are the only major difference. Another advantage of such an approach is that it introduces a mechanism which allows the policy to become closer and closer suited to the environment it controls. New information is constantly being added to the representation of the policy (e.g. in the case of DNN - to the neural network weights).

An approach, which also utilizes a simulated copy of the managed resources, called the *Digital Twin* or the *Virtual Twin* has been employed in industrial and manufacturing systems for over a decade [12]. In this paper we present an experimental monitoring and management system, which to the best of our knowledge, is a first attempt to apply the concept of a digital twin to cloud resources management. It is an extension of our previous research [5] which demonstrated how DRL techniques can be used to control cloud application's resources. It uses the newly acquired data to continuously re-train the control policy and then compare this with the currently used version. This allows the management system to respond to a potentially changing workload while addressing the issues described above. This paper's contribution includes a novel architecture of an autonomous management system which utilizes a continuous policy improvement loop, initial policy training procedure, implementation of the described concepts available as an Open Source project [6], experiments and analysis of their results.

The paper is organized as follows: in Sect. 2 we overview related work, Sect. 3 describes the system's architecture and Sect. 4 explains the policy training procedure. Section 5 discusses the design of the experiment, description of the environment it was executed in and evaluates the results of the experiment. Section 6 summarizes our research and outlines further work.

2   Related Work

Reinforcement Learning can be applied in the field of cloud resource autoscaling in various ways [8], e.g. to create a policy which changes the number of acquired resources (typically VMs) or a policy which assigns a computational task to a specific resource (typically VMs to physical servers).

In [16] authors aim to create a cloud resource scheduling framework, which uses the Deep Q-network (DQN) algorithm. The autonomous agent is assigning virtual machines, which execute computational tasks, to a set of physical servers. Its objective is to minimize both the submitted task execution timespan and the energy consumption of resources. The approach has been verified using a simulated experiment, in which the proposed approach has been compared to random, round robin and multi-objective particle swarm optimization allocation algorithms. The policy created using the DQN algorithm was able to find near-optimal allocation, what suggests that the presented approach can be considered as an efficient resource allocation and task scheduling strategy. A similar approach is used in [3]. In this case, however, the objective of the DQN-trained policy was to choose an assignment policy (e.g. first fit) for incoming VM placement requests. Authors performed a number of simulation experiments where they compared the proposed approach with traditional assignment heuristics. That analysis showed the effectiveness of the DRL-based approach, especially in the context of handling workloads with major fluctuations. In [20] a resource provisioning framework based on the concept of monitoring-analysis-planning-execution (*MAPE*) loop is introduced. It consists of two loops: the first one is responsible for provisioning resources from an IaaS provider and uses DRL techniques; the second loop is coordinating cloud services which use the provisioned resources. Using both loops allows to control the number of used VMs while reducing the waste caused by incorrectly predicting the specific task resource consumption. The approach has been verified using a simulated experiment which demonstrated its ability to increase utilization, decrease the total cost while avoiding SLA violations.

The mentioned papers suggest that autonomous control achieved by using DRL techniques can render good results. Unfortunately such conclusions are confirmed only by results of simulations. This raises a concern, whether the discussed approach can be applied to more complex, real-world infrastructures. In our previous work [5] we demonstrated how such a task could be addressed and presented a proof-of-concept of an autonomous resource provisioning system. That system used a policy, created by a DRL training algorithm, to control resources utilized by a sample application deployed to Amazon Web Services cloud [1]. In this paper we are extending this approach. We introduce a simulated copy of the managed resources (a so called *digital twin*) which is used to continuously improve the initially deployed policy.

The idea of using a virtual clone of a physical object or system is not new. It has been first proposed in 2003 [10] and since then applied primarily to manufacturing processes, aviation and healthcare [2]. The digital copy can be a source of information for production optimization, predictive maintenance, cost optimization and physical resource management. To the best of our knowledge, the presented system is the first attempt to apply this technique together with DRL to cloud resources management. In this context, a set of simulated resources becomes the *digitial twin* of the application infrastructure deployed to a public cloud. Due to the fact that the source environment is also digital and can be examined through a set of well defined APIs, its replication is relatively easy. The simulated behavior of the managed resources can be made quite accurate as they are governed by complex, yet precise and deterministic rules. By using a simulation we can create a safe environment in which on the one hand the training process can be performed safely (a policy making disastrous changes would not be copied to the real environment) and in a short amount of time (e.g. thanks to a speed up in the time flow).

3   Digital Twin System Architecture

The architecture of the described system consists of two loops. The first one is the feedback loop of the subsystem which embeds the control policy in the real cloud environment. The second one is formed of the components used to continuously update the policy, including the simulated copy of the controlled resources (the *digital twin*). The components of both loops are shown in Fig. 1.

The *first feedback loop* starts with collecting measurements about the resources which take part in executing the jobs. Each of them is configured to start reporting relevant measurements as soon as the resource becomes online. The measurements often differ in their nature what influences how often their values are provided, e.g. the amount of free RAM and CPU usage is reported every 10 s while the virtual machine (VM) count - once per minute. To simplify the implementation of collecting of those raw measurements, we introduced the Graphite monitoring tool [9]. Graphite aggregates all the collected values into a single interval to create a consistent snapshot of the environment. This interval in our case is set to one minute.

Next, the measurements are passed to the SAMM monitoring and management system [7]. SAMM enables experimenting with new approaches to management automation. It allows to easily add support for new types of resources, relevant metrics, to integrate new algorithms and technologies, and to observe their impact on the observed system. In our use case, SAMM is used to combine other elements of the system together. First, it periodically polls measurements which portray the current state of the system (e.g. the average CPU usage in the computation cluster, amount of used memory etc.). Then, SAMM aggregates the

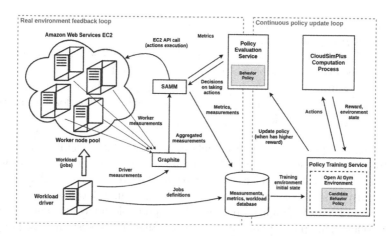

Fig. 1. Components of the real cloud environment under discussion. On the left side there is the environment-policy feedback loop. On the right side, the continuous policy update loop. Arrows denote interactions between the components.

measurements into metrics used by the decision policy. Finally, it communicates with the *Policy Evaluation Service*: provides the current state of the system in a form of metric values and retrieves decisions. The decisions are then executed through a cloud vendor API (e.g. Amazon Web Services API).

The *Policy Evaluation Service* provides decisions on how to change the allocation of resources based on the results of evaluation of the observed system state. The decisions are made according to the policy trained with the use of the PPO [18] algorithm. The results of the evaluation may include *starting a new small, medium or large VM* (deficient resources are used to handle the workload under the current system state), *removing resources - shutting down a small, medium, large VM* (excessive resources are used given the current state of the system), *doing nothing* (a proper amount of resources is allocated). One should remember that implementing the change is always subject to environment constraints. Not always it is possible to immediately execute an action. We might need to wait for a while because the system is in a *warm-up* or *cool-down* (a period of inactivity to allow to stabilize the metrics after the previous action has been executed), the previous request might still be being fulfilled, the request failed and needs to be retried in some time. In order to be able to train a policy which can cope with such limitations, the mentioned factors need to be involved in the simulation used for training.

For the described system we make a few assumptions about the workload under management:

- processing is organized into many independent tasks,
- the number of tasks which are yet to be executed can be monitored,
- the tasks which have been interrupted before their termination (e.g. in case the processing VMs are shutdown) are rescheduled,

- the tasks are considered idempotent, i.e. executing them multiple times does not change the end result,
- information about the currently executed tasks (e.g. schedule time, resources usage) needs to be available to the management system,
- resources administering the workload (e.g. accepting the input requests) are exempt from automatic management to prevent the workload from being accidentally terminated.

Fulfilling the monitoring requirements may require introducing *extensions* to the software which generates the workloads and *instrumenting the resources* which are used to create tasks. In our case, the workload driver has been enhanced with the capability to store relevant workload information in a database.

The *second loop* highlighted in Fig. 1 is responsible for continuously updating the policy. This part of the autonomous management system is responsible for ensuring that the decisions implemented in the real environment are made by the policy which has been retrained with the use of the most recent data. This loop starts with the *Policy Evaluation Service* which hosts the currently used *Behavior Policy*. Actions taken by the policy are implemented in the cloud environment and thus are observable in the measurements and metrics (e.g. in the number of used CPU cores) recorded in the database. The content of the database is then used by the *Policy Training Service*. It periodically retrieves a set of the most recently processed tasks and the specification of the resources which were available when those tasks were being executed. This allows the service to configure the simulated environment in which a *Candidate Behavior Policy* is being trained. Once the training is over, the driver compares the reward from the simulation and that from the real environment. If the former reward is greater, the candidate policy replaces the currently used one. The simulator has been implemented following the results of our prior research [4].

The policy is trained according to the procedure described in the next section.

4   Policy Training

The policy has been implemented as a neural network. We experimented with different architectures of the neural network used as a decision policy. The best results have been obtained with the use of the *long-short term memory (LSTM)* [11] architecture. LSTM is a type of recurrent neural network, which means it passes the output of a layer back to its input. This makes it well-suited to process data in form of sequences, as it has access to the previously made decisions. A basic building block in the LSTM networks is usually described as a *cell*. In our case the network consisted of 128 cells. For training we have used the *Proximal Policy Optimization* (PPO) [18] algorithm with parameters as shown in Table 1.

To avoid the cold start problem, we have trained the initial version of the policy in the above described simulator. As the workload we have used a set of 1551 jobs. The jobs have been organized into 21 batches (10 batches of 100 and 11 batches of 50 jobs) submitted at 8 min intervals. Every job requested

Table 1. Policy training process - parameters.

Parameter name	Parameter value	Parameter name	Parameter value
Value function coefficient	0.0005	Lambda	0.97
Gamma	0.99	Training timesteps	250000
Clipping factor	0.2	Learning rate	0.0003
Batch size	250	Simulator speedup	60

360 s on a single CPU core. The single job has been added 30 min after the final batch. This ensured that there would always be a cool-down period of time at the end. We chose such a workload because on the one hand it was small enough so that it allowed to conduct a full simulation in a short amount of time and on the other hand it was comprehensive enough to allow the policy to gather some valuable experience about batch processing applications. In our experiment we present a scenario where such an application is being automatically managed. The discussed approach is not limited to batch processing, though. If a different type of workload needs to be controlled, the policy can be adjusted by training it with the use of a different workload.

The agent objective was defined as minimizing the overall cost of resources, which has been expressed as maximizing the following reward function:

$$F(T_S, T_M, T_L, T_Q) = -\sum_{x \in V}(T_x \cdot C_x) - T_Q \cdot C_Q \qquad (1)$$

where:

- $F(T_S, T_M, T_L, T_Q)$ is the negative cost of resources used for processing,
- V denotes a set of possible VM sizes. In our experiments it includes S, M or L which represent *small*, *medium* or *large* VMs, accordingly,
- T_x denote the number of hours of running VMs of size x,
- C_x is the hourly cost of running a machine of size x. In our case $C_S = \$0.2$, $C_M = \$0.4$ and $C_L = \$0.8$,
- T_Q – the hours spent by tasks waiting for execution.
- C_Q – the hourly penalty for missing SLA targers when a task is waiting for execution. The cost 0.036 is accrued for every second of a delay between submitting task for execution and actual execution. There were no limitations on the waiting time or the waiting queue size.

5   Experiment

To evaluate our approach to the autonomous cloud resources control, we have conducted an experiment with the use of resources of a publicly available cloud environment. The overall objective was to quantify the impact of the continuous training loop on the management process. First, we ran the sample application 10 times and managed it using the *initial* version of control policy. Next, we

ran the same sample application 10 more times but managed it with the use
of a policy which was being continuously updated. Afterwards, we compared
the average resource costs and computation times. Finally, we analyzed how the
update process influenced the decisions made by the policy.

As a sample workload, we have used the *pytorch-dnn-evolution* tool [17].
This is a tool which attempts to discover an optimal structure of a Deep Neural Network (*DNN*) to solve a given problem (e.g. categorize images in a given
set) using a co-evolutionary algorithm. In our setup, the evolution process was
configured to search an optimal DNN architecture for recognizing the handwritten digits from the MNIST dataset [13]. Using *pytorch-dnn-evolution* also has
its drawbacks. The workload is CPU-intensive and very irregular. The number
of evaluated individuals can greatly change in subsequent evolution iterations,
what makes it hard to choose the proper amount of resources. On the other
hand, we have verified that such a workload met all the conditions outlined in
Sect. 4, which enabled using a dynamic scaling approach.

The experiment was carried out with the use of the Amazon Web Services [1]
infrastructure. The sample application has been using Virtual Machines (VMs)
of three types: *large* (2 core CPU and 8 GB of RAM), *xlarge* (4 core CPU
and 16 GB of RAM) and *2xlarge* (8 core CPU and 32 GB of RAM). Each
run started with 1 virtual machine of each type already provisioned and ran
until all the scheduled tasks were completed. We did not allow the autonomous
management policy to remove all VMs of a given type to avoid situations in
which the progress would have stalled completely. This would force us to predict
whether the policy is going to recover from such a state, which is a variant of the
halting problem. Shutting down all the virtual machines is also undesirable in
a production environment, therefore we have decided to exclude this possibility
from our tests. It is worth noting, however, that it is technically possible to
configure the presented system to allow the disposing of all of the provisioned
resources. All VMs were running in the same region (US North Virginia) and
the same availability zone to avoid introducing any additional network latency.
The components SAMM, Graphite and the workload driver have been running
on a separate VM.

Table 2. Raw measurements of subsequent workload runs.

Workload run	1	2	3	4	5	6	7	8	9	10
Resources cost, initial policy (USD)	7.86	8.10	8.07	7.82	8.43	8.15	8.29	8.04	8.25	7.41
Resources cost, policy updates (USD)	7.35	6.63	7.04	6.62	6.64	6.70	7.05	6.63	6.57	6.89
Workload time, initial policy (min.)	322	316	282	308	257	249	235	260	248	345
Workload time, policy updates (min.)	344	300	295	272	272	312	300	315	275	311

Table 2 presents raw observations of the total resources cost and the time
required to process all of the jobs for a given workload run. When the policy
remained unchanged, the average cost of resources was equal to 8.04 USD (standard deviation of 0.29). That value decreased to 6.81 USD (standard deviation

of 0.26) when the policy updates were activated. That can be interpreted as a 15.3% cost reduction. We have attempted to confirm that result with the use of the one-tail t-Student test, however we noticed that one of the value sets did not meet the near-normal criterion according to Shapiro-Wilk test. However, the observed cost averages show a strong difference while manifesting their low standard deviations. We reason that updating the control policy while a workload is being executed, rendered superior results.

It is also worth noting that the lowering of the resource cost seemed to increase the workload time (on average by 6.17%, from 282.20 to 299.6 min). The dynamically changed policy on the average showed slower overall execution, which shows that the policy traded off the execution time for the desirable cost reduction. We have analyzed a number of factors, which potentially might have affected the execution time, to confirm that the observed cost reduction resulted from introducing the changes in control policy.

- **The number of the fully executed jobs** (not interrupted by a VM termination) within a workload run. In both cases those numbers were very similar and thus would not affect the results.
- **Average computation time required for a single job.** We have noticed that the average amount of time required to finish a single job has been shorter by 0.98 s in the case of continuous policy updates. That can be caused by the workload driver generating jobs which require less computations to finalize. When considered in the context of a whole workload run, that factor could account for a reduction in the total used resource time by 184.69 min or in other words a reduction of $0.13 of monetary costs. Given that the difference between the averages of raw observations in the two considered scenarios (with continuous policy updates and without them) is equal to $1.23, we can estimate that at least $1.1 of the cost reduction can be attributed to the continuous policy updates. This allows to sustain the claim that policy updates reduce the overall monetary cost.
- **Environment factors.** Factors like network latency, VM start-up time, etc. had the same impact on both approaches (using a static policy and using that with continuous updates). These factors' effect has been reduced by running each variant of the policy multiple times. We also assume that given the small differences in the total used resource time measurements (e.g. 11221 min on average with a standard deviation of 403.98 min for runs without policy updates) the impact of the environment factors on the results of our experiment is very limited.

The summarized results of the conducted experiment are shown in Table 3.

To demonstrate the effects of continuous re-training and updating the policy, in Fig. 2 we present a single run of the *initial policy* versus a run of one of the policy versions obtained after a few iterations of the continuous training. The initial policy seems to focus on multiple changes to the count of small VMs. The *second* policy is more aggressive in the resource allocation: it launches multiple medium and large VMs, however the changes in VM counts seem to be less frequent. This results in a shorter total calculation time (189 min instead of 249 min

Table 3. Results of managing the sample application with and without the continuous policy updates. All values are averages over 10 runs.

Measured value	Without updates	With updates
Average resource cost (USD)	8.04 ($\sigma = 0.29$)	**6.81** ($\sigma = 0.26$)
Average workload time (min.)	**282.20** ($\sigma = 37.95$)	299.60 ($\sigma = 22.71$)
Average used resource time (min.)	11221	**9504**
Average single job time (seconds)	41.87	40.77
Average number of fully executed jobs	11422	11424

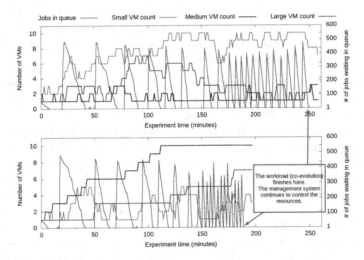

Fig. 2. Number of VMs running while the environment was being managed automatically. Top: initial policy, bottom: updated policy.

in the top chart). The number of the executed jobs and the average job execution times are very similar in both cases: 11424 and 41.76 for the initial policy vs. 11389 jobs and 41.34 s for the updated policy. This allows to conclude that the observed differences were primarily driven by the change in policy. As presented in the example above, the continuous re-training process is capable of introducing the versions of policy, which manifest significantly different behaviors, what translates to an optimization of costs.

Due to the use of the *digital twin* approach, the additional resources for the re-training of the control policy were very moderate in our test scenario. We could reuse the VMs which were already provisioned to support SAMM, Graphite, and other components of the management system. Since the additional cost introduced by the automatic resource management was equal in both experiment scenarios, we decided to exclude it from the final results.

6   Conclusions and Further Work

In this paper we have presented the use of the *digital twin* approach for the autonomous management of cloud resources. We created a digital, simulated version of an existing environment and used it to reduce the monetary cost of running it. We explained the architecture of a novel management system based on that idea and discussed its implementation which is based on the SAMM monitoring and management system. Finally, we have conducted an experiment to verify the presented approach, which empirically demonstrated the benefits of the used management method. We were able to reduce the average cost of resources from \$8.04 to \$6.83 (by 15.3%). The management policy was being updated using the new information coming from the managed environment, which allowed to respond to the situations to which it not been exposed before.

The continuous policy update loop proved to be an effective way of dynamically adjusting the management policy. At the same time this approach also has its disadvantages. Training an RL policy requires quite a significant amount of time. This means that, depending on the pace of changes to the actual workload, the update procedure might not be able to respond fast enough to changes in the workload or environment. Extending the management system with the continuous training loop increases its complexity and adds more parameters that need to be tuned. These parameters need to be tuned very carefully, otherwise one risks creating a policy which e.g. ignores historical data and only focuses on the most recent observations.

Our on-going work is focused on extending the presented approach. We plan to investigate the influence of different variants of the continuous training setup on the performance of the policy. We are working on introducing a parallelism of simulation, which would support more frequent re-training. We believe that neural network models which are used as the control policy can be further optimized, e.g. by using a bi-directional LSTM layer.

Acknowledgements. The research presented in this paper was supported by the funds assigned to AGH University of Science and Technology by the Polish Ministry of Education and Science. The experiments have been carried out on the PL-Grid infrastructure resources of ACC Cyfronet AGH and on the Amazon Web Services Elastic Compute Cloud.

References

1. Amazon Web Services Elastic Compute Cloud (2020). https://aws.amazon.com/ec2/. Accessed 30 Nov 2020
2. Barricelli, B.R., Casiraghi, E., Fogli, D.: A survey on digital twin: definitions, characteristics, applications, and design implications. IEEE Access **7**, 167653–167671 (2019). https://doi.org/10.1109/ACCESS.2019.2953499
3. Caviglione, L., Gaggero, M., Paolucci, M., Ronco, R.: Deep reinforcement learning for multi-objective placement of virtual machines in cloud datacenters. Soft Comput. **25**, 12569–12588 (2020). https://doi.org/10.1007/s00500-020-05462-x

4. Funika, W., Koperek, P.: Evaluating the use of policy gradient optimization approach for automatic cloud resource provisioning. In: Wyrzykowski, R., Deelman, E., Dongarra, J., Karczewski, K. (eds.) PPAM 2019. LNCS, vol. 12043, pp. 467–478. Springer, Cham (2020). https://doi.org/10.1007/978-3-030-43229-4_40
5. Funika, W., Koperek, P., Kitowski, J.: Automatic management of cloud applications with use of proximal policy optimization. In: Krzhizhanovskaya, V.V., et al. (eds.) ICCS 2020. LNCS, vol. 12137, pp. 73–87. Springer, Cham (2020). https://doi.org/10.1007/978-3-030-50371-0_6
6. Funika, W., Koperek, P.: Trainloop driver (2020). https://gitlab.com/pkoperek/trainloop-driver. Accessed 30 Apr 2021
7. Funika, W., Kupisz, M., Koperek, P.: Towards autonomic semantic-based management of distributed applications. Comput. Sci. **11**, 51–64 (2010)
8. Garí, Y., Monge, D.A., Pacini, E., Mateos, C., Garino, C.G.: Reinforcement learning-based application autoscaling in the cloud: a survey (2020)
9. Graphite Project (2011). https://graphiteapp.org/. Accessed 28 Nov 2020
10. Grieves, M.: Digital twin: manufacturing excellence through virtual factory replication. White Paper **1**, 1–7 (2014)
11. Hochreiter, S., Schmidhuber, J.: Long short-term memory. Neural Comput. **9**(8), 1735–1780 (1997)
12. Jones, D., Snider, C., Nassehi, A., Yon, J., Hicks, B.: Characterising the digital twin: a systematic literature review. CIRP J. Manuf. Sci. Technol. **29**, 36–52 (2020). https://doi.org/10.1016/j.cirpj.2020.02.002
13. LeCun, Y., Cortes, C.: MNIST handwritten digit database (2010). http://yann.lecun.com/exdb/mnist/
14. Mnih, V., et al.: Asynchronous methods for deep reinforcement learning. In: Proceedings of the 33rd International Conference on International Conference on Machine Learning, ICML 2016, vol. 48, pp. 1928–1937. JMLR.org (2016)
15. Mnih, V., et al.: Playing Atari with deep reinforcement learning (2013)
16. Peng, Z., Lin, J., Cui, D., Li, Q., He, J.: A multi-objective trade-off framework for cloud resource scheduling based on the Deep Q-network algorithm. Clust. Comput. **23**(4), 2753–2767 (2020). https://doi.org/10.1007/s10586-019-03042-9
17. PyTorch DNN Evolution (2018). https://gitlab.com/pkoperek/pytorch-dnn-evolution. Accessed 01 Dec 2020
18. Schulman, J., Wolski, F., Dhariwal, P., Radford, A., Klimov, O.: Proximal policy optimization algorithms. CoRR abs/1707.06347 (2017). http://arxiv.org/abs/1707.06347
19. Sutton, R.S.: Temporal credit assignment in reinforcement learning. Ph.D. thesis, University of Massachusetts Amherst (1984)
20. Zong, Q., Zheng, X., Wei, Y., Sun, H.: A deep reinforcement learning based resource autonomic provisioning approach for cloud services. In: Gao, H., Wang, X., Iqbal, M., Yin, Y., Yin, J., Gu, N. (eds.) CollaborateCom 2020. LNICST, vol. 350, pp. 132–153. Springer, Cham (2021). https://doi.org/10.1007/978-3-030-67540-0_8

A Distributed Game-Theoretic Approach to IaaS Cloud Brokering

Jakub Gąsior[(✉)] and Franciszek Seredyński

Department of Mathematics and Natural Sciences,
Cardinal Stefan Wyszyński University, Warsaw, Poland
{j.gasior,f.seredynski}@uksw.edu.pl

Abstract. We consider the problem of profit optimization for cloud brokerage service in the IaaS environment. We replace this optimization problem with a game-theoretic approach where players tend to achieve a solution by reaching a Nash equilibrium. We propose a fully distributed algorithm based on applying the Spatial Prisoner's Dilemma (SPD) game and a phenomenon of collective behavior of players participating in the game composed of two classes of automata-based agents - Cellular Automata (CA) and Learning Automata (LA). We introduce dynamic strategies like local profit sharing, mutation, and competition, which stimulate the evolutionary process of developing collective behavior among players to maximize their profit margin. We present the results of an experimental study showing the emergence of collective behavior in such systems.

Keywords: Collective behavior · Multi-agent systems · Spatial prisoner's dilemma game · Cellular automata · Infrastructure as a service

1 Introduction

Cloud Computing (CC) is a term used with increasing frequency in the past few years, as its popularity continues to grow. They can reduce the cost and complexity of owning and operating computers and networks. In an Infrastructure-as-a-Service (IaaS) cloud, this is achieved by using Virtual Machines (VMs), which can be dynamically assigned to the resources according to the demand and availability, as well as a possibility of consolidating several such VMs into the same virtual server.

As a result, an IaaS system can offer such on-demand computational services at a low cost. Cloud users usually pay for the usage (counted by the number of instance-hours incurred) in a pay-as-you-go model and are therefore freed from the prohibitive upfront investment on infrastructure, which is usually over-provisioned to accommodate peak demands [13].

Users may be charged in several different ways to access such resources. For example, it could be either a long-term reservation or a quick on-demand lease [13]. In long-term reservations, customers pay a fee to reserve a certain amount of

© Springer Nature Switzerland AG 2022
R. Chaves et al. (Eds.): Euro-Par 2021, LNCS 13098, pp. 81–90, 2022.
https://doi.org/10.1007/978-3-031-06156-1_7

computing resources for a period of one or several years. Then, they get charged extra for actually using the resource. While the extra payment may be lower than comparable on-demand service, it may not be desirable for each customer to pay for the more extended reservation period if their workload is relatively light or unpredictable [3].

One of the answers to this problem is cloud service brokering [4], a model in which a trusted third party matches the needs of customers with services of cloud providers. Typically, brokers' service is to find the best deals among a set of clouds that best fit the user requirements. Brokers consider the price and many other factors, such as privacy and security issues, Service Level Agreements (SLAs), performance, and they might offer solutions integrating services from multiple service providers [8].

In this paper, we analyze a game-theoretic approach to consider a problem of multi-broker job allocation and scheduling, aiming to optimize the brokers' profit while maintaining a Quality of Service (QoS) level acceptable to the customer. We propose a fully distributed approach based on converting this optimization problem into a game-theoretic one, where brokers representing users' demands will search for a solution in the form of a Nash equilibrium. For this purpose we will use a variant of SPD game proposed by [5] in the context of Cellular Automata (CA) space.

The remainder of this paper is organized as follows. In the next section, works related to the subject of our study are discussed. Section 3 describes the proposed Cloud Computing (CC) system model and defines the scheduling problem. Section 4 demonstrates the performance metrics, the input parameters, and the experimental results. Finally, Sect. 5 concludes the paper.

2   State of the Art

A multi-objective approach to the cloud brokering problem was recently proposed in [7], where authors provide a dichotomic approach to minimize the cost of service and a second - negatively correlated - objective. The novelty of the approach lies in considering services that can be sold in bundles, in which a set of services is sold together for a lower price than the sum of individual services' prices. In [6], the authors introduced a brokering system for scientific workflows, which optimizes a multi-criteria problem using an aggregated objective function. The brokering part of the system selects the length of the service period to minimize VMs lease cost.

The idea of broker exploitation of pricing model was also studied in [13] and solved using approximate dynamic programming. The theoretical study of users' requests aggregation under a concave cost function assumption and Randomized Online Stack-Centric Scheduling Algorithm (ROSA) was proposed in [14]. In their paper, authors proved the lower bound of the proposed solution's competitive ratio and evaluated its performance with trace-driven simulation using Google cluster data.

Aazam [2] proposed a dynamic broker, which predicts users' behavior based on the so-called relinquish probability, i.e., the likelihood that the user will cease to use the requested services. The study also involves an advanced refund mechanism based on multiple criteria. It is further extended to the Amazon cloud model and includes historical record integration in [1].

Similarly, in [10], the authors introduced an adaptive learning system that allows the analysis of the sequence of negotiation offers received by the broker for effectively learning the opponent's behavior over several stages of the negotiation process. They formulated this issue as the multi-stage Markov decision problem to suggest the broker with appropriate counter-offer tactics. Authors claim their solution can outperform the existing fixed behavioral learning schemes and maximize the utility value and success rate of negotiating parties without any break-offs.

Closer to our work, in [3] authors analyzed the scenario of user cost minimization in mobile cloud computing (MCC) networks, where multiple cooperative brokers assign cloud resources to mobile users. The work investigated two classes of cloud reservation strategies, i.e., a competitive strategy and a compete-then-cooperate strategy as a performance bound, showing that noticeable cooperative gains can be achieved over the pure competition in markets with only a few brokers. In contrast, the cooperative gain becomes marginal in more crowded markets.

A similar combinatorial auction-based algorithm was proposed in [9]. Authors aimed to solve the optimization problem where cloud users submit their requirements, and in turn, vendors submit their offers containing the price, QoS, and their prepared sets of resources. Results for procurement cost and scalability on a large number of cloud vendors were verified using various standard distribution benchmarks, including random, uniform, decay, and CATS.

3   Multi-objective Scheduling in Cloud Environment

3.1   Cloud Brokering Model

We assume that the Cloud Service Provider (CSP) offers abundant computing capacity at any given time. The Cloud Resource Broker (CRB) purchases computational resource from IaaS provider and has to pay for the resource cost. For the purpose of this paper we follow the specification of Compute Optimized VM series provided by Amazon EC2 and shown in Table 1[1]. Broker then offers to sell a set of VM instances $M_1, M_2, ..., M_m$, specified by several characteristics, including a number of cores $P(M_i)$, memory $M(M_i)$, storage space $S(M_i)$ and cost per hour $C^B(M_i)$.

Cloud Service Users (CSUs) $(U_1, U_2, ..., U_n)$ submit to the broker their workflow applications J_k^j for execution. Each application is the set of n tasks or jobs. Users are expected to pay appropriate fees to the broker dependent on the SLA requested. Job (denoted as J_k^j) is jth job produced (and owned) by user U_k. J_k stands for the set of all jobs produced by user U_k, while $n_k = |J_k|$ is the number of

---

[1] The price is for Linux Instances (EU Frankfurt) with full upfront payment on 1-year term reservation as of July, 2021.

Table 1. Compute Optimized Dedicated VM Instances in Amazon EC2.

	vCPU	Memory (GiB)	Price (Reserved)	Price (On-demand)
c4.large	2	3.75	$0.074	$0.114
c4.xlarge	4	7.5	$0.146	$0.227
c4.2xlarge	8	15	$0.293	$0.454
c4.4xlarge	16	30	$0.586	$0.909
c4.8xlarge	36	60	$1.173	$1.817

such jobs. Each task has varied parameters defined as a tuple $<r_k^j, size_k^j, t_k^j, d_k^j>$, specifying its release dates $r_k^j \geq 0$; its size $1 \leq size_k^j \leq m_m$, that is referred to as its processor requirements or *degree of parallelism*; its workload t_k^j and a deadline d_k^j.

The broker's cost function $C^B(M_i)$ is dependent on both the prices of reserved cloud resource instances and on-demand instances (as defined in Table 1). The cloud broker is capable of leveraging the pricing gap between reserved (C^R) and on-demand (C^{OD}) instances to reduce the expenses of all the users. To attract customers, CRBs should charge for a VM lease less than the on-demand pricing (C^{OD}) offered by the cloud provider. In order to ensure a reasonable profit for the broker, we assume that the broker's asking price $C^B(M_i)$ will be 25% lower than the on-demand price requested by the cloud provider.

We consider the multi-broker resource scheduling problem for IaaS clouds, where multiple customers may submit their job requests to a broker at random instants with a random workload that should be fulfilled before a specified deadline. We assume that the inter-arrival times for job requests are arbitrary. If the broker cannot accommodate the request to finish execution before the specified deadline, it must either use a larger VM instance offering more processing capacity or buy additional on-demand instances to fulfill the customer's request. Both solutions account for a negative impact on the broker's profit [8].

From a global system perspective, an appealing design objective is to find the allocation strategy for all brokers' submissions that minimizes all requests' average cost by cooperatively deciding on the reservation and task outsourcing strategies of all the brokers.

However, different brokers may be run by different organizations and may be selfish and only willing to maximize their profits. In other words, there is no incentive for the brokers to cooperate if the resulting profit is not higher compared with that achievable through pure competition [3].

4   A Game-Theoretic Approach to IaaS Multi-broker Scheduling

To mitigate this issue, we introduce an agent-based game-theoretic distributed scheduling scheme. We consider a two-dimensional CA lattice of the size $n \times m$. Each cell of the CA has a Moore neighborhood of radius r and a rule, which depends on its neighborhood state. Each cell of a 2D CA will be considered an agent (player) participating in the SPD game [5]. Each player (a cell of CA) has two possible actions: C (cooperate) and D (defect). The payoff function of the game is given in Table 2.

Table 2. Payoff function of a row player participating in the SPD game.

Player's action	Opponent's action	
	Cooperate (C)	Defect (D)
Cooperate (C)	$R = 1$	$S = 0$
Defect (D)	$T = b$	$P = a$

Each player associated with a given cell plays a game with each of his eight neighbors in a single round, collecting their total score. After a q number of rounds (iterations of CA), each cell (agent) of CA can change its rule (strategy). We assume that considered 2D CA is a non-uniform CA, with one of the following rules: *all-C* (always cooperate), *all-D* (always defect), and *k-D* (cooperate until no more than k $(0 \leq k \leq 7)$ neighbors defect).

A player may change his current strategy into another by comparing his total score collected during q rounds with his neighbors' scores. He selects as his new strategy the best performing neighbor's strategy, i.e., the player whose total collected score is the highest. This new strategy is used by a cell (player) to change its current state, and the value of the state is used in games during the following q rounds of interaction.

It is worth to notice that choosing the action D by all players corresponds to the Nash equilibrium (NE) point. Looking from the point of view of players' global collective behavior, this average total payoff of all players in NE point is low. Instead, we would expect the players to choose the action C, which provides the highest value of the average total payoff of all players equal to 1. For this instance of the game, it is the maximal value of a possible average total payoff of all players, and it will be achieved when all players decide to select the action C. We are interested in studying conditions when such behavior of players in iterated games is achievable.

4.1 CA–Based Players

We will be using CA–based agents as the first type of participant in the game. CAs are spatially and temporally discrete computational systems initially proposed by Ulam and von Neumann and today are a powerful tool used in computer science and natural science to solve problems and model different phenomena.

When a cell (i, j) is considered a CA-based player, it will be assumed that it is a part of the 2D array, and at a given discrete moment t, each cell is either in state C or D. The state's value is used by CA–based player as an action with an opponent player. For each cell, a local neighborhood is defined. Because we employ a 2D finite space, a cyclic boundary condition is applied.

In discrete moments, CA–based players will select new actions according to local rules (also called strategies or transition functions) assigned to them, which will change the states of the corresponding cells. We will be using several rules, among which one of them will be initially randomly assigned to each CA cell, so we deal with a non-uniform CA.

We will consider two types of CA–based players. To cells of the first type, one of the following rules: *all–C*, *all–D*, and *k–D* will be assigned. The second type of CA–based player uses probabilistic CA. To cells of this type, the following rule will be assigned: *cooperate* with probability p_{coop} or *defect* with probability $1 - p_{coop}$, where p_{coop} is some predefined value.

It is worth to notice that the considered 2D CA differs from a classical CA, where rules assigned to cells do not change during evolving CA in time. A CA with the possibility of changing its rules is called a second-order CA. In opposite to a classical CA, a second-order CA has the potential to solve various optimization problems.

4.2 LA–Based Players

We will also employ a deterministic ϵ–LA as the second group of players in the considered game. The ϵ–LA has $d = 2$ actions and acts in a deterministic environment $c = (c_1, c_2, ..., c_{2*d})$, where c_k stands for a reward defined by the payoff function from Table 2 obtained for its action and action of his opponent (CA or LA–based player) from the Moore neighborhood. It also has a memory of length h and a reinforcement learning algorithm that selects a new action. In our case, C and D are actions of an automaton, and they are associated with states of the array cells occupied by LA–based players.

Whenever ϵ–LA generates action, and its opponent from a neighborhood selects an action, the local environment (payoff function) sends it a payoff in a deterministic way. The objective of a reinforcement learning algorithm represented by ϵ–LA is to maximize its payoff in an environment where it operates.

The automaton remembers its last h actions and corresponding payoffs from the last h moments. As the next action ϵ–LA chooses its best action from the last h games (rounds) with the probability $1 - \epsilon$ ($0 < \epsilon \leq 1$), and with the probability ϵ/d any of its d actions.

4.3 Sharing, Mutation and Competition Mechanisms in the Game

In this paper, we are more interested in incorporating the global goal of the system into the local interests of individual brokers. In the following, we assume that action (C) is considered an equivalent of the cooperation in a classic PD game and denotes a situation where brokers are willing to share their unused allocation slots within their VMs while receiving a partial payment from other brokers. On the other hand, action (D) means that the broker declines to participate in resource sharing, which is considered an equivalent of the defection (D) in a classic PD game.

To study a possibility of the emergence of global collective behavior of players in the sense of the second class of the collective behavior classification [11] we introduce additional mechanisms of local interaction between players, which can be potentially spread or dismissed during the evolution.

The first mechanism is a competition, where after a q rounds (iterations), each agent compares its total payoff with its neighbors' total payoffs. If a more successful player exists in the neighborhood, this player replaces their own rule with the most successful one. This mechanism converts a classical CA into the *second-order* CA, which can adapt in time. When both players are CA-based players, a rule of a given player is replaced by a rule of the most successful players, and the value of the sharing tag is copied. If both players are LA-based players, then replacing happens only if the best player differs in at least one value of such parameters as h, ϵ, or a sharing tag. If one player is a CA-based player and the other one is an LA-based player, then a player of the most successful class replaces a given player.

The second mechanism used is a mutation of system parameters. With some predefined value of probability, a CA-based agent of the first type can change the currently assigned strategy (rule) to one of the two other strategies. Similarly, a CA-based agent of the second type can increase/decrease its probability of cooperation. Also, parameters h and ϵ of LA-based agents can be a subject of mutation.

The third mechanism called an *Income Sharing Mechanism* (ISM) provides a possibility of sharing payoffs between players. It is assumed that each player has a tag indicating whether he wishes (*on*) or not (*off*) to share his payoff with players from the neighborhood who also wish to share. Before starting the iterated game, each player turns on its tag with a predefined probability $p_{sharing}$. Due to the competition mechanism, rules with tags containing information about willingness to share incomes can be potentially spread or dismissed during the system's evolution.

5 Experimental Analysis and Performance Evaluation

In this section, we evaluate the performance of the considered classes of agents and introduced mechanisms of interactions (mutation, competition, sharing) and their impact on the emergence of cooperative behavior between brokers and their overall performance.

Optimal parameters for the SPD game were adapted from our earlier paper [12] and are as follows. A 2D array of the size of 4×4 cells (players) was used, with an initial state C or D (player action) set with the probability equal to 0.5. Initially, the rule k–D was assigned (if applied) to CA cells with probability 0.7, and the remaining three rules (all–C, all–D, probabilistic CA) with probability 0.1. When k–D was applied, k was randomly selected from the range 0–7. If the competition mechanism is turned on, updating the array cells (by a winner in a local neighborhood) is conducted after each iteration ($q = 1$). Parameters of the payoff function were set to $a = 0.3$ and $b = 1.4$, respectively. We incorporate these settings into the proposed scheduler to find a job allocation schedule maximizing the broker's income and minimizing the need for procuring additional resources on-demand.

We conduct simulations using the Google cluster trace data, which has been widely employed to perform cloud computing-related simulations. From the above dataset, we generate sample workload batches in the range of 1000–10000 jobs. The experimental scenarios are encoded as follows: $\{Agent, N, M\}$, where $Agent$ denotes the type of employed automata, N - number of brokers and M - number of VM instances, i.e., $\{CA, 4, 10\}$ denotes scenario employing $N = 4$ brokers in the system with $M = 10$ VM instances and CA–based players.

Jobs were then scheduled by independent brokering agents (in the range $N = \{2, 4, 8, 16\}$) on cloud infrastructure containing $M = 10$, 20, 30, and 40 reserved VM instances using a fast $Minimum\ Time\ Maximum\ Profit$ list heuristic [8] and a proposed game-theoretic space-sharing scheme.

We analyze two different performance metrics. First, the $Scheduling\ Success\ rate$, which denotes the ratio of completed job requests, i.e., without the need to procure additional on-demand resources. Similarly to [8], we do not count such events as SLA violations. In such cases, a broker will be forced to cover additional lease costs implying lower profits. The second analyzed metric is the aggregate profit improvement resulting from cooperation and multiplexing of job requests between individual brokers. Table 3 reports the average improvement over the results achieved using a simple list scheduling heuristic.

Let us start with a comparison between CA and LA–based agents. In most cases, LA–based players achieve better results than their CA–based counterparts. It might be because CA-based players do not have learning abilities, and the value of the average payoff is a result of the initial settings. In contrast to CA, LA–based players are aware of their environment, they can learn and adapt, and the average payoff depends upon a given memory size and the ϵ–value.

We can also notice that, as the congestion increases, the profit improvement decreases, i.e., the additional lease costs arise as the demand for resources increases. We also observe that ISM's benefits have a more significant impact on larger systems with a higher number of available VMs. As can be seen, the profit improvements increase on average by 8.6% points as the number of VM instances increases from 10 to 40. This means that cooperation is more beneficial in less crowded scenarios, while the benefit is only marginal if the number of job requests is high compared to a number of available VMs instances.

Table 3. Averaged Scheduling Success Rate and Profit Improvement results for multiple scheduling scenarios computed with SPD Scheduler (using Income Sharing and Mutation mechanisms) and Minimum Time Maximum Profit list heuristic.

Problem instance	Scheduling success rate [%]			Profit improvement [%]		
	MinTMaxP	SPD-ISM	SPD-Mut	MinTMaxP	SPD-ISM	SPD-Mut
{CA, 2, 10}	86.35	**89.24**	86.89	5.31	**5.78**	5.41
{CA, 4, 20}	89.78	91.31	**91.85**	7.51	**8.52**	7.89
{CA, 8, 30}	91.24	**92.21**	90.74	9.11	**9.52**	8.89
{CA, 16, 40}	92.45	**93.56**	91.56	12.41	**13.75**	13.24
{LA, 2, 10}	89.54	**90.78**	90.41	5.81	**6.07**	5.84
{LA, 4, 20}	91.44	**91.65**	90.97	9.44	9.26	**9.91**
{LA, 8, 30}	90.84	91.35	**91.57**	10.11	**10.86**	10.31
{LA, 16, 40}	93.33	**93.55**	92.89	13.58	13.76	**14.57**
{CA+LA, 2, 10}	89.98	**90.14**	89.74	5.75	**6.23**	5.89
{CA+LA, 4, 20}	91.24	**92.45**	91.45	8.42	**8.89**	8.74
{CA+LA, 8, 30}	92.98	**93.78**	92.48	8.11	9.89	**9.94**
{CA+LA, 16, 40}	95.54	95.75	**96.87**	14.41	15.37	**16.22**

This could also be attributed to the higher ratio of deadline violations in smaller-scale experiments. In such cases, due to a larger number of job requests, resource sharing between the brokers become less profitable due to the increasing number of additional on-demand leases required to meet the SLA requested by the customers.

6   Conclusion and Future Work

We have presented a theoretical framework to study the behavior of heterogeneous multi–agent systems composed of two classes of automata–based agents: CA and LA agents operating in an environment described in terms of a spatial PD game. This framework was defined to solve global optimization tasks in a distributed way by agents' collective behavior.

We incorporated this framework into the paradigm of a multi-broker job allocation scenario within the IaaS architecture to use the competition among the entities involved in the scheduling process to converge towards Nash equilibrium. It allowed us to account for often contradicting interests of the clients within the CC system without any centralized control and introduced several desirable properties such as adaptation and self-organization.

A set of conducted experiments has shown that these proposed solutions are promising building blocks that enable the emergence of global collective behavior in heterogeneous multi-agent systems. Conditions of the emergence of such systems' global behavior may depend on several additional parameters, and these issues will be a subject of our future work.

References

1. Aazam, M., Huh, E., St-Hilaire, M., Lung, C., Lambadaris, I.: Cloud customer's historical record based resource pricing. IEEE Trans. Parallel Distrib. Syst. **27**(7), 1929–1940 (2016). https://doi.org/10.1109/TPDS.2015.2473850
2. Aazam, M., Huh, E.N.: Cloud broker service-oriented resource management model. Trans. Emerg. Telecommun. Technol. **28**(2), 29–37 (2017). https://doi.org/10. 1002/ett.2937
3. Guan, Z., Melodia, T.: The value of cooperation: minimizing user costs in multi-broker mobile cloud computing networks. IEEE Trans. Cloud Comput. **5**(4), 780–791 (2017). https://doi.org/10.1109/TCC.2015.2440257
4. Guzek, M., Gniewek, A., Bouvry, P., Musial, J., Blazewicz, J.: Cloud brokering: current practices and upcoming challenges. IEEE Cloud Comput. **2**(2), 40–47 (2015). https://doi.org/10.1109/MCC.2015.32
5. Katsumata, Y., Ishida, Y.: On a membrane formation in a spatio-temporally generalized prisoner's dilemma. In: Umeo, H., Morishita, S., Nishinari, K., Komatsuzaki, T., Bandini, S. (eds.) ACRI 2008. LNCS, vol. 5191, pp. 60–66. Springer, Heidelberg (2008). https://doi.org/10.1007/978-3-540-79992-4_8
6. Kim, S., Kang, D., Kim, W., Chen, M., Youn, C.: A science gateway cloud with cost-adaptive VM management for computational science and applications. IEEE Syst. J. **11**(1), 173–185 (2017). https://doi.org/10.1109/JSYST.2015.2501750
7. Musial, J., et al.: Cloud brokering with bundles: multi-objective optimization of services selection. Found. Comput. Decis. Sci. **44**, 407–426 (2019). https://doi.org/ 10.2478/fcds-2019-0020
8. Nesmachnow, S., Iturriaga, S., Dorronsoro, B.: Efficient heuristics for profit optimization of virtual cloud brokers. IEEE Comput. Intell. Mag. **10**(1), 33–43 (2015). https://doi.org/10.1109/MCI.2014.2369893
9. Prasad, G.V., Prasad, A.S., Rao, S.: A combinatorial auction mechanism for multiple resource procurement in cloud computing. IEEE Trans. Cloud Comput. **6**(4), 904–914 (2018). https://doi.org/10.1109/TCC.2016.2541150
10. Rajavel, R., Thangarathanam, M.: Adaptive probabilistic behavioural learning system for the effective behavioural decision in cloud trading negotiation market. Futur. Gener. Comput. Syst. **58**, 29–41 (2016). https://doi.org/10.1016/j.future. 2015.12.007
11. Rossi, F., Bandyopadhyay, S., Wolf, M., Pavone, M.: Review of multi-agent algorithms for collective behavior: a structural taxonomy. IFAC-PapersOnLine **51**(12), 112–117 (2018). https://doi.org/10.1016/j.ifacol.2018.07.097. iFAC Workshop on Networked & Autonomous Air & Space Systems NAASS 2018
12. Seredyński, F., Gąsior, J.: Emergence of collective behavior in large cellular automata-based multi-agent systems. In: Rutkowski, L., Scherer, R., Korytkowski, M., Pedrycz, W., Tadeusiewicz, R., Zurada, J.M. (eds.) ICAISC 2019. LNCS (LNAI), vol. 11509, pp. 676–688. Springer, Cham (2019). https://doi.org/10.1007/ 978-3-030-20915-5_60
13. Wang, W., Niu, D., Liang, B., Li, B.: Dynamic cloud instance acquisition via IaaS cloud brokerage. IEEE Trans. Parallel Distrib. Syst. **26**(6), 1580–1593 (2015). https://doi.org/10.1109/TPDS.2014.2326409
14. Zhang, R., Wu, K., Li, M., Wang, J.: Online resource scheduling under concave pricing for cloud computing. IEEE Trans. Parallel Distrib. Syst. **27**, 1131–1145 (2015). https://doi.org/10.1109/TPDS.2015.2432799

Data Management Model to Program Irregular Compute Kernels on FPGA: Application to Heterogeneous Distributed System

Erwan Lenormand[1]([✉]) [iD], Thierry Goubier[1] [iD], Loïc Cudennec[2] [iD],
and Henri-Pierre Charles[3] [iD]

[1] Université Paris-Saclay, CEA, LIST, 91191 Gif-sur-Yvette, France
{erwan.lenormand,thierry.goubier}@cea.fr
[2] DGA Maîtrise de l'Information, BP 7, 35998 Rennes, France
loic.cudennec@intradef.gouv.fr
[3] Univ Grenoble-Alpes, CEA, LIST, 38000 Grenoble, France
henri-pierre.charles@cea.fr

Abstract. This paper presents a data management model targeting heterogeneous distributed systems integrating reconfigurable accelerators. The purpose of this model is to reduce the complexity of developing applications with multidimensional sparse data structures. It relies on a shared memory paradigm, which is convenient for parallel programming of irregular applications. The distributed data, sliced in chunks, are managed by a Software-Distributed Shared Memory (S-DSM). The integration of reconfigurable accelerators in this S-DSM, by breaking the master-slave model, allows devices to initiate access to chunks in order to accept data-dependent accesses. We use chunk partitioning of multidimensional sparse data structures, such as sparse matrices and unstructured meshes, to access them as a continuous data stream. This model enables to regularize memory accesses of irregular applications, to avoid the transfer of unnecessary data by providing fine-grained data access, and to efficiently hide data access latencies by implicitly overlaying the transferred data flow with the processed data flow.

We have used two case studies to validate the proposed data management model: General Sparse Matrix-Matrix Multiplication (SpGEMM) and Shallow Water Equations (SWE) over an unstructured mesh. The results obtained show that the proposed model efficiently hides the data access latencies by reaching computation speeds close to those of an ideal case (i.e. without latency).

Keywords: Distributed shared memory · Field programmable gate array · Irregular application

This work was supported by the LEXIS project, funded by the EU's Horizon 2020 research and innovation programme (2014–2020) under grant agreement no. 825532.

R. Chaves et al. (Eds.): Euro-Par 2021, LNCS 13098, pp. 91–103, 2022.
https://doi.org/10.1007/978-3-031-06156-1_8

1 Introduction

As a response to the power wall problem, High Performance Computing (HPC) systems heterogeneity is gradually increasing. Part of this heterogeneity comes from the association of processors with co-processors, mainly GPUs. These latter allow the execution of computational-intensive portions of applications, called compute kernels, with high FLOP/W efficiency. However, as illustrated by the efficiency on the High Performance Conjugate Gradient (HPCG) benchmark [11], these systems achieve only a fraction of their theoretical peak performance and do not show efficiency gains from their heterogeneity for irregular applications. This poor performance is due on one hand, to the random data access patterns generated by these applications, and on the other hand, to the complexity of porting irregular compute kernels to GPUs. Thanks to their reconfigurable architecture, Field-programmable gate arrays (FPGAs) are particularly suitable for processing irregular compute kernels [7]. The attractiveness of FPGAs for HPC systems is growing by means of their increasing computing power and the improvement of High Level Synthesis (HLS) tools. However, porting irregular compute kernels to FPGA remains a challenging task, because random data access patterns limit the abilities of HLS tools. Thus, designers must deal with low-level kernel design, optimization of data structures for FPGA memory systems and orchestration of distributed data transfers.

To address this issue, we propose a data management model for irregular compute kernels targeting heterogeneous distributed systems with reconfigurable accelerators. The latter is based on a shared-memory provided by a Software-Distributed Shared Memory (S-DSM). The application datasets are sliced in *chunks* managed by the S-DSM. The integration of reconfigurable accelerators in the S-DSM allows devices to initiate accesses to *chunks*. In this way, all the processing units can make fine-grained random data accesses. This unified data access model simplifies programming and meets the needs of irregular applications. By abstracting the data structure, *chunk* partitioning enables to prefetch the data as streams of *chunks*. This prefetching should make it possible to hide high data access latencies by implicitly overlaying the transferred data flow with the processed data flow. The efficiency of the proposed data management model relies on its ability to hide latencies. To assess this efficiency, we have used two case studies: General Sparse Matrix-Matrix Multiplication (SpGEMM) and a tsunami simulation code. These two applications generate a lot of irregular memory accesses, which are complex to optimize because they are data-dependent.

The paper is organized as follows: Sect. 2 presents the data management model, Sect. 3 describes the experiments conducted to validate the model, Sect. 4 gives some references on related work, finally, Sect. 5 concludes this paper.

2 Data Management Model

Shared memory is a convenient programming paradigm to develop multi-threaded applications, which randomly access data. Software-Distributed Shared

Memory can be used to aggregate distributed physical memories into a shared logical space. In this work, we consider a S-DSM for heterogeneous micro-server that has been proposed in previous work [5]. The latter is organized as a semi-structured super-peer network, where a set of clients are connected to a peer-to-peer network of servers. Clients execute the user code and servers manage the shared data and related metadata. The integration of reconfigurable accelerators in the S-DSM enables compute kernels to initiate access to distributed data. Obviously, this way to access the data can lead to high access latencies. To deal with this problem, the data management model aims to hide data access latencies by overlaying the transferred data flow with the processed data flow. This relies on the ability to access data as continuous streams. To do this we use *chunks*, a common object in computer science, whose concept is to use metadata to describe the data stored in it. *Chunks* are the atomic piece of data managed by the S-DSM. Each one has an unique identifier (*chunk ID*) and their maximum size can be set by the application. We use them to represent irregular data structures, as they are convenient objects for data management in distributed systems and their metadata allow to abstract the stored data. From the point of view of the compute kernels, the role of the S-DSM is to transparently provide the data and metadata corresponding to *chunk ID*. By partitioning the data structures according to the access granularity of the applications, data streams can be generated from sequences of *chunk ID*. Adapting the size of *chunks* to the granularity of access allows to avoid the transfer of unnecessary data. We have chosen two data structures widely used in irregular applications to illustrate the data management model: sparse matrix and unstructured meshes.

Sparse Linear Algebra consists in performing linear operations on matrices (or vectors) for which the majority of the elements are equal to zero. Sparse matrices are compressed to reduce their memory footprint and to accelerate access to their nonzero elements. The compressed sparse row format (CSR), shown in Fig. 1b, is one of the most used sparse matrix representations. The column indices and the values of elements are stored in row-major order in the arrays *Col* and *Val*. $RP[i]$ indicates the position of the first element of row i in the arrays and the operation $RP[i+1] - RP[i]$ is equal to the number of elements in the row. As shown in Fig. 1c, we have adapted the CSR format to the use of *chunks*. We colocalize the value and the column index of an element to form a pair. The set of pairs representing a row is stored in a *chunk*. Then we use *chunks*

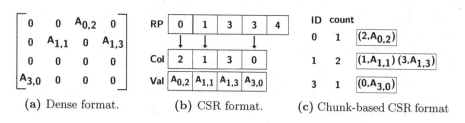

(a) Dense format.   (b) CSR format.   (c) Chunk-based CSR format

Fig. 1. Matrix representation.

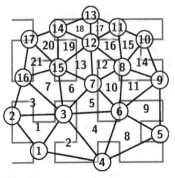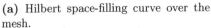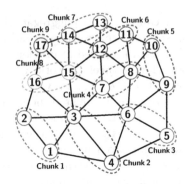

(a) Hilbert space-filling curve over the mesh.

(b) Chunk partitioning of the mesh with chunks of two elements.

Fig. 2. Reordering and partitioning of a 2D unstructured mesh.

metadata to indicate the number of elements per row. This structure reduces the number of memory accesses required to read or write a matrix row. It can be easily adapted to another compressed format (e.g. compressed sparse column format). Reading or writing a matrix involves to request access to each row and to request the transfer of rows data between the memory and the compute kernel. Decoupling the access request and the transfer request allows the prefetching of the data into the FPGA memory and thus hides the access latency. Considering that the kernel is developed as a pipeline of stages, which are separated by FIFOs, then the prefetching speed is implicitly limited by the size of the FIFOs. This prevents the FPGA memory from being overloaded due to too early data prefetching. In an ideal case prefetching speed corresponds to the speed of data consumption of the following stages in the pipeline.

Many HPC applications of Finite Element Method (FEM) work on unstructured meshes with triangular elements in 2D and tetrahedral elements in 3D. Typical kernels on such unstructured meshes proceed by mesh updates - updating all elements, nodes or edges of the mesh according to a function of neighbourhood values, applying a convolution or stencil and hence following indirections to both iterate over the mesh and to access neighbourhood information. Consequently, the topology of the mesh and indexing of data has a significant impact on data access locality and therefore application performance. Space-filling curves (SFC) allow to improve data access locality of the mesh [2]. We use this technique to do an efficient chunk partitioning of the mesh. As shown in Fig. 2a, a SFC is drawn in the geometric space of the mesh. Vertices are indexed according the order in which they meet the curve. As illustrated in Fig. 2b, we apply a basic partitioning along the curve, which consists in grouping the values of nodes of consecutive indices in *chunks* of constant size. The elements are numbered in order of the smallest index of their vertices. By following the path of the curve, most of the data of the mesh could be accessed through a sliding window, whose size would not be dependent of the mesh size. Thus, traversal of the mesh would be done through a continuous flow of data, where the majority of *chunks* would be accessed only once. Only the data of the elements located at the junction zones between the different spaces of the curve would not be accessible through the window. By following the curve, it is possible to identify the corresponding *chunks*. In this way, a *chunk ID* sequence corresponding to these data can be generated. We use these observations to design kernels iterating over unstructured meshes. The sliding window is implemented with an addressable FIFO. Buffers are used to access data not accessible through the sliding window.

3   Data Management Model Validation

To validate the proposed data management model and assess its ability to hide data access latencies, we have conducted experiments with a simulation tool. This tool makes it possible to evaluate the performance of the system from high level modeling without requiring a full FPGA synthesis. The experiments focused on sparse matrix-matrix multiplication and a tsunami simulation code.

3.1   Simulation Methodology

To conduct the experiments, we have chosen to use a simulation tool that we have developed [12]. The objective was to evaluate the performance of the system from a high-level modeling. The behavioral description of the kernels is modeled in *C++*. The irregularity of the applications we are studying and the distributed nature of the system we are targeting imply high and variable data access latencies. Thus, the main objective of this tool is to evaluate the effects of latency on the ability to speed up compute kernels using our data management model. Performance evaluation is based on the generation of data access latencies relating to the activity of the compute kernel. The tool uses a hybrid method: the activity of the compute kernel is generated by a simulation engine and latencies are produced by measuring the real latencies of S-DSM requests executed on the physical architecture, in order to produce faithful latencies. The simulation engine and the S-DSM server can be run on different nodes. This makes it possible to study different topologies associated with different latency profiles. In the rest of the section three topologies are used: *No Latency* which corresponds to the ideal case where all the data is stored in the FPGA memory, *Local* which corresponds to the case where the FPGA is connected by a local bus to the node running the S-DSM server and storing the data, and *Remote* which corresponds to the case where the FPGA and the S-DSM server are on two different nodes and are connected through an Ethernet network. Local node latencies are medium ($383\,\mu s$ for a read request and $207\,\mu s$ for a write request) and remote node latencies are high ($1311\,\mu s$ for read and $533\,\mu s$ for write). We have used a Xilinx Virtex VC707 as a reference FPGA to set up the simulation engine. Thus, the clock frequency was set to $200\,MHz$ and the theoretical peak memory bandwidth between the DDR and compute kernels was $12.8\,Gb/s$. The simulation being non-deterministic, the results presented are the median values of 10 runs.

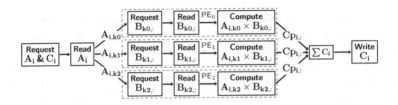

Fig. 3. Dataflow of the SpGEMM compute kernel using 3 PEs.

3.2 Case Study 1: General Sparse Matrix-Matrix Multiplication

SpGEMM is widely used to study acceleration methods for sparse linear algebra. This application generates irregular memory access patterns that makes it complex to optimize, with usually a low efficiency in terms of floating point operations per unit of time. We have designed the compute kernel by using the row-wise sparse matrix-matrix multiplication algorithm formulated by Gustavson [10]. Thanks to the row-wise traversal of the matrices, this algorithm is well suited to dataflow processing and is quite straightforward to parallelize. As illustrated in Fig. 3, to parallelize the computations, the kernel is implemented with several processing elements (PEs). The first stages of the kernel access the nonzero elements of the first input matrix and distribute them to the PEs. Each PE multiplies the elements received by the corresponding rows of the second input matrix. Finally, the last stages sum the partial results computed by the PEs and write the result matrix. The indices and the values of the matrix are encoded with 4 bytes (Single precision computations).

As the arithmetic intensity of SpGEMM is strongly data-dependent, we have chosen matrices, presented in Table 1, with varying sizes, densities and patterns. Thus, the experiments allow to evaluate the capacity of the data management model to adapt to irregularity. In order to limit the simulation time, the memory footprints of the matrices are smaller than a FPGA DRAM. To reproduce a situation where the capacity of the accelerator memory requires to transfer the data during the execution, we have adapted the simulated memory capacity accordingly to the dataset. Thus, the accelerator memory has been configured with 65536 locations of 1 kib (64 Mib). For each matrix, we have defined the theoretical peak computation speed by considering the processing time as the size of data transferred between the memory and the compute kernel divided by

Table 1. Square matrices, from [6], used for simulations. NNZ and density refer to the source matrix. The memory footprint includes the three operand matrices.

Name	Row	NNZ	Density (%)	Memory footprint	Peak GFLOP/s
consph	83334	6010480	0.087	294 Mb	2.99
cop20k_A	121192	2624331	0.018	182 Mb	2.52
F2	71505	5294285	0.10	383 Mb	2.93
m_t1	97578	9753570	0.10	427 Mb	3.07
s3dkt3m2	90449	3753461	0.046	134 Mb	2.94

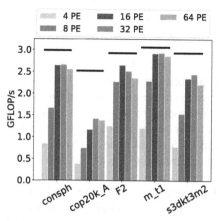

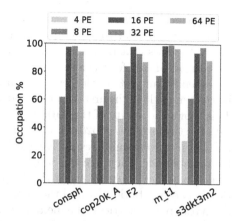

(a) Computation speed in GFLOP/s (higher is better). The horizontal lines are the theoretical peak computation speeds.

(b) Memory controller activity (occupancy percentage). Close to 100% means saturation.

Fig. 4. Performance according to the number of processing elements (PEs).

the FPGA memory bandwidth. These are represented by the horizontal black bars on Fig. 4a and Fig. 5.

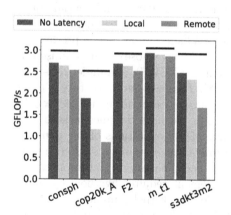

Fig. 5. Computation speed in GFLOP/s according the system topology (higher is better). The horizontal lines are the theoretical peak computation speeds.

For the first experiment, we varied the parallelism level of the compute kernel by implementing between 4 and 64 PEs on the local node. Figure 4a shows the computation speed obtained for this experiment. This shows that the increase in parallelism makes it possible to speed up computations, up to 16 PEs. The speed up obtained between 16 PEs and 32 PEs is low (between 1.04 and 1.22) or even negative. Between 32 and 64 PEs the speed ud is always negative. This efficiency limitation means that the PEs are under-exploited due to an insufficient supply of data (data starvation). The latter can be explained either by a data starvation in FPGA memory (due to excessive latencies), or by a FPGA memory bandwidth bottleneck. Figure 4b illustrates the occupancy rate of the FPGA memory controller. These results show that the controller is saturated for the configuration with 16 PEs. This information highlights that the FPGA memory bandwidth is the bottleneck for this kernel. This bandwidth limit is also one of the explanations for the nonlinear speed up between the configurations with 4 PEs and 16 PEs. The second experiment aimed to study the impact of topology on performance. For this we have used a configuration with 16 PEs, able to saturate the memory controller on the local node. The results obtained are illustrated in Fig. 5. It shows that for the matrices *consph*, *F2* and *m_t1* the performance gap with the ideal case for the local node (between 1% and 2%) and the remote node (between 2% and 6%) is very low. This small performance gap is mainly explained by the time to load the first data required to reach the nominal mode of the kernel. This shows the ability of the data management model to hide data access latencies. For the matrices *cop20k_A* and *s3dkt3m2*, the performance gap is larger, but remains relatively small, respectively 38% and 6% for local node and 54% and 32% for remote node. For these two latter, the performance gap with the theoretical peak is also the largest, even for the ideal case. These results highlight a correlation between data density and the ability to speed up computations. Indeed, for the most sparse matrices, the memory accesses at row granularity do not use all the width of the data bus. Therefore, sparsity amplifies the effect of memory bandwidth bottleneck. Moreover, the more the rows are sparse, more processing time is short. This limits the ability to overlay the processing flow with the data transfer flow. For the matrix *cop20k_A*, the low arithmetic intensity per row limits the ability to hide data access latencies.

3.3   Case Study 2: Shallow Water Equation

The Shallow Water Equations (SWE) are hyperbolic partial differential equations that describe a layer of fluid below a pressure surface. They can be solved with FEM. The code under study is the TsunAWI simulation code, a production code that implements the SWE with inundation, and whose results are used in the Indonesia Tsunami Early Warning System (InaTEWS), and under real-time constraints in the LEXIS European project [8]. The base data structure is a 2D unstructured mesh. This code has been optimized for performance, especially concerning the mesh ordering [9]. In this code, we have designed a kernel to speed up the calculation of the gradient, one of the operations of the tsunami simulation code. This operation is an interpolation of the sea surface height via barycentric coordinates. The barycentric coordinates are precomputed for each vertex element. The processing of an element requires five floating point operations, resulting in a low FLOP/byte ratio. The kernel is implemented with several independent processing elements (PEs). Each PE process a different part

Table 2. Characteristics of the set of meshes used for the experiments.

Region	Name	# Elements	# Vertices	Memory footprint
Indian ocean	Padang_C	460 119	231 586	14 Mb
	Padang_F	2 470 345	1 242 653	74 Mb
Pacific ocean	Coquibo_C	3 396 755	1 709 506	102 Mb
	Coquimbo_F	9 762 027	4 887 927	293 Mb
Mediterranean Sea	Mediterranean	9 917 645	4 999 404	298 Mb

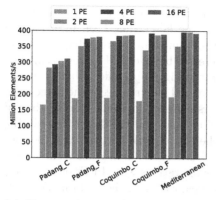
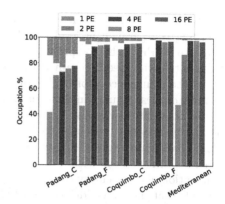

(a) Computation speed in MElements/s (higher is better).

(b) Memory controller activity (occupancy percentage). Gray bars correspond to the loading time of the first data.

Fig. 6. Performance according to the number of processing elements (PEs).

of the mesh. The size of the sliding window is 1024 words. For the experiments, we have used five meshes presented in Table 2. The FPGA memory have been configured with 32 Mib. This was defined according to the maximum number of processing elements implemented (16 PEs), in order to allow each PE to prefetch up to 512 chunks of 1 kib per stream of data. Considering the memory footprint of each mesh and the maximum memory bandwidth of the FPGA, the theoretical peak computation speed is approximately 426 MElements/s for all meshes.

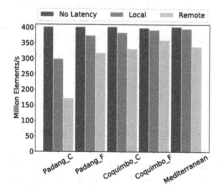
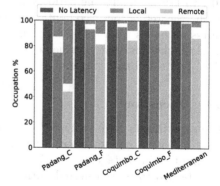

(a) Computation speed in MElements/s (higher is better).

(b) Memory controller activity (occupancy percentage). Gray bars correspond to the loading time of the first chunks.

Fig. 7. Performance according the system topology.

The first experiment aimed to study the speed up efficiency of the kernel according the parallelism level. To do this, the kernel has been implemented with 1 to 16 PEs. The computation speeds obtained are represented in Fig. 6a. It shows that the speed up gain sharply decreases beyond 2 PEs. The occupancy rate of the memory controller illustrated in the Fig. 6b provides a better understanding of these results. In this figure, the colored bars represent the percentage of time the controller is active, the gray bars correspond to the loading time of the first chunks as a percentage of simulation time, and the space between the colored bars and the gray bars represents the part of time during which the controller could have been used more. For the four largest meshes the results show a saturation of the memory controller for configurations with 4 PEs or more. We conclude that the bandwidth of the FPGA memory limits the performance scaling of the kernel. From 2 PEs onward, the controller occupancy rate is too high to efficiently speed up the processing by increasing the parallelism. Additionally, the smaller the mesh, the more the loading time of the first chunks represents a significant part of the total processing time, which reduces the computation speed.

For the second experiment, we have evaluated the kernel performance according to the topology with 4 PEs. Figure 7a and 7b respectively illustrate the computation speed obtained and the associated occupancy rate of the memory controller. These results show that increasing data access latency reduces computation speed and highlight a correlation between the size of the mesh and the slowdown. As shown in Fig. 7b, this effect can be explained by the proportion of the processing time spent to load the first chunks. For large datasets processing on the local node, where the load time is the least impacting, processing speeds almost reach those of the ideal case. For the remote node, where the read access latency is three times greater than on the local node, the slowing down of the computation speed is relatively low for the three largest meshes (from 10% to 17%). Finally, the performance of the *No Latency* configuration is close to the theoretical peak computation speed. The gap is due to the inability to access all nodes from the sliding window, which requires reading several times some chunks. Thus, we conclude that this mesh traversal method is almost ideal, given how small that gap is.

3.4   Discussion

The experiments have evaluated a data management model where accelerator tasks initiate access to distributed data. The experimental scenario used was the most disadvantageous, as the FPGA memory was empty at startup and all data had to be transferred during runtime. The results showed that thanks to prefetching, the programming model can efficiently hide the latencies of distributed data access. Nevertheless, this efficiency depends on the workload of the compute kernel. In practice, the observed workloads are huge. The size of the sparse matrices used in scientific applications can exceed ten gigabytes. The size of the complete datasets used for the tsunami simulation are at least ten times larger than the data subset used for the calculation of the gradient only. For the complete simulation each element of the mesh involves a hundred floating operation per iteration. Thus, the processing time of the largest meshes on a high end processor can exceed several hours, and this motivates to distribute the processing to an heterogeneous system with FPGAs. This work shows that an S-DSM can simplify the distributed data management thanks to *chunk* partitioning and that the presented data management model solves the data access latency issue. Experiments have shown how in this model an FPGA can be supplied with data. As each accelerator is master of its access to data, this model can be extended to a distributed system integrating several FPGAs.

4 Related Work

Prior work have been done to provide shared memory for distributed systems with accelerators. Willendberg et al. [16] have proposed an FPGA communication infrastructure compatible to GASNet. This enables processing elements implemented on an FPGA to initiate remote direct memory access to remote FPGAs. Unicorn [4] provides a distributed shared memory (DSM) for CPU-GPU clusters. This is achieved with transactional semantics and deferred bulk data synchronization. StarPU [1] uses a DSM to manage data replication for heterogeneous distributed systems, but this DSM is not directly exposed to users. Recent work has studied *chunk* partitioning applied to sparse matrix for acceleration of sparse linear algebra. Winter et al. [17] have proposed an adaptive *chunk*-based SpGEMM for GPU. This approach uses *chunks* to store the partial results of multiplication, then uses the *chunk* metadata for the merge stage. Rubensson and Rudberg [13] have proposed the Chunks and Tasks programming model for parallelization of irregular applications. In this model, matrices are represented by sparse quatrees of chunks. MatRaptor [15] and REAP [14] uses a chunk-based CSR format adaptation and the row-wise product to implement SpGEMM kernel on FPGA. Barrio et al. [3] have proposed an unstructured mesh sorting algorithm to enabling stream processing for finite element method applications. This algorithm was applied to study the acceleration of scientific codes on CPU-FPGA platform.

5 Conclusion

Increasing the energy efficiency of HPC systems has become a major issue. Thanks to their reconfigurable architecture, FPGAs could increase power efficiency for HPC applications with irregular compute kernels. However, due to their complexity of use, FPGAs are underemployed in HPC systems. In this paper we have proposed a data management model for irregular compute kernel acceleration on FPGA integrated in distributed system. This model relies on a S-DSM to allow accelerators to initiate access to distributed data and on *chunk* partitioning to abstract the irregular structure of the datasets. We have shown how this data management model could be applied to compute kernels of sparse linear algebra and finite element method. We have conducted experiments with a hybrid simulation tool, which exploits the physical system to provide accurate data. These experiments have shown that the data management model enables to efficiently hide high data access latencies. Finally, experiments have shown that memory bandwidth is a bottleneck. This phenomenon is normal since the studied applications are memory bound. High Memory Bandwidth (HBM) technologies as available on current and future FPGAs should help to remove this bottleneck and improving performance of compute kernels.

References

1. Augonnet, C., Thibault, S., Namyst, R., Wacrenier, P.A.: StarPU: a unified platform for task scheduling on heterogeneous multicore architectures. Concurr. Comput.: Pract. Exp. **23**(2), 187–198 (2011)
2. Bader, M.: Space-Filling Curves: An Introduction with Applications in Scientific Computing, vol. 9. Springer, Heidelberg (2013). https://doi.org/10.1007/978-3-642-31046-1
3. Barrio, P., Carreras, C., López, J.A., Robles, Ó., Jevtic, R., Sierra, R.: Memory optimization in FPGA-accelerated scientific codes based on unstructured meshes. J. Syst. Archit. **60**(7), 579–591 (2014)
4. Beri, T., Bansal, S., Kumar, S.: The unicorn runtime: efficient distributed shared memory programming for hybrid CPU-GPU clusters. IEEE Trans. Parallel Distrib. Syst. **28**(5), 1518–1534 (2017)
5. Cudennec, L.: Software-distributed shared memory over heterogeneous microserver architecture. In: Euro-Par 2017: Parallel Processing Workshops (2017)
6. Davis, T.A., Hu, Y.: The university of florida sparse matrix collection. ACM Trans. Math. Softw. **38**(1), 1:1–1:25 (2011)
7. Escobar, F.A., Chang, X., Valderrama, C.: Suitability analysis of FPGAs for heterogeneous platforms in HPC. IEEE Trans. Parallel Distrib. Syst. **27**(2), 600–612 (2016)
8. Goubier, T., et al.: Real-time model of computation over HPC/cloud orchestration - the LEXIS approach. In: Barolli, L., Poniszewska-Maranda, A., Enokido, T. (eds.) CISIS 2020. AISC, vol. 1194, pp. 255–266. Springer, Cham (2021). https://doi.org/10.1007/978-3-030-50454-0_24
9. Goubier, T., Rakowsky, N., Harig, S.: Fast tsunami simulations for a real-time emergency response flow. In: 2020 IEEE/ACM HPC for Urgent Decision Making, UrgentHPC@SC 2020, pp. 21–26. IEEE (2020)
10. Gustavson, F.G.: Two fast algorithms for sparse matrices: multiplication and permuted transposition. ACM Trans. Math. Softw. 4(3), 250–269 (1978)
11. High-Performance Conjugate Gradient (HPCG) Benchmark results, November 2020. https://www.top500.org/lists/hpcg/list/2020/11/
12. Lenormand, E., Goubier, T., Cudennec, L., Charles, H.P.: A combined fast/cycle accurate simulation tool for reconfigurable accelerator evaluation: application to distributed data management. In: 2020 International Workshop on Rapid System Prototyping (RSP) (2020)
13. Rubensson, E.H., Rudberg, E.: Chunks and tasks: a programming model for parallelization of dynamic algorithms. Parallel Comput. **40**(7), 328–343 (2014)
14. Soltaniyeh, M., Martin, R.P., Nagarakatte, S.: Synergistic CPU-FPGA acceleration of sparse linear algebra. CoRR abs/2004.13907 (2020)

15. Srivastava, N.K., Jin, H., Liu, J., Albonesi, D.H., Zhang, Z.: MatRaptor: a sparse-sparse matrix multiplication accelerator based on row-wise product. In: 53rd Annual IEEE/ACM International Symposium on Microarchitecture, MICRO, pp. 766–780. IEEE (2020)
16. Willenberg, R., Chow, P.: A remote memory access infrastructure for global address space programming models in FPGAs. In: Proceedings of the ACM/SIGDA International Symposium on Field Programmable Gate Arrays, pp. 211–220. ACM (2013)
17. Winter, M., Mlakar, D., Zayer, R., Seidel, H.P., Steinberger, M.: Adaptive sparse matrix-matrix multiplication on the GPU. In: Proceedings of the 24th Symposium on Principles and Practice of Parallel Programming, pp. 68–81. ACM (2019)

Towards an Efficient Sparse Storage Format for the SpMM Kernel in GPUs

Renzo Marini, Ernesto Dufrechou$^{(\boxtimes)}$ ⓘ, and Pablo Ezzatti ⓘ

Instituto de Computación (INCO), Facultad de Ingeniería,
Universidad de la República, Montevideo, Uruguay
{rmarini,edufrechou,pezzatti}@fing.edu.uy

Abstract. The sparse matrix-matrix multiply kernel (SpMM) gained significant interest in the last years due to its applications in data science. In 2018, Zhang and Gruenwald [15] proposed the bitmap-based sparse format *bmSparse* and described in detail the implementation of the SpMM for Nvidia GPUs. The novel format is promising in terms of performance and storage space. In this work, we re-implement the algorithm following the authors' guidelines, adding two new stages that can benefit performance. The experiments performed using nine sparse matrices of different sizes show significant accelerations with respect to cuSparse's CSR variant.

Keywords: Sparse matrix matrix multiplication · GPU · Sparse format

1 Introduction

The era of *big data* has brought about a major paradigm shift and the emergence of new problems in which the information is structured in large graphs. The connection between graphs and sparse matrices (those in which the vast majority of their coefficients are equal to zero) has been extensively studied and, because of it, there are important efforts that propose to express graph problems in terms of basic linear algebra operations on sparse matrices. These efforts have attracted the interest of part of the academic community, historically concentrated on the sparse matrix-vector product (SpMV) for its role in solving systems of linear equations, to other operations such as the sparse matrix-sparse matrix product (SpMM), which has important applications in data science. In particular, the most frequent goal is to find algorithms, implementations, and storage formats capable of running efficiently on parallel hardware.

In recent decades, the trend in computer architecture design has been to incorporate multiple cores on the same chip [2]. As a consequence, the use of throughput-oriented processors [7] to accelerate scientific applications has increased. A paradigmatic example is GPUs, which have been used heavily in the context of dense and sparse linear algebra for more than a decade, to the point where efficient implementations are publicly available for most of the standard operations [3,6,13].

© Springer Nature Switzerland AG 2022
R. Chaves et al. (Eds.): Euro-Par 2021, LNCS 13098, pp. 104–115, 2022.
https://doi.org/10.1007/978-3-031-06156-1_9

Sparse Matrix Multiplication (SpMM) operates on two matrices stored in a sparse storage format, that is, a format to avoid explicitly storing null coefficients. As the pattern of nonzero coefficients, and therefore the space necessary to store the result of the operation, will depend on the interaction between the nonzero coefficients of the operands, it must be estimated or calculated from them, which gives the SpMM a higher level of complexity than the SpMV.

In 2018, Zhang and Gruenwald [15] introduced a sparse block format called *bmSparse*, which adapts the bitmap indexing technique used in the context of relational databases (and also for some of the early sparse formats). Although the performance of similar formats has been studied in the context of SpMV [11], the work mentioned is the first to do so with SpMM. The results obtained for the (*WebBase-1M*) sparse matrix were promising, showing better performance than the libraries CUSP [1] and BHSPARSE [12].

This work focuses on re-implementing the algorithm proposed in [15] incorporating modifications to improve its performance. Among the optimizations considered, we explore the inclusion of two new stages. One avoids making the product of those blocks that will result in a null block due to their pattern of zeros (T_4). The other computes the final storage space and output nonzero pattern before the numerical multiplication stage (T_9). The experimental evaluation was carried out on a set of nine matrices from the SuiteSparse collection with different characteristics, showing that the new stage T_4 of the algorithm allows significant savings in the execution time of the subsequent stages.

The rest of the work is structured as follows. In Sect. 2, the main concepts about the sparse matrix multiplication operation are summarized. Then, in Sect. 3, the details of the SpMM kernel implementation using the *bmSparse* storage format are studied. Later, we present the main proposals in Sect. 4. The experimental evaluation of our proposals on a set of sparse matrices follows. Finally, the main conclusions drawn during the work and the lines of future work to be developed are presented in Sect. 6.

2   Sparse Matrix Multiplication (SpMM)

Sparse matrix multiplication (SpMM) is a very useful operation in various contexts of linear algebra and graph analysis, with applications such as solvers for algebraic multigrid methods (AMG) [8], triangle counting [4] and breadth-first search (BFS) with multiple sources [9]. Algorithm 1 presents a pseudocode of the row-wise SpMM method presented by [10]. In the case of other typical operations on sparse structures, such as SpMV, a common strategy to improve performance is to exploit prior knowledge about the sparse matrix's sparse pattern to minimize memory operations on global memory [14]. However, SpMM adds additional difficulties since the computational complexity of the problem does not depend solely on the nonzero structure of the separate inputs but on how they interact with each other. On the other hand, in most applications, the SpMM is usually executed only once for each pair of matrices. Therefore, the optimization techniques that are based on analyzing the nonzero patterns are less effective than in the case of the SpMV, which is usually part of the innermost loop of iterative solvers.

Algorithm 1: SpMM proposed by [10]

1: **for** $a_{i*} \in A$ **do**
2:    **for** $a_{ij} \in a_{i*}$ **and** $a_{ij} \neq 0$ **do**
3:       **for** $b_{jk} \in b_{j*}$ **and** $b_{jk} \neq 0$ **do**
4:          value $= a_{ij} * b_{jk}$
5:          **if** $c_{ik} \notin c_{i*}$ **then**
6:             $c_{ik} = 0$
7:          **end if**
8:          $c_{ik} = c_{ik} + value$
9:       **end for**
10:    **end for**
11: **end for**

The particularities above determine that the major design decisions to consider are how to partition the work to be done between different processing units (in the parallel case).

2.1 The *bmSparse* Storage Format

The *bmSparse* format represents sparse matrices using 8×8 blocks and the following data structures:

- *keys*: An array of integers (uint64_t) represents the position of a block in the block array. The first 32 bits encode the row number, while the last 32 bits encode the column number. The keys appear ordered by row and then by column. The choice of uint64_t to represent the keys makes it possible to represent arrays of up to 2^{32} blocks of columns and rows. For smaller arrays, memory usage could be reduced by modifying the format to allow 32 bits to represent keys.
- *bmps*: An array of integers (uint64_t) that stores in position i, a bitmap associated with the block in position $keys[i]$. Each element of the block is mapped to one bit of the bitmap. The bit is zero if the block element is null and one otherwise.
- *values*: Array with the nonzero values of the array ordered by rows and then by column.
- *offsets*: Array with the start position of each block in *values*.

3   The SpMM with bmSPARSE

Given two input matrices, A and B, stored in *bmSparse* format, the multiplication algorithm for this format performs two principal tasks. First, it has to build *task list* that determines which pairs of blocks of A and B must be multiplied and added to a block of the resulting matrix C. The task list can be seen as a list of (i, j, k) tuples, named *tasks*, obtained from the rule:

$$C_{ik} = \sum_j A_{ij} \times B_{jk}. \tag{1}$$

Once the task list is formed, the algorithm has to process the tasks and construct the output structure. The original algorithm [15] is divided into 7 stages, which are identified as $T_{1...7}$.

The stages T_1, T_2 and T_3 are in charge of creating the task list. Assuming that $A\_keys[n]$ stores the key (i, j), the task list is considered as the union of the sets $t'_n, n \in [0, size(A\_keys))$, of all the tuples in which the key (i, j) of A_keys participates. If $B\_row_j = \{x \mid x \in B\_keys \wedge row(x) = j\}$ is defined as the set of *keys* in row j from B, t'_n can be formally expressed as:

$$t'_n = \{ (i, j, k) \mid A\_keys[n] = (i, j) \wedge \exists x \in B\_row_j : col(x) = k\}. \tag{2}$$

Note that in the Definition 2, the tasks are represented as tuples of coordinates (i, j, k). However, if $(i, j) = A\_keys[n]$ and $(j, k) = B\_keys[m]$, the tasks can also be represented by the tuple of positions (n, m). In Eq. (3) the set t_n is defined, which uses the representation of tasks as tuple of positions. There is a one-to-one correspondence between the elements of t'_n and t_n.

$$t_n = \{ (n, m) \mid A\_keys[n] = (i, j) \wedge B\_keys[m] \in B\_row_j\} \tag{3}$$

We based our implementation on the latter representation, while [15] is based on the former. The main advantage of defining the task list as the union of sets t_n is that these sets can be easily calculated thanks to the characteristics of the format. On the one hand, observe that the second component of the t_n tasks represents positions of the same row of blocks in matrix B.

In stage T_5 the task list is ordered so that tasks associated with the same output block are contiguous. Using the representation of tasks as tuples of coordinates (i, j, k), the above is equivalent to ordering according to (i, k). Because the *task_list* array uses another representation of tasks, to determine the relative order between two items a conversion is done before comparing them.

The T_6 stage is in charge of determining which blocks of the resulting matrix will be non-null, which corresponds to the keys array of the format *bmSparse*. To achieve this, the *task_list* array is interpreted as an array of tasks represented as (i, j, k).

Stage T_7 processes the tasks to generate the resulting blocks. Processing a task involves building a dense version of the input blocks, performing the multiplication, and adding the partial block of results to the corresponding output block.

In stage T_8, the array of values generated in stage T_7 is taken as input, and a new array is created that contains only the non-null values of the original array. Relative orders remain.

Most of the implementation was performed using primitives from the *Thrust* API, with the exception of T_7 that required developing specific CUDA kernels.

4   Main Extensions

In addition to the variants made to the steps defined in [15], In this work, two new stages are proposed, T_4 and T_9 with the aim of improving performance, saving work in other stages.

Different versions of the algorithm are generated by including these stages, each one associated with a different sequence of stages. Valid sequences are represented by paths in the directed graph of Fig. 1. The layout followed by [15] is comparable to the one specified in the previous section, that is, $T_{1,2,3,5,6,7,8}$.

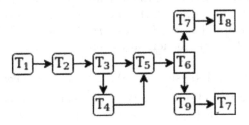

Fig. 1. Possible execution paths.

4.1 T_4: Null-Task Filtering

The result of executing a task is the product of two blocks, which will then be added to one of the blocks of the resulting matrix. If the bitmap of that product is null, that task will not affect the result of the SPMM and could be ignored. In [15], the bitmap of a task is calculated in stage T_7, once the product of the blocks has already been made. However, the bitmap of the product of two blocks can be obtained using only the bitmaps of those blocks, without the need for floating-point operations. Stage T_4 consists of calculating the bitmaps of each task, and eliminating from the task list those that do not contribute to the values of the resulting matrix. It is an optional stage in the sense that the correctness of the algorithm does not depend on it. The motivation for this step is to achieve higher performance in the later stages.

The filtering of tasks is performed using the primitive *thrust::remove_if*, which takes as input the array of tasks and a functor that determines if the bitmap that would be obtained when executing the task is null.

The functor implementation iterates over each dimension of the resulting bitmap, checking for possible intersections between the bits in each row of A and the corresponding column of B. The function returns false if a non-null bit is found.

4.2 T_9: Calculate C Bitmaps Based on A and B's Bitmaps

The stage T_9 computes the array of bitmaps of the resulting matrix using the input matrices' bitmaps.

For this purpose, the first step is to define an iterator of type *thrust::make_transform_iterator* to generate the bitmap resulting from executing a task with the incoming bitmaps. To calculate the output bit (i, k), the associated functor iterates over the dimension j of both input bitmaps. When determining which bit should be in 1 in each bitmap, it starts with a bitmap with 1 in the first position (0x8000000000000000) and shifts it to the right according to the row and column number. In case both corresponding bits are in 1, the results are accumulated in the *result* bitmap by a bitwise *or*, as shown in Listing 1.1.

Listing 1.1. Computation of the task bitmap.

```
#define F 0x8000000000000000;
...
uint64_t result = 0;
for (int i = 0; i < 8; i++)
  for (int k = 0; k < 8; k++)
    for (int j = 0; j < 8; j++) {
      const bool A_bit_set = A_bmp & (F >> (i * 8 + j));
      const bool B_bit_set = B_bmp & (F >> (j * 8 + k));
      if (A_bit_set && B_bit_set) result |= F >> (i * 8 + k);

    }
```

Once we have all the bitmaps associated with the block multiplications, *thrust::reduce_by_key* is used to perform a bitwise *or* between the bitmaps of the same output block. Computing the output bitmaps beforehand eliminates the need of the T_8 (compression) stage. However, since only the positions of the nonzero elements, and not their values, are taken into account, it is possible that some of the elements turn out to be null and some explicit zeros end up being stored.

5   Experimental Evaluation

This section makes an experimental evaluation of different variants of the SpMM algorithm based on *bmSparse* described previously.

5.1   Platform Setup and Test Cases

All testing is done on a system comprised of an Intel i7-9750H@2.60 GHz CPU and an NVIDIA GeForce GTX 1660 Ti GPU, Turing architecture. GPU programming is done using CUDA 10.2, and the associated Thrust [3] parallel algorithms library.

Square sparse matrices obtained from the *SuiteSparse Matrix Collection* [5] are used, identified with a number from 1 to 9. The matrices used store single-precision floating-point numbers (*floats*). The characteristics of each matrix are presented in Table 1.

Performance measured by runtime is compared to that of the cuSPARSE [3] library, also part of the CUDA Toolkit.

Table 1. Main characteristics of the matrices used. Arrays 1–3 have dimension close to 10^4, matrices 4–6 have dimension close to 10^5 and the remainder to 10^6.

Name	Id.	Blocks	NNZ	Dimension
cryg10000	1	8613	49699	10000
Goodwin_030	2	20728	312814	10142
ted_A_unscaled	3	13761	424587	10605
Goodwin_095	4	203725	3226066	100037
matrix_9	5	148928	2121550	103430
hcircuit	6	90082	513072	105676
webbase-1M	7	550761	3105536	1000005
t2em	8	572656	4590832	921632
atmosmodd	9	1410884	8814880	1270432

5.2 SpMM Algorithm Performance

We start the analysis by discussing the execution time of each stage. Table 2 details the base implementation (V_{base}) runtimes by multiplying each matrix by itself, broken down according to the stages of the method.

Table 2. Execution time (in µs) of multiplying sparse matrices using the base variant of the SpMM algorithm based on *bmSparse*. Arrays are assumed to be in device memory, that is, transfer time is not included.

Stage	Runtime by matrix								
	1	2	3	4	5	6	7	8	9
T_1	53	58	56	731	185	391	693	1084	2000
T_2	39	43	41	269	172	110	251	436	1858
T_3	202	536	339	1808	1668	1255	3788	2122	6238
T_5	318	1201	642	10355	8994	6906	25392	8505	42552
T_6	303	419	308	2284	2493	2130	5985	2515	7020
T_7	397	2036	965	19477	20618	17313	55158	19693	77953
T_8	58	1264	2659	14121	857	2238	46206	3155	5662
Total	1370	5557	5010	49045	34987	30343	137473	37510	143283

In this implementation, the T_1 stage calls the primitive *thrust::reduce_by_key* on the array of keys, so it is expected that the duration of T_1 depends mostly on the size of that array, which corresponds to the third column of Table 1. This hypothesis can be corroborated from Tables 1 and 2, where the duration of T_1 can be observed to increase with the number of blocks. Something similar happens in stage T_2, where the vector *B_count* is accessed for each element of *A_keys*.

The main goal of stage T_3 is to create the array *task_list*, Therefore, the times of T_3 should depend mainly on the number of tasks that are part of the task list. This hypothesis can be corroborated in Fig. 2, which shows a linear dependence between the number of tasks and execution times.

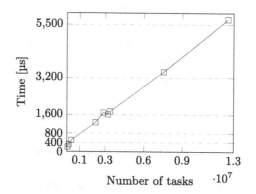

Fig. 2. Execution time (in μs) of T_3 stage as a function of the number of tasks in the task list.

Although the number of tasks is the variable that best predicts the duration of T_3, this information is typically not available before doing the multiplication. However, this duration could be estimated using the number of blocks and the dimension of an array. On the one hand, the more blocks, the more likely tasks will be formed between pairs of them. On the other hand, as the dimension increases, there are more possible positions for the blocks, which decreases the probability that they will form a task. This explains why, with a few exceptions, the T_3 times increase with the number of blocks.

In stages T_5, T_6 and T_7 a similar pattern is repeated between the execution times of each matrix, since the task list is also processed in these stages.

5.3   Impact of Executing T_4

Table 3 shows the runtimes corresponding to each stage of the variant that includes stage T_4 (V_{T4}). Comparing the results with Table 2, it can be observed that, despite the extra cost of including the T_4 stage, the overall performance does not deteriorate in any of the evaluated cases, obtaining execution time reductions of up to 40%.

Table 4 details, for each matrix, the number of tasks that are part of the *task_list* vector, built in stage T_3, and the percentage of tasks that are later discarded at stage T_4. It can be observed that for the selected set of matrices, the number of tasks eliminated varies significantly and that these can represent a high percentage of the tasks generated in T_3.

From Fig. 3, it can be seen that in stages T_5, T_6 and T_7, a linear reduction in execution time is obtained with respect to the amount of discarded tasks.

Table 3. Execution time (in µs) of multiplying sparse matrices using the V_{T4} variant. Arrays are assumed to be in device memory, that is, transfer time is not included.

Stage	Runtime by matrix								
	1	2	3	4	5	6	7	8	9
T_1	53	58	56	731	185	391	693	1084	2000
T_2	39	43	41	269	172	110	251	436	1858
T_3	202	536	339	1808	1668	1255	3788	2122	6238
T_4	42	91	58	592	492	385	1310	603	2249
T_5	167	1080	630	8947	7141	4199	14626	7944	33276
T_6	174	397	303	2106	1997	1391	3519	2387	6002
T_7	257	1731	949	16711	15938	10648	31330	17783	61583
T_8	57	1619	2635	17340	1017	3254	50965	4998	7945
Total	991	5555	5011	48504	28610	21633	106482	37357	121151

Table 4. Amount of tasks generated in T_3 and percentage of tasks eliminated in stage T_4.

Matrix	# tasks	% removed tasks
1	59512	36,3
2	346798	14,4
3	153486	1,6
4	3369528	13,4
5	3205366	20,0
6	2231426	38,5
7	7540274	42,6
8	2851764	7,8
9	12556668	22,1

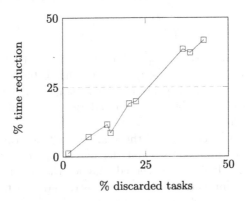

Fig. 3. Percentage of time reduction of stages T_5, T_6 and T_7 based on the percentage of tasks eliminated in stage T_4

On the other hand, and regarding the performance of the stage T_4 itself, it can be corroborated from the data in the Tables 3 and 4, that the execution times depend primarily on the size of the task list, as it happens in the T_3 stage.

5.4 Impact of Executing T_9

To answer whether it is convenient to perform (our variant of) the calculation of the array of bitmaps and offsets before the multiplication, Table 5 compares a variant that incorporates the previous calculation of the output bitmaps ($V_{T4\&T9}$) with the version V_{T4}. In this table, it can be seen that the time of the T_7 stage for the $V_{T4\&T9}$ version is less than that of the V_{T4} version in all cases. The main reason is that, in the first case, the calculation of the output offsets and bitmaps array is considered part of T_9, while in the second, it is considered part of T_7. However, when comparing the total time of both versions, the inverse relationship occurs. This is because stage T_8 in V_{T4} runs in less time than stage T_9 in $V_{T4\&T9}$. In the implementation used by $V_{T4\&T9}$, almost 90% the runtime of stage T_9 is spent executing the functor that generates bitmaps from tasks. This was easily verified replacing the functor by a trivial one in an informal experiment.

Table 5. Average duration (in μs) of the stages after T_6 in the V_{T4} and $V_{T4\&T9}$ variants. The last two rows show the sum of the times of the mentioned stages.

Stage	Versión	Runtime by matrix								
		1	2	3	4	5	6	7	8	9
T_7	V_{T4}	260	1730	952	16793	15985	10635	31320	17782	60671
	$V_{T4\&T9}$	226	1650	887	16099	14094	9381	28287	16105	53778
T_8	V_{T4}	76	225	222	1304	2399	1995	5464	2452	6727
T_9	$V_{T4\&T9}$	233	1002	621	8301	5723	3521	10750	5957	21081
Total	V_{T4}	336	1955	1174	18097	18384	12630	36784	20234	67398
	$V_{T4\&T9}$	459	2652	1508	24400	19818	12902	39038	22062	74860

Since the T_4 stage performs a job similar to that of T_9, a possible improvement is to calculate the bitmaps of those tasks that are non-null in the T_4 stage. In this way, the T_9 stage would only be in charge of reducing the bitmaps of the tasks that correspond to the same C block. As future work, it is interesting to study this change and possible optimizations to the functor that calculates the bitmaps of each task.

Comparison with CuSPARSE. Table 6 compares the execution times of the V_{T4} variant based on the *bmSparse* format and the implementation for the CSR format included in CUSPARSE. It is observed that V_{T4} has a better performance in all matrices except the first one, where there is a small difference that favors CUSPARSE. The matrix with the most significant difference is matrix 5, where the execution time of CUSPARSE is approximately 5× longer than that of *bmSparse*.

Table 6. Execution times (in µs) of the V_{T4} variant based on *bmSparse* and the implementation of cuSPARSE based on CSR. In both cases, values of type `float` and input arrays previously loaded into device memory are assumed.

	Matrix								
	1	2	3	4	5	6	7	8	9
Time cuSPARSE	882	3998	5841	46555	140496	22113	455073	48310	202372
Time bmSPARSE	991	5555	5011	48504	28610	21633	106482	37357	121151
Relative perf.	0.89×	0.72×	1.17×	0.96×	4.91×	1.02×	4.27×	1.29×	1.67×

6   Concluding Remarks

The SpMM is a sparse matrix operation that has interesting applications in data science. The *bmSparse* format, presented by Zhang and Gruenwald [15], is a novel bitmap-based sparse format, specially conceived to achieve high performance for the SpMM in throughput-oriented processors such as GPUs. The use of bitmaps effectively addresses one of the main challenges of the SpMM, which is to determine the nonzero pattern of the output matrix from the two input matrices, and the preliminary results presented by the authors are promising.

We have re-implemented the algorithm based on the directions of [15] and proposed two new stages that can improve its performance. T_4 stage removes unnecessary tasks from the task list based on the bitmaps of the blocks of A and B that form each task. The experimental results on a set of nine sparse matrices from the SuiteSparse Matrix Collection show that the savings on the time of subsequent stages greatly compensate for the addition of T_4, achieving interesting runtime reductions. The addition of T_9, which computes the resulting bitmaps from the bitmaps of A and B blocks, did not result in a performance gain, although several possible optimizations to this stage were identified. The variant that includes T_4 (V_{T4}) is superior to cuSPARSE in 6 out of 9 test cases and achieves up to 5× runtime reduction.

We intend to fine-tune each stage of the algorithm for future work, concentrating on optimizing the most time-consuming stages. We are also interested in adapting the implementation to harness GPUs equipped with Tensor Cores.

Acknowledgment. This work is partially funded by the ANII-MPI project *Efficient computational methods for numerical linear algebra on heterogeneus architectures*. Additionally, the authors thank PEDECIBA Informática and the University of the Republic, Uruguay.

References

1. Bell, N., Garland, M.: Cusp: generic parallel algorithms for sparse matrix and graph computations (2012). http://cusp-library.googlecode.com. Version 0.3.0
2. Blake, G., Dreslinski, R.G., Mudge, T.: A survey of multicore processors. IEEE Signal Process. Mag. **26**(6), 26–37 (2009). https://doi.org/10.1109/MSP.2009.934110

3. cuSPARSE: CUDA Toolkit Documentation. https://docs.nvidia.com/cuda/cusparse/index.html
4. Davis, T.A.: Graph algorithms via suitesparse: graphblas: triangle counting and k-truss. In: 2018 IEEE High Performance extreme Computing Conference (HPEC), pp. 1–6 (2018). https://doi.org/10.1109/HPEC.2018.8547538
5. Davis, T.A., Hu, Y.: The university of Florida sparse matrix collection. ACM Trans. Math. Softw. **38**(1), 1–25 (2011). https://doi.org/10.1145/2049662.2049663
6. Dufrechou, E., Ezzatti, P., Quintana-Ortí, E.S.: Selecting optimal SpMV realizations for GPUs via machine learning. Int. J. High Perform. Comput. Appl. **35**(3), 254–267 (2021). https://doi.org/10.1177/1094342021990738
7. Garland, M., Kirk, D.B.: Understanding throughput-oriented architectures. Commun. ACM **53**(11), 58–66 (2010). https://doi.org/10.1145/1839676.1839694
8. Georgii, J., Westermann, R.: A streaming approach for sparse matrix products and its application in Galerkin multigrid methods. Electron. Trans. Numer. Anal. **37**, 3–5 (2010)
9. Gilbert, J.R., Reinhardt, S., Shah, V.B.: High-performance graph algorithms from parallel sparse matrices. In: Kågström, B., Elmroth, E., Dongarra, J., Waśniewski, J. (eds.) PARA 2006. LNCS, vol. 4699, pp. 260–269. Springer, Heidelberg (2007). https://doi.org/10.1007/978-3-540-75755-9_32
10. Gustavson, F.G.: Two fast algorithms for sparse matrices: multiplication and permuted transposition. ACM Trans. Math. Softw. **4**(3), 250–269 (1978). https://doi.org/10.1145/355791.355796
11. Kannan, R.: Efficient sparse matrix multiple-vector multiplication using a bitmapped format. In: 20th Annual International Conference on High Performance Computing, pp. 286–294 (2013). https://doi.org/10.1109/HiPC.2013.6799135
12. Liu, W., Vinter, B.: A framework for general sparse matrix-matrix multiplication on GPUs and heterogeneous processors. J. Parallel Distrib. Comput. **85**(C), 47–61 (2015). https://doi.org/10.1016/j.jpdc.2015.06.010
13. Volkov, V., Demmel, J.W.: Benchmarking GPUs to tune dense linear algebra. In: SC 2008: Proceedings of the 2008 ACM/IEEE Conference on Supercomputing, pp. 1–11 (2008). https://doi.org/10.1109/SC.2008.5214359
14. Williams, S., Oliker, L., Vuduc, R., Shalf, J., Yelick, K., Demmel, J.: Optimization of sparse matrix-vector multiplication on emerging multicore platforms. In: SC 2007: Proceedings of the 2007 ACM/IEEE Conference on Supercomputing, pp. 1–12 (2007). https://doi.org/10.1145/1362622.1362674
15. Zhang, J., Gruenwald, L.: Regularizing irregularity: bitmap-based and portable sparse matrix multiplication for graph data on GPUs. In: Proceedings of the 1st ACM SIGMOD Joint International Workshop on Graph Data Management Experiences & Systems (GRADES) and Network Data Analytics (NDA). GRADES-NDA 2018. Association for Computing Machinery, New York (2018). https://doi.org/10.1145/3210259.3210263

Elastic Deep Learning Using Knowledge Distillation with Heterogeneous Computing Resources

Daxiang Dong[1], Ji Liu[1(✉)], Xi Wang[1], Weibao Gong[1], An Qin[1], Xingjian Li[1], Dianhai Yu[1], Patrick Valduriez[2], and Dejing Dou[1]

[1] Baidu, Beijing, China
{dongdaxiang,liuji04,wangxi16,gongweibao,qinan,lixingjian,
yudianhai,doudejing}@baidu.com
[2] Inria, University of Montpellier, CNRS, LIRMM, Montpellier, France
Patrick.Valduriez@inria.fr

Abstract. In deep neural networks, using more layers and parameters generally improves the accuracy of the models, which get bigger. Such big models have high computational complexity and big memory requirements, which exceed the capacity of small devices for inference. Knowledge distillation is an efficient approach to compress a large deep model (a teacher model) to a compact model (a student model). Existing online knowledge distillation methods typically exploit an extra data storage layer to store the knowledge or deploy the teacher model and the student model at the same computing resource, thus hurting elasticity and fault-tolerance. In this paper, we propose an elastic deep learning framework, EDL-Dist, for large scale knowledge distillation to efficiently train the student model while exploiting elastic computing resources. The advantages of EDL-Dist are three-fold. First, it decouples the inference and the training process to use heterogeneous computing resources. Second, it can exploit dynamically available computing resources. Third, it supports fault-tolerance during the training and inference processes within knowledge distillation. Our experimental validation, based on industrial-strength implementation and real datasets, shows that the throughput of EDL-Dist is up to 181% faster than the baseline method (online knowledge distillation).

Keywords: Knowledge distillation · Distributed computing · Deep neural network

1 Introduction

In recent years, Deep Neural Networks (DNNs) have achieved major success in various domains, such as computer vision [16] and natural language processing [15]. Bigger models with more layers, neurons and parameters generally improve

---

D. Dong and J. Liu—Equal contribution.

R. Chaves et al. (Eds.): Euro-Par 2021, LNCS 13098, pp. 116–128, 2022.
https://doi.org/10.1007/978-3-031-06156-1_10

the accuracy of a model. For instance, ERNIE [15] exploits large numbers of parameters, e.g., 10 billions parameters. With a large number of parameters, deep neural networks have high computational complexity and big memory requirements, which exceed the capacity of small devices (mobile phones or IoT devices) on which they are deployed for inference.

Knowledge distillation [6] is an efficient approach to distill the knowledge from a big model into a smaller model while retaining its accuracy. During knowledge distillation, a small model (a student model) is trained with the supervision of a large model (a teacher model). The teacher model is a cumbersome model, which could be an ensemble of separately trained models or a single very large model trained with a strong regularizer [6]. Compared with the teacher model, the student model is relatively small and compact.

Different from normal training, which does not rely on a trained teacher model, knowledge distillation requires a pre-trained teacher model. During knowledge distillation, the teacher model is used by the inference process to generate supervision knowledge while the student model is trained. These inference and training processes can be sequentially performed or in parallel. The training can be carried out offline or online. The offline approach exploits an extra data store to cache the knowledge distilled from the teacher model, which is used to train the student model separately [4]. This approach can decouple the inference of a teacher model and the training of a student model. However, this approach requires much storage and distilling the knowledge from the teacher model may take much time when the teacher model or input data are big. The online approach puts the teacher model and the student model into the same server and performs the training of the student model and the inference of the teacher model synchronously. When the teacher model is very big, the training of the student model gets limited by the synchronization of the inference of the teacher model, which takes much computing time. In addition, both the offline and online approaches do not support elastic computing resources or fault-tolerance.

The training of knowledge distillation typically exploits many computing resources, e.g., CPU cores or GPU cards. However, the availability of computing resources may vary dynamically as there may be concurrent users with same priority. Thus, some computing resources can be granted to a user for a long time while some other computing resources can only be used for a short time and may be dynamically withdrawn. During the long training of knowledge distillation with elastic computing resources, some will become unavailable, while some others will become available. Furthermore, these computing resources are heterogeneous, e.g., GPU cards with diverse computing capabilities.

In this paper, we address the problem of efficient knowledge distillation with heterogeneous computing resources. We assume a distributed environment with two kinds of computing resources: dedicated and elastic. The dedicated computing resources are provided by powerful servers, e.g., V100 GPU cards, for knowledge distillation only. The elastic computing resources are smaller servers, e.g., P4 GPU cards, and can be dynamically allocated to other tasks of higher priority or knowledge distillation. We propose an Elastic Deep Learning framework, i.e., EDL-Dist, with a distributed, fault-tolerant architecture. EDL-Dist provides an elastic service that manages multiple GPU cards, for inference of teacher models. It manages the training of knowledge distillation with multiple GPU cards on multiple servers (a server may have one GPU or more GPU cards). Furthermore, the type of GPU cards can be different depending on the process, e.g., training versus inference, which are decoupled in order to exploit elasticity. Our solution to fault-tolerance is based on a fail-over mechanism [14] using check-points and re-execution of tasks in Teacher. In addition, EDL-Dist comes with two main algorithms for scheduling and knowledge distillation. The scheduling algorithm is hybrid, i.e., combines static [9] and dynamic scheduling, and associates computing resources from different processes. The knowledge distillation algorithm, EDL-Dist algorithm, is distributed and enables decentralized training of the student model with the knowledge from the teacher model.

This paper is organized as follows. Section 2 introduces the related work of knowledge distillation. Section 3 describes the EDL-Dist framework. Section 4 presents the experimental results, which show the advantage of EDL-Dist compared with the baseline method (the online approach) and normal training. Finally, Sect. 5 concludes the paper.

2   Related Work

In this section, we first introduce knowledge distillation. Then, we discuss solutions for supporting knowledge distillation, with distributed or decentralized training, and elastic computing resources.

Knowledge distillation is based on the popular machine learning Softmax function and a temperature [6]. The Softmax output layer converts the logit computed for each class (predefined category associated to the input data) into a probability with a temperature T. The temperature indicates the impact of the output from the teacher model, where a higher value of T corresponds to a weaker impact of the output of the teacher model.

During the training of knowledge distillation, two neural networks are used: teacher model and student model. The student model is trained using the combination of two loss functions. One loss function is based on a soft prediction, which considers the soft labels from the teacher model. The other loss function is based on a hard prediction, which considers the ground truth label from the training data. The soft prediction corresponds to the outputs of the student model, while the hard prediction is the original output of the student model.

Knowledge distillation can be carried out based on two methods: offline and online. With the offline method, a teacher model is trained before distillation. Then, the knowledge of the teacher model can be extracted and stored in a cache [4]. This method requires large extra storage resources. With the online method [17], the inference of the teacher model and the training of the student model are performed in the same GPU card. Thus, when the teacher model is big, the training of the student model gets limited by the synchronization of the inference of the teacher model, which takes much computing time. Furthermore, these two approaches do not support elastic computing resources or fault-tolerance.

In order to accelerate the training of a deep learning network, multiple GPUs can be exploited using data parallelism. The model is replicated in each GPU while the data is distributed in different GPUs [1]. Ring all-reduce [3] is generally exploited to realize the distributed training process with the data parallelism method. However, the ring all-reduce method is only designed for the training without consideration of knowledge distillation. Furthermore, it cannot support elastic computing resources and do not provide fault-tolerance.

3   EDL-Dist

In this section, we present the EDL-Dist framework, its architecture, algorithms for scheduling and knowledge distillation, and our solution for fault-tolerance.

3.1   Architecture

The architecture of EDL-Dist (see Fig. 1) has three modules: Student, Teacher and Coordinator. Student is composed of dedicated computing resources, which are used to train a student model with a distributed or decentralized method. Teacher consists of dynamic computing resources. In the dynamic computing resources, the teacher models are deployed for the inference process. Coordinator coordinates data transfer and training in Student and inference in Teacher.

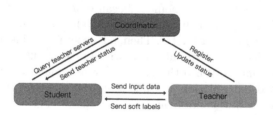

Fig. 1. Functional architecture.

We exploit a decentralized training algorithm, i.e., ring allReduce [3], to perform parallel training in Student. Since transferring data among different GPU cards is time consuming, the training data is partitioned and cached in the host memory of each server for fast data access. During training in Student, only the gradients are transferred among different servers. Within each iteration of the training process, each computing resource in the student model takes data, including the input training data, the hard labels and soft labels from a data service, DistilReader, to update the student mode.

DistilReader is a service that caches the input training data and the corresponding soft labels, generated from Teacher, in the host memory of each computing resource in Student. It provides an interface between a Student server and the Coordinator server or Teacher servers. The Student server, Coordinator server or Teacher server denotes a server that supports the corresponding module. This service is deployed in each Student server. As shown in Fig. 2, Distil-Reader sends the input data to Teacher and receives the soft labels from Teacher. In order to know which Teacher server to connect to, DistilReader retrieves the server information from Coordinator. In addition, DistilReader regularly queries Coordinator to know if the Teacher server is still alive. When a Teacher server becomes unavailable, DistilReader searches for available Teacher servers from Coordinator to replace the unavailable server.

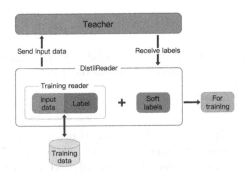

Fig. 2. DistilReader service.

Teacher is composed of multiple dynamic computing resources, each of which can become unavailable at any moment because of unexpected changes in the multiuser workload. When a dynamic server is alive and added as a Teacher server, it is registered in Coordinator. Then, a teacher model instance is deployed in the server in order to perform inference, which takes input data and generates corresponding soft labels. When the Teacher server remains available to be connected for knowledge distillation, it sends heartbeat messages to Coordinator in order to maintain its status until the end of the knowledge distillation task.

Coordinator has two components: a service manager and a database, which is an in-memory database for efficient data processing. The service manager can query the database in order to search for available computing resources in Teacher. The service manager answers the queries from DistilReaders in Student. The register information from Teacher is directly stored in the database. The alive status stored in the database has a time limit, i.e., Time to live (TTL). When the heartbeat information is sent from a Teacher server to the database, the corresponding alive status is prolonged, i.e., the corresponding TTL is updated. If the Teacher server does not send heartbeat messages to the database for a long time, when its TTL expired, its status will be considered unavailable.

3.2 Hybrid Scheduling Algorithm

In order to speed up the inference process, it is critical to schedule the workloads, i.e., the inference to generate soft labels for input data, requested from Student to computing resources in Teacher. A resource represents a computing unit that can perform training, e.g., a GPU card or a CPU care. The resource scheduling problem is NP-hard [12]. When a Student resource is scheduled to a smaller number of Teacher resources than an appropriate number, the throughput of the student model is restricted by the inference of its scheduled resources. Otherwise, when a resource in Student is scheduled to a bigger number of resources in Teacher, more and more soft labels and corresponding input data will be stored in the host memory of Student servers to be used. The accumulated stored soft labels and corresponding input data may occupy large amount of memory, which may block the training process. Thus, it is important to schedule the appropriate number of resources to each Student resource.

We propose a hybrid scheduling algorithm (see Algorithm 1), i.e., which combines static and dynamic scheduling methods. We assume historical information on the execution of the training and inference processes. For instance, the throughput of the training in a Student server, e.g., one GPU card in Student, is t_s and the throughput of the inference in a Teacher server, e.g., one GPU card in Teacher, is t_t. The throughput gives the number of images or the amount of input data that can be processed in the same resource per time unit by the student model (or the teacher model) without restriction of another module. We assume that the resources in the same module, e.g., Student or Teacher, are of the same type while the types of GPU cards in different modules can be different. We set the number of Teacher resources as $n = \frac{t_t}{t_s}$ for each Student resource, i.e., we schedule $\lceil n \rceil$ Teacher resources to each Student resource.

Algorithm 1. Hybrid Scheduling Algorithm

Require: number of Teacher resources n
Require: lower threshold of the volume of soft labels lt
Require: upper threshold of the volume of soft labels ut
  1: schedule n Teacher resources to the Student resource
  2: **while** knowledge distillation is not terminated **do**
  3:     volume = get_volume(unused soft labels)
  4:     **if** volume $> ut$ **then**
  5:         stop sending input data to Teacher servers
  6:     **end if**
  7:     **if** volume $== 0$ **then**
  8:         schedule an additional available Teacher resources to the Student resource
  9:     **end if**
 10:     **if** volume $< lt$ **then**
 11:         continue sending input data to Teacher resources
 12:     **end if**
 13: **end while**

During the training of knowledge distillation, when a Student resource searches for Teacher resources, it is scheduled $\lceil n \rceil$ Teacher resources (Line 1). As the execution environment may vary during the training of knowledge distillation, we dynamically adjust the scheduling (Lines 3–12). We use a monitoring task in each Student resource to monitor the number of combinations of soft labels and input data (Line 3). The occupied volume is calculated based on the number and average size of a combination of input data and soft labels, which can be measured with an offline method. When the growing volume exceeds a predefined upper threshold value (Line 4), the Student resource stops sending input data to the Teacher resource (Line 5) in order to consume the unused soft labels until the volume decreases to a smaller value than another lower bound threshold value (Lines 10–12). The upper threshold and the lower threshold can be set by the user based on the size of storage in the resource of Student. This mechanism ensures that the number of soft labels remains reasonable in each Student resource, which does not slow down the training or incur memory leaks in the Student resource. Otherwise, if the resources in Student stay idle in order to wait for the soft labels from Teacher, more Teacher resources are required by the Student resource in order to accelerate the inference in the teacher model (Lines 7–9). When there are available Teacher resources, they are scheduled to the Student resource.

3.3   EDL-Dist Algorithm

We now present our EDL-Dist Algorithm 2 for the parallel training in each Student resource during the training of knowledge distillation. The input data and the hard label y are retrieved from the host memory (Line 3), which can be done by DistilReader. Then, the soft labels are prepared by the DistReader service from Teacher in Line 4. Based on the hard label and the soft labels, the student model θ is updated in Line 5. The loss function in each server is a weighted function based on the loss function of the hard labels and the soft labels. λ is the learning rate, which can be set corresponding to the student model. Then, an average student model is calculated in Line 7.

Algorithm 2. EDL-Dist Algorithm

Require: hard loss function ϕ(hard label, hard prediction)
Require: soft loss function ψ(soft labels, soft predictions)
Require: hard prediction function $F(\theta, input)$
Require: soft prediction function $F'(\theta, input)$
Require: learning rate η
Require: weight for hard loss function α
Require: weight for soft loss function β
Require: number of Student resources N
1: **while** not converged **do**
2:    **for** θ_i in resource i **do**
3:        y, input = get_training_sample()
4:        soft_labels = get_soft_labels(input)
5:        $\theta_i = \theta_i - \eta \bigtriangledown_{\theta_i} \{\alpha\phi(y, F(\theta_i, input)) + \beta\psi(soft\_labels, F'(\theta_i, input)\}$
6:    **end for**
7:    $\theta = \frac{\sum_{j=1}^{N} \theta_j}{N}$
8: **end while**

3.4   Fault-Tolerance

We consider the fault-tolerance in Student and Teacher, assuming that Coordinator is always available. If the Coordinator server is not stable, fault-tolerance can be simply achieved by having multiple instances of the in-memory database deployed in multiple servers using existing frameworks, e.g., Zookeeper [7]. If a Teacher resource is not available, its status will become unavailable when its TTL expires in the database. The Teacher resource can become unavailable in three cases. The first case is before the resource is scheduled to a Student resource. In this case, EDL-Dist simply ignores this Teacher resource. The second case is when the Teacher resource is scheduled to a Student resource that does not send input data to it or does not wait for soft labels from it. In this case, the Student resource will search for another available Teacher resource that is not scheduled to any Student resource. The third case is when the Teacher resource is scheduled to a Student resource that sends input data to it and is waiting for soft labels from it. In this case, as presented in Sect. 3.1, the Student resource will search for another available Teacher resource. Once a Teacher resource is re-scheduled to it, the Student resource sends the input data to the Teacher resource again. When a new Teacher resource is available in Teacher, it is scheduled to a Student resource that is searching for Teacher resources. If there is no such Student resource, the Teacher resource will wait for such a Student resource.

To address fault-tolerance in Student, we exploit a fail-over mechanism [14] that uses check-points during the training of knowledge distillation. A checkpoint is a copy of the student model. Before the training process, a server is selected as a master node and saves the checkpoint at every certain iterations. The checkpoint is saved in a distributed file system, which is accessible to all the Student servers. Each Student server updates the student model in each iteration. Then, when a Student server becomes unavailable or a new Student server is added to Student, the training in all the Student servers stops. Afterward, each Student server loads the student model from the checkpoint and continues the training process. Thus, the consistency of the student model is ensured while addressing fault-tolerance.

4   Experimental Validation

In this section, we present our experimental validation of EDL-Dist in comparison with online knowledge distillation (Online) (baseline) and normal training (N-training). We present the experimental setup and then give the results.

4.1   Experimental Setup

EDL-Dist is implemented based on the PaddlePaddle framework [13] and publicly available at Github[1]. Student is based on Paddle FleetX[2], which implements

---

[1] https://github.com/elasticdeeplearning/edl.
[2] Paddle Fleet: https://github.com/PaddlePaddle/FleetX.

the ring allReduce algorithm using NCCL[3] for decentralized training. We use Redis[4] as the in-memory database in Coordinator [11].

We carry out three experiments to show the advantages of EDL-Dist compared with Online and N-training. Online deploys the teacher and student models in the same GPU server. N-training represents the training with GPU cards without knowledge distillation. In all experiments, we use real datasets, i.e., ImageNet data set [2]. In the first experiment, we combine CPUs and GPU cards, in order to show that EDL-Dist can efficiently exploit heterogeneous computing resources.

Table 1. Throughput for different approaches.

CPUcores	N-training	Online	EDL-Dist	Advantage
1	14.16	5.92	**14.34**	**142.23%**
2	28.44	11.51	**28.07**	**143.87%**
4	55.17	21.76	**54.92**	**152.39%**
8	101.59	37.87	**102.40**	**170.40%**
16	168.42	59.94	**168.42**	**180.98%**

Table 2. Throughput for different approaches.

CPUcores	N-training	Online	EDL-Dist	Advantage
8	57.14	46.04	35.68	−22.50%
12	57.14	46.04	**52.46**	**13.94%**
16	55.17	46.04	**57.65**	**25.22%**

In the next two experiments, we use ResNet101 [5] as the teacher model, ResNet50 [5] as the student model, and set the batch size as 32. The second experiment (Sect. 4.3) figures out the fine-tuned number of Teacher GPU cards (NVIDIA Tesla P4 GPU card) for each Student GPU card (NVIDIA Tesla V100 GPU card). The single-precision performance, which represents the speed to perform calculation, of P4 is 5.5 Teraflops while that of V100 is 14 Teraflops. The third experiment (Sect. 4.4) is performed with 8 v100 GPU cards in Student and various numbers of P4 GPU cards in Teacher for EDL-Dist. We compare the throughput and the training time to that of Online and N-training.

4.2   Comparison with Heterogeneous Resources

To validate that our solution is efficient with heterogeneous computing resources, we experiment with the combination of CPU and GPU cards for knowledge

---

[3] NCCL: https://developer.nvidia.com/nccl.
[4] Redis: https://redis.io/.

distillation. We take MobileNetV3_small [8] as the student model and Resnet50 [5] as the teacher model. We use Intel(R) Xeon(R) Gold 6148 CPU @ 2.40 GHz CPU cores and a P4 GPU card. We set the batch size as 64 in Student.

First, we take the P4 GPU card in Teacher and different numbers of CPU cores in Student. The results are shown in Table 1. The throughput of our proposed approach, i.e., EDL-Dist, is similar to that of N-training and significantly outperforms Online (up to 181%). Then, we take the P4 GPU card as the Student GPU card and different numbers of CPU cores as the Student resources. As shown in Table 2, the throughput of EDL-Dist is smaller than that of N-training and Online when Teacher resources are not enough (8). The throughput of EDL-Dist is similar to that of N-training and significantly outperforms Online (up to 25.22%) when the Teacher resources are enough (12 and 16).

4.3   Fine-Tuning of EDL-Dist

The throughput of EDL-Dist increases with the number of Teacher GPU cards. With enough Teacher GPU cards, the throughput of EDL-Dist can be similar to that of N-training. As we add more Teacher GPU cards, the throughput of EDL-Dist becomes a little bit lower as it takes some time to manage unused intermediate soft labels from Teacher. In order to validate this property of EDL-Dist, we also experiment using a v100 GPU card in Student and various numbers of P4 GPU cards as Teacher resources. The throughput of EDL-Dist is shown in Fig. 3a when using different numbers of P4 GPU cards. The training time is shown in Fig. 3b. Figures 3a and 3b indicate that the fine-tuned number of Teacher resources (P4 GPU card) is 5 when we use a single v100 GPU card as the Student resource. When the number of Teacher GPU cards is smaller than 5, the throughput increases linearly as number of P4 GPU cards increases, which shows the good scalability of EDL-Dist. When the number of Teacher GPU cards is greater than 5, the throughput slightly decreases as it takes time to manage unused soft labels in the Student server. Furthermore, we find that

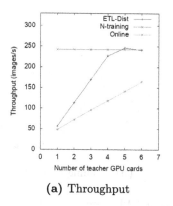

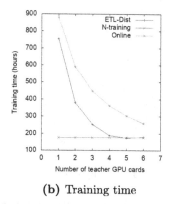

(a) Throughput   (b) Training time

Fig. 3. Fine-tuning with various numbers of P40 Teacher GPU cards.

the throughput of Online is much smaller (up to 93.0%) than that of EDL-Dist and the training time of the Online is much longer (up to 92.9%) than that of EDL-Dist when the number of Teacher GPU cards is smaller than 8.

4.4 Comparison with Multiple Student GPU Cards

In this experiment, we take 8 V100 GPU cards and 40–56 P4 GPU cards for different approaches. We compare the throughput between EDL-Dist, Online and N-training. We take 8 NVIDIA Tesla v100 GPU cards as dedicated Student GPU cards while using 48 P4 NVIDIA Tesla GPU cards as Teacher GPU cards as we find 48 is the appropriate number of Teacher GPU cards as shown in Table 3. Please note that some GPU servers are dynamically added and removed during the execution of the experiments.

Table 3 shows that the accuracy (1 and 5) of EDL-Dist is similar to that of N-training and Online. Accuracy 1 represents the accuracy of the predicted class with the highest probability. Accuracy 5 represents the accuracy of the top 5 ranked classes based on the probability. The accuracy of EDL-Dist can be slightly higher than that of N-training (Accuracy 5).

While the student model is trained with the training data and the soft labels with knowledge distillation, the trained student model from knowledge distillation can get more generalization information from the teacher model [6]. Thus,

Table 3. Experimental results (accuracy). Accuracy 1 is the accuracy of the predicted class with the highest probability. Accuracy 5 is the accuracy of the top 5 ranked classes based on the probability.

	N-training	Online	EDL-Dist (40)	EDL-Dist (48)	EDL-Dist (56)
Accuracy 1	77.1	79.0	**79.0**	**79.0**	**79.0**
Accuracy 5	93.5	94.3	**94.5**	**94.5**	**94.5**

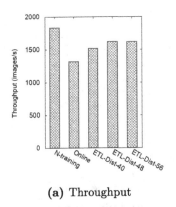

(a) Throughput

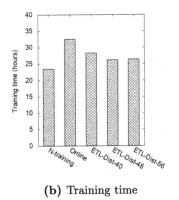

(b) Training time

Fig. 4. Experimental results with 8 Student v100 GPU cards and 40(EDL-Dist-40)/48(EDL-Dist-48)/56(EDL-Dist-56) P40 GPU cards.

we can efficiently train a student model with higher accuracy (compared with N-training) using EDL-Dist.

In Fig. 4a, the throughput of EDL-Dist is much higher (23.5% faster) than that of Online. This shows that EDL-Dist significantly speeds up training compared with the Online while not requiring extra storage resources. The throughput of EDL-Dist is slightly lower than that of N-learning because of some overhead when there are multiple Student GPU cards. The training time of N-training, Online and EDL-Dist is shown in Fig. 4b. The training time of EDL-Dist (48) is almost the same as that of EDL-Dist (56), which indicates that the bottleneck of the number of Teacher GPU cards is 48. With 48 Teacher cards, the training time of EDL-Dist is 19.4% shorter than that of Online. Compared with N-training, the training time of EDL-Dist is slightly longer (12.8%). As it takes time to transfer the data from Student servers to multiple Teacher servers, the training time of EDL-Dist is slightly longer than that of N-training.

5   Conclusion

In this paper, we proposed EDL-Dist, an elastic deep learning framework for large scale knowledge distillation. EDL-Dist has a distributed, fault-tolerant architecture that leverages heterogeneous computing resources. We did a thorough validation of our solution by implementing an industrial-strenght prototype of EDL-Dist (available at github) and experimenting with real datasets. The experimental results show that EDL-Dist can be 181% faster than online training while its accuracy is a little higher than that of normal training. In the future, we may exploit federated learning [10] to deal with the decentralized data in order to ensure the data security and privacy.

References

1. Anil, R., Pereyra, G., Passos, A., Ormándi, R., Dahl, G.E., Hinton, G.E.: Large scale distributed neural network training through online distillation. In: International Conference on Learning Representations (ICLR) (2018). https://openreview. net/forum?id=rkr1UDeC-

2. Deng, J., Dong, W., Socher, R., Li, L., Li, K., Li, F.: ImageNet: a large-scale hierarchical image database. In: IEEE Conference on Computer Vision and Pattern Recognition (CVPR), pp. 248–255 (2009). https://doi.org/10.1109/CVPR.2009. 5206848

3. Gibiansky, A.: Bringing HPC techniques to deep learning (2017). https://andrew. gibiansky.com/blog/machine-learning/baidu-allreduce/. Accessed 12 Aug 2020

4. Gou, J., Yu, B., Maybank, S.J., Tao, D.: Knowledge distillation: a survey. CoRR abs/2006.05525 (2020). https://arxiv.org/abs/2006.05525

5. He, K., Zhang, X., Ren, S., Sun, J.: Deep residual learning for image recognition. In: IEEE Conference on Computer Vision and Pattern Recognition (CVPR), pp. 770–778 (2016)

6. Hinton, G., Vinyals, O., Dean, J.: Distilling the knowledge in a neural network. In: NIPS Deep Learning and Representation Learning Workshop (2015). http:// arxiv.org/abs/1503.02531

7. Hunt, P., Konar, M., Junqueira, F.P., Reed, B.: ZooKeeper: wait-free coordination for internet-scale systems. In: USENIX Annual Technical Conference, p. 11 (2010)
8. Koonce, B.: MobileNetV3, pp. 125–144. Apress (2021)
9. Liu, J., Bondiombouy, C., Mo, L., Valduriez, P.: Two-phase scheduling for efficient vehicle sharing. IEEE Trans. Intell. Transp. Syst. **23**, 457–470 (2020)
10. Liu, J., et al.: From distributed machine learning to federated learning: a survey. arXiv preprint arXiv:2104.14362 (2021)
11. Liu, J., et al.: Efficient scheduling of scientific workflows using hot metadata in a multisite cloud. IEEE Trans. Knowl. Data Eng. **31**(10), 1940–1953 (2019). https://doi.org/10.1109/TKDE.2018.2867857
12. Liu, L., Yu, H., Sun, G., Luo, L., Jin, Q., Luo, S.: Job scheduling for distributed machine learning in optical wan. Futur. Gener. Comput. Syst. **112**, 549–560 (2020). https://doi.org/10.1016/j.future.2020.06.007
13. Ma, Y., Wu, T., Yu, D., Wang, H.: PaddlePaddle: an open-source deep learning platform from industrial practice. Front. Data Comput. **1**(1), 105 (2019). https://doi.org/10.11871/jfdc.issn.2096.742X.2019.01.011
14. Özsu, M.T., Valduriez, P.: Principles of Distributed Database Systems, 4th edn. Springer, Heidelberg (2020). https://doi.org/10.1007/978-3-030-26253-2
15. Sun, Y., et al.: ERNIE 3.0: large-scale knowledge enhanced pre-training for language understanding and generation. arXiv preprint arXiv:2107.02137 (2021)
16. Villegas, R., Yang, J., Zou, Y., Sohn, S., Lin, X., Lee, H.: Learning to generate long-term future via hierarchical prediction. In: International Conference on Machine Learning (ICML), vol. 70, pp. 3560–3569 (2017)
17. Zmora, N., Jacob, G., Zlotnik, L., Elharar, B., Novik, G.: Neural network distiller: a python package for DNN compression research. CoRR abs/1910.12232 (2019). http://arxiv.org/abs/1910.12232

Feasibility Study of Molecular Dynamics Kernels Exploitation Using EngineCL

Raúl Nozal[1](✉), Christoph Niethammer[2](✉), Jose Gracia[2](✉), and Jose Luis Bosque[1](✉)

[1] Computer Science and Electronics Department, Universidad de Cantabria, Santander, Spain
{raul.nozal,joseluis.bosque}@unican.es
[2] High Performance Computing Center Stuttgart (HLRS), University of Stuttgart, Stuttgart, Germany
{niethammer,gracia}@hlrs.de

Abstract. The ubiquity of heterogeneous systems facilitates the exploitation of scientific problems, such as molecular dynamics simulators, but their highly optimized codes for multi-core HPC architectures complicates porting. In this work, EngineCL is extended to enable efficient co-execution of molecular dynamics kernels. Contributions include support for a new execution core and a hybrid co-execution mode, solving the problems encountered when running only with OpenCL-based technologies. Experimental evaluation shows improvements in all the kernels studied, obtaining on average speedups of up to 1.38 in performance and 1.60 in energy efficiency over the current optimized version.

Keywords: Heterogeneous computing · Hybrid parallel computing · Co-execution · OpenCL · Performance portability · Load balancing · Molecular dynamics · Particle simulations

1 Introduction

Along the last three decades, computationally intensive scientific applications have generally been run in clusters composed of homogeneous multi-core computing nodes. Among these applications, ls1-MarDyn is a massively parallel Molecular Dynamics simulator for chemical engineering and energy technology applications for large systems, developed in the High-Performance Computing Center Stuttgart (HLRS) [14]. It is designed with a focus on performance and easy extensibility, targeting thermodynamics and nanofluidics simulations.

Ls1-mardyn has been deeply optimized to take advantage of the features of multi-core architectures, using OpenMP for efficient node-level performance. Data structures, such as linked cells, and algorithms have been defined to exploit the different levels of the memory hierarchy, prefetching, instruction level parallelism (ILP), as well as vector units (SIMD instructions) [15].

In this context, the emergence of heterogeneous systems and hardware accelerators, such as GPUS and FGPAs, offer a new chance to increase performance

© Springer Nature Switzerland AG 2022
R. Chaves et al. (Eds.): Euro-Par 2021, LNCS 13098, pp. 129–140, 2022.
https://doi.org/10.1007/978-3-031-06156-1_11

and reduce energy consumption. However, they also present a number of challenges, including programmability and performance portability. To overcome these problems OpenCL has been developed, extending C/C++ for heterogeneous systems, proposing a host-device programming model in which the CPU offloads the compute-heavy functions (kernels) to an accelerator.

However, given the great effort developed to optimize ls1-mardyn on CPUs, this paper proposes that the most suitable model for its implementation in heterogeneous systems is not the host-device model, but a co-execution model. In co-execution all the devices share the execution of a single massively data-parallel kernel to minimize its execution time. But co-execution presents a new challenge, because OpenCL does not offer equivalent performance to the CPU-optimized version of the kernels, significantly burdening the capacity of the system.

This paper presents a new hybrid co-execution mode for EngineCL, supporting two programming models for heterogeneous computing. This OpenCL-based runtime system outstandingly simplifies the co-execution of a single massive data-parallel kernel on all the devices of a heterogeneous system [2,9–11]. EngineCL performs a set of low level tasks regarding the management of devices, their disjoint memory spaces and scheduling the workload between the system devices while providing a layered API. In this work, it is also enhanced to allow the execution of native optimized kernels on the CPU as well as on-line compiled OpenCL kernels in the GPU, transparently to the programmer.

This topic has been studied previously from several points of view [3,4,7, 12]. For instance, [13] proposes a runtime system that splits work between the CPU and GPU. LaKomski et al. offers co-execution evaluation but uses a static work-sharing technique, not adapting to irregular problems [6]. Hybrid CPU-GPU implementation of particle simulations using OpenCL is proposed in [1,5], but they compute different kernels per device. The application field is close to our work but they do not perform co-execution among the devices. Finally, [8] address the same problem from another perspective for synthetic benchmarks.

Our work offers an independent runtime with a high-level API, facilitating the integration in real-world C++ applications. It offers two execution cores, including custom native parallelized and vectorized code execution. Moreover, it supports co-execution with a new hybrid mode running native code on the CPU combined with OpenCL code on the GPU. Nevertheless, we evaluate the scalability, along with its performance and energy efficiency when co-executing.

2   Motivation

The advent of heterogeneous systems has opened up new optimization opportunities for applications that have traditionally been optimized to run on clusters of CPUs, like ls1-mardyn. However, they give rise to three main challenges: programming complexity, inefficiency in balancing between CPUs and GPUs, and device performance portability issues as the programming model varies.

Firstly, OpenCL allows the execution of a kernel on different devices, through the host-device programming model, offering code portability but not always performance portability. Furthermore, it is a low-level language that is particularly difficult to use in complex software architectures, like ls1-mardyn.

Secondly, the host-device programming model leaves the CPU in charge of device management, work distribution and synchronization. This facilitates programming but the CPU continues consuming energy without contributing anything to the computation. Therefore, it is convenient to co-execute the problem to void harming both the performance and energy consumption of the system.

Thirdly, one of the key points of the performance of a device and the associated OpenCL programming model is determined by the quality of the driver and the optimizations provided by the vendor. This has been a serious problem encountered during the OpenCL technology applicability study in the kernels extracted from the ls1-mardyn simulator. The Intel Xeon processor requires a degree of optimizations not achievable by its driver regarding these molecular dynamics kernels, causing a performance penalty. Thus, the feasibility study only allowed a correct use by the GPU, but ruled out any possibility of exploiting the CPU.

The first two drawbacks are addressed by using EngineCL, a high-level co-executor runtime for heterogeneous computation tested on multiple architectures. It offers a layered and optimized design that enables high usability without penalizing performance. It facilitates incremental transformation of compute-intensive regions, thanks to its architecture, built-in schedulers and API design.

However, on the other hand, since EngineCL uses internally OpenCL technology, it still presents the third problem mentioned above. Ls1-mardyn uses parallelized and vectorized kernels, so OpenCL is not able to cope with such an optimized code, as it is depicted in Fig. 1. For this reason, it is necessary to adapt the runtime in order to maintain its premises and design principles, but to provide it with new computational capabilities more optimized for the CPU. To guarantee the first two issues mentioned above, the runtime must preserve a negligible overhead with respect to OpenCL, allow efficient co-execution and maintain a clean API design, while providing new execution methods that are independent of OpenCL and exploitable in the simulator. The goal is to be able to run molecular dynamics kernels on heterogeneous systems efficiently, taking advantage of as many devices as exist on the node and evaluating energy and performance tradeoffs with respect to the initial implementation.

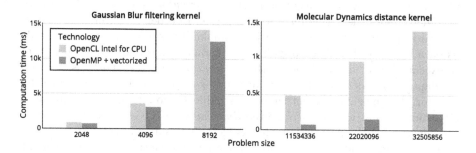

Fig. 1. CPU computation times for classical and ls1-mardyn kernels, using OpenCL and OpenMP technologies for a set of problem sizes.

3   Optimizations of EngineCL

The proposal of this article focuses on enhancing EngineCL [9,10] with more functionality, without compromising its usability. The runtime has experienced three innovations from the functional point of view. All of them with the main goal of providing support for hybrid heterogeneous computing model, which means combining different computing technologies for CPU-GPU co-execution.

First, the entire system has been adapted to support new execution engines. This has required an internal transformation, including the generation of new interfaces to encapsulate the distinct implementations of its behavior. Furthermore, it has also required a minimal modification of the external API, trying to preserve the high usability.

Secondly, a new execution core has been implemented, thanks to the architectural adaptation to support variants of the internal computational engine. This core is specialized in the execution of binary kernels for the CPU, as a native execution, instead of an execution core based on OpenCL.

Finally, the third innovation focuses on adapting the runtime to support hybrid co-execution, mixing native and OpenCL-based execution cores. In this way, the same kernel is computed simultaneously by two independent technologies, being EngineCL in charge of synchronization, workload distribution and resource management, regardless of the execution mode used.

3.1   Architecture

EngineCL offers a layered architecture in three tiers, increasing the functionality and degree of complexity the lower the tier [10]. Figure 2 shows the layers, tiered horizontally, and the main modules of EngineCL. Those modules that have been affected by the innovations presented in this paper have been highlighted, although new ones, such as Range or Executor, have also been included. This layered design allows encapsulating the functionality provided by the modules of the lower layers, while favoring functionality reuse and a simplified API design.

The adaptation of the runtime to support new execution paradigms has involved a refactoring of the execution engine, which until now was intended only for OpenCL. A new execution interface, *Executor*, has been incorporated, which determines the *execution core* of a device. In order to traverse the execution space, provided by the application domain (Program), the *Range* module has been introduced, which masks how the kernel is executed, independently of the execution core. In addition, both the *Runtime* and the *Work* distribution are adapted to understand the new abstract execution mechanism provided by Executor. The new component signatures influence how they are manipulated and instantiated by each *Device* and the *Runtime* itself. These structural changes have not affected the API design, thanks to the layered architecture.

On the other hand, with the addition of a new native execution core, a slight modification of Tier-1 has been facilitated. Variables and parameters provided to the Program class are internally associated to the structures needed by each internal execution core, regardless of the technology used.

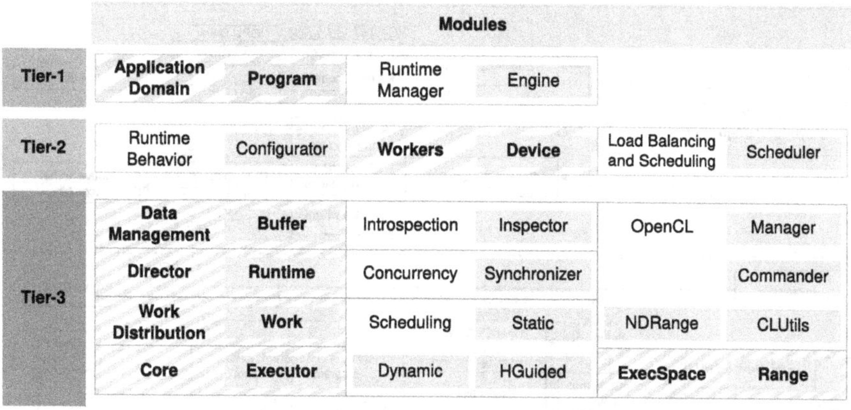

Modules					
Tier-1	**Application Domain**	**Program**	Runtime Manager	Engine		
Tier-2	Runtime Behavior	Configurator	**Workers**	**Device**	Load Balancing and Scheduling	Scheduler
Tier-3	**Data Management**	**Buffer**	Introspection	Inspector	OpenCL	Manager
	Director	**Runtime**	Concurrency	Synchronizer		Commander
	Work Distribution	**Work**	Scheduling	Static	NDRange	CLUtils
	Core	**Executor**	Dynamic	HGuided	**ExecSpace**	**Range**

Fig. 2. EngineCL main modules, highlighting those affected by the innovations.

Finally, new design principles have been provided to facilitate internal maintainability and extensibility. Three functionalities have been defined that can work independently of each other, the execution space (Range), the execution core (Executor) and the data management (Buffer). Since the behavior of each of the new interfaces depends on the instantiation of the chosen adapter, the *AbstractFactory* pattern is applied to simplify the composition of operating modes.

In this way, the mode of operation of the core does not determine the rest of the internal components on which it depends, the extensibility of the runtime and its internal execution mechanisms. *Abstract Factories* facilitate the construction of products with interchangeable parts. The NativeFactory builds the most optimal components for a native execution mode on CPU, instantiating an execution space based on C++ iterators, an execution core based on a executable code blob for CPU and a lightweight data management with direct access to host memory. Finally, OpenCLFactory offers the original EngineCL components, now refactored and encapsulated as independent instances. It builds an n-dimensional range-based execution space, an OpenCL-based execution kernel, and explicit reservation-based memory management with disjoint spaces.

3.2 Execution Model

The execution model is explained focusing on the divergent tasks regarding the execution cores, helping to understand the main differences that allow supporting distinct executors including the novel native CPU processor. To simplify the model, it is taken into account the compilation and execution phases of a program when using the runtime.

Figure 3 shows the kernel compilation stage in the upper part, while the lower one summarizes the stages produced during the execution phase. The starting point is a source code with an OpenCL kernel, while the offline compiler is used to prepare the binary kernels to be used later during runtime execution.

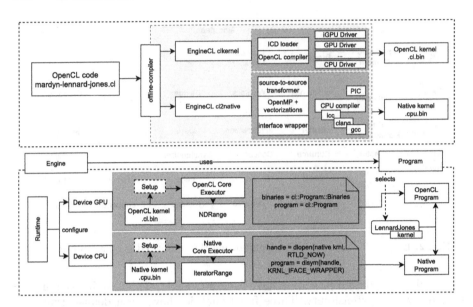

Fig. 3. Kernel source code compilation process (above) and initialization during the EngineCL execution phase (below).

The clkernel tool performs a compilation for the different devices present in the system, thanks to the *ICD loading mechanism* of OpenCL and the subsequent binary construction offered by its drivers. On the other hand, the cl2native tool performs a source code transformation to be compiled by the different backends present in the system. The programmer can include annotations to facilitate the conversion, provide his own optimized variant or even use his own binary file, as long as it maintains the appropriate signature to be consumed. In any case the code will be provided with a wrapper that establishes a common interface to be called. This signature will be consistent with the specification needed by EngineCL at runtime. The programming model chosen by cl2native is OpenMP, but the programmer is free to use any other strategy and model. Finally, one of the established compilers, such as icc or gcc, will be used, building an optimized binary kernel with *position-independent execution* and without *name mangling*, to be used directly by the runtime. In both cases, the resulting files contain the pre-compiled programs with the code ready to be consumed by the different devices of the heterogeneous node.

Subsequently, during the execution phase, as soon as the Engine module uses the Program, a series of steps occur that affect the chosen execution mode. The Runtime creates and configures the devices, starting to operate independently, configuring themselves. This behavior is hidden from the rest of the runtime, while they perform a series of steps depending on the chosen mode of operation determined by the instantiated components (the Factories). Figure 3 shows two paths at the bottom, one for the GPU and one for the CPU. The OpenCL binaries are initialized and assigned to the devices associated to the context managed by the Device, that is the GPU, who uses an execution engine based on OpenCL, an n-dimensional range and a program based on a low-level class of OpenCL. On the other hand, the CPU device uses the native execution core, its execution space is based on an iterator and initializes the program through a dynamic indirection mechanism. The previously constructed binary kernel is loaded dynamically in a blocking fashion, and the start function of the program is subsequently configured. Access to the appropriate symbol within the executable is provided by using a wrapper with a common signature.

3.3   Memory Model

The outline of the memory model, regarding the modifications performed in this work, is shown in Fig. 4. Originally there was only one Buffer class that encapsulated an OpenCL buffer, reserving one region of memory on the host and another on the device, except if it was the CPU, in which case there was only one region.

With the addition of the native mode and its optimizations, two new types of buffers have been offered for EngineCL. On the one hand, those based on memory region reservation, *BufferAlloc*, where two classes can be instantiated. The AllocOpenCLMemory acts as a Proxy pattern that delegates actions to an OpenCL buffer, preserving the initial EngineCL behavior for every OpenCL device. The AllocHostMemory provides a host buffer that can be used and manipulated exclusively by a native execution core.

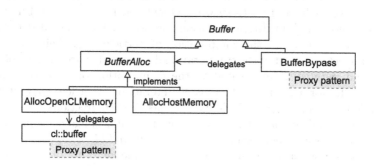

Fig. 4. New classes and interfaces as an abstraction of the EngineCL Buffer.

On the other hand, a *BufferBypass* class is provided as an optimization for the native core. This mechanism acts as a proxy with respect to the AllocHostMemory class, being able to configure the behavior depending on how the memory region is accessed. Considering ls1-mardyn and its kernels, it has been found that a pure bypass strategy is the most advantageous, since there is no reservation or copying of memory subregions. That is, the BufferBypass class configured by the runtime to always reuse host memory and never make instances of the AllocHostMemory class under any conditions. Thereby any memory request acts directly on the C++ containers or the host memory regions provided by the application domain (Program) itself. It is worth mentioning that the possibility of beneficial use of AllocHostMemory could be found in kernels that mutate buffer contents or where more sophisticated execution space strategies are performed, taking advantage of the memory hierarchy, such as in stencil algorithms.

Finally, it should be noted that the use of the native model reduces the memory requirements of the runtime, since the OpenCL-based operating mode includes multiple primitives and structures to be able to use this technology. This increase in memory occupation is not directly related to the application domain data, but is influenced by the use of this programming model and the number and architecture of the devices. Examples are contexts, command queues, events or the callback payloads themselves. Therefore, by using the native execution core, the runtime is being lightened, providing it with higher performance, less memory footprint, and facilitating a more beneficial co-execution, as will be seen in the Sect. 4.2.

4   Evaluation

4.1   Methodology

The experiments are carried out on a computer composed of an Intel Xeon E5-2620 with 24 threads and an AMD Rx5700XT GPU with 40 compute units. The first technology involved is the current ls1-mardyn implementation, labelled *CPU-icc*. It is parallelized with OpenMP, vectorized and compiled with the Intel compiler. Next, *GPU* and *CPU-ocl* when OpenCL drivers are used. Finally, the new hybrid mode and its native execution core for the CPU, labelled *CPU-hy*.

Five kernels related to the computation of particles and their interactions have been selected as part of the computational core of ls1-mardyn. Two of them, *md_dist* and *md_distn2* are related to the computation of distances between molecules. The former offers a flow-based interaction with low computational load, while the latter performs calculations based on indirections over all cells. On the other hand, *md_diststar* handles the minimum image convention while computing the distance between molecules. Finally, *md_bin* computes the associated indices for a set of cells in streaming mode, while *md_lj* obtains the potential and evaluates the force for the Lennard Jones 12-6 potential.

The validation of the proposal is done by analyzing the performance of the new native execution core and the hybrid co-execution compared with *CPU-icc*. The total response time is measured, including kernel computing and data transfer. Two EngineCL scheduling configurations are evaluated when co-executing, Static and HGuided [10], labelled as *St* and *Hg*, respectively.

Two metrics are used to evaluate the proposal, speedup and energy efficiency. The speedup is calculated as $S = \frac{T_{CPU-icc}}{T_{co-exec}}$, being $T_{CPU-icc}$ and $T_{co-exec}$ the execution times for the current CPU implementation and the coexecution, respectively. Finally, energies are measured using RAPL counters and sysfs system drivers, giving the total consumption in *Joules*. The Energy-Delay Product (EDP) is used to evaluate the energy efficiency, measured in *Js*.

4.2   Experimental Results

The execution times regarding single device execution are depicted in Fig. 5, showing how each device scales as the problem size is increased. For all the kernels, the CPU version of OpenCL obtains the worst results. These results are so poor that it limits the co-execution, penalizing the runtime management itself and preventing it from being competitive with respect to the *CPU-icc* version.

However, thanks to the contributions of this paper, a new execution kernel for EngineCL is provided that offers very similar performance to the CPU optimized ls1-mardyn version, as shown by *CPU-hy* and *CPU-icc*. On the other hand, the GPU obtains computation times close to these last two CPU modes, although being slightly slower except in the case of the *md_distn2* kernel. It computes 2.64 times faster than the best version of the CPU, when calculating the distances between one million molecules. These kernels are highly optimized for the CPU, taking advantage of the memory hierarchy and vectorizations. Thus, the GPU is not the fastest device, as has been the case in many other classical kernels.

It is now possible to properly exploit a heterogeneous environment thanks to the new execution core and the performance offered. These results show how the CPU with EngineCL is competitive and co-execution strategies may be possible.

Considering the co-execution in the heterogeneous system, Fig. 6 shows at the top the speedups when co-executing with respect to the CPU optimized version, *CPU-icc*. The abscissa axis shows the load balancing algorithms used for each of the kernels, including the geometric mean. EngineCL provides co-execution between the CPU and GPU devices. In the case of the CPU, it offers two different execution cores, OpenCL-based and the new native executor.

The results show that, using the right scheduler in each case, co-execution is always worthwhile, with the new hybrid execution model. The average speedup is of 1.38x, and up to 4.02x on the *md_distn2* kernel. This is due to the new architecture and optimizations enabled by the hybrid mode. Therefore, it allows concurrent operation without incurring overheads that slow down execution, as is the case with the purely OpenCL-based mode. The *GPU + CPU-ocl* setup only becomes competitive with the *CPU-icc* version with a single kernel, due to its computational overhead.

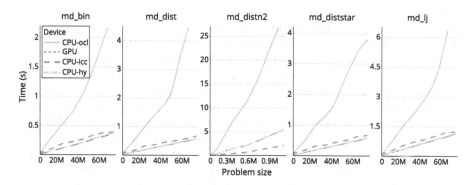

Fig. 5. Scalability when launching the computation in a single device.

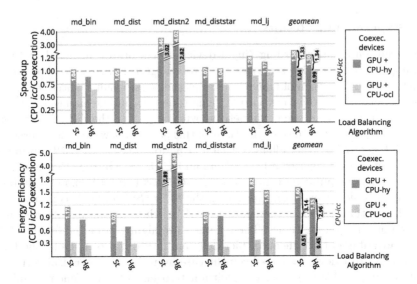

Fig. 6. Speedups (top) and energy efficiency (bottom) when co-executing compared with current ls1-mardyn technology (*CPU-icc*). The annotations of the most significant values have been rounded to the second decimal place.

It can be seen that the *md_distn2* and *md_lj* kernels are the ones that offer the highest performance in co-execution, due to the fact that they have a higher computational cost. The number and complexity of their operations, along with the memory regions used per kernel, increase the total computation time. On the other hand, kernels limited by memory or with a strong communication pattern compared with the computation time, are restricted in time. Therefore, dynamic balancing algorithms, such as *HGuided*, do not have enough time to amortize their cost by making decisions at runtime. The *Static* algorithm offers the best generalized performance, due to the simplification of management operations by the runtime, and the correct workload distribution. *Static* is adequate since the total computation time is low and the kernels present regular behaviors, balancing properly the workload. Since kernels are CPU intensive, it is counterproductive to take up management and scheduling time, as it slows down the final execution for such limited times. On the other hand, it is observed how in the case of *md_distn2*, where the execution is longer, the HGuided algorithm is able to amortize its synchronizations and CPU usage, obtaining shorter computation times than in the *Static* version. Since the total computation time is long enough, it benefits from the parallel operations provided by a strategy that generates multiple chunks at runtime, concurrently computing and doing data transfer. Therefore, it is important to highlight the advantage of having different scheduling algorithms, as each one offers beneficial exploitation situations.

Finally, Fig. 6 shows at the bottom the experimental results considering the energy efficiency of the co-execution with respect to the system using the *CPU-icc* version. Thus, it depicts the gains in EDP when co-executing compared to using the current optimized version. The conclusions observed in the performance evaluation are accentuated since both energy consumption and response time are taken into account. The GPU is a very energy efficient device, so that in kernels where there is a higher computational load, the improvements with respect to the CPU optimized version are intensified, reaching up to 4.94 in *md_disnt2* and 1.82 in *md_lj*. On average, improvements of 1.60x are obtained with *Static* and 1.35x with *HGuided*, with respect to the *CPU-icc*. Regarding the differences between the *CPU-hy* and *CPU-ocl* based co-execution, the performance is up to 1.34x better on average with the new hybrid mode, while in energy efficiency they increase to 3.14x with *Static* and 2.96x with *HGuided*.

5 Conclusions

Given the advantages of heterogeneous systems and their architectures, both in performance and energy efficiency, new opportunities are emerging to improve scientific applications. However, it is necessary to explore sophisticated solutions since they are complex to program and integrate in real applications.

In this work, ls1-mardyn, a highly optimized simulator for HPC processors, is chosen to exploit more efficient solutions that simultaneously take advantage of the different heterogeneous devices of a node, such as GPU and CPU.

Since the OpenCL technology for CPU does not have an appropriate performance for a set of molecular dynamics kernels, a number of innovations on the EngineCL runtime is carried out in order to exploit the co-execution efficiently. This paper describes the contributions made, such as the adaptation of the architecture to support new execution modes, the new native execution core for the CPU and a hybrid method of co-execution. An experimental evaluation is performed to compare both performance and energy efficiency with respect to the current parallelized and vectorized processing mode. Scalability analysis of the new CPU execution mode shows similar performance to the optimized mode used by ls1-mardyn, improving over the OpenCL version in all cases. When performing co-execution there is always at least one scheduling mechanism that offers improvements over the CPU version, both in performance and energy efficiency. On average, improvements of up to 1.38x in performance and 1.60x in energy efficiency are obtained with respect to the current optimized version.

In the future, behavioral studies will be performed regarding multi-node executions. Furthermore, strategies for integration of EngineCL inside the simulator will be provided, along with molecular dynamics multi-kernel experiments.

Acknowledgments. The work has been performed under the Project HPC-EUROPA3 (INFRAIA-2016-1-730897), with the support of the EC Research Innovation Action under the H2020 Programme; in particular, the author gratefully acknowledges the support of the SPMT Department of the HLRS. Moreover, this work has also been supported by the Spanish Ministry of Education (FPU16/ 03299 grant), the Spanish Science and Technology Commission under contract PID2019-105660RB-C22 and the European HiPEAC Network of Excellence.

References

1. Bergen, B.K., Daniels, M.G., Weber, P.M.: A hybrid programming model for compressible gas dynamics using OpenCL. In: 2010 39th International Conference on Parallel Processing Workshops, pp. 397–404. IEEE (2010)
2. Dávila Guzmán, M.A., Nozal, R., Gran Tejero, R., Villarroya-Gaudó, M., Suárez Gracia, D., Bosque, J.L.: Cooperative CPU, GPU, and FPGA heterogeneous execution with EngineCL. J. Supercomput. **75**(3), 1732–1746 (2019). https://doi.org/10.1007/s11227-019-02768-y
3. Ding, H., Huang, M.: A unified OpenCL-flavor programming model with scalable hybrid hardware platform on FPGAs. In: 2014 International Conference on ReConFigurable Computing and FPGAs (ReConFig14), pp. 1–7. IEEE (2014)
4. Gummaraju, J., Sander, B., Morichetti, L., Gaster, B.R., Houston, M., Zheng, B.: Twin peaks: a software platform for heterogeneous computing on general-purpose and graphics processors. In: 2010 19th International Conference on Parallel Architectures and Compilation Techniques (PACT), pp. 205–215. IEEE (2010)
5. Hofmann, M., Kiesel, R., Leichsenring, D., Rünger, G.: A hybrid CPU/GPU implementation of computationally intensive particle simulations using OpenCL. In: 17th IEEE International Symposium on Parallel and Distributed Computing, pp. 9–16 (2018)
6. LaKomski, D., Zong, Z., Jin, T., Ge, R.: Optimal balance between energy and performance in hybrid computing applications. In: 2015 Sixth International Green and Sustainable Computing Conference (IGSC), pp. 1–8. IEEE (2015)
7. Luk, C.K., Hong, S., Kim, H.: Qilin: exploiting parallelism on heterogeneous multiprocessors with adaptive mapping. In: 2009 42nd Annual IEEE/ACM International Symposium on Microarchitecture (MICRO), pp. 45–55. IEEE (2009)
8. Moreton-Fernandez, A., Gonzalez-Escribano, A., Llanos, D.R.: Multi-device controllers: a library to simplify parallel heterogeneous programming. Int. J. Parallel Prog. **47**(1), 94–113 (2019)
9. Nozal, R., Bosque, J.L., Beivide, R.: Towards co-execution on commodity heterogeneous systems: optimizations for time-constrained scenarios. In: 17th International Conference on High Performance Computing & Simulation, HPCS, Ireland, pp. 628–635. IEEE (2019). https://doi.org/10.1109/HPCS48598.2019.9188188
10. Nozal, R., Bosque, J.L., Beivide, R.: EngineCL: usability and performance in heterogeneous computing. Future Gen. Comp. Syst. **107**(C), 522–537 (2020). https://doi.org/10.1016/j.future.2020.02.016
11. Nozal, R.: Optimizing performance and energy efficiency in massively parallel systems. Universidad de Cantabria (2022)
12. Ravi, V., Ma, W., Chiu, D., Agrawal, G.: Compiler and runtime support for enabling generalized reduction computations on heterogeneous parallel configurations. In: Proceedings of the 2010 24th ACM International Conference on Supercomputing, pp. 137–146 (2010)
13. Scogland, T., Rountree, B., Feng, W.C., De Supinski, B.R.: Heterogeneous task scheduling for accelerated OpenMP. In: 2012 IEEE 26th International Parallel and Distributed Processing Symposium, pp. 144–155 (2012)
14. Seckler, S., Gratl, F., Heinen, M., Vrabec, J., Bungartz, H.J., Neumann, P.: AutoPas in ls1 mardyn: massively parallel particle simulations with node-level auto-tuning. J. Comput. Sci. **50**, 101296 (2021). https://doi.org/10.1016/j.jocs.2020.101296
15. Seckler, S., Tchipev, N., Bungartz, H.J., Neumann, P.: Load balancing for molecular dynamics simulations on heterogeneous architectures. In: IEEE 23rd International Conference on High Performance Computing (HiPC), pp. 101–110 (2016). https://doi.org/10.1109/HiPC.2016.021

Heterogeneous Voltage Frequency Scaling of Data-Parallel Applications for Energy Saving on Homogeneous Multicore Platforms

Pawel Bratek(⊠), Lukasz Szustak, Roman Wyrzykowski, Tomasz Olas, and Tomasz Chmiel

Department of Computer Science, Czestochowa University of Technology, Dabrowskiego 69, 42-201 Czestochowa, Poland
pawel.bratek@pcz.pl, {lszustak,roman,olas,tchmiel}@icis.pcz.pl

Abstract. In this paper, for the first time, we explore and establish the combined benefits of heterogeneous DVFS (dynamic voltage frequency scaling) control in improving the energy-performance behavior of data-parallel applications on shared-memory multicore systems. We propose to customize the clock frequency individually for the appropriately selected groups of cores corresponding to the diversified time of actual computation. In consequence, the advantage of up to 20% points over the homogeneous frequency scaling is achieved on the ccNUMA server with two 18-core Intel Xeon Gold 6240 containing 72 logical cores in total. The cost and efficiency of the proposed pruning algorithm for selecting heterogeneous DVFS configurations against the brute-force search are verified and compared experimentally.

Keywords: Data-parallel applications · Energy saving · Heterogeneous voltage frequency scaling · Multicore · ccNUMA

1 Introduction

Energy efficiency becomes one of the main challenges in the race of high-performance computing (HPC) to Exascale [11]. The scientific community is attempting to address this challenge in different ways on both hardware and software levels. State-of-the-art solution methods in this area can be generally divided [6] into system-level and application-level categories.

A widely accepted technique from the first category is dynamic voltage and frequency scaling (DVFS) [13]. It is known [8] as an efficient method to save energy for memory-bound applications when CPU cycles are being wasted as they are stalled on the main memory [8]. Using DVFS allows lowering the operational voltage/frequency at the cost of possibly higher execution time [3].

For multicore processors with shared memory, DVFS can be performed [9] at various level of granularity: (i) *per-chip* DVFS with changing the whole chip's

© Springer Nature Switzerland AG 2022
R. Chaves et al. (Eds.): Euro-Par 2021, LNCS 13098, pp. 141–153, 2022.
https://doi.org/10.1007/978-3-031-06156-1_12

frequency, (ii) *cluster-level* DVFS with multiple on-chip voltage regulators driving a set of DVFS domains, and (iii) per-core DVS with a separate regulator for each core. In particular, the per-core frequency control is available in more recent Intel processors (based on the Haswell architecture and later) by limiting the minimum and maximum frequencies for a given CPU core [18]. While the first level represents homogeneous voltage frequency scaling across the processor, the other two levels correspond to heterogeneous scaling, which can help [2] getting the most performance out of the system.

Data parallelism is the most common parallel decomposition strategy, by which an application's data domain is decomposed into as many data partitions as threads assigned to the computation. In data-parallel model, tasks are assigned to threads, and each task performs similar types of operations on different data. At an abstract programming level, data-parallel programs consist of a loop body executing on different parts of the input data [16].

Data-parallel programs are growing in importance, increasing in diversity, and demanding increased performance from hardware while preserving minimized energy consumption. In our previous works, we explore the usability of the DVFS technique as a tool for balancing energy savings with admissible performance losses for such data-parallel algorithms/applications as 3D MPDATA from computational fluid dynamics [14,17], and conjugate gradient [15].

Another example of using DVFS for data-parallel applications is presented in paper [4], which explores the relationship between task scheduling and energy constraints for stencil computation, a class of memory-bound applications that are quite common in scientific computing. This paper and our previous works apply homogeneous voltage frequency scaling for multicore CPUs, possibly combined with concurrency throttling. This solution seems to be a natural choice for homogeneous multicore and regular data-parallel applications structured with a uniform behavior when all cores or threads execute a similar type of work [2].

Typically, using heterogeneous DVFS across homogeneous multicore CPUs is justified [2] for irregular or unstructured applications when at a given time, cores might do different types of work. On the contrary, in this paper, *we explore and establish for the first time the combined benefits of heterogeneous DVFS control and performance heterogeneity in improving the energy-performance behavior of regular data-parallel applications on homogeneous multicore CPU systems with shared memory*, including ccNUMA (cache-coherent non-uniform memory access) ones. The rationale behind these benefits lies in the evolving relationship between feasible sizes of applications (determined by sizes of data sets) and increasing variety in the core number. The consequence is thread divergence within an application and load imbalancing across cores, resulting in deteriorating energy efficiency. The usage of heterogeneous DVFS allows us to mitigate the deterioration and reduce energy consumption without the performance loss.

The material of this paper is organized in the following way. Section 2 describes the basics of our approach, including a use case of application studied in the paper, as well as a more detailed motivation and the problem statement. A brute-force search and a pruning algorithm for selecting heterogeneous DVFS configuration across homogeneous multicore platforms are proposed in Sect. 3 and Sect. 4, respectively. Section 5 provides an overview of related work, while Sect. 6 presents conclusions.

2   Basics

2.1   Use Case of Data-Parallel Application: 3D Diffusion Problem

As the bulk of physics phenomena, the diffusion process is described [5] by a partial differential equation shown below:

$$\partial U/\partial t = \partial^2 U/\partial x^2 + \partial^2 U/\partial y^2 + \partial^2 U/\partial z^2 \tag{1}$$

In Eq. (1), the function $U = U(x, y, z, t)$ describes concentration of a physical quantity in point (x, y, z) at moment t. In some sense, this equation is universal. For example, it can describe the process of heat transfer where the unknown function $U(x, y, z, t)$ represents temperature. The studied application is based on the finite difference method [20], which results in the following equation:

$$U_{i,j,k}^{h+1} = \Delta t \big[(U_{i-1,j,k}^h - 2U_{i,j,k}^h + U_{i+1,j,k}^h)/\Delta x^2 + (U_{i,j-1,k}^h - 2U_{i,j,k}^h$$
$$+U_{i,j+1,k}^h)/\Delta y^2 + (U_{i,j,k-1}^h - 2U_{i,j,k}^h + U_{i,j,k+1}^h)/\Delta z^2 \big] + U_{i,j,k}^h \tag{2}$$

We focus on modeling 3D diffusion problems defined over the structured rectilinear domain of sizes $X \times Y \times Z$ in $i-$, $j-$, and $k-$dimensions, respectively. This iterative numerical algorithm is intended to run long simulations engaging even many thousands of time steps. Each step performs a single computing kernel - a 3D stencil code. The application code features a constant computation intensity for all steps, so the simulation time is proportional to their number.

In the basic code of the application (Listing 2.1), the computing kernel is implemented in parallel using the OpenMP standard. The parallelization strategy exploits data parallelism across $i-$dimension, based on distributing data across available resources by #pragma omp for directive, and then incorporates vectorization along $k-$dimension using #pragma vector directive.

The studied application is characterized by vector-friendly data structures that enable taking advantage of the vectorization process. However, the data traffic requirements constraint the parallel efficiency of the code by the main memory bandwidth. The performance bottleneck is mainly noticeable for rather large problems with domain sizes that significantly exceed the cache capacity.

In this work, all experiments are performed on the Intel-based ccNUMA server S2600WFT with two 18-core Intel Xeon Gold 6240 CPUs (Cascade Lake architecture) containing 72 logical cores in total. Each processor is equipped with 24.75 MB of L3 cache. The thermal and power limitations of the test platform permit setting the minimum clock frequency to 1.0 GHz and then sampling it at every 0.1 GHz to reach the maximum Turbo Boost speed of about 2.5 GHz.

All energy measurements are provided by the Yokogawa WT310 power meter [17], monitoring the entire platform. This power meter passes the power to the

Listing 2.1. Parallelization of data-parallel application using OpenMP

```
#pragma omp for
for(int i=0; i<X; i++) // i - dimension
  for(int j=0; j<Y; j++) // j - dimension
    #pragma omp simd
    for(int k=0; k<Z; k++) // k - dimension
      v(i,j,k) = u(i,j,k)
      v(i,j,k) += xS * (u(i-1,j,k) - 2*u(i,j,k) + u(i+1,j,k))
      v(i,j,k) += yS * (u(i,j-1,k) - 2*u(i,j,k) + u(i,j+1,k))
      v(i,j,k) += zS * (u(i,j,k-1) - 2*u(i,j,k) + u(i,j,k+1))
```

server under the load and measures the total energy consumption in real-time [6, 17]. It allows us to obtain maximally accurate and reliable energy measurements. Moreover, to make sure the experimental results for energy are trustworthy, we customize the number of time steps for every tested domain size to keep the execution time at the level of at least 700 s. As a result, the relative standard deviation (RSD) for all benchmarks does not exceed 1.5% and 2.5% for execution time and energy consumption measurements, respectively. Besides, we ensure the server is located in an air-conditioned server room providing stable temperature, as well as it is fully dedicated to our experiments.

2.2 Motivation for the Research and Problem Statement

The proposed parallelization (see Listing 2.1) splits up iterations within the first loop (i-dimension) and distributes them over the available threads corresponding to the OpenMP parallel region. As a result, the uniform workload distribution occurs only when the number X of iterations is equally divided among the number LC of logical cores. Otherwise, the parallelization scenario leads to workload imbalance and thread divergence. In this case, the load imbalancing percentage (LIP) corresponds to the ratio of total number of threads that perform more loop iterations to the total number of logical cores:

$$LIP = (X \bmod LC)/LC \cdot 100\% \tag{3}$$

Assuming $X > LC$, the more loaded threads perform R times more iterations than the rest of threads, where the parameter R can be expressed as:

$$R = \lceil X/LC \rceil / (\lceil X/LC \rceil - 1) \tag{4}$$

Figure 1 characterizes the execution time and energy consumption when solving the 3D diffusion problem with various domain sizes. In all examples, $R = 2$. This study assumes a limit of 2% performance losses to achieve energy savings.

The left parts of Fig. 1 present the execution time and energy consumption for various domain sizes, assuming the usage of homogeneous DFVS across cores for different frequencies. As shown in Fig. 1a and Fig. 1b, the optimal performance-energy trade-off (marked with red points) corresponds to the highest CPU frequency since reducing the frequency leads to energy savings but breaks the assumed limit for performance losses. The reason is that all required data reside in the cache hierarchy, and computing units are not waiting for loading data from the main memory.

In contrast, in Figs. 1c and 1d, we observe that reducing the clock frequency does not affect performance for large domain sizes. Now the execution time is practically constant despite decreasing the frequency from the highest to the lowest one. In this case, the performance depends primarily on the main memory speed, and frequency scaling does not affect the execution time. Consequently, the DVFS method allows reducing the total energy consumption up to 30% with negligible performance losses not exceeding 1–2% for all performed tests.

However, our experiments reveal a need for revisiting the DVFS technique even in this case that commonly assumes homogeneous frequency scaling across cores. To explain this, let us move on to the analysis of the right parts of Fig. 1a–d, which demonstrate the execution time distribution across threads for different domain sizes and a variety of workloads with varying values of LIP parameter, where $LIP \in \{8, 25, 50\}\%$. More precisely, these plots show the total execution time that every OpenMP thread spends on (i) computation (area marked in blue color) and (ii) synchronization. In turn, the synchronization costs are split into two stages: (i) the arrival stage that puts threads arriving at the barrier into a waiting state (area marked in red color), and (ii) the departure stage that releases from the barrier all waiting threads (marked in gray color).

The cost of the departure stage depends on the number of synchronization points, which in our study increases linearly with the number of time steps. As expected, the time required by this stage is practically uniform for every OpenMP thread. For a single synchronization point, this time mainly depends on the OpenMP implementation chosen and hardware limitations.

However, the cost of actual computation (see blue regions in the right parts of Fig. 1) differs across threads. The same is true for the cost of the arrival stage of synchronization. This heterogeneity results from non-uniform workload distributions over available cores/threads, described by LIP and R parameters.

Additionally, we observe a negative impact of the inter-socket data traffic on thread divergence. This undesirable effect becomes essential only when threads operate on data located in the cache hierarchy. As shown in the right parts of Figs. 1a and 1b, the threads pinned to cores located on the boundaries between sockets feature a higher time of actual computation even if they execute a fewer number of iterations. This time is mainly limited by the inter-socket data exchange overhead. On the contrary, the overhead is negligible or simply imperceptible for larger domains when the time of actual computation is constrained by the main memory speed (see Figs. 1c and 1d, respectively).

Summarizing our observations, the homogeneous variant of DVFS method allows selecting the performance-energy trade-off considering the total execution time that reflects the maximum computation time obtained across a pool of threads. Consequently, threads that process fewer loop iterations waste energy waiting at points of synchronization in the arrival stage. This disadvantage inten-

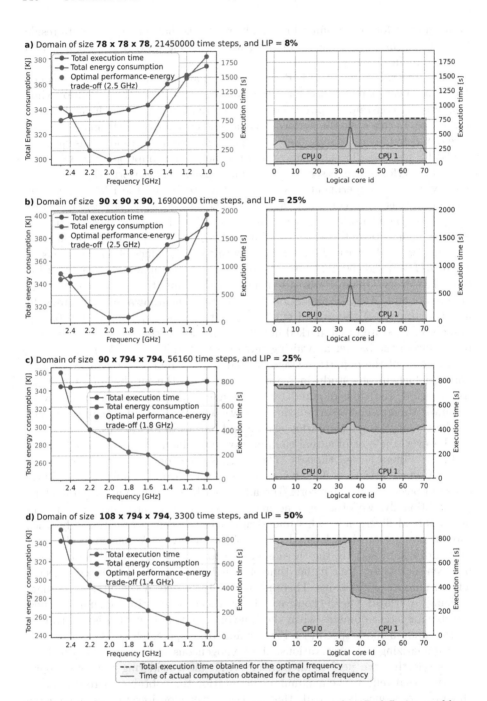

Fig. 1. Execution time and energy consumption for solving the 3D diffusion problem with various domain sizes, using homogeneous DFVS. (Color figure online)

sifies with a constantly increasing number of cores offered by modern shared-memory computing systems.

3   Heterogeneous DVFS: Brute-force Search

The analysis from Sect. 2 motivates us to adjust the frequency and supply voltage to individual cores. Our key idea is to customize the clock frequency individually for the appropriately selected groups of cores corresponding to the diversified time of actual computation. We distinguish two heterogeneous DVFS scenarios that prioritize the appropriately selected groups of cores.

The first scenario corresponds to smaller problem sizes (Figs. 1a and 1b), when we can identify cores with the time of actual computation limited by inter-socket data traffic overheads. In this case, we distinguish three groups of cores, including: (i) cores located on the boundaries between sockets; cores with a higher (ii) and a fewer (iii) number of loop iterations. The amounts of cores in the last two groups reflect the LIP parameter and depend on the domain size and number of cores. Based on the time of actual computation for every group, a higher voltage/frequency should be assigned to the first group, then for the second one, and the lowest for the last group. The second scenario assumes larger problem sizes where the main memory constraints result in performance degradation (Figs. 1c and 1d). Here, only two groups are indicated, including cores with a higher (ii) and a fewer (iii) number of loop iterations. Hence, a higher priority and thus a higher voltage/frequency are given to the first group.

To fully explore the heterogeneous DVFS approach, we test almost all frequency configurations for groups, considering various domain sizes. More precisely, while examining a given frequency for the group with a higher priority, we test different frequency combinations for the group with a lower priority by scaling down the frequency from a fixed level to the minimum, sampling it at every 0.2 GHz. For example, when setting clock speed to 2.0 GHz for cores in the first group, we combine it with the set $\{2.0, 1.8, ..., 1.0\}$ GHz of frequencies for the second group. We also reveal no need to scale down the clock speed for cores located on the boundaries between sockets. As expected, setting the maximum frequency/voltage for these cores guarantees to achieve the best results in terms of both performance and energy consumption.

The summary of performed tests is depicted in Figs. 2 and 3. The first one shows the best heterogeneous frequency setups determined for various domain sizes with up to 1–2% performance losses. We select three groups of clock speeds for domains of sizes not exceeding $138 \times 138 \times 138$ (these domains fit in the cache), while two groups are enough for larger domains.

Figure 3 presents the advantages of using heterogeneous voltage/frequency scaling compared to homogeneous scaling, achieved for different domain sizes. The proposed approach permits a maximum energy reduction of about 25% for the domain of size $150 \times 150 \times 150$, when the profit for homogeneous scaling is about 9% only. In general, the heterogeneous approach allows us to achieve better energy profits for all performed tests. The most significant energy improvement

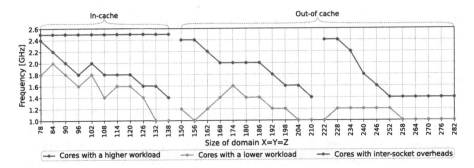

Fig. 2. The best heterogeneous frequency setups selected for various domain sizes.

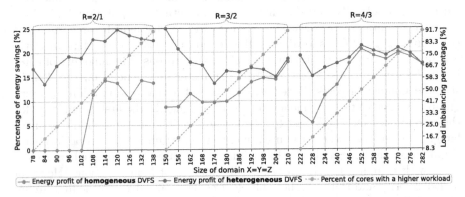

Fig. 3. Comparison of energy-savings for homogeneous and heterogeneous DVFS approaches applied to various domain sizes.

compared to the homogeneous solution is obtained for the size of $96 \times 96 \times 96$. In this case, we observe the advantage of about 20% points over the traditional frequency scaling, which does not bring any energy improvement.

4   Pruning Algorithm for Selecting Heterogeneous DVFS Configurations

The main disadvantage of the brute-force search is its high cost. Let us assume we begin tests with a clock speed equal to f_{max}. Then we decrease frequency starting from f_{start} up to f_{stop} by every f_{step}. Let $\mathbf{F} = \{f_{max}, f_{start}, \dots, f_{stop}\}$, where $|\mathbf{F}| = N$, be a set of tested frequencies. According to the brute-force technique of searching for frequencies for cores with higher and lower workloads, we combine each frequency f_i from the set $\mathbf{F}$ with a subset of $\mathbf{F}$ containing elements f_j such that $f_j \leq f_i$. As a result, the number TC of tested configuration is expressed as $TC = N(N+1)/2$, where the cardinality N of set $\mathbf{F}$ is as follows:

$$N = (f_{start} - f_{stop})/f_{step} + 2 \tag{5}$$

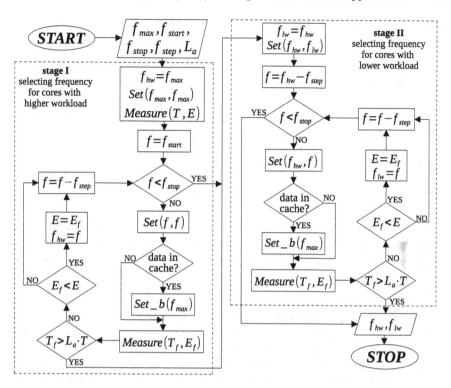

Fig. 4. Block diagram of the pruning algorithm for selecting heterogeneous DVFS configurations

For example, using the brute-force strategy with f_{max}, f_{start}, f_{stop}, and f_{step} equal to respectively 2.5, 2.4, 1.0, and 0.2 GHz, requires testing $TC = 45$ frequency configurations. In each of them, we perform energy consumption tests, and their run time should be long enough to ensure the stability of measurements. Therefore, finding the best frequency configuration in this way is a highly time-consuming task. In this section, we propose a pruning algorithm for selecting the best heterogeneous DVFS configuration. This algorithm allows us to significantly reduce the value of TC and speed up finding the best frequency configuration.

The proposed algorithm is shown in Fig. 4. It consists of two stages, the aim of which is to find the best frequencies f_{hw}, f_{lw} for cores with higher and lower workloads, respectively. The input parameters of the algorithm include L_a, which is an acceptable performance loss. For example, $L_a = 1.02$ allows the frequency to be reduced until a 2% increase in run time is achieved. We use the routine $Set(f_1, f_2)$ to examine frequency configurations - it sets clock speeds f_1 and f_2 for groups of cores with higher and lower workloads, respectively. Analogously, the routine $Set\_b(f)$ sets frequency f for cores located on the boundaries between sockets. In Fig. 4, the routine $Measure(T, E)$ is responsible for measuring the execution time T and energy consumption E for the current configuration. To

Table 1. Comparison of brute-force search (B-F) and proposed algorithm (A) for domains of various size $X = Y = Z$

R	LIP [%]	Domain size	f_{hw} [GHz]		f_{lw} [GHz]		TC		Energy reduction [%]		Efficiency r_E [%]
			B-F	A	B-F	A	B-F	A	B-F	A	
2	8	78	2.4	2.4	1.8	1.8	45	8	16.62	16.62	100.00
2	25	90	2.0	2.0	1.8	1.8	45	7	17.14	17.14	100.00
2	50	108	1.8	1.6	1.4	1.2	45	11	22.88	22.40	97.90
3/2	8	150	2.4	2.0	1.2	1.0	45	10	25.04	23.98	95.77
3/2	25	162	2.2	2.2	1.2	1.2	45	10	17.92	17.92	100.00
3/2	50	180	2.0	2.0	1.4	1.4	45	9	16.17	16.17	100.00
4/3	8	222	2.4	2.2	1.0	1.2	45	10	19.52	18.33	93.90
4/3	25	234	2.2	1.8	1.2	1.4	45	9	17.02	15.97	93.83
4/3	50	252	1.4	1.4	1.2	1.2	45	10	21.61	21.61	100.00

provide the accuracy of results, we repeat all measurements m times and calculate their median value ($m = 5$ as default). The algorithm checks if all data reside in the cache memory. When this condition is met, cores located on the boundaries between sockets have the highest time of actual computation (see Figs. 1a and 1b). In this case, the best strategy is to let these cores work with the maximum frequency to deal with data exchange overheads.

A set of tests is performed to explore the speed and efficiency of the proposed algorithm. Table 1 presents a comparison of results obtained using the brute-force search and pruning algorithm for different values of R and LIP. The comparison is based on the number TC of configurations tested by the pruning algorithm and efficiency r_E, where r_E is the ratio (in %) of energy reduction achieved by both techniques. In all tested cases, the algorithm's efficiency exceeds 90% and in more than half of them reaches 100%. At the same time, we significantly reduce the cost of selecting a heterogeneous DVFS configuration. While the brute-force search always requires exploring 45 frequency configurations, the pruning algorithm achieves the goal by examining only 7–11 configurations.

5 Related Works

The methods of improving energy efficiency in computing can be divided [6, 10] into hardware-level or system-level. The methods from the first category aim to optimize the energy efficiency of the environment where applications are performed. The solutions from the second category focus mainly on the optimization of applications for performance and energy. These methods use application-level models for predicting the performance and energy consumption of applications. The approach proposed in this work combines methods from both categories since it is based on DVFS and the application-level model.

For data-parallel applications, the combination of methods from both categories is also considered by Reddy and Lastovetsky in work [10]. They propose a method to solve the bi-objective optimization problem of an application for performance and energy on homogeneous clusters of modern multicore CPUs. This method gives a diverse set of Pareto-optimal solutions and can be combined with the DVFS technique to provide a better set of solutions. However, the proposed approach target only homogeneous DVFS policies.

At the same time, heterogeneous voltage frequency scaling is studied in a number of works that can be included into the first category. Unlike this paper, the studied methods employ application-agnostic models [7]. They are principally deployed at the operating system (OS) level [12] or as a runtime system extending the OS [2,19]. Therefore, they require changes to the OS [6]. Typically these methods propose asymmetry-aware or heterogeneity-aware schedulers that exploit the asymmetry [1,9] or heterogeneity [12,19] between sets of cores in a multicore platform to find optimal DVFS configurations. For example, work [1] studies a case when an application running on some cores coexists together with its co-runners (applications running on other cores), while paper [12] considers the heterogeneity of cores in ARM architectures.

6   Conclusions

This paper studies the benefits of heterogeneous DVFS control and performance heterogeneity in improving the energy-performance behavior of data-parallel applications on homogeneous multicore CPU systems. Using the 3D diffusion problem as a use case, we show that using heterogeneous voltage/frequency scaling permits significant energy improvement compared to the homogeneous solution. The advantage of up to 20% points over the homogeneous frequency scaling is achieved on the ccNUMA server with two 18-core Intel Xeon 6240.

The cost and efficiency of the proposed pruning algorithm for selecting heterogeneous DVFS configurations against the brute-force search are compared experimentally. In all tests, the efficiency of the pruning algorithm exceeds 90% and in more than half of them reaches 100%, which indicates that both techniques return the same energy saving. At the same time, we significantly reduce the cost of selecting a heterogeneous DVFS configuration. While the brute-force search always requires exploring 45 frequency configurations, the pruning algorithm achieves the goal by examining only 7–11 configurations.

Acknowledgments. This research was supported by the National Science Centre (Poland) under grant no. UMO-2017/26/D/ST6/00687.

References

1. Abera, S., Balakrishnan, M., Kumar, A.: Performance-energy trade-off in CMPs with Per-Core DVFS. In: Berekovic, M., Buchty, R., Hamann, H., Koch, D., Pionteck, T. (eds.) ARCS 2018. LNCS, vol. 10793, pp. 225–238. Springer, Cham (2018). https://doi.org/10.1007/978-3-319-77610-1_17

2. Acun, B., et al.: Fine-grained energy efficiency using per-core DVFS with an adaptive runtime systems. In: 2019 Tenth International Green and Sustainable Computing Conference (IGSC), vol. 1, pp. 1–8 (2019)

3. Calore, E., Gabbana, A., Schifano, S., Tripiccione, R.: Software and DVFS tuning for performance and energy-efficiency on Intel KNL processors. J. Low Power Electron. Appl. **8**(2), 18 (2018)

4. Ciznicki, M., Kurowski, K.: Resource management strategies with energy profiles for stencil computing. In: HiStencil 2015: 2nd International Workshop on High-Performance Stencil Computating, pp. 943–950 (2015)

5. Crank, J.: Mathematics of Diffusion, 2nd edn. Clarendon Press (1975)

6. Fahad, M., Shahid, A., Manumachu, R., Lastovetsky, A.: Energy predictive models of computing: theory, practical implications and experimental analysis on multicore processors. IEEE Access **9**, 63149–63172 (2021)

7. Gupta, M., Bhargava, L., Sreedevi, I.: Dynamic voltage frequency scaling in multicore systems using adaptive regression model. In: Proceedings of 4th International Conference on IoT in Social, Mobile, Analytics and Cloud (I-SMAC), pp. 1201–1206 (2020)

8. Haj-Yahya, J., et al.: Energy Efficient High Performance Processors: Recent Approaches for Designing Green High Performance Computing. Springer, Singapore (2018). https://doi.org/10.1007/978-981-10-8554-3

9. Kolpe, T., Zhai, A., Sapatnekar, S.: Enabling improved power management in multicore processors through clustered DVFS. In: 2011 Design, Automation & Test in Europe, pp. 1–6 (2011)

10. Lastovetsky, A., Manumachu, R.: Bi-objective optimization of data-parallel applications on homogeneous multicore clusters for performance and energy. IEEE Trans. Comput. **67**(2), 160–177 (2018)

11. Mair, J., Huang, Z., Eyers, D., Chen, Y.: Quantifying the energy efficiency challenges of achieving exascale computing. In: 15th IEEE/ACM International Symposium on Cluster, Cloud and Grid Computing, pp. 943–950 (2015)

12. Papadimitriou, G., et al.: Adaptive voltage/frequency scaling and core allocation for balanced energy and performance on multicore CPUs. In: 2019 IEEE International Symposium on High Performance Computer Architecture (HPCA), pp. 133–146 (2019)

13. Rauber, T., Rünger, G., Stachowski, M.: Performance and energy metrics for multithreaded applications on DVFS processors. Sustain. Comput.: Inform. Syst. **17**, 55–68 (2018)

14. Rojek, K., Ilic, A., Wyrzykowski, R., Sousa, L.: Energy-aware mechanism for stencil-based MPDATA algorithm with constraints. Concurr. Computat. Pract. Exper. **29**(8), e4016 (2017)

15. Rojek, K., Quintana-Ortí, E.S., Wyrzykowski, R.: Modeling power consumption of 3D MPDATA and the CG method on ARM and Intel multicore architectures. J. Supercomput. **73**(10), 4373–4389 (2017). https://doi.org/10.1007/s11227-017-2020-z

16. Sankaralingam, K., Keckler, S., Mark, W., Burger, D.: Universal mechanisms for data-parallel applications. In: Proceedings of 36th International Symposium on Microarchitecture (MICRO-36) (2003)

17. Szustak, L., et al.: Correlation of performance optimizations and energy consumption for stencil-based application on intel xeon scalable processors. IEEE Trans. Parallel Distrib. Syst. **31**(11), 2582–2593 (2020)

18. Technology Guide: Intel Speed Select Technology - Core Power, April 2021

19. Winter, J., Albonesi D.H. Shoemaker, C.: Scalable thread scheduling and global power management for heterogeneous many-core architecture. In: Proceedings of PACT 2010, pp. 29–40 (2010)
20. Zill, D., Wright, W.: Differential Equations with Boundary-Value Problems. 8th edn. Brooks/Cole Cengage Learning (2012)

Domain-Specific Runtime to Orchestrate Computation on Heterogeneous Platforms

Jared O'Neal[1]([✉])[iD], Mohamed Wahib[2], Anshu Dubey[1,3][iD], Klaus Weide[3],
Tom Klosterman[1], and Johann Rudi[1][iD]

[1] Mathematics and Computer Science Division, Argonne National Laboratory,
Lemont, IL 60439, USA
{joneal,adubey,tklosterman,jrudi}@anl.gov
[2] RIKEN Center for Computational Science, Kobe, Japan
mohamed.attia@riken.jp
[3] Department of Computer Science, University of Chicago, Chicago, IL 60637, USA
kweide@uchicago.edu

Abstract. Task-based runtime systems typically exploit asynchronicity inherent in applications to reduce overall execution time. In the past decade, focus shifted to supporting the heterogeneity that is increasingly prevalent in high-performance computing systems. Existing task-based runtime systems are designed to be general; thus, they come with challenges such as overheads and the complexity of abstractions. Much of the burden of exposing heterogeneous parallelism is placed on application developers, who must fit domain-specific code to general-purpose interfaces. This paper presents a different approach that targets heterogeneous systems through domain-specific runtimes. Our pipeline-based design presented here leverages the domain-specific knowledge of a focused class of scientific simulations to pragmatically orchestrate their computations. Promising, multi-GPU performance results obtained with the Oak Ridge Leadership Computing Facility's *Summit* are presented.

Keywords: Runtime system · Heterogeneous platforms ·
Asynchronous task execution · Domain-specific runtime · Performance portability

1 Introduction

Scientific workflows have evolved to the point where higher model fidelities create an axis of complexity that is orthogonal to the platform complexity, creating a new set of performance portability challenges. Most of the tools and abstractions that have been developed and deployed have attempted to be entirely transparent to the developers. Thus developers are often left with the choice of either embracing an entire abstraction (magic compiler) or shouldering the entire parallelization burden (ninja programmers). Neither choice is optimal. An abstraction that attempts to own the whole optimization must account for all corner cases, resulting in complex tools; on the other hand, leaving it all to the software developers is

© Springer Nature Switzerland AG 2022
R. Chaves et al. (Eds.): Euro-Par 2021, LNCS 13098, pp. 154–165, 2022.
https://doi.org/10.1007/978-3-031-06156-1_13

no longer viable for even modestly sized codes. Furthermore, leaving the domain knowledge on the table is likely to result in a suboptimal solution. A nascent movement in the programming models and compilers communities involves orthogonalizing the optimization of different aspects of scientific software as a way of making performance portability tractable. This approach takes the idea of separation of concerns in software architecture and applies it to program synthesis. We are using this approach in the multiphysics software Flash-X, where the orchestration system (OS) has individual tools that are simple, because each tool focuses on one aspect of program synthesis/optimization, but together they are intended to deliver a powerful performance portability solution.

A key design principle of the OS is to enable both domain-specific knowledge and platform knowledge to be utilized in the application configuration without placing undue burden on either the tool developers or the domain experts. The system relies on a pipeline consisting of assembly, configuration, transformation, and orchestration. The first three steps in the pipeline are static, and they are used to configure an instance of an application suited to a target platform. We refer to them as offline tools (OT). Note that these steps do not occur in the order specified; instead they are interspersed and work cooperatively. Along with the OT is an orchestration runtime (OR) in the system that carries out all the data movement between resources and orchestrates execution. In this paper we present the design and evaluation of the OR.

In Sect. 2 we discuss the background. Domain-specific structures and patterns that inform the design of our domain-specific runtime are presented in Sect. 3, and the design is described in Sect. 4. Section 5 presents results from a performance study executed as part of profiling and optimizing the current implementation of the OR. In Sect. 6 we discuss future work to be done so that OS can be used for our immediate science goals and beyond.

2   Background

Performance portability solutions throughout the history of high-performance computing (HPC) have relied on achieving separation of concerns. In the distributed-memory model it sufficed to keep the portions of the code that relied on communication separate from those that could be executed locally. One could then optimize the performance of a single processing element separately from the scaling performance (see [5] for an example of such an approach). With the advent of accelerators and heterogeneous nodes, the HPC community has been engaged in finding enduring solutions [13,17], and many solutions have been offered. These include domain-specific languages [3,7,9,15], abstractions based on C++ template metaprogramming [8,10], and other domain-specific solutions such as [18] providing an entire framework. Tools such as Kokkos [8] and Raja [10] provide the ability to express the computation at a high level, which can be specialized to the target device as needed. They also provide mechanisms for launching calculations on devices and accompanying data movement.

An orthogonal class of tools provide task-based runtime support. Some of these systems at the application execution level have been around since applications have deviated from lockstep parallelism or perfect load distribution.

Charm++ [12] and Uintah's runtime [14] have been among the longest-lived and are still in active use. Other more general-purpose asynchronous runtimes that have found variable degrees of success in HPC systems include HPX [11], StarPU [1], and Legion [2]. Except for Uintah, which is embedded, all the other systems subscribe to the idea of being transparent to the application programmer. They all rely on some form of implicit or explicit dependency analysis graph (DAG) to do their scheduling. Some of these provide a more complete solution (e.g., Legion [2]) while others focus just on tasking. To a large scientific software project, they present a collection of options that provide a part of the functionality but often no way of reasonably combining them. In addition they assume that dependencies become visible only at run time, and therefore they miss the opportunity of having significantly simpler static DAGs that exploit dependencies derived from domain knowledge. Our OS exploits this domain-specific knowledge of a relatively small space of dependencies and opportunities of overlapping executions. It has the possibility, therefore, to avoid unnecessary overheads and complexity that come from having to be conservative about dependency assumptions, corner cases, and dynamic analysis.

3   Domain-Specific Context for Runtime

The OS design targets applications for multiphysics simulations that are based on partial differential equations (PDEs). In particular, we focus on Flash-X, a new code derived from the FLASH code [4]. A major part of the execution time of such codes is spent in iterative cycles that advance the PDE solution. Examples are time-stepping methods as well as iterative linear and nonlinear solvers. In general, the high-level physics **operations** to be carried out at each time step is known when the simulation is specified (*i.e.*, at setup time). In addition the structure of these steps remains fixed during evolution. We target our runtime design at these iterative domain-specific structures and patterns.

The OR design is based on the assumption that the basic discretization is adaptive mesh refinement (AMR) with non-overlapping blocks and that physics operators are applied on blocks individually and concurrently in a predetermined sequence. We differentiate between two types of load distribution. Global distributed-memory mode is handled by MPI and is not relevant to this paper. Local distribution between various devices by a single MPI process is the focus of the OR and this article.

Because data locality and data movement are critical aspects of overall performance, the APIs of the physics solvers (referred to henceforth as **operators**) expose aggregate computations, called **task functions**, that run between any data movements and barriers that the operators need. This delineation enables maximization of local data reuse on devices. At the level of time stepping, explicit knowledge of task function interdependence within one operator and across operators results in simple graphs that enable the OR to use asynchronization and latency hiding for better performance.

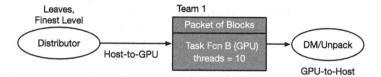

Fig. 1. Thread team configuration that applies a task function using a GPU with its own dedicated memory. Task function B is implemented to use a GPU, and the distributor will eventually enqueue with the team all leaf blocks at the finest AMR level in the form of data packets of blocks. We assume that the blocks' data resides in host memory and therefore that the distributor has an additional task of initiating asynchronous transfers of all packets to the GPU memory. The final runtime element in the configuration is responsible for asynchronous GPU-to-host data movement (DM) of packets of blocks and for unpacking these upon termination of each transfer. (Color figure online)

4   Design of the Orchestration Runtime

Our design assumes that each physics operator in each time step can be applied identically and concurrently to all active blocks. The OR implements scheduling and orchestration of the execution of necessary task functions for a number of well-understood arrangements of operators. Supported arrangements of operators are implemented via specific configurations built from components called **runtime elements**, which are described below.

4.1   Runtime Elements for Data Movement and Task Execution

The primary runtime elements are **thread teams**, which are created on the host when the simulation starts and persist throughout the application execution. The number of threads in each team is specified at run time. To apply a computation to a set of blocks in an arbitrary order, a thread team is assigned an associated task function along with all relevant data. The OR coordinates the asynchronous movement of data to the target memory systems as well as execution of all associated tasks. Note that task functions can execute code on any device without being aware of the specifics of the device so long as the required data is resident in the appropriate memory system.

Figure 1 shows a **thread team configuration** that uses a single thread team (in blue). The configuration begins with a runtime element called **distributor**, which for this configuration collects the blocks on which task function B will be applied, packages up the blocks into packets, and publishes each packet (the right arrow) with the team once the packet contains a specified number of blocks. The distributor also initiates an asynchronous host-to-GPU data movement. Ten of the team's threads are activated such that at any time each thread can have sole ownership of a single packet and apply task function B to the blocks in the packet by launching kernels on the GPU. The OR ensures that a data packet is available on the target device before the task function is applied to it.

Figure 1 also introduces the runtime element **data mover** (DM/Unpack), which is shown as the data subscriber of Team 1. When a thread in the team finishes applying task function B to a data packet, it publishes the packet by enqueueing it with DM/Unpack. In turn, the data mover is responsible for managing the asynchronous transfer of a data packet back to the host and its subsequent unpacking. The distributor and data mover allow for decoupling the thread team from data movements and therefore encapsulating low-level details associated with data movements on a particular platform.

This functionality of the configuration implies that a thread in the team can begin applying task function B to blocks in the data packet at the same time that the distributor can begin forming the next data packet. It follows that once the first data packet is sent, the OR is able to overlay data movements with computations to achieve latency hiding. Similarly, the latencies and overheads associated with the GPU-to-host data movement and unpacking are overlapped. The OR's ability to hide latencies is under the control of run time parameters that specify, for instance, sizes of data packets and numbers of active threads. This discussion hints at the notion of thread team configurations as pipelines, which is considered next.

4.2   Complex Orchestration of Multiple Thread Teams

Figure 2 depicts a more complex configuration with more than one task function. The distributor must now enqueue each block with both Teams 1 and 2 to enable parallel execution of different task functions. Here the distributor is multithreaded, which means that the set of blocks to which all task functions are to be applied are partitioned between two distributor threads working concurrently.

Since Teams 1 and 2 are assigned different data types and their task functions were written for different hardware (CPU and GPU, respectively), the distributor now gathers blocks on which task functions A, B, and C are to be applied, decomposes the blocks into tiles, and enqueues each tile with Team 1. It also aggregates those same blocks into data packets of a desired size (four blocks as drawn in the figure), and each of these is sent asynchronously to GPU memory before being enqueued with Team 2. This example demonstrates that thread team configurations allow the OR to run concurrently the same data items through multiple independent **pipelines**.

The inclusion of task function C in this example demonstrates that the composability of configurations allows for extending pipelines (green pipeline in Fig. 2), which can improve performance through increased overlapping of communication and computation as well as overlapping of computation at multiple levels in the hierarchy of parallelism. Note that this configuration is valid only if A is independent of B and C and if B and C are either independent, or C must be executed after B. Thus, the independence of the pipelines is important when mapping task functions onto configurations, in that two or more dependent task functions may be included in a mapping so long as dependent task functions are located in the same pipeline and in the correct order.

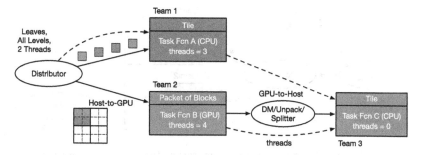

Fig. 2. A thread team configuration implementing two pipelines using three thread teams with CPU code for task functions A and C and GPU kernel launches for task function B. The task function A pipeline runs on the host with three threads. The B/C pipeline gives 4 threads to Team 2 for launching kernels on the GPU. Team 3 is initialized with with zero threads because it needs data items to first pass through Team 2. However, when a thread in Team 1 or Team 2 goes to sleep because its task function has been applied to all necessary data items, it informs Team 3 to activate a thread (thread migration is indicated by dashed lines).

The different data types between Teams 2 and 3 require the inclusion of a runtime element (DM/Unpack/Splitter) as a data subscriber for Team 2 and a data publisher for Team 3 that translates between types. Since the task functions assigned to these teams use different hardware, this element is also responsible for moving and unpacking of the data. In particular, when a thread in Team 2 finishes applying task function B to a data packet of blocks, the packet is enqueued with the new element. In turn, the element will transfer the packet asynchronously to the host, unpack its contents, decompose each block into its constituent tiles, and enqueue each of these with Team 3.

4.3   Load-Balancing with Data Movement and Thread Migration

The example in Fig. 2 also illustrates the OR's scheme for load balancing of thread resources of the host. This is accomplished by specifying a second relationship between runtime elements as **thread publishers** and **thread subscribers**. This relationship is indicated by dashed arrows. While a thread publisher can have at most one thread subscriber, there is no limit to the number of thread publishers that a thread subscriber can have. When a thread in a team with a thread subscriber determines that there is no more work to be done by the team in the current execution cycle, it goes to sleep only after informing the team's thread subscriber that the latter can now activate one of its threads.

The thread publisher/subscriber relationship explains, therefore, why Team 3 can be initialized with zero active threads. It is the thread subscriber of the other two teams (and of the distributor indirectly). Hence, by the end of the execution cycle, Team 3 can have nine threads activated for applying task function C. This thread setting prioritizes thread resources to transferring packets and launching kernels in task function B as quickly as possible to boost the occupancy of the

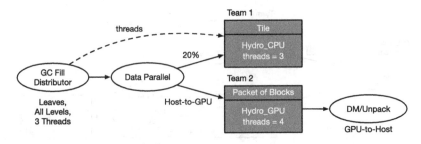

Fig. 3. A single-pipeline thread team configuration that enhances task-based parallelism with data parallelism *via* the inclusion of the data parallel runtime element and the mapping to two thread teams of CPU and GPU task functions that implement the same computation. As blocks flow into the data-parallel element, 20% of these will be decomposed into tiles and enqueued with the thread team assigned the CPU version of the function; the remaining blocks are aggregated into data packets, sent to the GPU, and enqueued with the team assigned the GPU version. Thus two thread teams work in tandem on different devices to apply a given computation to all necessary blocks.

GPU. Once threads are no longer needed to execute task functions A and B, they can be used to spin up the extension of the green pipeline.

We emphasize that while data publisher/subscriber connections are used to construct pipelines in a thread team configuration, thread publisher/subscriber connections are not. Rather, these connections resemble decorators added to a configuration in order to improve load balancing.

5   Evaluation

The orchestration runtime, which is implemented in C++ with pthreads, currently utilizes OpenACC only for offloading computations to accelerators and a CUDA backend for resource management and movement of data. The OR's design, however, does not preclude other offloading solutions or backends.

5.1   Experimental Configurations

For verification and early performance analysis of the OR, we use the Sedov explosion problem [16] with a simplified hydrodynamics solver used only for testing and development. While the solver is computationally simple, it is a stringent test of the efficacy of the OR because it has much lower arithmetic intensity than do most of the physics operators in Flash-X. Although AMReX (v20.08) provides the mesh, it is used in uniform grid mode to make reasoning about the performance easier in these early evaluations. The 3D domain is decomposed into a 16^3 array of 16^3 blocks, and the solution is evolved by 250 time steps.

The experiments were conducted on a single IBM Power System AC922 node on OLCF *Summit*.[1] Each node has two IBM POWER9 processors (42 usable

---

[1] https://www.olcf.ornl.gov/summit/.

cores with four HW threads per core) and six NVIDIA Volta V100 GPUs. The processors are connected to the GPUs via dual NVLink connections and have an aggregate 512 GB of DDR4 memory. The GPUs have 96 GB of high-bandwidth memory (HBM2) per node. We used the following test setups in our evaluation:

1. **MPI baseline** – 42 single-core MPI processes run without the OR and without OpenMP multithreading. At each time step, a loop over blocks applies the hydrodynamics physics operators to each block in series.
2. **OpenMP baseline** – 6 seven-core MPI processes run without the OR but with OpenMP multithreading over the AMReX block iterator. Each thread applies the hydrodynamics physics operator to its blocks in series. The number of OpenMP threads is a run time parameter.
3. **CPU-only OR** – 6 seven-core MPI processes with the orchestration runtime using a single-threaded distributor with a single team that is assigned a task function that applies the hydrodynamics operators using the CPU. The number of threads activated in the team is a run time parameter.
4. **GPU-only OR** – 6 seven-core MPI processes each using the orchestration runtime and each assigned a unique GPU. At each time step, the hydrodynamics physics operators are applied using the configuration in Fig. 1, where the distributor uses only a single thread and the team activates only a single thread. The number of blocks per packet is a run time parameter. Note that the single task function used in this case contains code that launches several computational kernels on the GPU.
5. **Data Parallel OR** – the same as for the GPU-only setup but using the configuration in Fig. 3. The distributor uses only a single thread, and Team 2 activates only a single thread. The number of threads activated in Team 1, the number of blocks per packet, and the splitting percentage are run time parameters.

Simulations were built with PGI (v19.9) with OpenACC and OpenMP activated where necessary. The IBM Spectrum MPI (v10.3.1.2-20200121) implementation was used. For GPU-based runs, CUDA (v10.1.243) was used to drive the OR backend. All host/GPU data movements were handled directly by the OR using CUDA and without using managed memory. Also, OpenACC is used solely for offloading computation to the GPU. In order to verify correct execution, the results of each test setup, which are executed independently of Flash-X, were compared against Flash-X results for the same problem.

5.2   Performance Analysis

The main figure of merit is the time a simulation spends applying hydrodynamics operators. This is reported as the maximum wall time across all MPI processes at a given time step (*Max Wall Time/Step*), or as the sum of the maximum wall time/step across all steps (*Max Wall Time*).

OpenMP baseline and CPU-only OR configurations were run once each for different values of the thread run time parameter. The results, shown in Fig. 4

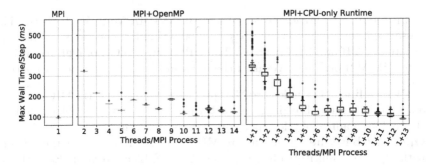

Fig. 4. Boxplots that summarize the per-time-step performance for a simulation run with the MPI baseline configuration (left), simulations run in the OpenMP baseline configuration each with a different number of threads over the AMReX block iterator loop (center), and simulations run in the CPU-only OR configuration each with a different number of threads activated in the team (right). $1 + X$ denotes one distributor thread and X team threads. Each box is associated with the max wall time per time step collected across the 250 time steps of a single simulation. These results have been used to fix run time parameter values and to compare the performance of these three CPU-only configurations.

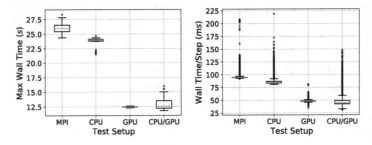

Fig. 5. Boxplots that summarize the performance of each of the principal test configurations. Each box in the left plot is associated with the total max wall time across 50 repeated trials of the given test configuration. Each box in the right plot is associated with the wall time/step reported by each MPI process across all time steps and all 50 repeated trials.

with the results from a single MPI run, indicate that 11 threads and 1 distributor thread with 13 team threads, respectively, give the best performance. A similar test for the GPU-only OR configuration found that 40 blocks per packet result in good performance. These results were used with a simplistic model to predict the best run time parameter values for the data-parallel configuration. A coarse grid search about these values revealed that using 55 blocks per packet, activating five threads in the CPU-based team, and sending 10 blocks to the CPU-based team for each packet yield reasonable results. With these run time parameters, 50 identical simulations were run for each of the four principal test configurations. The results are shown in Fig. 5.

Figure 4 shows that in general the CPU-only OR configuration is competitive with both the MPI configuration and the use of OpenMP to multithread the AMReX block iterator and therefore indicates that the implementation of thread teams is reasonably performant. One will need to understand, however, why the CPU-only performance has a much higher variance, which could be related to the observation that the GPU-only OR configuration has relatively little variance, as seen in both plots of Fig. 5. The left plot of the figure shows that roughly 50% of the data-parallel simulations (CPU/GPU) had total wall times that are better than or similar to those of the GPU-only configuration. However, it also shows that the remaining samples had significantly worse performance. The right plot shows that approximately 75% of all time-step executions in the data-parallel configuration were better than or similar to that of the GPU-only configuration. However, the variance in time-step performance is even stronger (indicated by black dots). This suggests that dividing the work between CPU and GPU for the same operation yields better performance than CPU-only or GPU-only approaches. However, the high variance implies that in a given time step a single MPI process may perform poorly and therefore result in a large max wall time, which could explain why the data-parallel configuration does not perform better than the GPU-only configuration in the left plot. Since this is the performance value that is important, suppressing the large tail of poorly performing time-step computations will be of fundamental importance in achieving good usage of heterogeneous platforms with GPUs and CPUs.

Since the Sedov test problem is computationally light and has low arithmetic intensity, the speedup of approximately 2 due to GPU usage seems reasonably good, especially since all data started in and was returned to the host memory. In order to help gauge the quality of the speedup, future performance studies should include a comparison with results obtained when all data movement and computation offloading to GPUs are executed by OpenACC or OpenMP. Profiling of the GPU-based configurations suggests that the Sedov task functions are executed faster by the GPU than it takes for the distributor to assemble a packet and for that packet to arrive at the GPU. Indeed, for one time step executed by the data-parallel configuration, the GPU was idle approximately 40% of the time. Therefore, multithreaded distributors should be used to stream data to the GPU and allow for overlapping more computation on the device. However, profiling also suggests that for this simple, quick task function, the interaction between the OR and the CUDA runtime was inefficient. This limitation impacts the OR's efficient use of the GPU and should be investigated further.

One possible source of the inefficient interaction is that for each packet, four kernels are launched in rapid succession. Three of these launches are to schedule-independent kernels for concurrent execution. If using multiple threads each launching four kernels in a short span of time is too overwhelming, then one should investigate whether avoiding optional concurrent kernel execution can lead to improved performance. Another possible solution is to use more MPI processes, each of which uses fewer cores, and assign more than one process to a given GPU. This could be an alternative scheme for streaming data to the GPU that might improve the interaction between runtimes.

6   Conclusions and Future Work

Our early investigations into the efficiency of the OR clearly indicate that this simplified approach to asynchrony as well as data movement and computation orchestration is promising for its target applications. The ultimate test will come when it is deployed in a production run at exascale. The class of applications that we are targeting have a few heavy-weight physics operators whose coarse-grained dependencies and potential for overlap between computations at different devices or between computation and communication are easy to infer. A complete DAG is neither needed nor practical for such applications that have a high degree of heterogeneity within their solvers and where the memory footprint of the state data changes dynamically because of adaptive mesh refinement. We leverage this characteristic of our applications to focus entirely on building the mechanics of making these overlaps and their corresponding data movements occur in heterogeneous computing environments without incurring the overheads of a general dynamic runtime scheduler. The dependencies are inferred at configuration time and informed by analytical performance models that we are simultaneously building. (See [6]; the offline toolchain can generate a relatively simple graph that is used for scheduling by the OR).

Aside from lines of investigation mentioned in the preceding section, our future work will consist of enabling OpenMP as an alternative means to offload computation to accelerators; implementing other OR backends with, for example, HIP; allowing for OR data movement paradigms beyond host-to-GPU-to-host; and implementing Fortran wrappers so that the OR can execute task functions written in Fortran. In terms of design, we would like to explore the idea of coupling global data movement operations, such as guardcell (GC) filling, with distributors (Fig. 3). At present, a simulation requests the global sharing of GC data and blocks further work. In particular, the distribution of blocks to pipelines for applying the hydrodynamics operators can begin only once all blocks have received their GC data. The coupling of GC fill with the distributor, however, would allow for immediately distributing a block upon receiving its GC data. Similarly, we would like to overlap MPI communications with computation and OR communication by integrating reductions into thread team functionality.

Acknowledgments. This work was supported by the U.S. Department of Energy Office of Science Office of Advanced Scientific Computing Research under contract number DE-AC02-06CH1137.

This research was supported by the Exascale Computing Project (17-SC-20-SC), a collaborative effort of two U.S. Department of Energy organizations (Office of Science and the National Nuclear Security Administration) that are responsible for the planning and preparation of a capable exascale ecosystem, including software, applications, hardware, advanced system engineering, and early testbed platforms, in support of the nation's exascale computing imperative.

This research used resources of the Oak Ridge Leadership Computing Facility at the Oak Ridge National Laboratory, which is supported by the Office of Science of the U.S. Department of Energy under Contract No. DE-AC05-00OR22725.

References

1. Augonnet, C., Thibault, S., Namyst, R., Wacrenier, P.A.: StarPU: a unified platform for task scheduling on heterogeneous multicore architectures. Concurr. Comput.: Pract. Exp. **23**, 187–198 (2011). Special Issue: Euro-Par 2009
2. Bauer, M., Treichler, S., Slaughter, E., Aiken, A.: Legion: expressing locality and independence with logical regions. In: Proceedings of SC12, pp. 1–11. IEEE (2012)
3. Clement, V., et al.: The CLAW DSL: abstractions for performance portable weather and climate models. In: Proceedings of PASC, pp. 1–10 (2018)
4. Dubey, A., et al.: Extensible component based architecture for FLASH, a massively parallel, multiphysics simulation code. Parallel Comput. **35**, 512–522 (2009)
5. Dubey, A., et al.: Pragmatic optimizations for better scientific utilization of large supercomputers. IJHPCA **27**(3), 360–373 (2013)
6. Dubey, A., Chawdhary, S., Harris, J.A., Messer, B.: Simulation planning using component based cost model. In: 2019 IEEE IPDPSW, pp. 683–688 (2019)
7. Earl, C., Might, M., Bagusetty, A., Sutherland, J.C.: Nebo: an efficient, parallel, and portable domain-specific language for numerically solving partial differential equations. J. Syst. Softw. **125**, 389–400 (2017)
8. Edwards, H.C., Trott, C.R., Sunderland, D.: Kokkos: enabling manycore performance portability through polymorphic memory access patterns. J. Parallel Distrib. Comput. **74**(12), 3202–3216 (2014)
9. Gysi, T., Osuna, C., Fuhrer, O., Bianco, M., Schulthess, T.C.: STELLA: a domain-specific tool for structured grid methods in weather and climate models. In: Proceedings of SC15, pp. 1–12 (2015)
10. Hornung, R., Keasler, J., et al.: RAJA: performance portability layer (2020). https://github.com/LLNL/RAJA
11. Kaiser, H., Diehl, P., et al.: HPX - the C++ standard library for parallelism and concurrency. JOSS **5**(53), 2352 (2020)
12. Kale, L.V., Bohm, E., Mendes, C.L., Wilmarth, T., Zheng, G.: Programming petascale applications with Charm++ and AMPI. Petascale Comput.: Algorithms Appl. **1**, 421–441 (2007)
13. Mittal, S., Vetter, J.S.: A survey of CPU-GPU heterogeneous computing techniques. ACM Comput. Surv. **47**(4), 1–35 (2015)
14. Parker, S.G.: A component-based architecture for parallel multi-physics PDE simulation. Future Gener. Comput. Syst. **22**(1–2), 204–216 (2006)
15. Ragan-Kelley, J., Barnes, C., Adams, A., Paris, S., Durand, F., Amarasinghe, S.: Halide: a language and compiler for optimizing parallelism, locality, and recomputation in image processing pipelines. ACM Sigplan Not. **48**(6), 519–530 (2013)
16. Sedov, L.I.: Similarity and Dimensional Methods in Mechanics. AP (1959)
17. Tate, A., et al.: Programming abstractions for data locality. Technical report, PADAL Workshop (2014)
18. Zhang, W., et al.: AMReX: a framework for block-structured adaptive mesh refinement. JOSS **4**(37), 1370 (2019)

A Novel Algorithm for Bi-objective Performance-Energy Optimization of Applications with Continuous Performance and Linear Energy Profiles on Heterogeneous HPC Platforms

Hamidreza Khaleghzadeh[1] , Ravi Reddy Manumachu[2(✉)] ,
and Alexey Lastovetsky[2]

[1] School of Computing, University of Portsmouth, Portsmouth, UK
hamidreza.khaleghzadeh@port.ac.uk
[2] School of Computer Science, University College Dublin, Belfield, Dublin 4, Ireland
{ravi.manumachu,alexey.lastovetsky}@ucd.ie

Abstract. Performance and energy are the two most important objectives for optimization on heterogeneous HPC platforms. This work studies a mathematical problem motivated by the bi-objective optimization of a matrix multiplication application on such platforms for performance and energy. We formulate the problem and propose an algorithm of polynomial complexity solving the problem where all the application profiles of objective type one are continuous and strictly increasing, and all the application profiles of objective type two are linear increasing. We solve the problem for the matrix multiplication application employing five heterogeneous processors that include two Intel multicore CPUs, an Nvidia K40c GPU, an Nvidia P100 PCIe GPU, and an Intel Xeon Phi. Based on our experiments, a dynamic energy saving of 17% is gained while tolerating a performance degradation of 5% (a saving of 106 J for an execution time increase of 0.05 s).

Keywords: Bi-objective optimization · Min-max optimization · Min-sum optimization · Performance optimization · Energy optimization

1 Introduction

Performance and energy are the two most important objectives for optimization on modern parallel platforms such as supercomputers, heterogeneous HPC clusters, and cloud infrastructures [3,5,7,18]. State-of-the-art solutions for the bi-objective optimization problem for performance and energy on such platforms can be broadly classified into *system-level* and *application-level* categories.

This publication has emanated from research conducted with the financial support of Science Foundation Ireland (SFI) under Grant Number 14/IA/2474.

System-level solution methods aim to optimize the performance and energy of the environment where the applications are executed. The methods employ application-agnostic models and hardware parameters as decision variables. The dominant decision variable in this category is Dynamic Voltage and Frequency Scaling (DVFS) [3,6,7,10,19,22].

The application-level solution methods proposed in [2,8,14,15] use application-level parameters as decision variables that include the number of threads, number of processors, loop tile size, and workload distribution. The solution methods proposed in [14,15] solve the bi-objective optimization problem of an application for performance and energy on homogeneous clusters of modern multicore CPUs. The solution method [2] considers the effect of heterogeneous workload distribution on bi-objective optimization of data analytics applications by simulating heterogeneity on homogeneous clusters.

Khaleghzadeh et al. [8] discover that moving from the single-objective optimization for performance or energy to the bi-objective optimization for performance and energy on heterogeneous processors results in a drastic increase in the number of optimal solutions in the case of linear performance and energy profiles, with practically all the solutions load imbalanced. They prove that for two processors with *linear* execution time and energy functions, the Pareto front is linear and contains an infinite number of solutions, out of which one solution is load balanced while the rest are load imbalanced. They then propose an algorithm that solves the bi-objective optimization problem for *discrete* execution time and dynamic energy functions with any arbitrary shape and returns the Pareto front of load imbalanced solutions and best load balanced solutions.

This work introduces a mathematical problem motivated by the bi-objective optimization of a matrix multiplication application on heterogeneous HPC platforms for performance and energy.

Consider the bi-objective optimization of a highly optimized matrix multiplication application on a heterogeneous computing platform for performance and energy. The application computes the matrix product, $C = \alpha \times A \times B + \beta \times C$, where A, B, and C are matrices of size $M \times N$, $N \times N$, and $M \times N$, and α and β are constant floating-point numbers. The application uses Intel MKL DGEMM for CPUs and Intel Xeon Phi and CUBLAS for Nvidia GPUs. The Intel MKL and CUDA versions used are 2017.0.2 and 9.2.148. Workload sizes range from 64×10112 to 19904×10112 with a step size of 64 for the first dimension m.

The platform consists of five processors: Intel Haswell E5-2670V3 multi-core CPU (CPU_1), Intel Xeon Gold 6152 multi-core CPU (CPU_2), NVIDIA K40c GPU (GPU_1), NVIDIA P100 PCIe GPU (GPU_2), and Intel Xeon Phi 3120P (XeonPhi_1).

Figure 1 shows the execution time functions $\{f_0(x), \ldots, f_4(x)\}$ and the dynamic energy functions $\{g_0(x), \ldots, g_4(x)\}$ of the processors against the workload size (x). Briefly, the total energy consumption during an application execution is the sum of dynamic and static energy consumptions. The static energy consumption is the idle power of the platform (without application execution) multiplied by the application's execution time. The dynamic energy consumption is the total energy consumed by the platform during the application execution

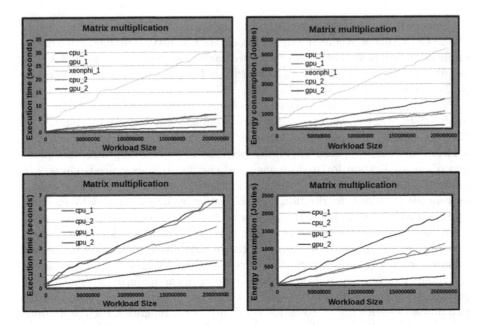

Fig. 1. The top two plots contain the execution time and energy profiles of the five heterogeneous processors employed in the matrix multiplication application. The bottom two plots do not contain the profiles for Xeon Phi. While the execution time profiles of the two CPUs are close to each other, the energy profile of CPU_1 is significantly higher than that of the CPU_2.

minus the static energy consumption. The dynamic energy consumption during an application execution is obtained using power meters, which is considered the most accurate method of energy measurement [9].

The execution time function shapes are continuous and strictly increasing. The energy function shapes can be approximated accurately by linear increasing functions. The execution time profiles of the two CPUs are close to each other but the energy profile of CPU_1 is significantly higher than that of the CPU_2. The optimization goal is to find workload distributions of the workload size n ($\{x_0, \ldots, x_4\}, \sum_{i=0}^{4} x_i = n$) minimizing the execution time ($\max_{i=0}^{4} f_i(x_i)$) and the total dynamic energy consumption ($\sum_{i=0}^{4} g_i(x_i)$) during the parallel execution of the application. We solve the optimization problem for such shapes of performance and dynamic energy functions in this work.

We first formulate the mathematical problem, which for a given positive real number n aims to find a vector $X = \{x_0, \cdots, x_{k-1}\} \in \mathbb{R}_{\geq 0}^k$ such that $\sum_{i=0}^{k-1} x_i = n$, minimizing the max of k-dimensional vector of functions of objective type one and the sum of k-dimensional vector of functions of objective type two. We then propose an algorithm solving the case where all the functions of objective type one are continuous and strictly increasing, and all the functions of objective type two are linear increasing. The algorithm exhibits polynomial complexity.

We employ the algorithm to solve the problem for the matrix multiplication application using the five heterogeneous processors. Based on our experiments, the maximum dynamic energy savings can be up to 17% while tolerating a performance degradation of 5% (an energy saving of 106 J for an execution time increase of 0.05 s).

The main original contributions of this work are:

- Mathematical formulation of the bi-objective optimization problem which for a given positive real number n aims to find a vector, $X = \{x_0, \cdots, x_{k-1}\} \in \mathbb{R}^k_{\geq 0}$, such that $\sum_{i=0}^{k-1} x_i = n$, minimizing the maximum of k functions of objective type one and the sum of k functions of objective type two.
- An exact algorithm of polynomial complexity solving the bi-objective optimization problem when all the functions of objective type one are continuous and strictly increasing, and all the functions of objective type two are linear increasing.

The rest of the paper is organized as follows. We discuss the related work in Sect. 2. The formulation of the bi-objective optimization problem is presented in Sect. 3. In Sect. 4, we propose our algorithm solving the bi-objective optimization problem. Section 5 contains the experimental results. Finally, we conclude the paper in Sect. 6.

2   Related Work

A bi-objective optimization problem can be mathematically formulated as [16,20]:

$$minimize \quad \{T(x), E(x)\}, \quad \text{Subject to} \quad x \in \mathcal{S}$$

where there are two objective functions, $T : \mathbb{R}^k \to \mathbb{R}$ and $E : \mathbb{R}^k \to \mathbb{R}$. We denote the vector of objective functions by $\mathcal{F}(x) = (T(x), E(x))^T$. The decision vectors $x = (x_1, ..., x_k)^T$ belong to the (non-empty) feasible region (set) $\mathcal{S}$, which is a subset of the decision variable space $\mathbb{R}^k$. We denote the image of the feasible region by $\mathcal{Z}$ ($=\mathcal{F}(\mathcal{S})$), and call it a feasible objective region. It is a subset of the objective space $\mathbb{R}^2$. The elements of $\mathcal{Z}$ are called objective (function) vectors or criterion vectors and denoted by $\mathcal{F}(x)$ or $z = (z_1, z_2)^T$, where $z_1 = T(x)$ and $z_2 = E(x)$ are objective (function) values or criterion values.

The objective is to minimize both the objective functions simultaneously. The objective functions are at least partly conflicting or incommensurable, due to which it is impossible to find a single solution that would be optimal for all the objectives simultaneously. Furthermore, there is no natural ordering in the objective space because it is only partially ordered. Therefore, the concept of optimality is handled differently from a single-objective optimization problem. The generally used concept is *Pareto optimality*.

Definition 1. *A decision vector $x^* \in \mathcal{S}$ is Pareto optimal if there does not exist another decision vector $x \in \mathcal{S}$ such that $T(x) \leq T(x^*), E(x) \leq E(x^*)$ and either $T(x) < T(x^*)$ or $E(x) < E(x^*)$ or both* [16].

An objective vector $z^* \in \mathcal{Z}$ is Pareto optimal if there is not another objective vector $z \in \mathcal{Z}$ such that $z_1 \leq z_1^*, z_2 \leq z_2^*$ and $z_j < z_j^*$ for at least one index j.

There are several classifications for methods solving bi-objective optimization problems [16,20]. Since the set of Pareto optimal solutions is partially ordered, one classification is based on the involvement of the decision-maker in the solution method to select specific solutions. There are four categories in this classification, *No preference, A priori, A posteriori, Interactive*. The algorithms solving bi-objective optimization problems can be divided into two major categories, *exact methods* and *metaheuristics*. While branch-and-bound (B&B) is the dominant technique in the first category, genetic algorithm (GA) is popular in the second category.

Bi-objective Optimization on High Performance Computing Platforms. There are two principal categories of methods for optimizing applications on high performance computing (HPC) platforms for performance and energy. The first category of system-level solution methods aims to optimize the performance and energy of the executing environment of the applications. The dominant decision variable in this category is Dynamic Voltage and Frequency Scaling (DVFS). DVFS reduces the dynamic power consumed by a processor by throttling its clock frequency. The methods proposed in [6,19,22] optimize for performance under a energy budget or optimize for energy under an execution time constraint. The methods proposed in [3,7,10] solve bi-objective optimization for performance and energy with no time constraint or energy budget.

The second category of application-level solution methods [2,8,11,14,15,17] use application-level decision variables and models. The most popular decision variables include the loop tile size, workload distribution, number of processors, and number of threads.

Reddy et al. [15,17] study bi-objective optimization of data-parallel applications for performance and energy on homogeneous clusters multicore CPUs employing only one decision variable, the workload distribution. They propose an efficient solution method. The method accepts as input the number of available processors, the discrete function of the processor's energy consumption against the workload size, the discrete function of the processor's performance against the workload size. It outputs a Pareto-optimal set of workload distributions. Khaleghzadeh et al. [8] propose exact solution methods solving bi-objective optimization problem for hybrid data-parallel applications on heterogeneous computing platforms for performance and energy.

Tarplee et al. [21] consider optimizing two conflicting objectives, the make-span and total energy consumption of all nodes in a HPC platform. They employ linear programming and divisible load theory to compute tight lower bounds on the make-span and energy of all tasks on a given platform. Using this formulation, they then generate a set of Pareto front solutions. The decision variable is task mapping. Aba et al. [1] present an approximation algorithm to minimize both make-span and the total energy consumption in parallel applications running on a heterogeneous resources system. The decision variable is task scheduling. Their algorithm ignores all solutions where energy consumption exceeds a given constraint and returns the solution with minimum execution time.

3   Formulation of the Bi-objective Optimization Problem

Given a positive real number $n \in \mathbb{R}_{>0}$ and two sets of k functions each, $F = \{f_0, f_1, \cdots, f_{k-1}\}$ and $G = \{g_0, g_1, \cdots, g_{k-1}\}$, where $f_i, g_i \colon \mathbb{R}_{\geq 0} \to \mathbb{R}_{\geq 0}, i \in \{0, \cdots, k-1\}$, the problem is to find a vector $X = \{x_0, \cdots, x_{k-1}\} \in \mathbb{R}_{\geq 0}^k$ such that $\sum_{i=0}^{k-1} x_i = n$, minimizing the objective functions $T(X) = \max_{i=0}^{k-1} f_i(x_i)$ and $E(X) = \sum_{i=0}^{k-1} g_i(x_i)$. We use $T \times E$ to denote the objective space of this problem, $\mathbb{R}_{\geq 0} \times \mathbb{R}_{\geq 0}$.

Thus, the problem can be formulated as follows:

BOPGVEC(n, k, F, G):

$$T(X) = \max_{i=0}^{k-1} f_i(x_i), E(X) = \sum_{i=0}^{k-1} g_i(x_i)$$

$$\underset{X}{\text{minimize}} \qquad \{T(X), E(X)\} \tag{1}$$

$$\text{s.t.} \qquad x_0 + x_1 + \cdots + x_{k-1} = n$$

We aim to solve BOPGVEC by finding both the Pareto front containing the optimal objective vectors in the objective space $T \times E$ and the decision vector for a point in the Pareto front. Thus, our solution finds a set of triplets $\Psi = \{(T(X), E(X), X)\}$ such that X is a Pareto-optimal decision vector, and the projection of Ψ onto the objective space $T \times E$, $\Psi \downarrow_{T \times E}$, is the Pareto front.

4   Bi-objective Optimization Problem for Max of Continuous Functions and Sum of Linear Functions

In this section, we solve BOPGVEC for the case where all functions in the set F are continuous and strictly increasing, and all functions in the set G are linear increasing, that is, $G = \{g_0, \cdots, g_{k-1}\}, g_i(x) = b_i \times x, b_i \in \mathbb{R}_{>0}, i = 0, \ldots, k-1$. Without loss of generality, we assume that the functions in G are sorted in the decreasing order of coefficients, $b_0 \geq b_1 \geq \cdots \geq b_{k-1}$.

Our solution consists of two algorithms, Algorithm 1 and Algorithm 2. The first one, which we call LBOPA, constructs the Pareto front of the optimal solutions in the objective space $\Psi \downarrow_{T \times E}$. The second algorithm finds the decision vector for a given point in the Pareto front.

The inputs to LBOPA (see Algorithm 1 for pseudo-code) are two sets of k functions each, F and G, and an input value, $n \in \mathbb{R}_{>0}$. LBOPA constructs a Pareto front, consisting of $k - 1$ segments $\{s_0, s_1, \cdots, s_{k-2}\}$. Each segment s_i has two endpoints, (t_i, e_i) and (t_{i+1}, e_{i+1}), which are connected by curve $P_f(t) = b_i \times n - \sum_{j=i+1}^{k-1} (b_i - b_j) \times f_j^{-1}(t)$ $(0 \leq i \leq k-2)$. Figure 2 illustrates the functions in the sets, F and G, when all functions in F are linear, $f_i(x) = a_i \times x$. In this particular case, the Pareto front returned by LBOPA will be piece-wise linear, $P_f(t) = b_i \times n - t \times \sum_{j=i+1}^{k-1} \frac{b_i - b_j}{a_j}$ $(0 \leq i \leq k-2)$, as shown in Fig. 2.

The main loop of the Algorithm 1 computes k points (Lines 3–7). In an iteration i, the minimum value of objective T, t_i, is obtained using the algorithm, solving the single-objective min-max optimization problem, $\min_X \{\max_{j=i}^{k-1} f_j(x_j)\}$.

Algorithm 1. Algorithm constructing the Pareto front of the optimal solutions.

```
1: function LBOPA(n, k, F, G)
2:     S ← ∅
3:     for i ← 0, k − 1 do
4:         tᵢ ← minₓ { maxⱼ₌ᵢᵏ⁻¹ fⱼ(xⱼ) }
5:         eᵢ ← bᵢ × n − Σⱼ₌ᵢ₊₁ᵏ⁻¹(bᵢ − bⱼ) × fⱼ⁻¹(tᵢ)
6:         S ← S ∪ (tᵢ, eᵢ)
7:     end for
8:     for i ← 0, k − 2 do
9:         Connect (tᵢ, eᵢ) and (tᵢ₊₁, eᵢ₊₁) by curve bᵢ × n − Σⱼ₌ᵢ₊₁ᵏ⁻¹(bᵢ − bⱼ) × fⱼ⁻¹(t)
10:    end for
11: end function
```

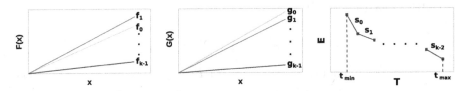

Fig. 2. Sets F and G of k linear increasing functions each. Functions in G are arranged in the decreasing order of slopes. LBOPA returns a linear piece-wise Pareto front shown in the bottom plot comprising a chain of $k-1$ linear segments.

We do not present the details of this algorithm. Depending on the shapes of functions, $\{f_0, \ldots, f_{k-1}\}$, one of the existing polynomial algorithms solving this problem can be employed [12,13].

The end point $(t_{min}, e_{max}) = (t_0, e_0)$ represents decision vectors with the minimum value of objective T and the maximum value of objective E, while the end point $(t_{max}, e_{min}) = (t_{k-1}, e_{k-1})$ represents decision vectors with the maximum value of objective T and the minimum value of objective E (as illustrated for the case of all linear increasing functions in Fig. 2).

Given an input $t \in [t_0, t_{k-1}]$, Algorithm 2 finds a decision vector $X = \{x_0, x_1, \cdots, x_{k-1}\}$ such that $\sum_{i=0}^{k-1} x_i = n$, $\max_{i=0}^{k-1} f_i(x_i) = t$, and $\sum_{i=0}^{k-1} g_i(x_i)$ is minimal. The algorithm first initialises X with $\{x_0, x_1, \cdots, x_{k-1} \mid x_i = f_i^{-1}(t)\}$ (Line 2) so that $f_i(x_i) = t$ for all $i \in [0, k-1]$. For this initial X the condition $\max_{i=0}^{k-1} f_i(x_i) = t$ is already satisfied but $\sum_{i=0}^{k-1} x_i$ may be either equal to n or greater than n. If $\sum_{i=0}^{k-1} x_i = n$, then this initial X will be the only decision vector such that $\sum_{i=0}^{k-1} x_i = n$ and $\max_{i=0}^{k-1} f_i(x_i) = t$ and hence the unique (Pareto-optimal) solution. Otherwise, $\sum_{i=0}^{k-1} x_i = n + n_{plus}$ where $n_{plus} > 0$. In that case, this initial vector X will maximize both $\sum_{i=0}^{k-1} x_i$ and $\sum_{i=0}^{k-1} g_i(x_i)$ in the set $\mathcal{X}_t$ of all vectors in the decision space satisfying the condition $\max_{i=0}^{k-1} f_i(x_i) = t$. The algorithm then iteratively reduces elements of vector X until their sum becomes equal to n. Obviously, each such reduction will also reduce $\sum_{i=0}^{k-1} g_i(x_i)$. To achieve the maximum reduction of $\sum_{i=0}^{k-1} g_i(x_i)$, the algorithm starts from vector element x_i, the reduction of which by an arbitrary amount Δx will result in the maximum reduction of $\sum_{i=0}^{k-1} g_i(x_i)$. In our case, it will be x_0 as the functions in G are sorted in the decreasing order of coefficients b_i. Thus, at the first reduction step, the algorithm will try to reduce x_0 by n_{plus}. If $x_0 \geq n_{plus}$, it will succeed and find a Pareto-optimal decision vector $X = \{x_0 - n_{plus}, x_1, \cdots, x_{k-1}\}$. If $x_0 < n_{plus}$, it will reduce n_{plus} by x_0, set $x_0 = 0$ and move to the second step. At the second step, it will try to reduce x_1 by the reduced n_{plus}, and so on. This way the algorithm minimizes $\sum_{i=0}^{k-1} g_i(x_i)$, preserving $\max_{i=0}^{k-1} f_i(x_i) = t$ and achieving $\sum_{i=0}^{k-1} x_i = n$.

Algorithm 2 . Algorithm finding a Pareto-optimal decision vector $X = \{x_0, x_1, \cdots, x_{k-1}\}$ for the problem $BOPGVEC(n, k, F, G)$.

```
 1: function PARTITION(n, k, F, G, t)
 2:     X = {x_0, ⋯, x_{k-1} | x_i ← f_i^{-1}(t)}
 3:     n_plus ← ∑_{i=0}^{k-1} x_i - n
 4:     if n_plus < 0 then
 5:         return (0, 0, ∅)
 6:     end if
 7:     i ← 0
 8:     while (n_plus > 0) ∧ (i < k - 1) do
 9:         if x_i ≥ n_plus then
10:             x_i ← x_i - n_plus
11:             n_plus ← 0
12:         else
13:             n_plus ← n_plus - x_i
14:             x_i ← 0
15:             i ← i + 1
16:         end if
17:     end while
18:     if n_plus > 0 then
19:         return (0, 0, ∅)
20:     end if
21:     e ← ∑_{i=0}^{k-1} b_i × x_i
22:     return (t, e, X)
23: end function
```

The correctness of these algorithms is proved in Theorem 1.

Theorem 1. *Consider bi-objective optimization problem $BOPGVEC(n, k, F, G)$ where all functions in F are continuous and strictly increasing and $G = \{g_i(x) \mid g_i(x) = b_i \times x, b_i \in \mathbb{R}_{>0}, i \in \{0, \cdots, k - 1\}\}$. Then, the piecewise function S, returned by LBOPA(n,k,F,G) (Algorithm 1) and consisting of $k - 1$ segments, is the Pareto front of this problem, $\Psi \downarrow_{T \times E}$, and for any $(t, e) \in \Psi \downarrow_{T \times E}$, Algorithm 2 returns a Pareto-optimal decision vector X such that $T(X) = t$ and $E(X) = e$.*

Proof. First, consider Algorithm 2 and arbitrary input parameters $n > 0$ and $t > 0$. If after initialization of X (Line 2) we will have $\sum_{i=0}^{k-1} x_i < n$, it means that t is too small for the given n, and for any vector $Y = \{y_0, y_1, \cdots, y_{k-1}\}$ such that $\sum_{i=0}^{k-1} y_i = n$, $\max_{i=0}^{k-1} f_i(y_i) > t$. In this case, there is no solution to the optimization problem, and the algorithm terminates abnormally.

Otherwise, the algorithm enters the *while* loop (Line 8). If $i < k - 1$ upon exit from this loop, then the elements of vector X will be calculated as

$$x_j = \begin{cases} 0 & j < i \\ n - \sum_{m=j+1}^{k-1} f_m^{-1}(t) & j = i \\ f_j^{-1}(t) & j > i \end{cases} \tag{2}$$

and therefore satisfy the conditions $\sum_{j=0}^{k-1} x_j = n$ and $\max_{j=0}^{k-1} f_j(x_j) = t$. More-over, the total amount of n will be distributed in X between vector elements with higher indices, which have lower G cost, $g_i(x)$, because $b_i \geq b_{i+1}, \forall i \in \{0, \cdots, k-2\}$. Therefore, for any other vector $Y = \{y_0, y_1, \cdots, y_{k-1}\}$ satisfying these two conditions, we will have $\sum_{i=0}^{k-1} g_i(y_i) \geq \sum_{i=0}^{k-1} g_i(x_i)$. Indeed, such a vector Y can be obtained from X by relocating certain amounts from vector elements with higher indices to vector elements with lower indices, which will increase the G cost of the relocated amounts. Thus, when the algorithm exits from the *while* loop with $i < k - 1$, it returns a Pareto-optimal vector X.

If the algorithm exits from the *while* loop with $i = k - 1$, it will mean that t is too big for the given n. We would still have $n_{plus} > 0$ to take off the last vector element, x_{k-1}, but if we did it, we would make $\max_{j=0}^{k-1} f_j(x_j) < t$. This way we would construct for the given n a decision vector, which minimizes $\sum_{i=0}^{k-1} g_i(x_i)$ but whose $\max_{j=0}^{k-1} f_j(x_j)$ will be less than t, which means that no decision vector X such that $\max_{j=0}^{k-1} f_j(x_j) = t$ can be Pareto optimal. Therefore, in this case the algorithm also terminates abnormally.

Thus, for any $t \in T$, Algorithm 2 either finds a Pareto-optimal decision vector X such that $T(X) = t$ and $E(X) = \sum_{i=0}^{k-1} b_i \times x_i = e$, or returns abnormally if such a vector does not exist. Let Algorithm 2 return normally, and the loop variable i be equal to s upon exit from the loop. Then, according to formula 2, $e = \sum_{i=0}^{k-1} b_i \times x_i = b_s \times (n - \sum_{i=s+1}^{k-1} f_i^{-1}(t)) + \sum_{i=s+1}^{k-1} (b_i \times f_i^{-1}(t)) = b_s \times n - \sum_{i=s+1}^{k-1} (b_s - b_i) \times f_i^{-1}(t)$, where s, n, b_i, b_s, a_i are all known constants. Therefore, the Pareto front $e = P_f(t)$ can be expressed as follows:

$$e = P_f(t) = b_s \times n - \sum_{i=s+1}^{k-1} (b_s - b_i) \times f_i^{-1}(t)$$

$$t_{min} = \min_X \{ \max_{j=i}^{k-1} f_j(x_j) \}, t_{max} = f_{k-1}(n)$$

$$t \in [t_{min}, t_{max}], \quad s \in \mathbb{Z}_{[0,k-2]},$$

which is the analytical expression of the piece-wise function constructed by Algorithm 1 (LBOPA). *End of Proof.*

Theorem 2. *LBOPA (Algorithm 1) and PARTITION (Algorithm 2) have polynomial time complexities.*

Proof. The *for* loop in LBOPA (Algorithm 1, Lines 3–7) has k iterations. At each iteration i, the computation of t_i has a time complexity of $\mathcal{O}(k^2 \times \log_2 n)$ [12], the computation of e_i has a time complexity of $\mathcal{O}(k)$, and the insertion of the point in the set S has complexity $\mathcal{O}(1)$. Therefore, the time complexity of the loop is $\mathcal{O}(k^3 \times \log_2 n)$. The time complexity of the loop (Lines 8–10) is $\mathcal{O}(k)$. Therefore, the time complexity of the Algorithm 1 is $\mathcal{O}(k^3 \times \log_2 n)$.

Let us consider the PARTITION Algorithm 2. The initialization of X (Line 2) and computation of n_{plus} has time complexity $\mathcal{O}(k)$ each. The while loop

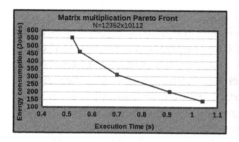
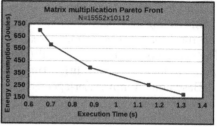

Fig. 3. Pareto front for the matrix multiplication application using five heterogeneous processors described earlier for two workloads. Each Pareto front contains four linear segments.

(Lines 8–17) iterates as long as $n_{plus} > 0$ and $i < k - 1$, of which $i < k - 1$ is the worst case scenario. The time complexity of the loop is, therefore, $\mathcal{O}(k)$. The time complexity of computation of e in Line 21 is $\mathcal{O}(k)$. Therefore, the time complexity of the Algorithm 2 is bounded by $\mathcal{O}(k)$. *End of Proof.*

5   Experimental Results

We employ the LBOPA and PARTITION algorithms to obtain the Pareto fronts for the matrix multiplication application using the five heterogeneous processors mentioned earlier. An automated tool, HCLWATTSUP [4], is used to determine the dynamic and total energy consumptions using system-level physical power measurements using power meters. HCLWATTSUP has no extra overhead and, therefore, does not influence the energy consumption of the kernel. The HCLWATTSUP interface is explained in the supplemental. Several precautions are taken in computing energy measurements to eliminate the potential disturbance due to components such as SSDs and fans. The input performance and dynamic energy functions, (F, G), to LBOPA and PARTITION are linear approximations of the profiles shown in the Fig. 1.

To obtain an experimental data point, the application is executed repeatedly until the sample mean lies in the 95% confidence interval and a precision of 0.025 (2.5%) has been achieved. For this purpose, Student's t-test is used assuming that the individual observations are independent and their population follows the normal distribution. We verify the validity of these assumptions using Pearson's chi-squared test.

Figure 3 shows the Pareto fronts for two workloads, 12352×10112 and 15552×10112. Each Pareto front contains four linear segments. Each segment is connected by two endpoints. All the points lying on a segment are the performance-energy optimal solutions in the objective space.

For the workload 12352×10112, 17% dynamic energy saving is gained while allowing 5% performance degradation. Similarly, for the workload 15552×10112, 13% energy saving is achieved while tolerating 5% performance degradation.

The first linear segment has a steep slope signifying a significant dynamic energy saving for a slight increase in execution time. The energy savings are 93 J and 106 J for execution time increases of 0.03 s and 0.05 s for the two workloads. The energy-performance tradeoff (that is, the gain in energy saving for a corresponding increase in execution time) decreases with each next linear segment.

Based on an input user-specified energy-performance tradeoff, one can selectively focus on a specific segment to return the Pareto-optimal solutions (workload distributions). The shapes of the two Pareto fronts are similar, suggesting that the qualitative conclusions apply for all workloads for this application.

6   Conclusion

Performance and energy are the two most important objectives for optimization on heterogeneous HPC platforms. This work introduced a mathematical problem motivated by the bi-objective optimization of a matrix multiplication application on heterogeneous HPC platforms for performance and energy. The application exhibits performance functions that are continuous and strictly increasing and energy functions that are linear increasing.

We first formulated the problem, which for a given positive real number n aims to find a vector $X = \{x_0, \cdots, x_{k-1}\} \in \mathbb{R}^k_{\geq 0}$ such that $\sum_{i=0}^{k-1} x_i = n$, minimizing the max of k-dimensional vector of functions of objective type one and the sum of k-dimensional vector of functions of objective type two. We then proposed an algorithm of polynomial complexity solving the problem for the case where all the functions of objective type one are continuous and strictly increasing, and all the functions of objective type two are linear increasing.

We solved the bi-objective optimization problem using the algorithm for the matrix multiplication application employing five heterogeneous processors, two Intel multicore CPUs, an Nvidia K40c GPU, an Nvidia P100 PCIe GPU, and an Intel Xeon Phi. Based on our experiments, 17% dynamic energy saving can be achieved while tolerating a performance degradation of 5% (a saving of 106 J for an execution time increase of 0.05 s).

References

1. Ait Aba, M., Zaourar, L., Munier, A.: Approximation algorithm for scheduling a chain of tasks on heterogeneous systems. In: Heras, D.B., Bougé, L. (eds.) Euro-Par 2017. LNCS, vol. 10659, pp. 353–365. Springer, Cham (2018). https://doi.org/10.1007/978-3-319-75178-8_29
2. Chakrabarti, A., Parthasarathy, S., Stewart, C.: A pareto framework for data analytics on heterogeneous systems: implications for green energy usage and performance. In: 2017 46th International Conference on Parallel Processing (ICPP), pp. 533–542. IEEE (2017)
3. Durillo, J.J., Nae, V., Prodan, R.: Multi-objective energy-efficient workflow scheduling using list-based heuristics. Futur. Gener. Comput. Syst. **36**, 221–236 (2014)

4. Fahad, M., Manumachu, R.R.: HCLWattsUp: energy API using system-level physical power measurements provided by power meters. Heterogeneous Computing Laboratory, University College Dublin, April 2021. https://csgitlab.ucd.ie/manumachu/hclwattsup

5. Fard, H.M., Prodan, R., Barrionuevo, J.J.D., Fahringer, T.: A multi-objective approach for workflow scheduling in heterogeneous environments. In: Proceedings of the 2012 12th IEEE/ACM International Symposium on Cluster, Cloud and Grid Computing (Ccgrid 2012), CCGRID 2012, pp. 300–309. IEEE Computer Society (2012)

6. Gholkar, N., Mueller, F., Rountree, B.: Power tuning HPC jobs on power-constrained systems. In: Proceedings of the 2016 International Conference on Parallel Architectures and Compilation, pp. 179–191. ACM (2016)

7. Kessaci, Y., Melab, N., Talbi, E.G.: A pareto-based metaheuristic for scheduling HPC applications on a geographically distributed cloud federation. Clust. Comput. **16**(3), 451–468 (2013)

8. Khaleghzadeh, H., Fahad, M., Shahid, A., Manumachu, R.R., Lastovetsky, A.: Bi-objective optimization of data-parallel applications on heterogeneous HPC platforms for performance and energy through workload distribution. IEEE Trans. Parallel Distrib. Syst. **32**(3), 543–560 (2021)

9. Khaleghzadeh, H., Fahad, M., Reddy Manumachu, R., Lastovetsky, A.: A novel data partitioning algorithm for dynamic energy optimization on heterogeneous high-performance computing platforms. Concurr. Comput.: Pract. Exper. **32**(21), e5928 (2020)

10. Kołodziej, J., Khan, S.U., Wang, L., Zomaya, A.Y.: Energy efficient genetic-based schedulers in computational grids. Concurr. Comput.: Pract. Exper. **27**(4), 809–829 (2015)

11. Lang, J., Rünger, G.: An execution time and energy model for an energy-aware execution of a conjugate gradient method with CPU/GPU collaboration. J. Parallel Distrib. Comput. **74**(9), 2884–2897 (2014)

12. Lastovetsky, A., Reddy, R.: Data partitioning with a realistic performance model of networks of heterogeneous computers. In: 2004 Proceedings of 18th International Parallel and Distributed Processing Symposium, p. 104 (2004)

13. Lastovetsky, A., Reddy, R.: Data partitioning with a functional performance model of heterogeneous processors. Int. J. High Perform. Comput. Appl. **21**, 76–90 (2007)

14. Lastovetsky, A., Reddy, R.: New model-based methods and algorithms for performance and energy optimization of data parallel applications on homogeneous multicore clusters. IEEE Trans. Parallel Distrib. Syst. **28**(4), 1119–1133 (2017)

15. Manumachu, R.R., Lastovetsky, A.: Bi-objective optimization of data-parallel applications on homogeneous multicore clusters for performance and energy. IEEE Trans. Comput. **67**(2), 160–177 (2018)

16. Miettinen, K.: Nonlinear Multiobjective Optimization. Kluwer (1999)

17. Reddy Manumachu, R., Lastovetsky, A.L.: Design of self-adaptable data parallel applications on multicore clusters automatically optimized for performance and energy through load distribution. Concurr. Comput.: Pract. Exper. **31**(4), e4958 (2019)

18. Rossi, F.D., Xavier, M.G., De Rose, C.A., Calheiros, R.N., Buyya, R.: E-eco: performance-aware energy-efficient cloud data center orchestration. J. Netw. Comput. Appl. **78**, 83–96 (2017)

19. Rountree, B., Lowenthal, D.K., Funk, S., Freeh, V.W., de Supinski, B.R., Schulz, M.: Bounding energy consumption in large-scale MPI programs. In: SC 2007: Proceedings of the 2007 ACM/IEEE Conference on Supercomputing, pp. 1–9 (2007)

20. Talbi, E.G.: Metaheuristics: from Design to Implementation, vol. 74. Wiley, Hoboken (2009)
21. Tarplee, K.M., Friese, R., Maciejewski, A.A., Siegel, H.J., Chong, E.K.: Energy and makespan tradeoffs in heterogeneous computing systems using efficient linear programming techniques. IEEE Trans. Parallel Distrib. Syst. **27**(6), 1633–1646 (2016)
22. Yu, L., Zhou, Z., Wallace, S., Papka, M.E., Lan, Z.: Quantitative modeling of power performance tradeoffs on extreme scale systems. J. Parallel Distrib. Comput. **84**, 1–14 (2015)

Accelerating FFT Using NEC SX-Aurora Vector Engine

Pablo Vizcaino$^{(\boxtimes)}$ ⓘ, Filippo Mantovani ⓘ, and Jesus Labarta ⓘ

Barcelona Supercomputing Center, Barcelona, Spain
{pablo.vizcaino,filippo.mantovani,jesus.labarta}@bsc.es

Abstract. Novel architectures leveraging long and variable vector lengths like the NEC SX-Aurora or the vector extension of RISCV are appearing as promising solutions on the supercomputing market. These architectures often require re-coding of scientific kernels. For example, traditional implementations of algorithms for computing the fast Fourier transform (FFT) cannot take full advantage of vector architectures. In this paper, we present the implementation of FFT algorithms able to leverage these novel architectures. We evaluate these codes on NEC SX-Aurora, comparing them with the optimized NEC libraries. We present the benefits and limitations of two approaches of RADIX-2 FFT vector implementations. We show that our approach makes better use of the vector unit, reaching higher performance than the optimized NEC library for FFT sizes under 64k elements. More generally, we prove the importance of maximizing the vector length usage of the algorithm and that adapting the algorithm to replace memory instructions with register shuffling operations can boost the performance of FFT-like computational kernels.

1 Introduction

Accelerated computing is becoming more and more relevant in High-Performance Computing (HPC). The limitation to the performance improvements imposed by the slow-down of Moore's law applied to general purpose CPUs has made HPC architects looking for solutions that can complement the computational power delivered by standard CPUs (i.e., accelerators). The most visible example of this are GP-GPU based systems, that populate 3 places within the first 5 most powerful supercomputers in the world (Top500).

GP-GPUs, however are not the only approach to acceleration: the use of vector or SIMD extensions is becoming more and more relevant in HPC systems. Beside the AVX-512 SIMD extension by Intel, we detect appearing on the market the first CPU implementing the Arm SVE extension (Fujitsu A64FX, ranked first in the Top500) and the NEC SX-Aurora vector engine, a discrete accelerator leveraging vector CPUs able to operate with registers of up to 256 double precision elements. On top of this market movements, we can not ignore the RISC-V architecture which recently ratified v1.0 of the V-extension, boosting vector computation from the academic world and the open-source community.

© Springer Nature Switzerland AG 2022
R. Chaves et al. (Eds.): Euro-Par 2021, LNCS 13098, pp. 179–190, 2022.
https://doi.org/10.1007/978-3-031-06156-1_15

The efficient use of vector accelerators often require to adapt or rewrite classical algorithms to exploit their full computing power. In most cases, vendor specific libraries coupled with optimized compilers allow to port large HPC codes to vector accelerators in a relatively smooth way. For portability reasons however, scientists often look for open-source libraries including kernels already optimized for specific architectures. The computation of the Fourier transformation using the FFT algorithms is an example of a relevant HPC kernel extremely used by the HPC community. For this reason we focused this paper on the design and the evaluation of non-parallel vectorized FFT implementations.

The main contributions of this paper are: *i)* we developed four implementations of the FFT algorithms targeting large vector architectures; *ii)* we evaluate our FFT codes on the NEC SX-Aurora accelerator, analyzing benefits and limitations of its architecture with an in depth study of hardware counters; *iii)* we compare our performance results with the vendor library distributed by NEC.

The remaining part of the paper is structured as follows: Sect. 2 compiles the related work in the field of FFT implementations for HPC systems; Sect. 3 briefly presents the NEC SX-Aurora accelerator; Sect. 4 analyzes the optimizations targeting large vector architectures; Sect. 5 includes the measurements gathered on NEC SX-Aurora; Sect. 6 closes the paper with general remarks and conclusions.

2   Related Work

FFT is a kernel of paramount importance in several algorithms of scientific computing. Therefore, a large body of research about FFT optimization on many architectures has been published in the last decades. The key reference publications used as background for our implementations are the book of E. Chu et al. [4], the paper of M. C. Pease [10] and the paper of P. N. Swarztrauber [11].

More recently, the research community is focusing on developing efficient FFT implementations targeting emerging architectures with different degrees of parallelism, e.g., high number of cores and long SIMD or vector units. Chow et al. [3] report their effort in taking advantage of the IBM Cell BE for the computation of large FFTs; Anderson et al. [1] make use of FPGAs for accelerating 3D FFTs; Wang et al. [13] present an FFT optimization for Armv8 architectures; Malkovsky et al. [9] evaluate FFTs on heterogeneous HPC compute nodes including GP-GPUs. Most of those studies are limited to up to 8-elements SIMD units in CPUs or high thread-level parallelism in GPUs while the implementations proposed in our paper are targeting wider vector units.

D. Bailey [2] and Paul N. Swarztrauber [11] studied various FFT algorithms, including Pease's and Stockham's, for the firsts vector computers which were limited by their inefficiency accessing non continuous data. The algorithms they propose have a minimum vector length of $\sqrt{N}$ at best, which is lower than our algorithm's $\frac{N}{8}$. Moreover, our implementations propose an exploitation of the data locality in the many vector registers that the SX-Aurora has, reducing the accesses to the main memory.

Furthermore, our method extends the approach of Franchetti et al. [5] since we explore larger FFT sizes as well as double precision data types.

Promising results for acceleration with the NEC SX-Aurora accelerator have been shown for SpMV in [6] and for spectral element method for fluid dynamics in [7]. We extend those evaluation efforts of NEC' accelerator with FFT. This paper continues the work done in the thesis from Pablo Vizcaino Serrano [12].

3   Hardware Platform: The NEC SX-Aurora

We implemented and evaluated our FFT codes targeting the NEC SX-Aurora VE (VE), the latest NEC's long vector architecture which combines SIMD and pipelining. Vector units and vector registers use a 32×64-bit wide SIMD front in an 8-cycles deep pipeline resulting in a maximum vector length of 256×64-bit elements or 512×32-bit elements. The VE10B processor used for this publication was presented at the IEEE HotChips 2018 [14], and the first performance evaluation was described in the same year [8].

Each of the 8 VE cores consists of a scalar processing unit (SPU) and a vector processing unit (VPU) and is connected to a shared last level cache (LLC) of 16 MB. Three fused multiply-add vector units deliver a peak performance of 269 GLFOPS (double precision) per core at 1.4 GHz. The peak performance of the used VE variant is 2.15 TFLOPS delivering a byte/FLOP ratio of 0.56.

Vector Engines are integrated as PCIe cards into their host machines. Programmers can use languages like C, C++, Fortran, and parallelize with MPI as well as OpenMP, while accelerator code can still use almost any Linux system call transparently. The proprietary compilers from NEC support automatic vectorization aided by directives. They are capable of using most features of the extensive vector engine ISA[1] from high-level languages loop constructs. For the work presented in this paper, we employed the open-source LLVM-VE project[2], which supports intrinsics allowing tight control over VE features to operate with complex numbers, control vector registers, and LLC cache affinity.

4   Implementation

There exist multiple algorithms for the computation of the FFT, each with its benefits and disadvantages from the computational point of view. In this paper, we focus on a subset of algorithms, those that are denominated RADIX-2. Considering an FFT with N being the number of transformed elements, a RADIX-2 FFT requires N to be a power of two and divides the required computation in $\log_2(N)$ phases. FFT algorithms are also split into *in-place* and *out-of-place*, with the latest requiring an additional buffer alongside the input and output arrays. All implementations proposed in this paper are out-of-place since our objective is an efficient vectorization and not a reduced memory footprint. Moreover, some FFT algorithms require a permutation of the resulting elements and others are self-sorting. In this paper we study both approaches.

---

[1] https://www.hpc.nec/documents/guide/pdfs/Aurora_ISA_guide.pdf.
[2] https://sx-aurora-dev.github.io/velintrin.html.

All implementations in this paper are designed for complex double-precision data. The visual representations of the algorithms shown in this paper are simplified, presenting only the real component because the computation of the imaginary component is conceptually equivalent to its real counterpart.

For the FFT calculation, we often refer to *twiddle factors*. W is the set of the twiddle factors, which are complex exponents computed as $\text{tf}(k, N) = e^{\frac{-2\pi i k}{N}}$, with $k \in \{0, N-1\}$.

4.1   Pease FFT

The first implementation with the potential to be efficiently vectorized is the FFT algorithm developed by Marshall C. Pease [10]. In terms of arithmetic operations, each phase of a naive Pease's FFT implementation requires $N/2$ additions, $N/2$ subtractions, and $N/2$ multiplications. One important downside of Pease's algorithm is the permutation requirement at the end of the last phase. Modern vector ISA offer instructions to load and store scattered data, but they are typically less efficient than those that operate on contiguous or constant-strided data.

Pease's algorithms is characterized by a constant geometry, that means that the same elements are operated in each of the $\log_2(N)$ phases. More specifically, the first half of the N elements operate with the second half of each phase. This leads to a potential $N/2$ elements that can be operated at the same time (i.e., vector length of $N/2$). Once a phase has been calculated, the vector registers no longer hold the first and second half of the N elements, so they must be shuffled. Due to the lack of instructions to perform this rearrangement on vector registers, this operation could be done storing all the elements in memory and loading them again in the correct order.

To mitigate the slowdown introduced by the need of accessing the memory in each phase, we propose an implementation of the Pease algorithm that distributes the N elements in eight registers instead of two. Sacrificing some potential vector length and using a precise distribution, this allows us for the computation of three phases before having to reorder the elements in memory.

A visualization of this technique is shown in the right of Fig. 1. This implementation is named *8-Pease* in the rest of the paper. It uses a potential vector length of $N/8$ and only accesses memory every three phases while still needing the data permutation at the final stage of the algorithm. The downside of having an upper limit on the vector length of $N/8$ instead of $N/2$ is supressed for large FFT sizes where $N/8$ is larger than the maximum vector length (256).

In Fig. 1 we also show that the twiddle factors are different in each phase; therefore, our first approach is to pre-compute them for each phase and to load them as the algorithm advances. The reason to not compute the twiddle factors during the execution is that they require the cosine operation, which is not present in the vector instruction set. Therefore, one needs to scalar compute them, store them in memory and load them in vector registers.

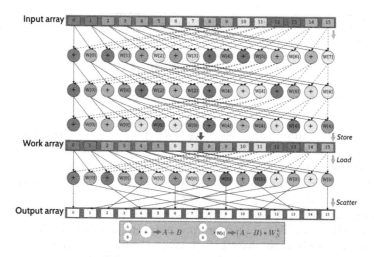

Fig. 1. *8-Pease* vectorization for N = 16. (Color figure online)

The pseudocode of the *8-Pease* implementation is given in Algorithm 1.

Algorithm 1. 8-Pease pseudocode

1: **procedure** $ft\_8Pease(Arr)$
2:     **for** $p \in [1:3:log2(N)]$ **do**
3:         $reg\_\{0,1..7\}\_r \leftarrow v\_ld(\&real(Arr[\{0,N/8..7*N/8\}]))$
4:         $reg\_\{0,1..7\}\_i \leftarrow v\_ld(\&imag(Arr[\{0,N/8..7*N/8\}]))$
5:         $3x4\_PairOperation()$
6:         **if** p < log2(N) **then**
7:             $v\_st\_strideds(res\_\{0,1..7\}\_r, \&real(Arr[\{0,1..7\}], 8)])$
8:             $v\_st\_strideds(res\_\{0,1..7\}\_i, \&imag(Arr[\{0,1..7\}], 8)])$
9:         **else**
10:             $vindex \leftarrow v\_load(\&indexes[0])$
11:             $v\_st\_scatters(res\_\{0,1..7\}\_r, real(Arr), vindex + \{0,N/8..7*N/8\})$
12:             $v\_st\_scatters(res\_\{0,1..7\}\_i, imag(Arr), vindex + \{0,N/8..7*N/8\})$

Note that unlike Fig. 1, the pseudocode shows the operation of the real and imaginary parts. The vector loads, the PairOperations and the stores have been grouped for simplicity. The dark red elements from Fig. 1 are loaded in *reg1*, the light reds in *reg2*, etc. The function *3x4_PairOperation* is equivalent to executing the function in Algorithm 2 for 3 phases with 4 *PairOperations* each. All vector instructions operate on N/8 vector elements. In reality, NEC limits the vector length to 256 elements, requiring our code to compute the phases in various iterations.

The function *PairOperation()* in Algorithm 2 takes advantage of fused operations to calculate the complex multiplication. Remember that the multiplication

---

Algorithm 2. PairOperation pseudocode

1: **procedure** $PairOperation(reg1\_r, reg1\_i, reg2\_r, reg2\_i)$
2:     $res1\_\{r,i\} \leftarrow reg1\_\{r,i\} + reg2\_\{r,i\}$
3:     $res2\_\{r,i\} \leftarrow (reg1\_\{r,i\} - reg2\_\{r,i\}) * W\_\{r,i\}$
4:     **return** $res1\_\{r,i\}, res2\_\{r,i\}$

---

of two complex numbers, $(a + b \cdot i) \cdot (c + d \cdot i) = (e + f \cdot i)$ normally requires 7 operations: $e = a \cdot c - b \cdot d$, and $f = a \cdot d + b \cdot c$. We can group operations to have 2 multiplications and 2 fused operations (operations calculated with a single instruction are encapsulated using parenthesis): $t_1 = (a \cdot c)$, and $t_2 = (a \cdot d)$, so that $e = (t_1 - b \cdot d)$ and $f = (t_2 + b \cdot c)$.

Looking at Fig. 1, it can be noted that there are only $N/2$ different twiddle factors $(W_0, W_1, ... W_{N/2-1})$. More precisely, the number of different twiddle factors to be used in each phase is half compared to the previous one.

The repetition of the twiddle factors across the FFT brings three important observations: *i)* we are wasting memory since we were storing all of them for each phase; *ii)* we are missing potential cache locality; *iii)* for advanced phases, we could access a single twiddle factor per register and then replicate it. In each batch of three phases in *8-Pease*, the twiddle factor of the second phase are identical for half the registers, and in the third one they are identical for all registers. This means that for the three phases, we only load 7 twiddle factor registers instead of 12.

Finally, another implementation of the Pease algorithm is proposed. Even with the twiddle factor access optimization, it still represents a slowdown.

To implement this optimization, we use gather vector instructions to load the twiddle factors. In reality, gather instructions offer a more general functionality than what we require since they are meant to load sparse data, while we need strided chunks of data. However, since no ad hoc instructions exist for our case, we decided to implement this version using gather instructions. In NEC architecture, gather operations require a vector with absolute addresses to index the memory. We use two registers, one holding the constant relative indexes that are reused and another temporarily holding the absolute indexes after adding the offset. A graphical representation of the use of gather operation is provided in Fig. 2, with its code equivalent in Algorithm 3. This implementation is named *8-Pease-gt* in the rest of the paper.

Algorithm 3. Gather access to twiddle factors pictured on Fig. 2.

1: $\_vr\ indexes = \_vel\_vseq\_vl(VL);$ ▷ 0, 1, 2, 3, ...
2: $indexes = \_vel\_vand\_vsvl(\ (0x1), indexes, VL);$ ▷ 0, 0, 2, 2, ...
3: $indexes = \_vel\_vsll\_vvsl(indexes, 3, VL);$ ▷ 0, 0, 8, 8, ...
4: $indexes = \_vel\_vaddul\_vsvl(addr, indexes, VL);$ ▷ 0xA000, 0xA000, 0xA008, ...
5: $\_vr\ W = \_vel\_vgt\_vvssvl(index, N/8, VL);$

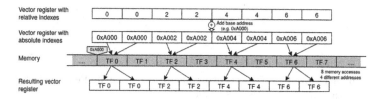

Fig. 2. Example of the proposed accesses to twiddle factors using gather operations

4.2   Stockham FFT

The other algorithm that has been studied for vectorization is Stockham's algorithm [11]. While the algorithm is still RADIX-2 and out-of-place, it has two main differences with Pease's algorithm. The first one is that it is a self-sorting algorithm, so it does not require a permutation at the last phase. The second difference is that Stockham's algorithm does not have constant geometry like Pease's. This complicates the algorithm and its vectorization, limiting the maximum vector length depending on the phase.

Using the same approach as with *8-Pease*, we can divide the N elements of each phase into eight vector registers to compute three phases before rearranging the elements in memory.

Due to the self-sorting nature of the algorithm, the process of storing and loading the elements changes for every three phases. With p being the phase where the loads occurs, the stores on $p + 3$ consist of $\frac{vector\_length}{2^p}$ groups of 2^p consecutive elements. Since an instruction that writes several consecutive elements before jumping a fixed stride does not exist in NEC's architecture, we have two options in the implementation. We can limit the vector length of the problematic phases to be equal to the size of the groups, 2^p. Since inside a group all the twiddle factors have the same value, we could use a broadcast operation to load them. The downside of this option is that for phases 3–5 and 6–8 this means limiting the vector length to 8 and 64. With SX-Aurora's maximum vector length of 256, this limit implies not taking full advantage of the vectorization potential.

If we do not want to limit the vector length, we can store values with a scatter operation and load twiddle factors with a gather. The initial interest in using the Stockham algorithm was removing this type of memory operations, so adding them again may seem counterproductive, even though the pattern of Stockham's scatter operations contain consecutive elements while Pease's is sparser. This difference is represented in a simplified example diagram in Fig. 3.

Regardless, using these long-latency instructions at the end of these special phases outperforms having up to 32 times more instructions during three phases when limiting the vector length to 8, so the final implementation uses scatters.

In terms of twiddle factors, we use the gather instruction that is also present in *8-Pease-gt* and we name this new implementation *8-Stockham-gt*.

A simplified pseudocode of this alternative is shown in Algorithm 4.

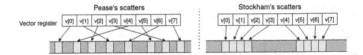

Fig. 3. Simplified example of the scatter operations used in Pease and Stockham's algorithms, with a vector length of 8 elements.

Algorithm 4. 8-Stockham pseudocode

1: **procedure** $fft\_8Stockham(Arr)$
2:     $reg\_\{0, 1..7\}\_r \leftarrow v\_ld(\&real(Arr[\{0, N/8..7 * N/8\}]))$
3:     $reg\_\{0, 1..7\}\_i \leftarrow v\_ld(\&imag(Arr[\{0, N/8..7 * N/8\}]))$
4:     $3x4\_PairOperation()$
5:     $v\_st\_strideds(res\_\{0, 1..7\}\_r, \&real(Arr[\{0, 1..7\}]), 8)$
6:     $v\_st\_strideds(res\_\{0, 1..7\}\_i, \&imag(Arr[\{0, 1..7\}]), 8)$
7:     $gsize = 8$
8:     **for** $p \in [4 : 3 : log2(N)]$ **do**
9:         $reg\_\{0, 1..7\}\_r \leftarrow v\_ld(\&real(Arr[\{0, N/8, ..., 7 * N/8\}]))$
10:        $reg\_\{0, 1..7\}\_i \leftarrow v\_ld(\&imag(Arr[\{0, N/8, ..., 7 * N/8\}]))$
11:        **if** $gsize <$ VL **then**
12:            $gatherW()$
13:            $3x4\_PairOperation()$
14:            $vindex \leftarrow v\_load(\&indexes[0])$
15:            $v\_st\_scatter(res\_\{0, 1..7\}\_r, real(Arr), vindex + \{0, gsize..7 * gsize\})$
16:            $v\_st\_scatter(res\_\{0, 1..7\}\_i, imag(Arr), vindex + \{0, gsize..7 * gsize\})$
17:        **else**
18:            $broadcastW()$
19:            $3x4\_PairOperation()$
20:            $v\_st(res\_\{0, 1..7\}\_r, \&real(Arr[\{0, N/8, ..., 7 * N/8\}]))$
21:            $v\_st(res\_\{0, 1..7\}\_i, \&imag(Arr[\{0, N/8, ..., 7 * N/8\}]))$
22:        $gsize = gsize * 8$

---

5   Evaluation

In this section we study the performance of our implementations in the vector accelerator from NEC, the SX-Aurora. We measure the real time used to compute the FFT, including the communication to the accelerator and other system interferences. The pre-computation is disregarded because it can be used for multiple FFT of the same size.

NEC has optimized math libraries called NEC Library Collection (NLC)[3]. Our usage of NLC is limited to *aslfftw*, a vectorized FFT whose interface is compatible with fftw. We have compared the performance of the proposed implementations in Sect. 4 with *aslfftw*, computing it as a speedup to a scalar (i.e., without vector instructions) fftw, compiled with NEC's compiler *ncc*.

---

[3] https://www.hpc.nec/documents/sdk/SDK_NLC/UsersGuide/main/en/.

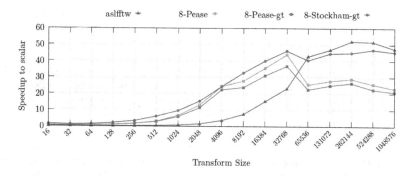

Fig. 4. Speedup in NEC of the proposed vectorized FFT implementations and *aslfftw*.

We see in Fig. 4 how our implementations outperform *aslfftw* until an FFT size of 65536 elements. From that point on, *aslfftw* doubles the performance of our Pease's implementations, while *8-Stockham-gt* only underperforms *aslffw* by less than 10%. In our best case, we reach 17% of the peak performance of one VE node. It is also notable that while *8-Pease-gt* was designed to improve *8-Pease*, it obtained a lower performance.

In Fig. 5 we show the number of total instructions and vector instructions with respect to *aslfftw*. NEC's implementation executes many more instructions than our implementations, with sizes up to 65536. From that point, we execute more instructions than *aslfftw*, except for the total instructions of *8-Stockham-gt*.

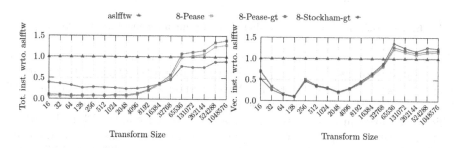

Fig. 5. Total (left) and vector (right) instructions with respect to *aslfftw*.

Figure 5 also shows us that *8-Pease-gt* executes approximately 10% more instructions than *8-Pease*. This is due to the gather instruction using absolute addresses in NEC, requiring additional operations to modify the indexes before the gathers.

To better understand the difference in instructions, we have to consider the number of elements being operated with each vector instruction. In Table 1 we display the average vector length used by the implementations, with greener colors indicating a higher vector length.

Table 1. Average vector length in elements for different FFT sizes and implementations.

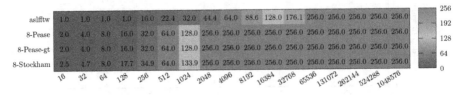

	16	32	64	128	256	512	1024	2048	4096	8192	16384	32768	65536	131072	262144	524288	1048576
aslfftw	1.0	1.0	1.0	1.0	16.0	22.4	32.0	44.4	64.0	88.6	128.0	176.1	256.0	256.0	256.0	256.0	256.0
8-Pease	2.0	4.0	8.0	16.0	32.0	64.0	128.0	256.0	256.0	256.0	256.0	256.0	256.0	256.0	256.0	256.0	256.0
8-Pease-gt	2.0	4.0	8.0	16.0	32.0	64.0	128.0	256.0	256.0	256.0	256.0	256.0	256.0	256.0	256.0	256.0	256.0
8-Stockham	2.5	4.7	8.0	17.7	34.9	64.0	133.9	256.0	256.0	256.0	256.0	256.0	256.0	256.0	256.0	256.0	256.0

We show that our proposed implementations are able to use the maximum vector length, 256 64-bit elements, with smaller problem sizes than *aslfftw*. This implies a better usage of the vector unit and a reduction in instructions since each is doing more operations.

A pair of relevant counters to understand the performance of the implementations is *vec_arith_cyc* and *vec_load_cyc*, which count the cycles spent in arithmetic vector instructions and load vector instructions respectively.

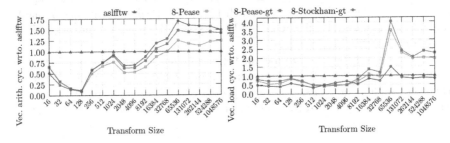

Fig. 6. Vec arith (left) and load (right) cycles of our implementations wrto. *aslfftw*.

In Fig. 6 we see the number of cycles used by arithmetic and load vector instructions with respect to *aslfftw*. There is a difference of 25%–70% in arithmetic cycles for larger FFT sizes. The finer grain of using a small vector length of *aslfftw* can allow it to be more precise with arithmetic optimizations, but the significant disparity in large sizes suggests a core difference in the FFT algorithm. In FFT computation, the number of floating-point operations is related to the used RADIX. These results suggest that *aslfftw* is using a different RADIX for bigger transforms.

A much larger difference is present in load vector cycles. We find a notable spike in the cycles spent by our Pease's algorithm in size 65536, taking 4 times more cycles loading vector elements. This is the exact size where *alsfftw* starts to outperform our implementations. We would also like to study the vector cycles spent in store operations, but these cycles are not mapped in any hardware counter present in the architecture.

To study if the increment in vector load cycles of our Pease's implementations is due to loading more elements or due to slower loads, in Fig. 7 we show how many vector elements are being loaded per each cycle spent in vector load instructions, as a metric of "efficiency" of the vector loads. We also show the vector load cache hit ratio of the implementations, since it can be related with slower loads.

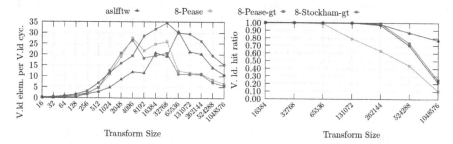

Fig. 7. Vec. load elements per vec. load cycle (left) and hit ratio (right)

We see that from size 65536 onwards *aslfftw* has greater vector load efficiency than our Pease's implementations, loading three times more elements per load cycle.

8-Pease-gt and *8-Stockham-gt* present a nearly identical hit ratio, and they load the same number of elements from memory. Considering that the vector load efficiency is not lowered for *8-Stockham-gt*, we can suggest that the difference in the efficiencies between implementations is caused by an unfavorable memory access pattern inherent to Pease's algorithm, presumably related to the scatter operations executed at the last phase of the implementation. We also note in the left plot of Fig. 7 that the usage of the gather instruction in *8-Pease-gt* does not accomplish its intended results since it lowers the efficiency of vector load instructions with respect to *8-Pease* instead of improving it. The theoretically better memory access of *8-Pease-gt* is reflected in the cache hit-ratio, when comparing it to *8-Pease*.

6   Conclusions

Our implementations of the FFT for the NEC SX-Aurora show an efficient usage of the vector engine, overtaking the highly optimized proprietary vendor implementation found in NEC Libary Collection for FFT sizes up to 65536 elements. We achieve 20× speedup for sizes under 1024 compared to NEC's FFT, and 2× speedup up to 65536 elements. We also discussed the performance of vector memory gather operations in our implementations, finding that optimizing memory accesses do not pay of because of their long latency.

We compared two algorithms for the FFT computation, Pease's and Stockham's. We found that for vectorized codes, the complex permutations needed by Pease's impact negatively the performance, notably with large FFT sizes. We argue in favour of more specific register shuffling and memory accessing vector instructions. We evinced the importance of avoiding memory instructions that FFT computation often requires, even if this implies more vector registers or reducing the vector length.

We also highlight two main weaknesses of our proposed implementations for larger FFT sizes when comparing them with NEC's implementation: *i)* both Pease and Stockham implementations spend ~25% more cycles executing floating-point operations, suggesting the need to explore different RADIX FFT algorithms. *ii)* Pease's implementation has a lower vector load efficiency.

We leave for future work the parallelization of our implementations, the exploration of different RADIX FFT algorithms and the evaluation on other vector architectures.

References

1. Anderson, M., Brodowicz, M., Swany, M., Sterling, T.: Accelerating the 3-D FFT using a heterogeneous FPGA architecture. In: Heras, D.B., Bougé, L. (eds.) Euro-Par 2017. LNCS, vol. 10659, pp. 653–663. Springer, Cham (2018). https://doi.org/10.1007/978-3-319-75178-8_52
2. Bailey, D.: A high-performance FFT algorithm for vector supercomputers. Int. J. High Perform. Comput. Appl. **2**, 82–87 (1987)
3. Chow, A.C., Fossum, G.C., Brokenshire, D.A.: A programming example: large FFT on the cell broadband engine. Glob. Signal Process. Expo (GSPx) (2005)
4. Chu, E., George, A.: Inside the FFT Black Box: Serial and Parallel Fast Fourier Transform Algorithms. CRC Press, Boca Raton (1999)
5. Franchetti, F., Puschel, M.: SIMD vectorization of non-two-power sized FFTs. In: 2007 IEEE International Conference on Acoustics, Speech and Signal Processing - ICASSP 2007, vol. 2, pp. II-17–II-20, April 2007
6. Gómez Crespo, C., et al.: Optimizing sparse matrix-vector multiplication in NEC SX-Aurora vector engine. In: Proceedings of the 26th Symposium on Principles and Practice of Parallel Programming (2021, accepted)
7. Jansson, N.: Spectral Element simulations on the NEC SX-Aurora TSUBASA. In: The International Conference on High Performance Computing in Asia-Pacific Region, pp. 32–39, January 2021
8. Komatsu, K., et al.: Performance Evaluation of a Vector Supercomputer SX-Aurora TSUBASA. In: SC18: International Conference for High Performance Computing, Networking, Storage and Analysis, pp. 685–696, November 2018
9. Malkovsky, S.I., et al.: Evaluating the performance of FFT library implementations on modern hybrid computing systems. J. Supercomput. **77**(8), 8326–8354 (2021). https://doi.org/10.1007/s11227-020-03591-6
10. Pease, M.C.: An adaptation of the fast fourier transform for parallel processing. J. ACM (JACM) **15**(2), 252–264 (1968)
11. Swarztrauber, P.N.: FFT algorithms for vector computers. Parallel Comput. **1**(1), 45–63 (1984)
12. Vizcaino Serrano, P.: Evaluación y optimización de algoritmos fast fourier transform en SX-Aurora NEC (2020)
13. Wang, Q., Li, D., Huang, X., Shen, S., Mei, S., Liu, J.: Optimizing FFT-based convolution on ARMv8 multi-core CPUs. In: Malawski, M., Rzadca, K. (eds.) Euro-Par 2020. LNCS, vol. 12247, pp. 248–262. Springer, Cham (2020). https://doi.org/10.1007/978-3-030-57675-2_16
14. Yamada, Y., Momose, S.: Vector engine processor of NEC's brand-new supercomputer SX-Aurora TSUBASA. In: Proceedings of A Symposium on High Performance Chips, Hot Chips, vol. 30, pp. 19–21 (2018)

Kernel Fusion in OpenCL

John A. Stratton[1,2]([⊠]), Jyothi Krishna V. S.[2], Jeevitha Palanisamy[2],
and Karthikadevi Chinnaraju[2]

[1] Whitman College, Walla Walla, WA 99362, USA
strattja@whitman.edu
[2] MulticoreWare Inc., Chennai, Tamil Nadu, India
{jkrishna,jeevitha,karthikadevi}@multicorewareinc.com

Abstract. Kernel Fusion is a widely applicable optimization for numerical libraries on heterogeneous systems. However, most automated systems capable of performing the optimization require changes to software development practices, through language extensions or constraints on software organization and compilation. This makes such techniques inapplicable for preexisting software in a language like OpenCL.

This work introduces an implementation of kernel fusion that can be deployed fully within the defined role of the OpenCL library implementation. This means that programmers with no explicit intervention, or even precompiled OpenCL applications, could utilize the optimization. Despite the lack of explicit programmer effort, our compiler was able to deliver an average of 12.3% speedup over a range of applicable benchmarks on a target CPU platform.

Keywords: OpenCL · Kernel fusion · Heterogeneous computing

1 Introduction

Good software design practices and good software performance practices are sometimes in tension. One tension exists between the desire for software portability and the optimization opportunities available when the target architecture is known ahead of time to the developer. OpenCL was designed to address this tension by deferring code generation of accelerator machine code until application execution, allowing each accelerator vendor to build appropriate optimizations into the compiler for that particular accelerator. Another common tension is between the design principle of modularity and the optimization opportunities enabled by interprocedural optimization. Function encapsulation allows useful units of code to be reused in a variety of different contexts. However, in any particular use case, performance would likely benefit from optimizations taking into account the particular mixture of functions used in that circumstance.

Recent efforts have turned towards generative frameworks where the host application explicitly constructs, at run-time, a complete description of the computation to be performed on the accelerator [2,2,13,14]. Such strategies are effective, but require applications to be rewritten for the newly developed language.

© Springer Nature Switzerland AG 2022
R. Chaves et al. (Eds.): Euro-Par 2021, LNCS 13098, pp. 191–202, 2022.
https://doi.org/10.1007/978-3-031-06156-1_16

In this work, we show how it is possible to implement inter-kernel optimizations entirely behind the OpenCL API. This strategy enables legacy software written with OpenCL C or already compiled into SPIR IR to take advantage of inter-kernel optimizations such as kernel fusion. While the extent of those optimizations can be limited by the information hidden by the narrow API, we find that in many examples, there is sufficient information for substantial performance improvements.

In this paper, we describe how the asynchronous nature of the OpenCL API can be exploited to perform inter-kernel optimizations without explicit intervention from the application programmer. Sections 2 and 3 cover the technical details of the opportunity and exploitation, respectively, of inter-kernel information in an OpenCL compiler through the OpenCL API. Section 4 show performance results demonstrating the impact of kernel fusion implemented with this strategy on a variety of applications. We conclude with a summary of related work in Sect. 5 and some final remarks in Sect. 6.

2   Background

While OpenCL is a widely supported standard, few implementations are available in open source. Portable OpenCL (POCL [8]) is one such actively supported open-source framework, so we will present our work in the context of that infrastructure. The POCL system is capable of executing OpenCL workloads on CPUs and supported GPUs with the main branch, and has been customized to a variety of other targets. This means that the architecture of POCL is likely to be representative of other OpenCL implementations as well, as many features are required by the OpenCL specification itself, as well as the constraints of discrete accelerators.

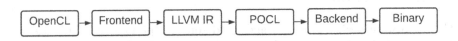

Fig. 1. POCL compilation chain.

The POCL implementation is divided into two layers, the host and device layer. The Host layer implements the portion of the OpenCL runtime that runs synchronously with the host application code. For our purposes, we will focus on the kernel compilation and execution portions of the system. The Host layer of the compiler comprises generic LLVM passes and optimization and is agnostic of the target hardware. The device layers include target specific implementations such as LLVM codegen and resource management that ensures proper sharing and synchronization of memory. The Fig. 1 shows the compilation path with POCL framework.

The POCL compiler uses clang as its frontend to generate LLVM IR or Standard Portable Intermediate Representation (SPIR [10]). POCL then proceeds by linking and inlining a target-specific builtin function library to the kernel. While targeting GPUs, POCL directly lowers the input OpenCL source code into SPIR code to target assembly code, as the GPU hardware and driver will manage the parallel work-item execution. The regions between barriers, will be executed by all work items before proceeding to the next region, are generated by the parallel region formation passes in POCL. For CPUs, POCL performs thread coarsening, instantiating explicit loops over work-item indexes within a work-group for those regions. POCL then adds target-specific optimizations such as vectorization and unrolling parallel regions. In the end, what was an LLVM-IR representation of the work of a single work-item becomes an LLVM-IR function encapsulating the computation of an entire work-group.

After compilation, when the application enqueues a kernel launch, the POCL compiler puts this command into its command queue to be sent to the asynchronously operating Device-runtime layer. For a CPU target, the device layer of the runtime manages the worker thread pool for parallel execution. The runtime dispatches work units to that worker pool when a kernel launch command is read from the queue. Even though some devices, such as the parallel cores of the host CPU itself, are capable of executing synchronously, the OpenCL standard mandates asynchrony between the host and device sides of the command queue. This design is beneficial for many systems, and can be exploited by our system to take advantage of the fact that kernels do not need to be eagerly executed when queued.

3   Kernel Fusion

In kernel fusion [2,3], we merge the code from multiple kernels to execute the code together as a single kernel. This process is expected to improve memory locality and can enable further instruction optimizations that only become apparent when optimizing the code across multiple kernels. In this section we describe our kernel fusion method. One of the salient features of our kernel-fusion framework is that our can perform kernel fusion even in the presence of loop-carried dependencies across multiple kernels if the compiler can determine the dependence to be bounded and deterministic.

Our entire fusion process is divided into two branches:

- **BRANCH A:** Which deals with total fusion. Here the participating kernels are either independent (i.e. they do not share I/O buffers) or there is no inter-work-item dependency. In such cases, the work of a given work-item in the first kernel can be immediately followed by the work of the work-item with the same index in the subsequent kernel, with no change in the computed results. The framework merges the kernels directly without any changes in kernel code or scheduling. The fusion framework makes use of the default POCL asynchronous scheduling.
- **BRANCH B:** deals with kernels with a non-zero loop-carry dependence. POCL kernels imply a global memory barrier in between them. This normally ensures all dependencies across the kernels are met. Our fusion framework

must ensure that the dependent work-items (or iterations) in the latter kernel are executed after all work-items from the former kernel on which they depend have been executed. The framework transforms the kernel code of the former kernel to merge the latest dependent iteration (for i-th iteration of the second kernel) of the kernel the i-th iteration of the latter kernel. The fused kernel, in such situation, mimics software pipelining in traditional loop fusion. In such cases, a few iterations of the predecessor kernel is executed before the merged kernel is executed, similar to how a software-pipelined loop may need to execute some startup iterations. Likewise, some of the work-items of the successor kernels will need to be executed after the merged kernel is executed. The number of iterations of the individual kernels and merged kernel executed will depend on scheduling and work-group sizes. In such cases, we transform the scheduling code to use work groups as large as possible to reduce the number of iterations of individual kernels executed. The framework reject the kernels as fusion candidates if a transformation to meet the dependencies cannot be applied.

Algorithm 1. Kernel Fusion algorithm. The *merged_kernel* list will contain the merged kernel along with the dependent iterations of individual kernels. We modify the *LAUNCH* function of the baseline POCL to check for inter-iteration dependency between the cached kernels.

```
 1: procedure LAUNCH(stack)        ▷ Launches with mergeable kernels in the stack
 2:     merged_kernel ← empty
 3:     carried_dependency ← none        ▷ Holds the dependency of merged kernel
 4:     arg_list ← empty                 ▷ Holds the argument list of merged kernel
 5:     for each kernel in stack do
 6:         kernel_args ← get_kernel_arguments(kernel)
 7:         kernel_dependency ← calculate_dependency(kernel)
 8:         if carried_dependency = none then
 9:             updated_kernel ← kernel
10:         else
11:             updated_kernel ← update_kernel(kernel, carried_dependency)
12:         end if
13:         merge_kernels(merged_kernel, updated_kernel, argList)
14:         update_carried_dependency(carried_dependency, kernel_dependency)
15:         update_argList(argList, kernel_args)
16:     end for
17: end procedure
```

Figure 2 describes our fusion framework. Our fusion framework extends from the compilation which handles the code transformation and merged kernel creation. The scheduling section requires some additional support to ensure the dependent iterations of individual kernels are executed for loop-carry dependent fusion. This scheduling is not used for total fusion to reduce the overhead in scheduling.

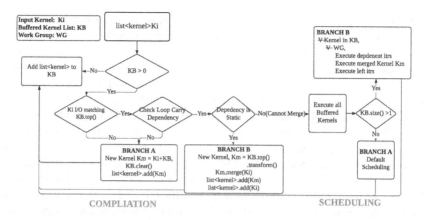

COMPLIATION   SCHEDULING

Fig. 2. The workflow of our fusion framework. The framework has two sections. The compilation section which handles the code transformation and merged kernel creation and the scheduling section which realizes the iteration scheduling for individual kernels and the merged kernel to handle the loop carry dependencies.

In our fusion compilation section the compiler follows a lazy loading policy. The compiler maintains a kernel buffer (KB) which will contain the kernels whose execution has been deferred so that fusion opportunities can be identified. When the first kernel received, it is directly moved from the command queue to the KB. For each additional kernel received, it is compared to the kernels already in the KB to determine whether the new kernel could be fused with the deferred kernels. If so, the fusion is performed, and the results of the fusion are put back in the KB in place of the kernels that were fused, potentially capable of being fused again with subsequent kernels. If not, or if a synchronization event is detected, all deferred and fused kernels are immediately executed with the appropriate scheduler.

To determine whether fusion is possible, for each new kernel, the compiler checks if there is a loop carry dependency with the previous kernels in the KB. The compiler also checks for the total number of iterations/work-items. If the total number of iterations are different, it considers the two kernels as non mergeable. Otherwise, if the kernels are fully independent (i.e. I/O buffers of the previous kernels is different from the I/O of the new kernels) or if there is no loop-carry dependency, the compiler will perform total fusion. In such cases, the compiler merges the incoming kernel with the existing kernel in the KB. The new merged kernel replaces the existing kernel in the KB. As the framework is able to achieve total fusion, the framework only schedules the merged kernel in the execution buffer. The merged kernel will be using the default POCL scheduling and the work-groups.

Branch B shows the path taken while merging kernels with a constant loop carry dependency. In such cases, the framework will not be able to do a complete fusion of the kernels. The compiler will find an upper bound for the loop-carry dependency distance and make the necessary transformation to the predecessor kernels before merging. The last dependent iteration of the predecessor kernel is merged with the iteration of the incoming kernel. The compiler will maintain all the individual kernels along with the merged kernel in the execution buffer. The compiler will also maintain the relative loop-carry dependence list for each kernel in the execution queue. The run-time module of Branch B will execute the dependent iterations of the independent kernels before it starts executing the merged kernel in the work group. The actual dependent-iterations will be contingent on the number of work-groups created. As more work-groups are created, the more fragmented the scheduling becomes and more individual dependent iterations needs to be executed. The default POCL scheduling for pthreads is dynamic with scheduling chunk size determined by the function $min(32, N/num\_threads)$ where N stands for max iterations and $num\_threads$ gives the total number of parallel threads. This limits the number for iterations executed in a work-group to 32. We need the size of the work-group to be as large as possible so that we execute the fewest individual iterations. Consequently, we use

$$(N - max\_loop\_dependence)/num\_threads \qquad (1)$$

as our work-group size. Here $max\_loop\_dependence$ stands for the maximum loop carry dependence across all merged kernels.

3.1   Loop Carry Dependent Fusion

Figure 3 explains the three stages involved in loop carry dependency fusion. The example contains three kernels (K_1, K_2 and K_3). Every iteration of K_2 has a loop carry dependency of a single iteration over K_1, and K_3 has a loop carry dependency of one iteration over K_2 The first stage in compilation involves identification of these dependencies using LLVM [6,11] analysis passes. Once the dependency is determined to be static, in the second stage the compiler transforms Kernel $K1$ to satisfy the dependency with $K2$ by simply updating the iterators used in the kernel. The compiler then merges the transformed kernel $K_1`$ with $K2$ to create a temporary merged kernel K_{12}. In the next iteration K_{12} is transformed to satisfy the dependency with K_3 before creating the final merged kernel K_{123}. We maintain individual Kernels ($K1, K2, K3$) and the merged kernel K_{123} in the execution queue.

In scheduling stage, the framework divide the iterations equally among all threads. Each thread will have its own iteration queue which will contain all kernels. Each will execute the dependent iterations of Kernels K_1 and K_2 for the iterations allocated to the thread. Once the dependents iterations are executed the allocated merged kernel iterations are scheduled.

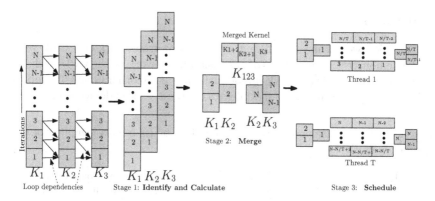

Fig. 3. Loop carry dependency Fusion. In Stage 1, we identify these dependency and if the value is deterministic we mark the kernels for fusion. In Stage 2, we try to merge the larges non-dependent chunks of Kernels K_1, K_2 and K_3 to create a new merged kernel K_{123}. In stage 3, scheduling For each thread i We will run all dependent iterations of Kernel K_1 and K_2 before executing the chunk of merged Kernel K_{123}.

3.2 Other Implementation Details

We have implemented our framework on top of POCL version 1.5. POCL has defined a set of optimizations such as barrier removal and autovectorization [7,8] for OpenCL kernels. Our Merge module is inserted before the these passes.

The overhead of analysis and code generation would substantially increase the apparent execution time of a set of kernels, given the relative complexity of the operations. However, many applications will regularly execute the same sequence of kernels with the same data dependencies, rather than shut down and start up the OpenCL environment for every new buffer. This is particularly applicable for applications processing consecutive frames of a video or a batch of images in a machine learning inference query. To take advantage of this, the first time a kernel is fused in the system, the fused kernel is cached and re-referenced when the same kernels with the same dependencies are seen again. This significantly decreases the effective cost of our transformations, but does not complete eliminate the runtime checking needed to verify the buffer dependencies between kernels in the queue every time.

We find that the default scheduling algorithm of POCL introduces a lot of fragmentation, which is counterproductive to the kernel merge. As a result, we were observing a lot of overhead in scheduling the kernels multiple times. We overcome this issue by introducing a new low-overhead scheduling based on the number of parallel threads (Function 1). This will also keep the number of iterations of individual kernels executed to minimum and we can extract more performance from the merged kernels. However, in such cases we are trading off the advantages of dynamic scheduling.

4   Results

In this section we discuss the efficacy of our fusion framework on POCL version 1.5. We demonstrate the efficacy of our fusion framework in the CPU backend of POCL. However, our framework can be easily ported to other OpenCL supported devices as only the scheduling module of the framework is device-specific.

Table 1. List of benchmarks used for evaluation, taken from a sampling of image processing operations.

Name (key)	Description	No of kernels	
		Before fusion	After fusion
Image Negatives (ImN)	Takes the negative of input image and performs jitter operation on it	3	2
Image Enhancement (ImE)	Enhance the input image using brightening and non max suppression filter	2	1
Intensity Transformation (Int)	Reduce the brightness of image, corrects it and modifies the color	3	1
Log Transformation Log	Log transform followed by grey-scaling the image and finally binarization of the image	4	1
Spatial Filtering (SpF)	It is a edge detection algorithm that uses convolutional filter	4	2
RGB2YUV (R2Y)	Converts an RGB image in interleaved format to a YUV image in interleaved format	3	1
HueContrastCrop (Con)	Modifies the input image color and crops it	3	1
Morphological Transforms (MT)	Dilate and erode a part of image	3	1
Gaussian (Gau)	Applying Gaussian Filter to the image	3	1
Canny Edge Detector (Can)	Applying Canny Edge detector algorithm on image	8	1
Image Transformation (ImT)	Apply log transformation on input image and convert them to single-channel grayscale. Performs binarization and crop the input image	4	2

We have tested our framework with a set of image processing benchmarks. Table 1 describes the set of benchmarks we have used for testing. In R2Y benchmark we do not have inter-iteration dependency across kernels. So we are able to do complete fusion for R2Y.

Our test machine is build with 16 GB RAM and AMD Ryzen 5 3600x with 6 cores and 12 threads. We used LLVM version 9 with Ubuntu 18.04. Table 2 provides the execution time of baseline POCL and POCL with kernel fusion in seconds. We observe an average improvement of 12.30% in overall execution time over the set of benchmarks.

Table 2. Execution time of various benchmarks in baseline POCL and POCL with kernel fusion in seconds.

Benchmark	Baseline POCL in s	Fused kernels in s
ImN	3.85	3.04
ImE	0.10	0.12
Int	17.59	16.64
Log	3.68	3.28
SpF	1.38	1.25
R2Y	2.94	1.65
Con	3.38	3.35
MT	4.08	4.20
Gau	1.50	1.11
Can	6.93	5.21

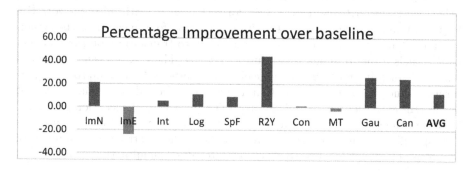

Fig. 4. Percentage improvement of our fusion compiler when compared to POCL baseline.

Figure 4 shows the percentage improvement in execution time for fusion framework over the baseline POCL. Some benchmarks show significant improvements, such as the R2Y benchmark where complete kernel fusion is possible, resulting in a 44% improvement in execution time. We can also see the overhead of our framework show in benchmarks with little potential from fusion and short kernels, such as the ImE benchmark. As a result of the additional overhead, we see a 20% increase in execution time for ImE. We can also the that kernel fusion is typically a memory locality optimization, so arithmetic-intensive benchmarks such as Int see little performance improvement. Other benchmarks generally saw improvements, with the magnitude of those improvements varying with the amount of kernel fusion opportunity and potential benefit, and the fixed overhead relative to the execution time of each individual kernel.

5 Related Works

Kernel Fusion is a widely known and extensively employed technique to improve execution time and reduce power consumption [1–3,12,15,17]. In [15] authors explain a kernel fusion framework for independent kernels in GPU to improve the power consumption. [2] explains a framework to automatically fuse GPU OpenCL kernels for Stan Math Library, using language extensions to drive the fusion optimizations. The framework was able to achieve performance comparable to the hand tuned fusion kernels. In [17] authors explain a runtime framework which will decide which kernel merges would result in faster code. The learning framework is based on the number of branches executed by each kernel which is especially costly in streaming processors such as GPUs. The OpenCL fusion described in [3] explains a framework to perform kernel fusion in CPUs where they explain data fusion for flow dependent kernels. In this work we have mostly concentrated on the data fusion with inter loop dependencies, however our framework can handle non dependent kernels. There has been a few compiler driven works for GPU devices [1,3–5], for SYCL cross-platform framework [12] for CUDA supported devices [1,4] to improve the performance across the kernels

In our work we are introducing a framework to transform loop carry dependent kernels to perform aggressive fusion in CPU. There have been some works which rely on scheduling [9,16] and avoid static kernel fusion to improve the performance and/or energy consumption. In [9], the authors describe three different concurrent execution of multiple kernels. The inner thread execution method is similar to the total fusion we elaborate as every thread in the warp executes the corresponding iteration of kernels. In [16] the authors introduces a framework to preempt a kernel at thread-block level to allow simultaneous execution of multiple kernels.

6 Conclusion

In this paper we described our kernel fusion framework in POCL. If the input kernels has no inter-loop dependencies, our framework performs a total fusion. When there is inter-loop dependencies our framework divides the input kernels to dependent iterations and independent iterations. The framework then transforms the independent iterations and fuses the kernels. The scheduling part of our framework executes the dependent iterations of the individual kernels before executing the fused kernel. We compared the performance of our kernel fusion framework and we observed an overall execution time improvement of 12.30% over the baseline POCL implementation. In future we want to optimize our fused kernel by eliminating the intermediate buffers which were primarily used to transfer data from one kernel to the next kernel in the baseline implementation. We would also want to implement compiler flags that a user could invoke to override the default behavior of the compiler, if the user can predict that kernel fusion is possible but detrimental. The will ensure that the users can weigh in to reduce the chances of the overhead dominating the gains of kernel fusion.

References

1. Aliaga, J.I., Pérez, J., Quintana-Ortí, E.S.: Systematic fusion of CUDA kernels for iterative sparse linear system solvers. In: Träff, J.L., Hunold, S., Versaci, F. (eds.) Euro-Par 2015. LNCS, vol. 9233, pp. 675–686. Springer, Heidelberg (2015). https://doi.org/10.1007/978-3-662-48096-0_52
2. Ciglarič, T., Češnovar, R., Štrumbelj, E.: Automated OpenCL GPU kernel fusion for Stan math. In: Proceedings of the International Workshop on OpenCL, IWOCL 2020. Association for Computing Machinery, New York (2020). https://doi.org/10.1145/3388333.3388654
3. Filipovic, J., Benkner, S.: OpenCL kernel fusion for GPU, Xeon Phi and CPU. In: 2015 27th International Symposium on Computer Architecture and High Performance Computing (SBAC-PAD), pp. 98–105 (2015). https://doi.org/10.1109/SBAC-PAD.2015.29
4. Filipovič, J., Madzin, M., Fousek, J., Matyska, L.: Optimizing CUDA code by kernel fusion: application on BLAS. J. Supercomput. 71(10), 3934–3957 (2015). https://doi.org/10.1007/s11227-015-1483-z
5. Gong, X., Chen, Z., Ziabari, A.K., Ubal, R., Kaeli, D.: TwinKernels: an execution model to improve GPU hardware scheduling at compile time. In: 2017 IEEE/ACM International Symposium on Code Generation and Optimization (CGO), pp. 39–49 (2017). https://doi.org/10.1109/CGO.2017.7863727
6. Jääskeläinen, P.O., de La Lama, C.S., Huerta, P., Takala, J.H.: OpenCL-based design methodology for application-specific processors. In: 2010 International Conference on Embedded Computer Systems: Architectures, Modeling and Simulation, pp. 223–230 (2010). https://doi.org/10.1109/ICSAMOS.2010.5642061
7. Jääskeläinen, P., et al.: Exploiting task parallelism with OpenCL: a case study. J. Signal Process. Syst. 91, 1–14 (2019)
8. Jääskeläinen, P., de La Lama, C.S., Schnetter, E., Raiskila, K., Takala, J., Berg, H.: POCL: a performance-portable OpenCL implementation. Int. J. Parallel Prog. 43(5), 752–785 (2014). https://doi.org/10.1007/s10766-014-0320-y
9. Jiao, Q., Lu, M., Huynh, H.P., Mitra, T.: Improving GPGPU energy-efficiency through concurrent kernel execution and DVFs. In: 2015 IEEE/ACM International Symposium on Code Generation and Optimization (CGO), pp. 1–11 (2015). https://doi.org/10.1109/CGO.2015.7054182
10. Kessenich, J., Ouriel, B., Krisch, R.: SPIR-V specification (2021)
11. Lattner, C., Adve, V.: LLVM: a compilation framework for lifelong program analysis & transformation. In: Proceedings of the 2004 International Symposium on Code Generation and Optimization (CGO 2004), Palo Alto, California, March 2004
12. Potter, R., Keir, P., Bradford, R.J., Murray, A.: Kernel composition in SYCL. In: Proceedings of the 3rd International Workshop on OpenCL, IWOCL 2015. Association for Computing Machinery, New York (2015). https://doi.org/10.1145/2791321.2791332
13. Ragan-Kelley, J., Barnes, C., Adams, A., Paris, S., Durand, F., Amarasinghe, S.: Halide: a language and compiler for optimizing parallelism, locality, and recomputation in image processing pipelines. In: Proceedings of the 34th ACM SIGPLAN Conference on Programming Language Design and Implementation. ACM, New York (2013). https://doi.org/10.1145/2491956.2462176
14. Rotem, N., et al.: Glow: graph lowering compiler techniques for neural networks. arXiv preprint arXiv:1805.00907 (2018)

15. Wang, G., Lin, Y., Yi, W.: Kernel fusion: an effective method for better power efficiency on multithreaded GPU. In: 2010 IEEE/ACM International Conference on Green Computing and Communications International Conference on Cyber, Physical and Social Computing, pp. 344–350 (2010). https://doi.org/10.1109/GreenCom-CPSCom.2010.102

16. Wang, Z., Yang, J., Melhem, R., Childers, B., Zhang, Y., Guo, M.: Simultaneous multikernel GPU: multi-tasking throughput processors via fine-grained sharing. In: 2016 IEEE International Symposium on High Performance Computer Architecture (HPCA), pp. 358–369 (2016). https://doi.org/10.1109/HPCA.2016.7446078

17. Wen, Y., O'Boyle, M.F.: Merge or separate? Multi-job scheduling for OpenCL kernels on CPU/GPU platforms. In: Proceedings of the General Purpose GPUs, GPGPU-10, pp. 22–31. Association for Computing Machinery, New York (2017). https://doi.org/10.1145/3038228.3038235

FPDAPP – International Workshop on Future Perspectives of Decentralized Applications

International Workshop on Future Perspectives of Decentralized Applications (FPDAPP)

Workshop Description

Blockchain technologies (BCTs) make agreement amongst untrusted parties possible, without the need for certification authorities. Proposed frameworks have been put forward in sector as diverse as finance, health-care, notary, intellectual property management, identity, provenance, international cooperation, social good, and security to cite but a few. Smart contracts, i.e. self-enforcing agreements in terms of executable software running on blockchains, have been developed in several contexts. Such an under-definition computational model introduces innovative aspects, such as the economics and trust of the decentralised computation relying on the shared contribution of peers and their decentralised consensus.

The fourth edition of the FPDAPP aimed to foster the cross-fertilisation between the blockchain and the distributed/parallel computing communities, which can strongly contribute to each other development.

FPDAPP workshop rigorously explored and evaluated the potentiality of such novel decentralised frameworks and applications. Of particular interest was the evaluation and comparison of killer applications that are showing evidence of how Distributed Ledger Technologies can revolutionize their domains or developing new application areas. Evaluation and comparisons are broadly understood, form technical aspects regarding the novel decentralised computer to the possible impact on society, business and the public sector.

In this on-line and pandemic year, we have received 6 articles for review; among these, 2 were submitted by members of the program committee. After a thorough peer reviewing process focused on quality, innovative contribution, applicability to real world scenarios, we have selected 4 articles for presentation at the workshop. Each paper has been revised by at least 3 independent reviewers. The workshop chairs have carefully supervised the review process and sometimes contributed with additional reviews. Final decision on the acceptance of the papers was the result of the reviewers' discussion and agreement. We believe that this process led to a high quality of the selected articles.

In addition to paper presentations, an interesting invited talk "Smart Contract Based Public Procurement to Fight Corruption" by prof. Tim Weingärtner – Lucerne University of Applied Sciences and Arts Computer Science and Information Technology, on blockchain and corruption in public administrations completed the program (http://fpdapp.di.unito.it/program.html).

Finally, we would like to thank all members of the FPDAPP Program Committee, the speakers, and the participants, as well as Euro-Par for hosting our new community and the workshop general chairs for the provided support.

Organization

Program Chairs

Andrea Bracciali   Stirling University, United Kingdom
Claudio Schifanella   University of Turin, Italy

Program Committee

Stefano Bistarelli   University of Perugia
Guido Boella   University of Turin
Annalisa Riccardi   Strathclyde University, UK
Nadia Fabrizio   Cefriel
Fadi Barbara   University of Turin
Monika Di Angelo   Technische Universitat, Wien, Austria
Yilei Wang   School of Computer Science, Qufu Normal University
Luca Mazzola   HSLU-I, Hoschschule Luzern – Informatik
Daniele Marazzina   Politecnico di Milano

Decentralisation over Privacy:
An Analysis of the Bisq Trade Protocol

Liam Hickey$^{(\boxtimes)}$ (iD) and Martin Harrigan (iD)

Department of Computing, Institute of Technology, Carlow,
Carlow, Republic of Ireland
liam.hickey@itcarlow.ie

Abstract. The Bisq trade protocol is a key component of the Bisq decentralised exchange, allowing users to trade with one another in a decentralised manner. However, the protocol publishes trade data to the Bitcoin blockchain. In this paper, we analyse the privacy risks this creates for users. Specifically, we present two new heuristics, one to identify Bisq trades on the Bitcoin blockchain and another to cluster the addresses used in those trades. We demonstrate that these heuristics are effective in identifying the trading activity of Bisq users and aggregating their trading activity across multiple trades. We conclude with suggestions as to how best to defeat these heuristics and improve the privacy aspects of the Bisq trade protocol.

Keywords: Decentralised exchange · Address clustering · Blockchain analysis · Privacy

1 Introduction

In recent years, a rise in both the value and applicability of many cryptocurrencies has led to substantial growth in various cryptocurrency communities. As one of the foremost ways in which cryptocurrencies are acquired and traded, this growth is reflected in the success of many centralised exchanges. While centralised exchanges are very accessible and easy to use, they are imperfect from a privacy perspective. Centralised exchanges often enforce identity checkpoints in accordance with KYC, or *know your customer*, law. These identity checkpoints combined with broad-based blockchain analysis techniques, can be a cause for concern.

Bisq is a decentralised cryptocurrency exchange that seeks to alleviate this concern. The Bisq exchange enables users to trade both cryptocurrencies and fiat currencies over a peer-to-peer network without the need for a trusted intermediary. Bisq allows traders to connect with each other directly, thereby eliminating identity checkpoints. However, while Bisq removes the need for a centralised clearing house, it relies on the Bitcoin blockchain to provide a degree of trust for its trading functions, consequently allowing for the application of blockchain analysis. In this paper, we use blockchain analysis techniques to analyse the Bisq trade protocol from a privacy perspective.

© Springer Nature Switzerland AG 2022
R. Chaves et al. (Eds.): Euro-Par 2021, LNCS 13098, pp. 207–218, 2022.
https://doi.org/10.1007/978-3-031-06156-1_17

Specifically, we present two heuristics that aid in the analysis of the Bisq trade protocol. Firstly, we use an *identification heuristic* that exploits the predictable structure of Bisq trade transactions in order to distinguish individual trades on the Bitcoin blockchain. Secondly, we use an *address clustering heuristic* to aggregate individual Bisq user activity. Address clustering heuristics are a commonly used technique in blockchain analysis: they allow for addresses on a blockchain to be grouped together, with each group, or *cluster*, representing a pool of addresses owned by a single individual or entity, see e.g., [5,9]. Our address clustering heuristic creates address clusters targeting Bisq traders.

This paper reviews related work (Sect. 2); introduces Bisq and the Bisq trade protocol (Sect. 3); presents our identification and address clustering heuristics (Sect. 4); details our analysis and results (Sect. 5); and concludes with suggestions to defeat the heuristics in the future (Sect. 6).

2   Related Work

In this paper, we divide related work into two fields, *address clustering* and *decentralised exchanges*.

Address clustering is a key analysis technique used in many high-level analyses of various blockchains, see, e.g. [3,5,6,8,9]. In this paper, we employ a specialised clustering heuristic in order to aggregate user activity in Bisq trades. Recently, specialised address clustering heuristics have been utilised in tracing transactions in "privacy coin" blockchains, such as ZCash shielded transactions [13] and Monero ring confidential transactions [10]. In our previous work, we used address clustering to highlight the privacy concerns surrounding participation in the Bisq DAO [4], a concern separate to the Bisq trade protocol.

Decentralised exchanges facilitate the exchange of cryptocurrencies and/or fiat currencies without the involvement of a trusted third party acting as a trade intermediary or central clearing house. While decentralised exchanges offer similar functionality to users, they vary widely in terms of technology, security and trustlessness, see [7]. Decentralised exchanges have been implemented using a variety of different technologies, such as the liquidity pools used by Uniswap [1] and order-book style trade protocol used by Bisq [2]. Bisq stands out from many decentralised exchanges in that it facilitates trades between blockchains, though it is not unique in this regard. THORChain is a decentralised liquidity protocol that facilitates cross-chain liquidity, see [15]. Due to the rising popularity of many different cryptocurrencies in recent years, there has been an increasing need for cross-blockchain exchange [12].

3   The Bisq Decentralised Exchange

Bisq is a decentralised cryptocurrency exchange that allows traders to connect and trade with one another directly without needing a trusted third party [2]. Bisq allows traders to trade bitcoins for altcoins (Ethereum, Litecoin, etc.) as well as fiat currencies (Euros, Dollars, etc.), with Bitcoin acting as a trade axis, i.e., every trade conducted on Bisq either buys or sells Bitcoin in exchange for some other asset. Bisq's use of Bitcoin as a trade axis will be discussed in Sect. 4. As of block height 670 026, over 90 000 trades have been completed using Bisq.

Similarly to Bitcoin and many other cryptocurrencies, decentralisation is a key driving force behind Bisq. Bisq's decentralised nature allows it to operate without the need for identity checkpoints or trusted third parties. Traders using Bisq need only divulge payment information directly with one another and on a trade-by-trade basis. Rather than acting as a central hub through which to trade, Bisq facilitates many individual trades. Additionally, Bisq's governance is managed decentrally through the Bisq DAO, or *decentralised autonomous organisation*. We investigated this aspect of Bisq in an earlier work [4] and omit the details here.

Bisq relies on the Bitcoin blockchain and its own peer-to-peer network to orchestrate trades. Bisq nodes connect to the peer-to-peer network in order to access an order-book. Traders wishing to buy or sell an asset broadcast their offer using the peer-to-peer network, which can then be accepted by other traders. Once an offer is accepted, traders connect with each other directly to complete the trade. The peer-to-peer network facilitates all communication between the traders and the Bitcoin blockchain provides security through the use of multi-signature transactions, which are used to lock funds until a trade has been completed successfully. We note that Bisq's reliance on the Bitcoin blockchain allows it to operate decentrally but requires it to publish data surrounding each trade.

3.1 The Bisq Trade Protocol

The Bisq trade protocol is a cornerstone of Bisq and is the mechanism by which a trade is performed decentrally. Essentially, the trade protocol sets out the steps performed on the Bisq peer-to-peer network and the Bitcoin blockchain over the course of a trade, allowing for the non-custodial transfer of funds between trading parties. The trade protocol is implemented by the Bisq software and executed on behalf of traders. Since its initial implementation, the protocol has changed over time with updated versions of the Bisq software. However, the underlying concepts behind the trade protocol have remained largely unchanged.

Over the course of a trade, the trade protocol uses both the peer-to-peer network and the Bitcoin blockchain. The peer-to-peer network facilitates communication between the traders, while the Bitcoin blockchain is used for a number of reasons including both trade security as well as the collection of trade fees. Bitcoin is also used as a trade axis, meaning every trade exchanges Bitcoin for some other asset, be it an altcoin or fiat currency. While the Bisq peer-to-peer network plays a key role in the protocol, we are more interested in the activity on the Bitcoin blockchain. For each successful trade, four transactions are added to the blockchain (see Fig. 1). These transactions are named the **maker fee** transaction, the **taker fee** transaction, the **deposit** transaction, and the **payout** transaction. These transactions are all linked, with transactions spending the outputs of previous transactions.

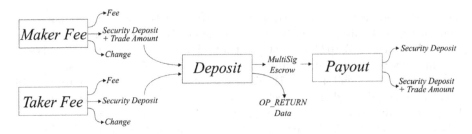

Fig. 1. A Bisq trade comprises four transactions on the Bitcoin blockchain: a maker fee transaction, a taker fee transaction, a deposit transaction and a payout transaction. The transaction outputs and transaction inputs of these four transactions are linked as shown, e.g., the second output of the maker fee transaction is redeemed by the first input of the deposit transaction.

Trade Flow. The Bisq trade protocol defines a number of steps that must be performed for each trade (see Fig. 2). First among these steps is the creation of an offer to trade. Any trader wishing to trade an asset will first broadcast an offer using the Bisq peer-to-peer network, after which the offer is added to the Bisq order-book. This coincides with the creation of a maker fee transaction on the Bitcoin blockchain. The purpose of this transaction is to collect a trade fee from the 'maker', or trader who created the offer to trade. This fee can be paid using either Bitcoin or a coloured-coin known as BSQ issued by the Bisq DAO. A coloured-coin is an amount of Bitcoin that has been marked, or 'coloured', as having some additional meaning, in this case, marking an amount of Bitcoin as being BSQ. For a more thorough explanation of coloured-coins, see [14]. The trade fee is collected from the first output of the maker fee transaction, while the second output comprises the security deposit for the trade, and, if the trader is selling Bitcoin, the trade amount to fund the Bitcoin side of the trade. Both traders provide a security deposit for each trade so as to disincentivise fraud, this deposit is refunded to both traders if a trade is completed successfully. Finally, the maker fee transaction may have a third output for change.

After an offer is created and added to the order-book, it can be accepted by another trader; this trader is known as the 'taker'. When a taker accepts an offer to trade, the peer-to-peer network is used to notify the maker and remove their offer from the order-book. This coincides with the creation of the taker fee transaction on the Bitcoin blockchain. This transaction is functionally identical to the maker fee transaction, with the outputs being used for the same purposes as before. When comparing the maker fee and taker fee from the perspective of a specific trade, only one of the transactions will include both the trade amount and the security deposit. This is due to the assignment of the maker and taker roles in a trade being irrespective of who is buying Bitcoin and who is selling. The seller is the party that adds the trade amount to the second output of their fee transaction regardless of whether they are the maker or the taker.

Once an offer is accepted and both fee transactions are confirmed, outputs from the fee transactions are used to create the deposit transaction. The

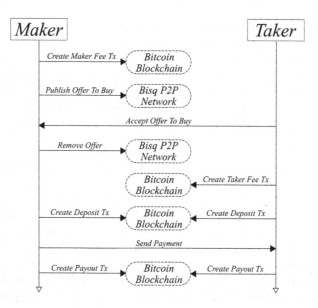

Fig. 2. Each Bisq trade consists of a number of steps involving both the Bitcoin blockchain and the Bisq peer-to-peer network. In this case, the 'maker', or trader creating the trade offer, is offering to buy bitcoins in exchange for some other asset. The taker accepts this offer, selling their bitcoins in exchange for that asset.

deposit transaction is a multi-signature transaction that is used to securely lock funds until a trade progresses. The deposit transaction uses the second output of both fee transactions as inputs, thereby combining the security deposits of both traders as well as the trade amount. These funds are then locked in the form of a 2-of-2 or 2-of-3 multi-signature transaction output. Additionally, the deposit transaction contains an OP_RETURN output containing the SHA256 hash of the trade contract agreed upon by the traders. The multi-signature output of the deposit transaction cannot be spent without the signature of both traders, preventing the transfer of funds without payment. In order to release the held funds, the buyer must confirm that they have sent payment via the agreed upon medium, e.g., bank transfer, altcoin trade, etc., and the seller must confirm that they have received said payment.

Finally, each successful trade concludes with a payout transaction to redistribute the locked funds to traders. Once payment for the trade amount has been sent and received, the payout transaction is created using the signatures of both traders. Each payout transaction has one input and two outputs, with the sole input being the multi-signature output of the deposit transaction. The two transaction outputs are used to distribute locked funds between traders, with both traders receiving a refund of their security deposit and the buyer receiving the Bitcoin trade amount. Once the payout transaction has been confirmed, the trade is complete, with the Bitcoin trade amount being transferred to the buyer and the seller being paid after the creation of the deposit transaction.

Mediation and Arbitration. Not all Bisq trades run smoothly. Occasionally, a dispute can arise between traders that requires the input or intervention of a third party. For this reason, Bisq integrates the capacity for mediation and arbitration into its trade protocol. If an issue arises over the course of a trade, either trader can open a dispute. Bisq implements a dispute escalation system where raised disputes are first addressed by a mediator, and, if mediation fails, an arbitrator. Mediators and arbitrators are bonded roles within the Bisq DAO, meaning that the holders of these roles have been approved by the Bisq DAO and have locked a required amount of BSQ. When a dispute arises, it is first brought to the attention of a mediator. Mediators can make suggestions as to how the dispute should be resolved, but do not have the authority to enforce these suggestions. Should no agreement be reached, disputes are then raised to arbitrators, who have the authority to implement their own solution as to how the dispute should be resolved. The way in which arbitrators have enforced their rulings has changed over time. Initially, arbitrators were provided a key for every 2-of-3 multi-signature deposit transaction, meaning the arbitrator only needed the agreement of a single trader in order to impose a solution. This functionality was removed in October 2019, introducing a new arbitration protocol. Now, traders sign a time locked transaction alongside the deposit transaction, which if published, forwards all funds to the Bisq donation address. Arbitrators can later reimburse traders as they deem fair.

4   Address Clustering

In this section, we demonstrate that the structure of transactions created by the Bisq trade protocol on the Bitcoin blockchain enables the creation of heuristics for identifying Bisq trades and clustering the addresses used by traders.

4.1   Identification Heuristic

The identification of Bisq trades on the Bitcoin blockchain is the starting point for any blockchain-based analysis of the Bisq trade protocol. The structure of the four transactions enables the creation of an identification heuristic. Specifically, each *deposit transaction* must meet the following criteria:

1. It must have at least two transaction inputs and two transaction outputs.
2. Both transaction inputs must reference the second output of a previous transaction.
3. The first output must be a 2-of-2 or 2-of-3 multi-signature transaction output using either P2SH *or* P2WSH.
4. The second output must be an OP_RETURN containing 32 bytes of data.

Once deposit transactions have been identified, the retrieval of the other Bisq trade transactions is trivial. The deposit transaction references both the maker fee and taker fee transactions, and is itself referenced by the payout transaction.

4.2 Address Clustering Heuristic

The identification of Bisq trades on the Bitcoin blockchain allows for a more in depth analysis of the Bisq trade protocol using blockchain analysis techniques. The inputs of the deposit transaction follow the same order as the outputs of the payout transaction, with the first ordinal belonging to the buyer, and the second to the seller. Due to this consistent ordering, addresses associated with the inputs of the deposit transaction and the outputs of the payout transaction can be added to address clusters corresponding to the buyer and seller. We can also add addresses referenced by the fee transactions to these clusters, as both inputs of the deposit transaction reference the second output of a fee transaction. This link allows for addresses referenced by the inputs of the fee transactions, as well as addresses referenced by any change outputs, to be added to the buyer and seller clusters alongside the address referenced by the second output of the fee transaction.

4.3 Arbitration Protocol

The Bisq arbitration protocol causes problems for our address clustering heuristic. While trades that have been mediated do follow the normal trade structure, arbitrated trades can deviate from this structure, leading to false positives in the heuristic. As such, arbitrated trades must be identified and removed. There are two arbitration protocols, as discussed in Sect. 3.1. Trades arbitrated using the newer arbitration protocol are easy to identify, as they use a time-locked transaction to forward all funds held in the deposit multi-signature output to the Bisq donation address. This creates a payout transaction with only one output as opposed to the two outputs of a non-arbitrated payout transaction.

It is more difficult to identify trades arbitrated using the older arbitration protocol. The older arbitration protocol uses a 2-of-3 multi-signature output rather than a 2-of-2 in the deposit transaction, with the third key belonging to the arbitrator. In order to identify arbitrated trades, we must know whether or not the arbitrator's key was used to sign the creation of the payout transaction. For each 2-of-3 multi-signature output created during a Bisq trade, the public keys authorised to sign a transaction spending the output are always added in the same order, with the arbitrator's key always being the first key, followed by the traders' keys. To recognise when a trade has been arbitrated, we need to know if this first key was used.

To identify which keys are used to spend a P2SH multi-signature output, we extract the `scriptSig` from the spending transaction, in this case the payout transaction. When a P2SH output is spent, the `OP_CHECKMULTISIG` operation is used to check whether or not the provided signatures match the public keys found in the P2SH redeem script. In the case of a 2-of-3 multi-signature output, the operation checks whether the two signatures provided match two of the three public keys provided in the redeem script. To check whether the first key is used, we execute the `scriptSig` as normal using `btcdeb`[1], the Bitcoin

---

[1] https://github.com/bitcoin-core/btcdeb.

Script Debugger. However, when the public keys are being added to the stack, we substitute the arbitrator's public key for a stand-in key. We then continue executing the script as normal to completion. Should the OP_CHECKMULTISIG operation execute successfully, we can assert that the arbitrator's public key was not used to create the payout transaction. However, should the operation fail, it will have done so due to the substitution of the arbitrator's key for a stand-in key, thereby proving that the arbitrator's key was used to create the payout transaction.

5   Analysis and Results

In this section, we apply[2] and analyse the results of both the identification (see Sect. 4.1) and address clustering heuristics (see Sect. 4.2). We illustrate the effectiveness of the clustering heuristic in classifying Bisq trade activity and we validate the results using data gathered from the Bisq peer-to-peer network.

Using the identification heuristic, we identified 90 801 Bisq trades[3] as of the end of Bisq DAO cycle 23, coinciding with block height 670 026 on the Bitcoin blockchain, i.e., the deposit transactions of all identified trades were included in or before block 670 026, with the first Bisq trade deposit transaction being identified in block 408 023.

The identification of Bisq trades allows for the application of the Bisq trade protocol-specific address clustering heuristic. Before the heuristic can be applied we must remove trades that cannot be clustered, such as arbitrated trades and incomplete trades. Such trades can be identified using the methods described in Sect. 4.3. We found that out of the 90 801 retrieved trades, the clustering heuristic could be applied to 87 326 trades. Of the trades that could not be clustered:

- 3003 were arbitrated using the older arbitration protocol.
- 353 were arbitrated using the newer arbitration protocol.
- 119 trades did not have an identified payout transaction, i.e., these trades may not have been completed.

We found that when the heuristic was applied to the 87 326 clusterable trades, 621 697 distinct addresses were identified. The clustering heuristic produced 40 801 address clusters, with each cluster representing a set of addresses that are likely controlled by the same Bisq trader. Here, the clustering heuristic produces clusters that contain on average 15.24 addresses. The clustering heuristic produces two address clusters for each trade, corresponding to the buyer and the seller. Should each cluster represent solely the activity of a single trader in a single trade, then we would expect to see two clusters per trade, or 174 652

---

[2] Source code implementing both heuristics can be found here: https://github.com/Liam-Hickey-Ire/BisqTradeProtocolAnalysisSource.

[3] https://github.com/Liam-Hickey-Ire/BisqTradeProtocolAnalysisSource/blob/master/Data/670026/our-deposit-tx-hashes.csv: This CSV file lists the deposit transaction hashes of every trade identified by our heuristic.

clusters. In practice, the clustering heuristic produces far fewer clusters; this means that the clustering heuristic not only follows the activity of traders on a per trade basis, but also aggregates trader activity across multiple Bisq trades, with each cluster including addresses used in, on average, 4.28 different trades. In this way, the clustering heuristic aggregates Bisq trading activity. The extent to which addresses used in trades, as well as trades themselves, can be linked using this clustering heuristic may be unexpected by Bisq users, and is a privacy risk.

5.1   Validation

In assessing the validity of a blockchain-based heuristic, the absence of a ground truth often poses a problem [11]. Fortunately for us, the Bisq peer-to-peer network offers a partial solution to validating the identification heuristic. Bisq stores a great deal of peer-to-peer sourced data using Protocol Buffers[4]. Specifically, Bisq uses Protocol Buffers to store data related to trade statistics in two files, TradeStatistics2 and TradeStatistics3.

Bisq uses these files to store data relating to each Bisq trade for the purpose of providing statistics. Formerly, TradeStatistics2 was used to store this data, which included the deposit transaction hash of each Bisq trade. TradeStatistics2 was deprecated in favour of TradeStatistics3, which only stores data relating to each trade that cannot be directly linked to the Bitcoin blockchain. To provide a ground truth against which to compare the identification heuristic, we extracted this data from TradeStatistics3 and an archived copy of TradeStatistics2.

We extracted 69 966 trade entries from TradeStatistics2. However, the data includes a number of incomplete and duplicate entries. Removing corrupted data yielded a total of 68 517 trade entries[5], with each entry containing a deposit transaction hash that can be compared with trades identified using the identification heuristic. We found that the identification heuristic successfully identified 99% of trades found in TradeStatistics2. Of the entries extracted from TradeStatistics2, 469 were not identified by the heuristic. However, we found that most of these trades did not actually exist on the Bitcoin blockchain, leaving just 18 trades that we failed to identify. Our heuristic identified approximately 503 trades that were not present in TradeStatistics2. However, at least some of these trades were confirmed to be valid due to the presence of BSQ trade fee transactions, implying that TradeStatistics2 contains inaccuracies.

We can perform a similar comparison using TradeStatistics3. Even though it no longer stores the deposit transaction hashes, it does contain an entry for

---

[4] Protocol Buffers is a data serialisation mechanism developed by Google, similar in function to other data serialisation mechanisms such as JSON or XML.

[5] https://github.com/Liam-Hickey-Ire/BisqTradeProtocolAnalysisSource/blob/ master/Data/670026/bisq-deposit-tx-hashes.csv: Each line of this CSV file lists the deposit transaction hashes of every Bisq trade retrieved from TradeStatistics2, with corrupted and duplicate entries removed.

each Bisq trade. After removing duplicate entries, `TradeStatistics3` contains 91 689 trade entries, compared to the 90 801 trades retrieved using the identification heuristic. This means that our identification heuristic falls short by some 888 trades, or 0.97% of the trades found in `TradeStatistics3`.

One of the motivating factors behind the removal of deposit transaction hashes from `TradeStatistics2` was an effort to hinder blockchain-based analysis of Bisq trades.[6] However, we have shown that Bisq trades can be identified on the Bitcoin blockchain with a high degree of accuracy using the identification heuristic. This shows that the identification heuristic reveals sensitive information even prior to the application of the clustering heuristic.

5.2   Case Study

In addition to the classification of Bisq user activity on a per-trade basis, clusters generated by the address clustering heuristic have the potential to aggregate Bisq user activity across multiple trades. Specifically, this scenario arises when a trader spends the output of a payout transaction when creating a maker or taker fee transaction, linking two separate trades in the process through a shared address. This situation also arises when a trader spends a change output of a prior maker or taker fee transaction, similarly linking two otherwise separate trades. In linking trades, users inadvertently merge address clusters, which are generated for each trade, thereby allowing their activity to be tracked across multiple trades.

This can best be seen in a specific example. Prior to our analysis, we performed numerous trades using the Bisq trade protocol. In doing so, we inadvertently linked trades by spending the outputs of payout transactions or change outputs in the creation of fee transactions. As the Bisq client software does not reuse addresses, we used 60 different addresses over the course of numerous trades. These address were partitioned into three clusters of size 29, 26, and 5 by our address clustering heuristic. Analysing the largest of these clusters, we find that the 29 addresses were used across 8 different trades. These trades were each linked in one of two ways. Firstly, as previously highlighted, trades can be linked when a trader spends the output of a payout transaction or a change output from a prior fee transaction to create a new maker or taker fee transaction. This occurs 6 times in the largest address cluster, 4 of which being due to the spending of change outputs. We also observe a single case of trades being linked through address reuse in the largest of our three clusters. Interestingly, this address is a BSQ address we used to pay trade fees. This points to the potential expansion of this address clustering heuristic to better contend with trades paying fees using BSQ. The analysis presented in this paper can be combined with other heuristics applicable to Bisq, see e.g., [4], as well as the wider Bitcoin blockchain.

Despite its anecdotal nature, from this example we can see how the clustering heuristic can be used to effectively aggregate Bisq user activity across multiple trades. This is due to the spending of transaction outputs resulting from previous

---

[6] https://github.com/bisq-network/bisq/issues/3893.

trades and address re-use, resulting, in this case, in only three known addresses being needed to retrieve clusters representing the entirety of our trading activity.

6   Conclusion

Bisq's reliance on the Bitcoin blockchain in decentralising many of its functions places it within the scope of blockchain analysis. In this paper, we performed such an analysis, focusing specifically on the Bisq trading functions. We illustrated the privacy risks associated with the Bisq trade protocol. Specifically, we used the structure of Bisq trade transactions on the Bitcoin blockchain to create a heuristic capable of identifying those trades with an accuracy level exceeding 99%, identifying 90 801 trades in total. We extended this analysis, again utilising the structure of Bisq trade transactions, to create a Bisq trade protocol-specific address clustering heuristic capable of partitioning addresses used in Bisq trades into clusters corresponding to the trading parties. We developed methods by which arbitrated Bisq trades can be identified. The heuristic partitioned 621 697 Bitcoin addresses found across 87 326 Bisq trades into 40 801 clusters, proving it to be effective in aggregating the activity of Bisq users across multiple trades. This can be seen in our case study, where our own Bisq trade activity was concentrated into only three address clusters by the clustering heuristic.

There are several approaches to remedying this situation. Both the identification heuristic and the address clustering heuristic rely on the structure of Bisq trade transactions. Any ambiguity introduced in this area could defeat both heuristics. This could be achieved by, for example, changing the order of inputs and outputs in Bisq deposit and payout transactions such that the addresses of the buyer and seller cannot be linked across transactions. This approach does not prevent addresses being linked by the value of their transaction outputs, as currently the trade amount is held alongside the security deposit allowing for the buyer and seller to be discerned by the value of their outputs. This could be addressed by separating the trade amount into its own transaction output, obfuscating the flow of Bitcoin between the buyer and the seller.

The effectiveness of the clustering heuristic can also be reduced by changing the behaviour of Bisq users. Many clusters aggregate user activity across multiple trades due to the output of a payout transaction or change output being spent in either a maker fee or taker fee transaction. Avoiding this behaviour would serve to increase the number of clusters generated by our heuristic while also reducing their size, thereby lessening its effectiveness.

Another way in which these heuristics can be defeated is by purposely triggering false positives. It is entirely possible to publish a set of transactions on the Bitcoin blockchain that mimic the characteristics of the transactions created during a Bisq trade. Creating such 'false' trades would trigger false positives in both heuristics. However, Bitcoin transaction fees make this a costly solution.

The Bisq trade protocol is an effective means by which the trading functions of Bisq are decentralised, allowing users to trade directly with one another without the need for a trusted third party. However, Bisq's reliance on the Bitcoin blockchain in achieving this level of decentralisation places the Bisq trade protocol under the purview of blockchain analysis providers, placing decentralisation ahead of user privacy. The heuristics described in this paper not only identify Bisq trades on the Bitcoin blockchain, but also aggregate user activity, often across multiple trades. The degree to which trades can be linked and addresses clustered within those trades may be unforeseen by Bisq's users who expect a higher standard of privacy. However, these privacy issues can be ameliorated as discussed, allowing the Bisq community to offer a more privacy focused decentralised exchange.

References

1. Adams, H., Zinsmeister, N., Robinson, D.: Uniswap V2 core, March 2020. https://uniswap.org/whitepaper.pdf
2. Bisq network documentation. https://docs.bisq.network
3. Harrigan, M., Fretter, C.: The unreasonable effectiveness of address clustering. In: The IEEE International Conference on Advanced and Trusted Computing (ATC), pp. 368–373. IEEE Computer Society (2016)
4. Hickey, L., Harrigan, M.: The Bisq DAO: on the privacy cost of participation. In: IEEE Symposium on Computers and Communications (2020)
5. Huang, D.Y., et al.: Tracking ransomware end-to-end. In: The IEEE Symposium on Security and Privacy, pp. 618–631. IEEE (2018)
6. Jourdan, M., Blandin, S., Wynter, L., Deshpande, P.: Characterizing entities in the Bitcoin blockchain. In: The International Workshop on Blockchain and Sharing Economy Applications (BlockSEA 2018) at the IEEE International Conference on Data Mining (ICDM). IEEE (2018)
7. Lin, L.X.: Deconstructing decentralized exchanges (2019). https://stanford-jblp.pubpub.org/pub/deconstructing-dex
8. Maesa, D.D.F., Marino, A., Ricci, L.: Data-driven analysis of bitcoin properties: exploiting the users graph. Int. J. Data Sci. Anal. **6**, 63–80 (2018)
9. Meiklejohn, S., et al.: A fistful of bitcoins: characterizing payments among men with no names. Commun. ACM (CACM) **59**(4), 86–93 (2016)
10. Möser, M., et al.: An empirical analysis of traceability in the Monero blockchain. In: Proceedings on Privacy Enhancing Technologies, pp. 143–163 (2018). https://doi.org/10.1515/popets-2018-0025
11. Nick, J.: Data-driven de-anonymization in Bitcoin. Master's thesis, ETH Zürich (2015)
12. Nieves, P.: Identification of cross blockchain transactions: a feasibility study. Master's thesis, Technical University of Munich (2018)
13. Quesnelle, J.: On the linkability of Zcash transactions (2017). https://arxiv.org/abs/1712.01210
14. Rosenfeld, M.: Overview of colored coins (2012). https://bitcoil.co.il/BitcoinX.pdf
15. THORChain: A decentralised liquidity network. https://github.com/thorchain/Resources/tree/master/Whitepapers

Towards a Graphical DSL for Tracing Supply Chains on Blockchain

Stefano Bistarelli[1], Francesco Faloci[2(✉)], and Paolo Mori[3]

[1] Dipartimento di Matematica e Informatica, University of Perugia, Perugia, Italy
[2] Dipartimento di Informatica, University of Camerino, Camerino, Italy
`francesco.faloci@unicam.it`
[3] Istituto di Informatica e Telematica, National Research Council, Pisa, Italy

Abstract. Nowadays, supply chain tracing notarization is among the most used non-financial blockchain applications. However, creating a blockchain based system for the management of a supply chain remains a complex task. In this paper, we propose a graphical domain specific language (DSL) and a tool allowing the supply chain domain expert to easily represent the supply chain he needs to trace. The graphical representation of the supply chain is then translated in automatic way in a set of solidity smart contracts implementing it. A small intervention of a programmer is required to customize and finalize such smart contracts. The obtained semi-automatic process of smart contract generation will boost the blockchain usage for supply chain traceability.

Keywords: Supply chain management · Blockchain · Smart contract · Graphical DSL

1 Introduction

According to the definition of Stadtler and Kilger [12], a supply chain (SC) is a "network of organizations that are involved, through upstream and downstream linkages, in the different processes and activities that produce value in the form of products and services in the hands of the ultimate consumer". From an analytic point of view, we can define a SC as a flow of goods or services generated by the processes that transform raw objects into intermediate objects, and such objects into final products. Hence, depending on the specific scenarios where they are applied, different types of SC can be defined, e.g., production, distribution, maintenance and sales supply chains. Several studies and applications propose to implement supply chain management systems exploiting the blockchain technology [1,9,11], but according to the same researches, they provide solutions that are not general enough.

This paper proposes a general model aimed at easily representing any specific SC. This model will be then exploited for automatizing SC management systems design and development over a blockchain. The design phase will be facilitated by a graphical interface enabling the SC manager to represent the objects (assets)

ⓒ Springer Nature Switzerland AG 2022
R. Chaves et al. (Eds.): Euro-Par 2021, LNCS 13098, pp. 219–229, 2022.
https://doi.org/10.1007/978-3-031-06156-1_18

involved in the supply chain process as basic components, the operations that can be done on these objects as relations among objects, and their constraints. The development phase will be facilitated because a set of smart contracts skeletons representing the objects, the operations, and the constraints of the supply chain are automatically derived from its graphical representation. Programmers will then finalize and customize these skeletons according to the specific supply chain features.

The paper is organized as follows. Section 2 describes SC features and typologies. In Sect. 3 we propose our model and framework for blockchain based SC design and development, while Sect. 4 describes a real use case exploiting our model. Section 5 describes the tool we developed which implements the model we defined. Finally, Sect. 7 draws the conclusions and describes possible future works.

2   Background

A SC is a system of organizations, people, activities, information and resources involved in the process of transferring or supplying a product or service from the supplier to the customers [12]. In this sense, a SC is a representation of a real system where some "agents" participate to fulfill the service. An agent is any entity involved in the SC including abstract or real subjects like: producers, vendors, warehouses, transportation companies, distributions centers, or retailers [8]. To analyze the definition of SC we study characteristics and properties of SC already classified in literature. **Production supply chains** are designed to organize the creation of a product. This type traces the phases in which the asset under analysis undergoes transformations: from the origin point to the end of the life cycle of production. This chain describes in detail the changes, the time required for transformations, the information required for production. These models generally include production of both goods and services [6]. Production supply chain is often represented by a flowchart, where there is always a well-known (defined) initial state, and possibly one or multiple final states. **Distribution supply chains** type aims to organize and manage the traceability of resources. A supply chain of this type highlights channels for each macro termination area, and specifies all the agents or the intermediaries involved an asset from the producer to the customer. Distribution channels can include wholesalers, retailers, deliverers, and even the Internet [5,13]. **Sales supply chains** describe the relationships between distribution nodes of an asset; it does not deal with changes in the asset or possible substantial changes, but only with the path chain that a product undergoes in its sales or delivery cycle: generally we speak of a finished product from producer to consumers [14]. This involves analysis such as market overview, production planning and financial strategies [2,15].

Distributed Ledger Technology (DLT) refers to systems and protocols that allow simultaneous access, validation, and updating with immutable data across a network. DLT, more commonly known as Blockchain Technology (BT), given its potential across industries and financial sectors. In simple words, the DLT is all about the idea of a "decentralized" network against the conventional monolithic centralized mechanism. The BT offers great potential to foster various sectors with its unique combination of characteristics as decentralization, immutability, and transparency. So far, the most prominent attention the technology received was through news from industry and media about the development of cryptocurrencies (such as Bitcoin[1], and Monero[2]), which all are having remarkable capitalization. BT, however, is not limited to cryptocurrencies; there are already existing blockchain based applications in industry and the public sector. Also, BT can have applications on non-financial sector, such as traceability problems and workflow organization. A smart contract is a self-executing contract (script) with the terms of the agreement between two actors, generally a buyer and a seller, directly written into lines of code. The code and the agreements contained in the script exist across a distributed decentralized blockchain system. One of the most popular coding languages for describing smart contracts is Solidity[3], widely used for Ethereum[4] systems.

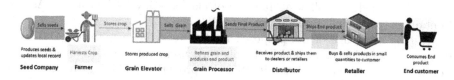

Fig. 1. Scheme of the supply chain used on soybeans traceability study [9]. (Color figure online)

Figure 1 shows an example of a real use case of supply chain representing the soybeans life cycle, from the seed production phase, to the end customer sell. This use case has been used in [9] to develop a blockchain based application able to represent supply chains for agricultural products. On the supply chain schema of Fig. 1 we can highlight different phases that describe three different type of supply chain: transitions from a point to another characterize moving operation (highlight in green); the passing from an owner to another represents sales phases (highlight in red); the various phases where the object under examination changes its properties are transformation phases (highlight in yellow).

3   Supply Chain Model and Graphical Representation

Our approach analyzes SC structures in order to highlight their typical elements and to identify recurrent patterns in the interactions among them. As a matter of fact, analysing the existing literature, we found out that there are a number of interaction patterns among the elements building up a SC that are general,

[1] Bitcoin project: https://bitcoin.org.
[2] Monero project: https://www.getmonero.org.
[3] Solidity white paper: https://docs.soliditylang.org/en/v0.8.6/.
[4] Ethereum project: https://ethereum.org/en/.

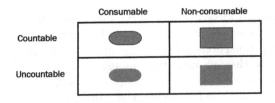

Fig. 2. Assets and containers graphical representation.

i.e., they are not strictly related to the specific business case represented by the supply chain. For instance, a typical pattern is the one which represents the packaging of a number of items in one single traceable package. The identified patterns are exploited to define the basic components of our model. The idea behind our model is to be able to define the workflow of a SC by simply composing the components representing the identified patterns.

We identified the following families of elements involved in a SC: Assets, Containers (packaging), Operations, and Roles.

To ease the usage of the proposed model, we define a graphical DSL representing a supply chain model. In this way, users will be able to define the workflow representing their specific SCs by properly combining the graphical components representing the constructs of our model.

Assets. They are the objects that the supply chain treats: they typically represent the goods involved in the operations on the supply chain. As a matter of fact, some goods are loaded in the supply chain at the beginning of the process (e.g., raw materials), some operations are applied to such goods to obtain semi-finished products, further operations are applied until the final product is obtained. The assets that, in order to be tracked, must be contained into containers are called *uncountable* (e.g., the milk needs to be stored in a bottle). If an asset involves any kind of destruction as a consequence of its use or transformation, it is called *"consumable"*.

Containers. Whenever an asset is inserted or accumulated into another object, the latter is referred as "container". Examples of containers are: silos, haulers, ships, and packagings. Containers are used in two cases: *i)* when an asset, for its own nature, must be necessarily contained in a support (for instance, the water must be contained in a bottle), this is the case of uncountable asset; *ii)* when an asset is contained into a package in order to be transported, stored or cataloged (for instance a case of water bottles) Containers are countable and traceable objects. Each asset or container on a supply chain can be *"consumable"* or *"non-consumable"*. An egg, a liter of milk, a bag of seeds, bucket of manure, are examples of consumable objects. A tree, a field, a vineyard, are instead examples of non-consumable objects.

Figure 2 shows a diagram of how assets and containers are graphically represented according to the proposed model, based on their properties.

Operations are the components of our model which allow to represent updates, modifications or transformations of an asset. Figure 3 shows some examples of the main operations defined in our model: each operation has specific properties, parameters, and outputs, all described in the following.

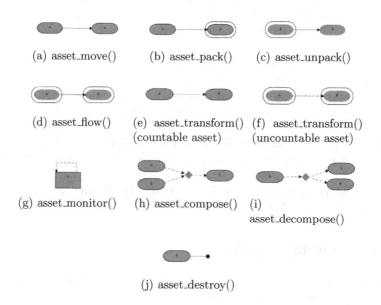

(a) asset_move()   (b) asset_pack()   (c) asset_unpack()

(d) asset_flow()   (e) asset_transform()   (f) asset_transform()
                    (countable asset)   (uncountable asset)

(g) asset_monitor()   (h) asset_compose()   (i)
                                              asset_decompose()

(j) asset_destroy()

Fig. 3. Examples of possible operations defined on the model.

- **asset_move** (Fig. 3(a)) this operation concerns the update of the position - or the geolocalization - of the asset. Figure 3(a) shows the operation applied over a countable asset, but it is also applicable to containers (with uncountable asset inside).
- **asset_pack** (Fig. 3(b)) This operation represents the packaging or collection of the asset inside an object suitable for transport or tracking. There is no change of original asset information. The asset is inserted into a further object which in turn can be a source of operations and traceability. This operation can obviously be repeated several times, with different container objects; it could be also applied to each pair formed by any object and any type of container.
- **asset_unpack** (Fig. 3(c)) In this case an asset is extracted from a container. When a non consumable container releases all the assets it contains, it is destroyed. The object contained is removed from the package.
- **asset_flow** (Fig. 3(d)) This operation represent the transfer of an asset from one package to another package.
- **asset_monitor** (Fig. 3(g)) This operation is used when an object requires a control operation. Therefore this operation does not change the traits of an asset, nor its geolocation: the operation keeps track of information of the asset, relevant for its traceability.

– **asset_transform** (Figs. 3(e) 3(f)) The transformation operations are meant to change features of an asset, and they are typically dependent on the specific asset and supply chain. Hence, transformations imply a substantial change of properties and traits of an asset. If the operation is applied to consumable assets, it has the main effect to destroy the original asset and to create the new one (or ones). Sometimes, a non consumable assets may generate assets: in this use, the "transform()" operation has the task of generating the new asset.

– **asset_compose and asset_decompose** (Fig. 3(h) 3(i)) Assembly operations exploits existing assets to create a new asset without destroying them. In the opposite way. the operation designed to disassemble objects previously assembled with a composition operation, is defined decomposition. Notice the similarly of the "asset_compose()" with the "asset_transform()": in both cases a new asset is created. However, the transform operation destroys the previous asset, while in the compose operation the original assets are still there.

– **asset_destroy** (Fig. 3(j)) when an object has to be destroyed and is no longer part of the supply chain, it is destroyed.

4   Representing a Real Case

This section shows how the proposed model can be exploited to represent the supply chain defined in [9] and represented in Fig. 1.

Here we suppose that the Soy Bean Producer, *SBP*, wants to track the soybean production process, from the acquisition of the seeds to their commercialization. For this reason, *SBP* exploits our framework to represent the main steps of the production process, thus automatically obtaining the skeletons of the smart contracts that represent each asset of the supply chain. Figures 4 and 5 show the graphical representation of the soybean production process using our framework.

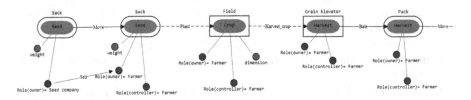

Fig. 4. Representation of the soybeans supply chain use case [9], seen in Fig. 1, with the proposed framework (part I).

The first asset of the supply chain represented in Fig. 4 is *Seed* (the leftmost box in the figure), which is an uncountable asset and hence it is enclosed in a container, called *Sack*. This asset does not have any incoming arrow. This means

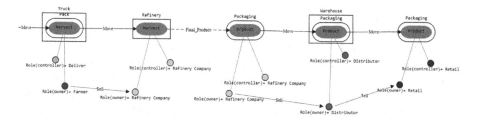

Fig. 5. Representation of the soybeans supply chain use case [9], seen in Fig. 1, with the proposed framework (part II).

that the production of this asset is not tracked using our framework, and this asset is simply created by a subject. Our framework allows to set constraints on the role of the subject who can create/buy an asset. In the reference example, the subjects allowed to create *Seed* assets must have the role *Seed Company*. As a matter of fact, in the figure we can see the constraint Role(owner) = *Seed Company* paired with the *Seed* assets. The operation that is done on the *Seed* asset is *Sell*, which is paired with the operation *Move*. Hence, in the graphical representation of the supply chain we have a second instance of the *Seed* asset on the right of the first instance, and these two instances are directly connected through a *Move* arrow, which represent the physical transfer of the asset and, at the same time, the owner properties of the two instances are connected with a red arrow representing the *Sell* operation. The framework, by default, imposes the constraint that only the owner of an asset can perform the *Sell* operation. This constraint is not explicitly reported in the supply chain graphical representation. In the reference example, a further constraint is defined on the role of the entity which can buy *Seed*. This constraint is represented in the Fig. 4 as Role(owner) = *Farmer*, and it is paired with the second instance of the *Seed* asset.

The second operation in the soybeans supply chain represented in Fig. 4 is the *Plant* one. This operation is a transformation (as shown by the dashed line) because the *Seed* asset is transformed in *Crop* asset when it is planted in the field. The *Crop* asset is uncountable as well, and hence it is included in a *Field* container, which represents the place where the seeds have been planted. The *Field* container is, obviously, *Non-consumable* and hence it is represented by a rectangle in the figure. More than one *Field* container can be defined in the supply chain, and the ID of the one to be used is specified in the invocation of the *Plant* operation. Our framework, by default, imposes the constraint that only the controller of an asset can perform an operation on such asset (with the exception of the *Sell* one which requires the invoking entity to be the owner, as previously explained). The reason is that the controller is the entity who have the physical availability of the asset. This constraint is automatically embedded in the smart contract representing the asset. Moreover, since the *Plant* operation can be executed only by entities having the role of *Farmer*, this additional constraint is explicitly paired with the *Plant* operation, and in Fig. 4 is represented by the constraint Role(controller) = *Farmer* paired with the *Crop* asset. However, differently from the *Sell* operation, in this case the constraint is imposed on the Controller of the asset, i.e., on the entity who has the physical availability of the asset. Another constraint that is imposed on this operation is that a given ratio between the weight of the seeds and the dimension of the field must be respected. Hence, a constraint taking into account the weight property of the *Seed* asset and the dimension property of the *Field* container is defined by the *SBP* on the *Plant* operation. More than one seed sack could be planted in the same field, generating multiple *Crop* assets included in the same *Field* container. Hence, the constraint will take into account the total weight of all the seed sacks already planted in the field to decide whether the *Plant* operation can be executed. Our framework, when producing the smart contract representing the assets, defines the methods representing the operations and the constraints, and the related invocations. The programmers will then customize such methods by writing the code implementing the required constraint checks. The third operation of the supply chain is *Harvest_crop*, and its features are very similar to the *Plant* operation. The result of the *Harvest_crop* operation applied to each *Crop* asset is a new asset, called *Harvest*. The *Harvest* assets are stored in a *Grain Elevator Non-consumable* container. More than one *Grain Elevator* containers can be defined in the supply chain, and the ID of the one to be used is specified in the invocation of the *Harvest_crop* operation. The next operations are very similar the ones we have already described, hence we will not provide a detailed description.

5   Describing the Tool

The developed tool point to describe the SC, and translate it into smart contracts. The user has only to draw the equivalent model of the supply chain: solid blocks that represent assets, linked particles for the properties of assets; arrows to represents the operations; roles and constraints that enrich each function specified with arrows. The tool translates the components into code suitable for creating smart contracts for a related framework. The smart contract structure is procedurally generated in solidity-like language, starting from blocks, arrows, constraints, and roles.

First set of available functions to the user is the representation of the assets: the three different classifications of an asset -described in the proposed model- are available through the "Asset" button. On this button selection, is possible to choose among the characteristic: uncountable or countable, consumable or non-consumable. Another basic feature is the "Package" draw option. In this case, there are only two options: consumable and non-consumable. Because a package is considered always a countable asset. Once a package object has been placed, any asset object could be dragged into it (or any other package object with its relative content). Another basic set of functions is operations. In this subset it is possible to draw each operation of the model according to each family: move, transform, compose. Also, it is possible to select the "sell" operation, which is

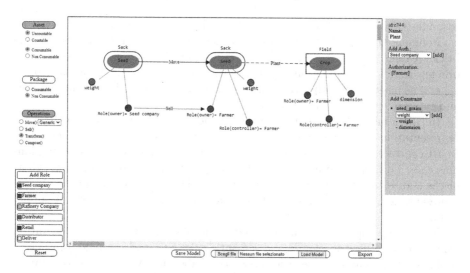

Fig. 6. A screenshot example of the proposed tool.

enabled only between two "owner properties" of the same asset in two different instances. To characterize the various operations of a SC it is possible to assign roles with and impose constraints on access to certain functions at a given time. Through the "roles" panel it is possible to build the set of roles necessary for the specific SC. Role constraints are only one specific constraint that can be defined. Interface prompt to set constraint and any defined property of the assets. Any object drawn in the main panel can be edited. By clicking on one of them, the green editing area will appear which the names and properties of each object can be changed: as already mentioned, selecting an operations it is possible in this area to add constraints an authorizations. Otherwise, in cases of the assets, packages, or properties, the editable options are limited to appearance, nomenclature, and handling properties.

To make the tool more user-friendly and to make the model easily editable over time, two functions allow saving and loading the drawn schema. The function "Save model" saves the drawing and the properties of the SC thus constructed, translated in JSON format. The function "Load model" loads a JSON file on the tool, then automatically redraws the schema. The function "Export" translates the model into smart contract prototypes, which is based on the recently released *solidity* standard. The translator parses the saves file JSON as a starting point. Based on assets, operations, roles, and constraints, it generates a Solidity code.

6 Relevant Related Work

One of the most similar study [7] presents a solution by a tool capable to design solidity code based on predetermined logic blocks: since models are usually easier to understand than software source code. This solution is based on a virtual environment that allows to build a smart contract, giving easily understandable bricks. Unlike this approach, our solution does not include a few pre-set bricks or a few common combinations of solidity code. Our graphical DSL aims to be as general as possible such that the framework can represent multiple combinations and types of supply chains.

In [10], a model based on the Business Process Model and Notation (BPMN) representation is shown. The developed graphical DLS translates blockchain smart contracts using the graphical representation of the DEMO modelling language [4]. This representation makes it easier for the user to represent a workflow or the transaction operations of the same asset. Due to the nature of the BPMN representation, through this is not possible to design various types of supply chains.

This study [3] presents an automatic smart contract template generation framework that uses ontologies and semantic rules to encode specific transaction problems. The template uses the structure of abstract syntax trees to organise the constraints in the generated template in a solidity script. The minimum atom of the constraint is the declaration of the owner and his/her ownership of an object. Similarly to our model, the study describes how the roles and minimum relations (atoms) can build more complex operations.

7   Conclusion and Future Work

Given the various natures of SCs, it is difficult to design a SCMS general enough to be able to represent all possible types of SCs. We present a universal model for SCs ; this model represents every aspect of the most used SC such as production processes or in business management. The model constitutes a graphical DSL for the representation of SCs. Through this model, we analyze and reconstruct a well-known use case: soybean traceability schema. its SC is translated through the presented model, also adding more detail to the original schema. Furthermore, we developed an easy-to-use graphic framework: the proposed tool allows a manager to design the various components of a CS and to specify their relationships and constraints.

As future work we plan to better analyze the proposed model, comparing it with several other general schemes, aiming to underline the differences in use or similarities. Our task is to refine the tool and make the graphical interface easier to handle, especially for inexperienced managers who lack specific knowledge of the model.

Also, we plan to analyze a specific use case such as "DOPUP: Dop Olive oil for a new Presence of Umbria on the Planet", about Umbria's olive supply chain.

As a successive step we plan to translate into other code languages for DLT, such as Chaincode[5].

---

[5] White paper of Chaincode: https://hyperledger-fabric.readthedocs.io/en/release-1.3/chaincode.html.

References

1. Azzi, R., Chamoun, R.K., Sokhn, M.: The power of a blockchain-based supply chain. Comput. Ind. Eng. **135**, 582–592 (2019). https://doi.org/10.1016/j.cie.2019.06.042

2. Brennan, L., Rakhmatullin, R.: Global value chains and smart specialisation strategy: thematic work on the understanding of global value chains and their analysis within the context of smart specialisation. JRC Working Papers JRC98014, Joint Research Centre (Seville site) (2015). https://doi.org/10.2791/44840, https://ideas.repec.org/p/ipt/iptwpa/jrc98014.html

3. Choudhury, O., Rudolph, N., Sylla, I., Fairoza, N., Das, A.: Auto-generation of smart contracts from domain-specific ontologies and semantic rules (2018). https://doi.org/10.1109/Cybermatics_2018.2018.00183

4. Dietz, J.L.: DEMO: towards a discipline of organisation engineering. Eur. J. Oper. Res. **128**(2), 351–363 (2001). https://doi.org/10.1016/S0377-2217(00)00077-1

5. Govindan, K., Soleimani, H., Kannan, D.: Reverse logistics and closed loop supply chain: a comprehensive review to explore the future. Eur. J. Oper. Res. **240**(3), 603–626 (2015). https://doi.org/10.1016/j.ejor.2014.07.012

6. Malik, S., Kanhere, S.S., Jurdak, R.: Productchain: scalable blockchain framework to support provenance in supply chains. In: 17th IEEE International Symposium on Network Computing and Applications, NCA 2018, Cambridge, November 1–3, 2018. pp. 1–10. IEEE (2018). https://doi.org/10.1109/NCA.2018.8548322

7. Mao, D., Wang, F., Wang, Y., Hao, Z.: Visual and user-defined smart contract designing system based on automatic coding. IEEE Access **7**, 73131–73143 (2019). https://doi.org/10.1109/ACCESS.2019.2920776

8. Rutner, S.M., Shepherd, C.D.: Is marketing still part of supply chain management, and should marketing academics and practitioners care? Atlantic Mark. J. **6**(1), 8 (2017)

9. Salah, K., Nizamuddin, N., Jayaraman, R., Omar, M.: Blockchain-based soybean traceability in agricultural supply chain. IEEE Access **7**, 73295–73305 (2019). https://doi.org/10.1109/ACCESS.2019.2918000

10. Skotnica, M., Klicpera, J., Pergl, R.: Towards model-driven smart contract systems–code generation and improving expressivity of smart contract modeling (2020)

11. Solarte-Rivera, J., Vidal-Zemanate, A., Cobos, C., Chamorro-Lopez, J.A., Velasco, T.: Document management system based on a private blockchain for the support of the judicial embargoes process in Colombia. In: Matulevičius, R., Dijkman, R. (eds.) CAiSE 2018. LNBIP, vol. 316, pp. 126–137. Springer, Cham (2018). https://doi.org/10.1007/978-3-319-92898-2_10

12. Stadtler, H., Kilger, C.: Supply Chain Management and Advanced Planning: Concepts, Models, Software, and Case Studies, 4th edn. Springer, Cham (2008). https://doi.org/10.1007/978-3-540-74512-9

13. Tetteh, A., Xu, Q.: Supply chain distribution networks: single-, dual-, & omni-channel. Interdis. J. Res. Bus. **2046**, 7141 (2014)

14. Trautmann, N., Fündeling, C.U.: Supply chain management and advanced planning in the process industries. In: Waldmann, K.H., Stocker, U.M. (eds) Operations Research Proceedings, vol. 2006. Springer, Heidelberg (2006). https://doi.org/10.1007/978-3-540-69995-8_80

15. Wang, T., Lan, Q., Chu, Y.: Supply chain financing model: based on China's agricultural products supply chain. Appl. Mech. Mater. **380–384**, 4417–4421 (2013). https://doi.org/10.4028/www.scientific.net/AMM.380-384.4417

DoS Attacks on Blockchain Ecosystem

Mayank Raikwar$^{(\boxtimes)}$ (ID) and Danilo Gligoroski (ID)

Norwegian University of Science and Technology (NTNU), Trondheim, Norway
{mayank.raikwar,danilog}@ntnu.no

Abstract. Denial of Service (DoS) attacks are a growing threat in network services. The frequency and intensity of DoS attacks are rapidly
increasing day by day. The immense financial potential of the Cryptocurrency market is a prevalent target of the DoS attack. The DoS attack
events are kept on happening in cryptocurrencies and the blockchain
ecosystem. To the best of our knowledge, there has not been any study
on the DoS attack on the blockchain ecosystem. In this paper, we identify ten entities in the blockchain ecosystem and we scrutinize the DoS
attacks on them. We also present the DoS mitigation techniques applicable to the blockchain services. Additionally, we propose a DoS mitigation
technique by the use of verifiable delay function (VDF).

Keywords: Denial-of-service · Verifiable delay function ·
Non-interactive · Blockchain

1 Introduction

Blockchain had brought a paradigm shift in digital innovation and the financial
world since the advent of Bitcoin [26]. Today, the cryptocurrency market consists of 5424 cryptocurrencies that all together built a financial market worth
around \$1.71 trillion (as of 26 May 2021) [9]. The immense financial potential
of the cryptocurrency market has become a growing concern for the targeted
attacks. Some of the well-known attacks in current blockchain systems are selfish
mining, blockchain forks, 51% attack, double spending, Sybil attack, and Denial-
of-service attacks [33]. A Denial-of-service (DoS) attack prevents legitimate user
requests and depletes the server's resources. Due to the various configurations
and decentralized features of blockchain, many of the attacks are preventable.
Nevertheless, DoS attacks, especially its distributed variant (DDoS), are still
prominent attacks on cryptocurrencies and blockchain-based applications.

Due to the increasing intensity and frequency of DoS attacks, it is con-
templated as one of the biggest and severe threats for the Internet industries.
One of the major DoS attacks was mounted on a DNS server in October 2016,
which manifested in a cut of access to major websites, including PayPal, Netflix,
and Twitter, for several hours [46]. The spectrum of DoS attacks can range
from DNS services, cloud providers, IoT devices to the cryptocurrency and
blockchain market. Nowadays, the cryptocurrency market is a popular target of

© Springer Nature Switzerland AG 2022
R. Chaves et al. (Eds.): Euro-Par 2021, LNCS 13098, pp. 230–242, 2022.
https://doi.org/10.1007/978-3-031-06156-1_19

DoS attacks, with the motivation of ransom, stealing funds, or business competition. In the past, many works [12,19,21] regarding the detection and prevention of DoS attacks have been carried out. Moreover, DoS/DDoS solutions based on blockchain are an emerging area of research. Applying the most recent advances of cryptographic research for the DoS/DDoS[1] problem can open new directions and avenues for addressing this ever-present problem.

In the general context of a DoS attack in blockchain, an adversary usually mounts a DoS attack when the cost of mounting an attack is very low. Therefore, various countermeasures, such as increased block size, increased transaction fees, or limiting transaction size have been proposed for mitigating the attacks. However, most of these countermeasures also force legitimate system users to invest their economic or computational power. This behavior shows a dire need to construct new methods for DoS prevention that do not require extra-economic or computational power of blockchain users. In this paper, we study and review DoS attacks on ten different entities in the blockchain ecosystem and possible mitigation techniques. In addition, we propose DoS mitigation by applying the astonishing functionality of verifiable random function (VDF) [8].

1.1 Related Work

Many DoS attacks have been mounted in the blockchain ecosystem and its services in the past few years. Some of these DoS attacks or threats on cryptocurrencies were disclosed a couple of years after they had been discovered. It requires new techniques to detect and counter the attack. Some of those new blockchain-based DoS mitigation techniques are devised from the decentralized nature and the deployed smart contracts of blockchain [30,36]. Even different machine learning techniques have been proposed to fight the DoS attack in cryptocurrency [14].

Specifically for the Bitcoin blockchain (as the blockchain of the most popular and valuable cryptocurrency), several DoS attacks have been mounted [40], which include mining pools, currency exchanges, eWallets, and financial services. Like most high visibility businesses, mining pools and currency exchanges are the primary DoS targets, which drives them to buy DDoS protection services such as Incapsula, CloudFlare, or Amazon Cloud. A report from September 2020 [18] revealed that the Bitcoin software implementation had a vulnerability for an uncontrolled memory consumption that was repeatedly used as a DoS vulnerability until it was patched in June 2018. This DoS vulnerability existed in many other branched Bitcoin implementations, including Litecoin and Namecoin.

Another major cryptocurrency, Ethereum [45] has also suffered from DoS attack [4]. In September 2016, a DoS attack against the Ethereum network was begun by exploiting a flaw in its client node. Furthermore, the same week, another DoS attack was mounted on the processing nodes of Ethereum [44]. A recent disclosure on Ethereum shows that a very cheap DoS attack could have brought down the Ethereum main net due to a bug in Geth Ethereum client [16].

---

[1] Throughout the paper, we use DoS to refer to both DoS and DDoS attacks, unless explicitly mentioned.

Recent work shows an Incentive-based blockchain denial of service attack (BDoS) [25] on Proof-of-work-based blockchains that exploits the reward mechanism to discourage the miner participation. This BDoS could theoretically be able to grind the (Bitcoin's) blockchain to a halt with significantly fewer resources (21% of the network's mining power). This attack raises a concern about the liveness of the Proof-of-work-based cryptocurrencies. This big concern and recent ongoing DoS attack disclosures compel researchers to find new ways to construct efficient DoS mitigation techniques.

1.2 Denial of Service Attack

A denial of service (DoS) attack targets to disrupt the availability of the network, server or application, and prevents legitimate requests from taking place. For a DoS attack to be successful, the attacker has to send more requests than the victim server can handle. These requests can be legitimate or bogus. The DoS attack depletes the server's resources such as CPU, memory, or network.

Definition 1. *(DoS): Let a server S be given, with the available resources $R_1, R_2, \ldots, R_n$ (R_i can be bandwidth, memory, CPU etc.). Let A or a set of $\{A_j\}$ are an attacker or a set of attackers and let the legitimate users are represented by the set $\{U_k\}$. A DoS attack on server S is expressed by a set of probabilities for successful resource-depletion $\{P_{R_1}, P_{R_2}, \ldots, P_{R_n}\}$. The total probability for a success of a DoS attack is then a probability the server S to refuse legitimate transactions from a user u, where $u \in \{U_k\}$ and is modeled as the probability of blocking the legitimate traffic in at least one of the resources:*

$$P_{DoS} = 1 - (1 - P_{R_1})(1 - P_{R_2}).\ldots.(1 - P_{R_n}) \tag{1}$$

Note that the situation when attacker(s) exhausts at least one resource R_i implies the attack probability is $P_{R_i} = 1$, which from Eq. (1) further leads to $P_{DoS} = 1$.

DoS attacks can be categorized into several categories based on network and application layers or volume and protocol attacks. Network-level DoS attacks aim to overload the server's bandwidth or cause CPU usage issues. However, application-level DoS attacks focus on applications, websites, or online services.

1.3 Our Contribution

The contributions of our work are as follows:

1. We thoroughly investigate the DoS attacks in the blockchain ecosystem.
2. We present different mitigation techniques of DoS attacks in the blockchain ecosystem.
3. We propose a VDF-based DoS resistant protocol by using the functionality of VDF.

The rest of the paper is as follows: Sect. 2 shows a detailed analysis of DoS attacks in the blockchain ecosystem. Further, Sect. 3 presents DoS mitigation techniques, including our VDF-based proposal. Finally, in Sect. 4, we conclude the paper and discuss the possible future directions.

2   DoS Attacks on Blockchain Ecosystem

The blockchain ecosystem has suffered from many DoS attacks in the past, and that situation is a continuing trend. The DoS attack can be launched against a specific entity or a network in the blockchain. We present a nonexclusive list of ten entities in the Blockchain ecosystem with their corresponding DoS attacks.

1. *On cryptocurrency wallets* A crypto wallet is a software program in which a user stores cryptocurrency. The wallet contains a set of signing keys for the user to sign new transactions. Wallets are also integrated with decentralized applications (DApps) to hold and manage users' signing keys and transactions securely. In a wallet service, a user is the sole owner of his account keys. However, if someone steals the signing keys, then the cryptocurrency held in that account can be spent. Therefore, hardware wallets (e.g., TREZOR) are ways to store cryptocurrency and the signing key in an offline manner. Nevertheless, online wallets are still a preferable choice for blockchain users. These online crypto wallets also suffer from DoS attacks [28] due to inconsistency in its smart contracts that further hinders the services of integrated DApps. Recently, a DDoS attack was mounted on the Wasabi bitcoin wallet [15].

2. *On cryptocurrency exchange services* A cryptocurrency exchange allows clients to buy, sell and store crypto-currencies at some exchange rate and leverages the clients to trade their currencies and earn some profit due to the fluctuations in the price of currencies. Besides, the exchange charges some fee for every trade made by its client and also converts the cryptocurrency into fiat currencies. Many exchange services also provide a wallet, but the wallet signing keys are controlled by the exchange service apart from the wallet user. Furthermore, these exchange services are online platforms, hence susceptible to DoS attacks that can cause the temporary unavailability of the platform. In the past, many of the crypto-currency exchange services were jeopardized by the DoS attacks (especially DDoS). One such example is the Bitcoin exchange platform, *Bitfinex* which has been a victim of DDoS attacks several times [2]. Another well-known bitcoin exchange service, Mt. Gox, was completely disrupted by DDoS attacks over time [17]. Over the years, many cryptocurrency exchange platforms have suffered DoS attacks. Recently, a UK-based exchange *EXMO* was hit by DDoS attack [10].

3. *On memory (transaction) pools* A memory pool (mempool) is a repository of unconfirmed transactions in a cryptocurrency blockchain, e.g., Bitcoin. Once a user creates a new transaction, it is broadcast to the network and stored in the mempool. In the mempool, the transaction waits to be picked by a miner to be added in a block and subsequently to the blockchain, therefore acquiring the transaction's confirmation. If a transaction remains unconfirmed for a long time in the mempool, it gets rejected eventually. As the transactions with high fees are most likely to be selected by a miner, it poses a threat to flood the mempool by small fee transactions, consequently affecting the mempool size. In that direction, it creates uncertainty among the users for their transactions and leads them to pay higher mining fees

to prevent the rejection of their transactions. The work [34] studies such an attack on Bitcoin mempool and proposes a few countermeasures. However, the proposed solutions have limitations regarding the minimum payable fee and rejection of fast transactions. A follow-up work [32] provides similar prevention measures for Proof-of-work-based blockchain but suffers from the similar problems.

4. *On mining pools* Mining pools are the major players in Proof-of-work-based cryptocurrencies, e.g., Bitcoin. The mining pool's goal is to accumulate miners' power and solve the Proof-of-work puzzles. As the difficulty of Proof-of-work puzzles gives a very low probability of solving the puzzle to a single miner, the miner usually prefers to join a mining pool where the miner gets a fair share of the reward proportional to his/her effort, if the mining pool finds the solution. Two kinds of entities can mount a DDoS attack on a mining pool: 1) A hacker whose aim is to make money by asking the ransom from the attacked mining pool with the promise of stopping the DDoS attack [22], 2) A competing mining pool whose goal is to increase his winning probability by undermining the power of competing mining pools. Few game-theoretic studies [47,48] are also conducted to analyze DoS attacks in mining pools.

5. *On layer-two blockchain protocols* Layer-two blockchain protocols are built on the top of the main blockchain that moves a sufficient amount of transaction load from the main blockchain to the off-chain in sub-seconds (instead of minutes or hours) with a reduced fee and similar security. Hence, these protocols are referred to as an orthogonal solution for the scalability problem in the blockchain. In recent years, there has been tremendous growth in constructing new layer-two protocols [20] for blockchain scalability such as channel networks. In a channel network, channels are established between the parties of the network and governed by the smart contracts of the main chain. It provides a fast and scalable approach for off-chain interactions. These protocols also suffered from DoS attacks in the past [39,42].

6. *On sharding protocols* Similar to layer-2 blockchain solutions, sharding protocols [41] also tackle the scalability issue of blockchain. The idea of sharding is to partition the blockchain state into multiple shards. Each shard processes a set of transactions; therefore, all shards can process the transactions parallelly and hence increases the blockchain throughput. The majority of the sharding protocols are built on the top of the Bitcoin blockchain, and some are built for the Ethereum blockchain. A sharding protocol deals with challenges involving the shard assignment to validators, transaction assignment to shard, and intra-shard consensus. A DoS attack can be mounted on sharding protocol by flooding a single shard which becomes the bottleneck for the whole system. A recent work [27] studies the DoS-attack on sharding protocols and proposes a Trusted Execution Environment (TEE) based countermeasure.

7. *On commit-chain operator* A commit-chain [23] is an off-chain scaling solution where the transactions are performed off-chain by a non-custodial and untrusted operator. The operator commits the balances of users periodically to the blockchain by computing a checkpoint and feeding it to an on-chain

smart contract. The scheme involves users publishing challenges to the smart contract in case of a dispute with the operator, which imposes a drawback where a malicious user can flood the smart contract with unwarranted challenges. Another significant issue is the operator being a central entity can become a victim of a DoS attack, resulting in collapsing the whole system.

8. *On smart contract* A smart contract is a transaction protocol in blockchain that takes actions according to the terms of the contract. In the Ethereum blockchain, each block has a maximum gas limit that is spent by executing a smart contract, and exceeding the gas limit causes a DoS attack. An attacker can mount a DoS attack on smart contract [4] in several possible ways such as: 1) By sending a computationally intensive transaction to a contract thus preventing other transactions from being included in a block; 2) By adding a couple of refund addresses at once that can end up smart contract exceeding the gas limit while refunding to those addresses; 3) By unexpected revert of refund to a legitimate user by using fallback function. A recent work [35] shows a method to detect DoS attacks caused due to unexpected revert in Ethereum smart contract. An example of a DoS attack on a smart contract is an auction contract where an attacker can constantly call the bidding function (e.g., *bid()*), preventing other legitimate users from making their bids. In the NEO blockchain, a vulnerability allowed attackers to invoke a malicious contract that created a DoS attack by crashing each node that tried to execute the contract [37]. Moreover, a DoS attack on a smart contract triggers stopping a node from executing the functions for all the DApps it hosts.

9. *On mixing services* A mixing service is a protocol that allows a cryptocurrency user to utilize its currency anonymously. It provides unlinkability of the user's input to its output and prevents the user's identification from being revealed. There are centralized [6] and decentralized [31] mixing services. Centralized mixing services being a single-point-of-failure are more vulnerable to DoS attacks (e.g. by competing services). However, both types of mixing services suffer from DoS due to different actions of its users, such as 1) By providing inconsistent input for the shuffle, leading the whole verification step of shuffle to fail; 2) By denying to perform some required task e.g., to sign a group transaction; 3) By several participation requests in the mixing transaction pool leading to the depletion of a precomputed pool by participants [49].

10. *On consensus participants* In the blockchain, consensus participants are the major players who decide on the blockchain's new block. Therefore, consensus participants are the usual DoS target for an attacker. In deterministic leader election protocols of consensus, the leader of the consensus round can be a primary target for DoS attacks which can make the whole system halt if the leader suffers a DoS attack. Other main targets can be stakeholders in Proof of Stake consensus mechanisms that hold some stake in the system, therefore attracting an attacker to mount DoS. A DoS attack can be mounted on PBFT-based permissioned blockchains and its participants, where a DDoS attack can be launched if an adversary controls over 33 %

of the replicas. As in the BFT-based blockchains, network size is known to the participants, an attacker creates the required number of Sybil replicas needed for a DoS attack. Hence, for each transaction sent by the primary, the Sybil replicas will not reply to their approvals, leading the whole system to halt.

3   DoS Mitigation Techniques for Blockchain Systems

In most of the DoS events, an attacker floods the network by creating multiple transactions in a short time period, hence maximizing his throughput. This kind of situation arises when the cost of creating a transaction is low. In most settings, these transactions are monetary payment transactions of a tiny value, but for some cases, these can be data transactions (e.g., IoT blockchain transactions). To mitigate the DoS attack, some cost should be imposed on the attacker to slow down or stop unnecessary requests in the blockchain system. Hence, following, we present the DoS mitigation techniques in the blockchain ecosystem.

- *Client Puzzles* Client puzzles are one of the most effective prominent techniques to defend against DoS attacks. In a client puzzle, a client has to solve a puzzle before being granted access to a service or a resource by a server. The initial introduction of the client puzzle was given by Dwork and Naor [13] to combat the spam attacks. Client puzzles can be categorized into different types based on the resource used by the client for solving the puzzle such as number of CPU cycles or a number of memory access, quantifying CPU-bound puzzles [5] and memory-bound puzzles [1] respectively. Several client puzzles such as Time-lock puzzles [29], Hash-chain [24] and Equihash [7] are employed in the blockchain ecosystem. A client puzzle scheme can be *Interactive* where server creates the puzzle for the client or *Non-Interactive* (NI) where the client creates a puzzle, solves the puzzle and sends it to the server.
- *Fee-based Approach* In many events of DoS attack, to disincentivize an attacker an extra or minimum fee can be introduced in the blockchain ecosystem. This fee can be of different types based on the underlying blockchain system. The fee can be a mining fee in mining pools, a mixing fee in mixing services, a transaction fee in transaction pools, a relay fee in a blockchain network, a registration fee for user registration (e.g. a user of a permissioned blockchain), etc. Therefore, with the introduction of a minimum fee, launching a DoS attack becomes costlier for an attacker. However, the fee-based approach adversely affects legitimate users who do not want to pay this minimum amount of fee.

Table 1 presents the possible DoS mitigation solutions for corresponding blockchain ecosystem. Fee-based approach can be applied in almost every case but will not be favorable for all blockchain users. In the table, for layer-2 and sharding protocols, the use of client puzzle will defeat the purpose of scalability due to its time consumption, therefore fee-based approach is a more viable option. For memory pools, mining pools, and mixing services, non-interactive client puzzle schemes can be applied where the miner/user presents a verifiable puzzle and its solution for the inclusion of its new transaction (Rewarding puzzle solution in case of mining pool). Apart from the above described techniques, other mechanisms such as packet filtering techniques or DoS protection services e.g. Incapsula can be used for DoS mitigation in some blockchain contexts.

Table 1. DoS mitigation techniques in blockchain ecosystem

Blockchain ecosystem	Applicable solutions
Cryptocurrency Wallets	Client Puzzle (Inside Smart Contract)
Cryptocurrency Exchange Services	Client Puzzle (On Exchange Clients)
Memory Pools	Fee-based Approach/NI-Client Puzzle
Mining Pools	Fee-based Approach/NI-Client Puzzle
Layer-2 Blockchain Protocols	Fee-based Approach
Sharding Protocols	Fee-based Approach
Commit-chain Operator	Client Puzzle (On Commit-chain Users)
Smart Contract	Client Puzzle (Inside Smart Contract)
Mixing Services	Fee-based Approach/NI-Client Puzzle
Consensus Participants	Client Puzzle (On Participant Registration)

3.1 VDF-Based DoS-Resistant Protocol

Most of the existing client puzzles lack public verifiability, non-parallelizability, non-interactivity, and easy verification. Therefore, the initial introduction of VDF [8] as a moderately hard function can be configured as a client puzzle for DoS mitigation achieving all these properties. A VDF can be described as a function $f : \mathcal{X} \to \mathcal{Y}$ which takes a predefined number of steps T to compute the output $y \in \mathcal{Y}$, given an input $x \in \mathcal{X}$ and a polynomial number of processors. Furthermore, the verification of the output is exponentially easy. VDF produces a unique output that is efficiently and publicly verifiable. There have been a few constructions of VDF. We employ the Wesolowski VDF scheme [43] to construct our client puzzle due to its fast verification and short proof size properties.

We define an Interactive VDF client puzzle, where a server $\mathcal{S}$ creates a puzzle p and asks for solution s of the puzzle from the client $\mathcal{C}$ before giving access to its resource. In the following construction, $\mathcal{K}$ is a key space, $\mathcal{P}$ is a puzzle space, $\mathcal{O}$ is a solution space, $\mathcal{D}$ is a puzzle difficulty space, and $\mathcal{I}$ is a puzzle input space.

- Setup(1^λ): Select $\mathcal{K} = \varnothing, \mathcal{D} \subseteq \mathbb{N}, \mathcal{P} \subseteq \{0,1\}^*, \mathcal{O} \subseteq \{0,1\}^*, \mathcal{I} \subseteq \{0,1\}^*$. Generate a group $\mathbb{G}$ of unknown order, an RSA modulus N, a hash function $H : \{0,1\}^* \to \mathbb{G}$ and $\mathcal{D} \leftarrow T$. Set $param \leftarrow (\mathcal{P}, \mathcal{O}, \mathcal{D}, \mathcal{I})$ and $pp \leftarrow (\mathbb{G}, N, H, T)$, return $(param, pp)$.
- GenPuz(T, i, pp): Server runs this algorithm to create a puzzle for the client. It generates an input $i \in \mathcal{I}$ for VDF-evaluation, samples $l \xleftarrow{\$} Primes(\lambda)$. Return a puzzle $p = l$ to the client.

- FindSol(i, p, pp): Client runs this algorithm to solve the puzzle p. Client computes $g = H(i)$, further computes $y \leftarrow g^{(2^T)} \bmod N$. It computes q, r such that $2^T = ql + r$ where $0 \leq r < l$, and computes a proof $\pi = g^q$. Send a solution $s = (y, \pi)$ to the server.
- VerSol(i, p, s, pp): Server computes $r \leftarrow 2^T \bmod l$ and accepts if $g, y, s \in \mathbb{G}$ and $y = \pi^l g^r \bmod N$.

An Interactive VDF-based DoS-resistant protocol can be designed using client puzzle as depicted in Fig. 1. The protocol construction follows from the Stebila et al. [38]. To define this interactive protocol, we assume server and client have public identities ID_S and ID_C. Our VDF-based client puzzle can also be made Non-Interactive where the client constructs a puzzle and its solution. The client and server share a common source of randomness (e.g. random beacon). The client creates publicly verifiable puzzles using randomness. Further, the non-interactive VDF client puzzle can be transformed into a DoS-resistant protocol that can be efficiently applied in the blockchain ecosystem during DoS events.

Interactive DoS-resistant Protocol

Client $\mathcal{C}$	**Server $\mathcal{S}$**

$SK_C, ID_C, N_C \xleftarrow{\$} \{0,1\}^k$ $\qquad\qquad\qquad$ SK_S, ID_S

$\xrightarrow{\quad (\text{Request} : ID_C, N_C) \quad}$

$N_S \xleftarrow{\$} \{0,1\}^k$
$i \leftarrow (ID_C, ID_S, N_C, N_S)$
$p \leftarrow \mathsf{GenPuz}(T, i, pp),$
$\sigma \leftarrow \mathrm{MAC}_{SK_S}(i, p)$

$\xleftarrow{\quad (\text{Challenge} : N_S, p, \sigma) \quad}$

$i \leftarrow (ID_C, ID_S, N_C, N_S)$
$s \leftarrow \mathsf{FindSol}(i, p, pp)$

$\xrightarrow{\quad (\text{Response} : s, p, i, \sigma) \quad}$

If $ID_C \in \{\text{List of Recorded IDs}\}$,
$\quad$ Reject
If $\sigma \neq \mathrm{MAC}_{SK_S}(i, p)$, Reject
If $\mathsf{VerSol}(i, p, s, pp) = 0$, Reject
Store ID_C

Fig. 1. Interactive DoS-resistant protocol

Following the implementation study of VDF [3], for 128-bit security and the difficulty between 2^{16} to 2^{20}, our DoS-resistant protocol can be efficiently employed for DoS mitigation in the blockchain. With the aforementioned setting, the running time for FindSol, VerSol algorithms are in order of minutes and order of milliseconds respectively. The verification time on the server side can be further optimized using Dimitrov's multiexponentiation method [11]. As a future work, we will put a demonstration of a proof-of-concept and initial experiments with Wesolowski VDF for DoS mitigation.

4 Conclusion

In this work, we offered a thorough study of DoS attacks in the blockchain ecosystem. To the best of our knowledge, this is the first investigation in the context of blockchain. As the frequency and intensity of DoS attacks are increasing rapidly, it raises a concern about efficient detection and mitigation techniques. Therefore, we listed out main mitigation approaches which can be used for DoS mitigation in the blockchain ecosystem. We also identify verifiable delay function as an effective primitive to mitigate DoS attacks. A proper construction of non-interactive VDF puzzle and experimental results will be provided in the continuation of this work. This paper will help academic and industrial researchers to study the possible venues and impact of the DoS attack in the blockchain context and to improve upon the existing solutions.

References

1. Abadi, M., Burrows, M., Manasse, M., Wobber, T.: Moderately hard, memory-bound functions. ACM Trans. Internet Technol. **5**(2), 299–327 (2005)
2. Abhishta, A., Joosten, R., Dragomiretskiy, S., Nieuwenhuis, L.J.M.: Impact of successful DDoS attacks on a major crypto-currency exchange. In: 2019 27th Euromicro International Conference on Parallel, Distributed and Network-Based Processing (PDP), pp. 379–384 (2019)
3. Attias, V., Vigneri, L., Dimitrov, V.: Implementation study of two verifiable delay functions. Cryptol. ePrint Arch. **2020**, 332 (2020)
4. Atzei, N., Bartoletti, M., Cimoli, T.: A survey of attacks on Ethereum smart contracts (SoK). In: Maffei, M., Ryan, M. (eds.) POST 2017. LNCS, vol. 10204, pp. 164–186. Springer, Heidelberg (2017). https://doi.org/10.1007/978-3-662-54455-6_8
5. Back, A., et al.: Hashcash - a denial of service counter-measure (2002). ftp://sunsite.icm.edu.pl/site/replay.old/programs/hashcash/hashcash.pdf
6. Bao, Z., Shi, W., Kumari, S., Kong, Z., Chen, C.-M.: Lockmix: a secure and privacy-preserving mix service for Bitcoin anonymity. Int. J. Inf. Secur. **19**(3), 311–321 (2019). https://doi.org/10.1007/s10207-019-00459-6
7. Biryukov, A., Khovratovich, D.: Equihash: Asymmetric proof-of-work based on the generalized birthday problem. Ledger **2**, 1–30 (2017)
8. Boneh, D., Bonneau, J., Bünz, B., Fisch, B.: Verifiable delay functions. In: Shacham, H., Boldyreva, A. (eds.) CRYPTO 2018. LNCS, vol. 10991, pp. 757–788. Springer, Cham (2018). https://doi.org/10.1007/978-3-319-96884-1_25

9. CoinMarketCap: Total market capitalization, May 2021. https://coinmarketcap. com. Accessed 26 May 2021
10. Crawley, J.: UK crypto exchange EXMO offline amid DDoS attack, Feb 2021. https://tinyurl.com/u8kk94ry. Accessed 08 June 2021
11. Dimitrov, V.S., Jullien, G.A., Miller, W.C.: Complexity and fast algorithms for multiexponentiations. IEEE Trans. Comput. **49**(2), 141–147 (2000)
12. Douligeris, C., Mitrokotsa, A.: DDoS attacks and defense mechanisms: classification and state-of-the-art. Comput. Netw. **44**(5), 643–666 (2004)
13. Dwork, C., Naor, M.: Pricing via processing or combatting junk mail. In: Brickell, E.F. (ed.) CRYPTO 1992. LNCS, vol. 740, pp. 139–147. Springer, Heidelberg (1993). https://doi.org/10.1007/3-540-48071-4_10
14. Sousa, J.E.A., et al.: Fighting under-price DoS attack in ethereum with machine learning techniques. SIGMETRICS Perform. Eval. Rev. **48**(4), 24–27 (2021)
15. Explica.co: Cryptocurrency: Wasabi bitcoin wallet servers suffered DDoS attack, June 2021. https://tinyurl.com/s6sbunam. Accessed 10 June 2021
16. Fadilpasic, S.: Disclosed: Ethereum 'lived' with a major threat for 18 months, May 2021. https://tinyurl.com/h7478aej. Accessed 07 July 2021
17. Feder, A., Gandal, N., Hamrick, J., Moore, T.: The impact of DDoS and other security shocks on Bitcoin currency exchanges: evidence from Mt. Gox. J. Cybersecur. **3**(2), 137–144 (2017)
18. Fuller, B., Khan, J.: CVE-2018-17145: Bitcoin Inventory Out-of-Memory Denial-of-Service Attack (2020). https://invdos.net/paper/CVE-2018-17145.pdf
19. Gasti, P., Tsudik, G., Uzun, E., Zhang, L.: DoS and DDoS in named data networking. In: 2013 22nd International Conference on Computer Communication and Networks (ICCCN), pp. 1–7 (2013)
20. Gudgeon, L., Moreno-Sanchez, P., Roos, S., McCorry, P., Gervais, A.: SoK: layer-two blockchain protocols. In: Bonneau, J., Heninger, N. (eds.) FC 2020. LNCS, vol. 12059, pp. 201–226. Springer, Cham (2020). https://doi.org/10.1007/978-3-030-51280-4_12
21. Gupta, B., Badve, O.P.: Taxonomy of DoS and DDoS attacks and desirable defense mechanism in a cloud computing environment. Neural Comput. Appl. **28**(12), 3655–3682 (2017)
22. Higgins, S.: Bitcoin Mining Pools Targeted in Wave of DDoS Attacks, March 2015. https://tinyurl.com/5jew979z. Accessed 07 July 2021
23. Khalil, R., Zamyatin, A., Felley, G., Moreno-Sanchez, P., Gervais, A.: Commit-chains: secure, scalable off-chain payments. Technical report, Cryptology ePrint Archive, Report 2018/642 (2018)
24. Mahmoody, M., Moran, T., Vadhan, S.: Publicly verifiable proofs of sequential work. In: Proceedings of the 4th Conference on Innovations in Theoretical Computer Science, pp. 373–388 (2013)
25. Mirkin, M., Ji, Y., Pang, J., Klages-Mundt, A., Eyal, I., Juels, A.: BDoS: blockchain Denial-of-Service. In: Proceedings of the 2020 ACM SIGSAC Conference on Computer and Communications Security, CCS 2020, pp. 601–619. ACM, New York (2020)
26. Nakamoto, S.: Bitcoin: a peer-to-peer electronic cash system (2009). http://bitcoin. org/bitcoin.pdf
27. Nguyen, T., Thai, M.T.: Denial-of-service vulnerability of hash-based transaction sharding: attacks and countermeasures. arXiv preprint arXiv:2007.08600 (2020)
28. Praitheeshan, P., Pan, L., Doss, R.: Security evaluation of smart contract-based on-chain ethereum wallets. In: International Conference on Network and System

Security, vol. 12570, pp. 22–41. Springer, Cham (2020). https://doi.org/10.1007/978-3-030-65745-1_2

29. Rivest, R.L., Shamir, A., Wagner, D.A.: Time-Lock Puzzles and Timed-Release Crypto. Massachusetts Institute of Technology, Laboratory for Computer Science (1996)

30. Rodrigues, B., Bocek, T., Stiller, B.: Multi-domain DDoS mitigation based on blockchains. In: Tuncer, D., Koch, R., Badonnel, R., Stiller, B. (eds.) AIMS 2017. LNCS, vol. 10356, pp. 185–190. Springer, Cham (2017). https://doi.org/10.1007/978-3-319-60774-0_19

31. Ruffing, T., Moreno-Sanchez, P., Kate, A.: CoinShuffle: practical decentralized coin mixing for bitcoin. In: Kutyłowski, M., Vaidya, J. (eds.) ESORICS 2014. LNCS, vol. 8713, pp. 345–364. Springer, Cham (2014). https://doi.org/10.1007/978-3-319-11212-1_20

32. Saad, M., Njilla, L., Kamhoua, C., Kim, J., Nyang, D., Mohaisen, A.: Mempool optimization for defending against DDoS attacks in PoW-based blockchain systems. In: 2019 IEEE International Conference on Blockchain and Cryptocurrency (ICBC), pp. 285–292. IEEE (2019)

33. Saad, M., et al.: Exploring the attack surface of blockchain: a systematic overview. arXiv preprint arXiv:1904.03487 (2019)

34. Saad, M., Thai, M.T., Mohaisen, A.: POSTER: deterring DDoS attacks on blockchain-based cryptocurrencies through mempool optimization. In: Proceedings of the 2018 on Asia Conference on Computer and Communications Security, pp. 809–811 (2018)

35. Samreen, N.F., Alalfi, M.H.: SmartScan: an approach to detect denial of service vulnerability in Ethereum smart contracts. preprint arXiv:2105.02852 (2021)

36. Singh, R., Tanwar, S., Sharma, T.P.: Utilization of blockchain for mitigating the distributed denial of service attacks. Secur. Priv. 3(3), e96 (2020). https://doi.org/10.1002/spy2.96

37. Sotnichek, M.: NEO smart contract vulnerabilities: DoS vulnerability, October 2018. https://tinyurl.com/faxjbby5. Accessed 07 July 2021

38. Stebila, D., Kuppusamy, L., Rangasamy, J., Boyd, C., Gonzalez Nieto, J.: Stronger difficulty notions for client puzzles and denial-of-service-resistant protocols. In: Kiayias, A. (ed.) CT-RSA 2011. LNCS, vol. 6558, pp. 284–301. Springer, Heidelberg (2011). https://doi.org/10.1007/978-3-642-19074-2_19

39. Tochner, S., Zohar, A., Schmid, S.: Route Hijacking and DoS in Off-Chain Networks, pp. 228–240. ACM, NY (2020)

40. Vasek, M., Thornton, M., Moore, T.: Empirical analysis of denial-of-service attacks in the Bitcoin ecosystem. In: Böhme, R., Brenner, M., Moore, T., Smith, M. (eds.) FC 2014. LNCS, vol. 8438, pp. 57–71. Springer, Heidelberg (2014). https://doi.org/10.1007/978-3-662-44774-1_5

41. Wang, G., Shi, Z.J., Nixon, M., Han, S.: SoK: sharding on blockchain. In: 1st ACM Conference on Advances in Financial Technologies, pp. 41–61 (2019)

42. Weintraub, B., Nita-Rotaru, C., Roos, S.: Exploiting Centrality: Attacks in Payment Channel Networks with Local Routing (2020)

43. Wesolowski, B.: Efficient verifiable delay functions. In: Ishai, Y., Rijmen, V. (eds.) EUROCRYPT 2019. LNCS, vol. 11478, pp. 379–407. Springer, Cham (2019). https://doi.org/10.1007/978-3-030-17659-4_13

44. Wilcke, J.: The Ethereum network is currently undergoing a DoS attack (2016). https://tinyurl.com/ww6kp2nu. Accessed 07 July 2021

45. Wood, G., et al.: Ethereum: a secure decentralised generalised transaction ledger. Ethereum Project Yellow Paper 151(2014), 1–32 (2014)

46. Woolf, N.: DDoS attack that disrupted internet was largest of its kind in history, experts say. Guardian **26** (2016)

47. Wu, S., Chen, Y., Li, M., Luo, X., Liu, Z., Liu, L.: Survive and thrive: A stochastic game for DDoS attacks in bitcoin mining pools. IEEE/ACM Trans. Netw. **28**(2), 874–887 (2020)

48. Zheng, R., Ying, C., Shao, J., Wei, G., Yan, H., Kong, J., Ren, Y., Zhang, H., Hou, W.: New game-theoretic analysis of DDoS attacks against bitcoin mining pools with defence cost. In: Liu, J.K., Huang, X. (eds.) NSS 2019. LNCS, vol. 11928, pp. 567–580. Springer, Cham (2019). https://doi.org/10.1007/978-3-030-36938-5_35

49. Ziegeldorf, J.H., Matzutt, R., Henze, M., Grossmann, F., Wehrle, K.: Secure and anonymous decentralized Bitcoin mixing. Future Gener. Comput. Syst. **80**, 448–466 (2018)

Towards a Broadcast Time-Lock Based Token Exchange Protocol

Fadi Barbàra[1(✉)], Nadir Murru[2], and Claudio Schifanella[1]

[1] Department of Computer Science, University of Turin, Turin, Italy
{fadi.barbara,claudio.schifanella}@unito.it
[2] Department of Mathematics, University of Trento, Trento, Italy
nadir.murru@unitn.it

Abstract. Many proposals for token exchange mechanisms between multiple parties have centralization points. This prevents a completely trustless and secure exchange between those parties. The main issue lies in the fact that communications in projects using a blockchain are asynchronous: classical result asserts that in an asynchronous system a secure exchange of secrets is impossible, unless there is a trusted third party. In this paper, we propose our preliminary results in the creation of our Broadcast Time-Lock Exchange (BTLE) protocol. The core of BTLE is the introduction of synchronicity in communications through the use of time-lock puzzles. This makes it possible to exchange secrets between two parties while eliminating the need for a trusted third party.

1 Introduction

Since the introduction of Bitcoin, a plethora of blockchain-based digital currencies have being created. These systems are very different in terms of design and purpose. Initially the projects tried to solve some of the problems in Bitcoin [21], such as increasing the number of transactions per second or creating a decentralized consensus method that would use less energy resources. This need has increased over the years, in particular with the rise of DeFi [25]. Because it is unlikely that there will emerge a token capable of solving all problems the different designs encounter, blockchain interoperability (also called *cross-chain communication*) is an important research problem.

The methods of cross chain communication to date can be divided into two macro categories [9]: centralized and decentralized. Centralized methods are methods in which participants send their funds to a central institution (e.g. an online exchange) that takes care of distributing them between the parties at a later date. The advantages of centralized methods are ease of implementation, easy of use and speed. Unfortunately, however, the disadvantages are greater: a central party can steal funds, deny access to funds and in general central parties cannot guarantee the privacy of users.

On the other hand, decentralized exchanges suffer from opposite problems. Although they do not depend on central entities that could jeopardize the safety

© Springer Nature Switzerland AG 2022
R. Chaves et al. (Eds.): Euro-Par 2021, LNCS 13098, pp. 243–254, 2022.
https://doi.org/10.1007/978-3-031-06156-1_20

of the participants, today these exchanges are difficult, slow to implement and require parties to be online for the whole duration of the exchange. An analysis of the different methods for Cross-Chain Communication is made in Zamyatin et al. [29]. As highlighted by the authors, all decentralized exchanges described in the literature involve only two parties. It is therefore assumed that the parties know each other beforehand: how to choose a partner is always left out of the protocol description. This makes it difficult to implement decentralized trades that mirror those of markets where a participant wants to exchange his tokens at an advantageous price, but is not interested in the identity of the partner. Solution for this problems are automatic market makers [28], non custodial exchanges with centralized order-books (also called *continuous* order books) and matching system [8]. Other proposals are decentralized order-books [13], but it's still unclear whether they can handle the liquidity of traditional centralized markets.

The impossibility result of Fair Exchange [2] states that in an asynchronous setting (as it is the one in blockchains) it is impossible to have secure fair exchange without a third party. Instead of relying on central parties or coordinators and to keep the protocol peer-to-peer, we decided to rely on synchronous communications. The idea is not new, and generally decentralized exchanges rely on Hash Time Locked Contracts (HTLCs), i.e. smart contracts that can be opened only by knowing a secret (in the form of an hash pre-image) after a certain time. The invention of these contracts is credited to Tier Nolan who explained its work on Bitcoin Forum [19] and it has been widely studied, for example in [10,16] in the context of atomic swaps. Interestingly, HTLCs are also the base of payment channels such as Lightning Network [24].

From the studies on Lightning Network, we know that one of the problems of HTLCs is that they require that both parties are constantly online for the protocol to be safe [18]. Also with HTLCs it is not possible to have more open channels. Only recently Malavolta et al. [14] have created a way to create multiple channels of exchange of funds from a single node, but these require that the available capital is divided between the various channels. It is not therefore possible to create general proposals of exchange of funds, as when orders are generated in an exchange market, but it is necessary to decide beforehand with whom to communicate/exchange funds.

To solve these problems, we decided to obtain synchronous communication between blockchains in a different way, namely by using time-lock puzzles [23]. Using a time-lock puzzle we can divide the exchange into two phases. In the first phase we use a time-lock puzzle to create an exchange proposal and collect the availability of different participants. In the second phase we make the actual exchange with the winner of the first phase. Here we could use an HTLC, since the parts have been reduced to two, but we decided to use the time-lock puzzle again to leave the possibility for the parts not to be constantly online. This gives the possibility to have a secure exchange even in case of network interruptions. The major contributions of our paper are:

- We present our preliminary results on Broadcast Time-Lock Exchange (BTLE): a new protocol for a broadcast (or multi-party) atomic exchange of token in a cross-chain scenario

– For optimization reasons, we investigated possible alternatives to the famous RSA-based time-lock puzzles [23]. In details, we propose a new time-lock puzzle based on the conic-based cryptosystem presented in [5], which can be of independent interest.

The structure of the paper is the following: in Sect. 2 we present the relevant literature on time release cryptography and cross chain communication, then in Sect. 3 we present briefly the classic RSA-based time-lock puzzle of Rivest et al. [23]. We use that to present the details of the inner working of our new conic-based RSA-like time-lock puzzle. On Sect. 4 we present BTLE. Finally in Sect. 5 we conclude.

2   Related Works

We use time-lock puzzles in a cross-chain communication protocol. For this reason it is useful to analyze the literature in two separate way. The first subsection analyzes the proposed time-related cryptosystems, while the second analyzes different cross-chain protocols.

2.1   Time Release Cryptography

On this topic there is a detailed survey by Jaques et al. [11]. In this sub-section we present only the fundamental results related to the BTLE protocol.

Timed primitives came up in several contexts. We can distinguish between a pre-blokchain phase and a post-blockchain phase. The first generation, pre-blockchain, includes "time capsules" for key escrowing as in Bellare et al. [4], time-based cryptographic secrets as Rivest et al. in [23] and contract signing as in Boneh et al. [7]. Of those, only the last two protocols are secure against parallel processing, i.e. they use what has been defined as *inherently secure* function [6].

After the introduction of Bitcoin [17], time based cryptography had a new wave of research. In particular, the post-blockchain study of time-based cryptographic protocols is focused on *verifiable delay functions* (VDF) and *time-lock puzzles* (TLP). The difference is that VDFs are time-lock puzzles whose solution is publicly verifiable without the need to solve the puzzle [6].

The majority of the newer studies have focused on VDFs. Some of them proposed new protocols, such as [15], while others extended the TLP in [23] making it a VDF. The works of the latter type are that of Wesolowski [26] and that of Pietrzak [20]. These works are compared in [6]. Interestingly, the new wave of research on time based cryptography has generally left aside the traditional time-lock puzzles. Still, because we do not need any outside verification of the result (our setting has an implicit verification: if the solution is right, then the user can retrieve the funds, otherwise it can not), we use the more heavily studied construct of time-lock puzzle.

2.2   Cross Chain Communication

In this paper, we focus on decentralized cross-chain exchanges, because centralized exchange are out of scope.

The first report on the interoperability issue is that of Buterin [9], in which describes the main methods of interoperability at the time. In many cases the realization of an interoperable system was leveraged to create a system that increased the scalability in terms of transactions of the blockchain in question. In fact, interoperability gave the possibility of rebalancing the loads between two blockchain and then divide the work between the two. In this sense we talk about sidechains, introduced for the first time in [3]. Several projects were born that aim to create "a blockchain of blockchains", such as Cosmos [12], Polkadot [27] and Plasma [22]. In both projects, the idea is to create a hierarchy of blockchains and each exchange of funds is approved through the blockchain at the head of all others. In these projects the exchange is neither atomic nor peer-to-peer.

To date, the peer-to-peer exchange methods are all based on the concept of Hash Time Lock Contract (HTLC), whose inventor is considered Nolan [19] and are analyzed for example by Herlihy [10] and by Miraz and Donald [16]. An HTLC is a contract that use hash-based and time-based locks to lock and unlock funds. Participants in this kind of contract have to manually redeem funds by generating cryptographic proof of payment before a certain date in order proceed with the protocol. This requires parties to stay online, which is difficult for power constrained devices of in places where continuos internet connectivity can't be assumed.

This type of contract is not implementable on any blockchain because it needs a scriptable blockchain and requires that different blockchain have the same hash function. These are not common requirements: for example the blockchain protocol in Monero does not have the concept of smart contract and can not implement HTLC, and it wouldn't be possible to make a HTLC between Tezos (which uses the Blake2b function as its principal hash function) and Bitcoin (which uses the SHA256 function to make hashing).

For a more detailed analysis see e.g. the work of Zamyatin et al. [29].

3   Two Time-Lock Puzzles

In this section we do a brief digression on how to measure time in a time-lock puzzle and then we present both the classic time-lock puzzle presented by Rivest et al. which we call it RSW-TL, and we present the new time-lock puzzle based on the RSA-like system in [5], which we call it BM-TL. Both systems use functions that are believed to be sequential, meaning they are not parallelizable. Therefore, given a particular type of CPU, there is no advantage in having more of them: all computations are necessarily done on only one core of the CPU. These time-lock puzzle can be classified as a CPU-bound puzzle with a timing function and an implicit verification [1].

On Time. Since computation is sequential, it's possible to predict the time to solve the puzzle. Given T the time such that A wants to keep B busy, and S the number of squaring per unit of time (either done by the RSW-TL method or the BM-TL method, see below), then $t = TS$ is the number of squaring needed. Obviously S depends mainly on the processor used. As of now, we are doing the necessary tests to see which of the two proposed methods is the best for the BTLE protocol, i.e. has the least variation based on the CPU.

RSA-TL. In [23], the authors proposed a simple yet effective time-lock puzzle exploiting repeated squares. A time-lock puzzle is used to encrypt a secret sk (which could be, e.g., the key of a symmetric cryptosystem) so that it could be decrypted only after a fixed amount of time T.

In particular, said A the entity that creates the time-lock puzzle, A encrypts sk as

$$c \equiv sk + a^{2^t} \pmod{n}$$

where $n = pq$, with p and q prime numbers, $0 < a < n$ a random number and t a positive number computed as before. The value of c can be efficiently computed if p and q are known. Indeed, in this case, one can compute $e \equiv 2^t \pmod{\varphi(n)}$ and then $a^e \pmod{n}$ exploiting Euler's totient theorem. The entity A sends (n, a, t, c) to the entity B that has to recover sk.

The entity B can not perform $a^e \pmod{n}$ efficiently because it doesn't know p and q, nor can it derive them from n. In fact, multiplication of "big" primes is the same trapdoor function used by the RSA cryptosystem. Therefore it has to perform t squarings, since the computation of a^{2^t} is believed not to be parallelizable.

BM-TL. The idea of Rivest et al. for creating time-lock puzzles can be easily adapted using different products for performing the powers. In [5], the authors developed an RSA–like cryptosystem based on a particular parametrization of the Pell conic. We recall here some details. The Pell conic is defined as

$$\mathcal{H} = \{(x, y) \in \mathbb{F} \times \mathbb{F} : x^2 - Dy^2 = 1\},$$

where $\mathbb{F}$ is a field and D square-free, meaning that there is no square in its prime decomposition. It is well known that $(\mathcal{H}, \otimes)$ is a group, where $\otimes$ is the Brahmagupta product defined by

$$(x_1, y_1) \otimes (x_2, y_2) = (x_1 x_2 + y_1 y_2 D, x_1 y_2 + x_2 y_1).$$

A set of parameters can be found using the line $y = \frac{1}{m}(x + 1)$, yielding to the group $(P, \odot)$ isomorphic to $(\mathcal{H}, \otimes)$, where

$$P = \mathbb{F} \cup \{\alpha\}, \quad a \odot b = \begin{cases} \frac{ab+D}{a+b}, & \text{if } a + b \neq 0 \\ \alpha, & \text{if } a + b = 0 \end{cases}$$

with $\alpha \notin \mathbb{F}$ the point at infinity. When $\mathbb{F} = \mathbb{Z}_p$, p prime, we have that

$$a^{\odot p+1} \equiv 1 \pmod{p}$$

for every $a \in P$, where the powers are evaluated with respect to the product $\odot$. The Pell conic $\mathcal{H}$ and the set of parameters P can be also constructed over rings and considering $P = \mathbb{Z}_n \cup \alpha$, with $n = pq$, p and q primes, we have an analogue of the Euler's totient theorem:

$$a^{\odot \Psi(n)} \equiv 1 \pmod{n}, \quad \forall a \in \mathbb{Z}_n^*,$$

where $\Psi(n) = (p+1)(q+1)$. Finally, we recall that the powers $z^{\odot n}$ can be evaluated by means of the Rédei rational functions:

$$z^{\odot n} = Q_n(D, z)$$

where $Q_n(D, z)$ is the n–th Rédei rational function defined by

$$Q_n(D, z) = \frac{A_n(D, z)}{B_n(D, z)}, \quad (z + \sqrt{D})^n = A_n(D, z) + B_n(D, z)\sqrt{D}$$

and the polynomials $A_n(D, z)$, $B_n(D, z)$ can be evaluated by

$$\begin{pmatrix} z & D \\ 1 & z \end{pmatrix} \begin{pmatrix} 1 \\ 0 \end{pmatrix} = \begin{pmatrix} A_n(D, z) \\ B_n(D, z) \end{pmatrix}.$$

For proofs and further details, see [5].

Thus, we can construct a time-lock puzzle following the idea of Rivest et al. [23], but exploiting the product $\odot$. In this case, the secret sk is encrypted by

$$c \equiv sk + a^{\odot 2^t} \pmod{n}.$$

Knowing the factorization of n, one can efficiently compute $a^{\odot 2^t}$ evaluating first $e \equiv 2^t \pmod{\Psi(n)}$ and then $a^e \pmod{n}$. Without knowing the factorization of n, one must perform t squarings with respect to the product $\odot$.

4   The Broadcast Time-Lock Exchange Protocol

We now explain how it is possible to use time-lock puzzles to create an alternative to order books and AMMs in decentralized token exchanges. We assume a decentralized platform where participants want to exchange tokens. We assume each participant has a client which follows the defined blockchain protocol. Because the setting is decentralized, it makes no sense speaking of synchronization between these clients. For this reason each participant has its own *view* of the current state of the decentralized market. Without loss of generality, we can say that the participant that initiates the process is selling its token in exchange of (or *to buy*) the other.

The Broadcast Time-Lock Exchange (BTLE) protocol needs two classes of participants. The first class is the *initiator*: this kind of participant is the one who initiates the exchange by proposing the deal, i.e. the selling of its token. Using the terminology of traditional centralized markets, this participant corresponds to a *market taker*. The other class of participants is that of *exchangers*: these participants are possible buyers interested in an equivalent deal but who do not want to start it. The analogue in traditional markets is that of *market makers*.

In this protocol there is a single initiator which we call Alice for simplicity and which we denote by A, and many possible exchangers. Since the exchangers represent Alice's partner, following the cryptography tradition we will call them all "Bobs". Moreover, supposing that they are indexed and that they are in finite number d, we will say that the potential exchangers are $\{B_1, B_2, \ldots, B_d\}$. Recall that we are in a decentralized environment and therefore there cannot be a temporal-based ordering of possible buyers: asynchronous systems imply the absence of a shared clocks.

Furthermore, we suppose the set $\{B_1, B_2, \ldots, B_d\}$ is completely determined by the view of A: since we are in an asynchronous environment, it is possible that Alice's view of potential buyers is not synchronized. This means that in some other nodes there are other potential exchangers or that some have withdrawn. In the protocol description we will see why neither of these two cases is a problem. Finally we assume that there are d secure channels of communication between A and each one of $\{B_1, B_2, \ldots, B_d\}$. Finally, we assume $\{B_1, B_2, \ldots, B_d\}$ compete at the same price level, as in traditional order books.

The BTLE protocol is divided into two rounds. In the first round Alice (the initiator) chooses from among the potential exchangers the one with whom the real token exchange will take place. In the second round the actual exchange takes place. In both stages a time-lock puzzle is used.

4.1   Choosing an Exchanger

In this round Alice has to choose the exchanger among $\{B_1, B_2, \ldots, B_d\} \leftarrow GetExchangersList()$. It will follow the routine explained in Fig. 1. In this subsection and in the following one we treat the time-lock puzzle TLP as a blackbox which takes two inputs and then outputs a cryptographic puzzle. The solution of the puzzle is the cleartext itself: that's why we chose time lock puzzles with implicit verification. Also, we see the modularity of BTLE that can support multiple types of time-lock puzzles, either from those presented in Sect. 3 or even different ones.

As seen in the Fig. 1, A generates a random message for each participant in $\{B_1, B_2, \ldots, B_d\}$ and associates this message to the intended receiver. The inputs of the time-lock puzzle are the message and a time in seconds. The output is a tuple that represent the cryptographic puzzle (See Sect. 3). A performs this subroutine for all $B_i, i = 1, \ldots, d$. Then it sends all the puzzles and waits for a solution. When A receives the first solution (i.e. the cleartext of the random message) from some B_j, it checks that is a valid message, i.e. the cleartext is equal to the message associated with B_j. If that is the case, A accepts the solution and B_j is the winner: A will proceed to communicate only with B_j and discards all other solutions. If the message isn't valid, A waits for another solution.

Note that in a time-lock puzzle $TB_i = TLP(rand_i, time)$, the random message is different for each B_i, but *time* is equal for all participants: all potential exchangers must have the same chance of being able to find the solution at the

---

Algorithm 1. Round 1: Choosing the Exchanger

1: $\{B_1, B_2, \ldots, B_d\} \leftarrow GetExchangersList()$
2: **for** $i = 1, \ldots, d$ **do**
3:     A generates $rand_i$
4:     $\{$map $rand_i \rightarrow B_i\}$
5:     A computes the time-lock puzzle $TB_i = TLP(rand_i, time)$ of B_i
6: **end for**
7: **for** $i = 1, \ldots, d$ **do**
8:     A sends TB_i to B_i
9: **end for**
10: accepted_solution=0
11: **while** accepted_solution==0 **do**
12:     wait_for_solution
13:     **if** verify_solution(sol)==1 **then**
14:         accepted_solution=1
15:         winner_sol=sol
16:     **end if**
17: **end while**
18: return map(sol)

---

same time. The randomness of the winner is determined by unpredictable factors such as network latency or puzzle real solving time.

From this we can see the equivalence with order books where the order is based on the order execution time: since there cannot be a shared clock due to the asynchronicity of the system, A bases its "order book" on the puzzle resolution time.

4.2   The Token Exchange

We call Bob the winner of the previous round and we denote him as B. From now on, Alice will only interact with Bob and will discard all other potential exchangers.

The goal of this second round is to obtain a token exchange protocol that is atomic. In particular, if A has 1 coin1, and B has 1 coin2[1] then there can be only two succesful ending of the protocol: either$A$ has 1 coin2 B has 1 coin1 or A has 1 coin1 B has 1 coin2.

Given the uncertainty of the real execution time to find a solution for a time-lock puzzle (the uncertainty is in the order of tens of seconds) it is not possible to carry out a simple exchange of keys between the parties. A few seconds are enough to issue two transactions, so the participant who first solves the assigned time-lock puzzle is able to take both the token associated with the solution and his token. Therefore the protocol would not be provably atomic. In the following we describe a method that allows to overcome this problem.

---

[1] The real exchange rates between the two tokens and how they are decided are beyond the scope of this paper.

Recall that given two secret keys sk_1 and sk_2, an elliptic curve generator g and the relative public key pk_1 and pk_2, then the key sum is homomorphic:

$$(sk_1 + sk_2)g = pk_1 + pk_2 = (sk_1 g) + (sk_2 g) \tag{1}$$

The Swap The actual exchange of tokens `coin1` and `coin2` is explained in Fig. 1, with notation in Table 1. A and B create the key pairs (sk_2^A, pk_2^A and sk_1^B, pk_1^B respectively) that represent the first of the two shares to redeem the exchanged funds. After this step, A and B exchange the public keys pk_2^A and pk_1^B. If this first part is successful, both A and B create ephemeral keys (sk_1^A, pk_1^A and sk_2^B, pk_2^B respectively) that represent the second of the two shares to redeem the exchanged funds. At this point A and B can create new public keys (called PK_1^B and PK_2^A respectively) to which they can send the funds. Because of the way the keys and consequently the addresses are built, neither of the two participants can redeem the funds in either blockchains at this point of the exchange. For example, A needs to know sk_2^B in order to redeem coins in the address for PK_2^A. For this reason in the second part of the exchange A and B exchange the time-lock puzzles TLP_A and TLP_B. Once the time-lock puzzles are opened/solved, A gets sk_2^B and B gets sk_1^A. Using λ as time unit, we see that the second time-lock puzzle is sent later with a smaller opening time (1/4 of the time unit). This is to make the two participants A and B open the puzzle at about the same time.

Table 1. Notation used in the explanation of the token exchange protocol

BC_1, BC_2	Blockchain 1 and 2 with tokens `coin1` and `coin2`
G_1, G_2	the base point for the elliptic curve of BC_1 and BC_2
l_1, l_2	the base point order for the elliptic curve of BC_1 and BC_2
PK_1^A	public key for the address on blockchain BC_1 where A has the coins
PK_1^B	public key for the address on blockchain BC_2 where B has the coins
PK_2^A	public key for the address on blockchain BC_1 where A has the coins
PK_2^B	public key for the address on blockchain BC_2 where B has the coins
$sk_{1,2}^A, pk_{1,2}^A$	shares created by A for blockchian $BC_{1,2}$
$sk_{1,2}^B, pk_{1,2}^B$	shares created by B for blockchian $BC_{1,2}$

4.3   Analysis of the BTLE Protocol

As in the HTLC case, BTLE is also atomic in the sense that either both participants get tokens from the other blockchain, or both participants can retrieve their tokens. This is possible if we assume that all participants are rational and thus incentivized to respect different timeouts, as in the case of HTLC. The only step where there is a possibility of stealing the secret and breaking the atomicity, is the one where participant A has the time-lock puzzle of participant B, but A has not yet sent his time-lock puzzle. In this case A could start working on the received time-lock puzzle and discover the secret without sending his

Alice (coin1→coin2)	Bob (coin2→coin1)
$sk_2^A \xleftarrow{\$} [1, l_2 - 1], pk_2^A = sk_2^A G_2$	$sk_1^B \xleftarrow{\$} [1, l_1 - 1], pk_1^B = sk_2^B G_1$

$$\xrightarrow{\ pk_1^A\ }$$
$$\xleftarrow{\ pk_1^B\ }$$

$sk_1^A \xleftarrow{\$} [1, l_1 - 1], pk_1^A = sk_1^A G_1$	$sk_2^B \xleftarrow{\$} [1, l_2 - 1], pk_2^B = sk_1^B G_2$
$PK_1^B = pk_1^A + pk_1^B$	$PK_2^A = pk_2^A + pk_2^B$
$hash_{A \to B} \leftarrow \text{SendTx}(PK_1^A \to PK_1^B)$	$hash_{B \to A} \leftarrow \text{SendTx}(PK_2^B \to PK_2^A)$
$T_1 \leftarrow TLP_A(sk_1^A, \frac{3}{4}\lambda)$	$T_2 \leftarrow TLP_B(sk_2^B, \lambda)$

$$\xleftarrow{\ (T_2, hash_{B \to A})\ }$$
$$\xrightarrow{\ (T_1, hash_{A \to B})\ }$$

| open TLP_B and redeem coin2 | open TLP_A and redeem coin1 |

Fig. 1. Protocol execution between Alice and Bob for a successful swap

own time-lock puzzle. This case, however, is covered by the protocol: B waits a limited amount of time (a quarter of the expected time to solve the time-lock puzzle) and in case it does not receive A's puzzle, he would proceed to recover his tokens assuming A is dishonest. The only requirement is that the time lambda be longer than the time for creating new blocks in the blockchains between which the exchange takes place: that to prevent participant A from solving the received time-lock puzzle and sending the solution to take the money before the block is created, preventing B from acting safely, i.e. sending a transaction to retrieve its token. In this case both the transaction of A and the one of B would appear in the mempool of the miners/validators and it is not possible to know in advance which of the two transactions will end up in the block (invalidating the atomicity of the system). By choosing a suitable lambda the problem does not arise and it is not possible for A to steal the tokens.

Another advantage of BTLE over traditional cross-chain swaps is that it does not require the use of hash functions. This is because the BTLE uses techniques at a lower level than other atomic swap methods. In fact, we use the fact that the sum between points in elliptic curves is homomorphic, so BTLE is not affected by the internal mechanics of a blockchain protocol. This means that our protocol can also be used on blockchains that do not use the same hash function.

Using only elliptic curve theory, BTLE can also be used on blockchains that do not have a scripting language, such as Monero and all blockchains that are derived from CryptoNote. This additional advantage gives the possibility to implement BTLE in all those cases for which to date there are no exchange methods.

Finally, since there is little communication between participants, it is not necessary for all parties to be constantly online, unlike other methods. In fact, they can stay offline for the duration of solving a time-lock puzzle without this creating security problems within the protocol.

5   Conclusions and Future Works

We presented in this paper the preliminary results of BTLE, a P2P and broadcast exchange protocol that creates an alternative to order-books and AMMs in a decentralized context. Unlike the other methods, it does not require the parties to be constantly online to finalize the exchange, thanks to the use of time-lock puzzles. We also proposed a new time-lock puzzle that is an alternative to the classical time-lock puzzle of Rivest et al.

At this moment, we are better investigating the two types of proposed time-lock puzzles with the goal of understanding which method is more suitable for short duration puzzles (in the order of seconds). We are also working on the implementation of the BTLE protocol to demonstrate its applicability on different blockchain technologies, like Bitcoin, Monero, Ethereum.

References

1. Ali, I.M., Caprolu, M., Di Pietro, R.: Foundations, properties, and security applications of puzzles: a survey. arXiv:1904.10164 [cs], April 2020
2. Asokan, N., Shoup, V., Waidner, M.: Asynchronous protocols for optimistic fair exchange. In: Proceedings of Security and Privacy-1998 IEEE Symposium on Security and Privacy, Oakland, CA, USA, 3–6 May 1998, pp. 86–99. IEEE Computer Society (1998). https://doi.org/10.1109/SECPRI.1998.674826
3. Back, A., et al.: Enabling blockchain innovations with pegged sidechains. Whitepaper, p. 25 (2014)
4. Bellare, M., Goldwasser, S.: Encapsulated key escrow. Technical report, Massachusetts Institute of Technology (1996)
5. Bellini, E., Murru, N.: An efficient and secure RSA-like cryptosystem exploiting Rédei rational functions over conics. Finite Fields Appl. **39**, 179–194 (2016). https://doi.org/10.1016/j.ffa.2016.01.011
6. Boneh, D., Bonneau, J., Bünz, B., Fisch, B.: Verifiable delay functions. In: Shacham, H., Boldyreva, A. (eds.) CRYPTO 2018. LNCS, vol. 10991, pp. 757–788. Springer, Cham (2018). https://doi.org/10.1007/978-3-319-96884-1_25
7. Boneh, D., Naor, M.: Timed commitments. In: Bellare, M. (ed.) CRYPTO 2000. LNCS, vol. 1880, pp. 236–254. Springer, Heidelberg (2000). https://doi.org/10.1007/3-540-44598-6_15
8. Borkowski, M., McDonald, D., Ritzer, C., Schulte, S.: Towards atomic cross-chain token transfers: state of the art and open questions within tast. Distributed Systems Group TU Wien (Technische Universit at Wien), report (2018)
9. Buterin, V.: Chain interoperability. R3 Research Paper (2016)
10. Herlihy, M.: Atomic cross-chain swaps. In: Proceedings of the 2018 ACM Symposium on Principles of Distributed Computing, pp. 245–254. ACM, Egham United Kingdom, July 2018. https://doi.org/10.1145/3212734.3212736
11. Jaques, S., Montgomery, H., Roy, A.: Time-release cryptography from minimal circuit assumptions. Technical report, 755 (2020)
12. Kwon, J., Buchman, E.: Cosmos whitepaper. https://cosmos.network/cosmos-whitepaper.pdf
13. m52go: Bisq whitepaper (2021). https://github.com/bisq-network/bisq-docs/blob/c3dc52fa62aa2bdfb5162cb6d7b147dcdc916055/exchange/whitepaper.adoc, original-date: 2017–09-06T18:19:27Z

14. Malavolta, G., Moreno-Sanchez, P., Schneidewind, C., Kate, A., Maffei, M.: Anonymous multi-hop locks for blockchain scalability and interoperability. In: 26th Annual Network and Distributed System Security Symposium, NDSS 2019, San Diego, California, USA, 24–27 February 2019. The Internet Society (2019). https://www.ndss-symposium.org/ndss-paper/anonymous-multi-hop-locks-for-blockchain-scalability-and-interoperability/

15. Malavolta, G., Thyagarajan, S.A.K.: Homomorphic time-lock puzzles and applications. In: Boldyreva, A., Micciancio, D. (eds.) CRYPTO 2019. LNCS, vol. 11692, pp. 620–649. Springer, Cham (2019). https://doi.org/10.1007/978-3-030-26948-7_22

16. Miraz, M.H., Donald, D.C.: Atomic cross-chain swaps: development, trajectory and potential of non-monetary digital token swap facilities. Ann. Emerg. Technol. Comput. **3**(1), 42–50 (2019). https://doi.org/10.33166/AETiC.2019.01.005

17. Nakamoto, S.: Bitcoin: a peer-to-peer electronic cash system. Whitepaper, p. 9 (2008)

18. Nisslmueller, U., Foerster, K.T., Schmid, S., Decker, C.: Toward active and passive confidentiality attacks on cryptocurrency off-chain networks [cs], February 2020. arXiv:2003.00003

19. Nolan, T.: Alt chains and atomic transfers. https://bitcointalk.org/index.php?topic=193281.msg2224949#msg2224949

20. Pietrzak, K.: Simple verifiable delay functions. In: 10th Innovations in Theoretical Computer Science Conference (ITCS 2019). Schloss Dagstuhl-Leibniz-Zentrum fuer Informatik (2018)

21. Poelstra, A.: On stake and consensus. Technical report, March 2015

22. Poon, J.: Plasma: scalable autonomous smart contracts (2017)

23. Rivest, R.L., Shamir, A., Wagner, D.A.: Time-lock puzzles and timed-release Crypto. Technical report (1996)

24. Rusty, R.: lightningnetwork/lightning-rfc September 2019. https://github.com/lightningnetwork/lightning-rfc/blob/3508e4e85d26240ae7492c3d2e02770cdc360fe9/02-peer-protocol.md, original-date: 2016–11-14T19:21:45Z

25. Werner, S.M., Perez, D., Gudgeon, L., Klages-Mundt, A., Harz, D., Knottenbelt, W.J.: SoK: decentralized finance (DEFI). CoRR abs/2101.08778 (2021). https://arxiv.org/abs/2101.08778

26. Wesolowski, B.: Efficient verifiable delay functions. J. Cryptol. **33**(4), 2113–2147 (2020). https://doi.org/10.1007/s00145-020-09364-x

27. Wood, D.G.: Polkadot: vision for a heterogeneous multi-chain framework. Whitepaper (2016)

28. Xu, J., Vavryk, N., Paruch, K., Cousaert, S., et al.: Sok: Automated market maker (AMM) based decentralized exchanges (DEXs). Technical report (2021)

29. Zamyatin, A., et al.: SoK: communication across distributed ledgers. ePrint IACR, p. 17 (2018)

Merging Real Images with Physics Simulations via Data Assimilation

Rossella Arcucci[1,2(✉)] , César Quilodrán Casas[2], Aniket Joshi[1],
Asiri Obeysekara[1], Laetitia Mottet[1], Yi-Ke Guo[2], and Christopher Pain[1]

[1] Department of Earth Science and Engineering,
Imperial College London, London, UK
r.arcucci@imperial.ac.uk
[2] Data Science Institute, Department of Computing,
Imperial College London, London, UK

Abstract. This work has started from the necessity of improving the accuracy of numerical simulations of COVID-19 transmission. Coughing is one of the most effective ways to transmit SARS-CoV-2, the strain of coronavirus that causes COVID-19. Cough is a spontaneous reflex that helps to protect the lungs and airways from unwanted irritants and pathogens and it involves droplet expulsion at speeds close to 50 miles/h. Unfortunately, it's also one of the most efficient ways to spread diseases, especially respiratory viruses that need host cells in which to reproduce. Computational Fluid Dynamics (CFD) are a powerful way to simulate droplets expelled by mouth and nose when people are coughing and/or sneezing. As with all numerical models, the models for coughing and sneezing introduce uncertainty through the selection of scales and parameters. Considering these uncertainties is essential for the acceptance of any numerical simulation. Numerical forecasting models often use Data Assimilation (DA) methods for uncertainty quantification in the medium to long-term analysis. DA is the approximation of the true state of some physical system at a given time by combining time-distributed observations with a dynamic model in an optimal way. DA incorporates observational data into a prediction model to improve numerically forecast results. In this paper, we develop a Variational Data Assimilation model to assimilate direct observation of the physical mechanisms of droplet formation at the exit of the mouth during coughing. Specifically, we use high-speed imaging, from prior research work, which directly examines the fluid fragmentation at the exit of the mouths of healthy subjects in a sneezing condition. We show the impact of the proposed approach in terms of accuracy with respect to CFD simulations.

Keywords: Data assimilation · CFD simulations · Coughing and sneezing simulations · Covid-19 diffusion

1 Introduction

Studies about the transmission of respiratory illnesses like influenza say that infections typically happen when a healthy person comes into contact with

© Springer Nature Switzerland AG 2022
R. Chaves et al. (Eds.): Euro-Par 2021, LNCS 13098, pp. 255–266, 2022.
https://doi.org/10.1007/978-3-031-06156-1_21

respiratory droplets from an infected person's cough, sneeze or breath [8]. Coughing is one of the most effective ways to transmit SARS-CoV-2, the strain of coronavirus that causes COVID-19. Cough is a spontaneous reflex that helps to protect the lungs and airway from unwanted irritants and pathogens, droplets are expelled at speeds close to 50 miles per hour. Unfortunately, it's also one of the most efficient ways to spread diseases, especially for respiratory viruses that need host cells in which to reproduce.

Computational Fluid Dynamics (CFD) is a powerful way to simulate droplets expelled by mouth and nose when people are coughing or sneezing. As for all numerical models, the CFD models for coughing and sneezing introduce uncertainty through the selection of scales and parameters. Taking into account these uncertainties is essential for the acceptance of any numerical simulation. Numerical forecasting models often use Data Assimilation (DA) methods for the uncertainty quantification in the medium to long-term analysis. DA is the approximation of the true state of some physical system at a given time by combining time-distributed observations with a dynamic model in an optimal way. DA incorporates observational data into a prediction model to improve numerically forecasted results. It allows for problems with uneven spatial and temporal data distribution and redundancy to be addressed such that models can incorporate information efficiently. DA tries to answer questions such as "what can be said about the value of an unknown variable x that represents the evolution of a system, if we have some measured data y and a model M of the underlying mechanism that generated the data?". This is the Bayesian context, where we seek a quantification of the uncertainty in our knowledge of the parameters that, according to Bayes' rule takes the form

$$p(x|y) = \frac{p(y|x)\,p(x)}{p(y)} \tag{1.1}$$

Here, the physical model is represented by the conditional probability (also known as the likelihood) $p(y|x)$, and the prior knowledge of the system by the term $p(x)$. The denominator is considered as a normalising factor and represents the total probability of y. There are many DA methods derived from this formulation [9, 10] which have been mostly custom-developed on the forecasting model with which they are combined. Those which have gained acceptance as powerful methods in the last ten years are the Variational DA (VarDA) approaches [1] based on the minimisation of a function which estimates the discrepancy between numerical results and observations assuming that the two sources of information, forecast and observations, have errors that are adequately described by error covariance matrices. To apply a DA approach to a CFD model for coughing and sneezing, real observations are needed.

2   Related Works and Contribution of the Present Work

In [16], a CFD analysis with an Eulerian-Lagrangian model was used to investigate the transport characteristics of evaporating droplets expelled into a ventilated room. This study aims to understand the transport and dispersal of droplets produced by coughing in a ventilated room with the help of Bayesian Data Assimilation. Experiments were conducted to measure the initial velocity and the duration of a coughing burst. In [17], an analytical approach instead of a CFD analysis is proposed. The authors model the detailed processes of cough jet flow, including droplet evaporation and motion, turbulent flow around the jet, and particle tracking to study the dispersion and deposition of expiratory droplets in a room during coughing. In [3], the authors present the results of a combined experimental and theoretical investigation of the fluid dynamics of such violent expiratory events. Direct observation of sneezing and coughing events reveals that such flows are multiphase turbulent buoyant clouds with suspended droplets of various sizes. Observations guide the development of an accompanying theoretical model of pathogen-bearing droplets interacting with a turbulent buoyant momentum puff. In [20], the transport characteristics of saliva droplets produced by coughing are examined in a calm indoor environment. The dispersion processes of saliva droplets of different diameters expelled during coughing are analysed using the Lagrangian equation. The results indicate that the transport characteristics of saliva droplets due to coughing change with size. In [15], the authors report the direct observation of physical mechanisms of droplet formation at the exit of the mouth during sneezing. Specifically, they use high-speed imaging to directly examine the fluid fragmentation at the exit of the mouths of healthy subjects.

In this work, we assimilate the real images provided in [15], in coughing and sneezing CFD simulations that we developed. To this aim, we implemented a 3D Variational DA model where an optimal parameter is introduced to balance the weight of the errors covariance matrices.

In summary, in this paper, we developed CFD models to simulate the droplet and aerosol size distributions and morphology at different positions, times, and exhalation conditions including coughing and sneezing. We use data assimilation to increase the accuracy of the CFD models using the observed data from the real experiments. This will provide more accurate data on the evolution of the particulate size distribution near the mouth.

The paper is structured as follows. In the next Section, the Data Assimilation problem is described and the definition of Variational approaches to solving it are presented. A description of the CFD simulations for sneezing and coughing are then presented. A Section that describes the pre-process of the resulting data, both from the CFD and the observed experimental results on realistic test cases is provided to show how DA performs on our test cases. A final Section presents the conclusions and describes future works.

3   Data Assimilation

Data Assimilation (DA) is an approach for fusing data (observations) with prior knowledge (e.g., mathematical representations of physical laws, model output) to obtain an estimate of the distribution of the true state of a process [18]. In order to perform DA, one needs observations (i.e., a data or measurement model), a background (i.e., a priori state or process model), and information about the distribution of the errors on these two. DA merges the estimated state $x_t \in \mathbb{R}^n$ of a discrete-time dynamic process at time t:

$$x_{t+1} = M_{t+1}x_t + w_t \tag{3.1}$$

with an observation $y_t \in \mathbb{R}^m$:

$$y_t = H_t x_t + v_t \tag{3.2}$$

where M_t is a dynamic system and H_t is called observation operator. The vectors w_t and v_t represent the process and observation errors, respectively. They are usually assumed to be independent white-noise processes with Gaussian probability distributions: $w_t \sim \mathcal{N}(0, Q_t)$, $v_t \sim \mathcal{N}(0, R_t)$, where Q_t and R_t are called error covariance matrices of the model and observation, respectively. DA is a Bayesian inference that combines the state x_t with y_t at each given time. The Bayes theorem conducts to the estimation of x_t^a which maximise a probability density function given the observation y_t and a prior from x_t. This approach is implemented in one of the most popular DA methods which is the three-dimensional Variational (3DVar) DA. The goal of 3DVar is to compute an optimal solution, x_t^a, that minimises a weighted difference between the actual measurement, y_t, and the measurement prediction.

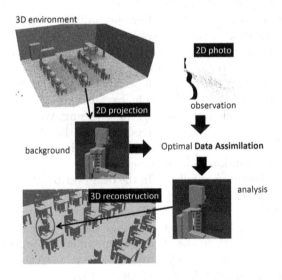

Fig. 1. 3D variational data assimilation framework.

The 3DVar problem can be described as following:

$$x_t^a = argmin_x J(x), \quad \text{with} \quad J(x) = J_1(x) + J_2(x) \tag{3.3}$$

where

$$J_1(x) = (x - x_t)^T Q^{-1}(x - x_t) \tag{3.4}$$

is called background or first-guess cost function and

$$J_2(x) = (H_t x - y_t)^T R^{-1}(H_t x - y_t) \tag{3.5}$$

is called observation cost function. If Eq. (3.3) is linearised around the background state [12], the 3DVar problem is formulated by the following form:

$$\delta x_t^a = argmin_{\delta x} J(\delta x), \quad \text{with} \quad J(\delta x) = J_1(\delta x) + J_2(\delta x) \tag{3.6}$$

and

$$J_1(\delta x) = \frac{1}{2}\delta x^T Q^{-1}\delta x, \quad J_2(\delta x) = \frac{1}{2}(H_t\delta x - d_t)^T R^{-1}(H_t\delta x - d_t) \tag{3.7}$$

where $d_t = [y_t - H_t x_t]$ is the misfit and $\delta x = x - x_t$ is the increment. The error covariance matrices Q_t and R_t in Eq. (3.7) are here designed to be correlated by a parameter α such that $Q_t = \alpha I$ and $R_t = (1 - \alpha)I$ with $0 < \alpha < 1$ and where I is the identity matrix. In this way we can decide the degree of fidelity we want to give to the observations with respect to the CFD simulation. As the weight of the covariance matrices in the DA process is given by the inverse of the matrices (see Eq. (3.4) and (3.5)) [2], with this choice of covariance matrices we can chose a bigger value of α if we assume that the observations are very reliable or a smaller value to α if the CFD model is a high fidelity model. With this choice Eq. (3.6) becomes

$$J(\delta x) = \frac{\delta x^T \delta x}{2\alpha} + \frac{(H_t\delta x - d_t)^T(H_t\delta x - d_t)}{2(1 - \alpha)} \tag{3.8}$$

As an important issue in Data Assimilation is to provide a result in real-time, the choice of an efficient method to compute the minimum of the functional J is a fundamental topic. In this paper, we compute the minimum of the functional J in Eq. (3.8) by the minimisation method proven to be faster for optimisation problems [11], i.e., the L-BFGS (Limited-Broyden Fletcher Goldfarb Shanno) method [19]. The L-BFGS method is a Quasi-Newton method that can be viewed as an extension of conjugate-gradient methods in which the addition of some modest storage serves to accelerate the convergence rate.

4   Coughing and Sneezing CFD Simulations

Numerical simulations of a cough respiratory event have been performed using an integrated computational fluid dynamics modelling framework known as IC-FERST, which is based on Fluidity [13]. The integrated approach includes a combination of an extended interface capturing model based on compressive advection method [14], with surface tension and hydrostatic force solvers for force-balancing, as well as adaptive mesh optimisation, to accurately predict complex droplet/ejecta transients and complex flow patterns.

To simulate a coughing respiratory event, a simple inlet is first modelled using assumed dimensions of a typical human mouth. Simplifying the mouth shape, a geometry can be designed with an angled and straight inlet of diameter 8 mm. To represent the surrounding, the inlet is modelled inside a domain of 5 m × 2.5 m. In [6] a model for the flow rate of air ejected after a single cough is presented. The male and female models are derived from a fit to results from 13 males and 12 females. We use the male relationships to establish boundary conditions for inlet velocity in our CFD simulations. The cough peak flow rate, CPFR (L/s), is related to the subjects' weight w (kg) and height h (m), as CPFR $= -8.8980 + 6.3952h + 0.0346w$, with the cough expiration volume, CEV (L), following as CEV $= 0.138$CPFR$+0.2983$, and the peak velocity time, PVT (s), as PVT $= (1.36$CPFR$+65.86)/1000$. Time is here non-dimensionalised as $\tau = t/$PVT, where t (s) is the time after the cough has begun, and the mass flow rate $\bar{M} = M/$CPFR, where M is the dimensioned mass flow rate (L/s). The dimensionless mass flow rate is computed to fit experimental results as: $\bar{M} = (a_1\tau^{b_1-1}\exp{(-\tau/c_1)})/(\Gamma(b_1)c_1^{b_1})$, where $a_1 = 1.680$, $b_1 = 3.338$, $c_1 = 0.428$, $a_2 = \frac{\text{CEV}}{(\text{PVT}\times\text{CPFR})} - a_1$, $b_2 = \frac{(-2.158\text{CEV})}{(\text{PVT}\times\text{CPFR})} + 10.457$, $c_2 = \frac{1.8}{b_2-1}$. and if $\tau \geq 1.2$ we must also add $\bar{M} \mathrel{+}= (a_2(\tau-1.2)^{b_2-1}\exp{(-(\tau-1.2)/c_2)})/(\Gamma(b_2)c_2^{b_2})$. We then compute the flow rate and given the area of our inlet (i.e., a mouth with size 3.4 cm^{-2}) compute the flow velocity through time for our inlet boundary conditions. A jet of fluid containing a water and air mixture can be used as an analogy for sneezing and coughing, characterised by a liquid jet that undergoes primary atomisation and further secondary droplet break-up [7] as an initial test case. Complex dynamic behaviour of high-speed jets, such as jet spreading and pressure decay, due to mass and momentum transfer [5] are well captured by the numerical schemes underpinning IC-FERST/Fluidity. Adaptive mesh optimisation and interface capturing are employed to model complex multi-phase jet flow physics such as nearnozzle instabilities, as well as droplet break-up, entrainment and droplet diffusion in the main region of the jet. The resolution of the mesh is focused on areas of highimportance physics, such as the interface and regions of high-vorticity. Adaptive implicit time-stepping, hydrostatic pressure and surface tension solvers additionally contribute to increasing the accuracy of the predicted droplet break-up and dispersion measurements.

Interface-Capturing Numerical Model: For multi-component flow modelling, one phase is generalised in an arbitrary number of phases (or fluid) components. If α_i is the volume fraction of component i and N_c is the number of components, where $i = 1, 2, 3..., N_c$, then a constraint of the system as $\sum_{i=1}^{N_c} \alpha_i = 1$ which can be used to define the conservation of mass for each component i as

$$\frac{\partial}{\partial t}\alpha_i\rho_i + \nabla \cdot (\alpha_i\rho_i\mathbf{u}) - Q_i = 0, \qquad i = 1, 2, 3..., N_c \qquad (4.1)$$

where ρ_i, t, $\mathbf{u}$, Q_i is the density of component i, time, velocity and mass source term, respectively. The equation of motion of an incompressible viscous fluid may be written as

$$\frac{\partial(\rho\mathbf{u})}{\partial t} + \nabla \cdot (\rho\mathbf{u} \times \mathbf{u}) = -\nabla p + \nabla \cdot [\mu(\nabla\mathbf{u} + \nabla^T\mathbf{u})] + \rho\mathbf{g} + \mathbf{F}_\sigma \qquad (4.2)$$

A compressive advection method based interface capturing scheme is employed.

5 Simulation, Data Pre-processing and Assimilation

Simulation: The domain size is 5 m × 2.5 m. A controlled water jet ejecta of size 0.03 mm is simulated from the 8 mm inlet. This corresponds to a total volume fraction of approximately 0.004. Results are shown in Fig. 2a and Fig. 2b. The mesh resolution varies from 10 μ to 5 mm. The lower limit of this resolution allows for the capturing of droplets at the interface which is important since numerous studies in the field of cough simulation estimate the droplets to vary from a few microns to 10 of microns. Figure 2a shows the mass fraction of water (log-scale) in the simulation at 63 ms and the ejecta has travelled approximately 23 cm. Figure 2b shows a zoomed-in version of the encircled area of Fig. 2a to illustrate the mesh adapting at the interface, with the minimum edge length observed to be 7 μ. This coughing simulation was subsequently used for data assimilation in the next Section.

(a) Water mass fraction of cough. Encircled area is zoomed-in and shown in Figure 2b.

(b) A zoomed-in view of the cough ejecta front, illustrating mesh adaptivity.

Fig. 2. Cough ejecta simulation

Real Images and data pre-processing: The images of real sneeze emissions were obtained from [15]. In order to assimilate sneezing images with a coughing CFD, we are here assuming that, in terms of velocity and mass fraction, the sneeze at a later time step corresponds to a cough at an earlier time step. The data was preprocessed using OpenCV Open Source Computer Vision Library) [4]. Two images of real observations were used: sneeze emissions after 5 ms recorded at 2000 fps fps (Fig. 3a); and sneeze ejecta at 8 ms recorded at 8000 fps fps (Fig. 3b). The images represent the observed data in the DA function (3.5); we have $y_t = y_{5ms}$ and $y_t = y_{8ms}$. The background data from the coughing CFD model are two images of simulated sneeze emissions: at an angle of 24 °C (Fig. 3c); and horizontal (Fig. 3d). This data represent $x_t = x_{5ms}$ and $x_t = x_{8ms}$ in (3.4). The images from the CFD simulation were scaled between 0 and 0.01 (for sneezing) and 0 and 0.02 (for coughing) with respect to their water mass fraction. The images from the simulations were cropped between 1.53 m and 1.63 m of height and a 0.12 m width. After this pre-process, the dimensions of the images from the CFD simulation (x_{5ms} and x_{8ms}) and the observations (y_{5ms} and y_{8ms}) match. All images were set at the same resolution and the

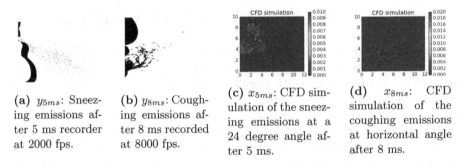

(a) y_{5ms}: Sneezing emissions after 5 ms recorder at 2000 fps.

(b) y_{8ms}: Coughing emissions after 8 ms recorded at 8000 fps.

(c) x_{5ms}: CFD simulation of the sneezing emissions at a 24 degree angle after 5 ms.

(d) x_{8ms}: CFD simulation of the coughing emissions at horizontal angle after 8 ms.

Fig. 3. Direct observations of the physical mechanisms of droplet formation at the exit of the mouth during sneezing [15] and CFD simulations of sneezing and coughing.

observations (interpolation) operator H_t in (3.2) is the identity function. The observation images (Fig. 3a and Fig. 3b) were also scaled between 0 and 0.01 (for sneezing) and 0 and 0.02 (for coughing) with respect to their water mass fraction to be consistent with to the simulation images.

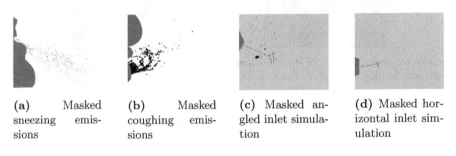

(a) Masked sneezing emissions

(b) Masked coughing emissions

(c) Masked angled inlet simulation

(d) Masked horizontal inlet simulation

Fig. 4. Different masks (in blue) applied to the CFD simulations and observations (Color figure online)

The four images in Fig. 3 were transformed to grayscale (ranged from 0 to 255 in one channel) using OpenCV. Additionally, a mask was drawn by hand on all images to eliminate the nose and mouth from the observations, and the inlets from the simulations. We chose a non-grayscale colour (blue) for the mask to avoid eliminating useful information. The mask allows us to perform the data assimilation only on the sneeze emissions and ejecta. The masked images are shown in Fig. 4. The backgrounds of all four images were set to white. Since the observations do not include a water mass fraction associated with them, we assumed a value of 0.01 (for sneezing) and 0.02 (for coughing) for pixels in black and 0 for pixels in white, in order to complement the simulations.

Data Assimilation: The algorithm has been implemented using Python 2.7.15 and tested on 3 high-performance nodes equipped with bi-Xeon E5-2650 v3 CPU and 250 GB of RAM. The execution time of the algorithm for assimilating y_{5ms} (Fig. 3a) in x_{5ms} (Fig. 3c) is 0.38 s. The execution time of the algorithm for assimilating y_{8ms} (Fig. 3b) in x_{8ms} (Fig. 3d) is 0.42 s. These values of the execution times have been computed as mean values of 50 runs of the algorithm on the same machine and the same data set and for different values of $0 < \alpha < 1$.

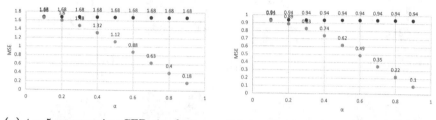

(a) $t = 5ms$, sneezing CFD simulation.   (b) $t = 8ms$, coughing CFD simulations.

Fig. 5. Values of MSE, for the coughing and sneezing CFD simulations, computed with respect to the observed data y_t before x_t (blue dots) and after x_t^a (orange dots) the assimilation process for different values of the parameter α. (Color figure online)

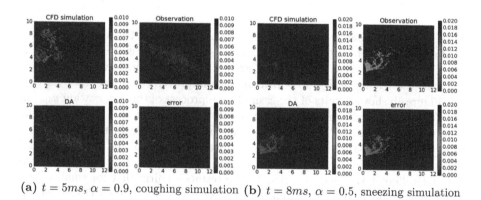

(a) $t = 5ms$, $\alpha = 0.9$, coughing simulation   (b) $t = 8ms$, $\alpha = 0.5$, sneezing simulation

Fig. 6. Results of the assimilation of y_t (observation) and x_t (CFD simulation) for a fixed t and a specific value of α

Figure 5 shows value of Mean Square Error (MSE) defined as $MSE(x) = \frac{\|x - x_C\|_{L^2}^2}{\|x_C\|_{L^2}^2}$ where x_C denotes a control variable. The MSE is here computed with respect to the observed data before and after the assimilation process for different values of the parameter α. As expected, for bigger values of α, the result of the assimilation come closer to the observations and it presents a smaller value of

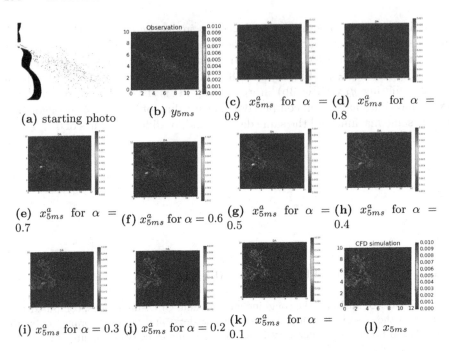

(a) starting photo

(b) y_{5ms}

(c) x^a_{5ms} for $\alpha = $ 0.9

(d) x^a_{5ms} for $\alpha = $ 0.8

(e) x^a_{5ms} for $\alpha = $ 0.7

(f) x^a_{5ms} for $\alpha = 0.6$

(g) x^a_{5ms} for $\alpha = $ 0.5

(h) x^a_{5ms} for $\alpha = $ 0.4

(i) x^a_{5ms} for $\alpha = 0.3$ (j) x^a_{5ms} for $\alpha = 0.2$

(k) x^a_{5ms} for $\alpha = $ 0.1

(l) x_{5ms}

Fig. 7. Results of the assimilation of y_{5ms} in the CFD sneezing simulation x_{5ms} for different values of α

MSE. Figure 6a shows results of the assimilation process of the observation y_{5ms} in the CFD sneezing simulation x_{5ms} for $\alpha = 0.9$. The Figure shows also the error computed as $|x_{5ms} - y_{5ms}|$; the error is here zero almost everywhere. This confirms the results in Fig. 5b which show an improvement in accuracy for $\alpha = 0.9$. Figure 6b shows results of the assimilation process of the observation y_{8ms} in the CFD sneezing simulation x_{8ms} for $\alpha = 0.5$. This choice of α means that the observation and the CFD simulation have the same weight in the assimilation process. In this case, the assimilation completely merges the data with an equal balance between the two. Figure 7 shows how the DA technology merges the two data for different values of $0 < \alpha < 1$. The results confirm that for small values of α the solution x^a of the assimilation process is closer to the CFD simulation. The assimilation of those data can have a big impact on real case applications to evaluate "safe" distances. In the presented case, for example, the CFD says that the spread of the droplets after 5 ms has a radius of almost 4 cm with almost 6 cm of distance from the mouth (Fig. 8b). The observation shows a smaller radius near the mouth but the droplets reach 12 cm from the mouth (Fig. 8a). The fusion of these pieces of information (Fig. 8c) is important in the evaluation of safe distances for people interactions. In fact, the technology and the model we presented are general and can be applied to other kinds of computational fluid dynamic systems which simulate other scenarios.

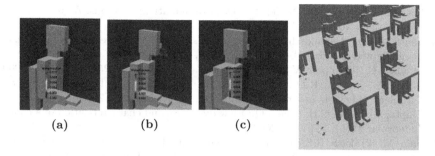

Fig. 8. Real world scenario: students in a classroom: (a) result from the real observation, (b) result from the CFD simulation, (c) result from the DA of observation and CFD

6   Conclusions and Future Work

In this study, we implemented a 3D Variational DA model to merge real images with numerical results of a physics simulation. In particular, we use a coughing CFD simulation at varying inlet geometries and assimilate its results with experimental results from [15] of sneezing and coughing. For this initial test case, we have considered only the mouth as the source of ejecta. We have also hypothesised that considering a sneeze simulation at a later timestep as compared to a cough simulation may be able to provide comparable and interchangeable results thereby also testing the versatility of the DA techniques. To this aim, we implemented the DA model where an optimal parameter is introduced to balance the weight of the error covariance matrices in the assimilation function. The benefits of this study are highlighted by the demonstration of DA's versatility in effectively using the experimental sneezing results in the coughing CFD simulation. This versatility can be leveraged to provide for a robust methodology that can assist in modelling various COVID-19 spread scenarios which involve ventilation airflows (indoors or outdoors) while also reserving the potential to model crowd airflow dynamics. These simulations run High Performance Computing infrastructure. The computing resources and the related technical support used for future work have been provided by CRESCO/ENEAGRID High Performance Computing infrastructure and its staff http://www.cresco.enea.it/englishforinformation.

Acknowledgements. This work is supported by the EP/V036777/1 Risk EvaLuatIon fAst iNtelligent Tool (RELIANT) for COVID19 and the EP/T000414/1 PREdictive Modelling with QuantIfication of UncERtainty for MultiphasE Systems (PREMIERE).

References

1. Arcucci, R., Mottet, L., Pain, C., Guo, Y.K.: Optimal reduced space for variational data assimilation. J. Comput. Phys. **379**, 51–69 (2019)

2. Asch, M., Bocquet, M., Nodet, M.: Data Assimilation: Methods, Algorithms, and Applications, vol. 11. SIAM, Philadelphia (2016)
3. Bourouiba, L., Dehandschoewercker, E., Bush, J.W.: Violent expiratory events: on coughing and sneezing. J. Fluid Mech. **745**, 537–563 (2014)
4. Bradski, G.: The openCV library. Dr. Dobb's J. Softw. Tools **25**(1), 120–123 (2000)
5. Guha, A., Barron, R.M., Balachandar, R.: Numerical simulation of high-speed turbulent water jets in air. J. Hydraul. Res. **48**(1), 119–124 (2010)
6. Gupta, J.K., Lin, C.H., Chen, Q.: Flow dynamics and characterization of a cough. Indoor Air **19**(6), 517–525 (2009)
7. Jain, M., Prakash, R.S., Tomar, G., Ravikrishna, R.: Secondary breakup of a drop at moderate weber numbers. Proc. Roy. Soc. Math. Phys. Eng. Sci. **471**(2177), 20140930 (2015)
8. Jayaweera, M., Perera, H., Gunawardana, B., Manatunge, J.: Transmission of covid-19 virus by droplets and aerosols: a critical review on the unresolved dichotomy. Environ. Res. **188**, 109819 (2020)
9. Kalman, R.: A new approach to linear filtering and prediction problems. Trans. ASME J. Basic Eng. **82**(1), 35–45 (1960)
10. Kalnay, E.: Atmospheric Modeling, Data Assimilation and Predictability. Cambridge University Press, Cambridge (2003)
11. Liu, D.C., Nocedal, J.: On the limited memory BFGS method for large scale optimization. Math. Program. **45**(1–3), 503–528 (1989). https://doi.org/10.1007/BF01589116
12. Lorenc, A.: Development of an operational variational assimilation scheme. J. Meteorol. Soc. Japan **75**, 339–346 (1997)
13. Pain, C., Umpleby, A., De Oliveira, C., Goddard, A.: Tetrahedral mesh optimisation and adaptivity for steady-state and transient finite element calculations. Comput. Methods Appl. Mech. Eng. Comput. Methods Appl. Mech. Eng. **190**(29), 3771–3796 (2001)
14. Pavlidis, D., Gomes, J.L.M.A., Xie, Z., Percival, J.R., Pain, C.C., Matar, O.K.: Compressive advection and multi-component methods for interface-capturing. Int. J. Numer. Meth. Fluids **80**(4), 256–282 (2016). https://doi.org/10.1002/fld
15. Scharfman, B.E., Techet, A.H., Bush, J.W.M., Bourouiba, L.: Visualization of sneeze ejecta: steps of fluid fragmentation leading to respiratory droplets. Exp. Fluids **57**(2), 1–9 (2015). https://doi.org/10.1007/s00348-015-2078-4
16. Sun, W., Ji, J.: Transport of droplets expelled by coughing in ventilated rooms. Indoor Built Environ. **16**(6), 493–504 (2007)
17. Wei, J., Li, Y.: Enhanced spread of expiratory droplets by turbulence in a cough jet. Build. Environ. **93**, 86–96 (2015)
18. Wikle, C.K., Berliner, L.M.: A bayesian tutorial for data assimilation. Physica D **230**(1–2), 1–16 (2007)
19. Zhu, C., Byrd, R.H., Lu, P., Nocedal, J.: Algorithm 778: L-BFGS-B: fortran subroutines for large-scale bound-constrained optimization. ACM Trans. Math. Softw. (TOMS) **23**(4), 550–560 (1997)
20. Zhu, S., Kato, S., Yang, J.H.: Study on transport characteristics of saliva droplets produced by coughing in a calm indoor environment. Build. Environ. **41**(12), 1691–1702 (2006)

Data Management in EpiGraph COVID-19 Epidemic Simulator

Miguel Guzmán-Merino[1], Christian Durán[1], Maria-Cristina Marinescu[2],
Concepción Delgado-Sanz[3,4], Diana Gomez-Barroso[3,4], Jesus Carretero[1],
and David E. Singh[1(✉)]

[1] Department Computer Science, Universidad Carlos III de Madrid, Leganés, Spain
dexposit@inf.uc3m.es
[2] Barcelona Supercomputing Center, Barcelona, Spain
[3] CIBER en Epidemiología y Salud Pública (CIBERESP), Madrid, Spain
[4] National Centre for Epidemiology, Carlos III Institute of Health, Madrid, Spain

Abstract. The transmission of COVID-19 through a population depends on many factors which model, incorporate, and integrate many heterogeneous data sources. The work we describe in this paper focuses on the data management aspect of EpiGraph, a scalable agent-based virus-propagation simulator. We describe the data acquisition and pre-processing tasks that are necessary to map the data to the different models implemented in EpiGraph in a way that is efficient and comprehensible. We also report on post-processing, analysis, and visualization of the outputs, tasks that are fundamental to make the simulation results useful for the final users. Our simulator captures complex interactions between social processes, virus characteristics, travel patterns, climate, vaccination, and non-pharmaceutical interventions. We end by demonstrating the entire pipeline with one evaluation for Spain for the third COVID wave starting on December 27th of 2020.

Keywords: Epidemiological simulation · COVID-19 · Heterogeneous data processing · Parallel tool

1 Introduction

The transmission of the COVID-19 virus through a population depends on many factors that reflect the makeup of the community, the characteristics and behaviours of the individuals, as well as the effect of the measures taken to curb its propagation. The larger the community, the more difficult it becomes to predict

This work has been supported by the Spanish Instituto de Salud Carlos III under the project grant 2020/00183/001, the project grant BCV-2021-1-0011, of the Spanish Supercomputing Network (RES) and the European Union's Horizon 2020 JTI-EuroHPC research and innovation program under grant agreement No. 956748. We would like to thank to Diego Fernandez Olombrada for his support in the early collection of part of the data of this work.

© Springer Nature Switzerland AG 2022
R. Chaves et al. (Eds.): Euro-Par 2021, LNCS 13098, pp. 267–278, 2022.
https://doi.org/10.1007/978-3-031-06156-1_22

the outcomes. To tackle this problem, we have implemented EpiGraph, a scalable, parallel agent-based simulator. This paper centres on data management, which turns out to be quite complex, given that EpiGraph implements several modules that reproduce the different aspects which have an impact on the virus propagation. The interplay of these modules simulates a complex phenomenon that takes many heterogeneous sources and data types as input by mapping them to the different parameters of the agent model. The aim of this work is two-fold, on one hand we aim to contribute to a better understanding on the modelling for the epidemic simulation to coronavirus pandemic, and on the other, we describe methodologies for an efficient integration of heterogeneous data.

Figure 1 shows the different stages involved in EpiGraph simulation. The input data is first obtained from multiple sources ranging from research papers, to public and private databases. These data are highly heterogeneous and have to be processed in a second stage using multiple technologies. Section 2 describes in detail these two stages.

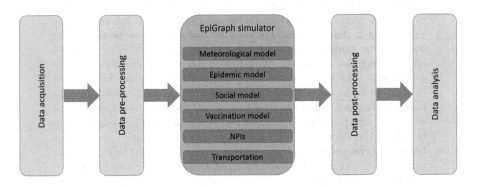

Fig. 1. Stages involved in EpiGraph simulations.

The third stage of the figure corresponds to the simulation process. EpiGraph is an agent-based simulator that includes multiple models that realistically reproduce the environment where the infection spreads. The Meteorological model uses meteorological data to increase or reduce the disease's R0s values based on each particular weather condition. The Epidemic model is a compartmental stochastic extended SEIR model. Rather than the more common analytic models based on differential equations, Epigraph computes, for each infected individual, the duration of the different compartments and the transition probabilities.

The social model reproduces the social habits of four different main group types: students, workers, stay-at-home people, and elders. A group can represents a certain number of individuals that interact during work hours - for instance, groups are the students belonging to the same classroom, workers of the same company. Note that an interaction involves the co-location in time at a distance that is small enough to make disease transmission possible. EpiGraph model interaction during work hours, school-time, family time, and leisure, including multiple professions. See [16, 24] for additional details. The risk of infection, given by the specific R_0 value of the infected individual, also depends on two factors that reduce the transmission risk: the vaccination of the susceptible individual that is in contact with the infected one, and the use of non-pharmaceutical intervention (NPIs), like the use of face masks. These factors are modelled by the Vaccination and NPI models included in the simulator. Finally, the transportation model computes the number of travellers between the urban areas that are being simulated based on the geographical distance between them.

There is a large amount of output data produced during the simulation (we have simulated up to 200M individuals and 650 cities). In order to provide a comprehensive analysis of the results, a post processing stage (fourth stage) is carried out. Then, the fifth stage uses this information to generate different statistical data that summarize the simulation output and graphically displaying the results. Section 2.3 describes more in detail the analysis and visualization stage.

2   Epigraph Data Management

This section provides a description of the data used and produced by the simulator, as well as how these data are processed. Figure 2 shows the different data sources involved in a simulation and how they interact with the different software components. Epigraph consists of two main software pieces that are used in combination with several auxiliary programs. The first component is the Scenario generation in which the different urban areas used in the simulation are created. Note that these urban areas only contain information about the characteristics of the individual in the population and the way they interact with other individuals. The input data sources (upper part in the figure) are geolocation provided by web applications that are used to identify the geographic coordinates of each city, its related NUTS code, as well as the distances between each pair of cities. The second data source are the Eurostat, and Spanish-equivalent INE, that provide the demographic data used by the simulator. This information, depicted in Sect. 2.1, includes among other, the population pyramid and the distribution of employment related to each city. Two different social-network graphs are used for generating the contact patterns of each individual. Finally, contact matrices, extracted from public surveys, are used to provide statistical information of the average number of contacts between individuals of certain age ranges.

The Epigraph generator is an MPI program written in C that creates, for each urban area, the characteristics (age, profession, etc.) of all individuals belonging to the same urban area as well as the related contact patterns[1]. We call this *social fabric*, and we store it as sparse matrices, in which each node is an individual and each edge is a time-dependent interaction with other person.

The social fabric created in the scenario generation stage is used as input in the scenario simulation (lower part of Fig. 2). Note that this information can be reused among multiple simulations when the social fabric (i.e. the simulated urban areas) do not change. Regarding the data sources shown in the figure,

---

[1] Note the EpiGraph employs static and dynamic contact patterns, and in this section we are referring to the static one.

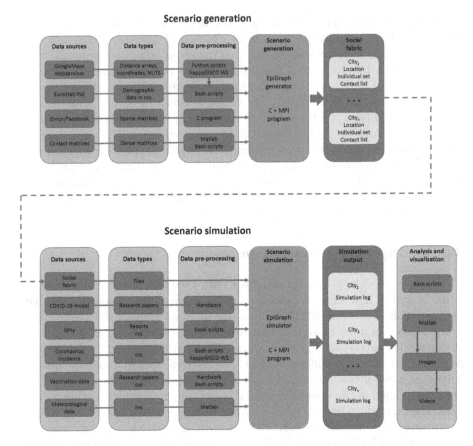

Fig. 2. Overview of the data flow related to EpiGraph simulation. In the scenario generation stage (upper part figure) the social fabric is generated and stored in files. In a second stage this information is used in combination with other sources of data (lower part figure) to perform the simulation.

the COVID-19 model parameters were taken from the existing literature. The non-pharmaceutical interventions (NPIs) applied in each region and the coronavirus incidence were processed using Excel and Bash scripts. The vaccination data is a combination of the different parameters used in vaccine efficacy models and data for the existing doses administrated in each region. This information was taken from the existing literature and government databases, respectively. Finally, the meteorological data consists of a collection of meteorological measurements (pressure, temperature, etc.) of each urban area that was processed using Matlab.

All the previous data is used by EpiGraph to perform the scenario simulation. The simulator output is a collection of trace files with the state of each individual for each simulated time step in each urban area. Note that this information is very rich in contents, because it includes, in combination with the individual characteristics (health, age, occupation, etc.), the actions taken or applied to the person (vaccination, use of NPIs, travel, etc.) for each time step. The following sections provide details about the data sources involved in the simulations and how these data were processed.

2.1   Scenario Generation

Geographical Data. EpiGraph simulations comprises one or multiple urban areas, that are identified by names, coordinates and NUTS codes. The first two parameters are used by the transport model for calculating the distance between the cities, i.e., the number of individuals in a population that travel between the cities. The latter parameters is used to carry out database search.

– The city's latitude and longitude were obtained from online databases, based on these coordinates, and using Google Maps services. By means of these services it was possible to obtain the distances of each city with the other ones -which is needed by EpiGraph's transport model-.
– NUTS codes represent a three-levels division of the European territory [14]. We use the happyGISCO tool [10] (which is an interface to Eurostat Gisco web services) in combination with Python scripts to obtain the city NUTS codes from their coordinates. The red arrow in Fig. 2 highlights that the city NUTS codes are used by shell scripts for selecting the related demographic data of each city.

Demographic Data. This set of data defines the characteristics of the simulated population. For Spain, the data was taken from the Spanish National Statistics Institute (INE) [19] with an aggregation level of province. For the rest of European countries, the source of data was EuroStat [11] with an aggregation level of country.

Demographic data include the following attributes related to the social activity: percentage of the people for the collectives of students, elderly people, workers and unemployed; Regarding the elderly people we distinguish the sub-collectives that live in nursing homes or at home. The worker collectives are broken down by the following sub-collectives: industry, building, catering, services, security forces, education, front-line-health, non-front-line-health, social-health and transport. Note that each collective and profession has a different social pattern. The household size is percentage of homes with one to five members that is used to model the family contacts.

Demographic data also includes: the population and population pyramid related to each simulated city; The percentage of essential workers; and the collective group sizes that includes a normal distribution comprising the minimum and maximum number of people involved in the same collective. For instance, the number of students in the same classroom or the number of workers in a company[2].

---

[2] Note that each collective and sub-collective has different group sized based on the activity that they perform.

Population-Mixing Data. This data is used to generate the social pattern, i.e. the social interactions, between the simulated individuals. In epidemic simulations, population mixing is a crucial factor that determines the realism and accuracy of the simulations. The sources of information for the social model are described below:

- Social network graphs: we have employed the Enron Email Corpus graph [7] (70,578 nodes and 312,620 edges) for generating the work, elderly and informal meetup contacts, and a Facebook graph [2] (250,000 edges and 3,239,137 edges) for the school contacts. We have developed in [16] a variation of the Random Walk algorithm [18] which generates scaled sub-graphs from the Enron and Facebook data-sets, with an specific average connectivity $<k>$ provided as input argument. This value of connectivity is obtained from the contract matrices that are explained next.
- Contact matrices [6] are dense matrices in which each element $A_{i,j}$ represents average number of daily interactions between individuals of ages i and j. The contact matrix repository includes data for various countries and some regions of these countries, including sub-contact matrices for school, work, and community contacts. These contact matrices were processed using Matlab and Bash scripts. The school contact matrix was used to generate the student's school contacts (using the Facebook graph), with a number of interactions per age specified by the matrix. In a similar way, the work contact matrix was used to define the age distribution of the work, stay-at-home and elders interactions. Finally, the community contact matrix was used to generate the connectivity related to the leisure contacts.
- Daily Contacts of health professional with patients: according to the Spanish National Health System, on average a health professional is in contact with 30 patients per day on average. Due to the lack of data, we have used this value for all the simulated countries.
- Average contacts of health professional with COVID-19 patients. We estimate this value considering, on one hand, 180,000 health professionals in Spain. On the other, given a 10% of SARS-CoV-2 prevalence among the Spanish population at the end of the second wave, and the number of suspects per day, based on the number of diagnostic tests performed (1M per day, scaled by 1.3 in order to consider the tests not performed on suspects) will result in an average of 4.2 contacts with suspects per day, and a estimation of 0.4 contacts with COVID-19 patients per day, per health professional. According to [21] the hazard ratio for front-line health professionals is 3.3, so we assume that front-line health professional have a larger number of about 1.4 contacts with COVID-19 patients per day. Data are stored in configuration files formatted in xml.

– Catering contacts per hour. In our experiments we consider three levels of catering contacts: pre-pandemic, pandemic with a more reduced number of contacts per hour, and lockdown with catering services closed. Related data are stored in configuration files formatted in xml.

2.2   Scenario Simulation

SARS-CoV-2 Infection Data. These data were extracted from research papers. They include the basic reproduction numbers (R0s) related to each disease stage, the state transition probabilities (for instance, the probability of an infected individual of being asymptomatic), the hospitalized and death probabilities, and the duration of each infection stage. Please refer to [24] for a detailed description of these parameters.

Non-pharmaceutical Intervention Data. This category includes different sources of heterogeneous data that record the NPIs imposed by each country during the pandemic.

– Social distancing policies consider three distancing measures collected from the Data on country response measures to COVID-19 database [9]: the closure of schools, the closure of public spaces of any kind, and the workplace closure. In this work we use the existing social distance measures for each European country in a simulation starting on December 27th of 2020.
– Face mask use. EpiGraph models the use of both surgical and ffp2-grade face masks, with different efficacies [24]. The results provided in this work are related to the simulation period at the beginnings of 2021 in which the entire European population was using mask outside the family circle.
– Sampling strategies [16] are modelled by the number of daily tests performed, the minimum time between two consecutive tests carried out to the same individual, the quarantine time, and the percentage of quarantine breakers, i.e. the fraction of people who do not comply with social distancing during quarantine time. These data was provided by the Spanish Ministry of Health.

COVID-19 Incidence. We use the ECDC's weekly sub-national 14-day notification rate of new COVID-19 cases [9] for setting the initial percentage of infected population in each urban area (this value is only used at the beginning of the simulation). ECDC database provides sub-regional data for European countries, so the cities are set with regional values -instead of average country values-. These data are automatically loaded using bash scripts that leverage the city's NUTS code to identify the incidence region values in the ECDC database.

We obtain the seroprevalence information related to each country from [20]. This information, which is uploaded using bash scripts, is only needed for setting the initial conditions at the beginning of the simulation.

Vaccination Data. [23] presents the EpiGraph's vaccination model in detail. It includes both the vaccine effectiveness model, that depends on the individual age and the SARS-CoV-2 variant, and the vaccination strategy that is simulated, that defines aspects such as prioritization among target groups, and the time between the administration of the doses. The vaccination model was obtained from research papers and the vaccination strategy was provided by the Spanish Ministry of Health[3]. Please see [23] for further details about this model.

Meteorological Data. In the current development of the simulator the meteorological data is provided by the Spanish Meteorological Agency (AEMET) [1] and is only used for Spanish-level simulations. The input data consists of cvs files with 10-min samples taken during one year by all the meteorological stations in Spain. Data was processed by Matlab using interpolation algorithms (for estimating lost values) and collecting and processing the desired meteorological parameters of temperature, pressure and humidity for each city in Spain [22].

2.3 Analysis and Visualization

EpiGraph generates simulation traces for each urban area, that contain, for each time step, the number of individuals each state of the infection and additional information as the number of vaccinated individuals (for each vaccine type and time when the doses have been administrated), use of masks, number of quarantined and hospitalized individuals, use of other NPI interventions. This information is processed in parallel and is combined with the population demographic and social data in order to generate both global and collective-specific statistics. For example, it is possible to obtain for a certain urban area, how many catering workers are infected or how many of the infected ones are vaccinated. In addition, we employ Matlab for providing overall statistics and graphical display of the results by means of images and videos.

3 Evaluation

In this section we provide simulation results for a national scenario related to Spain. The simulations were executed on the Tirant supercomputer, which is made up of 336 nodes each with two Intel Xeon processors Sandy Bridge E5-2670 and 32 GB RAM, interconnected with an Infiniband 40 Gbps network. In this section we provide simulation results for Spain. We simulate the third wave starting on December 27th of 2020.

This scenario simulates a population of 19,574,086 individuals related to the 63 most populated cities of Spain, using 109 processes. The simulation starts on December 27th of 2020, which was the starting date for the COVID-19 vaccination campaign. It reproduces the Spanish COVID-19 vaccination campaign and includes a given number of daily tests of 0.25% over the simulated population,

---

[3] Note that the vaccination prioritization strategy is similar for all European countries.

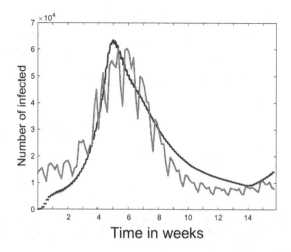

Fig. 3. Spain third wave: daily real (in red colour) and simulated (in blue colour) data related to the number of infections of the COVID-19. Simulation starts on December 27th of 2020. (Color figure online)

and a percentage of positive tests of around 9% (which corresponds to the real testing rate and detection efficacy). Figure 3 shows in red colour the daily real reported cases for Spain and in blue colour the aggregated simulated cases for the considered cities. Real cases have been scaled by a factor of 1.42 in order to include the non-reported cases. Simulated cases represent the median of 10 different simulations.

A more detailed results of the simulation output is shown in Fig. 4 (left) in which the results are broken down by Spanish provinces. We can observe that both the real cases (in red) and the simulated ones (in blue) are similar although there are some differences for some of them. Note the high complexity of the problem that we are tackling. Figure 4 (left) shows the geographic location of each one of the urban areas.

Note that this baseline simulation scenario is being used to evaluate different alternative scenarios. Examples of them are the scenarios where we introduce changes in the vaccination strategy (for instance, introducing changes in the prioritization process). Other interesting question is to assess alternative NPIs. For instance, evaluate school closing (instead of being opened, as has happened in Spain), reducing the activity in the catering sector, lifting up the imposition of using face masks in open spaces, etc.

4   Related Work

There are many approaches to model the COVID-19 propagation. A starting approach is the SEIR model based on solving the differential equations like in [4]. More complex versions of the SEIR model include, for instance, a quarantine

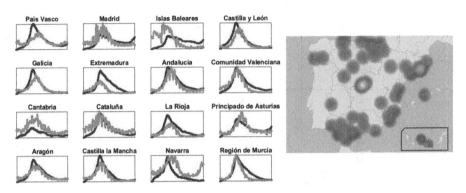

Fig. 4. (Left) Simulations results of the Spanish third wave, broken down by communities. Red line represents the real infected and the blue ones the simulated. Simulation starts on December 27th of 2020. (Right) Infected dispersion map of the 64 simulated cities. (Color figure online)

class and a class of isolated (hospitalized) members [3,17]. The main limitation of this approach is the lack of details in the simulation. An alternative way of modelling the infection spread are the models based on machine learning [15]. The work in [12], developed in the Imperial College of London introduces an extension of a semi-mechanistic Bayesian hierarchical model that infers the impact of interventions and estimates the number of infections over time. In [13], the authors use the discrete renewal equation as a latent process for the modelling of infections and propose a generative mechanism to connect infections to death data. They use this joint Bayesian hierarchical model to produce short-term predictions, and they apply their model to 11 different countries.

The European Centre for Disease Prevention and Control (ECDC) [8] has built a Monte-Carlo based model of COVID-19 that they use for forecasting. To model the behaviour of the people and how well they are responding to the measures, they compare the predictions with Google data about mobile phone use and they use the daily confirmed COVID-19 cases and daily deaths to calibrate it. It is interesting to note that some models perform forecast, like COFFEE model from Los Alamos National Laboratory [5], and other are also capable of performing projections. A projection involves simulating alternative hypothetical scenarios. In the case of EpiGraph, this tool belongs to the models that perform projection.

5   Conclusion

This work describes the data management of EpiGraph, an agent-based simulator for influenza and COVID-19 propagation. The approach followed in Epi-Graph is to combine several models that reproduce the different aspects of the environment where the disease spreads. This involves the simulation of complex phenomena that are modelled by employing different, complex and heterogeneous data sources. This work provides a description of the data management involved in EpiGraph's simulations including both the input data acquisition and pre-processing, and the output data post-processing and analysis. In our simulation framework, the use of Python and Bash scripts allows to quickly gather and perform simple processing (as data filtering or, specific data gathering) from many heterogeneous sources. Alternatively, Matlab was used for computing more complex tasks. This tool permits using advanced processing algorithms, because of the large number of toolboxes that includes, although its performance (considered as execution time) is low. We used Matlab for tasks that are usually performed once (like meteorological data interpolation) or for data visualization where data that was already processed. C programming language was employed for complex, computational-intensive tasks, like the social contact generation (that involves processing Enron/Facebook graphs) and the simulation processes. Given the particular characteristics of EpiGraph, it was possible to divide this data-intensive processing into different tasks, related to different sections of urban areas. In this way, several processing scripts can be simultaneously executed in order to speed-up the pre-processing and post-processing stages. For both the scenario generation and the simulation, MPI was used to execute the C program in parallel on multiple compute nodes.

References

1. AEMET: Agencia estatal de meteorología (aemet) (2021). https://www.aemet.es
2. Batra, S.: Facebook data (2018). https://www.kaggle.com/sheenabatra/facebook-data
3. Brauer, F., Castillo-Chavez, C.: Mathematical Models in Population Biology and Epidemiology. Springer, New York (2012). https://doi.org/10.1007/978-1-4614-1686-9
4. Carcione, J.M., Santos, J.E., Bagaini, C., Ba, J.: A simulation of a COVID-19 epidemic based on a deterministic SEIR model. Front. Public Health **8**, 1–13 (2020)
5. Castro, L., Fairchild, G., Michaud, I., Osthus, D.: COFFEE: COVID-19 Forecasts using Fast Evaluations and Estimation. Los Alamos National Laboratory, LA-UR-20-28630 (2020)
6. Chinazzi, M., Mistry, D.: Mixing patterns (2021). https://github.com/mobs-lab/mixing-patterns
7. Cukierski, W.: The Enron email dataset (2015). https://www.kaggle.com/wcukierski/enron-email-dataset
8. The European Centre for Disease Prevention and Control: Updated projections of COVID-19 in the EU/EEA and the UK. Technical report, ECDC, Stockholm (2020)
9. European Centre for Disease Prevention and Control (ECDC): Home-ECDE (2021). https://www.ecdc.europa.eu/en
10. European Commission (EC - DG ESTAT): HappyGISCO Python interface to GISCO web-services (2021). https://happygisco.readthedocs.io/en/latest/
11. Eurostat: Home-Eurostat (2021). https://ec.europa.eu/eurostat
12. Flaxman, S., et al.: Estimating the effects of non-pharmaceutical interventions on COVID-19 in Europe. Nature **584**, 257–261 (2020)

13. Flaxman, S., Mishra, S., et al.: Estimating the number of infections and the impact of non-pharmaceutical interventions on COVID-19 in European countries: technical description update. arXiv:2004.11342 (2020)
14. Grazzini J., Museux J.-M., Hahn M.: Eurostat (2021). https://ec.europa.eu/eurostat/web/nuts/background
15. Gu, Y.: COVID-19 projections using machine learning (2020). https://covid19-projections.com
16. Guzmán-Merino, M., et al.: Assessing population-sampling strategies for reducing the COVID-19 incidence. Preprint (2021)
17. Li, M.L., et al.: Overview of DELPHI Model V3 - COVID Analytics (2020)
18. Lovasz, L.: Random walks on graphs: a survey. Bolyai Soc. Math. Stud. **2**, 46 (1993). https://web.cs.elte.hu/~lovasz/erdos.pdf
19. Ministry of Economic Affairs and Digital Transformation (MINECO): National Statistics Institute (INE) (2021). http://www.ine.es
20. Rostami, A., et al.: First "snap-shot" meta-analysis to estimate the prevalence of serum antibodies to SARS-CoV-2 in humans. Clin. Microbiol. Infect. **27**(3), 331–340 (2021)
21. Shah, A.S.V., et al.: Risk of hospital admission with coronavirus disease 2019 in healthcare workers and their households: nationwide linkage cohort study. BMJ **371** (2020). https://doi.org/10.1136/bmj.m3582
22. Singh, D.E., Marinescu, M.C., Carretero, J., Delgado-Sanz, C., Gomez-Barroso, D., Larrauri, A.: Evaluating the impact of the weather conditions on the influenza propagation. BMC Infect. Dis. **20**, 265 (2020)
23. Singh, D.E., et al.: Evaluation of vaccination strategies for Spain. Preprint (2021)
24. Singh, D.E., et al.: Simulation of COVID-19 propagation scenarios in the Madrid metropolitan area. Front. Public Health **9**, 172 (2021). https://doi.org/10.3389/fpubh.2021.636023

Resilience – Fourteenth Workshop on Resiliency in High Performance Computing in Clouds, Grids, and Clusters

Resilience 2021: Fourteenth Workshop on Resiliency in High Performance Computing in Clouds, Grids, and Clusters

Workshop Description

Resilience is a critical challenge as high performance computing (HPC) systems continue to increase component counts, individual component reliability decreases (such as due to shrinking process technology and near-threshold voltage (NTV) operation), hardware complexity increases (such as due to heterogeneous computing) and software complexity increases (such as due to complex data- and workflows, real-time requirements and integration of artificial intelligence (AI) technologies with traditional applications).

Correctness and execution efficiency, in spite of faults, errors, and failures, is essential to ensure the success of the HPC systems, cluster computing environments, Grid computing infrastructures, and Cloud computing services. The impact of faults, errors, and failures in such HPC systems can range from financial losses due to system downtime (sometimes several tens-of-thousands of Dollars per lost system-hour), to financial losses due to unnecessary overprovision (acquisition and operating costs of underutilized machines), to financial losses and legal liabilities due to erroneous or delayed output.

The emergence of AI technology opens up new possibilities, but also new problems. Using AI technology for operational intelligence that enables resilience in HPC systems and centers is a complex control problem, while designing resilient AI technology for HPC applications is a difficult algorithmic problem. Resilience for HPC systems encompasses a wide spectrum of fundamental and applied research and development, including theoretical foundations, error/failure and anomaly detection, monitoring and control, end-to-end data integrity, enabling infrastructure, and resilient algorithms.

This workshop brought together experts in the community to further research and development in HPC resilience and to facilitate exchanges across the computational paradigms of extreme-scale HPC, cluster computing, Grid computing, and Cloud computing. The Resilience 2021 workshop program included presentations of four (4) high-quality peer-reviewed papers, a keynote by Dr. Christian Engelmann of the Oak Ridge National Laboratory, titled Faults, Errors and Failures in Extreme-Scale Supercomputers, and varying opportunities for discussions among the participants from research, academia, and industry.

Organization

Workshop Chairs

Stephen L. Scott — Tennessee Tech University, USA
Christian Engelmann — Oak Ridge National Laboratory, USA

Workshop Program Chairs

Thomas Naughton — Oak Ridge National Laboratory, USA
Ferrol Aderholdt — Middle Tennessee State University, USA

Workshop Chair Emeritus

Chokchai (Box) Leangsuksun — Louisiana Tech University, USA

Program Committee (PC)

Wesley Bland — Intel Corporation, USA
Hans-Joachim Bungartz — Technical University of Munich, Germany
Marc Casas — Barcelona Supercomputer Center, Spain
Zizhong Chen — University of California at Riverside, USA
James Elliott — Sandia National Laboratories, USA
Kurt Ferreira — Sandia National Laboratories, USA
Saurabh Hukerikar — NVIDIA, USA
Ignacio Laguna — Lawrence Livermore National Laboratory, USA
Scott Levy — Sandia National Laboratories, USA
Rolf Riesen — Intel Corporation, USA
Yves Robert — ENS Lyon, France
Thomas Ropars — Universite Grenoble Alpes, France
Martin Schulz — Lawrence Livermore National Laboratory, USA
Keita Teranishi — Sandia National Laboratories, USA

RDPM: An Extensible Tool for Resilience Design Patterns Modelling

Mohit Kumar$^{(\boxtimes)}$ and Christian Engelmann$^{(\boxtimes)}$

Computer Science and Mathematics Division, Oak Ridge National Laboratory,
Oak Ridge, TN 37831, USA
{kumarm1,engelmannc}@ornl.gov

Abstract. Resilience to faults, errors, and failures in extreme-scale high-performance computing (HPC) systems is a critical challenge. Resilience design patterns offer a new, structured hardware and software design approach for improving resilience. While prior work focused on developing performance, reliability, and availability models for resilience design patterns, this paper extends it by providing a Resilience Design Patterns Modeling (RDPM) tool which allows (1) exploring performance, reliability, and availability of each resilience design pattern, (2) offering customization of parameters to optimize performance, reliability, and availability, and (3) allowing investigation of trade-off models for combining multiple patterns for practical resilience solutions.

Keywords: High-performance computing · Resilience · Design patterns · Tool

1 Introduction

Resilience ensures successful execution of application running on HPC systems with thousands of nodes prone to several software and hardware failures. Next generation of HPC systems, contending for exaflops speed, will see more of these software and hardware failures, requiring more rigorous resiliency techniques. Recent unexpected issues in HPC systems such as bad solder, dirty power, and early wear-out [10,17] calls for better resiliency measures.

This work was sponsored by the U.S. Department of Energy's Office of Advanced Scientific Computing Research. This manuscript has been authored by UT-Battelle, LLC under Contract No. DE-AC05-00OR22725 with the U.S. Department of Energy. The United States Government retains and the publisher, by accepting the article for publication, acknowledges that the United States Government retains a non-exclusive, paid-up, irrevocable, world-wide license to publish or reproduce the published form of this manuscript, or allow others to do so, for United States Government purposes. The Department of Energy will provide public access to these results of federally sponsored research in accordance with the DOE Public Access Plan (http://energy.gov/downloads/doe-public-access-plan).

© Springer Nature Switzerland AG 2022
R. Chaves et al. (Eds.): Euro-Par 2021, LNCS 13098, pp. 283–297, 2022.
https://doi.org/10.1007/978-3-031-06156-1_23

Resilience design patterns [12,13] present a structured hard- and software design approach to tackle resilience problems in next generation HPC systems. Prior work focus on (1) identifying and standardizing the resilience design patterns in production high-performance computing (HPC) systems [11–13], (2) developing a proof-of-concept prototype for demonstrating the resilience design pattern concept using a fault-tolerant generalized minimal residual method (FT-GMRES) linear solver with portable resilience [1,2], (3) describing performance, reliability, and availability models for all structural patterns with flowcharts and state diagrams, and (4) introducing initial Resilience Design Pattern Modeling (RDPM) tool to study the characteristics of patterns [15].

This paper extends the previous work by (1) exploring each resilience design pattern models with parameter values customization, and (2) advancing RDPM tool to study combination of resilience design patterns.

2   Background

This section describes the metrics and resilience design patterns necessary to understand models implemented in RDPM.

2.1   Terminology and Metrics

The glossary in this work is mostly derived from our prior work in computing systems [3,13,14,19].

A fault is a flaw in a system that can result in an error. It may not cause any error when hidden, but once activated it can result in an error that can put a system in an illegal state. Once the error gets to the system service interface, it becomes a failure and makes the system inconsistent.

Reliability of a system is the probability of it not running into a fault, error, or failure $0 \leq t$ (Eq. 1). The fault, error, or failure distribution is the system reliability probability during $0 \leq t$ (Eq. 2). Its relative possibility is probability density function (PDF) $f(t)$. The rate at which a system encounters fault, error, or failure is λ. The mean-time to error (MTTE) is its anticipated time to error, while the mean-time to failure (MTTF) is its anticipated time to failure (Eq. 3).

$$R(t) = 1 - F(t) = \int_t^\infty f(t)dt \quad (1)$$

$$F(t) = 1 - R(t) = \int_0^t f(t)dt \quad (2)$$

$$MTTF = \int_0^\infty R(t)dt \quad (3)$$

$$A = \frac{t_{pu}}{t_{pu} + t_{sd} + t_{ud}} \quad (4)$$

$$MTBF = MTTF + MTTR \quad (5)$$

$$A = \frac{MTTF}{MTTF + MTTR} \quad (6)$$
$$= \frac{MTTF}{MTBF}$$

Availability is the part of the time a system works correctly, with planned uptime (PU) t_{pu}, scheduled downtime (SD) t_{sd}, and unscheduled downtime (UD) t_{ud} (Eq. 4). Performance is the time in which a task is executed successfully, including PU, SD, and UD. The mean-time to repair (MTTR) is the anticipated time to repair. It can be used with the MTTF to determine the mean-time between failures (MTBF) (Eq. 5). Availability can be determined using MTTR, MTTF, and MTBF (Eq. 6), if there is no SD.

2.2 Resilience Design Patterns

Resilience design patterns [12] specifically tackle the problem of handling faults, errors, and failures in extreme-scale HPC. They help in finding the problem induce by faults, errors, and failures and provide solutions to resolve them. Architects and developers can use resilience design patterns catalog [13] to create next generation resilient systems. Resilience design patterns allow investigation of design options to study the cost-benefit trade-offs between performance, protection coverage, and power consumption of different resilience solutions.

The current resilience design patterns catalog has 21 behavioral patterns: 4 strategy, 7 architectural, and 15 structural (Fig. 1). It also contains 5 state patterns. This paper extends the prior work [15], by introducing RDPM tool to explore performance, reliability, and availability of each structural resilience design pattern and investigate trade-off models for combining multiple patterns for practical resilience solutions.

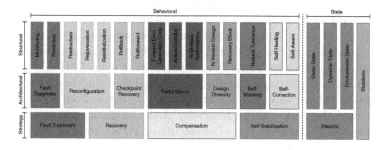

Fig. 1. Classification of resilience design patterns

3   Related Work

Reliability modeling, analysis and optimization proposes three types of models [18]: structural, state-space, and hierarchical. Structural models use block diagrams, reliability graphs, and fault trees to show the relation between systems. State-space models use Markov chains to show dependency between systems. Hierarchical models combine abstract structural models with Markov models to balance the speed of analysis and model accuracy. Additionally, Trivedi et.al. [21] propose performability analysis to model the interaction between performance and failure recovery behavior.

Rollback pattern represents Checkpoint/restart (C/R), which is one of the main resiliency strategies in HPC. In C/R, most of the reliability and performance models have been about optimum checkpoint interval [4, 22] and its application to systems with a non-constant MTBF [20], different failure distributions [16], and multilevel C/R solutions [5].

In production HPC, modular redundancy is still not in use. Modular redundancy research is mostly concentrated on solutions and models at the Message Passing Interface (MPI) [7, 9]. For the first time, Elliott et al. combine two different resilience mechanisms, C/R and modular redundancy [6], to explore performance and reliability trade-offs. This paper implements and further investigates the performance, reliability, and availability trade-off models.

4 RDPM

RDPM tool simplify the modeling of performance, reliability, and availability of patterns and their combination. Each pattern has its own models and parameters, which makes it hard to understand the performance, reliability, and availability for different parameters values under different implementations. Things get more complex when multiple patterns are combined horizontally or vertically for resiliency. The RDPM tool allows calculation of performance, reliability, and availability with ease for individual or combined patterns.

The Python-based RDPM[1] tool allows calculation, plotting, and storing of performance, reliability, and availability values for patterns and patterns combination. It has five components - RDP, Extract, Plot, CSV, and Patterns. RDP is the main class. It allows extraction of parameters from XML file and calculation, storing, and plotting of performance, reliability, and availability values. Extract allows extraction of individual pattern parameters from XML[2] file. Patterns calculate the performance, reliability, and availability values and pass to Plot to draw line/3D scatter plot. The calculated values are also passed to CSV for storing as CSV files.

4.1 Structural Patterns

Next, we will define the parameters, calculate performance, reliability, and availability values, and plot it for all the structural patterns. The performance, reliability, and availability models for all the structural patterns can be found in [15].

Monitoring: The monitoring pattern uses a monitoring system to recognize a defects or anomalies. Figure 2 demonstrates performance, reliability and availability of the Monitoring pattern. The task's execution time T_E is 168 h (7 days), MTTF M is 24–168 h (1–7 days). t_m, T_a, and T_n is 1 s. Reliability remains low with wrong results as the pattern just monitor the system.

---

[1] https://code.ornl.gov/6hk/rdpm.

[2] https://code.ornl.gov/6hk/rdpm/-/blob/master/xml/patterns.xml.

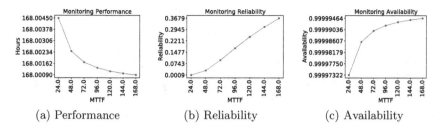

(a) Performance   (b) Reliability   (c) Availability

Fig. 2. Monitoring pattern performance, reliability, and availability

Prediction: The prediction pattern uses a monitoring system to recognize the potential of future defect or anomaly. Figure 3 demonstrates performance, reliability and availability of the Prediction pattern. The task's execution time T_E is 168 h (7 days), MTTF M is 24–168 h (1–7 days). t_{mon}, t_f, t_r, and t_{mod} is 2 s. T_n is 1 s. Reliability remains low with wrong results as the pattern just monitor the system to predict potential defect or anomaly.

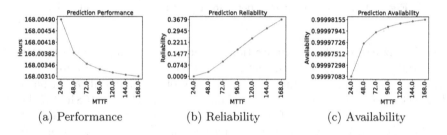

(a) Performance   (b) Reliability   (c) Availability

Fig. 3. Prediction pattern performance, reliability, and availability

Restructure: The restructure pattern changes the interconnection between the systems to reduce the impact of a fault, error, or failure. Figure 4 demonstrates performance, reliability and availability of the Restructure pattern. The task's execution time T_E is 168 h (7 days), MTTF M is 24–168 h (1–7 days). t_d, T_i, and T_r is 2 s. The MTTF M_u of the unprotected part of the system is 720 h (30 days). Reliability increases as the pattern resolve the fault, error, or failure.

Rejuvenation: The rejuvenation pattern restores the affected system to reduce the impact of a fault, error, or failure. Figure 5 demonstrates performance, reliability and availability of the Rejuvenation pattern. The task's execution time T_E is 168 h (7 days), MTTF M is 24–168 h (1–7 days). t_d and $T_l + T_r$ is 2 s. $T_{e,f}$ is 0.5 h. T_s is 1, 5 and 10 min. The MTTF M_u of the unprotected part of the system is 720 h (30 days). Restoring the affected system results in higher execution time.

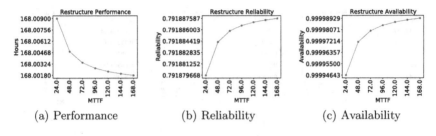

(a) Performance   (b) Reliability   (c) Availability

Fig. 4. Restructure pattern performance, reliability, and availability

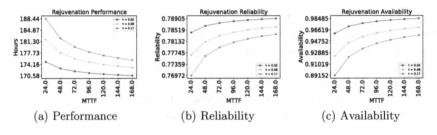

(a) Performance   (b) Reliability   (c) Availability

Fig. 5. Rejuvenation pattern performance, reliability, and availability

Reinitialization: The reinitialization pattern restores the affected system to its initial state to reduce the impact of a fault, error, or failure. Figure 6 demonstrates performance, reliability and availability of the Reinitialization pattern. The task's execution time T_E is 168 h (7 days), MTTF M is 24–168 h (1–7 days). t_d, T_i, and T_r is 2 s. The MTTF M_u of the unprotected part of the system is 720 h (30 days). Execution time increases significantly as the application executes from the start whenever required.

Rollback: The rollback pattern restores the system to the last checkpoint before a fault, error, or failure. Figure 7 demonstrates the performance, reliability, and availability of the Rollback pattern. The task's execution time T_E is 168 h (7 days), MTTF M is 24–168 h (1–7 days), the time to save system state/progress to storage T_s is 1, 5 and 10 min, $T_l + T_r$ is 1 s, and the MTTF M_u of the unprotected part of the system is 720 h (30 days). Faster storage results in better performance, reliability, and availability.

Rollforward: The rollforward pattern restores the system to the time when a fault, error, or failure. Figure 8 demonstrates the performance, reliability, and availability of the Rollforward pattern. The task's execution time T_E is 168 h (7 days), MTTF M is 24–168 h (1–7 days), the time to save system state/progress to storage T_s is 1, 5 and 10 min, $T_l + T_r$ is 1 s, and the MTTF M_u of the unprotected part of the system is 720 h (30 days). Rollforward results in better performance, reliability, and availability than rollback as the system restores to the point when a fault, error, or failure occur.

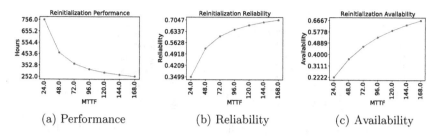

(a) Performance   (b) Reliability   (c) Availability

Fig. 6. Reinitialization pattern performance, reliability, and availability

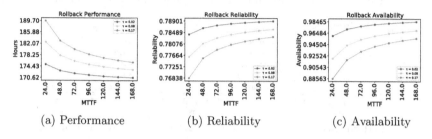

(a) Performance   (b) Reliability   (c) Availability

Fig. 7. Rollback pattern performance, reliability, and availability

Forward Error Correction Code: The Forward Error Correction Code (FECC) pattern applies redundancy to system state or resources to reduce the impact of a fault, error, or failure. Figure 9 demonstrates performance, reliability and availability of the Forward Error Correction Code pattern. The task's execution time T_E is 168 h (7 days), MTTF M is 24–168 h (1–7 days). $T_a, t_{en} + t_d$, and T_c is 2 s. The MTTF M_u of the unprotected part of the system is 720 h (30 days). Redundancy allows better performance, reliability, and availability than other patterns discussed till now. However, reliability is still low as the pattern doesn't employ redundancy fully.

Active/Standby: The Active/Standby pattern applies redundancy in the form of N functionally identical replicas to reduce the impact of a fault, error, or failure. Figure 10 demonstrates the performance, reliability and availability of the Active/Standby pattern. The task's execution time T_E is 168 h (7 days). To demonstrate performance, redundancy N is 1, 2 or 3 and in time and space, α between 0 and 1, and MTTF M is 24–168 h (1–7 days). T_a is 1 s, $t_i + t_d + t_r$ is 2 s, and T_f is 1 min. To demonstrate reliability and availability, redundancy N is 1, 2 or 3 and in space with $\alpha = 1$, the MTTF M is 48–336 h (2–14 days in 1 day increments). Reliability increases significantly but redundant systems overhead increases execution time significantly.

N-modular Redundancy: The N-modular redundancy pattern applies redundancy in the form of N functionally identical replicas to maintain continuous

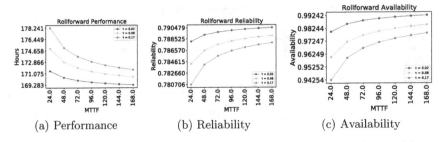

Fig. 8. Rollforward pattern performance, reliability, and availability

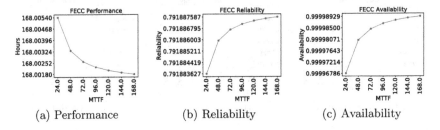

Fig. 9. Forward Error Correction Code pattern performance, reliability, and availability

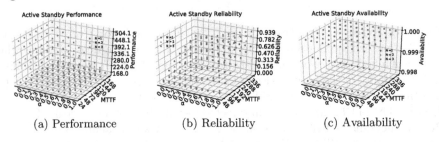

Fig. 10. Active/Standby pattern performance, reliability, and availability

correct operation of a system. Figure 11 demonstrates the performance, reliability and availability of the N-modular Redundancy pattern. The task's execution time T_E is 168 h (7 days). To demonstrate performance, redundancy N is 1, 2 or 3 and in time and space, α between 0 and 1, and MTTF M is 24–168 h (1–7 days). T_a is 1 s, $t_i + t_o$ is 1 s, and T_r is 1 min. To demonstrate reliability and availability, redundancy N is 1, 2 or 3 and in space with $\alpha = 1$, the MTTF M is 48–336 h (2–14 days in 1 day increments). Performance, reliability, and availability remain same as the active/standby pattern as the parameters remain almost same.

N-Version Design: The N-version design applies redundancy as N functionally equivalent alternate system implementations to handle a fault, error, or failure. Figure 12 demonstrates the performance, reliability and availability of

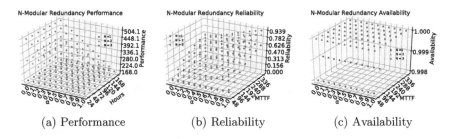

(a) Performance   (b) Reliability   (c) Availability

Fig. 11. N-modular Redundancy pattern performance, reliability, and availability

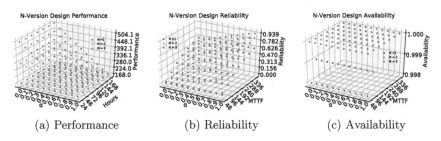

(a) Performance   (b) Reliability   (c) Availability

Fig. 12. N-Version Design pattern performance, reliability, and availability

the N-Version Design pattern. The task's execution time T_E is 168 h (7 days). To demonstrate performance, redundancy N is 1, 2 or 3 and in time and space, α between 0 and 1, and MTTF M is 24–168 h (1–7 days). T_a is 1 s, $t_i + t_o$ is 1 s, and T_r is 1 min. To demonstrate reliability and availability, redundancy N is 1, 2 or 3 and in space with $\alpha = 1$, the MTTF M is 48–336 h (2–14 days in 1 day increments). Performance, reliability, and availability are same as the active/standby pattern as the parameters are almost same.

Recovery Block: The recovery block pattern applies redundancy as a functionally equivalent alternate system implementation encapsulated in a recovery block. Figure 13 demonstrates the performance, reliability and availability of the Recovery Block pattern. The task's execution time T_E is 168 h (7 days). To demonstrate performance, redundancy N is 1, 2 or 3 and in time and space, α between 0 and 1, and MTTF M is 24–168 h (1–7 days). T_a is 1 s, $t_i + t_o$ is 1 s, and T_r is 1 min. To demonstrate reliability and availability, redundancy N is 1, 2 or 3 and in space with $\alpha = 1$, the MTTF M is 48–336 h (2–14 days in 1 day increments). Performance, reliability, and availability are same as the active/standby pattern as the parameters are almost same.

Natural Tolerance: The natural tolerance pattern uses implicit error/failure detection and self-masking to reach a correct system state from an illegal system state. Figure 14 demonstrates the performance, reliability and availability of the Natural Tolerance pattern. The task's execution time T_E is 168 h (7 days). To

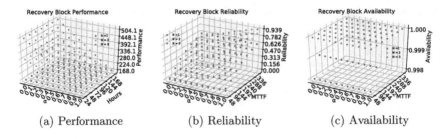

(a) Performance   (b) Reliability   (c) Availability

Fig. 13. Recovery Block pattern performance, reliability, and availability

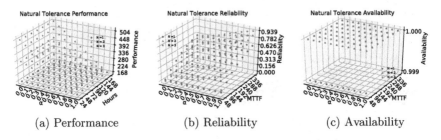

(a) Performance   (b) Reliability   (c) Availability

Fig. 14. Natural Tolerance pattern performance, reliability, and availability

demonstrate performance, redundancy N is 1, 2 or 3 and in time and space, α between 0 and 1, and MTTF M is 24–168 h (1–7 days). T_a is 1 s, t_d is half second, and T_m is 30 s. To demonstrate reliability and availability, redundancy N is 1, 2 or 3 and in space with $\alpha = 1$, the MTTF M is 48–336 h (2–14 days in 1 day increments). Performance, reliability, and availability improve a little from the active/standby pattern as the parameters T_m improve by 30 s as compared to T_f.

Self-healing: The self-healing pattern uses explicit error/failure detection and self-correction to reach a correct system state from an illegal system state. Figure 15 demonstrates the performance, reliability and availability of the Self-Healing pattern. The task's execution time T_E is 168 h (7 days). To demonstrate performance, redundancy N is 1, 2 or 3 and in time and space, α between 0 and 1, and MTTF M is 24–168 h (1–7 days). T_a is 1 s, t_d is half second, and T_c is 30 s. To demonstrate reliability and availability, redundancy N is 1, 2 or 3 and in space with $\alpha = 1$, the MTTF M is 48–336 h (2–14 days in 1 day increments). Performance, reliability, and availability are same as the natural tolerance pattern as the parameters remain almost same.

Self-aware: The self-aware pattern uses explicit error/failure detection and self-correction to reach a correct system state from an illegal system state. Figure 16 demonstrates the performance, reliability and availability of the Self-Aware pattern. The task's execution time T_E is 168 h (7 days). To demonstrate perfor-

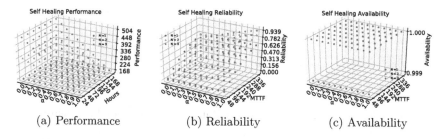

(a) Performance   (b) Reliability   (c) Availability

Fig. 15. Self-Healing pattern performance, reliability, and availability

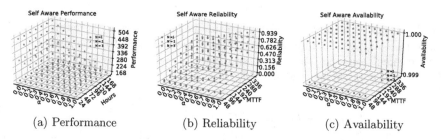

(a) Performance   (b) Reliability   (c) Availability

Fig. 16. Self-Aware pattern performance, reliability, and availability

mance, redundancy N is 1, 2 or 3 and in time and space, α between 0 and 1, and MTTF M is 24–168 h (1–7 days). t_m, T_a, and T_o is 1 s. T_c is 30 s. To demonstrate reliability and availability, redundancy N is 1, 2 or 3 and in space with $\alpha = 1$, the MTTF M is 48–336 h (2–14 days in 1 day increments). Performance, reliability, and availability remain same as the natural tolerance pattern as the parameters remain almost same.

4.2 Pattern Combinations

Multi-level Rollback: Recent work [8] detailed prior solutions and proposed a new approach for offering a separate resilience strategy for computation offloaded to a general-purpose computing graphics processing unit (GPGPU) accelerator. While the application itself is employing the Rollback pattern (level $l = 0$), an additional Rollback pattern is employed for the offloaded computation (level $l = 1$) to contain and mitigate GPGPU errors and failures using a more efficient strategy. The GPGPU computation is rolled back to a locally stored checkpoint upon an error or failure. The performance, reliability, and availability are calculated based on the parameters for each pattern, making the GPGPU resilience pattern a subsystem of the application resilience pattern.

While the application is waiting for the offloaded computation to finish, it is assumed that no other computation takes place and there is no need to save system state and progress to storage at level 0. Therefore, the application's failure free performance $T_{f=0}$ and performance under failure T are composed of the corresponding performances at level 0 and 1 (Eqs. 7 and 8). The reliability $R(t)$

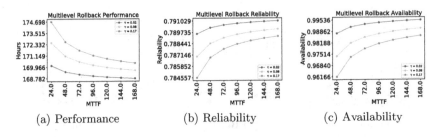

(a) Performance   (b) Reliability   (c) Availability

Fig. 17. Multi-level Rollback performance, reliability, and availability

can be obtained using the performance under failure T and the failure rate λ_u (or MTTF M_u) of the unprotected part of the system (Eq. 9). The availability A can be calculated using the task's execution time without any resilience strategy T_E and the performance under failure T (Eq. 10).

$$T_{f=0} = T_{f=0,l=0} + T_{f=0,l=1} \quad (7)$$

$$T = T_{l=0} + T_{l=1} \quad (8)$$

$$R(t) = e^{-\lambda_u T} = e^{-T/M_u} \quad (9)$$

$$A = \frac{T_E}{T} = \frac{T_E}{T_{l=0} + T_{l=1}} \quad (10)$$

Figure 17 shows the performance, reliability and availability of 2-level Rollback using the parameters from in Fig. 7 with 80% of the task's execution time T_E offloaded to a GPGPU, the time to save GPGPU state/progress to node-local storage $T_{s,l=1}$ of 1 s and the time to load it and to roll it back the same. Multi-level rollback provides better performance, reliability, and availability than normal rollback pattern.

Rollback and N-modular Redundancy: The recent work OpenMP target offload resilience [8] also considered employing the N-modular Redundancy pattern. In this case, GPGPU errors and failures are detected and potentially corrected using redundancy. The performance, reliability, and availability are calculated similarly to the multi-level Rollback based on the parameters for each pattern (Eqs. 7–10).

Figure 18 shows the performance, reliability, and availability of this solution using the parameters from Fig. 7, where 80% of T_E offloaded to a GPGPU. GPGPU redundancy N is 1, 2, or 3 and in time ($\alpha = 1$), the times to replicate the input T_i and to compare the outputs T_o are 0. The time to reboot a GPGPU and use it again for redundancy T_r and the MTTR R are 1 min. Inclusion of redundancy further improves performance, reliability, and availability than rollback pattern.

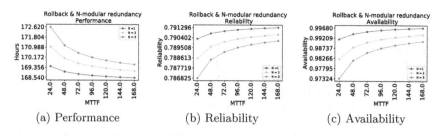

(a) Performance   (b) Reliability   (c) Availability

Fig. 18. Rollback and N-modular Redundancy performance, reliability, and availability

5 Conclusion

We introduced the RDPM tool, which allows exploring the design space for resilience solutions in HPC systems. It applies the resilience design pattern concept and models the performance, reliability and availability of resilience solutions. The parameterized resilience patterns can be employed horizontally, i.e., covering different parts of the system, or vertically, i.e., covering subsets of each other. The tool is easily extensible to new patterns and provides results in plots and CSV files. Future work involves extending the RDPM tool with power consumption models. The ultimate goal of this longer-term effort is to enable hardware/software codesign for performance, resilience and power consumption.

Acknowledgements. This work was supported by the U.S. Department of Energy, Office of Science, Office of Advanced Scientific Computing Research, program managers Robinson Pino and Lucy Nowell. This manuscript has been authored by UT-Battelle, LLC under Contract No. DE-AC05-00OR22725 with the U.S. Department of Energy.

References

1. Ashraf, R., Hukerikar, S., Engelmann, C.: Pattern-based modeling of multiresilience solutions for high-performance computing. In: ACM/SPEC International Conference on Performance Engineering, pp. 80–87 (2018). https://doi.org/10.1145/3184407.3184421
2. Ashraf, R., Hukerikar, S., Engelmann, C.: Shrink or substitute: handling process failures in HPC systems using in-situ recovery. In: Euromicro International Conference on Parallel, Distributed, and Network-Based Processing, pp. 178–185 (2018). https://doi.org/10.1109/PDP2018.2018.00032
3. Avizienis, A., Laprie, J., Randell, B., Landwehr, C.: Basic concepts and taxonomy of dependable and secure computing. IEEE Trans. Depend. Secure Comput. **1**(1), 11–33 (2004). https://doi.org/10.1109/TDSC.2004.2
4. Daly, J.T.: A higher order estimate of the optimum checkpoint interval for restart dumps. Future Gener. Comput. Syst. **22**(3), 303–312 (2006). https://doi.org/10.1016/j.future.2004.11.016

5. Di, S., Bautista-Gomez, L., Cappello, F.: Optimization of a multilevel checkpoint model with uncertain execution scales. In: IEEE/ACM International Conference for High Performance Computing, Networking, Storage and Analysis, pp. 907–918 (2014). https://doi.org/10.1109/SC.2014.79

6. Elliott, J., Kharbas, K., Fiala, D., Mueller, F., Ferreira, K., Engelmann, C.: Combining partial redundancy and checkpointing for HPC. In: International Conference on Distributed Computing Systems, pp. 615–626 (2012). https://doi.org/10.1109/ICDCS.2012.56

7. Engelmann, C., Ong, H.H., Scott, S.L.: The case for modular redundancy in large-scale high performance computing systems. In: IASTED International Conference on Parallel and Distributed Computing and Networks, pp. 189–194 (2009)

8. Engelmann, C., Vallée, G.R., Pophale, S.: Concepts for OpenMP target offload resilience. In: Fan, X., de Supinski, B.R., Sinnen, O., Giacaman, N. (eds.) IWOMP 2019. LNCS, vol. 11718, pp. 78–93. Springer, Cham (2019). https://doi.org/10.1007/978-3-030-28596-8_6

9. Fiala, D., Mueller, F., Engelmann, C., Ferreira, K., Brightwell, R., Riesen, R.: Detection and correction of silent data corruption for large-scale high-performance computing. In: IEEE/ACM International Conference on High Performance Computing, Networking, Storage and Analysis, pp. 78:1–78:12 (2012). https://doi.org/10.1109/SC.2012.49

10. Geist, A.: How to kill a supercomputer: dirty power, cosmic rays, and bad solder. IEEE Spectr. **10**, 2–3 (2016)

11. Hukerikar, S., Engelmann, C.: A pattern language for high-performance computing resilience. In: European Conference on Pattern Languages of Programs, pp. 12:1–12:16 (2017). https://doi.org/10.1145/3147704.3147718

12. Hukerikar, S., Engelmann, C.: Resilience design patterns: a structured approach to resilience at extreme scale. J. Supercomput. Front. Innov. **4**(3), 4–42 (2017). https://doi.org/10.14529/jsfi170301

13. Hukerikar, S., Engelmann, C.: Resilience design patterns: a structured approach to resilience at extreme scale (version 1.2). Technical Report. ORNL/TM-2017/745, Oak Ridge National Laboratory, August 2017. https://doi.org/10.2172/1436045

14. Koren, I., Krishna, C.M.: Fault-Tolerant Systems. Morgan Kaufmann, Burlington (2007)

15. Kumar, M., Engelmann, C.: Models for resilience design patterns. In: 2020 IEEE/ACM 10th Workshop on Fault Tolerance for HPC at eXtreme Scale (FTXS), pp. 21–30. IEEE (2020)

16. Levy, S., Ferreira, K.B.: An examination of the impact of failure distribution on coordinated checkpoint/restart. In: Workshop on Fault-Tolerance for HPC at Extreme Scale, pp. 35–42 (2016). https://doi.org/10.1145/2909428.2909430

17. Ostrouchov, G., Maxwell, D., Ashraf, R., Engelmann, C., Shankar, M., Rogers, J.: GPU lifetimes on Titan supercomputer: survival analysis and reliability. In: Proceedings of the International Conference on High Performance Computing, Networking, Storage and Analysis (SC), 15 –20 November 2020 (2020)

18. Pham, H.: Reliability Modeling, Analysis and Optimization. World Scientific, Singapore (2006)

19. Snir, M., et al.: Addressing failures in exascale computing. Int. J. High Perform. Comput. Appl. **28**(2), 127–171 (2014). https://doi.org/10.1177/1094342014522573

20. Tiwari, D., Gupta, S., Vazhkudai, S.S.: Lazy checkpointing: exploiting temporal locality in failures to mitigate checkpointing overheads on extreme-scale systems. In: IEEE/IFIP International Conference on Dependable Systems and Networks, pp. 25–36 (2014). https://doi.org/10.1109/DSN.2014.101

21. Trivedi, K.S., Malhotra, M.: Reliability and performability techniques and tools: a survey. In: Walke, B., Spaniol, O. (eds.) Messung, Modellierung und Bewertung von Rechen- und Kommunikationssystemen. INFORMAT, pp. 27–48. Springer, Heidelberg (1993). https://doi.org/10.1007/978-3-642-78495-8_3
22. Young, J.W.: A first order approximation to the optimum checkpoint interval. Commun. ACM **17**(9), 530–531 (1974). https://doi.org/10.1145/361147.361115

Exploring the Impact of Node Failures on the Resource Allocation for Parallel Jobs

Ioannis Vardas$^{(\boxtimes)}$ [ID], Manolis Ploumidis [ID], and Manolis Marazakis [ID]

Institute of Computer Science (ICS), Foundation for Research
and Technology – Hellas (FORTH) Greece, 100 N. Plastira Av.,
Vassilika Vouton, Heraklion 70013, Greece
{vardas,ploumid,maraz}@ics.forth.gr

Abstract. Increasing the size and complexity of modern HPC systems also increases the probability of various types of failures. Failures may disrupt application execution and waste valuable system resources due to failed executions. In this work, we explore the effect of node failures on the completion times of MPI parallel jobs. We introduce a simulation environment that generates synthetic traces of node failures, assuming that the times between failures for each node are independently distributed, following the same distribution but with different parameters. To highlight the importance of failure-awareness for resource allocation, we compare two failure-oblivious resource allocation approaches with one that considers node failure probabilities before assigning a partition to a job: a heuristic that randomly selects the partition for a job, and Slurm's linear resource allocation policy. We present results for a case study that assumes a 4D-torus topology and a Weibull distribution for each node's time between failures, and considers several different traces of node failures, capturing different failure patterns. For the synthetic traces explored, the benefit is more prominent for longer jobs, up to 82% depending on the trace, when compared with Slurm and a failure-oblivious heuristic. For shorter jobs, benefits are noticeable for systems with more frequent failures.

Keywords: Impact of node failures on MPI parallel jobs · Fault-aware resource allocation · Synthetic node failure trace generation

1 Introduction

HPC systems grow in size to meet the increased demand for both capability and capacity. At the same time, heterogeneity and complexity also increase to keep pace with application demand for performance. Several studies have outlined that the higher scale and complexity of HPC systems comes at the cost of more frequent failures [1, 15, 20, 23]. Furthermore, larger scale and more complex systems will introduce more complex software stacks to exploit their resources, with

© Springer Nature Switzerland AG 2022
R. Chaves et al. (Eds.): Euro-Par 2021, LNCS 13098, pp. 298–309, 2022.
https://doi.org/10.1007/978-3-031-06156-1_24

more frequent software-related errors [4,23]. To further motivate the importance of fault-tolerance, authors in [4,15,23] argue that reliability, along with resource management and energy efficiency, will be among the main obstacles towards robust exascale. Error resilience has been recognized to be one of the major technical research priorities for the next years, in the European Technology Platform for HPC (ETP4HPC) strategic research agenda [8].

By combining failure logs and traces with workload logs, several studies have outlined the impact of various system failures on system resource utilization. Authors in [5] report that in a large-scale HPC system, 20% or more of the computing resources are wasted due to failures and recovery. For one of Google's multipurpose clusters, it was found that a large fraction of time is spent for jobs that do not complete successfully [4]. The authors in [18] show that system related errors cause an application to fail once every 15 min. What is more, failed applications, although few in number, account for approximately 9% of total production hours. Authors in [20] examine node failure rate in the dataset collected during 1995–2005 at LANL. The number of failures per year per system can be as high as 1100, implying that an application requiring the entire cluster is expected to fail more than two times per day.

Therefore, node failures in a HPC system need to be considered both from the point of view of job completion times (a main concern for application owners) and from the point of view of potential resource wastage (one of the main concerns of system owners and operators). To mitigate the impact of failures, different approaches have been proposed including checkpointing [13,25,27], scheduling methods [3,12] and methods for resource allocation and resource management [9,10,17,30]. For evaluating the effectiveness of these approaches, failures traces and logs acquired from a real HPC system or cluster have been used. However, traces constitute merely a *snapshot* of a real system, corresponding to a specific size and period of operation. Moreover, several studies have shown that failures are affected by the workload [21,28].

It is therefore important to be able to explore the efficiency of fault tolerance methods under different failure conditions in a controllable and configurable manner. In this work, we present a simulation environment based on a synthetic trace generator for node failures. Further to the evaluation of fault tolerance methods, this work is a tool for system operators to assess the cost of failures, expressed in node-hours lost, either due to failure-oblivious resource allocation, or the overhead of fault-tolerance methods. We assume that for each node time-to-failure (TTF) is independently distributed, with all nodes following the same distribution, but with different parameters for each node.

To highlight the importance of failure aware resource allocation, we compare three different approaches with two of them being failure oblivious. The first one is based on a simple heuristic that searches for different contiguous and rectangular partitions of a torus topology. Then, based on the findings of [11], we estimate for each such partition the probability of failing during the upcoming job. This approach is compared against Slurm's [29] linear resource allocation, and to a heuristic that selects a partition for each job in a random manner. Both of these comparison baselines are oblivious to the probability of node failures. Finally, we illustrate the potential benefits of the failure-aware resource allocation approach with a set of simulation results for a case study concerning a 4D-torus topology with 4096 nodes. The mean time between failures for each node is independently distributed, and follows the Weibull distribution [10,11]. The scale and shape parameters of the corresponding distribution for each node are determined by two separate Gaussian distributions. Results derived with our simulation environment suggest that the benefit achieved by a failure-aware resource allocation approach depends on the system failure pattern. Specifically, the benefit is more prominent for larger jobs (job duration ≥24 h) in systems with less frequent failures. This benefit is up to 82%, depending on the simulated trace. For shorter jobs, the benefit becomes notable only on systems with more frequent failures.

2 Simulation Environment

In this section we describe our simulation environment and its main components. *Fail-stop* errors cause the execution of an application to terminate due to a hardware or software fault, whereas *silent errors* can impact the result of an application without causing termination. In this paper, we focus on *Fail-stop* type of failures. Moreover, with the term *failure* we refer hardware- or software-related deviation from nominal operating behavior. We further assume that a node restart is enough to fix transient failures, and that nodes fail independently of each other. Our simulation environment is not meant to offer the same level of simulation accuracy like Simgrid [2] or xSim [7]. In the current version we do not rely on any networking or processor model for deriving an accurate job duration; instead, we assume that job durations are known and explore three resource allocation approaches under different failure patterns. Job durations can be specified either through a distribution a post-processed trace.

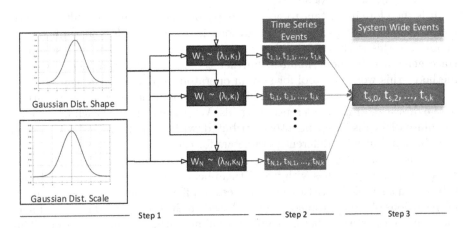

Fig. 1. Synthetic failure generation process.

2.1   Generator of Node Failure Traces

The key component of our simulated environment is the node failure trace generator. It assumes that the time to failure (TTF) for each node are independently distributed and characterized by the same distribution, but with each node having different distribution parameters. The synthetic node failure generator assigns the parameters to each node's TTF distribution. Each such parameter value is a sample drawn from a normal distribution. The main idea behind this assignment is that appropriate choices for the mean and standard deviation of the normal distribution lead to a predictable range of generated parameters for the TTF distribution of each node, and provide a degree of control on the way in which node parameters are distributed within this range. To make the above failure trace generation method more clear, we use as an example the case study presented in Sect. 3. We assume a topology of N nodes where TTF for node i is modeled with a Weibull distribution $W_i \sim (\lambda_i, k_i)$, where λ_i denotes the scale and k_i the shape of the corresponding distribution, respectively. Figure 1 summarizes the trace generation flow for this case study. In step 1, scale and shape parameter values are assigned to each node's TTF distribution. $G_\lambda \sim (\mu_\lambda, \sigma_\lambda)$ denotes the normal distribution from which samples are drawn to provide the scale parameter. The corresponding distribution for the shape parameter is $G_k \sim (\mu_k, \sigma_k)$. In the second step, K different failure times are generated for each node. The jth failure time for node i is estimated as $t_{i,j} = t_{i,j-1} + w_{i,j}$ where $w_{i,j}$ is the jth sample of $W_i \sim (\lambda_i, k_i)$ and $t(i,0) = 0$. In the third step, all different $t_{i,j}$ are merged into a single time-series and then sorted to derive the time of system failures, denoted as $(t_{s,1}, t_{s,2}, \ldots)$.

2.2   Resource Allocation Alternatives

The second major component of the simulation environment presented in this paper consists of the different resource allocation approaches. The first, denoted as *Slurm-linear*, is the resource allocation implemented by Slurm's linear selection plugin [22]. Nodes are arranged in an one-dimensional array, and for a request for k nodes with no overcommit requirement, the first k consecutive available nodes are allocated to the job. The other two approaches are specific to 4D-torus topologies, and are based on a heuristic that extracts a contiguous and rectangular partition from the 4D-torus topology. Its goal is to avoid contention from other partitions. If static routing is further assumed, this heuristic also ensures that failures of nodes that do not belong to the selected partition will not affect any job running on that. In the current version of the simulation environment, we rely on a simple heuristic for extracting such a partition. However, more elaborate approaches that also consider fragmentation may also be used [14,19]. The second resource allocation approach implemented is *random partition selector (RPS)*. When emulation of a new job's execution is needed, our heuristic populates a list of available contiguous and rectangular topology partitions, and then RPS selects one of them randomly, without consideration of any information or estimate about node failure probabilities. Both *Slurm-linear* and *RPS* are failure-oblivious approaches, and serve as comparison baselines.

The third approach implemented, will be denoted as *failure aware partition selection - FAPS* hereafter. It is based on the finding of [11] and consists of two steps. First, it utilizes the aforementioned heuristic to get a list of available contiguous and rectangular torus partitions, with P_i denoting the ith partition. In the second step, the goal is to select the partition that is the least probable to fail during that the execution duration of the job being scheduled. Let us assume a topology of $n = 1...N$ nodes where resources needed to be allocated for the jth with duration d_j. As per the case study presented in Sect. 3, we assume that each node's TTF follows a Weibull distribution. For simplicity, let t denote the uptime of the nth node after its last failure. Following the findings of [11], the probability that a node n will fail in d_j given that it has survived until t is expressed through Eq. 1, where k_n denotes the shape parameter of the nth node's TTF distribution and λ_n the corresponding scale parameter.

$$p_n^f = P(T \le d_j + t | t) = 1 - e^{\frac{t^{k_n} - (d_j + t)^{k_n}}{\lambda_n^{k_n}}} \tag{1}$$

Then, the probability of a partition P_i failing in d_j is derived via Eq. 2, which enables the proposed resource allocation approach to identify the partition with the lowest failure probability ($\underset{i}{\mathrm{argmin}} P_i^f$).

$$P_i^f = 1 - \prod_{n=1}^{N} (1 - p_n^f) \tag{2}$$

2.3   Impact of Node Failures to a Batch of MPI Parallel Jobs

The third component of the simulation environment is the logic that schedules jobs for execution. This component checks if the synthetic node failure generator has generated any fault on any node that belongs on the partition assigned to that job. The input to this component is a batch of jobs, where jobs durations are assumed to be known. More precisely, job durations can be specified through a post-processed trace of a distribution. In the current version of our simulation environment, no concurrent job execution is emulated. Instead, each job j_{k+1} is assigned resources and scheduled for execution only after job j_k completes. When a node failure occurs at some point in time, the uptime of that node is set to 0. If this node is assigned to the job whose execution is currently emulated, then this job is marked as aborted. When the job is aborted, both RPS and FAPS rerun their corresponding scheduling logic to determine a new partition to assign the job to.

3   Evaluation Case Study

In this section we present a case study of a system consisting of 4096 nodes, arranged in an $8 \times 8 \times 8 \times 8$ 4D-torus topology. The TTF of every node follows a Weibull distribution, with different parameters for each node. We use our simulation environment to compare the time required to complete a batch of jobs in the presence of failures, when resources are allocated according to the approaches discussed in Sect. 2: the two failure-oblivious ones (*Slurm-linear*, *RPS*), and the failure-aware approach FAPS. We consider different simulation scenarios by using different parameters for the normal distributions depicted in Fig. 1, thus controlling the combination of shape and scale parameters assigned to the Weibull distribution characterizing the TTF of each node.

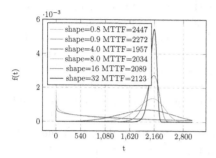

Fig. 2. Impact of shape on node TTF.

Table 1. Normal distribution parameters for scale & shape, and resulting MTTF (hours).

tid	Scale μ_λ	σ_λ	Shape μ_k	σ_k	Avg node MTTF	System MTTF
1	5800	0.1	8	0.1	5462	1.37
2	5800	0.1	32	0.1	5700	1.42
3	8500	0.1	8	0.1	8004	2.04
4	8500	0.1	32	0.1	8345	2.13
5	16000	0.1	8	0.1	15068	4.04
6	16000	0.1	32	0.1	15726	4.27
7	22000	0.1	8	0.1	20718	5.36
8	22000	0.1	32	0.1	21623	5.72

Figure 2 shows how the corresponding shape parameter affects a node's TTF, with the scale value set to a value corresponding to 2160 h (i.e. uptime of approximately 3 months). Each curve corresponds to a different pdf. As shape values become larger, a single node's MTTF approaches the corresponding scale value. Each of the 8 main rows in Table 1 corresponds to a different node failure trace. For each trace, we derive scale and shape parameters for the TTF distribution of 4096 nodes following the process depicted in Fig. 1. Columns 2 and 3 are, respectively, the mean and standard deviation of the normal distribution that generates the values for the scale parameter of each node. Columns 4 and 5 are the mean and standard deviation parameters of the normal distribution that generates the corresponding shape values for each node. Each pair of scale and shape values defines the parameters of each node's TTF following the Weibull distribution. Following the process described in Sect. 2.1, time series of failures for each node are generated. Merging and sorting the time series of all nodes, for a period of 10 years, allows us to extract the system-wide MTTF. For the experiments discussed in the rest of this section, for both normal distributions we set the standard deviation to a rather small number compared to the mean, resulting in an homogeneous cluster of nodes (in terms of their scale and shape parameters). For the normal distribution that generates scale values, we have used two alternative settings for the mean: 5800 and 22000. These settings correspond to average scale values over all nodes. From the first two traces in Table 1, we notice that, when the average scale value is 5800, the corresponding average MTTF over all nodes is 5700 for the higher average shape value, and

5462 for the setting of 8. So, the average scale value used in the first normal distribution, when combined with large shape values, directly affects each node's MTBF. Another observation is that, although average MTBF over all nodes is as high as 5800 in the first two traces, the corresponding system wide MTTF to failure is 1.37 h, suggesting that, there is at least one node failure every 1.37 h. Even when the average node MTBF is 21623 h which corresponds to one failure per 2.46 years approximately, the system wide MTTF is 5.72 h.

Next, we present results for each one of the simulated scenarios explored. The description of each simulated scenario consists of the following information: (a) number of jobs in the batch, (b) job duration for each job instance, (c) job size in terms of number of processes, and finally (d) a synthetic trace of failures. For the case study presented in this section, we use one of the eight traces listed in Table 2. For each simulated scenario, before emulating each job's execution, a resource allocation is carried out using the three methods described in Sect. 2.2. To determine whether a job execution fails, we extract all nodes that belong to the partition assigned to that job, for each allocation method. If the corresponding failure trace indicates a failure for one or more nodes, the job is considered aborted. Then, batch completion time is augmented by $t_{j,i} + rt$ where rt denotes the node repair time and $t_{j,i}$ job's j execution time until the failure. After a node is rebooted and considered fixed, its uptime is reset to 0. The aborted job is rescheduled for execution, i.e. the resource allocation step is repeated until its execution completes. For the simulation results presented here, the topology size is set to 4096 nodes, arranged in an $8 \times 8 \times 8 \times 8$ 4D-torus. Job size is set to 256 processes, and we assume batches of homogeneous jobs, i.e. jobs of the same duration. However, different simulation scenarios are possible with different job sizes and durations drawn from traces. Batch size is set to 1000 jobs, and we consider 5 different job durations: 4, 8, 24, 48, and 72 h. Repair time (rt) for a failed node is set to 9 min. The simulation environment discussed though, also allows to specify a distribution for deriving node repair times.

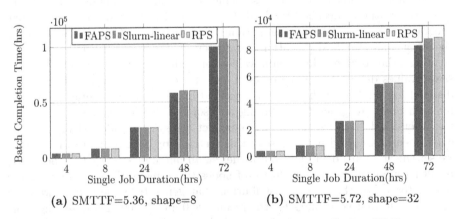

(a) SMTTF=5.36, shape=8   (b) SMTTF=5.72, shape=32

Fig. 3. Completion time for 1000 jobs, 256 processes, Scale = 22000.

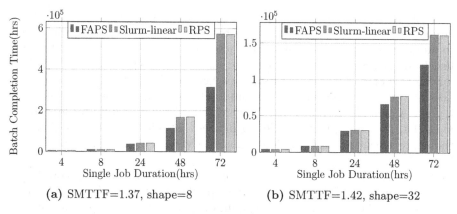

Fig. 4. Completion time for 1000 jobs, 256 processes, Scale = 5800.

Due to space limitations, we focus only on the traces that resulted in the lower and higher system MTTF (denoted as *SMTTF*). These 4 traces are enough to describe the key patterns observed in all our simulated scenarios. A common observation for Figs. 3a, 3b is that for the shorter duration jobs emulated (4, 8, 24 h), the benefit of the failure aware resource allocation (*FAPS*), in terms of batch completion time, is rather limited. More on that, for the scenario in Fig. 3a that corresponds to an average shape value of 8, it is marginally worse than the two failure-oblivious approaches (*Slurm-linear, RPS*). There are two main reasons for that. First, for larger scale values of the node's TTF Weibull distribution, failures become more rare over time, and thus more shorter jobs may *fit* between two successive system failures. Moreover, a batch of 1000 72-h long jobs, runs for longer and thus, more errors accumulate during the batch's lifetime on the cluster. In such scenarios, there is more room for a failure-aware approach to show benefit. Figures 3a, 3b also show that with longer jobs the failure aware resource allocation approach offers notable benefit. For the case of a batch of 48 h long jobs and an average shape of 32, it achieves 1.4% and 1.6% lower batch completion when compared to *Slurm-linear* and *RPS*, respectively. Although this reduction might not seem much, the failure aware approach achieves to save 768 and 895 h respectively. The corresponding improvements are even higher for the case of 72 h-long jobs (6.3% and 7.3%). There is another interesting observation regarding the effect of the average shape parameter. Comparing the benefit of *FAPS* over *RPS*, for the scenarios in Figs. 3a and 3b, we observe that it is higher for the case of the lower average shape value. The corresponding benefit is 5.6% for an average shape value of 8, and 5.1% for a value of 32. As Fig. 2 shows, smaller shape values imply a more *flattened* curve for the TTF distribution which in turns implies that node failures are more *dispersed* over time. A larger shape value suggests that TTF samples are more *clustered* around the scale value; many nodes are expected to fail in close-by points in time. Under such conditions, all the partitions explored by *FAPS* are expected to have similar failure probabilities, leaving little room for a beneficial selection. An observation that further supports this assumption is that the difference in benefit would be larger in a trace with more frequent faults, where *FAPS* is more often incapable to find a *good* partition to assign to a job. Indeed, Figs. 4a, 4b reveal that the benefit of *FAPS* over *RPS* is 23.5% for an average shape value of 8 and 79% for the case of 32. Our partition selection heuristic is a rather simple one, as it does not perform an exhaustive search for all possible partitions. Consequently, it yields a limited set of partitions in which *FAPS* will search for the less probable to fail. We are currently exploring further the validity of this intuition, and the improvement potential with an enhanced variant of the partition selection heuristic.

Figures 4a and 4b cover another pair of interesting scenarios. They correspond to traces 1 and 2 in Table 1 and describe a platform with more frequent failures. For the two different average shape values explored, the corresponding system MTTF are 1.37 and 1.42 h, respectively. Following the pattern observed before, for jobs of shorter durations, such as, 4 and 8 h, the failure aware resource allocation method achieves the same batch completion time with the failure oblivious ones. However, *FAPS* offers a notable benefit even for jobs with a 24 h duration. Following the pattern regarding shape's effect before, this benefit is larger for the smaller average shape value explored. At the scenario with 48-h long jobs and an average shape value of 8, *FAPS* achieves 46.8% and 48.4% lower batch completion time when compared to *Slurm-linear* and *RPS*. This benefit remains significant for the scenario depicted in Fig. 4b where the average shape value is larger (32). These results indicate that the type of jobs (in terms of duration) that benefit from failure-aware resource allocation is affected by the system failure pattern. In the paragraphs above, we discussed results from simulation scenarios with 256 process. We have also derived results for scenarios with 512 processes; however, due to space limitations, the corresponding graphs are omitted. Our results correspond to traces 5 and 6 from Table 1. Again, we observe marginal or not benefit with the failure-aware resource allocation method for job durations up to 24 h. For longer jobs and an average shape value of 8, we observe a more notable benefit. However, for the larger shape value, the benefit over the failure-oblivious approaches, even for 72-h long jobs is limited. We are currently exploring which of two factors contributes the most to this effect: limited number of partitions enumerated by our heuristic, and implications of a large shape value on node failures.

4   Related Work

Simulations of parallel applications have been a valuable tool for exploring their performance and scalability in large scale setups. They also allow to evaluate applications in setups that are different than the real HPC platforms that are available, offering the advantages of a controlled and configurable environment. Towards this direction, several simulators have been proposed. Simgrid [2] allows the simulation of unmodified applications, while xSim [6] allows running an application at a scale of up to millions of concurrent threads. LogGOPSim [6] allows the simulation of parallel algorithms at large scale relying on an extended version of the *LogGPS* model. For systems of growing size and complexity, a large number of studies have outlined the importance and effect of various failures [1,15,20,23] apart from performance. For mitigating the effect of failures several approaches have been proposed including checkpoint/restart [13,25,27], failure aware scheduling and resource allocation [3,9,10,12,17,30]. The resource allocation approach explored in this study is heavily based on the findings of [11] and follows a similar path for the resource allocation with [10]. More precisely, authors in [10] present algorithms that allocate resources for MPI jobs, such that system reliability is maximized. They take into account the probability of nodes failing during the execution time of each job. A common approach for evaluating the effectiveness of fault tolerance mechanisms relies on failure logs and traces acquired from real HPC systems. It is important though, to be able to evaluate such approaches in larger scales and under different system configurations and failure patterns. Towards this direction several studies have proposed simulators aimed at evaluating fault tolerance mechanisms (apart from performance and scalability). The work in [7] extends xSim [6] adding support to inject MPI process failures and explore the efficiency of checkpoint/restart. Authors in [24] discuss a simulator that aims at exploring proactive and reactive fault tolerance mechanisms, as well as a combination of the two. For its evaluation, they replay traces from failure logs. With a focus on coordinated and uncoordinated checkpoint/restart protocols, authors in [16] suggest a simulation framework based on LogGOPSim [6]. The work in this study does not target a full system simulator. Our main focus is on different failure patterns and their effect on resource allocation for parallel jobs. Our key contribution is a configurable mechanism that generates different traces of node failures.

5   Conclusions and Future Work

This paper is an early exposition of our modeling and simulation approach towards quantifying the impact of node failures on the completion times of MPI parallel jobs. We generate synthetic traces of node failures in a case study that assumes a 4D-torus topology and a Weibull distribution for each node's mean time between failures. For the synthetic traces explored, benefit is more prominent for the longer jobs. It can be up to 82% depending on the failure trace, when compared with Slurm and a failure-oblivious heuristic. For shorter jobs, benefit is notable for systems with more frequent failures.

Our research plan going forward includes more comprehensive case studies for larger-scale supercomputers incorporating more nodes and more complex interconnection topologies (such as 6D-torus and Dragonfly). We also plan to extend the scheduling logic for concurrent job execution and explore different distributions for the time to failure. Furthermore, we plan to incorporate node failure prediction in Slurm, by taking advantage of its software plug-in architecture. This extension will be building upon the software infrastructure created in our prior work towards adding failure awareness to resource allocation in Slurm [26].

Acknowledgments. This research has received funding from the European Union's Horizon 2020/EuroHPC research and innovation programme under grant agreements 955606 (DEEP-SEA) and 754337 (EuroEXA). National contributions from the involved state members match the EuroHPC funding.

References

1. Cappello, F., Al, G., Gropp, W., Kale, S., Kramer, B., Snir, M.: Toward exascale resilience: 2014 update. Supercomput. Front. Innov.: Int. J. **1**(1), 5–28 (2014)
2. Casanova, H., Giersch, A., Legrand, A., Quinson, M., Suter, F.: Versatile, scalable, and accurate simulation of distributed applications and platforms. J. Parallel Distrib. Comput. **74**(10), 2899–2917 (2014)
3. Dogan, A., Ozguner, F.: Matching and scheduling algorithms for minimizing execution time and failure probability of applications in heterogeneous computing. IEEE Trans. Parallel Distrib. Syst. **13**(3), 308–323 (2002)
4. El-Sayed, N., Zhu, H., Schroeder, B.: Learning from failure across multiple clusters: a trace-driven approach to understanding, predicting, and mitigating job terminations. In: 2017 IEEE 37th International Conference on Distributed Computing Systems (ICDCS), pp. 1333–1344 (2017)
5. Elnozahy, E.N.: System resilience at extreme scale. Technical report. Defense Advanced Research Project Agency (2008)
6. Engelmann, C., Lauer, F.: Facilitating co-design for extreme-scale systems through lightweight simulation. In: 2010 IEEE International Conference on Cluster Computing Workshops and Posters (CLUSTER WORKSHOPS), pp. 1–8 (2010)
7. Engelmann, C., Naughton, T.: Toward a performance/resilience tool for hardware/software co-design of high-performance computing systems. In: 2013 42nd International Conference on Parallel Processing, pp. 960–969 (2013)
8. ETP4HPC-SRA 4: Strategic Research Agenda for High Performance Computing in Europe. https://www.etp4hpc.eu/pujades/files/ETP4HPC_SRA4_2020_web.pdf
9. Fu, S.: Failure-aware resource management for high-availability computing clusters with distributed virtual machines. J. Parallel Distrib. Comput. **70**(4), 384–393 (2010)
10. Gottumukkala, N.R., Leangsuksun, C.B., Taerat, N., Nassar, R., Scott, S.L.: Reliability-aware resource allocation in HPC systems. In: 2007 IEEE International Conference on Cluster Computing, pp. 312–321 (2007)
11. Gottumukkala, N.R., Nassar, R., Paun, M., Leangsuksun, C.B., Scott, S.L.: Reliability of a system of k nodes for high performance computing applications. IEEE Trans. Reliab. **59**(1), 162–169 (2010)
12. Hakem, M., Butelle, F.: Reliability and scheduling on systems subject to failures. In: 2007 International Conference on Parallel Processing (ICPP 2007), pp. 38–38 (2007)
13. Heien, E., LaPine, D., Kondo, D., Kramer, B., Gainaru, A., Cappello, F.: Modeling and tolerating heterogeneous failures in large parallel systems. In: SC 2011: Proceedings of 2011 International Conference for High Performance Computing, Networking, Storage and Analysis, pp. 1–11 (2011)
14. Choo, H., Yoo, S.-M., Youn, H.Y.: Processor scheduling and allocation for 3D torus multicomputer systems. IEEE Trans. Parallel Distrib. Syst. **11**(5), 475–484 (2000)

15. Jauk, D., Yang, D., Schulz, M.: Predicting faults in high performance computing systems: an in-depth survey of the state-of-the-practice. In: Proceedings of the International Conference for High Performance Computing, Networking, Storage and Analysis, SC 2019, pp. 30:1–30:13. ACM, New York (2019)
16. Levy, S., Topp, B., Ferreira, K.B., Arnold, D., Hoefler, T., Widener, P.: Using simulation to evaluate the performance of resilience strategies at scale. In: Jarvis, S.A., Wright, S.A., Hammond, S.D. (eds.) PMBS 2013. LNCS, vol. 8551, pp. 91–114. Springer, Cham (2014). https://doi.org/10.1007/978-3-319-10214-6_5
17. Machida, F., Kawato, M., Maeno, Y.: Redundant virtual machine placement for fault-tolerant consolidated server clusters. In: 2010 IEEE Network Operations and Management Symposium - NOMS 2010, pp. 32–39 (2010)
18. Martino, C.D., Kramer, W., Kalbarczyk, Z., Iyer, R.: Measuring and understanding extreme-scale application resilience: a field study of 5,000,000 HPC application runs. In: 2015 45th Annual IEEE/IFIP International Conference on Dependable Systems and Networks, pp. 25–36 (2015)
19. Oliner, A.J., Sahoo, R.K., Moreira, J.E., Gupta, M., Sivasubramaniam, A.: Fault-aware job scheduling for BlueGene/L systems. In: Proceedings of the 18th International Parallel and Distributed Processing Symposium, p. 64 (2004)
20. Schroeder, B., Gibson, G.: Understanding failures in Petascale computers. J. Phys.: Conf. Ser. **78** (2007)
21. Schroeder, B., Gibson, G.A.: A large-scale study of failures in high-performance computing systems. IEEE Trans. Depend. Secure Comput. **7**(4), 337–350 (2010)
22. Slurm Resource Selection Plugin. https://slurm.schedmd.com/selectplugins.html
23. Snir, M., et al.: Addressing failures in exascale computing. In: ICiS Workshop ANL/MCS-TM-332, April 2013
24. Tikotekar, A., Vallee, G., Naughton, T., Scott, S.L., Leangsuksun, C.: Evaluation of fault-tolerant policies using simulation. In: 2007 IEEE International Conference on Cluster Computing, pp. 303–311 (2007)
25. Tiwari, D., Gupta, S., Vazhkudai, S.S.: Lazy checkpointing: exploiting temporal locality in failures to mitigate checkpointing overheads on extreme-scale systems. In: 2014 44th Annual IEEE/IFIP International Conference on Dependable Systems and Networks, pp. 25–36 (2014)
26. Vardas, I., Ploumidis, M., Marazakis, M.: Towards communication profile, topology and node failure aware process placement. In: 2020 IEEE 32nd International Symposium on Computer Architecture and High Performance Computing (SBAC-PAD), pp. 241–248 (2020)
27. Li, Y., Lan, Z.: Exploit failure prediction for adaptive fault-tolerance in cluster computing. In: Sixth IEEE International Symposium on Cluster Computing and the Grid (CCGRID 2006), vol. 1, pp. 8 p. 538 (2006)
28. Yigitbasi, N., Gallet, M., Kondo, D., Iosup, A., Epema, D.: Analysis and modeling of time-correlated failures in large-scale distributed systems. In: 2010 11th IEEE/ACM International Conference on Grid Computing, pp. 65–72 (2010)
29. Yoo, A.B., Jette, M.A., Grondona, M.: SLURM: simple Linux utility for resource management. In: Feitelson, D., Rudolph, L., Schwiegelshohn, U. (eds.) JSSPP 2003. LNCS, vol. 2862, pp. 44–60. Springer, Heidelberg (2003). https://doi.org/10.1007/10968987_3
30. Zhang, Y., Squillante, M.S., Sivasubramaniam, A., Sahoo, R.K.: Performance implications of failures in large-scale cluster scheduling. In: Feitelson, D.G., Rudolph, L., Schwiegelshohn, U. (eds.) JSSPP 2004. LNCS, vol. 3277, pp. 233–252. Springer, Heidelberg (2005). https://doi.org/10.1007/11407522_13

Characterizing Memory Failures Using Benford's Law

Kurt B. Ferreira$^{(\boxtimes)}$ and Scott Levy

Center for Computing Research, Sandia National Laboratories, Albuquerque, USA
{kbferre,sllevy}@sandia.gov

Abstract. Fault tolerance is a key challenge as high performance computing systems continue to increase component counts, individual component reliability decreases, and hardware and software complexity increases. To better understand the potential impacts of failures on next-generation systems, significant effort has been devoted to collecting, characterizing and analyzing failures on current systems. These studies require large volumes of data and complex analysis in an attempt to identify statistical properties of the failure data.

In this paper, we examine the lifetime of failures on the Cielo supercomputer that was located at Los Alamos National Laboratory, looking specifically at the time between faults on this system. Through this analysis, we show that the time between uncorrectable faults for this system obeys Benford's law, This law applies to a number of naturally occurring collections of numbers and states that the leading digit is more likely to be small, for example a leading digit of 1 is more likely than 9. We also show that a number of common distributions used to model failures also follow this law. This work provides critical analysis on the distribution of times between failures for extreme-scale systems. Specifically, the analysis in this work could be used as a simple form of failure prediction or used for modeling realistic failures.

Keywords: Failure characterization · DRAM memory failure · Benford's law

1 Introduction

Fault tolerance is a key challenge as high performance computing systems continue to increase component counts, individual component reliability decreases, hardware complexity increases, and software complexity increases. To better understand the potential impacts on next-generation systems, significant effort has been devoted to collecting, characterizing and analyzing failures [15,16,19,25,26]. These studies require large volumes of data, typically gathered over many years, and utilizing complex analysis in an attempt to identify the underlying probability distribution and its statistical properties.

Several mitigation methods have been developed to address memory failures. A popular method of fault tolerance in today's large-scale production systems is

© Springer Nature Switzerland AG 2022
R. Chaves et al. (Eds.): Euro-Par 2021, LNCS 13098, pp. 310–321, 2022.
https://doi.org/10.1007/978-3-031-06156-1_25

coordinated checkpoint/restart. The overheads of checkpoint/restart are determined, in part, by the duration of the checkpoint interval. Determining the optimal checkpoint interval requires an understanding of failure statistics on a given system in order to minimize lost work and checkpoint overheads [8]. Therefore, to better understand checkpoint overheads, one must understand the failure rate on a system. Checkpointing can also be coupled with failure prediction [14] to minimize time lost in the *rework* stage, but current prediction-based mechanisms have relatively poor performance or exceedingly high overheads. Therefore, having a cheap method to determine when faults are likely could improve application performance.

In this paper we examine faults on the entire lifetime of the Cielo supercomputer that was located at Los Alamos National Laboratory, looking specifically at the time between memory faults on this system. We undertake several simple analytical studies and make the following contributions. We show that:

- The time between uncorrectable memory faults over the lifetime of Cielo obey Benford's Law: the leading digit is more likely to be small (Sect. 3.2);
- The correctable faults from Cielo do *not* appear to obey Benford's law. We also outline a few suggestions as to why this is not true (Sect. 3.2); and
- Several common theoretical distributions used in HPC to model failures also appear to obey Benford's Law (Sect. 3.3).

To the best of our knowledge, this is the first work to demonstrate that memory faults from an large-scale HPC system obey a Benford distribution. It also provides critical analysis on the occurrence of memory failures on extreme-scale systems. Specifically, our analysis could be used to improve existing failure prediction mechanisms or to make models of memory failures more realistic.

2   Background

2.1   System Description

Cielo was a leadership-class HPC system located in Los Alamos, New Mexico. It was a Cray XE6 system running Linux that was operated from March 2011 to May 2016. At the time of its decommissioning, it was comprised of approximately 8,500 compute nodes. Each compute node contained 32 GB of DRAM and two processor sockets, each occupied by an AMD Opteron^{TM} 8-core processor. Cielo consisted of 96 *racks* of compute nodes arranged in 6 rows. Each rack contained 96 compute nodes arranged in a three-level hierarchy. Each rack was composed of three *chassis*. Each chassis was composed of eight *slots*. Each slot hosted four compute nodes.

2.2   Terminology: Faults and Errors

Throughout this paper, we distinguish between faults and errors, *cf.* [2]. A **fault** is the underlying cause of an error (e.g., stuck-at bits or high-energy particle strikes). An **error** is incorrect system state due to an active fault. Errors are *detected* and possibly *corrected* by higher-level mechanisms such as parity or error correcting codes (ECC). They may also be *uncorrected* or, in the worst case, *undetected*.

2.3 Terminology: Transient vs. Permanent Faults

Hardware faults can be classified as *transient, intermittent,* or *hard* [3,6,7]. *Transient faults*, which cause incorrect data to be read from a memory location until the location is overwritten with correct data. These faults occur randomly and are not indicative of device damage [3]. Particle-induced upsets ("soft errors"), which have been extensively studied in the literature [3,27], are one type of transient fault. Distinguishing a hard fault from an intermittent fault in a running system requires knowing the exact memory access pattern to determine whether a memory location returns the wrong data on every access. In practice, this is impossible in a large-scale field study such as ours. Therefore, we group intermittent and hard faults together in a category of *permanent* faults.

2.4 Memory Failure Logs

All of the DRAM on Cielo is protected by chipkill-correct ECC. When the memory controller detects a memory error, it is designed to use ECC to correct the error. If it is able to correct the error, the error is recorded as a *correctable error* (CE). If it is unable to correct the error, the error is recorded as a *detected, uncorrectable error* (DUE). Correctable errors are recorded in registers provided by the x86 Machine Check Architecture (MCA) [1]. The contents of these registers are polled periodically and written to the console log. Uncorrectable errors are recorded in an event log after the node is rebooted. For both correctable and uncorrectable errors, detailed information about each error is recorded. This information includes the physical address where the error occurred and ECC syndrome data that describes the cause of the error. Decoding the recorded information about each error allows us to identify the physical location of each logged error. We examined the memory error logs collected on Cielo from May 2011 to May 2016. Additional details can be found elsewhere [16,23].

2.5 Benford's Law

Benford's law, also called the Newcomb-Benford law, the law of anomalous numbers, or the first-digit law, is an observation about the frequency distribution of leading digits in many real-life sets of numerical data. The law states that in many naturally occurring collections of numbers, the leading digit is likely to be small. In sets that obey the law, the number 1 appears as the leading significant digit about 30% of the time, while 9 appears as the leading significant digit less than 5% of the time. The law is named after physicist Frank Benford, who proposed the law in 1938 [4], although it had been previously observed by Simon

Newcomb in 1881 [20]. Benford's Law has been shown to apply to a wide variety of data sets, including electricity bills, street addresses, stock prices, house prices, death rates, lengths of rivers, and physical and mathematical constants.

Mathematically, the probability distribution of the leading digit d ($d \in \{1, \cdots, 9\}$ is:

$$P(d) = \log_{10}(d+1) - \log_{10}(d) = \log_{10}\left(\frac{d+1}{d}\right) \tag{1}$$

Figure 1 shows both the probability distribution function (PDF) and the cumulative distribution function (CDF) for a theoretical Benford distribution.

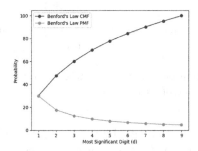

Fig. 1. Probability mass function for Benford distribution and cumulative mass function (CMF)

3 Experimental Results

3.1 Methodology

In the following sections we calculate the probability mass function of the leading digit and compare with a theoretical Benford distribution. For this calculation we use the time between memory faults in seconds. If the first digit of the time between faults begins with a zero, we use the first non-zero digit in the calculation.

The choice of seconds is arbitrary as the properties of this distribution is independent of the representations (*i.e.*, if an observation obeys Benford's Law it does not matter how that metric is represented). More formally, Benford's Law has been shown to be sum-invariant, inverse-invariant, and addition and subtraction invariant [5, 13].

3.2 Cielo System Lifetime Data Benford Analysis

Figure 2 shows the empirical distribution of the first digit of the time between faults in DRAM and SRAM over the lifetime of Cielo, measured in seconds. Figure 2a shows the data for uncorrectable memory faults. Figure 2b shows the data for correctable memory faults. From this figure, we make a few important observations. First, the intervals between uncorrectable memory faults follows a Benford distribution: memory fault intervals are much more likely to have a small first digit. However, Fig. 2b shows that while the interval between correctable memory faults are more likely to have a small first digit, they do *not* follow a Benford distribution as closely as the uncorrectable memory faults do.

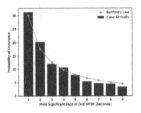

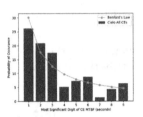

(a) All Uncorrectable Faults on Cielo

(b) All Correctable Faults on Cielo

Fig. 2. Benford distribution of fault time for all correctable faults and uncorrectable faults over the entire lifetime of Cielo

This difference may be explained by the mechanics of how errors are logged on the system. As described in Sect. 2.4 correctable memory faults on Cielo were logged in a ring buffer. Therefore, it is possible that some of these errors were lost when the ring buffer overflowed during computation. This is due, at least in part, to the fact that a correctable memory fault can produce a very large number of correctable errors, depending on the system's memory access patterns. If errors are lost, the calculation of the fault time may be affected. In contrast, it is less likely that uncorrectable memory faults are lost because the affected node halts and the single fault is recorded.

To understand how these data are affected by memory technology, Fig. 3 shows the leading digits of our uncorrectable memory fault data divided into two groups: memory faults in Static Random Access Memory (SRAM) (Fig. 3b); and memory faults in Dynamic Random Access Memory (DRAM) (Fig. 3a). Investigating these differences are important to developing a complete understanding of how memory faults occur because these two memory technologies use different protection mechanisms on Cielo; Chipkill [9] is used to protect DRAM, and memory parity is used to protect SRAM.

From the data in these figures. we make several observations. First, the SRAM uncorrectable fault times in Fig. 3b appear to follow a Benford distribution. The likely reason for this is due to total number of faults in each of these two scenarios. Because some of the logs we analyzed contain confidential information, we cannot comment on the total number of DRAM or SRAM faults, but over its lifetime, Cielo experienced more SRAM errors in comparison to DRAM. This is related to the fact that the SRAM structures are typically protected only by parity. Recent AMD processors provide much stronger SRAM protection. Finally, we observe that although the Benford distribution does not appear to be a good match for the intervals between uncorrectable DRAM faults, they do exhibit a similar trend: leading digits are still likely to be small.

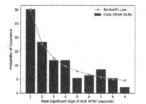 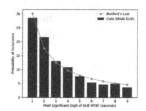

(a) DRAM Uncorrectable Faults on Cielo

(b) SRAM Uncorrectable Faults on Cielo

Fig. 3. Benford distribution of uncorrectable fault time for Static Random Access Memory (SRAM) and Dynamic Random Access Memory (DRAM) on Cielo

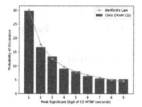 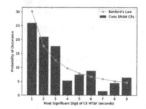

(a) DRAM Correctable DRAM Faults on Cielo

(b) SRAM Correctable DRAM Faults on Cielo

Fig. 4. Benford distribution of correctable fault times for Static Random Access Memory (SRAM) and Dynamic Random Access Memory (DRAM) on Cielo

In Fig. 4, we examine the same data for correctable memory faults. Interestingly, we observe a trend that is the opposite of what we observed with uncorrectable memory faults. Specifically, the Benford distribution is a good match for the time between DRAM correctable faults while the match between the Benford distribution and the time between correctable SRAM faults is not particularly good. In this case, these differences in SRAM cannot be attributed to the size of the data sample (*i.e.*, the total number of correctable memory faults in our dataset). Correctable faults are much more common than uncorrectable faults. As a result, we do not believe that these results can be attributed to the size of the sample. We are currently investigating the source of this phenomenon. As with uncorrectable memory faults, it might be related to the differences of logging and reporting the correctable errors. However, further study is needed.

Finally, Fig. 5 shows the distribution of failure interarrival times for both permanent and transient faults. For the data in these figures, we only distinguish between faults based on whether they are transient or permanent. All other distinctions are ignored; each dataset includes SRAM and DRAM faults, and correctable and uncorrectable memory faults). From this figure we observe that the permanent errors more closely follow a Benford distribution. This result may not be surprising given the fact that the majority of permanent faults are uncorrectable and transient faults are more likely to be correctable. However, it suggests that further analysis is needed to understand if the processes behind these faults obey a Benford distribution. Although the Benford distribution is not a particularly fit for the intervals between transient memory faults, these intervals do exhibit the same general trend: small leading digits are more common than large leading digits.

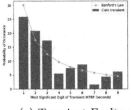
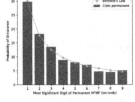

| (a) Transient Faults | (b) Permanent Faults |

Fig. 5. Benford distribution of the interarrival times for permanent and transient faults on Cielo.

3.3   Theoretical Distributions

In the previous section, we observed that fault interarrival time for Cielo appeared to follow closely a Benford distribution. In addition to characteriz- ing and tabulating failures, fitting failures to known distributions is common in fault tolerance. In this section, we examine the relationship between Ben- ford's Law and three probability distributions that are commonly used to model failures on HPC systems: exponential, Weibull, and gamma.

Mathematically, the probability mass function of the leading digit d ($d \in \{1, \cdots, 9\}$ for a theoretical probability distribution is:

$$P(d) = \sum_{k=-\infty}^{\infty} \Big(F((d+1) \cdot 10^k) - F(d \cdot 10^k)\Big)$$

where $F(x)$ is a cumulative density function (CDF).

Figure 6a shows the probability of the leading digit of a random variable drawn from exponential distributions. The solid lines represent the probabilities based on the theoretical distribution. The dashed lines represent the probability predicted by Benford's Law. Figure 7a and 7c show the same data for two differ- ent groups of Weibull distributions, corresponding to two different values of the shape parameter (0.25 and 0.75). Figure 8a and 8c show the same data for two different groups of gamma distributions, corresponding to two different values of the shape parameter (0.25 and 0.75).

Figure 6b shows the the sum of squared errors (SSE) of the leading digit probabilities based on theoretical exponential distributions relative to the probability predicted by Benford's Law. Figure 7b and 7d show the same data for two

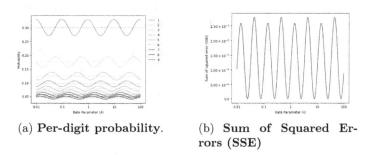

(a) **Per-digit probability.**   (b) **Sum of Squared Errors (SSE)**

Fig. 6. Exponential Distribution. Comparison of the probability leading digits from data drawn from exponential distributions to the results predicted by Benford's Law. In subfigure (a), solid lines represent values for the theoretical exponential distributions. Dashed lines represent the values predicted by Benford's Law.

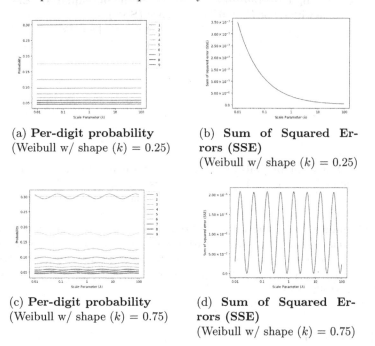

(a) **Per-digit probability** (Weibull w/ shape $(k) = 0.25$)

(b) **Sum of Squared Errors (SSE)** (Weibull w/ shape $(k) = 0.25$)

(c) **Per-digit probability** (Weibull w/ shape $(k) = 0.75$)

(d) **Sum of Squared Errors (SSE)** (Weibull w/ shape $(k) = 0.75$)

Fig. 7. Weibull Distribution. Probability of leading digits from data drawn from two groups of Weibull distributions (each with a different value of the shape parameter) to the results predicted by Benford's Law. In subfigures (a) and (c), solid lines represent values for the theoretical Weibull distributions. Dashed lines represent the values predicted by Benford's Law.

different groups of Weibull distributions, corresponding to two different values of the shape parameter (0.25 and 0.75). Figure 8b and 8d show the same data for two different groups of gamma distributions, corresponding to two different values of the shape parameter (0.25 and 0.75).

These figures show that the probability of leading digits for random variables drawn from these theoretical distributions closely match the values predicted by Benford's Law. Because these distributions have been shown to be a reasonable fit for memory errors on Cielo [16], these data help explain why Benford's Law accurately predicts the leading digits of these intervals on Cielo.

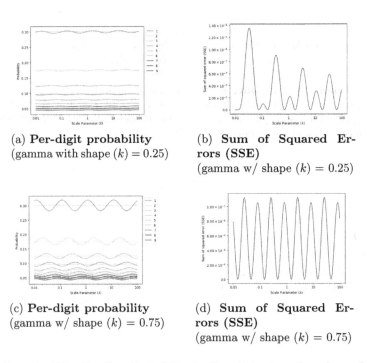

(a) **Per-digit probability** (gamma with shape $(k) = 0.25$)

(b) **Sum of Squared Errors (SSE)** (gamma w/ shape $(k) = 0.25$)

(c) **Per-digit probability** (gamma w/ shape $(k) = 0.75$)

(d) **Sum of Squared Errors (SSE)** (gamma w/ shape $(k) = 0.75$)

Fig. 8. Gamma Distribution. Probability leading digits from data drawn from two groups of gamma distributions (each with a different value of the shape parameter) to the results predicted by Benford's Law. In subfigures (a) and (c), solid lines represent values for the theoretical gamma distributions. Dashed lines represent the values predicted by Benford's Law.

4   Related Work

Failures characterization on large computer systems has been ongoing for over a decade. These studies have focused both on failures in HPC centers [10–12, 16,21,23–26] and industry datacenters [12,17,18,22]. These studies cover a wide diversity of systems of varying sizes and hardware/software configurations, yet many common failure trends are observed across all these systems.

Our work distinguishes itself from the existing studies in a number of important ways. First, to the best of our knowledge this is the first study to examine Benford's law and the interarrival times of failures for an HPC system. Second, this work is critical to both those modeling faults for HPC and those studying failures as it provides a simple methodology for verifying failure times. Finally, the results of this work may be of use to the those trying to mitigate or predict failures as this Benford property might be utilized to aid failure prediction.

5   Conclusions

In this paper, we have provided a study of the time interval between memory faults for both correctable and uncorrectable errors on the Cielo supercomputer that was located at Los Alamos National Laboratory. Through this analysis, we show that the time between uncorrectable faults for this system obeys Benford's law – a law that states that the leading digits of some naturally occurring datasets is more likely to be small in value. We also show that correctable errors do not appear to follow this law, possibly due to the fact that the logging of correctable errors is done by polling mechanism and therefore many errors can be missed or logged with times that vary significantly from the actual fault time. Finally, we show that many common distributions used in literature to model failures also follow a Benford distribution.

Acknowledgment. Sandia National Laboratories is a multimission laboratory managed and operated by National Technology & Engineering Solutions of Sandia, LLC, a wholly owned subsidiary of Honeywell International Inc., for the U.S. Department of Energy's National Nuclear Security Administration under contract DE-NA0003525.

References

1. AMD64 architecture programmer's manual volume 2: system programming, revision 3.23 (2013). http://developer.amd.com/wordpress/media/2012/10/24593_APM_v21.pdf
2. Avizienis, A., Laprie, J.C., Randell, B., Landwehr, C.: Basic concepts and taxonomy of dependable and secure computing. IEEE Trans. Depend. Secure Comput. **1**(1), 11–33 (2004). https://doi.org/10.1109/TDSC.2004.2
3. Baumann, R.: Radiation-induced soft errors in advanced semiconductor technologies. IEEE Trans. Device Mater. Reliab. **5**(3), 305–316 (2005). https://doi.org/10.1109/TDMR.2005.853449
4. Benford, F.: The law of anomalous numbers. Proc. Am. Philos. Soc. **78**(4), 551–572 (1938)
5. Berger, A., Hill, T.P.: Benford's law strikes back: no simple explanation in sight for mathematical gem **33**(1), 85–91 (2011). https://doi.org/10.1007/s00283-010-9182-3
6. Constantinescu, C.: Impact of deep submicron technology on dependability of VLSI circuits. In: Proceedings of the International Conference on Dependable Systems and Networks, DSN 2002, pp. 205–209 (2002). https://doi.org/10.1109/DSN.2002.1028901

7. Constantinescu, C.: Trends and challenges in VLSI circuit reliability. IEEE Micro **23**(4), 14–19 (2003). https://doi.org/10.1109/MM.2003.1225959
8. Daly, J.T.: A higher order estimate of the optimum checkpoint interval for restart dumps. Future Gener. Comput. Syst. **22**(3), 303–312 (2006). https://doi.org/10.1016/j.future.2004.11.016
9. Dell, T.J.: A white paper on the benefits of Chipkill-correct ECC for PC server main memory. IBM Microelectron. Div. 1–23 (1997)
10. Di Martino, C., Kalbarczyk, Z., Iyer, R.K., Baccanico, F., Fullop, J., Kramer, W.: Lessons learned from the analysis of system failures at Petascale: the case of Blue Waters. In: International Conference on Dependable Systems and Networks (2014)
11. Gupta, S., Patel, T., Engelmann, C., Tiwari, D.: Failures in large scale systems: long-term measurement, analysis, and implications. In: Proceedings of the International Conference for High Performance Computing, Networking, Storage and Analysis, SC 2017, pp. 44:1–44:12. ACM, New York (2017). https://doi.org/10.1145/3126908.3126937
12. Hwang, A.A., Stefanovici, I.A., Schroeder, B.: Cosmic rays don't strike twice: understanding the nature of DRAM errors and the implications for system design. In: Proceedings of the 17th International Conference on Architectural Support for Programming Languages and Operating Systems, ASPLOS XVII, pp. 111–122. ACM, New York (2012). https://doi.org/10.1145/2150976.2150989
13. Jamain, A.: Benford's Law. Master's thesis, Department of Mathematics, Imperial College of London and ENSIMAG, London, UK (2001), http://www.math.ualberta.ca/~aberger/benford_bibliography/jamain_thesis01.pdf. Not found in Imperial College Library or COPAC Catalogs on 16 February 2013. URL link is broken too
14. Jauk, D., Yang, D., Schulz, M.: Predicting faults in high performance computing systems: an in-depth survey of the state-of-the-practice. In: Proceedings of the International Conference for High Performance Computing, Networking, Storage and Analysis, SC 2019. Association for Computing Machinery, New York (2019). https://doi.org/10.1145/3295500.3356185
15. Kondo, D., Javadi, B., Iosup, A., Epema, D.: The failure trace archive: enabling comparative analysis of failures in diverse distributed systems. In: 2010 10th IEEE/ACM International Conference on Cluster, Cloud and Grid Computing (CCGrid), pp. 398–407. IEEE (2010)
16. Levy, S., Ferreira, K.B., DeBardeleben, N., Siddiqua, T., Sridharan, V., Baseman, E.: Lessons learned from memory errors observed over the lifetime of Cielo. In: Proceedings of the International Conference for High Performance Computing, Networking, Storage, and Analysis, SC 2018. IEEE Press (2018)
17. Li, X., Huang, M.C., Shen, K., Chu, L.: A realistic evaluation of memory hardware errors and software system susceptibility. In: Proceedings of the 2010 USENIX Conference on USENIX Annual Technical Conference, USENIXATC 2010, pp. 6–20. USENIX Association, Berkeley (2010). http://dl.acm.org/citation.cfm?id=1855840.1855846
18. Li, X., Shen, K., Huang, M.C., Chu, L.: A memory soft error measurement on production systems. In: 2007 USENIX Annual Technical Conference on Proceedings of the USENIX Annual Technical Conference, ATC 2007, pp. 21:1–21:6. USENIX Association, Berkeley (2007). http://dl.acm.org/citation.cfm?id=1364385.1364406
19. Liu, Y., Nassar, R., Leangsuksun, C., Naksinehaboon, N., Paun, M., Scott, S.L.: An optimal checkpoint/restart model for a large scale high performance computing system. In: IEEE International Symposium on Parallel and Distributed Processing, IPDPS 2008, pp. 1–9. IEEE (2008)

20. Newcomb, S.: Note on the frequency of use of the different digits in natural numbers. Am. J. Math. **4**(1–4), 39–40 (1881). http://www.jstor.org/stable/2369148
21. Schroeder, B., Gibson, G.A.: A large-scale study of failures in high-performance computing systems. In: Proceedings of the International Conference on Dependable Systems and Networks, DSN 2006, pp. 249–258. IEEE Computer Society, Washington (2006). https://doi.org/10.1109/DSN.2006.5
22. Schroeder, B., Pinheiro, E., Weber, W.D.: DRAM errors in the wild: a large-scale field study. Commun. ACM **54**(2), 100–107 (2009). https://doi.org/10.1145/1897816.1897844
23. Siddiqua, T., et al.: Lifetime memory reliability data from the field. In: 2017 IEEE International Symposium on Defect and Fault Tolerance in VLSI and Nanotechnology Systems (DFT), pp. 1–6, October 2017. https://doi.org/10.1109/DFT.2017.8244428
24. Sridharan, V., et al.: Memory errors in modern systems: the good, the bad, and the ugly. In: Proceedings of the Twentieth International Conference on Architectural Support for Programming Languages and Operating Systems, ASPLOS 2015, pp. 297–310. ACM, New York (2015). https://doi.org/10.1145/2694344.2694348
25. Sridharan, V., Liberty, D.: A study of DRAM failures in the field. In: Proceedings of the International Conference on High Performance Computing, Networking, Storage and Analysis, SC 2012, pp. 76:1–76:11. IEEE Computer Society Press, Los Alamitos (2012). http://dl.acm.org/citation.cfm?id=2388996.2389100
26. Sridharan, V., Stearley, J., DeBardeleben, N., Blanchard, S., Gurumurthi, S.: Feng Shui of supercomputer memory: positional effects in DRAM and SRAM faults. In: Proceedings of the International Conference on High Performance Computing, Networking, Storage and Analysis, SC 2013, pp. 22:1–22:11. ACM, New York (2013). https://doi.org/10.1145/2503210.2503257
27. Ziegler, J., Lanford, W.: The effect of sea level cosmic rays on electronic devices. J. Appl. Phys. **52**(6), 4305–4312 (1981). https://doi.org/10.1063/1.329243

Energy-Efficient Execution of Streaming Task Graphs with Parallelizable Tasks on Multicore Platforms with Core Failures

Jörg Keller and Sebastian Litzinger[✉]

FernUniversität in Hagen, Hagen, Germany
{jorg.keller,sebastian.litzinger}@fernuni-hagen.de
https://www.fernuni-hagen.de/pv

Abstract. Real-time applications often take the form of streaming applications, where a stream of inputs such as camera images is processed by an application represented as a task graph. The workload together with the required throughput often necessitates processing on a multicore system and also demands parallelization of large tasks. We extend a scheduling algorithm for such applications, originally devised to handle varying task workloads, to also cover varying core count, e.g. caused by failure of a core. We use frequency scaling to accelerate processing when the necessity to re-execute tasks from the crashed core arises, to maintain throughput. We evaluate the algorithm by scheduling synthetic task graphs that represent corner cases and a real streaming application.

Keywords: Fault-tolerant execution · Task scheduling · Energy efficiency

1 Introduction

Data stream processing is an important paradigm in embedded and edge computing [4], where a stream of data elements, e.g. camera images from a sensor, arrive and are processed by an application arranged as a task graph. Different instances of the task graph are overlapped, cf. Fig. 1, leading to a sequence of *rounds* with identical workloads. Real-time throughput requirements determine the maximum length of such a round. Scheduling the tasks of a round can be done statically, i.e. before actual execution, as a large sequence of identical rounds amortizes this investment. If the throughput is fixed, the target to optimize is energy per round, i.e. average power consumption, which has become as important as throughput for mobile systems. Executing such applications often necessitates multicore platforms because of tight deadlines, and sometimes tasks must be parallelized to reduce processing times of large tasks.

As such platforms and applications are running for long times, a fault may occur in a core, so that it fails. In this case, the application cannot be continued with the previous schedule. Litzinger and Keller have presented a scheduling

© Springer Nature Switzerland AG 2022
R. Chaves et al. (Eds.): Euro-Par 2021, LNCS 13098, pp. 322–333, 2022.
https://doi.org/10.1007/978-3-031-06156-1_26

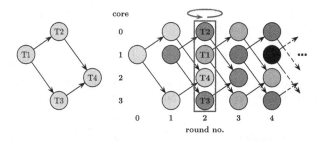

Fig. 1. Left: Task graph, with tasks T1 to T4 which communicate via links. Right: Streaming pipeline on 4 cores, with one round of execution marked with a rectangle and steady state indicated by a circular arc, Task graph and steady state of streaming pipeline, with marked round, adapted from [12]. (Color figure online)

algorithm that can adapt a (statically computed) schedule in case of varying workload [12]. We apply this algorithm to re-schedule tasks onto the remaining cores in case of a core failure. We discuss several scenarios how to handle the task graph from which a task was processed during the fault. Variants trade additional energy to handle the fault for delay of output. We evaluate our proposal with synthetic task graphs which represent corner cases to give upper and lower bounds on increase in workload and energy consumption for subsequent rounds. Furthermore, we implement a real-world image processing application to demonstrate applicability. Naturally, this approach cannot be used if all cores are running at maximum frequency in the fault-free case, as no processing resources will be left to handle the increased workload per core on fewer cores after a core failure. For example, even if workload w per round can be perfectly balanced, then a core failure will increase the workload per core by a factor $p/(p-1)$ and thus the (average) frequency in the fault-free case can be at most $f_{\max} \cdot (p-1)/p$, and will be lowered by an additional factor $1/\alpha$ if repetition of a lost task increases the workload by αw. Please note that this argument also holds in case of a spare core, the only difference being starting from $p+1$ cores.

The remainder of this article is structured as follows. In Sect. 2, we provide background information on static scheduling of moldable tasks for energy efficiency, and fault tolerance. In Sect. 3, we combine the scheduling algorithm from [12] with fault tolerance to continue applications in the presence of a core failure, with minimum energy overhead. Section 4 reports on our preliminary evaluation, while Sect. 5 gives conclusions and an outlook to future work.

2 Background

Scheduling Parallelizable Tasks. In the streaming pipeline of Fig. 1, n independent tasks are given with their workload τ_j (measured in cycles) and their speedup profile $s_j(q)$ when executed on q cores. All these tasks have to be completed before a given deadline D, the length of the round. To schedule these tasks

Fig. 2. Left: 4 equal-sized tasks on 4 cores, each with allocation $a_j = 1$. Right: 4 tasks with exponentially increasing workloads on 4 cores with allocations 0.5, 0.5, 1, 2, resp.

(cf. e.g. Melot [14]), an allocation, i.e. a number of cores is computed for each task to run on. This means that tasks are moldable [11], i.e. the degree of parallelism is fixed before actual task execution. Furthermore, an assignment, i.e. a subset of cores where the task is to run on, is specified, as well as a starting time and an operating frequency. The schedule must be feasible, i.e. no two task executions may overlap on a core. The platform is a multicore machine with p cores which can be scaled individually to K discrete operating frequencies f_1 to f_K. Thus, the runtime of task j on q cores running at frequency f_k is $t_{j,k,q} = \tau_j/(s_j(q) \cdot f_k)$. Runtime can also be influenced by memory access patterns, which might depend on the scheduling decision. However, we do not include this in our model. For each frequency level k and each task j (or task type), the power profile $pow_j(f_k)$ of the cores is known. Thus, the energy consumption of task j on q cores running at frequency f_k is $E_{j,k,q} = t_{j,k,q} \cdot pow_j(f_k) \cdot q$. Please note that $pow_j(f_k)$ is not total power consumption, but idle power pow_{idle} is subtracted. Thus, the total energy per round is the sum of the task execution energies plus $D \cdot p \cdot pow_{\text{idle}}$. This term is a constant for given D and thus not influencing scheduling decisions.

Litzinger and Keller [12] present such a scheduling algorithm for independent, parallelizable tasks. Each task is assigned an allocation $a_j = 2^{b_j}$ where $b_j \in \{-\max\{\lceil \log_2(\frac{n}{p}) \rceil, \log_2(p)\}, \ldots, \log_2(p)\}$. If a_j is integral, then task j has exclusive use of a_j cores for the time interval between 0 and D. If a_j is a fraction, then task j is sequential and runs for a time interval of length at most $a_j \cdot D$, i.e. the maximum runtime of a task with allocation a_j is $T(a_j) = \min(1, a_j) \cdot D$. The execution frequency for task j is set to the minimum f_k such that $t_{j,k,\max(a_j,1)} \leq T(a_j)$. Obviously, the allocations must be set that such a frequency exists. Allocations are set such that $\sum_j a_j \leq p$, and that the energy consumption resulting from these settings is minimized. Figure 2 depicts two examples with the 4 tasks from Fig. 1, yet with different workload distributions.

Allocations need not necessarily be powers of two, it is sufficient to have a small number of allocations. Also, for fractional allocations, i.e. sequential tasks mapped to the same core, using powers of 2 makes it always possible to find allocations that sum up to 1, i.e. utilize that core completely. The task runtimes are derived by benchmarking and include a 3% buffer for variation in task runtime, e.g. due to interrupt processing, to exclude late tasks. In the following, we assume that a feasible schedule with above structure exists for given task set and deadline. The scheduling algorithm from [12] is able to adapt allocations in case of varying task workload. Yet, alternatively to changing workloads, also the number of cores could change and necessitate an adapted schedule.

Scheduling for Fault Tolerance. A reason for such a change in core count could be the failure of a core due to a hardware or software bug or some bit flip from radiation. We consider the fail-stop model for cores [15], i.e. the failed core is assumed to be silent. Our work tries to improve system time to failure by overcoming core failures. Other works (cf. e.g. [3]) rely on a runtime system for failure notification. We consider a task that does not write its results until the deadline as lost, and the corresponding core reported as failed. In order to continue an application in this case, either task duplication or task repetition can be used [16]. We will consider task repetition in the sequel. Thus, besides the number of cores, also the workload may change after a failure.

Related Work. Kicherer and Karl [9] combine dynamic scheduling of multi-variant tasks on a heterogeneous system for performance with fault tolerance. In contrast, we target streaming applications without task variants or heterogeneity. Eitschberger [3] computes static schedules for tasks with dependencies on parallel machines with speed scaling and considers the trade-off between runtime, energy efficiency and fault tolerance. However, he treats fault-free and fault cases separately. Moreover, we use quasi-static scheduling instead of static scheduling. Marahatta et al. [13] present a dynamic scheduler that minimizes response time and simultaneously improves energy consumption and degree of fault tolerance. By contrast, we target task sets with a common deadline. Izosimov [8] considers transient faults, which are overcome by re-execution. In contrast, we consider permanent faults, i.e. we also consider re-mapping of tasks. Ajwani et al. [1] investigate the generation of synthetic but realistic streaming task graphs for benchmarking purposes, while we target corner cases and real applications for illustration. Benoit et al. [2] consider scheduling of moldable jobs on platforms with core failures, however they do not address frequency scaling nor energy consumption, but minimize makespan for one execution.

3   Scheduling Moldable Tasks for Fault-Tolerance

We consider the case that a core fails at an arbitrary point of time within a round. We assume that it fails near to the end, as this is a worst case scenario. We notice the failure because this core does not write the results of its task computation to the shared memory and late tasks do not occur, cf. Sect. 2. Hence, we do not rely on a runtime system to notice a core fault. In particular, we consider a fail-stop model [15], i.e. a core that fails is silent, and does neither memory accesses nor disturbs other cores from this point on. While a fail-stop model sounds quite restricted, we note that this is only the model exposed to the scheduler level. Within task execution, more evolved fault models and detection strategies can be used, cf. e.g. [5,6,10]. As we do not consider task duplication, the task that has been executed on that core is considered lost. If the application allows that processing of one input packet is skipped, then the cure is simple. In the following rounds, the tasks dependent on the lost task (i.e. the rest of the task graph instance) are skipped, and from the following round on the tasks to be executed only use $p - 1$ instead of p cores. As the scheduling algorithm from

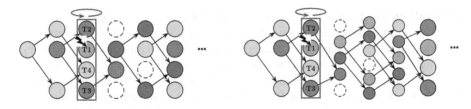

Fig. 3. Streaming pipeline from Fig. 1 with a core running task T1 (yellow) getting faulty. Left: T1 (yellow) is lost due to a core failure, and all dependent tasks are skipped, leading to reduced workload for the two rounds following the core failure. Right: T1 (yellow) is lost due to a core failure, and repeated in the subsequent round. All dependent tasks are delayed by one round, leading to workload fluctuations in the three rounds following the core failure. (Color figure online)

Sect. 2 can adapt the mapping prior to each round, and considers the number of cores as a parameter just as it considers the task count, it can cope both with the changed workload and with the changed platform. If e.g. task T1 from the yellow task graph instance is lost in the marked round in Fig. 1, then tasks T2 and T3 (yellow) will be skipped in the following round, and T4 (yellow) will be skipped in the next-but-one round, cf. Fig. 3 (left).

Another, also straightforward scenario is when the processing of an input packet can be delayed by one round. In that case, the lost task is repeated in the next round. To realize this, we only need to store task inputs until the task is successfully executed. Note that also all tasks dependent on the lost task in the respective task graph instance will be delayed by one round. Thus, the next s rounds show a variation in workload, if the lost task has a distance s from the sink of the task graph, and a change in platform in all following rounds, because only $p - 1$ instead of p cores are available. Yet, there is no change beyond the higher energy consumption that comes with higher load and frequency. We consider again the fault from the previous example. If T1 (yellow) is lost in the marked round, then it must be repeated in the following round, while T2 and T3 (yellow) will be delayed to the next but one round, cf. Fig. 3 (right).

In the following, we thus concentrate on a more ambitious scenario. We want to avoid the jitter in output production, i.e. we want to maintain a throughput of one completed sink task per round even after a core failure. Mind that this is not possible if a sink task runs until the end of a round: if a core it runs on fails, this is detected by the end of the round, and the sink task must be repeated. Therefore, we divide a round into two *half-rounds*. Accordingly, we divide the task set into two half-sets, where each half-set has approximately half of the workload from the complete task set. Even if the workload cannot be split exactly, the tasks can be divided evenly by allocation, as all allocations are powers of 2. We schedule each half-set in a half-round, putting the half-set with the sink task first. Allocations in the half-rounds can be derived from allocations in the full round by multiplying with 2. Still, a division into two half-rounds will already increase energy consumption in the fault-free case because of reduced parallel efficiency at higher degrees of parallelism.

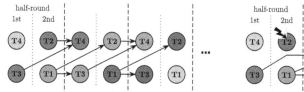 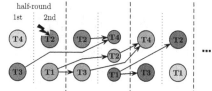

Fig. 4. Streaming pipeline from Fig. 1 mapped onto two half-rounds (assuming equal workloads). Left: no fault. Right: fault in second half-round on core running task T2. (Color figure online)

If a core fails, we will notice this at the end of a half-round because the task that ran on this core did not write its results, i.e. it is lost. The lost task is then repeated in the next half-round. Please note that due to our requirement, the next half-round can only belong to a subsequent round if the lost task is *not* the sink task. In this case, it might be necessary to delay some dependent task, as in the delay scenario discussed above. Thus, we can apply the same solution, however with half-rounds instead of rounds.

We demonstrate our approach with the two examples from Fig. 2. These examples can be considered corner cases. In the first example (best case) we have identical workload and allocation thus the additional work due to repeating a lost task is bounded. In the second example (worst case), the lost task is the biggest and its repetition doubles the workload in a half-round. In the first example, the 4 tasks with equal workload from Fig. 2 (left) can be evenly divided into two half-rounds (T3 and T4 in the first half-round, T1 and T2 in the second half-round), each with an allocation of 2 cores, see Fig. 4 (left). If core 3 fails in the second half-round, then T2 (red) must be repeated in the next half-round, which belongs to the subsequent round. Hence, T4 (red), which is dependent, must be delayed into the second half-round of the subsequent round, see Fig. 4 (right). This example can be considered a best case, as the task workloads are well balanced, and the fault occurs towards the end of a round. Still, as the number of cores reduces to 3, some task allocations reduce from 2 to 1, which leads to an increase in operating frequency and hence energy consumption.

The second example assumes an exponential workload distribution, i.e. $\tau_4 = 2\tau_3 = 4\tau_2 = 8\tau_1$. Scheduling into two half-rounds means that T4 runs in the first half-round with allocation 4, and T1, T2 and T3 run in the second half-round with allocations 0.5, 1 and 2, respectively. If a core fails in the first half-round, then this means that all tasks must execute in the second half-round, with only three cores left. This is kind of a worst-case scenario, where the workload of a half-round doubles, and the number of cores is reduced. Figure 5 illustrates this example.

If the workload in a half-round gets very high after a fault, then it might be worthwhile to treat jitter for energy by prolonging this half-round. In the extreme, the length of the half-round could be doubled, which is equivalent to

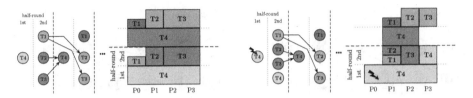

Fig. 5. Streaming pipeline from Fig. 1 mapped onto two half-rounds (assuming exponential workloads) and corresponding schedules. Left: no fault. Right: fault in first half-round on core 0 running T4.

having an additional half-round to repeat the lost task. In Sect. 4, we mention both ways, but any half-round length in-between these two extremes is possible.

While our examples only comprise a small number of tasks, our approach can be scaled to much larger task sets. First, the underlying scheduling heuristic from [12] is not computationally intensive. Second, if there are many tasks (compared to the number of cores), then most or all tasks will be sequential. This simplifies scheduling, and results in only $1/p$ of the total workload being affected by a core failure at most, in contrast to parallel tasks. For example, the fault in Fig. 5 affects more than half of the workload.

Please also note that our approach is not restricted to using two half-rounds. Using three (or even more) partial rounds would allow more freedom of task placement, e.g. to place a sink task in either first or second partial round. Furthermore, if the sink task is in the first partial round, then we would have the freedom to move some tasks of a task graph either to next or next-but-one partial round, and thus possibly achieve a better workload balance. On the other hand, using more partial rounds for a given task set results in fewer tasks per partial round and shorter partial rounds, which reduces energy efficiency and workload balance between partial rounds already in the fault-free case. Moreover, also the length of the half-rounds or partial rounds need not be identical, they could be scaled in proportion to their workloads.

4   Evaluation

To evaluate our approach, we have computed schedules for the two cases discussed in Sect. 3 as well as for a real-world application from the image processing domain. To this end, we have adopted the scheduler in [12]. In order to obtain realistic results even for the synthetic task sets considered in Sect. 3, scheduling is based on power and runtime characteristics which have been experimentally determined. In [12], these are provided for a floating-point multiplication task from the epEBench benchmark [7] running on an Intel Xeon E5-1620 v3 processor with four physical cores and 15 discrete operating frequencies between 1.2 GHz and 3.5 GHz. Furthermore, we take parallelization to be perfect (i.e. $e(q) = 1, 1 \leq q \leq p$) in the best case scenario (equal workload distribution), while parallel efficiency is assumed to decline with increasing core count and set as $e(1) = 1$, $e(2) = 0.9$, $e(4) = 0.85$, $e(8) = 0.8$ for the scenario with exponentially increasing workload. Deadlines are chosen in such a way that a feasible solution exists under a single core failure in all considered situations.

We will first examine the scenario where we have tasks with equal workloads, cf. Fig. 4. The scheduler computes the following schedules (for $p = 4$ initially, as we assume a system as specified above):

1. schedule for a full round ($n = 4$, $p = 4$, deadline D),
2. schedule for the regular 1st half-round (T3, T4, $p = 4$, deadline $D/2$),
3. schedule for the regular 2nd half-round (T1, T2, $p = 4$, deadline $D/2$),
4. schedule for the 1st half-round immediately succeeding a single core failure (T2, T3, $p = 3$, deadline $D/2$),
5. schedule for the 2nd half-round immediately succeeding a single core failure (T1, T2, T4, $p = 3$, deadline $D/2$),
6. schedule for the 1st half-round thereafter (T3 and T4, $p = 3$, deadline $D/2$),
7. schedule for the 2nd half-round thereafter (T1 and T2, $p = 3$, deadline $D/2$).

After the core failure has been accommodated in the subsequent round, scheduling for the remaining rounds is very similar to scheduling prior to the occurrence of a core failure, the only difference being $p = 3$ instead of $p = 4$. Scheduling yields the following results:

1. all tasks: $q = 1$, $f = 2.0\,\text{GHz}$,
2. T3, T4: $q = 2$, $f = 2.0\,\text{GHz}$,
3. T1, T2: $q = 2$, $f = 2.0\,\text{GHz}$,
4. T2: $q = 2$, $f = 2.0\,\text{GHz}$, T3: $q = 1$, $f = 3.5\,\text{GHz}$,
5. T1, T2, T4: $q = 1$, $f = 3.5\,\text{GHz}$,
6. T3: $q = 2$, $f = 2.0\,\text{GHz}$, T4: $q = 1$, $f = 3.5\,\text{GHz}$,
7. T1: $q = 2$, $f = 2.0\,\text{GHz}$, T2: $q = 1$, $f = 3.5\,\text{GHz}$.

Scheduling all four tasks over a full round under deadline D leads to an allocation of one core for each task, which is not surprising as workloads are equal among the tasks. Furthermore, each task can be executed prior to the deadline at a rather low operating frequency ($2.0\,\text{GHz}$). Scheduling in half-rounds leads to an increase in allocation to two cores per task, while operating frequencies can be kept at the same low level. A core fault during the execution of T2 in the second half-round leads to the necessity of repeating T2's execution in the upcoming round, cf. Fig. 3. Accordingly, T2 and T3 are run in the first half-round immediately succeeding the core failure. As only three cores are in working condition, there can be no allocation of two cores to both T2 and T3. One of them must make do with one core, which leads to a higher operating frequency of $3.5\,\text{GHz}$ for the core in question. In the second half-round immediately after the core failure, three tasks must be run in parallel on the three available cores to uphold throughput. Each task is allocated one core and operating frequency is adjusted to prevent a deadline violation. In the remaining rounds after the core failure, the assignment of tasks to half-rounds reverts to the status quo ante. Yet, scheduling has to take into account that only three cores are operational,

Table 1. Relative energy consumption for equal and exponentially increasing τ_j

Situation	Rel. energy consumption	
	Equal τ_j	Exp. incr. τ_j
Full round, no fault	1.00	1.00
Half rounds, no fault	1.00	1.06
Half rounds, immediately after fault	1.74	1.86
Half rounds, afterwards	1.25	1.06

thus in each half-round, one of the two tasks is allocated one core instead of two. Consequently, it is executed at a higher operating frequency.

Table 1 shows relative energy consumption values for the various situations encountered here. The full round fault-free case serves as a reference. Scheduling in half-rounds does not lead to an increase in energy consumption despite the larger allocations, the reason being a parallel efficiency of 1. For the round immediately succeeding the single core failure, an energy overhead of 74% is predicted by the scheduler for executing the majority of tasks on a higher frequency level. This overhead could be reduced by stretching the second half-round, which is where total workload peaks, leading to a trade-off. The energy overhead drops to 25% for the half-rounds thereafter.

For the scenario with exponentially increasing task workloads, computing schedules for all the relevant situations (cf. Fig. 5), leads to the following results:

1. (full round, no fault, $n = 4$, $p = 4$) T1: $q = 0.25$, $f = 1.7\,\text{GHz}$, T2: $q = 0.5$, $f = 1.7\,\text{GHz}$, T3: $q = 1$, $f = 1.7\,\text{GHz}$, T4: $q = 1$, $f = 2.0\,\text{GHz}$,
2. (1st half-round, no fault, $n = 1$, $p = 4$) T4: $q = 2$, $f = 2.0\,\text{GHz}$,
3. (2nd half-round, no fault, $n = 3$, $p = 4$) T1: $q = 0.5$, $f = 1.7\,\text{GHz}$, T2: $q = 1$, $f = 1.7\,\text{GHz}$, T3: $q = 1$, $f = 2.0\,\text{GHz}$,
4. (2nd half-round, immediately after fault, $n = 4$, $p = 3$) T1: $q = 0.5$, $f = 1.7\,\text{GHz}$, T2: $q = 0.5$, $f = 2.0\,\text{GHz}$, T3: $q = 1$, $f = 2.0\,\text{GHz}$, T4: $q = 1$, $f = 3.5\,\text{GHz}$,
5. (1st half-round, afterwards, $n = 1$, $p = 3$) T4: $q = 2$, $f = 2.0\,\text{GHz}$,
6. (2nd half-round, afterwards, $n = 3$, $p = 3$) T1: $q = 0.5$, $f = 1.7\,\text{GHz}$, T2: $q = 1$, $f = 1.7\,\text{GHz}$, T2: $q = 1$, $f = 2.0\,\text{GHz}$.

When scheduling for a full round, for the most part allocations are chosen according to the workload distribution, the exception being T4 with $a_4 = 1$, although additional resources are available. Scheduling T4 to two cores would reduce energy efficiency due to a worse parallel efficiency and despite $a_4 = 1$ requiring a higher operating frequency of 2.0 GHz. Scheduling in half-rounds leads to T4 being run on two cores in parallel in the first half-round to keep operating frequency low. In the second half-round, T3 is allocated one core instead of two. Utilizing two cores more accurately represents workload distribution but decreases efficiency. Core operating frequency is raised slightly to match the half-round's deadline. A core failure during T4's execution (1st half-round) leads to the necessity of executing all four tasks in the second half-round on three cores, cf. Fig. 5. While this is not critical for the small tasks, T4 can be completed without a deadline violation only by increasing the operating frequency to the maximum value of 3.5 GHz. Again, this could be mitigated by stretching. Subsequently, the original task assignment to half-rounds is restored without modification, as only three cores were occupied already in the fault-free case.

With regard to energy consumption, we can gather from the rightmost column of Table 1 that scheduling for half-rounds instead of full rounds introduces a slight penalty of 6% to energy efficiency, which can be partially attributed to higher operating frequencies and to some extent also to the higher degree of parallelism invoked when scheduling tasks in half-rounds. In the round where the core failure occurs, energy efficiency takes a massive hit as all tasks must be executed in the second half-round, having one core run at maximum frequency. Thereafter, the energy overhead reverts to 6% for the execution in half-rounds, as the schedule matches the one from before the core failure.

To evaluate our technique for a real-world streaming application, we have adopted the image processing application in [12] with slight modifications to raise the fraction of computationally intensive tasks. In particular, the application consists of 7 tasks: (0) load image, (1) enhance contrast, (2) sharpen image, (3) vertical edge detection, (4) horizontal edge detection, (5) combine images, and (6) write image. Each task j depends on the output of task $j-1$, except for task 4, which processes task 2's output, and task 5, combining the results of tasks 3 and 4. In contrast to the application in [12], we have created an additional task (sharpen image), and the edge detection tasks work with a 5×5 kernel instead of a 3×3 one. For the tasks remaining unchanged, power and runtime characteristics as well as parallel efficiency values when running on an Intel Xeon E5-1620 v3 are taken from [12], while for the others we have performed runtime and energy measurements ourselves. All tasks are parallelizable on up to four cores except for the I/O tasks, which run sequentially. Parallel efficiencies are derived from runtime measurements. When scheduling, the deadline for a full round is computed as

$$D = \frac{\frac{\sum_j t_{j,1,1}}{p} + \frac{\sum_j t_{j,K,1}}{p}}{2}.$$

Tasks 2, 4, and 6 are assigned to the first half-round. Accordingly, tasks 0, 1, 3, and 5 are executed in the second half-round. Scheduling in half-rounds introduces an energy overhead of 0.3% versus scheduling for a full round, which reaches 8.0% after a core failure has been compensated for (i.e. for the regular schedule in half-rounds on $p-1$ cores). As it turns out, a failure of any of the seven tasks cannot be accommodated under D as computed above. If a looser deadline is not an option (e.g. in case a certain throughput is to be upheld), one of the upcoming half-rounds may be stretched so the failed task can be repeated and a regular execution thereafter is granted. Due to dependencies, tasks may have to be postponed over several upcoming half-rounds. As we are interested in avoiding output jitter, we have determined the minimum half-round lengths after a core failure until the task graph instance the failed task belongs to is

Table 2. Minimum half-round lengths yielding a feasible schedule for the half-rounds succeeding a core failure (image processing application, Intel Xeon E5-1620 v3)

Failed task		0	1	2	3	4	5	6
Min. half-round length (ms)	#1	64	38	32	64	64	24	67
In half-round after core	#2		64	65		24	67	
Failure	#3		65			67		
	Σ	64	167	97	64	155	91	67
Cumulative deadline transgression (ms)			24	48	18	24	36	12	27

completed (afterwards, execution proceeds as before, the only difference being $p-1$ instead of p available cores). Table 2 shows the results.

Note that $D = 79.4$ ms, i.e. the deadline for a half-round is $D/2 = 39.7$ ms. In the worst case (failure of task 1), we have a cumulative deadline transgression of 48 ms $> D/2$. Here, avoiding output jitter may not be possible, depending on when exactly the sink task completes or whether other measures to speed up execution can be taken. The situation is less critical for all the other tasks, with a shorter delay ($<D/2$) at the end of the task graph instance's execution suffering the core failure. In fact, the first half-round can be completed in <37.4 ms on three cores, and the second one in <33.2 ms. This leaves the opportunity to make up for the delay once execution has reverted to the regular pattern.

In summary, we have seen that the concept of scheduling task sets in half-rounds can provide significant fault tolerance and even maintain the original throughput in cases of single core failures for different task workload distributions, a natural requirement being that deadlines are not too tight in the first place.[1] As can be expected, this comes at a price in the form of a small detriment to energy efficiency in the fault-free case.

5   Conclusion and Future Work

We have presented an approach to continue processing in a streaming application after a core failure. Throughput requirements are maintained, and jitter of result production is avoided, both at the cost of increased core operating frequencies. The choice of frequencies seeks to restrict additional energy consumption as much as possible. We have evaluated our approach based on synthetic task sets and a real application with parameters measured on an Intel multicore platform.

---

[1] If this is not the case—as e.g. for the image processing application treated here—one can stretch the half-round(s) right after the core failure in which the failed task is repeated while its dependent tasks are postponed as necessary, potentially recovering the time lost in the subsequent rounds by slightly tightening the deadline. This procedure will not lead to output jitter if the initial delay is kept reasonably short. Another option could be to decrease task runtime following a core failure by executing a less computation-intensive implementation, e.g. performing edge detection with a 3×3 kernel instead of a 5×5 one.

Future work will comprise actual fault experiments on a real system and a comparison of throughput and energy consumption from model and experiment.

References

1. Ajwani, D., et al.: Generating synthetic task graphs for simulating stream computing systems. J. Parallel Distrib. Comput. **73**(10), 1362–1374 (2013)
2. Benoit, A., Fèvre, V.L., Perotin, L., Raghavan, P., Robert, Y., Sun, H.: Resilient scheduling of moldable jobs on failure-prone platforms. In: 2020 IEEE International Conference on Cluster Computing (CLUSTER), pp. 81–91 (2020)
3. Eitschberger, P.: Energy-efficient and fault-tolerant scheduling for manycores and grids. Ph.D. dissertation, FernUniversität in Hagen, Germany (2017)
4. Gordon, M.I., Thies, W., Amarasinghe, S.: Exploiting coarse-grained task, data and pipeline parallelism in stream programs. In: Proceedings of the 12th International Conference on Architectural Support for Programming Languages and Operating Systems (ASPLOS XII), pp. 151–162 (2006)
5. Haas, F.: Fault-tolerant execution of parallel applications on x86 multi-core processors with hardware transactional memory. Ph.D. thesis, University of Augsburg, Germany (2019). https://opus.bibliothek.uni-augsburg.de/opus4/frontdoor/index/index/docId/59566
6. Höger, M.: Fault tolerance in parallel data processing systems. Ph.D. thesis, Technical University of Berlin, Germany (2019). https://nbn-resolving.org/urn:nbn:de:101:1-2019103000573284581309
7. Holmbacka, S., Müller, R.: epEBench: true energy benchmark. In: Merelli, I., Lio, P., Kotenko, I.V. (eds.) 25th Euromicro International Conference on Parallel, Distributed and Network-Based Processing (PDP), pp. 426–429, March 2017
8. Izosimov, V.: Scheduling and optimization of fault-tolerant distributed embedded systems. Doctoral dissertation, Linköping University (2009)
9. Kicherer, M., Karl, W.: Automatic task mapping and heterogeneity-aware fault tolerance: the benefits for runtime optimization and application development. J. Syst. Archit. - Embed. Syst. Des. **61**(10), 628–638 (2015). https://doi.org/10.1016/j.sysarc.2015.10.001
10. Kulkarni, S.S., Arora, A.: Low-cost fault-tolerance in barrier synchronizations. In: Proceedings of the 1998 International Conference on Parallel Processing (ICPP 1998), pp. 132–139. IEEE Computer Society (1998). https://doi.org/10.1109/ICPP.1998.708472
11. Leung, J.Y.T. (ed.): Handbook of Scheduling: Algorithms, Models, and Performance Analysis. CRC Press, Boca Raton (2004)
12. Litzinger, S., Keller, J.: Code generation for energy-efficient execution of dynamic streaming task graphs on parallel and heterogeneous platforms. Concurr. Comput.: Pract. Exp. (2020). https://doi.org/10.1002/cpe.6072
13. Marahatta, A., et al.: Energy-aware fault-tolerant dynamic task scheduling scheme for virtualized cloud data centers. Mob. Netw. Appl. **24**, 1063–1077 (2019)
14. Melot, N.: Algorithms and framework for energy efficient parallel stream computing on many-core architectures. Ph.D. thesis, Linköping University, Sweden (2017)
15. Schlichting, R., Schneider, F.: Fail-stop processors: an approach to designing fault-tolerant computing systems. ACM Trans. Comput. Syst. **1**(3), 222–238 (1983)
16. Siewiorek, D.P., Swarz, R.S.: Reliable Computer Systems—Design and Evaluation, 3rd edn. A K Peters, Natick (1998)

ParaMo – Workshop on Parallel Programming Models in High-Performance Cloud

Workshop on Parallel Programming Models in High-Performance Cloud (ParaMo)

Workshop Description

ParaMo is a forum for researchers working on programming models, networking, resource management, and runtime to solve the problems on parallel computing in high-performance cloud. The notion of cloud computing has changed the way how we utilize computing resources. Since High-Performance Computing (HPC) has long been suffered from under- or over-utilization of resources, many HPC researchers are trying to adapt HPC applications to the cloud environment. With proper adaptation, HPC applications are able to enhance their resource utilization ratio and scalability by using virtualized and on-demand resources on clouds. While we discuss HPC on clouds, we should discuss the parallel programming models as well. Various parallel programming models and their frameworks (e.g., TensorFlow, PyTorch, MapReduce, MPI, OpenMP, OpenCL, CUDA) has been proposed for parallel computing. For example, the MapReduce programming model has been used for various big data processing applications since it helps to reduce the complexity of problem parallelization such as decomposition, communication, and scheduling. However, a parallel programming model should be carefully selected for HPC applications to achieve high-performance and efficient resource usage because their target hardware architectures (e.g., accelerators, multi-core CPUs, memory hierarchy, etc.) are different as well as the abstraction levels. For example, MapReduce may not be a suitable selection of parallel programming model for a large-scale graph data processing problem. In addition, since traditional parallel programming models, such as MPI, are implemented for a single tenant cluster environment, applying these models to HPC applications on the cloud is challenging in terms of resource management.

The third International Workshop on Parallel Computing Models in High-Performance Cloud (ParaMo 2021) was held as a virtual event in Lisbon, Portugal. The workshop was organized in conjunction with the Euro-Par annual series of international conference. The format of the workshop was the technical presentation of research papers. Around twenty people attended the online sessions.

This year, we have received four articles for review, from European and Asian countries. After a thorough peer-reviewing process, we have selected three articles for presentation at the workshop (75% of acceptance ratio). The review process focused on the quality of the papers, their innovative ideas and soundness of the presentation. In addition to regular papers, we had an invited keynote paper, which also followed the same review process with regular papers.

We would like to thank the ParaMo Advisory Committee, the Program Committee, and the sub-reviewer who made the workshop possible. We would also like to thank Euro-Par for hosting our community, and the Euro-Par workshop chairs, Prof. Ricardo Chaves and Prof. Dora B. Heras for their help and support.

Organization

Program Co-chairs

Sangyoon Oh   Ajou University, South Korea
Hyun-Wook Jin   Konkuk University, South Korea

Advisory Committee

Geoffrey C. Fox   University of Virginia, USA
Dhabaleswar K. Panda   Ohio State University, USA

Publicity Chair

Sangho Yeo   Ajou University, South Korea

Program Committee

Seung-Hee Bae   Intel, USA
Jee Choi   University of Oregon, USA
Jong Choi   Oak Ridge National Lab., USA
Cheol-Ho Hong   Chung-Ang University, South Korea
Xiaoyi Lu   University of California at Merced, USA
Carmine Spagnuolo   Univ. of Salerno, Italy
Lauritz Thamsen   TU Berlin, Germany
Wenjun Wu   Beihang University, China
Beytullah Yildiz   Atilim University, Turkey
Weikuan Yu   Florida State University, USA

DepCon: Achieving Network SLO for High Performance Clouds

Eunsook Kim, Kyungwoon Lee, and Chuck Yoo$^{(\boxtimes)}$

Korea University, Seoul, South Korea
{eskim,kwlee,chuckyoo}@os.korea.ac.kr

Abstract. As containers run in a distributed manner in clouds, it is important to satisfy network service level objectives (SLOs) for containers. In addition, it has been known that containers utilize more CPU resources for network processing than native processes because of the long networking stack of containers. Thus, for achieving network SLOs, containers require sufficient CPU resources as well as network resources, which we call inter-resource dependency. However, existing cloud schedulers have limitations in that they do not take CPU into account for the network SLO. This paper proposes DepCon that controls CPU resources for containers to satisfy network SLOs. DepCon consists of DepCon scheduler that works in the cloud-level and DepCon agent at each node. We implement DepCon in the most popular container orchestration platform, Kubernetes. Our evaluation results show that DepCon reduces the network performance variance by 20 times while improving the network throughput by 40%. In addition, DepCon reduces the scheduling overhead by 20 times compared to the representative multi-resource scheduling technique like DRF.

1 Introduction

Cloud applications have performance requirements such as throughput and latency and the requirements are expressed as service level objectives (SLOs) that are defined by tenants [11,22]. In particular, SLO guarantee in terms of network performance is of paramount importance. This is because recent cloud applications tend to run as containers in a distributed manner and provide user-facing service by communicating with each other [9,13,15,29]. However, it remains challenging to satisfy network SLOs for containers [3,11,22,25,28].

The challenge comes partly from the fact that containers share the same operating system (i.e., host OS) [17,24]. The networking stack of the same host OS is shared among containers. Therefore, containers can interfere with each other, which makes difficult to achieve network SLOs. Furthermore, the network processing of containers consumes higher CPU resources than the native processes [13,18,26]. This is because containers require additional packet processing in a network bridge [18]. This means that satisfying network SLOs needs to have both network and CPU resources. For example, if a container does not receive enough CPU resources, the network performance of the container can be degraded despite the sufficient network resources allocated to the container [26].

© Springer Nature Switzerland AG 2022
R. Chaves et al. (Eds.): Euro-Par 2021, LNCS 13098, pp. 339–351, 2022.
https://doi.org/10.1007/978-3-031-06156-1_27

However, existing container scheduling techniques do not consider the dependency between the network and CPU resources. For example, the most popular container orchestration platform, Kubernetes, does not take into account the required CPU resources for containers to achieve specific network performance. We find that containers running on Kubernetes experience performance degradation (by 51% on average) and performance variance (by 41% on average) when containers with different network SLOs run on multiple servers (Sect. 4.2).

This paper proposes DepCon that addresses the performance degradation and performance variance in Kubernetes by taking the dependency between network and CPU resources into account in satisfying network SLOs. First, we devise DepCon scheduler that assigns a proper host server to satisfy network SLOs of containers. DepCon scheduler acquires network SLOs for containers from users and examines host servers in the system to find a host server with sufficient network and CPU resources. When the DepCon scheduler assigns a host server for a container, DepCon agent on the host server dynamically allocates CPU resources for the container. DepCon agent adaptively adjusts the CPU allocation depending on the actual network performance and SLOs of containers. Such hybrid architecture of DepCon that consists of DepCon scheduler and DepCon agent reduces the scheduling overhead by dividing container placement and resource allocation into cloud-level DepCon scheduler and server-level DepCon agent. This is different from existing multi-resource scheduling that conducts both container placement and resource allocation in a centralized scheduler. We implement DepCon in the most popular container orchestration platform, Kubernetes [7], and conduct performance evaluation. Our evaluation results show that DepCon improves performance by 40% while reducing performance variance by 20 times compared to Kubernetes. In addition, DepCon reduces scheduling overhead by 20 times compared to the existing multi-resource scheduling technique.

2   Background and Motivation

Kubernetes consists of servers called nodes, and a cluster consists of a master node that manages the cluster and worker nodes where pods are actually created and operated. The smallest deployable unit in Kubernetes is a pod, which consists of one or more containers[1]. By default, Kubernetes allocates computing resources for the pod CPU and memory via Linux cgroups [23], and network bandwidth via tc [10].

We conduct an experiment to demonstrate the limitation of container scheduling in Kubernetes, which cannot satisfy the network SLOs of containers. For the experiments, we utilize two servers equipped with an Intel Xeon CPU E5-2650v3@2.3 GHz (10 cores), 128 GB memory, and 256 GB SSD. The servers are connected using an Intel 82599 10 GbE network interface. The host OS is Ubuntu 18.04 and kernel version is 5.3. We construct container environments using Docker 19.03 and Kubernetes 1.18.3. For Kubernetes, we configure one server as a master node while running one worker node on another server.

---

[1] In this paper, we put one container per pod for simplicity.

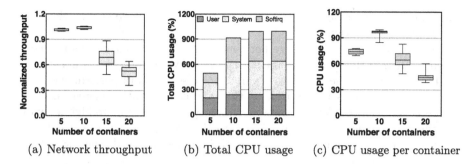

(a) Network throughput   (b) Total CPU usage   (c) CPU usage per container

Fig. 1. Performance by increasing the number of containers with tc

We utilize Netperf [19] benchmark to measure the network performance of containers and configure the containers running on the worker node to transmit 64 B TCP packets to the master node. Then, we assign 300 Mbps of network bandwidth as SLO to each container and increase the number of containers from five to 20. We run Netperf benchmark on each container for two minutes and measure the network throughput and CPU usage.

Figure 1(a) shows the normalized and average network throughput (y-axis) of containers when the number of containers increases (x-axis). The normalized throughput 1.0 means the configured network SLOs, 300 Mbps of network bandwidth. When the number of containers running on the worker node is less than 10, all containers satisfy the network SLO simultaneously. However, as the number of containers increases larger than 15, all containers experience performance degradation that achieves lower throughput than the SLOs. The network capacity is 10 Gbps, which is sufficient for 20 containers running concurrently (i.e., 6 Gbps in total), but the throughput of containers decreases by 48% on average. In addition, we find that when 15 containers run concurrently, the performance variance of containers increases by 14% on average. This means that the containers achieve varied throughput even though the same network bandwidth is allocated to the containers.

Figure 1(b) depicts the reason of the performance degradation is insufficient CPU resources. When the number of containers running on the worker node increases to 15, the total CPU usage becomes 1000% that is the total CPU capacity of the worker node. However, the container scheduling of Kubernetes does not consider the required CPU resources for the containers to achieve 300 Mbps on the worker node and allow the containers to contend for CPU resources. This leads to the performance degradation of the containers, which results in SLO violation. In addition, we divide the CPU usage into different categories such as User, System, and Softirq. Note that User and System indicate the CPU usage in user-level and kernel-level respectively, while Softirq means the CPU usage to process software interrupts (i.e., softirq). Especifically, when the number of containers increases from 5 to 20, the CPU usage of Softirq increases by 3.2 times. This is because the network processing of containers (i.e., pods) requires a larger amount of CPU resources from additional IP forwarding and NAT [16,18,21,30] in kernel-level compared to native processes. Moreover, the network bandwidth allocation by tc increases the CPU overhead from frequent lock operation and packet header inspection [13].

Figure 1(c) depicts CPU usage per container. When 15 containers run concurrently, we find that the CPU usage variance between the containers increases by 14% on average. The CPU usage variance causes network performance variance in Fig. 1(a). This means that as the overhead of softirq increases, CPU performance variance between containers increases, which leads to high network performance variance. As a result, to address the problem of performance degradation and high performance variance in Kubernetes, we need a new scheduler that achieves network SLO.

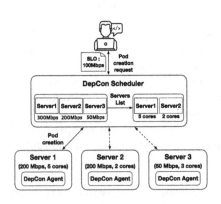

Fig. 2. DepCon design

Algorithm 1 Pod placement

$S=\{s_1...s_N\}$: set of host servers
$AS=\{as_1...as_N\}$: set of available servers
C_{SLO}: network SLO of container request
$netIdle, cpuIdle$: idle network and CPU

1: $count \leftarrow FW \leftarrow 0$
2: $FS \leftarrow \emptyset$
3: $AS \leftarrow S$
4: **for** $i \in 1..N$ **do**
5:     $idle \leftarrow s_i.netIdle$
6:     **if** $idle > C_{SLO}$ **then**
7:         $as_{count++} \leftarrow s_i$
8:     **end if**
9: **end for**
10: **while** $AS \neq \emptyset$ **do**
11:     **if** $FS = \emptyset \parallel FW < as_i.cpuIdle$ **then**
12:         $FS \leftarrow as_i$
13:         $FW \leftarrow as_i.cpuIdle$
14:     **end if**
15: **end while**

3   Design and Implementation

This paper proposes DepCon that is designed to satisfy the network SLO. A goal of DepCon is to overcome the limitations of Kubernetes as follows: 1) DepCon considers CPU for the network SLO to select the suitable server to create pods. 2) To achieve network SLO, DepCon allocates "proper" CPU to containers. So, DepCon scheduler performs the cloud-level pod placement and the DepCon agent node-level CPU allocation. The DepCon scheduler first searches host servers with sufficient network resources, which means that the amount of available network resources is larger than the network SLO. Then, among the servers, the DepCon scheduler selects a server with the largest CPU resources in order to ensure network SLO. At last, the DepCon agent on the selected server allocates CPU resources dynamically for achieving the network SLO.

Figure 2 depicts the design of DepCon. The DepCon scheduler runs as a centralized controller and performs pod placement. For example, the DepCon scheduler receives a request to create a pod with 100 Mbps network SLO from a tenant. Then, the DepCon scheduler creates a list of servers with available network bandwidth more than 100 Mbps among 3 servers, which are Server 1 ($S1$)

and Server 2 ($S2$). Note that this is different from Kubernetes that only offers admission control for CPU and memory resources. Between $S1$ and $S2$, the DepCon scheduler selects a server with the larger amount of available CPU resources. So, $S1$ is selected as the server. In Fig. 2, when the container is created on $S1$, the node changes the available bandwidth reduces to 200 Mbps (from 300 Mbps). DepCon agent on $S1$ receives the network SLO of the container from the DepCon scheduler. Then the DepCon agent monitors the network performance of the container and dynamically adjusts CPU allocation for the container to achieve the network SLO 100 Mbps.

We implement DepCon in Kubernetes and Linux kernel. First, we modify the scheduling plugin of Kube-scheduler to assign a higher weight to servers with more available CPUs and also modify the Kubernetes agent (i.e., Kubelet) to communicate with the DepCon agent (the LoC is 96). Second, we implement the DepCon agent as a loadable kernel module (the LoC is 317). The DepCon agent retrieves the information of containers from Kubelet such as network SLO and performs CPU allocation for containers by exploiting the Linux functionality, cgroups [23].

3.1 DepCon Scheduler

Algorithm 1 shows the pod placement of the DepCon scheduler. First, DepCon scheduler creates a list of servers that have larger amount of available network resources than the requested network SLO (lines 4–9). The scheduler rejects the pod creation request when the available network resources are less than the network SLO. Second, it assigns a weight on each server in the list based on the amount of available CPU resources (lines 10–15). DepCon scheduler does not have knowledge on how much CPU resources are needed for achieving network SLOs. Therefore, the scheduler assigns higher weight to the server with more CPUs. Finally, the scheduler selects a host server (FS) with the highest weight (FW) to place the pod.

3.2 DepCon Agent

DepCon agent runs dynamically to adjust CPU allocation for the container in order to satisfy network SLOs. As DepCon obtains the network SLO, the DepCon agent tries to find a proper amount of CPU resource for achieving the network SLOs in the host server. For simplicity, we assume that network SLO is given as network bandwidth.

DepCon agent periodically monitors network bandwidth of the container and compares the bandwidth with the network SLO. When the bandwidth is less than the SLOs, the DepCon agent increases CPU allocation for the container. The degree of increase and decrease is designed to be in proportion to the difference between the SLO (N_S) and the actual bandwidth (N_P) as in Eq. 1. This is based on a closed-loop control algorithm. Note that CPU_{prev} and CPU_{alloc} indicate the CPU allocation in previous period and current period, respectively. In Eq. 1, k is a tunable parameter that has an impact on the overall performance of the

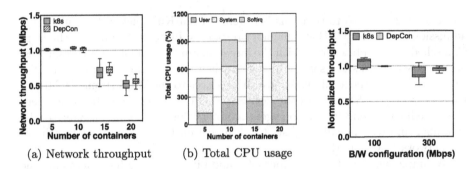

(a) Network throughput   (b) Total CPU usage

Fig. 3. Containers have the same SLO, 300 Mbps   **Fig. 4.** Network throughput with two SLOs

DepCon agent. For example, the large value of k reduces the time for achieving the SLOs by increasing the CPU allocation in big steps. However, this can result in the large variance of container performance. On the other hand, when k is small, the performance of containers does not fluctuate much. But, the CPU allocation is changed at a slow pace, which leads to slow convergence to the network SLO.

$$CPU_{alloc} = CPU_{prev} + CPU_{prev} * k * \frac{N_S - N_P}{N_S} \tag{1}$$

4   Evaluation

We evaluate DepCon in three sets of experiments. First, we measure the network throughput and CPU utilization when the containers are configured with the same network SLO, and compare them with that of Kubernetes. Second, we measure the network throughput for containers configured with different network SLOs. At last, we compare the scheduling overhead of DepCon with that of DRF, representative multi-resource scheduling technique.

4.1   Motivating Example Evaluation

For the experiments, we measure the network throughput and CPU usage under DepCon using the same experimental setup as in Sect. 2. In DepCon agent, k is set to 0.05, which is empirically determined, and the monitoring period is set to 100000 μs.

Figure 3 shows the network throughput (see Fig. 3(a) and total CPU usage (see Fig. 3(b)) with DepCon. The network throughput of DepCon is compared to that of k8s (k8s stands for native Kubernetes). With DepCon, the network performance variance between 15 containers reduces by 43% on average compared to k8s. This is because DepCon agent adjusts the CPU resources for the containers to satisfy the network SLOs. We also find that all containers achieve a similar level of CPU utilization. This is different from k8s where containers

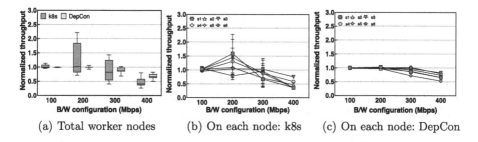

(a) Total worker nodes   (b) On each node: k8s   (c) On each node: DepCon

Fig. 5. Normalized throughput of containers with four SLOs using 10 servers

utilize different amounts of CPU resources owing to softirq processing. In addition, when 20 containers run concurrently, DepCon reduces the CPU usage for softirq processing by 12% on average. This is because DepCon does not utilize tc so that reduces the packet processing overhead caused by tc. By reducing the CPU usage in softirq, DepCon improves average network throughput by 7% by increasing the amount of CPU that the container of each container can utilize (see Fig. 3). However, the containers still cannot satisfy the network SLOs when the number of containers increases larger than 15 because the CPU resources of the worker node become saturated similar to Fig. 1(b). Even so, the DepCon guarantees network SLO as much as possible by adjusting the CPU to reduce network performance variance.

4.2   Support for Different Network SLOs on Multiple Servers

Now, we evaluate DepCon when containers with different network SLOs run on multiple servers. We conduct two experiments with the different numbers of host servers when the servers have the same hardware specification as Sect. 4.1.

For the first experiment, we utilize four servers in total. We configure the experimental environment with one master node, two worker nodes, and an evaluation machine. We create 30 containers on the two workers and the containers have two different SLOs in a random manner (100 Mbps or 300 Mbps). We present normalized average network throughput (y-axis) in Fig. 4. With k8s, Fig. 4 shows that the network performance decreases by 9% and the performance variance increases by 10%. There are two reasons. First, k8s does not take into account the CPU resources required to achieve network SLO. As a result, this leads to run containers with insufficient CPU resources. Second, k8s performs fair CPU scheduling by the default Linux CPU scheduler, CFS, even though the containers have different network SLOs such as 100 Mbps, 300 Mbps. Thus, the containers receive the same amount of CPU, which is not sufficient for the container with 300 Mbps of network SLOs. On the other hand, DepCon adjusts the CPU allocation of containers to converge to the SLO. As a result, DepCon enables the containers to achieve 300 Mbps by reducing the performance variance between containers by 3 times compared to k8s. Additionally, network performance improves on average by 5% compared to k8s.

For the second experiment, we utilize 10 servers in total and assign one master node, six worker nodes, and three traffic reception machines. We create 100 containers on the six workers and the containers have four different SLOs in a random manner from 100 Mbps to 400 Mbps. Figure 5(a) shows the SLO achievement of 100 containers under the k8s and DepCon, respectively. We present normalized and average network throughput (y-axis). At the network SLO of 200 Mbps, the k8s suffer from performance variance of up to 103 Mbps. This is because the containers with 200 Mbps of SLO do not receive sufficient CPU as k8s do not consider the CPU usage of the containers and results in CPU contention in the worker nodes. In addition, we illustrate the performance distribution of containers per worker node with k8s and DepCon, respectively, in Fig. 5(b) and Fig. 5(c) to observe the difference in satisfying SLOs depending on worker nodes. Note that x-axis indicates the configured SLO per container while y-axis means the normalized throughput to the value of SLOs. Figure 5(b) shows that the containers with k8s suffer from performance degradation and performance variance regardless of the worker node they are running on. At the network SLO of 400 Mbps, the network performance of k8s decreases by an average of 51%. On the other hand, Fig. 5(c) depicts that DepCon resolves performance variance in all worker nodes and satisfies the SLOs ranging from 100 Mbps to 300 Mbps. DepCon reduces the average performance variance of servers by 16x compared to k8s by scheduling containers on servers with sufficient CPU and adjusting CPU to achieve network SLO. In addition, in Fig. 5(a), the performance variance of containers at SLO of 200 Mbps decreases by an average of 20 times (98 Mbps) compared to k8s which has a performance variance by 41% on average.

However, we find that the containers with 400 Mbps of SLO experience performance degradation compared to the configured SLOs. The reason is that the CPU capacity of six worker nodes is insufficient to support 100 containers with different SLOs from 100 Mbps to 400 Mbps. The total CPU utilization of worker nodes is 973% on average, which means that the CPU resources are fully utilized in all worker nodes. This allows the containers with 400 Mbps of SLO not to receive sufficient CPU resources to achieve 400 Mbps. Even though the containers with 400 Mbps of SLO achieve lower performance than the configured SLO by 32% on average, DepCon improves the network performance by 40% on average compared to k8s.

4.3   Scheduling Overhead Analysis

Because container scheduling deals with numerous numbers of servers, low scheduling overhead is important for high scalability [4]. This evaluation shows the scheduling overhead of DepCon compared with Dominant Resource Fairness (DRF) [6], the well-known multi-resource scheduling technique.

DRF is a fair sharing model that is designed to achieve the max-min fairness to multiple resource types. DRF receives the resource demand that includes the amount of computing resources such as CPU and memory required for a job from tenants, which is similar to the container scheduling in Kubernetes. Then, based on the resource demand, DRF finds a dominant resource that has a larger

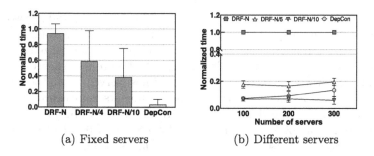

(a) Fixed servers   (b) Different servers

Fig. 6. Scheduling overhead of DepCon and DRF in different conditions

fraction among multiple resources as follows. DRF-based scheduling algorithm iterates resource allocation over the number of tenants (T) and resource types (R). Hence, the time complexity of the DRF-based algorithm is $O(R^2T)$ [12] and its scheduling overhead increase with the number of tenants and resource types. On the other hand, DepCon scheduler does not iterate resource allocation for the numbers of tenants or resource types, only for the number of host servers (N) (see Algorithm 1). Therefore, the worst-case time complexity of DepCon scheduler is $O(N)$.

We run two experiments to compare the scheduling completion time of Dep-Con and DRF using simulations. Note that scheduling completion time indicates the time spent to determine the appropriate host server to place containers. First, We measure scheduling completion time with fixed number of servers by utilizing a representative cloud simulator, CloudSim [20]. Then, we measure the scheduling completion time of DepCon and DRF under various experiment environments that have different numbers of tenants and host servers.

In the first experiment, we measure scheduling overhead in a simulation environment consisting of 400 host servers. We compare the scheduling completion time of DepCon and DRF for the 300 container creation requests with varying the number of tenants. Figure 6(a) shows the scheduling overhead of DepCon and DRF in the CloudSim environment. The x-axis is the DepCon and DRF experimented with changing the number of tenants. For example, in DRF-#, # means the number of tenants where N denotes the number of containers. In other words, DRF-$N/4$ indicates that the number of tenants is $\frac{300}{4}$. The y-axis is the normalized total scheduling time. On CloudSim, DepCon takes 0.032 as average normalized scheduling time and DRF takes average normalized scheduling time from 0.38 to 0.94 as the number of tenants increases from $N/10$ to N. So, DepCon reduces scheduling overhead by 29x on average compared to DRF-N, and decreases scheduling overhead by 20x on average compared to overall DRF.

In the second experiment, we measure the scheduling overhead of DepCon with the different numbers of host servers and containers, and compare the results with DRF. Also, we divide the evaluation of DRF into three cases such as DRF-N, DRF-$N/5$, and DRF-$N/10$. N, $N/5$, and $N/10$ indicate the number of tenants in each experiment where N means the number of total containers to be created. We construct the simulation environment using DepCon simulator, our own simulator due to the difficulty of CloudSim because it did not work with more than 700 containers. Note that we measure the scheduling completion time that takes to determine proper host servers and present normalized scheduling time where one indicates the results of DRF-N. Figure 6(b) shows normalized scheduling time with the increasing number of host servers when the number of containers is fixed as 2,000. As the number of tenants increases from $N/10$ to N, the scheduling overhead of DRF dramatically increases by 15x. In contrast, the scheduling time of DepCon increases by 1.8x from 0.072 to 0.135, as the number of servers increases from 100 to 300. This is because the time complexity of pod placement algorithm depicted in Algorithm 1 is only dependent on the number of host servers. Even though the number of host servers increases, DepCon offers lower scheduling overhead than DRF-N and DRF-$N/5$. With 300 host servers, DepCon reduces the scheduling time by 640% and 45% compared to DRF-N and DRF-$N/5$, respectively. However, DepCon has a higher overhead than DRF-$N/10$ because the number of servers that affect the scheduling overhead of DepCon is larger than the number of tenants which is related to the time complexity of DRF.

5   Discussion

Kubernetes allows tenants to assign CPU for their pods using *CPU request* and *CPU limit*. The CPU request indicates the minimum CPU allocation for pods, which is applied to the `cpu.shares` in cgroup. The CPU limit means the maximum CPU allocation for pods and is applied to `cpu.cfs_quota_us`. As DepCon agent also configures `cpu.cfs_quota_us`, the configuration of CPU limit by tenants can interfere with the operation of the DepCon agent. This is because DepCon agent adjusts the `cpu.cfs_quota_us` of containers while CPU limit configured the `cpu.cfs_quota_us` of pods. As Kubernetes subordinates containers to pods, the `cpu.cfs_quota_us` of a container cannot exceed the `cpu.cfs_quota_us` of a pod where the container belongs. This means that DepCon agent cannot increase the value of `cpu.cfs_quota_us` more than that of pods. As a result, DepCon allows tenants not to specify a CPU limit for the pod to prevent interference with the operation of the DepCon agent.

6   Related Work

Multi-resource scheduling techniques have been actively researched for efficient resource utilization because the resource sharing (e.g., CPU, memory, and network bandwidth) between jobs (e.g., containers) results in several issues such as performance interference and SLO violation.

DRF [6] and H-DRF [2] are representative multi-resource schedulers. The schedulers aim at providing fairness in resource allocation by applying the generalization of max-min fairness that maximizes the minimum allocation received by a user in the system for multiple resource types. DRF considers the heterogeneous data center applications and allocates the same dominant share, which is the maximum among all shares of a user, to all jobs. H-DRF applies a hierarchical structure to DRF in order to offer multi-resource scheduling for Hadoop frameworks [1]. However, both DRF and H-DRF have high computational complexity because they calculate resource allocation for every tenant and resource [12].

Other studies [8,12,14,27] achieve fairness in resource allocation while solving several issues such as utilization or overhead of DRF. DC- DRF [12] is the adaptive approximation of DRF to reduce the time complexity for multi-resource allocation at a centralized controller. It presents several optimization techniques such as parallelism and NUMA-awareness to improve the scheduling performance of the controller. PS-DSF [14] is a server-based DRF extension for the fair resource allocation of multiple resources in heterogeneous servers with placement constraints. PS-DSF proposes the max-min fairness of virtual dominant shares for tenants associated with each server to improve resource utilization. Carbyne [8] is an altruistic approach that focuses on long-term fairness rather than immediate fairness. It improves average job completion time and cluster resource utilization by re-locating the leftover resources without violating fairness. TSF [27] is a new sharing policy that considers multi-resource shares for data center jobs with placement constraints. TSF suggests to remove the placement constraint and allocates the maximum amount of resources. Even though it increases resource utilization by providing idle resources to users, it increases scheduling overhead when there are more than 100 tasks configured to run the job, which increases the total runtime of the job.

At last, HUG [5] is a DRF-based scheduling technique that not only increases resource utilization but also guarantees minimal performance, which is similar this paper. HUG limits the bandwidth utilization of each tenant to ensure optimal isolation and high network utilization for multiple tenants. Also, HUG can satisfy the network SLOs, as it reserves and allocates the minimum network resources to each tenant. Even though the technique can offer minimum network bandwidth through resource reservation, it cannot guarantee sufficient CPU resources for achieving specific network SLOs.

7 Conclusion

This paper proposes a new cloud scheduler that achieves the network SLO in the Kubernetes environment. DepCon overcomes the limitations of Kubernetes by providing admission control for containers and by adjusting CPU resources for the network SLO. We design and implement DepCon in Kubernetes and measure network performance in different environments. Our evaluation results show that DepCon reduces the network performance variance by 20x and improves the network performance by 40%. In addition, in terms of the scheduling overhead, DepCon decreases the scheduling completion time by 20 times compared to DRF (Dominant Resource Fairness). In future work, we plan to adopt learning approaches to predict the required computing resources for various workloads to satisfy the network SLOs of containers.

References

1. Apache Hadoop. http://hadoop.apache.org/
2. Bhattacharya, A.A., et al.: Hierarchical scheduling for diverse datacenter workloads. In: Proceedings of the 4th Annual Symposium on Cloud Computing, pp. 1–15 (2013)
3. Boucher, S., et al.: Putting the "micro" back in microservice. In: 2018 USENIX Annual Technical Conference (USENIX ATC 2018), pp. 645–650 (2018)
4. Burns, B., et al.: Borg, omega, and kubernetes. Queue **14**(1), 70–93 (2016)
5. Chowdhury, M., et al.: HUG: multi-resource fairness for correlated and elastic demands. In: 13th USENIX Symposium on Networked Systems Design and Implementation (NSDI 2016), pp. 407–424 (2016)
6. Ghodsi, A., et al.: Dominant resource fairness: fair allocation of multiple resource types. In: NSDI, vol. 11, pp. 24–24 (2011)
7. Google Container Engine. http://Kubernetes.io/
8. Grandl, R., et al.: Altruistic scheduling in multi-resource clusters. In: 12th USENIX Symposium on Operating Systems Design and Implementation (OSDI 2016), pp. 65–80 (2016)
9. Guo, Y., Yao, W.: A container scheduling strategy based on neighborhood division in micro service. In: NOMS 2018–2018 IEEE/IFIP Network Operations and Management Symposium, pp. 1–6. IEEE (2018)
10. Hubert, B., et al.: Linux advanced routing & traffic control HOWTO. Netherlabs BV 1 (2002)
11. Kannan, R.S., et al.: GrandSLAm: guaranteeing SLAs for jobs in microservices execution frameworks. In: Proceedings of the Fourteenth EuroSys Conference 2019, pp. 1–16 (2019)
12. Kash, I.A., et al.: DC-DRF: adaptive multi-resource sharing at public cloud scale. In: Proceedings of the ACM Symposium on Cloud Computing, pp. 374–385 (2018)
13. Khalid, J., et al.: Iron: isolating network-based CPU in container environments. In: 15th USENIX Symposium on Networked Systems Design and Implementation (NSDI 2018), pp. 313–328 (2018)
14. Khamse-Ashari, J., et al.: Per-server dominant-share fairness (PS-DSF): a multi-resource fair allocation mechanism for heterogeneous servers. In: 2017 IEEE International Conference on Communications (ICC), pp. 1–7. IEEE (2017)
15. Kim, D., et al.: FreeFlow: software-based virtual RDMA networking for containerized clouds. In: 16th USENIX Symposium on Networked Systems Design and Implementation (NSDI 2019), pp. 113–126 (2019)
16. Lei, J., et al.: Tackling parallelization challenges of kernel network stack for container overlay networks. In: 11th USENIX Workshop on Hot Topics in Cloud Computing (HotCloud 2019) (2019)
17. Moga, A., et al.: OS-level virtualization for industrial automation systems: are we there yet? In: Proceedings of the 31st Annual ACM Symposium on Applied Computing, pp. 1838–1843 (2016)
18. Nakamura, R., et al.: Grafting sockets for fast container networking. In: Proceedings of the 2018 Symposium on Architectures for Networking and Communications Systems, pp. 15–27 (2018)
19. Netperf. https://hewlettpackard.github.io/netperf/
20. Piraghaj, S.F., et al.: ContainerCloudSim: an environment for modeling and simulation of containers in cloud data centers. Softw.: Pract. Exp. **47**(4), 505–521 (2017)

21. Qi, S., et al.: Assessing container network interface plugins: functionality, performance, and scalability. IEEE Trans. Netw. Serv. Manag. **18**(1), 656–671 (2020)
22. Qiu, H., et al.: FIRM: an intelligent fine-grained resource management framework for SLO-oriented microservices. In: 14th USENIX Symposium on Operating Systems Design and Implementation (OSDI 2020), pp. 805–825 (2020)
23. Rosen, R.: Resource management: Linux kernel namespaces and cgroups, vol. 186, p. 70. Haifux, May 2013
24. Soltesz, S., et al.: Container-based operating system virtualization: a scalable, high-performance alternative to hypervisors. In: Proceedings of the 2nd ACM SIGOPS/EuroSys European Conference on Computer Systems 2007, pp. 275–287 (2007)
25. Sriraman, A., et al.: μtune: auto-tuned threading for OLDI microservices. In: 13th USENIX Symposium on Operating Systems Design and Implementation (OSDI 2018), pp. 177–194 (2018)
26. Suo, K., et al.: An analysis and empirical study of container networks. In: IEEE INFOCOM 2018-IEEE Conference on Computer Communications, pp. 189–197. IEEE (2018)
27. Wang, W., et al.: Multi-resource fair sharing for datacenter jobs with placement constraints. In: SC 2016: Proceedings of the International Conference for High Performance Computing, Networking, Storage and Analysis, pp. 1003–1014. IEEE (2016)
28. Wu, M., et al.: Platinum: a CPU-efficient concurrent garbage collector for tail-reduction of interactive services. In: 2020 USENIX Annual Technical Conference (USENIX ATC 2020), pp. 159–172 (2020)
29. Xu, C., et al.: NBWGuard: realizing network QoS for kubernetes. In: Proceedings of the 19th International Middleware Conference Industry, pp. 32–38 (2018)
30. Zhuo, D., et al.: Slim: OS kernel support for a low-overhead container overlay network. In: 16th USENIX Symposium on Networked Systems Design and Implementation (NSDI 2019), pp. 331–344 (2019)

Rafiki: Task-Level Capacity Planning in Distributed Stream Processing Systems

Benjamin J. J. Pfister[1]([✉]), Wolf S. Lickefett[1], Jan Nitschke[1], Sumit Paul[1],
Morgan K. Geldenhuys[1], Dominik Scheinert[1], Kordian Gontarska[2],
and Lauritz Thamsen[1]

[1] Technische Universität Berlin, Berlin, Germany
{benjamin.pfister,wolf.lickefett,jan.nitschke,
sumit.paul}@campus.tu-berlin.de,
{morgan.geldenhuys,dominik.scheinert,lauritz.thamsen}@tu-berlin.de
[2] Hasso Plattner Institute, University of Potsdam, Potsdam, Germany
kordian.gontarska@hpi.de

Abstract. Distributed Stream Processing is a valuable paradigm for reliably processing vast amounts of data at high throughput rates with low end-to-end latencies. Most systems of this type offer a fine-grained level of control to parallelize the computation of individual tasks within a streaming job. Adjusting the parallelism of tasks has a direct impact on the overall level of throughput a job can provide as well as the amount of resources required to provide an adequate level of service. However, finding optimal parallelism configurations that fall within the expected Quality of Service requirements is no small feat to accomplish.

In this paper we present Rafiki, an approach to automatically determine optimal parallelism configurations for Distributed Stream Processing jobs. Here we conduct a number of proactive profiling runs to gather information about the processing capacities of individual tasks, thereby making the selection of specific utilization targets possible. Understanding the capacity information enables users to adequately provision resources so that streaming jobs can deliver the desired level of service at a reduced operational cost with predictable recovery times. We implemented Rafiki prototypically together with Apache Flink where we demonstrate its usefulness experimentally.

Keywords: Distributed Stream Processing · Capacity planning ·
Resource optimization · Quality of Service · Parallelization · Profiling ·
Performance modeling

1 Introduction

Distributed Stream Processing (DSP) enables the processing of large volumes of unbounded streams of data with high throughput rates and low end-to-end latencies. Streams of data are generated in a growing number of contexts including IoT sensor networks, social media, and online transactions [5,9]. In order to

© Springer Nature Switzerland AG 2022
R. Chaves et al. (Eds.): Euro-Par 2021, LNCS 13098, pp. 352–363, 2022.
https://doi.org/10.1007/978-3-031-06156-1_28

meet Quality of Service (QoS) requirements regarding performance and availability, DSP systems must be configured and allocated a sufficient amount of resources to provide an adequate level of service. Determining configurations, how many resources to allocate to a DSP system, and what levels of throughput those resources and configurations can provide is challenging. Finding optimal configurations is typically time-consuming and requires expert-level knowledge of the DSP system and streaming job [1,10]. However, uncovering this information is important for all users of these systems, and providing an approach that automates and speeds up this process is necessary.

In the stream processing model, a series of tasks are performed on a stream of data, and each item in the data stream is processed by a task as soon as it becomes available [5]. Given an infinitely large stream of data, tasks will process as many items as possible using the available resources. To increase overall throughput and reduce end-to-end latency, the computation of tasks in DSP jobs can be run in parallel. Because each task performs a different function and can therefore process a different maximum number of messages per second, one of the most important configurations to adjust to match available resources to stream processing workloads is the number of parallel computations, or parallelism, of tasks.

By gaining insights into the capacity of a DSP job on a fine-grained level, resource allocation can be better optimized and QoS requirements can be more easily met. Finding optimal parallelism configurations and the capacity of a DSP job is often used for dynamic autoscaling. These reactive approaches typically profile running jobs and automatically rescale tasks when certain thresholds are reached [6]. Though useful for running applications, there is value in proactively profiling a DSP job in order to understand task-level capacity and set utilization targets.

In this paper we present Rafiki, an approach which automatically determines the processing capacities of individual tasks for any selected streaming job. Rafiki takes advantage of cloud computing, OS-level virtualization, and container orchestration technologies to deploy duplicate DSP pipelines and test their maximum capacity under realistic conditions. By running a series of proactive profiling runs, Rafiki finds optimal parallelism configurations at a task level and reports the maximum throughput possible for those configurations. With the insights gained from the profiling runs, a user can allocate sufficient resources to a DSP job in order to reach utilization targets, which allows for a more accurate estimation of recovery times as well as the identification and removal of performance bottlenecks. Additionally, our method provides an interface for monitoring the capacity utilization for any targeted job after profiling runs have been completed. We provide a prototype and evaluate its effectiveness experimentally with two DSP jobs.

The remainder of this paper is organized as follows. In Sect. 2 we explain our approach. In Sect. 3 we outline Rafiki's design and evaluate our approach with two DSP jobs. We conclude with related work in Sect. 4 and a brief conclusion in Sect. 5.

2   Approach

In order to measure task-level capacity and apply the gained insights to a given DSP job, we propose Rafiki, a three-step solution. First, a set of profiling runs are iteratively executed with increasing and optimal parallelism configurations to obtain maximum capacities across the different tasks. Second, the capacity information for all tasks is deduced based on the metrics gathered from the profiling runs of the tested parallelism configurations. Third, the gathered capacity information is applied to a running job to target a specific utilization. Additionally, real-time insights are provided into the potential effects of changing task parallelisms in an interactive dashboard. An overview can be seen in Fig. 1. We have implemented this approach to validate it and promote its usability.[1]

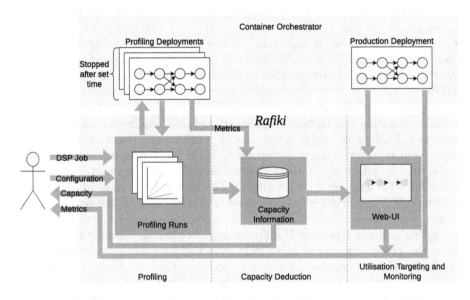

Fig. 1. Overview of the architecture and interactions

2.1   Profiling Runs

The main goal of this step is to calculate the maximum capacity for each task at a given level of parallelism. We achieve this by executing a set of brief profiling runs while stressing the system's processing capacity in every iteration. By ensuring a sufficient amount of messages are available to be consumed, we can flood the entire pipeline to detect tasks that are unable to process messages at the rate they are received. These tasks cause backpressure and indicate the maximum processing capacity of the task at the current parallelism configuration. In each

---

[1] https://github.com/ciklista/rafiki.

run, the essential idea is to detect tasks that are the bottleneck given the current configuration and increase their parallelism in the next iteration.

A set of profiling runs is always started with all tasks having a parallelism of one. We then subsequently increase the parallelism of certain tasks, one at a time, until no more bottlenecks can be enforced, or a user-defined maximum parallelism has been reached. With each profiling run, we take advantage of cloud computing and container orchestration technologies to deploy duplicate DSP jobs with increasing parallelism configurations that read from the same Apache Kafka source. Messages are replayed from the same offset to ensure that each experiment iteration receives the same message sequence.

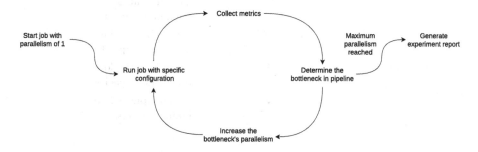

Fig. 2. Profiling run loop

Figure 2 illustrates the experiment loop as well as the decision process of which task parallelism to increase for the next iteration. After a run has successfully completed and metrics have been collected, we check if backpressure was detected on any task throughout the run. If this was not the case, we can assume none of the tasks reached its maximum capacity and no bottleneck was found within the system. In this case, we increase the parallelism on the source task, allowing messages to be consumed at a larger rate. This process is repeated until backpressure is found on any task. Once that happens, we can then deduce which task parallelism needs to be increased in order to resolve this bottleneck. If backpressure is reported for a single task, the subsequent task is not able to consume messages at the same rate at which they are produced. Following this reasoning, we therefore increase the parallelism of the task following the task that experienced backpressure. If we see multiple tasks experiencing backpressure, we will increase parallelism on the task subsequent to the last task that experienced backpressure, in the order of the data flow. We repeat this process until increasing the parallelism of a certain task would exceed the predefined maximum allowed parallelism. This upper bound is set by the user and is derived from financial or host system constraints.

2.2 Deducing Capacity

After each profiling run, throughput and backpressure metrics are collected and used to define the maximum throughput of individual tasks. Based on observed backpressure, we can deduce different types of information for any task x with any task parallelism configuration y as shown in Table 1. Rafiki assumes, that all tasks are isolated and that parallel instances of an operator are similar, i.e. receive a similar share of messages, and that the underlying system operates without failures.

Table 1. Capacity assumptions for task x at parallelism y

Case	Task $x - 1$ under backpressure	Task x under backpressure	Assumption
1	✓	✗	Throughput is maximum capacity
2	✗	✓	Throughput is lower bound for capacity
3	✗	✗	Throughput is lower bound for capacity
4	✓	✓	Throughput is lower bound for capacity

One additional special case is a source task, as it does not have a preceding task to monitor in order to determine its capacity. There are two approaches to solving this issue. First, one could identify a metric that follows the concept of backpressure in the system generating the input stream of the DSP job. Alternatively, one could simply aggregate capacity information across all runs for a given parallelism configuration of the source task. By design of the profiling runs, this provides a lower bound for the given configuration. Further, under the assumption of infinite messages at the time of a profiling run, maximum capacity for source tasks is defined as the capacity observed when none of the tasks experienced backpressure. It can then be assumed, that the source task operated at its maximum capacity.

2.3   Utilization Targeting

After successfully completing the profiling runs, the maximum, or at least a lower bound for the maximum, number of messages that a task can process at a specific parallelism has been recorded in the database. With this throughput table we can monitor a running job and deduce the current capacity to achieve a target utilization. A DSP job should typically be run at a percentage of the maximum capacity in order to be able to recover from failures that will likely occur over the lifespan of a long-running job. Effective DSP systems use fault tolerance mechanisms such as checkpointing to periodically create consistent states to recover from in case a failure occurs. Upon failure, messages since the last saved state must be reprocessed in addition to the messages that continue to arrive. Targeting a specific utilization allows a DSP system enough processing capacity to be able to recover from failure. For example, a job processing incoming messages at 100% has no additional capacity for recovery, but a job running at 70% of the maximum capacity has 30% processing capacity for recovery. Having insights into the processing capacity and target utilization also make it possible to estimate recovery times. It is crucial that the running job we monitor is the same as the job we run our experiments with since the capacity depends on the implementation.

3   Evaluation

In this section, we show through experiments that using Rafiki is both practical and beneficial for obtaining the task-level capacity information of DSP jobs.

3.1   Prototype Implementation

To evaluate our approach, we implemented Rafiki prototypically to work with Apache Flink. The prototype consists of three main components, a Java application, a database, and a web UI. All components ship as docker containers. The core is a Java Spring Boot application that triggers the profiling runs. It publishes an API that can start the execution of jobs on a remote DSP system and supervises the profiling loop. After completing a profiling run, it records and stores the metrics in a PostgreSQL database.

The web UI, depicted in Fig. 3, is a React application that enables a user to upload a custom Java executable to Flink and to set parameters relevant for the profiling runs such as the highest level of parallelism. The web UI calls the APIs exposed by the Java application. Once results are available, the web UI allows for real-time monitoring of a running job and applies the capacity information to single tasks of that job, indicating current capacity via color codes. The web UI also features a sandbox mode that enables users to simulate a different level of parallelism on their job and observe changes in capacity.

3.2   Experiment Setup

Profiling runs were conducted on the Google Cloud Platform[2] in a three node Kubernetes [14] cluster using the Google Kubernetes Engine.[3] Hardware and software specifications are shown in Table 2. Flink was deployed natively in Kubernetes with HDFS [12] being used for the storage of Flink checkpoints. All streaming jobs were configured to consume messages from the Kafka [7] streaming platform. Based on the cluster setup, a maximum parallelism of six

---

[2] https://cloud.google.com/.
[3] https://cloud.google.com/kubernetes-engine.

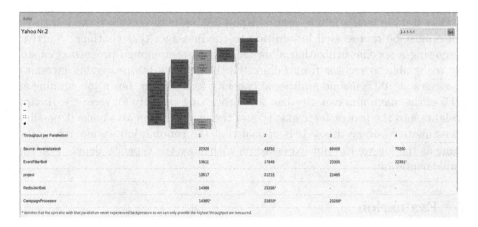

Fig. 3. Rafiki UI. Task-level capacity is indicated via different colors. (Color figure online)

was used. The duration of a profiling run iteration was set to two minutes to allow enough time for messages to accumulate and be processed in windowing periods. Each job was profiled with four successive runs with the mean being used for the evaluation.

Table 2. Cluster specifications

Resource	Details
OS	Ubuntu 18.04
CPU	4 vCPU
Memory	16 GB RAM
Software	Java v1.11, Flink v1.12, Kafka v2.6, ZooKeeper v3.6, Redis v5.0, Prometheus v2.25, Docker v19.3, Kubernetes v1.18, HDFS v2.8

3.3 DSP Jobs

Rafiki was tested with two DSP jobs, the Yahoo Streaming Benchmark [2] and an IoT Vehicles Experiment [3]. Source code for both jobs can be found in the Rafiki repository.[4] The Yahoo Streaming Benchmark is an advertising analytics use case that counts how many times ads from an ad campaign were viewed in a given time window. In the benchmark, ad campaigns with corresponding ad events are synthetically generated at a constant rate. The stream processing job then deserializes events from Kafka, filters them based on an ad type, matches the ad id to a campaign id, and counts how many times ads from a campaign

---

[4] https://github.com/ciklista/rafiki.

were viewed in a 10-s window. The IoT Vehicles Experiment is an IoT traffic sensor use case that detects speeding vehicles. The experiment uses pregenerated vehicle data that includes the positional data of the vehicles. The data stream is filtered based on certain points of interest and then collected in a window. The vehicle speed is calculated based on the window time and the update interval of the vehicles. Vehicles that exceed a predefined speed are then reported to a different Kafka sink.

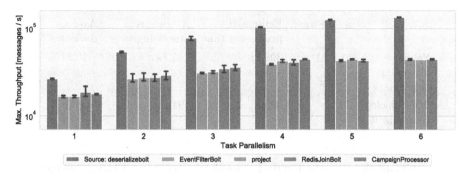

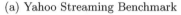

(a) Yahoo Streaming Benchmark

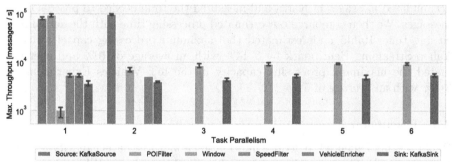

(b) IoT Vehicles Experiment

Fig. 4. Profiling results of experiments conducted with our two DSP jobs. For each job, task, and task parallelism, we report the average maximum throughput and the corresponding standard deviation across all conducted runs. For most tasks, it can be observed that the influence of the task parallelism on the maximum throughput is fairly linear.

3.4 Results

Rafiki tested on average 25 configurations for the Yahoo Streaming Benchmark and 17 configurations for the IoT Vehicles Experiment on each run. The results depicted in Fig. 4 show the highest measured throughput for each level of parallelism. Cases where throughput was not recorded indicate that the task could adequately handle the overall throughput at a lower parallelism, and that overall throughput was limited by another task. With a maximum parallelism of 6, each task shows a linear increase in processing capacity with additional task parallelism. Despite slight variance across runs, repeated profiling experiments found the same bottlenecks and generally tested configurations in the same order. We therefore conclude that Rafiki proved its ability to measure task-level capacity and identify bottlenecks that would benefit most from increased parallelism.

Table 3. Validation results

Job	# Messages	Estimated processing time	Average real processing time	Average deviation
Yahoo Streaming Benchmark	51.8 M	398.7 s	445.3 s	−10.31%
IoT Vehicles Experiment	56 M	625.8 s	594 s	5.38%

To validate the measured capacity results, we compared the predicted processing time against the actual processing time, as seen in Table 3. To do this, we accumulated messages in Kafka and measured the time needed to process these messages. We then compared our estimated processing time with the actual processing time. Rafiki underestimated the maximum processing capacity in the Yahoo Streaming Benchmark by 5–14% with an average of 10% and overestimated the maximum processing capacity in the IoT Vehicles Experiment by 3–6% with an average of 5%.

3.5   Discussion

Rafiki was implemented to deduce information about task-level capacity in order to make it possible to monitor and reach utilization targets. While the results for the IoT Vehicles Experiment also show the same relation, we cannot observe as high of a capacity gain per parallelism as in the Yahoo Streaming Benchmark experiment. Although we can still use the capacity information to set a utilization target, the results indicate that the limiting factor for this job is likely not the parallelism. While Rafiki is able to reveal such bottlenecks, it cannot show its source.

The current implementation of Rafiki is limited by a few aspects. External factors such as failing nodes or a bottleneck in the underlying network are not detectable by Rafiki and would alter the results. This issue could be solved in future iterations by extending the range of collected metrics to include these factors and for Rafiki to react to the events. Another limitation is jobs that have multiple sources. If Rafiki does not detect backpressure in the system, it would increase the parallelism for all the sources, likely resulting in a higher parallelism than needed for a subset of the sources. This issue could also be solved by extending our approach.

4 Related Work

Our approach is inspired by previous work in DSP capacity planning. Related work that assesses the maximum capacity of a DSP system typically uses analytical models to predict capacity or profiling techniques to monitor actual capacity in a running system. Profiling-based approaches have been shown to be more accurate. Roy et al. use both analytical modeling and profiling to find the capacity of distributed systems [11]. They find that the accuracy of their models decrease as system activity increases. Bilal and Canini [1] argue that using analytical modeling to predict throughput and latency reduces the accuracy of results as assumptions must be simplified to create models and these models must be regularly updated to reflect changing environmental conditions.

Kalavri et al. [6] use task processing rates to create a model to automatically scale a DSP job according to the current workload. Theirs is a reactive profiling-based approach that works on running systems. Rafiki, by contrast, uses parallel profiling runs to determine the capacity information of a chosen DSP job so that utilization targets can be easily set by a user for different throughput rates thus ensuring any QoS requirements are met.

In [8], the authors propose a prototype called Flink-ER which represents the DSP execution graph as a flow network. Here each task has a capacity and a flow representing the maximum message processing rate and current processing rate respectively. Flink-ER uses graph theory and partitions to identify performance bottlenecks, using network bandwidth and latency as the basic capacity measurement.

To automate finding optimal parameters in DSP systems, Bilal and Canini [1] propose a framework that compares the results of various optimization algorithms. Their profiling-based approach focuses on minimizing latency while providing a minimum level of throughput to obtain realistic results.

Tang and Gedik [13] use an estimation of each task's CPU utilization to generally measure capacity at a task level. The tasks with the highest CPU utilization are identified as bottlenecks and are allocated more resources. After increasing the parallelism of the bottleneck task, it is then tested to see if the throughput increased. In contrast, Rafiki directly identifies bottleneck tasks using backpressure metrics.

Stela [15] identifies bottleneck tasks based on their input and output rate to dynamically scale individual tasks of a DSP system up or down. Congestion is found when the input rate of the data stream is higher than the number of messages that can be processed. This measure of capacity is used by Rafiki, however, it is obtained as a metric directly from backpressure metrics. Stela is an online, reactive application, while Rafiki duplicates configurations pipelines in parallel and intentionally overloads the system to find bottlenecks.

Our overall approach borrows from Chiron [4]. Chiron uses a profiling-based approach to measure the capacity of DSP jobs with QoS requirements to find optimal checkpoint intervals. OS-virtualization, container orchestration, and IaC methods are used to deploy isolated and duplicated pipelines with varying checkpoint interval configurations. In order to test the maximum capacity and increase the number of events processed by the DSP job, events are read from an earlier timestamp. All duplicate pipelines read from the same Kafka topic to increase accuracy [4]. Chiron builds on Timon [3], which tests alternate DSP configurations by deploying parallel pipelines that read from production data streams.

5   Conclusion

Finding optimal parallelism configurations for DSP jobs and determining the maximum throughput those configurations can provide is no easy feat. In this paper we proposed Rafiki, an automated approach for finding optimal configurations and gaining insights into the task-level capacity of a DSP job. A number of proactive profiling runs are conducted where Rafiki uncovers capacity information for individual tasks. This capacity information is collected and makes the process of allocating sufficient resources to meet QoS requirements easier for users. It can be used to estimate recovery times through selecting specific utilization targets, thus helping to create more efficient and reliable DSP jobs. Rafiki was tested experimentally using two DSP jobs and found to accurately measure capacity within an average of 5–10%. Rafiki offers increased usability by providing a web UI that allows for real-time capacity monitoring and experiment evaluation. Future work could enhance and build upon the proposed solution in a number of ways. Though tested prototypically with Apache Flink, the concepts of task parallelism and bottlenecks in stream processing pipelines are common across most DPS systems. Mapping these abstractions to different systems would increase Rafiki's versatility. Bottlenecks could also be defined by metrics other than backpressure, such as processing rates, latency, or CPU utilization.

Acknowledgment. This work has been supported through grants by the German Ministry for Education and Research (BMBF) as BIFOLD (funding mark 01IS18025A) and WaterGridSense 4.0 (funding mark 02WIK1475D).

References

1. Bilal, M., Canini, M.: Towards automatic parameter tuning of stream processing systems. In: SoCC 2017, pp. 189–200. Association for Computing Machinery, New York, NY, USA (2017)
2. Chintapalli, S., et al.: Benchmarking streaming computation engines: storm, flink and spark streaming. In: IPDPSW. IEEE (2016)
3. Geldenhuys, M.K., Thamsen, L., Gontarska, K.K., Lorenz, F., Kao, O.: Effectively testing system configurations of critical IoT analytics pipelines. In: Baru, C., et al. (eds.) Big Data, pp. 4157–4162. IEEE (2019)
4. Geldenhuys, M.K., Thamsen, L., Kao, O.: Chiron: optimizing fault tolerance in QoS-aware distributed stream processing jobs. In: Wu, X., et al. (eds.) Big Data, pp. 434–440. IEEE (2020)
5. Isah, H., Abughofa, T., Mahfuz, S., Ajerla, D., Zulkernine, F.H., Khan, S.: A survey of distributed data stream processing frameworks. IEEE Access **7**, 154300–154316 (2019)

6. Kalavri, V., Liagouris, J., Hoffmann, M., Dimitrova, D., Forshaw, M., Roscoe, T.: Three steps is all you need: fast, accurate, automatic scaling decisions for distributed streaming dataflows. In: OSDI, pp. 783–798. USENIX Association, Carlsbad, CA (2018)
7. Kreps, J.: Kafka: a distributed messaging system for log processing (2011)
8. Li, Z., et al.: Flink-ER: an elastic resource-scheduling strategy for processing fluctuating mobile stream data on flink. Mob. Inf. Syst. **2020**, 5351824:1–5351824:17 (2020)
9. Nasiri, H., Nasehi, S., Goudarzi, M.: Evaluation of distributed stream processing frameworks for IoT applications in smart cities. J. Big Data **6**, 52 (2019)
10. Röger, H., Mayer, R.: A comprehensive survey on parallelization and elasticity in stream processing. ACM Comput. Surv. **52**(2), 36:1–36:37 (2019)
11. Roy, N., Dubey, A., Gokhale, A., Dowdy, L.: A capacity planning process for performance assurance of component-based distributed systems. In: ICPE 2011, pp. 259–270. Association for Computing Machinery, New York, NY, USA (2011)
12. Shvachko, K., Kuang, H., Radia, S., Chansler, R.: The Hadoop distributed file system. In: Khatib, M.G., He, X., Factor, M. (eds.) MSST, pp. 1–10. IEEE Computer Society (2010)
13. Tang, Y., Gedik, B.: Autopipelining for data stream processing. IEEE Trans. Parallel Distrib. Syst. **24**(12), 2344–2354 (2013)
14. Verma, A., Pedrosa, L., Korupolu, M., Oppenheimer, D., Tune, E., Wilkes, J.: Large-scale cluster management at Google with Borg. In: Réveillère, L., Harris, T., Herlihy, M. (eds.) EuroSys, pp. 18:1–18:17. ACM (2015)
15. Xu, L., Peng, B., Gupta, I.: Stela: enabling stream processing systems to scale-in and scale-out on-demand. In: IC2E, pp. 22–31. IEEE Computer Society (2016)

Extracting Information from Large Scale Graph Data: Case Study on Automated UI Testing

Ramazan Faruk Oguz[1]([✉]), Mert Oz[1], Erdi Olmezogullari[2],
and Mehmet Siddik Aktas[1]

[1] Yildiz Technical University, Davutpasa Campus, Istanbul, Turkey
{ramazan.faruk.oguz,mert.oz}@std.yildiz.edu.tr, aktas@yildiz.edu.tr
[2] Development Center, Microsoft, Oslo, Norway
erdi.olmezogullari@ozu.edu.tr

Abstract. Even though a large-scale graph structure is a powerful model to solve several challenging problems in various applications' domains today, it can also preserve various raw essences regarding user behavior, especially in the e-commerce domain. Information extraction is a promising research area in deep learning algorithms using large-scale graph data. This study focuses on understanding users' implicit navigational behavior on an e-commerce site that we can represent with the large-scale graph data. We propose a GAN-based e-business workflow by leveraging the large-scale browsing graph data and the footprints of navigational users' behavior on the e-commerce site. With this method, we have discovered various frequently repeated clickstream data sequences, which do not appear in training data at all. Therefore, We developed a prototype application to demonstrate performance tests on the proposed business e-workflow. The experimental studies we conducted show that the proposed methodology produces noticeable and reasonable outcomes for our prototype application.

Keywords: Deep learning · Large scale graph data · GAN · Distributed e-business workflows · Distributed systems

1 Introduction

We have been observing the increasing importance of e-commerce websites worldwide since the beginning of the Covid-19 outbreak. As the number of e-commerce users and their interactions with e-commerce websites increase, we would say that the volume of record files associated with users' interaction also significantly overgrows. Meanwhile, understanding user needs and intents will also be challenging because the volume of data increases massively. However, this new difficulty can bring new opportunities to understand users' behavior more deeply

---

M. Oz and E. Olmezogullari—The authors conducted this work while they were working in R&D Center at Testinium, Istanbul.

R. Chaves et al. (Eds.): Euro-Par 2021, LNCS 13098, pp. 364–375, 2022.
https://doi.org/10.1007/978-3-031-06156-1_29

with scalable approaches. One of the existing scalable approaches is learning from large-scale graph data that we can adapt to represent the user's navigational behavior as a graph network. There exist studies that have successfully shown that they can model navigational browsing behavior data as graph data [10,11]. We observe this research problem in various domains, such as telecom [1], internet of things [3], and social networking [5,14]. This study focuses on learning from navigational behavioral data generated in e-commerce websites.

This study focuses on analyzing and learning from browsing graph data for enabling automating UI testing. Software testing includes requirement analysis, test case design, test case writing, test code development, test execution, test report preparation [2]. In the test phase, there are too many scenarios for the software to be tested. Usually, business analysts create these scenarios. Then, the testers perform the tests semi-automatically or automatically by utilizing the software. Selenium is an example of software that automatically performs tests. It tests all of the operations for the functional requirements on the interface. The testing process of the UI interfaces must follow specific steps in the user interface so that it can test some of the functional requirements [16]. For example, to buy a dress, the user must first enter the dress category, put the dress in the basket, and then complete the buying steps. Hence, automating the testing process and generating the testing scripts is highly important in UI testing for efficiency and time savings. To address this need, we propose a workflow that can learn from the large-scale graph data to generated automated testing scripts.

In e-commerce web applications, the user interfaces are constantly changing. Conversely, the processing steps and services at the back-engine of these e-commerce websites are generally less subject to change. As a result, alternatives are continually increasing from the beginning to the last desired page. Due to these changes and the complexity of the business processes at the user interfaces, the need to renew or re-create new test data as the page changes appear. Hence, there is a need for automated testing methodologies that can learn user behavior from large-scale behavioral data.

This study addresses the predicament mentioned above by investigating the following research problem: How do the deep learning algorithms create clickstream-based data sequences in automated UI testing? We investigate an e-business workflow design that can generate automated user test codes for e-commerce websites to address this research problem. Our proposed e-business workflow collects many examples of UI browsing scenarios, i.e., clickstream-based data sequences, from the e-commerce website by running the application that crawls the websites according to their page structures. We use the page structures (URL structures) available on websites to create large-scale browsing graph data to train the deep learning algorithm. We use one of the deep learning methods, i.e., GAN (Generative Adversarial Networks) [15], which has proven successful. GAN architectures generally produce new indistinguishable examples very similar to the given input. After using these examples as training data for the GAN architecture, we then create many new scenarios. Next, we determine whether these scenarios are usable or not. We eliminate data sequences that are not valid from the collected dataset. Finally, we transfer the newly generated data sequences to the next step in the proposed workflow to create test scripts for the sequences successfully selected by the workflow.

Motivation: We argue that automating the testing process and generating the testing scripts is highly important in software engineering. Based on the standard software development practices, we already know that the user interface is constantly changing. On the other hand, the logical flow of the back-engine codes and services does not change that frequently. Due to the changes in user interfaces, there is a need to generate new click-stream-based data sequences that the end-users can use and then provide automating testing of the data sequences in advance. Our motivation is to design and implement an e-business workflow that can automate UI testing by dynamically generate and test new data sequences that the end-user might use.

Research Problem: In this study, we propose an e-business workflow for automating user interface testing. We propose the architecture of an e-business workflow. We also realize the prototype implementation. The most crucial function of our business workflow is whether the synthetic sequences it has created are successfully created or not. The research questions we are interested in are as follows. 1) How can such a business workflow be realized and learn from large-scale graph data? 2) What might be the deep learning algorithms in this proposed e-business workflow process? What should be the approach used for this learning algorithm to learn from the page in the best way? 3) How can the success and correct outcomes of the selected deep learning algorithms be observed?

Contributions: We propose an e-business workflow on generating artificial test scripts over the data obtained by crawling the structure of an e-commerce website. The proposed workflow creates synthetic sequences by getting the URL structure of the website. Furthermore, to facilitate testing of the proposed approach, we implement a prototype application. We test the prototype application via an e-commerce website and dataset collected from the website. The experimental study results are promising and show the usability of the proposed approach.

Organization: Section 2 presents the literature review on automated UI testing and deep learning approaches. Section 3 describes the proposed methodology, while Sect. 4 presents the details of the prototype of the proposed methodology. Section 5 presents the evaluation of the proposed methodology. Finally, Sect. 6 concludes the article and discusses future work.

2   Literature Review

Automatic determination of scenarios, such as our motivation mentioned in the introduction, becomes more and more important day by day. There are different approaches in the literature for determining scenarios automatically. For example, in a patent obtained in the USA, a tool can produce test scripts based on rules (US8850407B2). After this, a research group work on [4] automatically generates test cases and codes using pre-existing UML sequence diagrams. Thus, many operations can be performed in the user interface in large-scale desktop and web applications. Considering that these processes come one after another, in a subsequent study to find these scenarios, these many possible scenarios are created by using genetic algorithms [13]. In another study in [8], allows users and developers to automatically save the tests they want to be performed automatically for android applications. Unfortunately, these can be quite costly to obtain.

From this point of view, the algorithms that use the basis of the GAN algorithm selected and proceeded [6]. The purpose of the algorithms and other deep learning algorithms selected here in the flow we propose is to produce synthetic flows that are not included in the training dataset and contain actions that the user can perform.

The data we use in our system is the flow data that may occur on the website. Websites are kept graphically due to their structure. Motivated by the growing need for fast distributed processing of large-scale graphics such as website graphics and various social networks, the researchers wanted to introduce lower limits to keep calculations distributed. Therefore, they set a lower bound to calculate the spanning tree (ST) value in the website graph. As a result of their work, they determined algorithms and lower limits for distributed computation of various graph problems [9]. In the proposed system, we use GPU-supported processors and a flow to work on multiple GPUs to provide training.

3   Methodology

To address the research problem discussed in the introduction, we propose an e-business workflow that can process large-scale browsing graph data and generate UI testing scripts. Figure 1 depicts the proposed workflow. The proposed e-business workflow is designed to be a distributed system. Therefore, its components are implemented on distributed software development platforms. The proposed workflow consists of several components: The Crawling Module, The Browsing Graph Data Clustering Module, The Mapping Based Data Representation Module, The GAN Based Sequence Generator Module, The Filtering Module, and The Sequence2Script Module. We explain these modules in great detail below.

3.1   Crawling Module

This module takes the starting page of the e-commerce website to be tested as to its input and generates all possible URL sequences. The starting page of the website is the first page that users can interact. The crawler module generates clickstream data sequences that represent the user's browsing behaviors on the website. We record each clickstream data sequence as graph data. Figure 2 depicts an example browsing graph data.

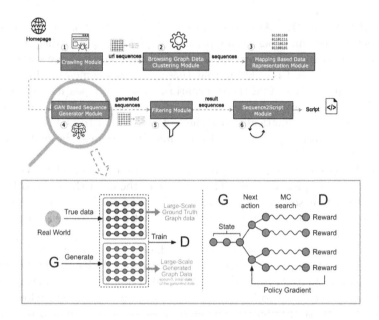

Fig. 1. Overview of the proposed pipeline

Fig. 2. An example of the browsing data. The figure on the left represents the large scale browsing graph data. The figure on the right represents the one particular browsing graph data that belongs to a user. Note that the user browsing graph data is referred as clickstream data sequence throughout the manuscript.

Table 1. The best clustering evaluation result

Algorithm	Distance measure	n	s	Window size	V-measure
Bisecting K-means	Euclidean	6	4.63	3	90%

Browsing data can take very large steps. Here we can talk about 3 quintillion data for a 6-step graph. As the number of steps and topic values increases, the number of data also increases.

3.2   Browsing Graph Data Clustering Module

This module is responsible for processing the clickstream data-sequences data to map each URL to a related topic. In this module, we apply clustering algorithms on the clickstream data sequence graph data to categorize them and determine the appropriate topic label for each category. To do this, we use the word2vec embedding approach to represent each URL as encoded feature vectors. We cluster the URLs encountered in clickstream data sequences using different clustering algorithms such as partition-based clustering algorithms (e.g., k-means) and hierarchical clustering algorithms (e.g., bisecting k-means). We obtain the web site's URL tree structure by crawling the website.

To validate the results of the clustering algorithms, we also create ground truth data. Here, we utilize regular expressions and map each URL into a topic to obtain ground truth data. Then, we use the ground truth data to analyze the quality of the clustering results. The experimental study results indicate that the clustering algorithms can group the URLs in the collected data successfully. Table 1 shows the results where s is the characteristic of the Zipf distribution and n is the number of cluster [16]. The empirical study shows that the bisecting k-means algorithm gives the best results with euclidean space as the distance metric.

After completing the clustering, The Browsing Graph Data Clustering Module also determines the label for each cluster. This module maps each URL within a cluster to the corresponding topic of that cluster. This way, we use the topics to represent the URLs. As an output, this module produces "topic sequences" that correspond to URL sequences. Table 2 shows the example topic labels.

Table 2. Sample dataset. The first column indicates the URL which the user visits during browsing the website. The second column indicates the topic, which is associated to each URL.

Input data: URL	Output data: Label
https://www.site1.com/path-to-a/product-page?pid=123456	Product
https://www.site1.com/path-to-a/search-result?q=query	Search

3.3   Mapping Based Data Representation Module

The results we get after applying regular expressions to streams are sequences. In this module, we use a vocabulary-based mapping methodology to represent "topic sequences." Here, we create a vocabulary dictionary from all the unique keywords found in the sequences. By using this vocabulary dictionary, we map each keyword in sequence dataset to its corresponding numerical value. Figure 3. represents the way we represent the topic sequences with numerical values.

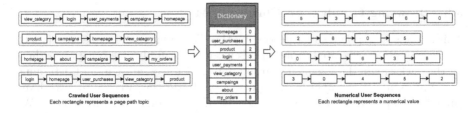

Fig. 3. The mapping process used in the system

3.4 GAN Based Sequence Generator Module

In this module, we use a GAN-based deep learning algorithm to generate new data sequences. There are many different versions of GAN [15] based deep learning algorithms in the literature. The SeqGan network proposed by Yu et al. inspires the method used in this study [17]. Figure 1 depicts our deep learning approach. GAN (Generative adversarial networks) [6] architectures consist of two neural networks. These two nerves are called heavy Generator and Discriminator. When GAN is given a training set, it learns to create new data with the same statistics as the training set. Here, the generator tries to trick the discriminator into producing new artifacts. And the discriminator will gradually make the distinction better.

Since our study aims in sequence production, we decided to use GAN networks, a new production model that has proven successful. In this study, we use a customized SeqGAN network for sequence generation. In our approach, LSTM and CNN are used respectively in generator and discriminator networks that form SeqGAN. The additional information about how sequences are generated using SeqGan can be found in [17]. The steps of generating sequences using SeqGan are explained in detail by the author [17]. First, the generator is trained to generate negative samples for training the discriminator network. This generator training and the discriminator training using these negative samples are called pre-training of generator and discriminator. Until SeqGan converges, the following two producers take place: (1) generate a sample from the generator and then compute a Q value and update the generator parameters via policy gradient g-steps times. (2): Generate a group of negative samples and combine them with the positive samples to train the discriminator network k epoch and apply this procedure d-steps.

We use the ground truth data sequences created in the previous steps by the clustering module to train the model. At each iteration of the GAN-based neural network, we also produce generated data sequences to trick the discriminator into creating new data sequences. Table 3 lists the details of the datasets used in this study. This table represents the counts of large scale ground truth data and generated sequences on the Mother & Baby products clickstream data. 239,570 of the 426,781 sequences produced here have passed through hashmap and are marked as valid browsing graph data.

As an output of this module, the new data sequences (i.e., topic sequences) are produced.

Table 3. Number of browsing graph data (1-node, 2-node, 3-node browsing graph data) in dataset

Counts	Large-scale ground truth data	Large-scale generated data
All	813,430	655,356
Uniques	22,141	426,781

3.5 Filtering Module

In this module, we implement two important features in our workflow for data sequence generation. These features are 1) eliminate the sequences in the dataset produced by the proposed e-business workflow and 2) check if a page path-topic sequence is valid. In this context, valid sequences are those sequences that can be executable using a test executor probably. Figure 4 illustrates the construction of Trie and HashMap data structures on a example training sequences Fig. 4. We use Trie data structure to eliminate duplicated sequences generated by the model. At the end of the filtering module, the sequences that are not eliminated are used to generate test scripts.

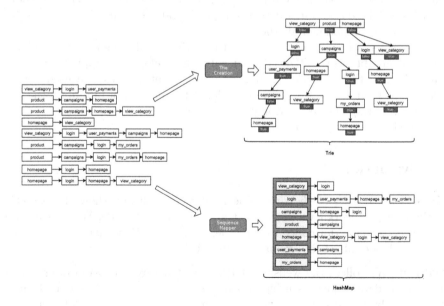

Fig. 4. Building Trie and HashMap on example training sequences

3.6 Sequence2Script Module

The purpose of our last module in the system is to generate executable test scripts using sequences from the previous module. Up to now, we create data sequences with a deep learning approach using GAN architecture for representing possible website topics that can be sequentially visited. To create executable test scripts, we need website URLs and the identifiers of elements showing which element interacts with the generated sequences on those websites. This is a concept module for creating test scripts from giving data sequence.

4 Prototype

To facilitate testing of the proposed e-business workflow, we provide a prototype implementation. We implement a crawler to collect data on the website. The Scrapy library in Python is used to implement a crawler. Here, for tracking the pages where the crawler goes, we used the topics of the website whose following page structure we know and extracted regular expressions [16]. After the URL sequence data was obtained, the URL sequences were clustered with the k-means and bisecting k-means algorithms in Python. Then the v-measure scores were calculated. We choose the best performing clustering methodology based on the v-measure values. Here, we use Apache Spark ML library to implement the clustering module [16]. We use Sagemaker on the AWS machine to train the deep learning model and determine its results. Here, KernelGateway-ml.g4dn.xlarge was selected for the kernel, and the training was completed with GPU support. We selected the data-sequence length as three and the batch parameter as 100 and during the experimental study.

We created a Dom tree while generating scripts. Following this, we produced scenarios suitable for the BDD (Behavior-driven development) approach by using Cucumber. In this way, we created a UI test script that can be used for the relevant flow, and as a result, we completed the process of obtaining the test scenarios. During the test script production we perform here, these codes are generated with negligible periods.

5 Evaluation

To facilitate testing of the prototype implementation and show the usability of the proposed workflow, we conduct an experimental study. We measure the proposed system performance with Perplexity and BLEU evaluation metrics. We describe the details of the evaluation study below.

Dataset: We collect the website's URL tree structure using a crawler. Then, we created data sequences using this tree structure as the ground truth data. Note that browsing data sequences can include a high number of steps. For example, we can talk about three quintillion possible data sequences for a 6-step browsing data sequence. As the number of elements in a datasequence increases, the total number of possible data sequence will also increase. To facilitate testing of the proposed approach, in this study, we only focused on up to 3-node data sequences. Since we divide sequences including at least one duplicated token into subsequences, we generally obtain smaller sequences. Therefore we account up to 3-node data sequences. Table 3 lists the details of the datasets used in this study. Figure 2 depicts an example browsing graph data.

Note that, by crawling the website we are not able to capture all possible paths in the website's URL tree structure. The reason for this that the e-commerce websites limit crawlers' activities within the sites for various reasons such as they don't allow robots to crawl the websites for security purposes. Hence, we only have a partial picture of the URL tree structure. Based on the obtained URL structure, we generate the possible 1-node, 2-node, ... n-node data sequences as the ground truth data. By utilizing the proposed workflow, we try to generate new data sequences that do not exists in the ground truth dataset and that can be used to create new UI testing scripts.

Experimental Study Design: To understand the usability of the proposed workflow, we compared the final output generated data-sequences against the training dataset (i.e., ground truth browsing data-sequences). We investigate that whether the proposed workflow can find new data sequences that the system has not seen before. After that, the new datasequences should represent the same browsing behavior that one would encounter in the initial input of the ground truth browsing data sequence dataset. We run the whole workflow and generated new synthetic sequences by utilizing the SeqGan algorithm. The proposed workflow used the Trie and HashMap data structures to make generated sequences valid and non-duplicated. We compared the final generated data sequence against the initial dataset by using perplexity and BLUE metrics. The tests were conducted on Jupyter in AWS Sagemaker employed a Tesla T4 GPU.

Evaluation Metrics: There are so many metrics to compute similarity, difference, distance, and so on. We take the two metrics to evaluate our generated graph data sequences: Bleu score metric and Perplexity metric.

By using Blue score we evaluate our generated sequences over training sequences. Results close to zero mean that it is not good enough for translations in data sequences and results close to 1 mean better translations [12].

We also use perplexity to evaluate the generated sequences over training sequences. The perplexity metric does not have a range like the blue score. It is particularly used for evaluating language models [7]. We take inverse probability to calculate this metric. Since we take inverse probability, a lower perplexity score means that we produce better data sequences.

Evaluation Results: The results we obtained have been arranged in order to find answers to the questions of the system we mentioned above in the research motivation and the third research problem. We calculate the BLEU and Perplexity scores for a random number of data sequences generated as the output of the whole workflow. After these calculations, we compute an average of Perplexity and BLUE metrics separately for the sequences to obtain the overall system scores. Table 4 shows the result for the evaluation. The results show that the proposed workflow can generate new data sequences successfully.

Table 4. Results for perplexity and BLEU score analysis based on unigram and bigram

Score metric	Unigram	Bigram
Perplexity	43.51	28.71
BLEU	0.798	0.606

Threads to Validity: The results we obtained in this study depend on the website URL structure of the e-commerce website we have carried out. However, the e-business workflow we use constitutes a step-by-step mechanism independent of data. This e-business workflow can also be applied to different datasets.

6   Conclusion and Future Work

In this study, an e-business workflow has been proposed where UI testing can be automated. The proposed workflow utilizes a GAN-based deep learning approach, which allows the system to generate new clickstream-based data sequences after training on the large-scale graph data. In the proposed workflow, to represent the graph data, we use a vocabulary-based mapping approach. We reckon that embedding approaches such as word2vec and node2vec can also be used and integrated with the proposed workflow. To facilitate testing of the system, we implement a prototype application. We evaluate the prototype application via an experimental study. The results of the empirical research results indicate that the proposed approach can generate new synthetic data sequences. In turn, these data sequences can be used to create UI test scripts automatically.

In the future work, we plan on expanding on the number of e-commerce websites in which we can test the prototype application. Furthermore, we also plan on utilizing different hyperparameter algorithms for finding the best parameter suite for the GAN-based deep learning algorithm.

Acknowledgment. We thank TUBITAK for supporting this research (under project id: 3191534) and Saha Bilgi Teknolojileri Egitim Danismanlık San. Tic. A.S. R&D Center for providing the computational facilities that made this study possible. We are grateful to Caner Kaya and Ekin Oncu for their supports. We encouraged by their perspectives.

References

1. Afrassa, K.W., Cosgun, G., Gursoy, U.F., Yildiz, E.M., Aktas, M.S.: On the community discovery methods for complex networks: a case study. In: 2020 15th Conference on Computer Science and Information Systems (FedCSIS), pp. 473–477. IEEE (2020)

2. Akpinar, P., Aktas, M.S., Keles, A.B., Balaman, Y., Guler, Z.O., Kalipsiz, O.: Web application testing with model based testing method: case study. In: 2020 International Conference on Electrical, Communication, and Computer Engineering (ICECCE), pp. 1–6. IEEE (2020)
3. Aktas, M.S., Astekin, M.: Provenance aware run-time verification of things for self-healing internet of things applications. Concurr. Comput.: Pract. Experience **31**(3), e4263 (2019)
4. Anbunathan, R., Basu, A.: Automation framework for test script generation for android mobile. In: 2017 2nd IEEE International Conference on Recent Trends in Electronics, Information & Communication Technology (RTEICT), pp. 1914–1918. IEEE (2017)
5. Baeth, M.J., Aktas, M.S.: An approach to custom privacy policy violation detection problems using big social provenance data. Concurr. Comput.: Pract. Experience **30**(21), e4690 (2018)
6. Goodfellow, I., et al.: Generative adversarial nets. In: Advances in Neural Information Processing Systems, vol. 27 (2014)
7. Jelinek, F., Mercer, R.L., Bahl, L.R., Baker, J.K.: Perplexity—A measure of the difficulty of speech recognition tasks. J. Acoust. Soc. Am. **62**(S1), S63–S63 (1977)
8. Kaasila, J., Ferreira, D., Kostakos, V., Ojala, T.: Testdroid: automated remote UI testing on android. In: Proceedings of the 11th International Conference on Mobile and Ubiquitous Multimedia, pp. 1–4 (2012)
9. Klauck, H., Nanongkai, D., Pandurangan, G., Robinson, P.: Distributed computation of large-scale graph problems. In: Proceedings of the Twenty-Sixth Annual ACM-SIAM Symposium on Discrete Algorithms, pp. 391–410. SIAM (2014)
10. Olmezogullari, E., Aktas, M.S.: Representation of click-stream datasequences for learning user navigational behavior by using embeddings. In: 2020 IEEE International Conference on Big Data (Big Data), pp. 3173–3179. IEEE (2020)
11. Olmezogullari, E., Aktas, M.S.: Pattern2Vec: representation of clickstream data sequences for learning user navigational behavior. Concurr. Comput.: Pract. Experience **34**, e6546 (2021)
12. Papineni, K., Roukos, S., Ward, T., Zhu, W.J.: BLEU: a method for automatic evaluation of machine translation. In: Proceedings of the 40th Annual Meeting of the Association for Computational Linguistics, pp. 311–318 (2002)
13. Rauf, A., Anwar, S., Jaffer, M.A., Shahid, A.A.: Automated GUI test coverage analysis using GA. In: 2010 Seventh International Conference on Information Technology: New Generations, pp. 1057–1062. IEEE (2010)
14. Riveni, M., Nguyen, T.D., Aktas, M.S., Dustdar, S.: Application of provenance in social computing: a case study. Concurr. Comput.: Pract. Experience **31**(3), e4894 (2019)
15. The Gan Zoo. https://github.com/hindupuravinash/the-gan-zoo. Accessed 15 Apr 2021
16. Uygun, Y., Oguz, R.F., Olmezogullari, E., Aktas, M.S.: On the large-scale graph data processing for user interface testing in big data science projects. In: 2020 IEEE International Conference on Big Data (Big Data), pp. 2049–2056. IEEE (2020)
17. Yu, L., Zhang, W., Wang, J., Yu, Y.: SeqGAN: sequence generative adversarial nets with policy gradient. arxiv e-prints. arXiv preprint arXiv:1609.05473 (2016)

Parallelizing Automatic Model Management System for AIOps on Microservice Platforms

Ruibo Chen$^{(\boxtimes)}$ and Wenjun Wu

State Key Laboratory of Software Development Environment, Beihang University,
Beijing, China
{chenruibo,wwj09315}@buaa.edu.cn

Abstract. With the gradual increase in the scale of applications based on microservice architecture, the complexity of system operation and maintenance is also significantly increasing. The emergence of AIOps makes it possible to automatically detect the state, allocate the resources, warn and detect the anomaly of the system through some machine learning models. Given dynamic online workloads, the running state of a production microservice system is constantly in flux. Therefore, it is necessary to continuously train, encapsulate and deploy models based on the current system status, so that the AIOps model can dynamically adapt to the system environment. To address this problem, this paper proposes a model management pipeline framework for AIOps on microservice platforms, and implements a prototype system based on Kubernetes to verify the framework. The system consists of three components: model training, model packaging and model deploying. Parallelization and parameter search are introduced in the model training process to support rapid training of multiple models and automated model hyperparameter tuning. Rapid deployment of models is supported by the model packaging and deploying components. Experiments were performed to verify the prototype system, and the experimental results illustrate the feasibility of the proposed framework. This work provides a valuable reference for the construction of an integrated and streamlined AIOps model management system.

Keywords: Model management pipeline · AIOps · Parallel model training · Microservice · MLOps

1 Introduction

With the wide adoption of the microservice architecture [2,18] in a variety of enterprise information system, the complexity of system management significantly arises for large-scale microservice platforms. Recently AIOps (Artificial Intelligence for IT Operations) [4,14] is emerging as a promising solution to this challenge on microservice system management. Under the framework of

© Springer Nature Switzerland AG 2022
R. Chaves et al. (Eds.): Euro-Par 2021, LNCS 13098, pp. 376–387, 2022.
https://doi.org/10.1007/978-3-031-06156-1_30

AIOps, system designers are able to integrate machine learning and data analytic technologies to build intelligent microservice management systems. By leveraging container orchestration frameworks such as Kubernetes, AIOps enhanced microservice systems can easily collect their real-time monitoring data streams [8] and execution logs, and adopt machine learning models to provide proactive insights and management decisions to effectively detect system anomaly, meditate resource allocations, and prevent potential system failures.

Under this architecture, AIOps machine learning (ML) models play a critical role of implementing decisions related to autonomous system management. It is not a trivial task to train accurate AOps models across different circumstances and deploy them in the microservice systems. Generally speaking, there are two major issues to be addressed:

(1) Fast model training to adopt to the dynamics of running context Different from static classification scenarios, it is often impractical to directly deploy an AIOps model for anomaly detection or root cause location in a microsystem [22] without onsite calibration. An open micro-service system may exhibit changing dynamics under different workloads. Therefore, AIOps needs to continually train [5,19] and update models so as to represent the dynamics of a running system. Furthermore, During the runtime of the system, system administrators and reliability engineers regularly check the outputs of the models and assess their performance. In case of low accurate prediction or poor decision, they may want to kick off the re-training process for the models with the newly collected data. Given the complexity of training a modern Deep Neural Network model for AIOps [12], it is a challenge to efficiently run the training process with sufficient computing resources.

(2) Encapsulation and deployment of model code as microservice A natural way to deploy an AIOps model in a the microservice system is to containerize the model code into a docker image, and then deploy the model image. To implement such a model-as-service approach, we need to streamline and automate many relevant processing steps including model training, verification, packaging and deployment. Clearly, Continuous Integration and Continuous Deployment (CI/CD) [10,16] is the right design pattern to support model-as-service in AIOps. Most existing CI/CD pipelines are designed for integrating software code rather than machine learning models. To support model encapsulation and deployment, we must introduce customized model metadata description and deployment scripts.

In order to solve the problems mentioned above, this paper proposes a new AIOps model management pipeline framework and implemented a prototype system built on Kubernetes to verify this framework. This framework consists of the following steps:

(1) Model training: It is often time consuming to run an iterative training process for a DNN models with many weight parameters. Therefore, we adopt state-of-the-art parallel training method to accelerate this process for updating the AIOps models.

(2) Model packaging: Building reproducible container images from model source code and supporting libraries, and creating model registry to implement version control and storage of model mirroring.

(3) Model deploying: Handling single or more complex deployments for installing model images on kubernetes.

The final outcome of this framework is a ML pipeline [23] that trains multiple AIOps models, explores the metrics to pick the best, packages the model as a docker image, and deploys it as a Rest API.

The rest of the paper is organized as follows. Section 2 discusses the related work, Sect. 3 introduces the details of the Microservice-oriented model management system. Section 4 describes some verification experiments of the system. Section 5 concludes the paper and discusses future work.

2   Related Work

2.1   Parallel Model Training

In general, the methods for parallel training of deep learning models [1,15] can be divided into two categories. The first one is data parallelism [17], and the second is model parallelism [3]. Before introducing the parallel model training method, we briefly describe the traditional deep learning model training process [11]. As shown in Fig. 1, In each round of the iterative training algorithm, the values of current weight parameters and a batch of train data need to be injected into the model, and the current loss values are obtained through the forward propagation process. After that, the backpropagation algorithm [9] calculates the gradient of the parameters according to the loss function and update the weight parameters. In the next round, the updated parameters go through the forward propagation process of the model with the new batch data again.

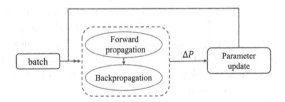

Fig. 1. Traditional model training process

Model Parallelism: A deep neural network model is divided into multiple components according to their functions. These components can be trained respectively by different devices (GPU/CPU, etc.) in the distributed system. As shown in Fig. 2 and Fig. 3, different network layers of the neural network model are assigned to multiple computing devices, or different parameters within the same layer are assigned to these devices.

Data Parallelism: We allow multiple computing devices to have their own copies of the same model, and partition the training dataset into multiple groups. Each device is only responsible for training the model with their share of the dataset. After they finish the training, the calculation results of all the devices are combined in a certain way.

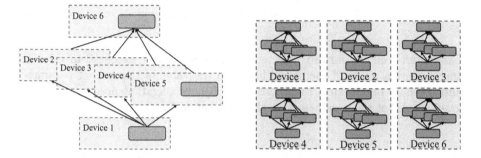

Fig. 2. Model parallelism   **Fig. 3.** Data parallelism

In current AIOps implementations, most models are not very large and many-layer DNN models. Instead, they tend to be medium size and moderate numbers of parameters. Therefore, it is more suitable to adopt data parallelism approach because it is better for handling large amount of training data. Data-parallel distributed training stores a backup of a model on each worker node, and processes different parts of the data set on each node. The data parallelization training method needs to combine the results of each worker node and synchronize the model parameters between them. This paper mainly discusses data parallelism from two aspects: synchronous and asynchronous [13, 20].

Data parallelism in synchronous mode is shown in the Fig. 4. It can be seen that at the beginning of each iteration, the training data will be divided into different mini-batch. All devices will first uniformly read the values of the current parameters and acquire a mini-batch data. After that run the forward propagation process on different devices to get the prediction results of the model, and then run the backpropagation process to get the gradient ΔP of the parameters on the respective mini-batch. Because each work node processes its own partition of the training dataset, the gradients of their parameter copies are always different from each other. Thus, after all the worker nodes have completed back propagation computation, a shared parameter server needs to collect the parameter gradients from them, calculate the average value of the gradients, and update the parameters based on the average value. Finally, the parameter server transmitted the updated parameters to each worker node for the next round of the iterative training.

Data parallelism in asynchronous mode is shown in the Fig. 5. The biggest difference between it and synchronization mode is the method of parameter update. In each iteration, different devices will read the current value of the

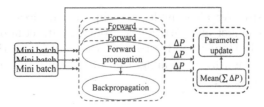

Fig. 4. Data parallelism in synchronous mode

parameter. And the forward propagation process will be executed to calculate the prediction result of the model based on the value of the current parameter and the mini-batch data. Finally, run the backpropagation process to get the gradient ΔP of the parameters on the mini-batch.

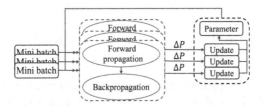

Fig. 5. Data parallelism in asynchronous mode

Different from synchronous mode, the process of updating parameters in asynchronous mode is also independent of each other, although each device reads the parameters from the same place. In asynchronous mode, different devices are completely independent. Each device uses different data for training, and updates the parameters according to the gradient value which acquired by itself. Note that different devices training the same model often consume different time, and due to the independence of each device, it may lead to the different reading time of the parameters. This will cause the differences between parameter values obtained by these devices. This problem is called gradient interference in asynchronous mode. The more serious problem caused by this is that the deep learning model trained in asynchronous mode may not be able to achieve better training results.

2.2 MLOps

In order to establish a standard machine learning model development and deployment process, MLOps was proposed [21]. MLOps is a practice in the ML field that applies DevOps principles [6,24] to ML systems for unifying the ML system development and operation. The main target of MLOps is to shorten the iterative cycle of model development and deployment, and to improve the overall efficiency of model delivery through more standardized and automated processes. The main principles of MLOps are automation and continuity. Automation requires that all automated links in the entire workflow from data access to final model deployment should be automated. Continuity requires the addition of continuous training and updating of the model on the basis of CI/CD, that is, when new data arrives or the performance of the model decreases, the model needs to be triggered to retrain to improve its performance [7]. On the basis of the above-mentioned MLOps, AIOps model management for microservice systems needs to introduce a model encapsulation process, and encapsulate the training model as a docker image for deployment and operation in the microservice system.

There are already some tools for MLOps and model encapsulation for microservice platforms. Kubeflow is an open source pipelined machine learning platform based on Kubernetes. It provides end-to-end lifecycle management of ML applications by leveraging TFX components such as data validation, model evaluation, and model services. Because it can be deployed in various Kubernetes clusters, Kubeflow enables ML workflows to work in any Kubernetes-based microservice platform where Kubeflow is installed. Source-to-Image (S2I) is a toolkit for building reproducible container images from source code. S2I produces ready-to-run images by injecting source code into a container image and enabling the container to prepare necessary code and scripts for execution. It takes a base "builder" image with all the libraries and adds tools needed to compile an application or install dependencies and a set of scripts for testing and running the applications.

3   The Framework of the Model Management System

The model management system proposed in this article is composed of three main components, including Model training, Model packaging and Model deploying component (Fig. 6).

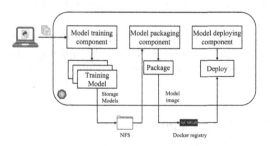

Fig. 6. Workflow diagram of the model management system

3.1   Model Training Component

The model training component adopts the synchronous data parallel method to carry out the model training in a distributed way. The implementation of data parallelism of the model training consists of a group of workers that are assigned to independent computing accelerators. Each worker is responsible for maintaining a copy of the model parameters (weights being trained) and synchronizing between all workers before each training starts. The process of distributed model training is described as follows:

Step1: Every worker node performs a forward and backward propagation computation of the model on its mini-batch of data from the entire dataset. After it finishes the backward propagation pass computation, every worker node generates a set of updates to the weight parameters based on the data it processed.
Step2: All the worker nodes exchange their parameter updates with each other, so that they can gather all the updates from Step 1.
Step3: Every worker node calculates the average values of the updates by the number of nodes.
Step4: Every worker node applies the averaged updates to its own copy of the model parameters.
Loop: Return to Step 1.

Reducing Computation and Communication Overheads: In the process of distributed model training, steps 1, 2, and 3 introduce computation and communication overhead. Specifically, step 1 and step 2 result in the majority of the computational overhead. We use the maximum batch size suitable for memory to make more efficient utilization of the GPU to reduce the computational overhead incurred in these two steps. For the reason of deep learning models typically perform dense updates. In this way, model parameters are updated for every training sample, and batch size does not affect the communicate updates time that the workers take. However, changing the batch size affects the number of cycles of the above training process. Therefore, we can reduce the number of process executions by increasing the batch size and reduce the total communication overhead.

In addition, when there are more available computing resources, the model training component can launch multiple parallel training experiments to search for optimal hyperparameters, and using multiple GPUs to accelerate a single experiment.

3.2   Model Packaging Component

After the training model is obtained, the model needs to be packaged as a docker image for management and deployment. We implement the system model packaging and management components based on open source tools including Source-to-Image, Argo and Gitlab. Source-to-Image (S2I) is a container image packaging tool that can build container images in a fast, flexible and reproducible way.

Next, we need to construct a CI pipeline to automate the packaging process. In our framework, we adopt Argo, an open-source workflow manager for Kubernetes, to do this work. Moreover, we also built a docker image registry based on Gitlab to save the packaged models.

The Argo pipeline orchestrates the packaging process in the three steps: First, it runs S2I to generate a new image for the model. Second, it mounts three resources in the generated docker image, including the volume to access the model data, the docker socket and credentials to upload the image onto the docker image repository. Third, it actually pushes the image to the repository and informs the model deployment component.

3.3   Model Deploying Component

The model deploying component in this system is responsible for installing model images in a Kubernetes platform and converting ML models into production REST microservices. In addition, the component also takes care of scaling the model and keeping it running with a standard API. Model deploying component uses Kubernetes CRD for image deployment. We configure the deployment CRD of the component through a configuration file in the Yaml format. This configuration file specifies the relevant information such as the name, the docker image and the namespace of the service to be deployed. The model deploying component needs to creates Kubernetes Pods with the specific model image on the Kubernetes cluster according to the specification of the Yaml file.

In order to achieve the timely update of the model in the AIOps system, we have designed model monitoring and feedback functions within the model deploying component. The model monitoring mainly implements the performance evaluation of the deployed model. Through regular performance evaluation, the system can detect the performance degradation of the deployed model in time. When such a degradation occurs, the feedback mechanism of the model management system kicks in to automatically retrain the new version of the model and package it to ensure the high adaptability of the AIOps model in the microservice platform.

4   Experiments

Based on the self-built Kubernetes cluster, we have conducted experiments to verify the prototype system. Since the entire system is not fully implemented at present, we only performed some preliminary tests on the main functional components of the system. The Kubernetes version corresponding to the cluster is v1.20.6. We manage the Kubernetes cluster based on Rancher and use Single Node Filer (NFS) for model storage. We utilize the MNISTdataset to train the image classification model to test the model training components. We have configured two configuration files, "const" and "adaptive" for the model. The former is used for training and testing a single model, and the latter is used for training and testing multiple models in hyperparameter search. In the training experiment of a single model, our model learning rate is 0.5, and the model contains three layers, the dropout for layer 1 and 2 is 0.25, and 0.5 for layer 3. Totally, eight times of single model trainings were performed in this experiment, and the average training time was recorded. The validation loss changes of the model in a single model training is shown in Fig. 7 and the final validation loss value is 0.044, validation accuracy is 0.986.

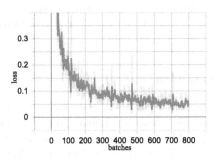

Fig. 7. Validation loss curve of single model training experiment

We conducted 8 hyperparameter search experiments and ensured that at least one experiment had the same validation accuracy as a single model training experiment. The model structure of the hyperparameter search experiment is the same as that in the single model experiment. The difference is that the corresponding parameter of the hyperparameter search experiment is a variable range, rather than a fixed value as a single experiment. The validation loss curve of the best hyperparameter search experiment is shown in Fig. 8, and the result of the complete hyperparameter search experiment is shown in the Fig. 9. One can see that the best validation loss and accuracy value among the 8 hyperparameter search experiments is 0.056 and 0.982, and it took 227 s in total.

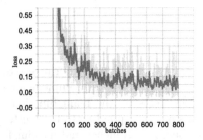

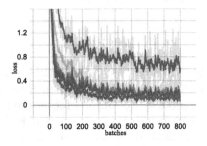

Fig. 8. Validation loss curve of optimal hyperparameter

Fig. 9. Validation loss curve of complete hyperparameter

Table 1 shows the training time and validation loss results of a single experiment and a hyperparameter search experiment. From the results, one can clearly see that the average training time of multiple hyperparameter search experiments using parallel training is lower than that of a single experiment. The main reason is that hyperparameter search only requires at least one experiment to achieve the same accuracy as a single model experiment, so some experiments may end early. The time to complete 8 parallel experiments is 250 s, which is far less than the time for serial completion, which shows the feasibility of the parallel training we have achieved.

Table 1. Performance of different model training experiments

	Number	1	2	3	4	5	6	7	8	Average value
Single model training	Training time (s)	130	237	148	196	148	192	148	221	177.5
	Val loss	0.046	0.05	0.044	0.046	0.048	0.05	0.051	0.051	0.0495
	Val Acc	0.985	0.983	0.986	0.986	0.984	0.985	0.984	0.984	0.985
Hyperparameter search	Training time (s)	118	241	115	94	135	53	135	54	118.1
	Val loss	0.056	0.065	0.074	0.078	0.159	0.212	0.228	0.285	0.1446
	Val Acc	0.982	0.98	0.976	0.975	0.952	0.944	0.938	0.919	0.958

We also carried out packaging and deployment tests on the three models of MINIST, ARIMA and TRANSFORMER. Each model executed the complete process three times, recorded and calculated the average packaging and deployment time of each model. The specific results are shown in Table 1. The time consumption of the entire process is mainly concentrated in the model packaging stage. Since models have different dependencies, that leads to differences in the packaging time (Table 2).

Table 2. Average package and deploy time of different models

Model	Average package time (s)	Average deploy time (s)
MINIST	457	10
ARIMA	228	10
TRANSFORMER	543	10

5   Conclusion

In this paper, we introduce an AIOps model management prototype system based on Kubernetes, the system consists of three main components, which are used to implement the functions of model training, model packaging and model deploying in the model management for AIOps on the microservice system. However, the system we proposed is still in the early stage of design and implementation, we only conducted some simple experiments to test the basic functions of the system. The preliminary experimental results show the feasibility of implementing an integrated and streamlined AIOps model management with the components we have developed.

In future work, we will further integrate the entire system on the basis of current work, implement phased performance testing of deployed models, and develop feedback mechanisms to ensure that models in the production environment can be updated in time when their performance declines. We plan to make further verification of the system in real operation and maintenance scenarios, ensuring that the framework we proposed can truly serve the real AIOps systems.

Acknowledgements. This paper was supported by National Key R&D Program of China (Funding No. 2018YFB1402800), State Key Laboratory of Software Development Environment (Funding No. SKLSDE-2020ZX-01).

References

1. Ben-Nun, T., Hoefler, T.: Demystifying parallel and distributed deep learning: an in-depth concurrency analysis. ACM Comput. Surv. (CSUR) **52**(4), 1–43 (2019)
2. Cerny, T., Donahoo, M.J., Trnka, M.: Contextual understanding of microservice architecture: current and future directions. ACM SIGAPP Appl. Comput. Rev. **17**(4), 29–45 (2018)
3. Chen, C.C., Yang, C.L., Cheng, H.Y.: Efficient and robust parallel DNN training through model parallelism on multi-GPU platform. arXiv preprint arXiv:1809.02839 (2018)
4. Dang, Y., Lin, Q., Huang, P.: AIOps: real-world challenges and research innovations. In: 2019 IEEE/ACM 41st International Conference on Software Engineering: Companion Proceedings (ICSE-Companion), pp. 4–5. IEEE (2019)
5. Diethe, T., Borchert, T., Thereska, E., Balle, B., Lawrence, N.: Continual learning in practice. arXiv preprint arXiv:1903.05202 (2019)
6. Ebert, C., Gallardo, G., Hernantes, J., Serrano, N.: DevOps. IEEE Softw. **33**(3), 94–100 (2016)
7. Fontenla-Romero, Ó., Guijarro-Berdiñas, B., Martinez-Rego, D., Pérez-Sánchez, B., Peteiro-Barral, D.: Online machine learning. In: Efficiency and Scalability Methods for Computational Intellect, pp. 27–54. IGI Global (2013)
8. Haselböck, S., Weinreich, R.: Decision guidance models for microservice monitoring. In: 2017 IEEE International Conference on Software Architecture Workshops (ICSAW), pp. 54–61. IEEE (2017)
9. Hecht-Nielsen, R.: Theory of the backpropagation neural network. In: Neural Networks for Perception, pp. 65–93. Elsevier (1992)
10. Humble, J., Farley, D.: Continuous Delivery: Reliable Software Releases Through Build, Test, and Deployment Automation. Pearson Education, London (2010)
11. LeCun, Y., Bengio, Y., Hinton, G.: Deep learning. Nature **521**(7553), 436–444 (2015)
12. Li, Y., et al.: Predicting node failures in an ultra-large-scale cloud computing platform: an AIOps solution. ACM Trans. Softw. Eng. Methodol. (TOSEM) **29**(2), 1–24 (2020)
13. Littman, M.S., Metcalf, C.D.: An exploration of asynchronous data-parallelism. Personal communication (1990)

14. Masood, A., Hashmi, A.: AIOps: predictive analytics & machine learning in operations. In: Cognitive Computing Recipes, pp. 359–382. Springer, Berkeley (2019). https://doi.org/10.1007/978-1-4842-4106-6_7
15. Park, J.H., et al.: HetPipe: enabling large {DNN} training on (Whimpy) heterogeneous {GPU} clusters through integration of pipelined model parallelism and data parallelism. In: 2020 {USENIX} Annual Technical Conference ({USENIX} {ATC} 2020), pp. 307–321 (2020)
16. Schneider, R.: Continuous integration: improving software quality and reducing risk. Softw. Qual. Prof. **10**(4), 51 (2008)
17. Shallue, C.J., Lee, J., Antognini, J., Sohl-Dickstein, J., Frostig, R., Dahl, G.E.: Measuring the effects of data parallelism on neural network training. arXiv preprint arXiv:1811.03600 (2018)
18. Singh, V., Peddoju, S.K.: Container-based microservice architecture for cloud applications. In: 2017 International Conference on Computing, Communication and Automation (ICCCA), pp. 847–852. IEEE (2017)
19. Stocco, A., Tonella, P.: Towards anomaly detectors that learn continuously. In: 2020 IEEE International Symposium on Software Reliability Engineering Workshops (ISSREW), pp. 201–208. IEEE (2020)
20. Subhlok, J., Stichnoth, J.M., O'hallaron, D.R., Gross, T.: Exploiting task and data parallelism on a multicomputer. In: Proceedings of the Fourth ACM SIGPLAN Symposium on Principles and Practice of Parallel Programming, pp. 13–22 (1993)
21. Tamburri, D.A.: Sustainable MLOps: trends and challenges. In: 2020 22nd International Symposium on Symbolic and Numeric Algorithms for Scientific Computing (SYNASC), pp. 17–23. IEEE (2020)
22. Wang, L., Zhao, N., Chen, J., Li, P., Zhang, W., Sui, K.: Root-cause metric location for microservice systems via log anomaly detection. In: 2020 IEEE International Conference on Web Services (ICWS), pp. 142–150. IEEE (2020)
23. Zhou, Y., Yu, Y., Ding, B.: Towards MLOps: a case study of ML pipeline platform. In: 2020 International Conference on Artificial Intelligence and Computer Engineering (ICAICE), pp. 494–500. IEEE (2020)
24. Zhu, L., Bass, L., Champlin-Scharff, G.: DevOps and its practices. IEEE Softw. **33**(3), 32–34 (2016)

LSDVE – Eighth Workshop on Large Scale Distributed Virtual Environments

Eighth Workshop on Large Scale Distributed Virtual Environments (LSDVE 2021)

Workshop Description

The Eighth International Workshop on Large Scale Distributed Virtual Environments (LSDVE 2021) was held in online, on 31th of August, 2021. For the eighth time, this workshop was organized in conjunction with the Euro-Par annual series of international conferences.

The recent advances in networking have determined an increasing use of information technology to support distributed networked cooperative applications. Several novel applications have emerged in this area: distributed social networks and media, blockchain-based social media, token economies, and collaborative applications. In particular, this workshop aims to provide a venue for researchers to present and discuss important aspects of large-scale networked collaborative applications and of the platforms supporting them, with a particular focus on distributed social networks and media. Social Networks are dynamic and evolving in nature and involve a huge amount of users and this makes it challenging to design distributed platforms for social networks/media. Important challenges are the design of user interfaces, coordination protocols, and proper middle-ware and architectures. The workshop's aim is to provide the opportunity for scientists, engineers, researchers, and entrepreneurs to discuss and exchange novel ideas, results, and experience on all the aspects of Distributed Social Networks design and their deployment on distributed architectures.

This year, the workshop has provided three sessions. In the first session, the paper "Consistency Analysis of Distributed Ledgers in Fog-enhanced Blockchains" shows how a blockchain deployed in the fog layer outperforms a blockchain deployed in the end-user layer, in terms of block finality and storage. The paper addresses the problem of reliability of fog-enhanced blockchain systems by analyzing the forking phenomenon in integrated fog-blockchain systems under different conditions.

The second session "Trust and Reputation in social Media" includes the paper "SMART: a Tool for Trust and Reputation Management in Social Media", which proposes a data-driven tool called SMART whose aim is to provide a decision-making methodology to compute weighted trust content ratings to classify them as trustworthy or not. The tool has been developed within the European ARTICONF project.

The second session "Cloud Infrastructures" includes two papers. The first one, "Towards Generating Realistic Trace for Simulating Functions-as-a-Service", addresses the problem of generating realistic traces for simulating serverless computing platforms. The generated traces are based on the Azure Functions dataset and they are applicable in an already available versatile and high performance simulator (DISSECT-CF). The paper "SPIRIT: A microservice-based framework for interactive Cloud infrastructure planning" proposes an open framework named SPIRIT, which allows a user to include cloud infrastructure planning algorithms and to evaluate and compare their solutions.

We wish to thank all who helped to make also this eighth edition of the workshop a success: authors submitting papers, colleagues who refereed the submitted papers, the numerous colleagues who attended the sessions, and finally the Euro-Par 2021 organizers whose invaluable support greatly helped in the organization of the workshop.

Organization

Program Chairs

Laura Ricci	Department of Computer Science, Pisa, Italy
Barbara Guidi	Department of Computer Science, Pisa, Italy
Radu Prodan	University of Klagenfurt, Austria

Program Committee

Damiano Di Francesco Maesa	University of Pisa, Italy
Marco Furini	University of Modena and Reggio Emilia, Italy
Ombretta Gaggi	University of Padova, Italy
Barbara Guidi	Department of Computer Science, University of Pisa, Italy
Mohammad Hammoudeh	Manchester Metropolitan University, UK
Dragi Kimovski	University of Klagenfurt, Austria
Kevin Koidl	Trinity College, Dublin, Ireland
Javier Marìn Morales	Universitat Politècnica de València, Spain
Pietro Manzoni	Universitat Politècnica de València, Spain
Filippo Marozzo	University of Calabria, Italy
Andrea Michienzi	University of Pisa, Italy
Silvia Mirri	University of Bologna, Italy
Paolo Mori	IIT, CNR, Pisa
Valtteri Niemi	University of Helsinki, Finland
Claudio Palazzi	University of Padova, Italy
Dana Pectu	University of Timisoara, Romania
Radu Prodan	University of Klagenfurt, Austria
Laura Ricci	University of Pisa, Italy
Nishant Saurabh	University of Klagenfurt, Austria

Consistency Analysis of Distributed Ledgers in Fog-Enhanced Blockchains

Attila Kertesz$^{(\boxtimes)}$ ⑩ and Hamza Baniata ⑩

University of Szeged, Dugonics ter 13, Szeged 6720, Hungary
{keratt,baniatah}@inf.u-szeged.hu

Abstract. Both revolutionary technologies of Fog Computing (FC) and Blockchain (BC) serve as enablers for enhanced, people-centric trusted applications, and they do meet in the provision of higher standards and expectations. In this paper, we address the reliability of fog-enhanced BC systems by analyzing the forking phenomenon under different conditions, and provide a reliable Distributed Ledger (DL) consistency assessment. We use the FoBSim tool that is specifically designed to mimic and emulate realistic FC-BC integration, in which we deploy the Proof-of-Work (PoW) consensus algorithm and analyze the forking probability under fluctuating conditions. Based on our results, we propose an inconsistency formula, which can quantitatively describe how consistent the DL in a BC system can be. Finally, we show how to deploy this formula in a decision making model for indicating optimal deployment features of a BC network in a Fog-enhanced system.

Keywords: Distributed Ledger · Consistency · Blockchain · Fog Computing

1 Introduction

Blockchain (BC) is the technology proposed by Nakamoto [24] in 2009 as the backbone of the famous Bitcoin network. BC proposed many simple solutions for different problems that faced a successful distributed digital currency system for years. A major component of a BC-based system is the Distributed Ledger (DL), whose consistency is a problem that describes the unreliability of DLs in dense and highly dynamic networks [7]. This problem concerns maintaining exact copies of the DL, as the appearance of different DL versions is trivially expected in realized scenarios. Reasons for such issue include both, the transmission delay between network entities and the continuous and concurrent alteration of DL data. The concept of Finality is usually related to the DL consistency, which is the state of the BC, under which the transaction cannot be canceled, reversed or changed by any of the participants in this network under any circumstances [4]. Although Nakamoto's model did not perfectly solve the consistency problem, it proposed a highly accurate, probabilistic solution. Specifically, a next block of data is introduced into the network when its previous block had, most likely,

ⓒ Springer Nature Switzerland AG 2022
R. Chaves et al. (Eds.): Euro-Par 2021, LNCS 13098, pp. 393–404, 2022.
https://doi.org/10.1007/978-3-031-06156-1_31

sufficient time to be confirmed by the DL (i.e. synchronized between the majority of network entities). The occurrence of two pieces of information at the same time would lead to a temporary inconsistent state of the ledger, which is termed forking [13].

The enforced delay between blocks depends mainly on the ability of system entities to find a puzzle solution. The difficulty of the puzzle is indeed updated through time according to the design requirements (e.g. Bitcoin's predefined delay is 10 min). Such model is classified as a 'Probabilistic Finality System' since the system continuously lowers the probability of concurrent DL updates, yet the probability never reaches zero. Examples of algorithms belonging to this class include the Proof-of-Work (PoW) and the Proof-of-Elapsed-Time (PoET). The other class is the 'Absolute Finality Systems', where the system allows its entities to produce a next block, only when the previous block is confirmed. Examples of algorithms belonging to this class include the PBFT and some versions of the Proof-of-Stake (PoS) [14].

The mechanisms deployed in BCs to decrease the probability of forking can be concluded by three main approaches. First, a gossiping protocol to synchronize confirmed blocks/ledgers. Second, the continuous increment of the puzzle difficulty, which gives a window to network entities to gossip, leading to increased total energy consumption of the system, and/or decreased total throughput. Third, the utilization of full and light nodes in the network [27], so that gossiping is performed by fewer network entities. Accordingly, data propagation through the network shall consume less time.

Fog Computing (FC) [21] is the distributed extension of the cloud at the edge of the network. FC provides enhanced services closer to end-users in terms of time, energy, and network load. The integration of FC with BC had been recently discussed by many researchers [2]. On one hand, more efficient services can be provided by FC over clouds, mostly required by Internet of Things (IoT) systems. On the other hand, the BC technology can be deployed for reliable, TTP-free, and secure Transactions (TXs) ledger in such distributed environments.

We have previously shown in [3] how a BC deployed in the fog layer outperforms a BC deployed in the end-user layer, in terms of block finality and storage. This paper aims at analyzing the forking phenomenon in integrated FC-BC systems that utilizes a probabilistic finality mechanism. Specifically, we use the PoW algorithm to represent the class of probabilistic finality. As we perform our analysis under different conditions, we contribute a method for evaluating the consistency of the DL, by finding the ratio of forks appearing within the DL to the maximum possible number of chain versions. Additionally, we study the effect of different BC deployment scenarios in the fog and end-user layer. Consequently, we propose a decision making model that may help practitioners choose the optimal deployment approaches of BCs in Fog-enhanced environments. Such assessment approach can clarify the path for a reliable and consistent construction of DLs, deployed at both the fog and end-user layers. It also determines the conditions under which a BC deployed in the fog layer outperforms a BC deployed in the end-user layer, in terms of DL consistency.

The remainder of this paper is organized as follows: Sect. 2 presents the previous research efforts that targeted the analysis of forking in PoW-based BCs. Section 3 presents the terminology, the proposed methods and parameters, and the implementation we used for conducting our research. Section 4 presents and discusses our results. Finally, Sect. 5 concludes our paper.

2   Related Work

It was proven by Brewer [6] that a DL system cannot guarantee ledger consistency, nodes availability and partition tolerance, altogether. Accordingly, any attempt for decreasing the inconsistency levels in a given BC system, would either decrease the availability level of the system, or decrease the overall tolerance against network partitioning. Later, the Trust property was added to these three characteristics of a DL [10]. In this work the authors quantified the trust in a BC system by referring to the average number of orphaned blocks in one day, leading to the probability of discarding a proposed TX. Similarly, we proposed the Un-Reliability metric of PoW-based BCs in [1]. This metric describes how reliable shall a BC system be according to the probability of discarding a generated TX relatively to the throughput (in terms of TXs per given time) of that BC.

Kiffer et al. [16] analyzed the consistency of Nakamoto's BC from a security point of view. In their study, the block delay, puzzle difficulty, and the adversarial fraction out of the total network size, were the considered parameters. The proposed method aimed at presenting the probability of some versions of the delay attacks, that may alter data saved on the DL. Under similar conditions, Zhao et al. [30] have recently proposed a formula for ensuring the consistency property against the delay attacks.

Misic et al. [23] presented some ledger forking probability analysis depending on the absence hours of miners and the network size. They have discussed the optimization of mean delivery time of TXs, while the network size is fluctuating. Accordingly, the effects of varying properties of their proposed network model, namely different types of blocks, and different number of TCP connections per node, were analyzed. The authors also analyzed the BC forking events, BC partitioning, and duration of inconsistent state of the ledger in a Bitcoin delivery network [22]. Using a probabilistic model, they computed the probability distribution of two- and three-way forks, the forked partition sizes, and the duration of ledger inconsistency until the resolution.

Lan et al. [18] proposed consistency maintenance techniques for P2P networks (e.g. BC networks), based on push, pull, and hybrid gossiping algorithms. They found that a push-based approach achieves near-perfect consistency in stable P2P networks, although the flooding of messages through the network was found a burden, while a hybrid approach is very good for highly dynamic networks.

Wang et al. [29] compared their proposed CMV algorithm with the rumor spreading based scheme, and the Update Propagation Through Replica Chain (UPTReC) scheme, in terms of finality time and messages overhead. Similar benchmarks were used in [15,28] and [18] to evaluate the consistency of the DL.

In light of this short literature review, our present work addresses the open issue regarding the factors that affect the consistency of probabilistic finality-based BCs. We also noted that all previous works targeted a binary output of their proposed models/analysis. Such models answer: "What is the probability that a fork appears in a given scenario?". However, our proposed models and analysis aims at quantifying the output by answering the question on "How many chain versions may appear out of the maximum possible number of chains in a given scenario?".

3   Methods

To obtain accurate measures for our analysis, we used the FoBSim tool [3] for mimicking BC operations both in the end-user and fog layers. The main advantage of FoBSim is that it provides means for investigating integrated BC-FC systems using different deployment options and different consensus mechanisms.

FoBSim uses a hybrid gossiping protocol to trigger all miners to share new blocks and adopt the longest chain that is confirmed by the majority of the network. Using this functionality in FoBSim, one can decrease the number of different DL versions occurring at the end of a simulation run. To detect the appearance of a fork during a simulation run, however, we deactivated this gossiping function. That is, more forks appearing in the ledger indicate higher levels of DL inconsistency under the simulated scenario conditions. Manipulating the conditions, leading to higher or lower levels of inconsistency, facilitates the detection of direct effects of such conditions on DL consistency.

To enforce the required abstraction of different conditions, we designed several simulation scenarios. In each scenario, we oscillate the configuration of one condition and stabilize the others. Furthermore, for each case within a scenario, we performed five consequent runs under the same conditions and computed the average number of chain versions. The five parameters that were oscillated are the number of miner nodes in the BC network M, the number of neighbors per miner N, the puzzle difficulty Ω, the number of simultaneously mined blocks β, and the average transmission delay between neighbors τ. Table 1, and the second column of Table 2 present the configuration of different parameters for each simulation scenario. All parameters can be directly configured in the *Sim_parameters.json* file (i.e. the input file for FoBSim). We define the set $P(\beta)$ as a set containing all chain versions that can be possibly formed, independently, out of all confirmed blocks. By referring to the Probability Theory and the principles of Enumerative Combinatorics, the number of elements in $P(\beta)$ can be computed according to Eq. 1. Note that the order of blocks in a given chain matters, which increases the number of elements in $P(\beta)$ even more than $\beta!$.

$$|P(\beta)| = \sum_{k=0}^{\beta} \frac{\beta!}{(\beta - k)!} \tag{1}$$

We notate the number of chain versions obtained at the end of a simulation run as δ, and the maximum possible number of chain versions that can appear at

Table 1. FoBSim configuration parameters

Scen.	(M)	(N)	(Ω)	(β)	(τ) (in ms)
1	100, 500, 1000, 1500	2	20	10	0
2	500	2, 3, 5, 8, 15	5	10	0
3	1500	2	5, 10, 15, 20, 25	10	0
4	500	2	15	2, 3, 5, 8, 12, 18	0
5	1500	2	25	10	0, 5, 10, 15

the end of a simulation run as ξ. It is trivial that $\delta = \xi$ in a given scenario is the worst case in terms of DL consistency, while $\delta = 1$ is the best case. Naturally, ξ shall be equal to the number of miners. However, if M is large enough and β is relatively small, ξ shall be equal to the number of elements in the set $P(\beta)$. Consequently, as long as $M > 0$ and $\beta > 0$, ξ is determined according to Relation 2:

$$\xi = \min\{M, |P(\beta)|\} \tag{2}$$

Quantitative conclusions, then, can be drawn regarding the inconsistency Y of a DL by calculating the ratio δ to ξ. This can be formalized using Eq. 3.

$$Y = \delta/\xi \tag{3}$$

Note that, even if there was only one chain version, one cannot obtain an inconsistency level of 0% using Eq. 3. To solve this, we can further develop Eq. 3 into Eq. 4.

$$Y' = \frac{\delta - 1}{\xi - 1} \tag{4}$$

Generally, a BC puzzle is a computational challenge $f(.)$, whose solution S must fulfill the condition Ω. In order for S to be sufficiently hard to find, yet easy to verify, Ω should be set moderately according to the network conditions (e.g. the avg. computational capacity C of miners or the avg. transmission delay T between neighbors). S shall be coupled with every newly mined block so that other miners can verify it referring to Ω. A probabilistic finality based system requires several miners to search for S at the same time, while an absolute finality-based system requests one selected miner to find S. Thus, β in our analysis may be >1.

We attempt to simulate a probabilistic finality system represented by the PoW algorithm. This is because it is useless to assess the consistency of an absolute finality system as it offers a perfect consistency with the cost of lower security. Accordingly, Ω is the number of Zero's at the beginning of $f(x)$, where $f(x) = H(x \oplus S)$ ($H(.)$ is a hash function, x is data being mined, and S is a random integer being searched for by the miner).

We conducted our experiments on the Google Cloud Platform using an E2-standard-32 VM instance (up to 3.8 GHz, 32 vCPUs, 128 GB memory) running a Ubuntu 20.10 OS.

4   Results, Implications and Discussion

In this section we present and discuss the results we obtained after executing the identified scenarios. We executed all scenarios five times, and we also provide the average results of each scenario run. Table 2 concludes the results we obtained, where δ and Avg. δ are presented. The table also concludes the general observed effect of each factor oscillation on δ. Next, we discuss those results and further assess their effect on Y. Accordingly, we propose a decision model that can determine optimal deployment of a given BC application.

For Scenario-1, simulation shows that δ is proportional to the number of miner nodes participating in the BC network. For Scenario-2, simulation shows that δ is inversely proportional to the number of neighbors per miner, as long as the ratio $N : M \leq 1\%$. This result is similar to the results presented in [18], because the impact of N (on the distributed DB consistency, although was studied with different consistency metric model), was studied for a maximum of four, and with a network size of 500. However, we found that for the case where the ratio $N : M > 1\%$, one can notice that δ is directly proportional to N. This observation is somewhat consistent with the observations presented in [25]. That is, it was argued that $N < \log M$ may increase the number of forks in a given BC, due to several weak links acting as bottlenecks. Accordingly, it was recommended that N shall be set to $\geq \frac{M-1}{M} \log M$. Taking the Bitcoin network as an example, the authors argued that it is safe, with regards to N, since it operates within a stable range of 22–99 connections (per Full miner nodes). However, we argue that although such range is safe to guarantee network connectivity, it is not optimized in terms of forking. As [25] sets the recommended lower bound of N for safety, our results recommend the upper bound of N, for optimization, to be $N \leq \lceil M/100 \rceil$.

For Scenario-3, simulation shows that δ is inversely proportional to the puzzle solution difficulty. As discussed earlier, such result is naturally expected for a system with a probabilistic finality. Increasing Ω is the BC solution to decrease the probability of $\beta > 1$. Additionally, the increment of Ω provides sufficient window for miners to spread the word, and compensates for the continuous enhancement of mining machines. That is, such continuous enhancement (predicted by Moore's law [26]) may lead to faded effect of a static Ω through time. From another point of view, compensating the advancement of computational capacities of mining machines only by increasing Ω implies higher energy consumption through time.

For Scenario-4, the simulation shows that δ is directly proportional to the number of blocks simultaneously mined and broadcast in the BC network.

Lastly, for Scenario-5, the simulation shows that δ is directly proportional to the average transmission delay between neighboring miners. These results conform with the proportionality characteristic presented in [20], where higher transmission delays predicted higher forking probability. Furthermore, it agrees with [12], where it was shown that lower delay between BC miners implies higher efficiency in terms of consistency.

Table 2. Number of chain versions at the end of each simulation run, the average number of chain versions for each scenario, and the observed effect of oscillating the corresponding factor on the average number of chain versions

Scenario	Oscillated factor	Run-1	Run-2	Run-3	Run-4	Run-5	Average δ	Effect
Scenario-1	$M = 100$	1	1	1	1	3	1.4	
	$M = 500$	5	1	4	2	2	2.8	↑
	$M = 1000$	37	11	4	2	9	12.6	↑
	$M = 1500$	26	57	54	28	24	37.8	↑
Scenario-2	$N = 2$	91	105	78	69	91	86.8	
	$N = 3$	87	66	42	65	79	67.8	↓
	$N = 5$	45	50	53	65	64	55.4	↓
	$N = 8$	117	73	71	45	71	75.4	↑
	$N = 15$	417	418	409	374	413	406.2	↑
Scenario-3	$\Omega = 5$	138	125	142	134	144	136.6	
	$\Omega = 10$	143	123	128	126	142	132.4	↓
	$\Omega = 15$	129	135	125	140	136	133	↑
	$\Omega = 20$	22	14	20	9	31	19.2	↓
	$\Omega = 25$	1	1	1	8	1	2.4	↓
Scenario-4	$\beta=2$	3	3	3	3	3	3	
	$\beta=3$	4	3	4	4	3	3.6	↑
	$\beta=5$	66	72	42	52	89	64.2	↑
	$\beta=8$	38	51	39	62	58	49.6	↓
	$\beta=12$	393	376	389	405	379	388.4	↑
	$\beta=18$	459	461	469	466	460	463	↑
Scenario-5	$\tau = 0$ ms	2	5	2	1	17	5.4	
	$\tau = 5$ ms	26	47	7	24	6	22	↑
	$\tau = 10$ ms	21	46	2	6	40	23	↑
	$\tau = 15$ ms	31	72	37	11	103	50.8	↑

According to our results, we can accumulate our findings in Relation 5, where η is $1/N$ if $N/M \leq 1\%$ and is N otherwise.

$$\delta \propto \frac{M \times \eta \times \tau \times \beta}{\Omega} \qquad (5)$$

Solving for Y using Eqs. 1, 2 and 3, we can compute Y as a percentage. That is, 100% level of inconsistency indicates the lowest level of DL consistency. In other words, the lower the value of Y, the lower the number of logical forks. For δ values, we use the average values in Table 2. We educe the relevant values of M and β, and compute ξ accordingly.

Figure 1 present the results we obtained from each scenario assessment, in terms of percentage Y. According to these results we can deduce that Relation 6 applies, where λ is M if $M \leq |P(\beta)|$, and is $1/|P(\beta)|$ otherwise.

$$Y \propto \frac{\lambda \times \eta \times \tau \times \beta}{\Omega} \qquad (6)$$

Specifically, one can notice that highest consistency levels can be achieved when deploying 500 miners, while each is connected to no more than 8 neighbors. Furthermore, the puzzle difficulty is extremely effective as hardening the puzzle solution results in a decreased value of β. However, Scenario-4 shows that, in the case where $M \leq 500$, simultaneous blocks appearing in the network are tolerated in terms of Y up to $\beta = 8$. This can be justified by the exponential growth rate of ξ, which compensates the linear growth of δ and M, and almost hides the effect of the increasing β. Once the value of ξ is switched to be equal to M (according to Eq. 2), the actual effect of β can be clearly noted. Finally, Scenario-5 shows that the DL has the highest consistency levels with lower average transmission delays between miners.

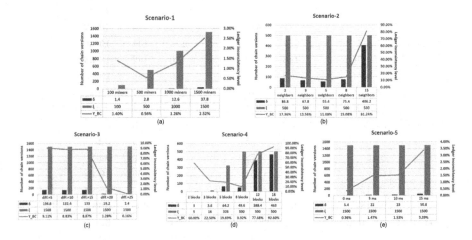

Fig. 1. Average number of chain versions according to the simulation of Scenarios 1–5, and maximum possible number of chain versions that could appear during the simulation, represented by blue bars and orange bars, respectively (correlated with the primary y-axis on the left). And the percentage value of Ledger inconsistency, represented by the grey curve (correlated with the secondary y-axis on the right) (Color figure online)

One can also notice the individual relative effect of each analyzed factor. That is, adding more miners can indeed decrease the ledger consistency level, yet it is not as effective as increasing the number of neighbors per miner (e.g. adding 500 miners to the network increases Y with about 1%, while changing the number of neighbors per miner from 8 to 15 increases Y with about 60%). Furthermore, adding more miners to the BC network (i.e. increasing M) leads to increasing both δ and ξ in case $\xi = M$, while it only leads to increasing δ in case $\xi = |P(\beta)|$. Such notion can particularly justify that increasing M does not strongly affect Y as M increases and decreases Y at the same time. Additionally, it justifies the results of Scenario-4, where β increases yet Y decreases. According to the results of Scenario-1, increasing M can guarantee higher ledger consistency (in the cases where $M \leq 500$), as the effect of M is higher on ξ than it is on δ.

Fog Computing Enhancement for DL Consistency

BC technology can provide services that map to some of the services that Fog-enhanced systems are expected to provide. Depending on the expected characteristics of the fog layer, one can evaluate the benefits of deploying BC in the fog, so that FC services can be extended beyond data pre-processing, monitoring and storage. For example, fog components are expected to be directly connected to each other, which lowers the transmission delay, while the BC nodes, deployed in the end-user layer, are connected through the internet, in a P2P fashion. Thus, it is trivial to expect the enhancement of a BC application in terms of ledger consistency, when deployed in the fog layer instead of the end-user layer.

To evaluate these expectations, we assume two cases, where probabilistic finality based BC is deployed in the end-user layer, and in the fog layer. In both cases, $M = 500$, $N = 5$ and $\Omega = 20$. Meanwhile, the size of the message to be sent to neighbors is unified. Recalling the results presented in [5] and [19], the average transmission delay τ can be set between miners in the first case to 1000 ms, and between miners in the second case to 12 ms, while no jitter is considered in both cases.

The computational power C of fog nodes and end-user miners need to be also considered as described in [30]. That is, mining devices used by end users to mine new blocks have more computational power than it is expected for fog nodes. This is due to the fact that end-user miners deploy their Graphics Processing Units (GPUs) for mining new blocks and providing BC services. On the other hand, fog nodes usually use their CPUs to perform tasks and provide fog services.

Since M, N and Ω are equal in both cases, τ and C, are the effective factors on Y in both deployments. The current state-of-the-art is unclear regarding the exact fog node architecture and whether they have built-in GPUs, the comparison results remain dependant on the individual case parameters at the time of application. Additionally, some PoW versions, that are described as Memory Hard Puzzles [9], may indeed present fogs to have higher ability to solve the puzzle. That is, even if they actually have less computational power than the average computational power of end-user miners, they may offer higher memory. An example of a BC system with Memory Hard Puzzle scheme is *Chia*, the most recently launched Chinese cryptocurrency [11]. In such a case C represents memory capacity, rather than computational capacity, of compared miners.

To help making the right deployment decision in such situations, we propose the evaluation in terms of Y. That is, one can find the ratio between Y_f and Y_e, where f is fog layer and e is end-user layer. This shall result in a positive value Ψ. As C is, by definition, proportional with β, and inversely proportional with Ω [17], a modified version of Eq. 6 gives:

$$\Psi = \frac{Y_f}{Y_e} = \frac{T_f \times C_f}{T_e \times C_e} \tag{7}$$

where $T = \varsigma \times \tau$ is the average total time of propagation and ς is a constant that reflects different communications criteria between miners. Those criteria may cause additional delays related to average processing/routing delay, average queuing delay, link distance/type/quality, block/packet size, resources allocation, etc.

Equation 7 can be used then to make a reliable decision regarding the deployment of the BC in e or f. Assuming all factors other than τ and C are equal, if the value of Ψ is less than 1, then the BC is better be deployed in f, because such deployment guarantees higher DL consistency. Otherwise, the BC is better be deployed in e. The single critical point, where both e and f deployments are expected to provide equivalent Y measures, can be utilized as follows:

$$1 = \frac{12 \times C_f}{1000 \times C_e} \Rightarrow 12 \times C_f = 1000 \times C_e \Rightarrow C_e = \frac{1.2}{100} \times C_f$$

Consequently, if average C_e is less than 1.2% of average C_f, then it is better, in terms of Y, to deploy the BC in e. Otherwise, the BC is better be deployed in f (we assumed that ς is equal in both deployment options, although it is expected that the fog will provide super high connectivity that outperforms typical P2P communications through classical internet).

On one hand, Eq. 7 describes a trade-off between T and C, as T is expected to decrease, which strengthens DL consistency, while C is expected to increase, which weakens DL consistency (or at least triggers reactions for maintaining it, such as increasing Ω). Similar exclusive trade-off observations were discussed in [8], where the relation between mining costs and queuing delays was discussed. On the other hand, Eq. 7 describes a race condition between the technology enhancement in e devices against f devices, which shall boost the optimization of BC deployment in terms of DL consistency.

5   Conclusion

In this paper, we have discussed and analyzed the concepts and effective factors of the consistency of Distributed Ledgers (DLs) in Blockchain (BC) systems. We designed various simulation scenarios to accurately capture why and how data in a DL becomes consistent or inconsistent. We used the FoBSim tool to simulate our proposed scenarios, which was originally implemented to mimic Fog-BC integrated applications. We conducted extensive simulation runs providing a window for measuring maximum possible number of chain versions in a given BC. Accordingly, we proposed a quantitative method to describe the inconsistency of its DL, using the principles of enumerative combinatorics in probability theory, and we updated the conditions under which the experiments were conducted. We further deployed this method to contribute to a decision making model, which can determine the optimal deployment features of a BC in a fog-enhanced system, depending on information regarding the average computational power or memory capacity C, and the average transmission delay between miners T. The proposed model describes the trade-off between T and C, and the race between technologies deployed in the fog layer versus the end-user layer.

Acknowledgment. This research was supported by the Hungarian Scientific Research Fund under the grant number OTKA FK 131793, and by the national project TKP2021-NVA-09 implemented with the support provided by the Ministry of Innovation and Technology of Hungary from the National Research, Development and Innovation Fund, financed under the TKP2021-NVA funding scheme.

References

1. Baniata, H., Kertész, A.: PF-BVM: a privacy-aware fog-enhanced blockchain validation mechanism. In: CLOSER, pp. 430–439 (2020)
2. Baniata, H., Kertesz, A.: A survey on blockchain-fog integration approaches. IEEE Access **8**, 102657–102668 (2020)
3. Baniata, H., Kertesz, A.: FoBSim: an extensible open-source simulation tool for integrated fog-blockchain systems. PeerJ Comput. Sci. **7**, e431 (2021)
4. Bano, S., et al.: Consensus in the age of blockchains. arXiv preprint arXiv:1711.03936 (2017)
5. Bi, W., Yang, H., Zheng, M.: An accelerated method for message propagation in blockchain networks. arXiv preprint arXiv:1809.00455 (2018)
6. Brewer, E.: Cap twelve years later: how the "rules" have changed. Computer **45**(2), 23–29 (2012)
7. Carrara, G.R., Burle, L.M., Medeiros, D.S., de Albuquerque, C.V.N., Mattos, D.M.: Consistency, availability, and partition tolerance in blockchain: a survey on the consensus mechanism over peer-to-peer networking. Ann. Telecommun. **75**, 1–12 (2020)
8. Fang, M., Liu, J.: Toward low-cost and stable blockchain networks. In: ICC 2020 - 2020 IEEE International Conference on Communications (ICC) (2020)
9. Feng, Z., Luo, Q.: Evaluating memory-hard proof-of-work algorithms on three processors. Proc. VLDB Endow. **13**(6), 898–911 (2020)
10. Finlow-Bates, K.: Adding trust to cap: blockchain as a strong eventual consistency recovery strategy (2017)
11. Hoffman, G.: The Chia business whitepaper. Technical report, Chia Network (2021). chia.net/assets/Chia-Business-Whitepaper-2021-02-09-v1.0.pdf
12. Hu, Q., Xu, M., Wang, S., Guo, S.: Sync or fork: node-level synchronization analysis of blockchain. In: Yu, D., Dressler, F., Yu, J. (eds.) WASA 2020. LNCS, vol. 12384, pp. 170–181. Springer, Cham (2020). https://doi.org/10.1007/978-3-030-59016-1_15
13. Jameel, F., Nabeel, M., Jamshed, M.A., Jäntti, R.: Minimizing forking in blockchain-based IoT networks. In: 2020 IEEE International Conference on Communications Workshops (ICC Workshops), pp. 1–6. IEEE (2020)
14. Jaroucheh, Z., Ghaleb, B., Buchanan, W.J.: SklCoin: toward a scalable proof-of-stake and collective signature based consensus protocol for strong consistency in blockchain. In: 2020 IEEE International Conference on Software Architecture Companion (ICSA-C), pp. 143–150. IEEE (2020)
15. Khasmakhi, N.N., Jamali, S., Chenaghlu, M.A.: A solution for replica consistency maintenance in unstructured peer-to-peer networks. Int. J. Res. Comput. Appl. Robot. **4**, 43–49 (2016)
16. Kiffer, L., Rajaraman, R., Shelat, A.: A better method to analyze blockchain consistency. In: Proceedings of the 2018 ACM SIGSAC Conference on Computer and Communications Security, pp. 729–744 (2018)

17. Kraft, D.: Difficulty control for blockchain-based consensus systems. Peer-to-Peer Network. Appl. **9**(2), 397–413 (2015). https://doi.org/10.1007/s12083-015-0347-x
18. Lan, J., Liu, X., Shenoy, P., Ramamritham, K.: Consistency maintenance in peer-to-peer file sharing networks. In: Proceedings the Third IEEE Workshop on Internet Applications, WIAPP 2003, pp. 90–94. IEEE (2003)
19. Li, J., Zhang, T., Jin, J., Yang, Y., Yuan, D., Gao, L.: Latency estimation for fog-based Internet of Things. In: 2017 27th International Telecommunication Networks and Applications Conference (ITNAC), pp. 1–6. IEEE (2017)
20. Ma, Z., Zhao, Q., Yuan, J., Zhou, X., Feng, L.: Fork probability analysis of PoUW consensus mechanism. In: 2020 IEEE International Conference on Smart Internet of Things (SmartIoT), pp. 333–337. IEEE (2020)
21. Mahmud, R., Kotagiri, R., Buyya, R.: Fog computing: a taxonomy, survey and future directions. In: Di Martino, B., Li, K.-C., Yang, L.T., Esposito, A. (eds.) Internet of Everything. IT, pp. 103–130. Springer, Singapore (2018). https://doi.org/10.1007/978-981-10-5861-5_5
22. Misic, J., Misic, V., Chang, X.: On ledger inconsistency time in bitcoin's blockchain delivery network. In: 2019 IEEE Global Communications Conference (GLOBECOM), pp. 1–6. IEEE (2019)
23. Misic, J., Misic, V.B., Chang, X.: Performance of Bitcoin network with synchronizing nodes and a mix of regular and compact blocks. IEEE Trans. Netw. Sci. Eng. **7**, 3135–3147 (2020)
24. Nakamoto, S.: Bitcoin: a peer-to-peer electronic cash system. Technical report, Manubot (2019)
25. Shahsavari, Y., Zhang, K., Talhi, C.: A theoretical model for fork analysis in the bitcoin network. In: 2019 IEEE International Conference on Blockchain (Blockchain), pp. 237–244. IEEE (2019)
26. Shalf, J.: The future of computing beyond Moore's law. Phil. Trans. R. Soc. A **378**(2166), 20190061 (2020)
27. Simplified payment verification (2020). en.bitcoinwiki.org/wiki/Simplified_Payment_Verification
28. Song, G.: Dynamic data consistency maintenance in peer-to-peer caching system. Ph.D. thesis, School of Computing, National University of Singapore (2004)
29. Wang, Z., Datta, A., Das, S.K., Kumar, M.: CMV: file consistency maintenance through virtual servers in peer-to-peer systems. J. Parallel Distrib. Comput. **69**(4), 360–372 (2009)
30. Zhao, J., Tang, J., Zengxiang, L., Wang, H., Lam, K.Y., Xue, K.: An analysis of blockchain consistency in asynchronous networks: deriving a neat bound. arXiv preprint arXiv:1909.06587 (2019)

SPIRIT: A Microservice-Based Framework for Interactive Cloud Infrastructure Planning

Spiros Koulouzis[1,2]([⊠]) [iD], Riccardo Bianchi[1,2], Robin van der Linde[1], Yuandou Wang[1], and Zhiming Zhao[1,2] [iD]

[1] Multiscale Networked Systems Research Group, University of Amsterdam, Amsterdam, The Netherlands
z.zhao@uva.nl
[2] LifeWatch ERIC, Virtual Lab Innovation Center, Amsterdam, The Netherlands
s.koulouzis@uva.nl

Abstract. The IaaS model provides elastic infrastructure that enables the migration of legacy applications to cloud environments. Many cloud computing vendors such as Amazon Web Services, Microsoft Azure, and Google Cloud Platform offer a pay-per-use policy that allows for a sustainable reduction in costs compared to on-premise hosting, as well as enable users to choose various geographically distributed data centers. Using state-of-the-art planning algorithms can help application owners to estimate the size and characteristics of the underlying cloud inveterate. However, it's not always clear which is the optimal solution especially in multi-cloud environments with complex application requirements and QoS constraints. In this paper, we propose an open framework named SPIRIT, which allows a user to include cloud infrastructure planning algorithms and to evaluate and compare their solutions. SPIRIT achieves this by allowing users to interactively study infrastructure planning algorithms by adjusting parameters via a graphical user interface, which visualizes the results of these algorithms. In the current prototype, we have included from the IaaS Partial Critical Path algorithm. By taking advantage of SPIRIT's microservice-based architecture and its generic interfaces a user can add to the framework, new planning algorithms. SPIRIT can transform an abstract workflow described using the CWL to a concrete infrastructure described using the TOSCA specification. This way the infrastructure descriptions can be ranked on various key performance indicators.

Keywords: Virtual infrastructure planning · IaC · Microservice · IaaS · Workflow · IC-PCP

1 Introduction

The cloud computing paradigm allows for on-demand IT service delivery via the internet. The main benefits of cloud computing are dynamic scalability and elasticity, which is achieved via virtualized resources [3].

© Springer Nature Switzerland AG 2022
R. Chaves et al. (Eds.): Euro-Par 2021, LNCS 13098, pp. 405–416, 2022.
https://doi.org/10.1007/978-3-031-06156-1_32

The IaaS model enables enterprises to migrate their in-house software stack to remote cloud data centers. The IaaS model also provides virtual infrastructures for applications with specific performance requirements [8]. However, selecting Cloud infrastructure services and configuring them for specific objectives is time-consuming for an enterprise. It can also be costly when an enterprise consumes more resources than its application requires.

Most cloud providers offer a pay-per-use policy, which allows for a substantial reduction in costs compared to on-premise hosting. However, cloud providers do not offer tools for estimating and comparing the cost of an application as a function of its requirements, QoS, QoE, etc., and the size of the infrastructure. For instance, Azure[1], Google[2], and Oracle[3] offer similar pricing calculators, that allow for the estimation of costs given a selection of cloud services. The cost of each service is displayed as well as the total costs. However, these tools are limited to just calculating the total costs and cost per service. They only work for their corresponding providers and therefore are not cloud-agnostic. Additionally, they do not help decide which services are needed for an application to preserve performance or other QoS demands. Moreover, the choice of services and their characteristics have to be done manually, since there is not an automated infrastructure recommendation. Moreover, some services may be only available in specific data centers.

The process of designing and formally describing a customized Cloud infrastructure for an application with specific requirements can be described as Virtual Infrastructure planning [2,7,13]. Virtual infrastructure planning is also often referred to as Infrastructure as a Service planning or even simply *infrastructure planning*. To elaborate on this definition, application developers want to select cloud resources while optimizing certain QoS, such as performance and costs. Furthermore, they want to do this is in a time-efficient way. Within infrastructure planning, resource utilization is an important objective. This is usually achieved by: resource sharing, minimum resource allocation, and load balancing [6].

Infrastructure planning is important in various contexts, such as the cloud computing context, and scientific computing context. There are many approaches to tackle this problem that depends on the context. The most obvious way is manual configuration. This usually involves running the application in the cloud, and keeping adding resources until the performance of the application meets the requirements specified. This method is not efficient, as it requires several time-consuming manual iterations. Also, for more complex applications, such as a complex workflow with many tasks, this approach becomes even less viable [18]. If infrastructure planning is used to migrate an existing on-premise application to the cloud, one can pick services in the cloud with similar specifications as the on-premise services. This is often referred to as resource mapping[4]. Nevertheless, this approach is only viable if there is already an on-premise solution available.

---

[1] https://azure.microsoft.com/en-us/pricing/calculator/.

[2] https://cloud.google.com/products/calculator/.

[3] https://www.oracle.com/cloud/cost-estimator.html.

[4] https://cloud.google.com/solutions/resource-mappings-from-on-premises-hardware-to-gcp.

For other types of applications, such as (scientific) workflows, it is often the case that a list of interdependent tasks needs to be executed. These tasks usually process large data sets and require a specific amount of servers with certain properties [14]. This problem requires a different IaaS planning approach, such as estimating required resources through the use of scheduling algorithms, such as the partial critical path algorithm [13]. We will be looking at existing solutions more extensively in this research.

Aside from the planning itself, it is can also be difficult to effectively compare two IaaS solutions and make decisions suitable for a specific application and its context [10]. This is because there may be differences in performance and QoS in each solution, which can be hard to evaluate [5].

To tackle the above issues, we propose an open framework with the following requirements: 1. the proposed open-framework should allow various infrastructure planning algorithms to be used and analyzed simultaneously, 2. it should be user-centered with an intuitive user interface, 3. it should adhere to DevOps principles by outputting IaC, 4. and it should implement a model to rank the generated infrastructure plans.

Analyzing the above requirements we offer an implementation with the following key contributions: 1. A framework that via its intuitive user interface, allows users to interactively study infrastructure planning algorithms. 2. A framework that can generate multiple infrastructure descriptions for time-critical applications. 3. A framework that is extendable by allowing developers to add their planning algorithms. This allows for a wide range of application types to be planned for. 4. A framework that allows the user to dynamically compare planning results.

The remainder of this paper is organized as follows. Section 2 reviews state-of-the-art infrastructure planning and workflow scheduling algorithms. Section 3 presents the requirements and architecture design of our proposed tool, namely SPIRIT. In Sect. 4, we focus on our usability study results. Finally, Sect. 5 presents our conclusions and a description of future work.

2   State-of-the-Art

The infrastructure planning problem can be approached via the use of scheduling algorithms. Workflow scheduling tries to solve the problem of mapping each task in a workflow to a suitable resource and to order the tasks on each resource to satisfy some performance criterion [1]. However, in this paper, we will use workflow scheduling only to generate infrastructure solutions instead of mapping tasks to virtual machines at run-time.

Abishami et al. [1] introduce the IC-PCP and the IC-PCPD2 algorithms. Where the critical path, is the longest of all execution paths from the beginning to the end in a task graph. [11]. Both algorithms are workflow scheduling algorithms for the cloud.

Taal et al. [13] proposed different implementations, greedy and more stringent, of the IC-PCP algorithm designed by [1]. The paper focuses on getting the cheapest cloud infrastructure while adhering to the deadline of the workflow.

Wang et al. [16] proposed a machine learning-based approach called deep-Q-network to schedule multi-workflows in the cloud. To improve the completion time and user's cost of this approach, a Markov game model is applied, which has the number of workflow applications and VM's as state input and the maximum completion time and cost as rewards. The proposed model is tested via scientific workflows and Amazon EC2, as well as several other algorithms such as non-dominated sorting genetic algorithm-II, multi-objective particle swarm optimization, and game-theoretic-based greedy algorithms.

Rimal et al. [12] proposed a workflow scheduling algorithm for multi-tenant cloud computing environments. The algorithm focuses on minimizing the makespan of workflows, tardiness, cost of execution of workflows, and make use of idle cloud resources.

Wu et al. [17] proposed a task scheduling algorithm based on QoS-driven for cloud computing. The algorithm works by creating a sorted list of tasks based on task attributes, including user privilege, expectation, task length, and the pending time of task in the queue. Then the algorithm will traverse the list and assign the tasks to the services that will complete them the fastest.

Jain et al. [9] compare four static workflow scheduling algorithms, FCSS, Round-Robin, Min-Min, and Max-Min. These algorithms are compared based on a set of parameters, such as makespan, and costs such as communication cost and computation cost. The algorithms are compared by the use of workflows generated by the Pegasus workflow generator and cloud resources.

Visheratin et al. [15] introduce a new, improved algorithm for workflow scheduling called CDCGA. They compared their algorithm to the IC-PCP [1] and the LDD-LS algorithms by running it on the same workflows.

Workflow scheduling algorithms generally require performance models to do their calculations. A performance model contains the execution time, for each task in the workflow, on one of the available machines. So to get useful calculations, we need to make sure that this model is accurate. These performance models are quite ambiguous in the sense that it is hard to predict these for tasks without actually running them. There are existing benchmarking solutions that can be used to obtain performance values [4]. The user of these algorithms might want to know how much of an impact a change in this parameter has on the overall costs and makespan. This is something we will further analyze during the design of our framework.

3   SPIRIT: A Microservice-Based Framework for Interactive Cloud Infrastructure Planning

In this section, we describe requirements and system architecture.

3.1   Requirements

From a developer's perspective, we identified which features to be included in the open framework by identifying user stories. To be specific, the tool should offer one or more IaaS solutions for planning applications. Since we are building an open framework that should provide value to application developers, we need to identify what features should be included from their point of view. This can be achieved by identifying user stories. As a developer, I want: – one or more IaaS solutions for my application, to I save time and costs. – to apply QoS constraints on the provided solution, so my application will behave as intended when it is run on the generated infrastructure. – to generate IaaS solutions that are cloud agnostic, so I can deploy it on various cloud providers. – several IaC solutions, so I have the option to run my application on a different infrastructure. – to add my planning algorithm to the tool, so if I have a better planning approach for my application. – IaaS solutions, in the form of an IaC template,so it can be automatically deployed. – to compare various price and performance models so I can evaluate the impact of these parameters on the result(s). – to customize the virtual machines used by the planning algorithms. – to compare the results on one or more key performance indicators so I can select the solution that is best suited. – to automatically generate planning parameters so I can use the planner without having this data.

Functional Requirements. Here we list the functional requirements that we want our framework to fulfill. These requirements describe the desired behavior of our system. We did a MoSCoW analysis on these functional requirements, such that the requirements have an assigned priority. Therefore the system: 1. must integrate planning approaches for at least one type of application, 2. must have a web interface that is accessible via most common browsers, 3. must use common standards for APIs, such as REST, 4. must apply at least two different planning approaches, 5. must provide an IaaS solution in the form of IaC if the QoS demands can be satisfied, 6. must allow the user to configure virtual machines to be considered by the planner, 7. must provide a ranking scheme, in which a recommendation can be made based on KPIs, 8. should allow users to specify the preferred cloud provider, 9. could allow users to insert their planning approach, 10. should allow the user to generate planning parameters based on empirical values, 11. could automatically select the correct planning algorithm based on user input, 12. could visualize the recommended infrastructures.

Non-Functional Requirements. Besides the functional requirements we also designed some non-functional requirements for our system. These requirements focus on the technical aspects of our system. 1. The graphical user interface should focus on accessibility and usability. 2. The web interface should load within 10s, given an internet speed of ≥ 10 mb/s 3. The system should be able to handle at least 1000 simultaneous requests. 4. The system should provide solutions at least 70% of the time if the parameters are within acceptable boundaries. 5. The processing time of the systems should not exceed 5s. 6. The software will be open source and adhere to the software design principles that are included in SOLID.

3.2   Architecture

To fulfill the proposed requirements, we designed an architecture of our system, as can be viewed in Fig. 1 and is composed by the elements listed below:

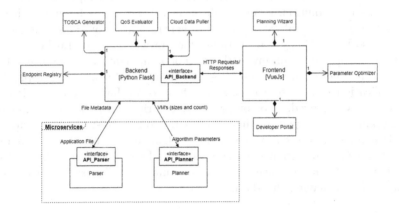

Fig. 1. Architecture diagram

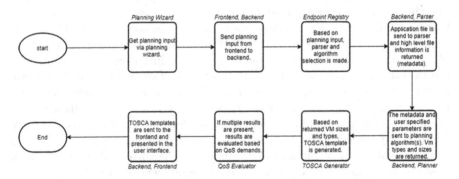

Fig. 2. Process flow and architectural components

Backend: It provides a RESTful API to the Frontend and allows for the registration of infrastructure planning algorithms

Frontend: This is the web user interface that allows the user to select the type of application they want to plan for (workflow application, time-constrained workflow application, microservice-based application, IOT based application), specify their performance model, and present to the user the results of the planning algorithm. Developers can register additional planning services via the developer portal.

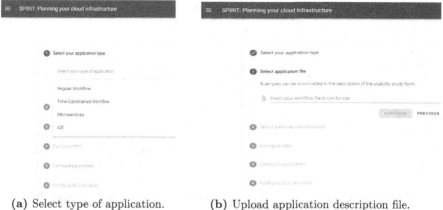

(a) Select type of application.   (b) Upload application description file.

Fig. 3. SPIRIT wizard for selecting application type and description.

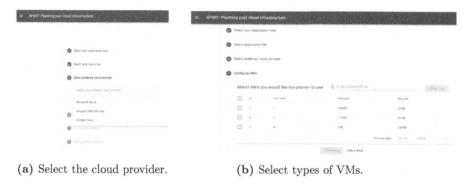

(a) Select the cloud provider.   (b) Select types of VMs.

Fig. 4. SPIRIT wizard for selecting cloud provider and VMs.

Parser: This component is responsible for analyzing the application description and extracting the parameters need for the planning algorithm. In our proof of concept, we implemented a parser for the CWL.

Planner: This component generates the infrastructure plans. In our proof of concept, we implemented two versions of the IC-PCP algorithm: A greedy version and a greedy version with a repair cycle, as proposed by Zhao et al. [13].

Cloud Data puller: This component retrieves available virtual machines and corresponding prices from several cloud providers. Data are displayed in the user interface, from which the user can make a selection. The selection will be used by the planning algorithms.

QoS Evaluator: It has the responsibility to process QoS demands from the user. The component will find infrastructure solutions that comply with the specified QoS demands. If there is no solution available that complies, the user will be notified accordingly.

(a) Select (optional) configuration param-eters.   **(b)** Select (optional) the relevant parameters for the planning algorithm.

Fig. 5. SPIRIT wizard for selecting parameters for the planning algorithm.

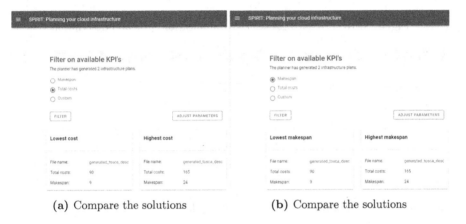

(a) Compare the solutions   **(b)** Compare the solutions

Fig. 6. The SPIRIT infrastructure plan results

TOSCA Generator: This component is responsible for generating a TOSCA description based on the output from the planning algorithms. This information can be used by a provisioner to automatically set up the infrastructure.

Endpoint Registry: It is used to store the available (external) services.

To illustrate how the components are used and interact with each other, we describe a process flow which is shown in Fig. 2, for planning a cloud infrastructure for an application.

According to the flow diagram in Fig. 2 a user takes the flowing steps to generate an infrastructure plan: 1. Select type of application you want to plan for (Fig. 3a) 2. Upload the application description file. Currently that is a CWL file (Fig. 3b). 3. Select the cloud provider (Fig. 4a). 4. Select type of VMs for in the infrastructure plan (Fig. 4b). 5. Select (optional) configuration parameters to generate a planning input model. This model contains the costs and the performance characteristics of the VMs (Fig. 5a). 6. Select (optional) the parameters for the planning algorithms. In the current version, this includes the price and performance model (Fig. 5b). 7. Compare the solutions, based on the selected KPIs. In our proof of concept, the user can compare the available solutions on makespan and costs (Fig. 6a and 6b).

4   Usability Study

To evaluate the usability of our GUI we surveyed Cloud and DevOps experts. By following the presented guidelines, the user was expected to complete a planning process. The planning process is considered complete when the user has downloaded at least one of the proposed infrastructure descriptions. We also expected the participants to use our ranking scheme to rank the presented output on the available key performance indicators. After completion of the planning process, the user was asked to answer the questions in the survey.

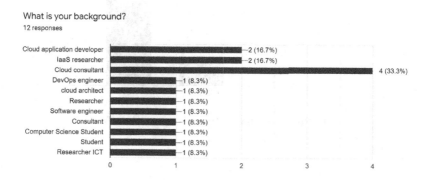

Fig. 7. Survey participants background information.

A total of twelve people participated in the experiment. Although the overall volume of participants is low, nearly all the participants have a background relevant to work. As can be seen in Fig. 7, most participants work in the field of Cloud consultancy, or they are Cloud application developers or even IaaS researchers.

Figure 8 indicates that the majority of users were able to complete the planning process except one. According to that user, they did not have enough information to complete the task.

Figure 9 shows how intuitive the user interface is considered by the participants. A score of 1 means it is not intuitive, and a score of 5 means it is very intuitive.

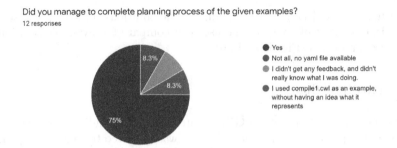

Fig. 8. Results on completed planning task.

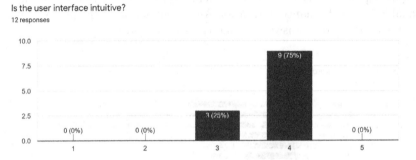

Fig. 9. Results on how intuitive the user interface is.

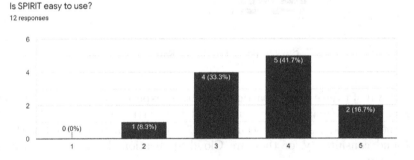

Fig. 10. Results on how easy to use the user interface is.

Figure 10 presents the results considering the ease of use of SPIRIT. A linear scale is applied, where a score of 1 means it is hard to use, and a score of 5 very easy to use. The majority is in the range from 3 to 5, which can be considered positive.

5 Conclusion and Future Work

In this paper, we elaborated and implemented an open framework with a user-friendly GUI that can create cost-effective infrastructure plans for various application types. Our proof of concept can transform an abstract workflow defined in CWL to a concrete infrastructure defined using the TOSCA standard. Our microservice-based architecture and generic interfaces make our framework extendable for other planning algorithms, and thus other application types. Our tool also allows for the ranking of the generated infrastructures on various key performance indicators, therefore, allowing for essayer migration of in-house applications to the Cloud while reducing operating costs. In this paper, we have implemented two versions of the IC-PCP algorithm: A greedy version and a greedy version with a repair cycle. In the future, we aim to use SPIRIT as a platform to integrate and compare more planning algorithms.

Acknowledgment. This work has been partially funded by the European Union's Horizon 2020 research and innovation programme by the project CLARIFY under the Marie Sklodowska-Curie grant agreement No 860627, by the ARTICONF project grant agreement No 825134, by the ENVRI-FAIR project grant agreement No 824068, by the BLUECLOUD project grant agreement No 862409, by the LifeWatch ERIC.

References

1. Abrishami, S., Naghibzadeh, M., Epema, D.H.: Deadline-constrained workflow scheduling algorithms for infrastructure as a service clouds. Future Gener. Comput. Syst. **29**(1), 158–169 (2013)
2. Anastasopoulos, M.P., Tzanakaki, A., Georgakilas, K.: Virtual infrastructure planning in elastic cloud deploying optical networking. In: 2011 IEEE Third International Conference on Cloud Computing Technology and Science, pp. 685–689. IEEE (2011)
3. Carroll, M., Van Der Merwe, A., Kotze, P.: Secure cloud computing: benefits, risks and controls. In: 2011 Information Security for South Africa, pp. 1–9. IEEE (2011)
4. Elzinga, O., et al.: Automatic collector for dynamic cloud performance information. In: 2017 International Conference on Networking, Architecture, and Storage (NAS), pp. 1–6. IEEE (2017)
5. Frisch, J.: Comparison of IaaS solutions: how companies find the right solution (2017). https://docs.microsoft.com/en-us/learn/modules/predict-costs-and-optimize-spending/2-estimate-costs-with-the-azure-pricing-calculator. Accessed 15 May 2020
6. Georgakilas, K.N., Tzanakaki, A., Anastasopoulos, M., Pedersen, J.M.: Converged optical network and data center virtual infrastructure planning. J. Opt. Commun. Netw. **4**(9), 681–691 (2012)
7. Hu, Y., et al.: Deadline-aware deployment for time critical applications in clouds. In: Rivera, F., Pena, T., Cabaleiro, J. (eds.) Euro-Par 2017: Parallel Processing. LNCS, vol. 10417, pp. 345–357. Springer, Cham (2017). https://doi.org/10.1007/978-3-319-64203-1_25
8. Hu, Y., Zhou, H., de Laat, C., Zhao, Z.: Concurrent container scheduling on heterogeneous clusters with multi-resource constraints. Future Gener. Comput. Syst. **102**, 562–573 (2020). https://doi.org/10.1016/j.future.2019.08.025
9. Jain, A., Kumari, R.: A review on comparison of workflow scheduling algorithms with scientific workflows. In: Modi, N., Verma, P., Trivedi, B. (eds.) Proceedings of International Conference on Communication and Networks. AISC, vol.

508, pp. 613–622. Springer, Singapore (2017). https://doi.org/10.1007/978-981-10-2750-5_63

10. Koulouzis, S., et al.: Time-critical data management in clouds: challenges and a dynamic real-time infrastructure planner (drip) solution. Concurr. Comput. Pract. Exp. **32**, e5269 (2019)

11. Rahman, M., Venugopal, S., Buyya, R.: A dynamic critical path algorithm for scheduling scientific workflow applications on global grids. In: Third IEEE International Conference on e-Science and Grid Computing (e-Science 2007), pp. 35–42. IEEE (2007)

12. Rimal, B.P., Maier, M.: Workflow scheduling in multi-tenant cloud computing environments. IEEE Trans. Parallel Distrib. Syst. **28**(1), 290–304 (2016)

13. Taal, A., Wang, J., de Laat, C., Zhao, Z.: Profiling the scheduling decisions for handling critical paths in deadline-constrained cloud workflows. Future Gener. Comput. Syst. **100**, 237–249 (2019)

14. Vahi, K., Rynge, M., Juve, G., Mayani, R., Deelman, E.: Rethinking data management for big data scientific workflows. In: 2013 IEEE International Conference on Big Data, pp. 27–35 (2013)

15. Visheratin, A.A., Melnik, M., Nasonov, D.: Workflow scheduling algorithms for hard-deadline constrained cloud environments. Procedia Comput. Sci. **80**, 2098–2106 (2016)

16. Wang, Y., et al.: Multi-objective workflow scheduling with deep-q-network-based multi-agent reinforcement learning. IEEE Access **7**, 39974–39982 (2019)

17. Wu, X., Deng, M., Zhang, R., Zeng, B., Zhou, S.: A task scheduling algorithm based on QoS-driven in cloud computing. Procedia Comput. Sci. **17**, 1162–1169 (2013)

18. Zhao, Z., Grosso, P., van der Ham, J., Koning, R., de Laat, C.: An agent based network resource planner for workflow applications. Multiagent Grid Syst. **7**(6), 187–202 (2011). https://doi.org/10.3233/MGS-2011-0180

SMART: A Tool for Trust and Reputation Management in Social Media

Nishant Saurabh[1]([⊠])(iD), Manuel Herold[1], Hamid Mohammadi Fard[2](iD),
and Radu Prodan[1](iD)

[1] Distributed and Parallel Systems Group, Institute of Information Technology,
University of Klagenfurt, Klagenfurt 9020, Austria
`nishant.saurabh@aau.at`
[2] Department of Computer Science, Technical University of Darmstadt,
Darmstadt, Germany

Abstract. Social media platforms are becoming increasingly popular
and essential for next-generation connectivity. However, the emergence
of social media also poses critical trust challenges due to the vast amount
of created and propagated content. This paper proposes a data-driven
tool called SMART for trust and reputation management based on community engagement and rescaled sigmoid model. SMART's integrated
design adopts a set of expert systems with a unique inference logic for
trust estimation to compute weighted trust ratings of social media content. SMART further utilizes the trust ratings to compute user reputation and represent them using a sigmoid curve that prevents infinite accumulation of reputation ratings by a user. We demonstrate the SMART
tool prototype using a pilot social media application and highlight its
user-friendly interfaces for trustworthy content exploration.

Keywords: Social media · Trust · Reputation · Sigmoid model ·
Community engagement

1 Introduction

Social media platforms gained prominence as an essential technology for next-
generation connectivity. Typically, social media are centralized platforms that
allow users to create, publish, and share content across an interconnected network. This poses critical issues of trust [17] over the created content and the
authentication of users who publish them. This is particularly problematic when
fake news, trolling, and misinformation are a regular phenomenon across popular social media platforms such as Facebook and Twitter [8]. Moreover, the
integration of privacy-by-design [18] features in social media platforms such as
pseudonymized or anonymized identity systems that enable users to control their
digital identity access aggravates this problem further. While such platforms

ARTICONF receives funding from the European Union's Horizon 2020 research and
innovation program under grant agreement number 825134.

R. Chaves et al. (Eds.): Euro-Par 2021, LNCS 13098, pp. 417–427, 2022.
https://doi.org/10.1007/978-3-031-06156-1_33

improve upon privacy violations, they pose traceability challenges, for example, in identifying users publishing fake content.

To prevent the propagation of malicious information in electronic networks requires innovative decision-making solutions at the user level (i.e., content creation, propagation, consumption) [1] and the underlying social media environment. The essential need is to explore trust and reputation management solutions [3] that involve social media users and allow them to be a part of decision-making. Such a process facilitates trustworthy and authenticated content creation and consumption and empowers users to tackle disinformation [4] and foster a positive engagement with fast-evolving technologies.

To achieve these goals, we propose a data-driven tool called SMART developed in the European ARTICONF [12] project, which provides a decision-making methodology engaging community experts [6] in computing weighted trust content ratings and classifying them as trustworthy or not. The trust ratings employ the rescaled sigmoid model [13] to compute the reputation ratings of a social media user who created them. Additionally, SMART associates each user with a contextualized local and global reputation, where the local rating reflects a user's trust for the created content within the same context. The global reputation, in contrast, provides the weighted trust ratings of a user across all contexts. Such a design allows SMART to provide fair and democratic decision-making for content trust management and prevents infinite accumulation of reputation by any user.

We developed a pilot social media application similar to Reddit[1] [2] called SocialApp to demonstrate SMART's trust and reputation management methodology. We highlight the current status of the SMART prototype and its interfaces, where a SocialApp user can perform trustworthy content exploration based on interesting topics, endorsements, and their time of creation.

The paper has five sections. Section 2 presents the SMART tool architecture and trust and reputation methodology. Section 3 demonstrates the SMART tool prototype and its interfaces using the sample social media application SocialApp. Section 4 briefly discusses the related works and industry-based trust and reputation management systems. Section 5 concludes the paper.

2   SMART Architecture

Figure 1 describes the SMART architectural workflow for trust and reputation management through a pseudonymized user who creates and publishes several posts in the science and technology community. Furthermore, SMART provides a list of trust oracles to the community members, representing expert systems with a unique knowledge base and an inference logic to compute the content trust ratings. The community members can choose one or more trust oracles by consensus to compute intermediary trust values for each content based on a particular inference logic. Afterward, SMART computes the weighted average of the trust ratings obtained from each oracle and labels the trustworthy or fake content. Finally, SMART aggregates the intermediary trust values of all posts created by the user and generates its reputation.

---

[1] https://www.reddit.com/r/socialmedia/.

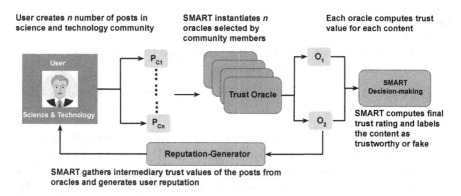

Fig. 1. SMART architectural workflow for trust and reputation management.

2.1   Trust Oracle

SMART computes the trust ratings and their content using a set of oracles with their own unique inference logic. SMART currently supports two types of trust oracles by design and plans to integrate several others in the future (e.g., online fact-checker tools).

Community voting based oracle O_1 utilizes the percentage of upvotes gathered by a post P_{Ci} in a community C to compute its trust rating rescaled between $[-1, 1]$ as follows:

$$O_1(P_{Ci}) = 2 \cdot \frac{Upvotes\,(P_{Ci})}{Votes\,(P_{Ci})} - 1, \tag{1}$$

where $Upvotes\,(P_{Ci})$ and $Votes\,(P_{Ci})$ are the number of endorsements and total votes of the post P_{Ci}.

ML classification based oracles O_2 represent binary machine learning models that classify a post P_{Ci} as trustworthy $(O_2\,(P_{Ci}) = 1)$ or fake $(O_2\,(P_{Ci}) = 0)$:

Trust $T(P_{Ci})$ computed by SMART decision-maker represents the aggregated normalized trust ratings of each oracle for a post P_{Ci} in a community C:

$$T\,(P_{Ci}) = \frac{O_1\,(P_{Ci}) + O_2\,(P_{Ci})}{2}. \tag{2}$$

The average trust computation is easily extensible to more oracles. A positive trust indicates trustworthy content, while a negative value suggests the opposite.

2.2   Reputation Generator

The SMART reputation generator computes the reputation rating of a user and classifies it as trustworthy and not. We define two types of reputation ratings.

Local reputation rating represents the trustworthiness of a user in a community C.

Global reputation rating reflects the accumulated trust of a user across all the communities of a social application.

The reputation generator follows three stages to compute the local and global reputation of a user.

Intermediary reputation RI_C is the first stage that initially gathers the final trust ratings $T(P_{Ci})$ (computed using Eq. 2) of all posts P_{Ci} of a user in a community C. Essentially, each post created by the user varies in quality and trust and contributes to the intermediary reputation differently. Hence, we utilize content volume $V(P_{Ci})$ (measured in the number of characters) to distinguish the quality of different posts, assuming that a larger and more detailed content has a higher contribution to the user reputation:

$$RI_C = \frac{\sum_i T(P_{Ci}) \cdot V(P_{Ci}) \cdot \delta(P_{Ci})}{\alpha_C}, \tag{3}$$

where α_C is the maximum content volume threshold V of a post in a community C, and $\delta(P_{Ci})$ represents a weighted bias that rewards trustworthy and penalises fake posts using two weights p and r, respectively:

$$\delta(P_{Ci}) = \begin{cases} p, & T(P_{Ci}) < 0; \\ r, & T(P_{Ci}) > 0; \\ 0, & T(P_{Ci}) = 0. \end{cases} \tag{4}$$

We use $p = -2$ to penalize the fake posts and $r = 1$ to reward trusted ones in the current implementation. However, our design allows the community members to freely decide the reward and penalty weights based on consensus.

Local reputation RL_C of a user in a community combines the intermediary reputation rating RI_C with a rescaled sigmoid [13,19] function. We use the sigmoid function due to its capability to model natural growth and decay rate in the non-deterministic environment such as social media platforms and compute the local reputation of a user as follows:

$$RL_C = \frac{2}{1 + e^{-RI'_C}} - 1, \tag{5}$$

where $R'_I \in [-\gamma, \gamma]$ is the *reputation growth and decay constraint* that prevents infinite accumulation of trust:

$$RI'_C = \begin{cases} -\gamma, & RI_C < -\gamma; \\ RI_C, & RI_C \in [-\gamma, \gamma]; \\ \gamma, & RI_C > \gamma. \end{cases} \tag{6}$$

We utilize a *reputation threshold* β decided by community members with consensus to classify a user into three categories:

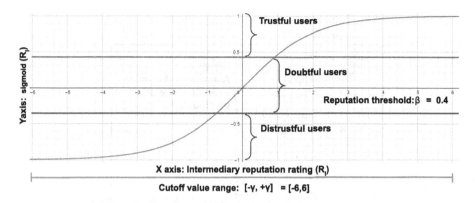

Fig. 2. Sigmoid representation of user reputation.

Trustful with a high positive local reputation: $RL_C > \beta$;
Distrustful with a low negative local reputation: $RL_C < -\beta$;
Doubtful with a local reputation in the range $RL_C \in [-\beta, \beta]$.

Figure 2 illustrates a sigmoid curve initialized with a reputation threshold $\beta = 0.4$ and a reputation growth and decay range $\gamma \in [-6, 6]$. We observe that a trustful user has a local reputation rating $RL_C > 0.4$, while $RL_C < -0.4$ classifies a user as distrustful. Additionally, we observe that the reputation growth and decay constraint γ prevents infinite accumulation of reputation by a user and instead limits a finite range of values.

Global Reputation RG of a user averages the local reputations RL_C across all communities C weighted by the volume of the total posts in each community:

$$RG = \frac{\sum_{\forall C} V_C \cdot RL_C}{\sum_{\forall C} V_C}, \tag{7}$$

where $V_C = \sum_i V(P_{Ci})$ is the total content volume of all posts P_{Ci} published by a user in a community C.

3   Implementation

We developed a social media application similar to Reddit named `SocialApp` to pilot our research and development. Figure 3 shows a sample instance of the `SocialApp` application with two communities labeled `science and technology`, and `international politics`. A `SocialApp` user can join one or more communities based on topics of interest. For example, the users in the `international politics` community discuss ongoing affairs and the latest news across the world. In contrast, the `science and technology` community users create research and innovation-related content.

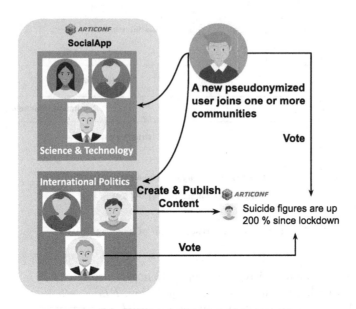

Fig. 3. SocialApp pilot use case application.

A SocialApp user can create and publish content in the form of text or multimedia. SocialApp also allows users to vote for content in their own community, reflecting their opinion about the content authenticity and quality. In its current form, SocialApp offers three basic functionalities to pseudonymized users as any other generic social media platform:

Post functionality allows a SocialApp user to create and publish content in its own community. SocialApp does not allow a user to post content in a community without joining it.

Vote functionality allows a SocialApp user to either upvote or to downvote a published post across the associated community. Similar to post functionality, a user cannot vote a content without joining it.

Comment functionality allows a SocialApp user to comment on a post either in the form of text or multimedia.

Each post in SocialApp has a data schema consisting of ten fields: the unique identifier, pseudonymized user identifier, community label, title, content, timestamp, comments, as well as the number of votes, endorsements, and dislikes. To demonstrate the SMART prototype, we integrated the Mockaroo[2] random data generator into the SocialApp interface. Mockaroo enables the creation of realistic test data in CSV, JSON, and SQL formats, which we used to generate 2000 users and 12 000 posts according to this schema.

Figure 4 shows the SMART cluster visualization with four interfaces:

---

[2] https://www.mockaroo.com/.

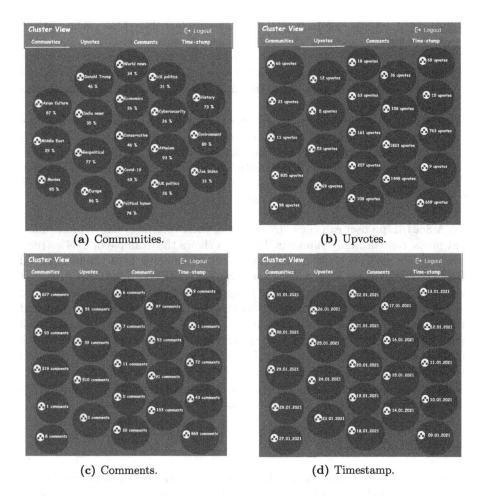

(a) Communities.

(b) Upvotes.

(c) Comments.

(d) Timestamp.

Fig. 4. SMART cluster visualization snapshots.

Communities interface provides an aggregated view of the posts based on the community labels and identifiers. Figure 4a shows the clustered visualization of 12 000 SocialApp posts across 19 communities with unique labels. Each community label represents the context and type of the social media posts created by its members based on their interest topics. Social media users who are not members of a specific community cannot post content.

Upvotes interface shows the clustered posts based on the number of endorsements and dislikes by SocialApp users in their respective communities. Figure 4b shows 12 000 posts clustered across categories with upvotes ranging between 1893 and 5. The upvotes interface enables users to find the posts with the most positive reviews and contemplate if they match the content trust ratings. Such an interface aggregates the most endorsed SocialApp posts and promotes trustworthy content propagation.

Comments interface depicts the aggregated posts based on their number of comments, reflecting the general interest across community members. Figure 4c shows the clustered visualization of `SocialApp` posts based on the number of comments, ranging between zero and 800. This visualization allows users to obtain awareness of the trending posts and topics of discussion, generating higher interest.

Timestamp interface shows the clustered posts based on their creation date and time across different communities. Figure 4d shows the `SocialApp` posts clustered with different timestamp across 23 d. This clustered view allows `SocialApp` users to understand the timeliness of the content contained within each post. Additionally, this visualization indicates up-to-date or expired content and focuses on recent events.

A `SocialApp` user can click any cluster in these interfaces and explore different posts, content, and comments. Figure 5a shows the example of a 44% trustworthy post published in the `conservative` community by a pseudonymized user `itsanoobsgame`. This enables `SocialApp` users to check the trust ratings of a post and track the user who created the post and its corresponding community.

SMART also links each content to the user who published the post and their local and global reputation ratings. Figure 5b shows the snapshot of a pseudonymized `SocialApp` user `scorpio05foru` with a local reputation rating 0.11 in community `conservative` and a global reputation −0.17 across all joined communities. Additionally, SMART links other posts created by the same user along with their trust ratings. This allows a `SocialApp` user to get a historical overview of the content quality created and published by the user.

4   Related Work

Trust and reputation management is an extensively studied problem across many disciplines, including sociology [11], psychology [5], economics [7], and computer science [9,16]. Each discipline defined trust from different perspectives that may not fit into the diversified and digital social networks. In this section, we briefly describe some of the trust models across academia and industry.

Marsh et al. [10] proposed one of the earliest theoretical models for computational trust classified in three categories: basic, general, and situational. They characterize collaboration in digital networks, where a user who tends to trust others yields a higher reputation. Similarly, Sebater et al. [15] classify trust across four dimensions: the information source and the granularity that reflect the type and context of content for trust computation, the behavioral assumption that identifies manipulative activities by a social media user for trust enhancement, and the reliability that refers to the accuracy of the trust model.

In the industrial sphere, the eBay trust model is quite popular across online marketplaces. Online marketplaces such as Amazon use the eBay trust model to rate users and publicly reflect the historical users' activity and behavior in an online digital network public [14,15]. The eBay computational trust model

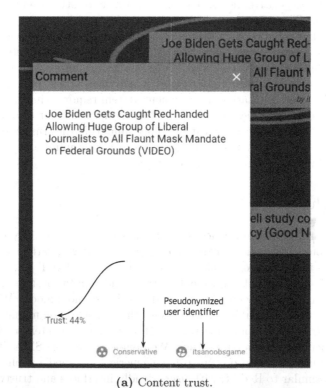

(a) Content trust.

(b) User local and global reputation.

Fig. 5. SMART trust and reputation visualization snapshots.

accumulates the positive, negative or neutral rating of other users over a period of six months. There are several potential problems with the eBay trust model. Firstly, the user reputation ratings are unbound and allow infinite accumulation of trust. As a consequence, new users find it difficult to compete with existing highly reputed ones. This also allows malicious users to accumulate high reputations by first performing trustworthy activities and scamming afterward. Hence, a trust and reputation management system requires time sensitivity and prioritizes recent activities. Sporas [20] trust model is similar to eBay but only considers the last user activity instead of accumulating the trust and reputation ratings over six months. However, Sporas also allows infinite accumulation of reputation by a user, similar to the eBay model.

5   Conclusion

Mitigating misinformation concerns and provisioning trustworthy content creation and propagation is essential for realizing next-generation social media. We propose in this paper a data-driven tool called SMART developed in the ARTICONF project that implements a trust and reputation management system based on community engagement and rescaled sigmoid model. We presented the SMART decision-making methodology that engages community experts in computing trust and reputation ratings of social media content and users and classifies them as trustworthy or not. We demonstrated the SMART trust and reputation management prototype using a generic social media application called SocialApp similar to Reddit, with user-friendly interfaces and trustworthy content exploration. In the future, we plan to integrate online fact-checkers to the SMART tool to improve fairness across computation of trust and reputation ratings. We also aim to validate its trust and reputation management for content co-creation, news marketplace, and other real industrial applications.

Acknowledgement. This work received funding from the European Union's Horizon 2020 research and innovation programme, grant agreement 825134, "Smart Social Media Ecosytstem in a Blockchain Federated Environment (ARTICONF)".

References

1. Al Qundus, J., Paschke, A.: Investigating the effect of attributes on user trust in social media. In: Database and Expert Systems Applications, vol. 903, pp. 278–288. Springer, Cham (2018). https://doi.org/10.1007/978-3-319-99133-7_23
2. Buntain, C., Golbeck, J.: Identifying social roles in reddit using network structure. In: 23rd International Conference on World Wide Web, pp. 615–620 (2014)
3. Chen, B.C., Guo, J., Tseng, B., Yang, J.: User reputation in a comment rating environment. In: Proceedings of the 17th ACM SIGKDD International Conference on Knowledge Discovery and Data Mining, pp. 159–167 (2011)
4. Cohen, R., et al.: Addressing misinformation in online social networks: diverse platforms and the potential of multiagent trust modeling. Information **11**(11), 539 (2020)

5. Cook, K.S., Yamagishi, T., Cheshire, C., Cooper, R., Matsuda, M., Mashima, R.: Trust building via risk taking: a cross-societal experiment. Soc. Psychol. Q. **68**(2), 121–142 (2005)

6. Habibi, M.R., Laroche, M., Richard, M.O.: The roles of brand community and community engagement in building brand trust on social media. Comput. Hum. Behav. **37**, 152–161 (2014)

7. Huang, F.: Building social trust: a human-capital approach. J. Inst. Theor. Econ. (JITE)/Zeitschrift für die gesamte Staatswissenschaft 552–573 (2007)

8. Kim, Y.A., Ahmad, M.A.: Trust, distrust and lack of confidence of users in online social media-sharing communities. Knowl.-Based Syst. **37**, 438–450 (2013)

9. Maheswaran, M., Tang, H.C., Ghunaim, A.: Towards a gravity-based trust model for social networking systems. In: 27th International Conference on Distributed Computing Systems Workshops (ICDCSW 2007), p. 24. IEEE (2007)

10. Marsh, S.P.: Formalising trust as a computational concept (1994)

11. Möllering, G.: The nature of trust: from Georg Simmel to a theory of expectation, interpretation and suspension. Sociology **35**(2), 403–420 (2001)

12. Prodan, R., et al.: ARTICONF: towards a smart social media ecosystem in a blockchain federated environment. In: Schwardmann, U., et al. (eds.) Euro-Par 2019: Parallel Processing Workshops. LNCS, vol. 11997, pp. 417–428. Springer, Cham (2020). https://doi.org/10.1007/978-3-030-48340-1_32

13. Ren, J., McIsaac, K.A., Patel, R.V., Peters, T.M.: A potential field model using generalized sigmoid functions. IEEE Trans. Syst. Man Cybern. Part B (Cybern.) **37**(2), 477–484 (2007)

14. Resnick, P., Zeckhauser, R.: Trust among strangers in internet transactions: empirical analysis of eBay's reputation system. In: The Economics of the Internet and E-commerce. Emerald Group Publishing Limited (2002)

15. Sabater, J., Sierra, C.: Review on computational trust and reputation models. Artif. Intell. Rev. **24**(1), 33–60 (2005)

16. Sikder, O., Smith, R.E., Vivo, P., Livan, G.: A minimalistic model of bias, polarization and misinformation in social networks. Sci. Rep. **10**(1), 1–11 (2020)

17. Tang, J., Liu, H.: Trust in social media. Synth. Lect. Inf. Secur. Priv. Trust **10**(1), 1–129 (2015)

18. Wahlstrom, K., Ul-haq, A., Burmeister, O., et al.: Privacy by design. Australas. J. Inf. Syst. **24** (2020)

19. Weisstein, E.W.: Sigmoid function (2002). https://mathworld.wolfram.com/

20. Yu, W.: Analysis on trust influencing factors and trust model from multiple perspectives of online auction. Open Phys. **15**(1), 613–619 (2017)

Towards Generating Realistic Trace for Simulating Functions-as-a-Service

Dilshad Hassan Sallo[1,3]([✉]) and Gabor Kecskemeti[1,2]

[1] Institute of Information Technology, University of Miskolc, Miskolc, Hungary
{sallo,kecskemeti}@iit.uni-miskolc.hu
[2] Department of Computer Science, Liverpool John Moores University,
Liverpool, UK
g.kecskemeti@ljmu.ac.uk
[3] Department of Computer Science, College of Science, University of Duhok,
Duhok, Iraq
dilshad.sallo@uod.ac

Abstract. Serverless computing is a step forward to provide a cloud environment that responds to user requests by mainly focusing on managing infrastructure, resources and configurations. Despite the widespread use of cloud simulators, they are still mainly focused on supporting more traditional Infrastructure-as-a-Service scenarios and this reduces their applicability in the serverless and function as a service domains. Moreover, workload traces typically employed by IaaS simulators to represent user behaviour, are not well adoptable for serverless model. More realistic and serverless-like traces are essential to simulate and predict the behaviour of functions in serverless systems. Therefore, this paper focuses on generating realistic traces for simulating serverless computing platforms. The generated traces produced by our approach are based on the Azure Functions dataset and they are readily applicable in an already available versatile and high performance simulator (DISSECT-CF). We validated the generated approach using the coefficient of determination (R^2), which shows very good values for the average and percentiles of the execution time and memory. To demonstrate the benefits of the generated traces we introduced a rudimentary model for serverless systems to DISSECT-CF. Our evaluation shows that our workloads are realistic and closely follow the behaviour of Azure's function as a service component.

Keywords: Serverless computing · Serverless workload · Serverless trace · FaaS · DISSECT-CF

1 Introduction

Numerous cloud simulators have been built to support the IaaS model. They offer an environment for easy evaluation of algorithms and scenarios in the field of infrastructure management. However, these simulators are not designed to take responsibility for managing the necessary infrastructure, complex provisioning, and configurations on behalf of a user, which is how users are expected to deal

© Springer Nature Switzerland AG 2022
R. Chaves et al. (Eds.): Euro-Par 2021, LNCS 13098, pp. 428–439, 2022.
https://doi.org/10.1007/978-3-031-06156-1_34

with serverless systems. Moreover, there are features essential to support the serverless model that are missing from most IaaS frameworks. Among others these include the following features: sharing low-level computing, support loading and managing several trace file formats and imitate the configuration of a real serverless provider. Thus, with these simulators, the burden is on the users to ensure good quality results when they intend to test or evaluate the behaviour of serverless functions.

Instead of creating dedicated serverless simulators, it is beneficial to create them on top of already existing IaaS simulators as they can reveal detailed information about resource consumption and pricing. DFaaSCloud [3] is a simulator developed as an extension of CloudSim, for simulating FaaS in distributed cloud architecture. However, DFaaSCloud includes several limitations such as low-level computing resource sharing is not supported to reduce the usage of resources, and unable to generate and simulate realistic traces. OpenDC Serverless [4] simulator is developed based on Open DC framework, to model and test custom FaaS patterns. The main restriction of this simulator is not supporting auto-scaling approach that acts in response to the number of invocations.

As a foundation for the serverless simulators, the main contribution of this work is to generate realistic traces resembling behaviour observable in the Azure Functions dataset. Alongside this trace generation approach we introduce a simple evaluation framework for it that mimics basic features of the serverless model. The model automatically provisions resources and calculates the expected price of simulated functions calls, while also discloses information regarding the behaviour of the simulated workload. Our generator and serverless model was devised by extending the DISSECT-CF simulator [5].

We have generated several traces to evaluate our approach. These traces involved functions with arbitrary invocation numbers to demonstrate the usability of our approach under different circumstances. We then validated our generated approach using the coefficient of determination (R^2) of the reported execution time and memory utilisation averages and percentiles between both the original Azure Functions trace as well as our generated ones. Finally, using these generated traces, we imitated the behaviour of Azure's function provider and made several estimates and predictions of cost and utilisation of our serverless extension of DISSECT-CF.

To validate that our trace generation approach provides realistic function invocation behaviour, we have compared the generated trace to the originals on the following way. First, we have randomly selected five thousand functions to generate the traces for. The generated invocations were analysed for CPU time and memory utilisation, namely, we have collected averages and percentiles for both of these. We then compared the already available averages and percentiles from the original trace with the generated ones with the help of R^2. Our approach provided very good R^2 (>0.99) values for predicting averages, in terms of percentiles it fallen behind a bit but it still produces traces with relatively well matching behaviour to the originals found in the azure traces.

The remainder of this paper is structured as follows. In Sect. 2, we discuss related work to proposed model. In Sect. 3, we focus on the methodology of generating functions and implementing serverless model. Section 4 covers the evaluation of proposed model and Finally, Sect. 5 concludes the paper and suggests future work.

2   Related Work

Over the last two decades, several IaaS simulation frameworks have been built to offer elasticity to evaluate algorithms and scenarios. These frameworks introduced many features and concepts to handle the challenges accompanying cloud computing field. Each framework was built in mind to focus on specific purpose, functionality or aspect to handle unaddressed challenges.

On one hand, some simulators have been built to focus on specific aspects such as energy aware provisioning, middleware supervision as the best solution in this sub-field. For example, GreenCloud [6] is a simulator specifically built for estimating the energy consumption of cloud data centres. Or, SPECI [10] is a simple simulator that was built to investigate middleware supervision protocols of data centres. Finally, GroudSim [8] is a platform mainly focused on scientific application modelling (e.g., workflows) in cloud and grid computing. As these simulators are too focused on a particular purpose, they are problematic to adapt to support serverless concepts.

On the other hand, some simulators have been built to suit wider cloud modelling scenarios with extensibility in mind to support comprehensive features. Thus, they provide essential architecture and significant concepts as foundation to other. These include CloudSim [2] which is one of the well-known frameworks designed to mimic general cloud behaviour. CloudSim built with the ability to extend for introducing new features that support modelling and simulation of cloud computing environments and its extensibility has been demonstrated with numerous extensions over the years. Mostly, general purpose simulators such as CloudSim are suitable to provide solid-foundation to support serverless model. However, CloudSim's performance is not sufficient, for instance, compared with DISSECT-CF [7] (which is another general purpose simulator), to provide a robust-extension able to foster analysis of billions of simulated serverless functions invocations.

As most IaaS simulators lack crucial features to simulate FaaS, several new simulators have been designed. First, DFaaSCloud [3] addressed the missing serverless functionalities of CloudSim by adding basic FaaS components on top of the simulated distributed cloud architecture. However, this new simulator is unable to utilise large scale generated realistic serverless traces. It also not fully establishing and managing the virtual infrastructure backing function platforms. Another simulator, called OpenDC [4], followed the same step: they also modelled and tested custom FaaS patterns. However, the major limitation of this simulator is neglecting auto-scaling approach that responds to workloads.

Based on this research, there is a clear gap in realistic, large scale trace generation for serverless platforms. Thus this paper aims at presenting a good quality trace generator as well as a rudimentary simulation framework that can handle the modelling of larger scale serverless workloads.

3   Methodology

3.1   Overview of DISSECT-CF Simulator

DISSECT-CF is an IaaS simulator that brought distinct features to foster improvements of cutting-edge computing technology. As this paper builds on top of DISSECT-CF, here we briefly provide an overview of the simulator, its capabilities and ecosystem.

The core of the DISSECT-CF consists of five major subsystems that implement concepts around clouds and distributed systems. The lowest subsystem, event system takes responsibility to manage the behaviour of regular and irregular events as well as controlling the basic state of the simulation in a given time instance. Next, its unified resource sharing subsystem establishes a shared resource provisioning framework usable by all other components in the simulator. Then, the energy modelling subsystem introduces a unique decoupled approach to energy modelling which is not integrated into resource simulation (i.e., allows performance gains by only focusing the energy model on parts of the simulated system). On a top of these foundational components, the Infrastructure simulation subsystem, offers a comprehensive set of infrastructure components like: virtual machines, physical machines, storage and networking. Finally, the infrastructure management subsystem is the highest layer of abstraction that enables the user of simulator to interact with particular components such as Repository and the IaaS service. This layer contains major IaaS components such VM scheduler and PM scheduler that simulate the management of users requests and fosters the creation of custom internal IaaS behaviours.

Along the core DISSECT-CF, there are several extensions and projects that enrich the simulator's feature set. The most relevant to this paper is the auto scaling framework presented in the dissect-cf-examples project[1]. This framework enables the modelling of virtual infrastructure management tools and job schedulers on these virtual infrastructures. This allows simulations where the virtual infrastructure built up on top of DISSECT-CF core components are following the workload patterns pushed to the job scheduler.

The other relevant extension to the simulator is its workload representation focused DistSysJavaHelpers project[2]. This project provides abstractions to represent arbitrary workloads. Offers ways to produce even generated workloads with the help of its GenericTraceProducer. Finally, it also enables the loading of several well known workload trace formats to foster realistic simulations.

3.2   Architecture of Proposed Model

Supporting serverless computing model by IaaS simulators necessitate the introduction of additional features. One of the significant features is to enable the simulator to generate realistic-trace and predict the behaviour of such realistic serverless workloads. We introduced our serverless architecture based on

---

[1] https://github.com/kecskemeti/dissect-cf-examples.

[2] https://github.com/kecskemeti/DistSysJavaHelpers.

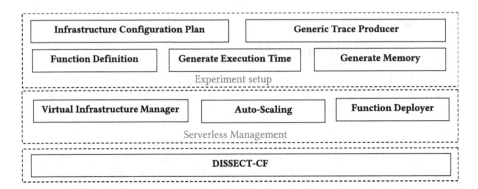

Fig. 1. Architecture of proposed model

DISSECT-CF that is aimed at offering automated management of function as a service workloads (by building on top of the pre-existing auto-scalers), as well as providing realistic models for such serverless models in order to enable building large scale simulations. This architecture consists of two layers built on the top of DISSECT-CF as shown in Fig. 1.

The first step towards generating and executing serverless functions, is selecting the workload file and type of provider by a user of simulator, which will then be passed to the experiment setup layer.

The experiment setup layer handles the user options by establishing proper infrastructure based on the selected plan and generates serverless-trace for simulation. It consists of the following main components:

Infrastructure configuration plan contains preset configurations that mimic a particular functions provider (in the current case, it was focused on Azure functions [1]). The configurations offered focus on resource options (e.g., storage and memory) for functions as well as pricing and energy model details.

Realistic execution time and memory utilisation generators are built on top of the GenericTraceProducer of the previously mentioned DistSys-JavaHelpers project. These allow the generation of function invocations to be simulated following the desired amount and distribution specified by the simulator's user. The way the function invocations are generated are governed by trace files (in our case the Azure functions trace). These components are further detailed in the next subsection.

The serverless management layer is responsible for managing virtual infrastructure (that backs the serverless computing platform), as well as providing just-enough resources for all the function invocations. This layer consists of following main components:

The virtual infrastructure manager is responsible for providing and managing the virtual infrastructure that backs the function invocations. It is used to offer a unified interface towards the auto-scalers and abstract the cloud infrastructure so the virtual machine requests or destruction requests are handled uniformly. This component is also responsible of collecting information on the provisioned resources during the simulation (e.g., the total amount of memory used at a particular moment).

The auto-scaling approach provides several, extensible mechanisms that observes the previously collected information and makes sure the virtual infrastructure is increased or decreased in size according to the ongoing and future function invocations. When a decision is made to change the infrastructure, the auto-scaler will notify the Virtual Infrastructure Manager class to request or destroy VMs.

The function deployer gets all generated functions and dispatches them to available VMs for execution. For example, when the number of functions needs to be dispatched simultaneously is increased, auto-scaling class will observe the utilization of VMs and request more.

3.3   Generating Realistic Serverless Traces from the Azure Functions Trace

The first official real-world FaaS workload trace was publicly released on June 17th 2020 [9] by Microsoft Azure Functions on Github[3]. In this subsection, we demonstrate our approach of generating realistic trace from the Azure dataset, to be the foundation for our introduced architecture. The azure trace consists of 14 sets of three files representing 14 d of execution history. Each file includes real detailed information regarding a particular aspect of Azure functions provider.

The first one contains a history of invocations per function. The file contains 1440 columns (1440 min, a full day) per function due to the invocations were binned at 1-min intervals. The second file contains distributions of execution time and the number of invocations per function. Moreover, it includes average, minimum and maximum execution times over the number of invocations across 24-h. The third and last file contains distributions of allocated memory per application, which is able to host the execution of individual functions. For this metric, each application's memory was sampled every 5 s, which they then averaged every minute. In addition to this, the trace discloses the percentiles for the distribution of average allocated memory and execution time. We combined the three files into a single file, representing one day, by matching hash of the owner's ID, the function's ID and the application ID.

Generating Invocations. When a user selects the azure trace file, it will be processed by `Generic Trace Producer`. This loads the previously discussed files and analyses its contents.

---

[3] https://github.com/Azure/AzurePublicDataset.

The `Generic Trace Producer` class reads each line from the trace file (which represent one unique function and its invocations over a 24 h period) and imitates the behaviour of function according to invocations as shown in Fig. 2. This is done by extracting the necessary percentile information to be passed for generating execution time and memory. It also collects how many times this function is invoked in one day. For each invocation, the `Function Definition` will be instantiated with the previously extracted values (e.g., amount of memory). The Function Definition is responsible for populating the corresponding task definition in the simulation. These fields determine the behaviour of function by including a unique ID, submitted time that function is invoked in real systems, as well as the execution time and memory need for this invocation. Function Definition will continue the generation of the tasks of the selected function according to its total number of invocations. After generating all the required function invocations for the simulator, the Generic Trace Producer proceeds reading the next line from the trace. This process continues till we finish generating all requested functions and their invocations. Once these are generated the workload is ready to be used by the simulator's further components (this is achieved with the Function Deployer).

Generating Execution Times and Allocated Memory. Generating the execution time and amount of memory for each function and its invocations, is mainly based on the values of the trace file's percentile related columns. The minimum and maximum values determine the range for the invocations. The count value specifies the total number of invocations for single function in a day of the original trace's recording. Our approach offers customisation options for the count value in order to allow the simulator's user to generate traces which are similar but have different number of invocations. The percentile values that existed under percentile ranks, which determines how execution time and memory are distributed over one day. The execution time came with 1, 25, 50, 75, 99 and 100 percentile ranks, whereas the percentile ranks of memory are 1, 5, 25, 50, 75, 95, 99 and 100.

When the functions are defined, as a first step we calculate how many invocations should fall in each percentile rank by using Eq. 1.

$$Value = \frac{count * percnetileRank}{100} \tag{1}$$

Thus, the total number of invocations will be divided into six and eight values for execution time and memory, respectively, according to the percentile ranks. As the percentile is a value score below which a given percentage of scores in its frequency distribution falls, each calculated value will be subtracted from its previous one, except the first value that falls under percentile rank 1. Thus, the total number will be equal the count value (total number of invocations).

The second step of our approach is generating execution time and memory values from the percentile values according to the number of invocations for each percentile rank. Here, `Generate Execution Time` and `Generate Memory`

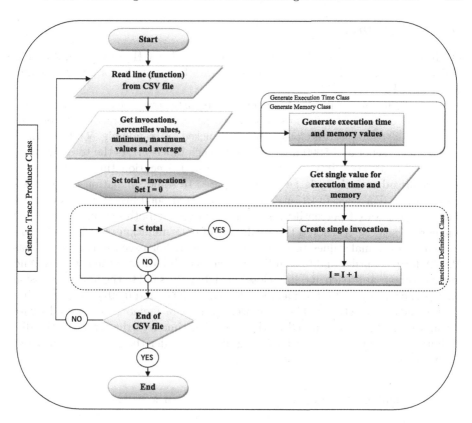

Fig. 2. Flowchart for process of generating trace by `Generic Trace Producer` class

classes take percentile values that provided in the original file, and then generates execution time and memory values within the range (considering minimum and maximum values for each function) of percentile values.

When the count value is customized the characteristics of the invocations are maintained from the original trace. Let us take an arbitrary number of invocations such as 89434 with percentile values 10, 230, 550, 650, 800, 950 for percentile ranks 1, 25, 50, 75, 99 and 100, respectively. As the first step, our approach calculates the invocations fall within each percentile rank using Eq. 1. As result of first step, we will have 894, 21464, 22359, 22358, 21464 and 895 for percentile ranks 1, 25, 50, 75, 99 and 100 respectively. After getting total invocations for each percentile rank, the second step is generating execution time values for invocations. Our approach will generate randomly (with a uniform PRNG) 894 execution time values within the range of min (that came with original file) and 10 that located under percentile rank 1. Then, it generates 21464 execution time values within the range of 10 and 230 located under percentile ranks 1 and 25, respectively, and so on. This process will continue till generating execution values for all invocations and the same approach will be used for memory values.

4 Evaluation

A laptop (Intel (R) Core (TM) i7-4600U CPU @ 2.10 GHz (4 CPUs), 2.7 GHz, 8 GB) was used for the evaluation of our approach and model for generating and simulating FaaS.

To validate our approach of generating realistic trace that used as a foundation for evaluation serverless model, we have chosen a trace that contains around 36000 unique functions. Then we picked up randomly 5000 functions and we have generated 5000 invocations for each function. As the total, we have generated 25,000,000 invocations with generated execution time and memory (this is already relatively large scale compared to some simulation framework's capabilities). For each function that has generated 5000 invocations, we calculated the generated percentile values and average for both execution time and memory. Then, we measured the coefficient of determination (R^2) between generated and original values to show data accuracy. For execution time, R^2 was 0.8438 for percentiles and 0.9956 for average, which indicates the accuracy (and realism) of our approach and how close the data points fall to the fitted regression line as shown in Fig. 3a. For memory, R^2 were 0.9999 and 0.9977 for percentiles and average, respectively. The generated average of memory is more adequate as shown in Fig. 3b, compared to the execution time and the reason is the distribution of execution time values is significantly wider than the distribution of memory usage.

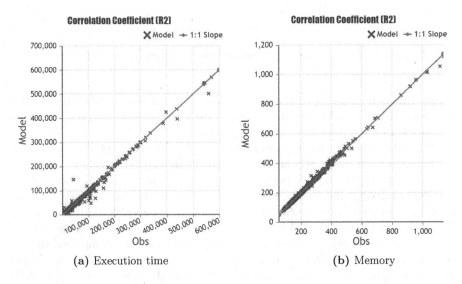

(a) Execution time   (b) Memory

Fig. 3. Coefficient of determination evaluation for generated execution time and memory

There are many applications areas that are able to use our generated realistic trace, but we used Azure provider as scenario to demonstrate the advantage of our model. The configurations to simulate serverless functions are different in FaaS providers. Azure functions provider offers several plans to be selected by a user for their workload. Our model is able to support consumption and premium plans, which have different resources such as the memory, price and storage. We have provided a measurement using the consumption plan, to simulate our generated serverless functions and predict the internal behaviour of azure provider in our model.

We have conducted the measurement that simulates several generated functions with around 2 million invocations. This scenario demonstrates how our model responds to rapid increase or decrease in demand of invocations during the simulation. The Fig. 4 shows how our model imitates the Azure provider by utilising dynamic allocation of memory based on the number of invocations at each time instance. Our model was able to estimate the total price for simulated functions (based on the pricing plans of Azure). In Azure, the cost of functions invocations consists of two parts based on an execution count and a resource consumption.

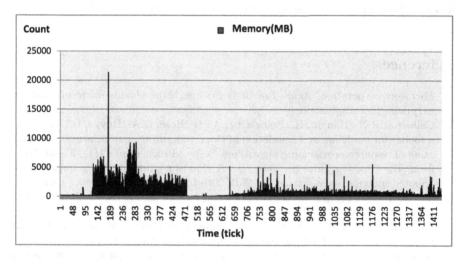

Fig. 4. Dynamic memory allocation of our model

The part of execution count is straightforward based on total number of invocations. Thus, every call of function counts and the bill charged $0.20 per million executions. In Fig. 4, our model executed various functions with 1,995,727 invocations and estimated the cost of execution count which was $0.3991. Resource consumption billing depends on both completion time and memory consumption. It is metered in GB-seconds and charged $16 per million GB-seconds. Our model calculated the consumption cost in Fig. 4, which was $0.1487. Thus, the total cost of simulation will be sum of execution count cost and resource consumption cost, which was $0.5478. These results demonstrate the realism and scaling of our approach.

5 Conclusion and Future Work

IaaS simulators play a critical role in evaluating and testing several scenarios by providing easy-setup and reproducible environments. However, with existing features, they are problematic to use for modelling serverless environments due to lack of ready-to-use environment and realistic workload models. We extended DISSECT-CF to generate realistic trace from Azure functions dataset as foundation step towards simulating serverless functions. Our approach produced accurate and realistic results regarding the execution time and memory. Based on the outcomes, we imitated azure provider as scenario to demonstrate the usability of the generated traces. Our model demonstrated the capability of estimating the total cost for simulated serverless functions. Future work will focus on exploiting our approach to shift generated realistic trace other formats allowing reuse of the previously generated traces. This could result in alternative ways to simulate serverless behaviours with IaaS simulators that do not natively serverless model.

Acknowledgements. This research was supported by the Hungarian Scientific Research Fund under the grant number OTKA FK 131793.

References

1. Microsoft corporation. Azure functions pricing. https://azure.microsoft.com/en-us/pricing/details/functions/
2. Calheiros, R.N., Ranjan, R., Beloglazov, A., De Rose, C.A., Buyya, R.: Cloudsim: a toolkit for modeling and simulation of cloud computing environments and evaluation of resource provisioning algorithms. Softw.: Pract. Exp. **41**(1), 23–50 (2011)
3. Jeon, H., Cho, C., Shin, S., Yoon, S.: A cloudsim-extension for simulating distributed functions-as-a-service. In: 2019 20th International Conference on parallel and distributed computing, applications and technologies (PDCAT), pp. 386–391. IEEE (2019)
4. Jounaid, S.: OpenDC Serverless: Design, Implementation and Evaluation of a FaaS Platform Simulator. Ph.D. Thesis, Vrije Universiteit Amsterdam (2020)
5. Kecskemeti, G.: DISSECT-CF: a simulator to foster energy-aware scheduling in infrastructure clouds. Simul. Modell. Pract. Theor. **58**, 188–218 (2015)
6. Kliazovich, D., Bouvry, P., Khan, S.U.: GreenCloud: a packet-level simulator of energy-aware cloud computing data centers. J. Supercomput. **62**(3), 1263–1283 (2012)
7. Mann, Z.Á.: Cloud simulators in the implementation and evaluation of virtual machine placement algorithms. Softw.: Pract. Exp. **48**(7), 1368–1389 (2018). https://doi.org/10.1002/spe.2579
8. Ostermann, S., Plankensteiner, K., Prodan, R., Fahringer, T.: Groudsim: an event-based simulation framework for computational grids and clouds. In: Euro-Par 2010 Parallel Processing Workshops, vol. 6586, pp. 305–313. Springer, Cham (2010). https://doi.org/10.1007/978-3-642-21878-1_38

9. Shahrad, M., et al.: Serverless in the wild: characterizing and optimizing the server-less workload at a large cloud provider. In: 2020 {USENIX} Annual Technical Conference ({USENIX}{ATC} 20), pp. 205–218 (2020)

10. Sriram, I.: SPECI, a simulation tool exploring cloud-scale data centres. In: Jaatun, M.G., Zhao, G., Rong, C. (eds.) Cloud Computing, vol. 5931, pp. 381–392. Springer, Cham (2009). https://doi.org/10.1007/978-3-642-10665-1_35

AMTE – Asynchronous Many-Task systems for Exascale

Asynchronous Many-Task systems for Exascale (AMTE)

Workshop Description

The workshop, Asynchronous Many-Task systems for Exascale (AMTE) 2021, was held at x in conjunction with the 27th International European Conference on Parallel and Distributed Computing (EuroPar) as a virtual event. The goal of the workshop was to explore the advantages of task-based programming on modern and future high performance systems. It gathered developers, users, and proponents of these models and systems to share experiences, discuss how they meet the challenges posed by Exascale system architectures, and explore opportunities for increased performance, robustness, and full-system utilization.

The workshop was organized by Irina Demeshko, Patrick Diehl, Steven R. Brandt, Zahra Khatami, and Parsa Amini. The keynote was given by Thomas Fahringer, and the invited talk by Daisy Hollman. The panel discussion was moderated by Irina Demeshko with the following panellists: Hartmut Kaiser, Laxmikant (Sanjay) Kale, Martin Berzins, Mike Bauer, and Thomas Fahringer.

This volume of LNCS compromises selected contributions of attendees from this event. The contributed papers range from optimization of asynchronous many-task runtime systems to applications. This workshop has shown that AMTs are widely used in academia and national laboratories, and researchers are working to address some challenges posed by Excascale system architectures.

Organization

Organizing Committee

Patrick Diehl	Center for Computation and Technology at Louisiana State University, USA
Steven R. Brandt	Center for Computation and Technology at Louisiana State University, USA
Parsa Amini	Center for Computation and Technology at Louisiana State University, USA
Zahra Khatami	NVIDIA, USA
Irina Demeshko	Los Alamos National Laboratory, USA

Program Committee

Metin H. Aktulga	Michigan State University, USA
Bryce Adelstein Lelbach	NVIDIA, USA
John Biddiscombe	Swiss National Supercomputing Centre, Switzerland
Gregor Daiss	University of Stuttgart,
Vassilios Dimakopoulos	University of Ioannina, Greece
Patricia Grubel	Los Alamos National Laboratory, USA
Jeff Hammond	NVIDIA, USA
Adrian Lemoine	AMD, USA
Roman Lakymchuk	Fraunhofer ITWM, Germany
Thomas Heller	Exasol, Germany
Kevin Huck	University of Oregon, USA
Daisy Hollman	Sandia National Laboratories, USA
Laxmikant (Sanjay) V. Kale	University of Illinois at Urbana-Champaign, USA
Hartmut Kaiser	Center for Computation and Technology at Louisiana State University, USA
Erwin Laure	Max Planck Computing and Data Facility, Germany
Andrew Lumsdaine	Northwest Institute for Advanced Computing, USA
Pat McCormick	Los Alamos National Laboratory, USA
Dirk Pleiter	Jülich Supercomputing Centre, Germany
Brad Richardson	Sourcery Institute, USA
Galen Shipman	Los Alamos National Laboratory, USA

Shahrzad Shirzad   Center for Computation and Technology
                                         at Louisiana State University, USA
Mikael Simberg   Swiss National Supercomputing Centre,
                                         Switzerland
Sean Treichler   NVIDIA, USA
Didem Unat   Koç University, Turkey
Nanmia Wu   Center for Computation and Technology
                                         at Louisiana State University, USA

OpenMP Target Task: Tasking and Target Offloading on Heterogeneous Systems

Pedro Valero-Lara$^{(\boxtimes)}$ (ID), Jungwon Kim (ID), Oscar Hernandez,
and Jeffrey Vetter (ID)

Oak Ridge National Laboratory, Oak Ridge, TN 37830, USA
{valerolarap,kimj,oscar,vetter}@ornl.gov
https://www.ornl.gov/

Abstract. This work evaluated the use of OpenMP tasking with target GPU offloading as a potential solution for programming productivity and performance on heterogeneous systems. Also, it is proposed a new OpenMP specification to make the implementation of heterogeneous codes simpler by using OpenMP target task, which integrates both OpenMP tasking and target GPU offloading in a single OpenMP pragma. As a test case, the authors used one of the most popular and widely used Basic Linear Algebra Subprogram Level-3 routines: triangular solver (TRSM). To benefit from the heterogeneity of the current high-performance computing systems, the authors propose a different parallelization of the algorithm by using a nonuniform decomposition of the problem. This work used target GPU offloading inside OpenMP tasks to address the heterogeneity found in the hardware. This new approach can outperform the state-of-the-art algorithms, which use a uniform decomposition of the data, on both the CPU-only and hybrid CPU-GPU systems, reaching speedups of up to one order of magnitude. The performance that this approach achieves is faster than the IBM ESSL math library on CPU and competitive relative to a highly optimized heterogeneous CUDA version. One node of Oak Ridge National Laboratory's supercomputer, Summit, was used for performance analysis.

Keywords: Tasking · Heterogeneity · OpenMP · CUDA · Linear
algebra · TRSM · BLAS

© Springer Nature Switzerland AG 2022
R. Chaves et al. (Eds.): Euro-Par 2021, LNCS 13098, pp. 445–455, 2022.
https://doi.org/10.1007/978-3-031-06156-1_35

1   Introduction

The motivation of this work was to analyze the OpenMP 4.5 specification for programming productivity and performance on heterogeneous systems via the integration of tasking and target GPU offloading. Triangular solve (TRSM) was used as a motivating example because it is one of the most popular Basic Linear Algebra Subprograms (BLAS) routines. The authors also included a highly optimized Compute Unified Device Architecture (CUDA) code in their analysis to compare not only the performance but also the programming productivity.

Many other studies efficiently used task-based programming models for linear algebra computations. Examples include CPU-only math libraries, such as Parallel Linear Algebra Software for Multicore Architectures (PLASMA) [7], which is based on OpenMP and Quark [10]; Chamaleon, which is based on StarPU [2]; and Linear Algebra routines on OmpSs (LASs) [18], which is based on OmpSs [8].

Tasking [19,20] is an efficient tool for addressing irregular problems, such as sparse [3,4] and dense [17,18] linear algebra kernels. Unlike conventional directive-based clauses used for a uniform work sharing (i.e., decomposition) of loops, tasking provides the flexibility, transparency, and programming productivity necessary for handling irregular and nonbalanced applications in which each task has a different computational cost. Tasking is also well positioned to address the heterogeneity of the current and upcoming high-performance computing systems [2,16]. Since OpenMP 4.0, it is possible to use target GPU offloading in OpenMP codes. Using GPU offloading in OpenMP tasking could be a transparent and simple way to implement heterogeneous codes without compromising performance. Multiple implementations of the OpenMP 4.5 specification are found in multiple vendor compilers, such as Intel [12], NVIDIA [15], AMD [1], Cray [5], and IBM [11], as well as in open-source compilers [9,13], which would make OpenMP a portable specification among many different heterogeneous CPU+GPU systems. However, this study should be extended by using other architectures, such as AMD and Intel GPUs, to verify the portability of OpenMP 4.5.

The parallel algorithm of the TRSM routine comprises two main components: TRSM and general matrix-matrix multiplication (GEMM). Although GEMM can reach a very high—nearly peak—performance on GPU, TRSM is a more complex routine, reaching a lower performance on GPUs. In terms of the percentage of the peak performance reached, TRSM works better on CPUs than on GPUs, reaching about 75–80% of the CPU peak performance but only about 50% of the GPU peak performance. To achieve high performance on GPU and CPU, the authors propose to use CPU to compute the TRSM blocks while using GPU for the GEMM blocks. The use of heterogeneous (i.e., CPU+GPU) systems for linear algebra solvers is not new. For example, the MAGMA library [14] has different linear algebra factorizations (i.e., LAPACK routines), such as LU factorization/solve and Cholesky factorization/solve. These routines are distributed and computed on CPU and GPU by using vendor programming models, such as CUDA or HIP on NVIDIA and AMD GPUs and math libraries, such as cuBLAS/hipBLAS on NVIDIA/AMD GPUs or MKL on Intel CPUs.

Unlike MAGMA, which uses CUDA or HIP, the authors propose to use OpenMP tasking with target GPU offloading as the orchestrator of the blocks and tasks. Unfortunately, there is not a heterogeneous TRSM implementation in MAGMA that can be compared with this. Thus, the authors included a highly optimized asynchronous and heterogeneous CUDA implementation of TRSM in their analysis, following the same programming approach used by MAGMA. Like MAGMA and many other math linear algebra libraries, the authors used vendor libraries—IBM ESSL on CPU and NVIDIA cuBLAS on GPU—to compute the different components or blocks of the algorithms. To the best of the authors' knowledge, this is the first time that target GPU offloading within OpenMP tasking has been used for heterogeneous linear algebra operations on heterogeneous systems.

The remainder of the paper is structured as follows. Section 2 describes the main characteristics of TRSM. Section 3 explains the main details of the OpenMP and CUDA implementations. Section 4 evaluates these implementations and Section 5 presents the proposal for a novel OpenMP construct which integrates OpenMP tasking and target offloading in a single OpenMP pragma. Finally, Sect. 6 summarizes the conclusions and future directions.

2   Motivating Example: TRSM BLAS Level-3 Routine

The TRSM BLAS Level-3 routine is one of the most popular and widely used BLAS routines. It is used in multiple applications and in some of the most important LAPACK operations, such as LU and Cholesky solve. It solves a triangular system, which can be defined as:

$$op(A) \cdot X = ALPHA \cdot B, or X \cdot op(A) = ALPHA \cdot B. \tag{1}$$

TRSM has a triangular matrix as input and a regular dense matrix as output. Matrix A is a triangular matrix, which can be "lower" or "upper," depending on the locations of the nonzero elements within it. The result of this operation is stored in matrix X. This matrix can be positioned on the left or right of matrix A, which affects the order of the operations to be computed. Matrix B is a dense matrix, and $ALPHA$ is a scalar matrix. $Op(A)$ can be a transposed (i.e., A^T) or nontransposed matrix. For clarity and simplicity, the remainder of this document will focus only on one of the possible cases of this operation, which consists of computing a triangular system in which matrix A is a lower triangular matrix, is not transposed, and is positioned to the left of matrix X. More information about this operation and other BLAS Level-3 operations can be found in Dongarra et al. [6] or on the BLAS website.[1]

3   Task-Based Implementation of TRSM

One of the most common ways to parallelize this type of operation is to decompose the matrix into tiles of the same size, defining the dependencies between the tiles and operations to be computed on each tile. This can be efficiently implemented via tasking [7,17,18].

---

[1] http://www.netlib.org/blas/.

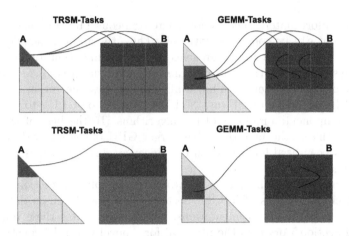

Fig. 1. Uniform (top) and nonuniform (bottom) tiled TRSM decomposition.

The top image in Fig. 1 illustrates the dependencies among the tiles and operations to be computed on the tiles. The algorithm computes TRSM on the diagonal tiles of the input and triangular tiled matrix A and the tiles of the first row of the output and regular dense tiled matrix B. Once complete, a set of GEMM operations must be run by using the output (i.e., tiles) of the previous TRSM operations and the tiles of the column below the diagonal tile as input. The output corresponds to the tiles located in the second row through the last row of the output tiled matrix. This process is repeated until the last diagonal tile of the input matrix is computed.

3.1   OpenMP

Figure 2 shows a pseudocode for the tiled TRSM decomposition, which is illustrated in the top image in Fig. 1, on a CPU-GPU heterogeneous system. The algorithm used in this implementation is identical to the one used by the PLASMA, Chameleon, and LASs math libraries. As mentioned previously, the goal is to compute TRSM blocks on CPU and GEMM blocks on GPU. The data and task dependencies are defined by using the #pragma omp task depend clause. A few more lines of code must be provided to compute GEMM on GPU and encapsulate target GPU offloading into OpenMP tasking. These new lines consist of (1) describing the data moving from CPU and GPU via #pragma omp target enter data map, (2) specifying that the pointers used in the GEMM call are GPU pointers via #pragma omp target data use_device_ptr, and (3) identifying which data must be copied back to CPU via #pragma omp target exit data map.

Unlike the previous OpenMP code (Fig. 2) in which the matrices are decomposed into square tiles of the same size, the authors propose a different and irregular decomposition and/or parallelization, as shown in the bottom image of Fig. 1, in which matrix A is decomposed into square tiles, but matrix B is

```
1   aSIZE = TILE_SIZE*TILE_SIZE;
2   for(d = 0; d < dt; d++) {
3     for(c = 0; c < ct; c++) {
4       #pragma omp task depend(in:TILE_A[d][d]) \
5                        depend(inout:TILE_B[d][c])
6       CPU-TRSM(L, L, N, N,
7               TILE_SIZE, TILE_SIZE,
8               ALPHA, TILE_A[d][d], TILE_SIZE,
9                      TILE_B[d][c], TILE_SIZE);
10    }//End for c
11    for(r = d+1; r < rt; r++) {
12      for(c = 0; c < ct; c++) {
13        #pragma omp task depend(in:TILE_A[r][d]) \
14                         depend(in:TILE_B[d][c]) \
15                         depend(inout:TILE_B[r][c]) {
16        TILE_A=TILE_A[r][d];TILE_B=TILE_B[d][c];TILE_C=TILE_B[r][c];
17        #pragma omp target enter data map
          ↪   (to:TILE_A[0:aSIZE],TILE_B[0:aSIZE],TILE_C[0:aSIZE])
18        #pragma omp target data use_device_ptr(TILE_A,TILE_B,TILE_C) {
19          GPU-GEMM(N, N,
20                   TILE_SIZE, TILE_SIZE, TILE_SIZE,
21                   -1.0, TILE_A, TILE_SIZE,
22                         TILE_B, TILE_SIZE,
23                   ALPHA, TILE_C, TILE_SIZE);
24        }//End pragma target
25        #pragma omp target exit data map(from:TILE_C[aSIZE])
26      }//End pragma task
27      }//End for c
28    }//End for r
29  }//End for d
```

Fig. 2. CPU-GPU OpenMP code of the tiled TRSM decomposition.

```
1   aSIZE = TILE_SIZE*TILE_SIZE;
2   bSIZE = TILE_SIZE*MATRIX_SIZE;
3   for(d = 0; d < dt; d++) {
4     #pragma omp task depend(in:TILE_A[d][d]) \
5                      depend(inout:TILE_B[d])
6     CPU-TRSM(L, L, N, N,
7             TILE_SIZE, MATRIX_SIZE,
8             ALPHA, TILE_A[d][d], TILE_SIZE,
9                    TILE_B[d], TILE_SIZE);
10    for(r = d+1; r < rt; r++) {
11      #pragma omp task depend(in:TILE_A[d][r]) \
12                       depend(in:TILE_B[d]) \
13                       depend(inout:TILE_B[r]) {
14      TILE_A=TILE_A[r][d];TILE_B=TILE_B[d];TILE_C=TILE_B[r];
15      #pragma omp target enter data map
        ↪   (to:TILE_A[0:aSIZE],TILE_B[0:bSIZE],TILE_C[0:bSIZE])
16      #pragma omp target data use_device_ptr(TILE_A,TILE_B,TILE_C) {
17        GPU-GEMM(N, N,
18                 TILE_SIZE, MATRIX_SIZE, TILE_SIZE,
19                 -1.0, TILE_A, TILE_SIZE,
20                       TILE_B, TILE_SIZE,
21                 ALPHA, TILE_C, TILE_SIZE);
22      }//End pragma target
23      #pragma omp target exit data map(from:TILE_C[bSIZE])
24      }//End pragma task
25    }//End for r
26  }//End for d
```

Fig. 3. CPU-GPU OpenMP code of the optimized tiled TRSM decomposition.

decomposed into rectangular matrices. This different decomposition, which is illustrated in Fig. 1 and implemented in the code shown in Fig. 2, allows the occupancy of the CPU and GPU to be maximized, as well as helps overlap more of the CPU-GPU communication and computation. Also, a lower number of tasks is necessary, which minimizes the scheduler overhead. These modifications in the code (Fig. 3) consists of (1) removing those for loops related to the columns of matrix B, (2) using a unidimensional array for the tiles of matrix B, and (3) changing the input of the BLAS calls in which a whole block of rows of matrix B is computed instead of a square tile. These modifications also reduce the number of lines of code relative to the previous approach.

3.2 CUDA

The CUDA code uses the same matrix decomposition used in the optimized OpenMP code shown in Fig. 3. To overlap communication with computation—as well as CPU computation with GPU computation, when possible—the asynchronous application programming interface of the cuBLAS library and CUDA streams must be used. Also, CUDA events must be used to guarantee the data dependencies among those blocks of the algorithm computed on the CPU and on GPU. The use of async memory transfers between CPU and GPU requires the use of pinned memory. This is done by using `cudaHostAlloc` to allocate host CPU memory. Finally, a stream must be associated with the CUDA handle before running GEMM via `cublasSetStream`. To achieve fully overlapping computation and communication, the authors used a different stream in each consecutive GEMM block.

Figure 4 shows a pseudocode corresponding to the first iteration of the CUDA CPU-GPU asynchronous TRSM code. The authors implemented this code to minimize the overhead of CPU-GPU communication as much as possible, as well as to maximize CPU and GPU use. During the first iteration of the code, all rectangular tiles of matrix B must be transferred from CPU to GPU. Once these tiles are in GPU memory, only these must be copied back to the CPU after the computation of the first GEMM block of each iteration because TRSM must compute them on the CPU at the beginning of the following iteration (Fig. 4).

4 Evaluation

The authors conducted the performance evaluation by using one node of Oak Ridge National Laboratory's heterogeneous supercomputer, Summit, which is currently listed on the TOP500 list as the second fastest supercomputer in the world. Summit features 2× IBM Power9 8335-GTH at 2.4 GHz, 32 GB RAM memory, and 6× NVIDIA V100 (Volta) GPU with 16 GB HBM2 and NVLink2 for high-bandwidth communication between CPU and GPU. In this study, the authors used one IBM Power9 CPU (21 cores) and one NVIDIA GPU (V100); all computations were done in double precision. The math libraries IBM ESSL (6.1.0-2) and NVIDIA cuBLAS (CUDA version 10.1.243) were used to compute

```
1    cuStream_t stream0, stream1;
2    cuEvent_t event;
3    cuHandle_t handle;
4    //First iteration
5    cblas_dtrsm(L, L, N, N,
6              TILE_SIZE, MATRIX_SIZE,
7              ALPHA, TILE_A[0][0], TILE_SIZE,
8                    TILE_B0, TILE_SIZE);
9    cudaEventRecord(event);
10   cudaEventSynchronize(event);
11   cublasSetMatrixAsync(TILE_SIZE,MATRIX_SIZE,sizeof(precision),
12                    TILE_B[0], TILE_SIZE,
13                    TILE_BGPU0, TILE_SIZE, streams[0]);
14   //First GEMM block
15   cublasSetMatrixAsync(TILE_SIZE, TILE_SIZE, sizeof(precision),
16                    TILE_A[1][0], TILE_SIZE,
17                    TILE_AGPU1, TILE_SIZE, streams[0]);
18   cublasSetMatrixAsync(TILE_SIZE,MATRIX_SIZE,sizeof(precision),
19                    TILE_B[1], TILE_SIZE,
20                    TILE_GPUB1, TILE_SIZE, streams[0]);
21   cublasSetStream(handle, streams[0]);
22   GPU-GEMM(N, N,
23              TILE_SIZE, MATRIX_SIZE, TILE_SIZE,
24              -1.0, TILE_GPUA1, TILE_SIZE,
25                    TILE_GPUB0, TILE_SIZE,
26              ALPHA, TILE_GPUB1, TILE_SIZE);
27   cublasGetMatrixAsync(TILE_SIZE,MATRIX_SIZE,sizeof(precision),
28                    TILE_GPUB1, TILE_SIZE,
29                    TILE_B[1], TILE_SIZE, streams[0]);
30   //Second GEMM block
31   cublasSetMatrixAsync(TILE_SIZE, TILE_SIZE, sizeof(precision),
32                    TILE_A[2][0], TILE_SIZE,
33                    TILE_AGPU2, TILE_SIZE, streams[1]);
34   cublasSetMatrixAsync(TILE_SIZE,MATRIX_SIZE,sizeof(precision),
35                    TILE_B[2], TILE_SIZE,
36                    TILE_GPUB2, TILE_SIZE, streams[1]);
37   cublasSetStream(handle, streams[1]);
38   cublasDgemm(N, N,
39              TILE_SIZE,MATRIX_SIZE,TILE_SIZE,
40              -1.0, TILE_GPUA2, TILE_SIZE,
41                    TILE_GPUB0, TILE_SIZE,
42              ALPHA, TILE_GPUB2, TILE_SIZE);
43   ...
```

Fig. 4. CUDA code of the optimized tiled TRSM decomposition.

the different components of the algorithm (i.e., CPU-TRSM and GPU-GEMM in the codes illustrated in Figs. 2 and 3). The IBM compiler xl 16.1.1-5 was also used.

The performance analysis corresponds to a set of runs by using different square matrix sizes ranging from 512 to 16,384. In every run, the authors used a tile size that was $1/8$ the size of the matrix. For example, for a matrix size of 512^2, a tile size of 64^2 was used for matrices A and B in the OpenMP version (Figs. 2 and 5) in which the matrices are uniformly decomposed (top image in Fig. 1). Additionally, a tile size of 64×512 was used for matrix B in the other OpenMP implementation (Figs. 3 and 5) and CUDA code (Fig. 4). Thus, depending on the matrix decomposition used, the authors used the same number of tasks and blocks. For comparison and completeness, two different CUDA implementations were included: one synchronous and one asynchronous. These are shown as CUDA-sync and CUDA-async in Fig. 5. This helps show the impact of using asynchronous CPU-GPU communication and computation.

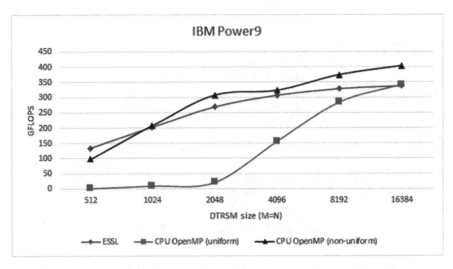

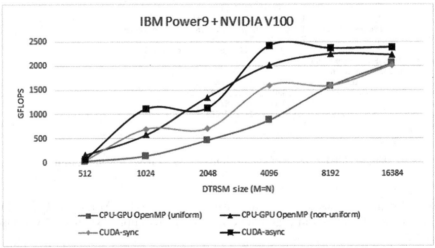

Fig. 5. Performance in terms of giga-floating point operations per second of the different implementations on CPU (top) and CPU+GPU (bottom).

First, the results were evaluated on CPU only, as shown in the top image of Fig. 5. The OpenMP uniform code is based on the implementations of the CPU-only math libraries, including PLASMA [7] and LASs [18] libraries. As shown in Fig. 4, the use of a nonuniform decomposition can outperform the OpenMP uniform code, achieving a speedup of up to one order of magnitude in some cases (23× for a matrix size of 1,024 and 15× for a matrix size of 2,048). An irregular distribution of the workload can achieve a high performance, even on relatively small matrix sizes. Finally, as expected, both variants achieved the best performance on the biggest matrix tested, being the OpenMP nonuniform code about 1.2× faster. Also, this code is faster than the multithreading IBM ESSL library in most cases, performing up to a 1.2× speedup.

Except for the smallest matrix size computed, all heterogeneous versions are faster than using CPU only. As in the CPU case, using OpenMP tasking with OpenMP target via a nonuniform decomposition of the matrices, as shown in the bottom image of Fig. 5, achieves a better result than using a uniform matrix decomposition. As in the CPU case, the OpenMP nonuniform code can achieve better results, even on small and medium matrices. The OpenMP nonuniform code was 4.3× faster on a matrix size of 1,240, 2.3× faster on a matrix size of 4,096, and 1.1× faster on a matrix size of 16,384. Also, the OpenMP nonuniform code surpasses the CUDA synchronous implementation in most experiments because it is about 2× faster. Finally, although the asynchronous version of the CUDA implementation, as shown in the bottom image of Fig. 5, is faster than the heterogeneous OpenMP nonuniform code, the performance of the OpenMP code is competitive with respect to the performance reached by the CUDA code because OpenMP tasking with the target offloading code achieved about 85–95% of the asynchronous CUDA code performance.

5 A Proposal for OpenMP Target Tasking

Given the good results shown in the previous section by using target offloading in OpenMP tasks, we propose the integration of both OpenMP tasking and target

```
1   //Current specification
2   #pragma omp task depend(in:TILE_A[d][r]) \
3                    depend(in:TILE_B[d]) \
4                    depend(inout:TILE_B[r]) {
5     TILE_A=TILE_A[r][d];TILE_B=TILE_B[r];TILE_C=TILE_B[r];
6     #pragma omp target enter data map
      ↪ (to:TILE_A[0:aSIZE],TILE_B[0:bSIZE],TILE_C[0:bSIZE])
7     #pragma omp target data use_device_ptr(TILE_A,TILE_B,TILE_C) {
8       GPU-GEMM(N, N,
9               TILE_SIZE, MATRIX_SIZE, TILE_SIZE,
10              -1.0, TILE_A, TILE_SIZE,
11              TILE_B, TILE_SIZE,
12              ALPHA, TILE_C, TILE_SIZE);
13    }//End pragma target
14    #pragma omp target exit data map(from:TILE_C[bSIZE])
15  }//End pragma task
16  //Proposed specification
17  #pragma omp target task depend(in:TILE_A[d][r]) \
18                    depend(in:TILE_B[d]) \
19                    depend(inout:TILE_B[r]) {
20    GPU-GEMM(N, N,
21            TILE_SIZE, MATRIX_SIZE, TILE_SIZE,
22            -1.0, TILE_A[d][r], TILE_SIZE,
23            TILE_B[d], TILE_SIZE,
24            ALPHA,   TILE_B[r], TILE_SIZE);
25  }//End pragma target task
```

Fig. 6. Proposal for OpenMP target task.

offloading by using a new OpenMP construct: OpenMP target task. An example of this new construct with respect to the current OpenMP specification can be seen in Fig. 6. As shown, the use of OpenMP target tasking would simplify the implementation of heterogeneous codes considerably. Additionally, a better CPU-GPU communication could be performed by keeping the data in GPU memory when other GPU tasks need to access to the same data.

6   Conclusions and Future Work

This paper proposes a new parallel approach for the BLAS Level-3 routine TRSM by using a nonuniform data decomposition that better matches the characteristics of heterogeneous systems. This new approach can achieve an important acceleration compared with the reference implementations by using a nonuniform data decomposition on both CPU and the heterogeneous CPU+GPU implementations. The authors implemented two different codes using a nonuniform data decomposition: one based on OpenMP tasking and target GPU offloading and one based on CUDA. Although slower than the asynchronous CUDA code, the OpenMP code can achieve about 85–95% of the performance achieved by the CUDA code with a much lower programming effort, reaching a high programming productivity without compromising much performance. To simplify the implementation of heterogeneous codes, we propose OpenMP target tasking, a new OpenMP construct which combines OpenMP tasking and target offloading in a single OpenMP pragma.

In future work, the authors plan to (1) extend this work to other dense and sparse linear algebra kernels and other heterogeneous systems and (2) achieve better problem tuning by using and including algorithm and hardware factors that are susceptible to tuning in the code and OpenMP specification.

References

1. AMD: AOMP, June 2021. https://rocmdocs.amd.com/en/latest/Programming_Guides/aomp.html
2. Augonnet, C., Thibault, S., Namyst, R., Wacrenier, P.: StarPU: a unified platform for task scheduling on heterogeneous multicore architectures. Concurr. Comput. Pract. Exp. **23**(2), 187–198 (2011). https://doi.org/10.1002/cpe.1631
3. Catalán, S., Martorell, X., Labarta, J., Usui, T., Díaz, L.A.T., Valero-Lara, P.: Accelerating conjugate gradient using OmpSs. In: 20th International Conference on Parallel and Distributed Computing, Applications and Technologies, PDCAT 2019, 5–7 December 2019, Gold Coast, Australia, pp. 121–126. IEEE (2019). https://doi.org/10.1109/PDCAT46702.2019.00033
4. Catalán, S., Usui, T., Toledo, L., Martorell, X., Labarta, J., Valero-Lara, P.: Towards an auto-tuned and task-based SpMV (LASs library). In: Milfeld, K., de Supinski, B.R., Koesterke, L., Klinkenberg, J. (eds.) OpenMP: Portable Multi-Level Parallelism on Modern Systems, IWOMP 2020, LNCS, vol. 12295, pp. 115–129. Springer, Cham (2020). https://doi.org/10.1007/978-3-030-58144-2_8
5. Cray: CCE OpenMP, June 2021. https://pubs.cray.com/bundle/Cray_Fortran_Reference_Manual_S-3901_11-0/page/OpenMP_Overview.html

6. Dongarra, J.J., Croz, J.D., Hammarling, S., Duff, I.S.: A set of level 3 basic linear algebra subprograms. ACM Trans. Math. Softw. **16**(1), 1–17 (1990). https://doi.org/10.1145/77626.79170

7. Dongarra, J.J., et al.: PLASMA: parallel linear algebra software for multicore using OpenMP. ACM Trans. Math. Softw. **45**(2), 16:1-16:35 (2019). https://doi.org/10.1145/3264491

8. Duran, A., et al.: OmpSs: a proposal for programming heterogeneous multi-core architectures. Parallel Process. Lett. **21**(2), 173–193 (2011). https://doi.org/10.1142/S0129626411000151

9. GNU: GCC OpenMP, June 2021. https://gcc.gnu.org/wiki/Offloading

10. Haidar, A., Ltaief, H., Dongarra, J.J.: Parallel reduction to condensed forms for symmetric eigenvalue problems using aggregated fine-grained and memory-aware kernels. In: Lathrop, S.A., Costa, J., Kramer, W. (eds.) Conference on High Performance Computing Networking, Storage and Analysis, SC 2011, 12–18 November 2011, Seattle, WA, USA, pp. 8:1–8:11. ACM (2011). https://doi.org/10.1145/2063384.2063394

11. IBM: XLC OpenMP, June 2021. https://www.ibm.com/docs/en/xl-c-and-cpp-linux/13.1.6?topic=gpus-programming-openmp-device-constructs

12. Intel: OneAPI, June 2021. https://software.intel.com/content/www/us/en/develop/documentation/get-started-with-cpp-fortran-compiler-openmp/top.html

13. LLVM: OpenMP, June 2021. https://llvm.org/docs/AMDGPUUsage.html#target-triples

14. Nath, R., Tomov, S., Dongarra, J.J.: An improved magma GEMM for fermi graphics processing units. Int. J. High Perform. Comput. Appl. **24**(4), 511–515 (2010). https://doi.org/10.1177/1094342010385729

15. NVIDIA: NVCC OpenMP, June 2021. https://docs.nvidia.com/hpc-sdk/compilers/hpc-compilers-user-guide/index.html#openmp-use

16. Planas, J., Badia, R.M., Ayguadé, E., Labarta, J.: Self-adaptive OmpSs tasks in heterogeneous environments. In: 27th IEEE International Symposium on Parallel and Distributed Processing, IPDPS 2013, 20–24 May 2013, Cambridge, MA, USA, pp. 138–149. IEEE Computer Society (2013). https://doi.org/10.1109/IPDPS.2013.53

17. Valero-Lara, P., Catalán, S., Martorell, X., Labarta, J.: BLAS-3 optimized by OmpSs regions (LASs library). In: 27th Euromicro International Conference on Parallel, Distributed and Network-Based Processing, PDP 2019, 13–15 February 2019, Pavia, Italy, pp. 25–32. IEEE (2019). https://doi.org/10.1109/EMPDP.2019.8671545

18. Valero-Lara, P., Catalán, S., Martorell, X., Usui, T., Labarta, J.: sLASs: a fully automatic auto-tuned linear algebra library based on OpenMP extensions implemented in OmpSs (LASs library). J. Parallel Distrib. Comput. **138**, 153–171 (2020). https://doi.org/10.1016/j.jpdc.2019.12.002

19. Valero-Lara, P., Sirvent, R., Peña, A.J., Labarta, J.: MPI+OpenMP tasking scalability for multi-morphology simulations of the human brain. Parallel Comput. **84**, 50–61 (2019). https://doi.org/10.1016/j.parco.2019.03.006

20. Valero-Lara, P., Sirvent, R., Peña, A.J., Martorell, X., Labarta, J.: MPI+OpenMP tasking scalability for the simulation of the human brain: human brain project. In: Proceedings of the 25th European MPI Users' Group Meeting, 23–26 September 2018, Barcelona, Spain, pp. 5:1–5:8. ACM (2018). https://doi.org/10.1145/3236367.3236373

Understanding the Effect of Task Granularity on Execution Time in Asynchronous Many-Task Runtime Systems

Shahrzad Shirzad[1]([✉])(iD), R. Tohid[1](iD), Alireza Kheirkhahan[1](iD), Bibek Wagle[2](iD), and Hartmut Kaiser[1](iD)

[1] Louisiana State University, Baton Rouge, LA, USA
{sshirz1,akheir1}@lsu.edu, hkaiser@cct.lsu.edu
[2] The STE||AR Group, Baton Rouge, USA
bibek@alumni.lsu.edu

Abstract. Task granularity is a key factor in determining the performance of asynchronous many-task (AMT) runtime systems. The overhead of scheduling an excessive number of tasks with smaller granularities causes performance degradation, while creating a few larger tasks leads to starvation and therefore under-utilization of resources. In this paper, we developed an analytical model of the execution time of an application with balanced parallel *for-loops* in terms of grain size, and number of cores. The parameters of this model mostly depend on the runtime and the architecture. We introduce an approach to suggest a range of possible grain sizes to achieve the best performance based on the proposed model. To the best of our knowledge, our analytical model is the first to explain the relationship between the execution time in terms of grain size, runtime, and physical characteristics of the machine in an asynchronous runtime system.

Keywords: Task granularity · Analytical model · AMTs · HPX

1 Introduction

Achieving exascale computing relies on computing environments with complex architectures, deeper memory hierarchies, heterogeneous hardware and complex networks [7]. Asynchronous many-task (AMT) models and their corresponding runtimes are the solution to keep application developers safe from the upcoming architectures by mitigating exascale difficulties to runtime level [3]. New runtime systems rely on lightweight threads to avoid expensive context switching. Therefore, the cost of thread creation is relatively low, e.g., HPX threads are created in a few cycles. However, if millions of lightweight threads are created so each carry out a small task of a few cycles, then the overhead of task creation will be significant. On the other hand, if only a few tasks carry out the entire execution, resources

© Springer Nature Switzerland AG 2022
R. Chaves et al. (Eds.): Euro-Par 2021, LNCS 13098, pp. 456–467, 2022.
https://doi.org/10.1007/978-3-031-06156-1_36

will most likely not be utilized to the full extent. Therefore, the amount of work assigned to each task, *grain size*, requires meticulous analyses.

We have developed a model by carefully studying the relationship between the total execution time and the grain size. Based on the analytical model, we recommend a range of grain sizes that would lead us to lowest possible execution times. The model depends on two mostly architecture-specific parameters. Identifying these parameters on one system would then help us to improve the performance of other similar balanced for-loop applications on the same system.

The contribution of this work includes:

- Developing an analytical model to predict the total execution time of a balanced parallel for-loop. To our knowledge, this is the first analytical model in terms of both grain size and number of cores.
- A method has been offered to estimate the range of grain sizes to achieve minimum execution time for a particular number of cores.
- Building a microbenchmark on top of HPX to evaluate the model. The data collected through this microbenchmark is used to estimate model parameters on each machine architecture. The obtained parameters could then be utilized to predict the optimum range of grain sizes for minimum execution time, and consequently improve the performance of any other balanced parallel for-loop application executed on the same system.

2 Background

This section provides a brief overview of the concepts and technologies that are building blocks of this work.

2.1 HPX

HPX[11] is a C++ runtime system for parallel and distributed applications. HPX provides users with lightweight user-level threads with fast context switching [12]. When a thread is blocked, the scheduler picks up another one from the ready queue in order to hide latency, avoid starvation and therefore improve the utilization of the computation resources [12].

2.1.1 Execution Model
HPX's execution model mainly holds four factors responsible for performance degradation in parallel applications: Starvation, Latency, Overheads, and Waiting (also known as contention) [10].

Starvation refers to the situation where there is not enough work to keep the computing resources busy- this could be due to an insufficient total amount of work available, or unbalanced distribution of work among resources [12].

Latency is the time distance, usually measured in processor clock, between requesting and accessing remote data or services [4].

Overhead refers to the effort taken to manage parallel resources and actions on the critical path but are not necessarily needed by the application itself [12].

Waiting is the contention over shared physical or logical resources when one or more threads try to access the same resource and all get blocked [4].

Table 1. Table of notations

Parameter	Definition	Parameter	Definition
N	Number of cores	t_{seq}	Sequential execution time
n_t	Total number of tasks created	t_i	Execute time of one iteration
p_s	Total amount of work	n	Number of loop iterations
M	Number of utilized cores	c_s	Chunk size
t_{max}	Execution time of w_{max}	g	Grain size
w_{max}	Maximum amount of work assigned to a single core		

2.2   Analytical Modeling of Parallel Programs

The performance of a parallel program mostly depends on its underlying algorithm and the architecture it is run on [5]. Amdahl's law [2], Equation (1), shows that there is a limit on maximum speed-up achievable in a parallel application. This limit is imposed by the sequential fraction of the program denoted by σ.

$$S(p) = \frac{p}{1 + \sigma(p-1)} \tag{1}$$

Gunther [9] extends Amdahl's law by incorporating effects of three factors: *concurrency*, *contention*, and *coherency*, as shown in Eq. 2.

$$S(p) = \frac{p}{1 + \sigma(p-1) + \kappa p(p-1)} \tag{2}$$

In this equation, known as the Universal Scalability Law (USL), concurrency (p) represents the linear speed-up in the absence of interactions among parallel processors, contention (σ) represents the serialization effect of shared writable data, and finally coherency or data consistency (κ) represents the cost imposed for keeping shared writable data consistent [9].

Several models have been proposed to model scalability, including the Geometric model [9], and the Quadratic model [8]. These models are mainly non-physical, and not applicable for large number of processors [8].

3   Methodology

In this section we provide an overview of the methodology used to analyze the effect of *grain size*, i.e., the workload of each runtime thread, on the execution time in AMT runtime systems. Table 1 shows the notations used throughout this section. It should be noted that the amount of work could be measured in terms of execution time or floating point operations depending on the application. Chunk size is defined as the number of iterations included in one task, while grain size is the amount of work contained in a task and is executed by a single user-level thread.

The total execution time is then defined as the maximum of the execution times of each individual core. In general this is the amount of time it takes for the core with maximum amount of work to finish execution of its task. Here the maximum expected amount of work to be assigned to a core is denoted as w_{max}, and the time it takes to execute this amount of work as t_{max}.

With this assumption, the key factors contributing to the execution time are, the overhead of scheduling tasks on the core with maximum amount of work, the time it takes to run w_{max} amount of work, denoted with t_{max}, and the number of cores executing the work(M). Depending on the amount of work available, either all N cores or less than N cores will be performing the work.

Equation (3) shows the expected formula in its simplest form.

$$execution\_time = t_{overhead} + t_{max} \tag{3}$$

$t_{overhead}$ represents the penalty that has to be paid for running the program in parallel. We hold two major factors accountable for this overhead.

The first factor is the overhead of scheduling the tasks. Although this overhead is negligible for a small number of tasks, it becomes significant as the number of created tasks becomes larger.

In the ideal case, when n_t tasks are created, $\lceil \frac{n_t}{N} \rceil$ of them would be scheduled on the core with the maximum amount of work. If we represent the overhead of scheduling one task on a core with α, then $\alpha \lceil \frac{n_t}{N} \rceil$ would be the scheduling overhead associated with $\lceil \frac{n_t}{N} \rceil$ tasks.

The second factor is the overhead due to contention and coherency based on USL. Equation (4) shows how USL models the effect of the overheads due to contention(σ) and coherency(κ) in the overall execution time t, with sequential execution time of t_{seq}, on N cores, when $\frac{t_{seq}}{N}$ is the expected execution time on N cores in ideal case when the mentioned overheads are not present.

$$speedup = \frac{t_{seq}}{t} = \frac{N}{1 + \sigma(N-1) + \kappa N(N-1)} \Rightarrow$$
$$t = \frac{t_{seq}}{N} + \sigma(N-1)\frac{t_{seq}}{N} + \kappa N(N-1)\frac{t_{seq}}{N} \tag{4}$$

Based on Eq. (4), the term $\sigma(N-1)t_{seq}$ represents the overhead observed due to contention, and $\kappa N(N-1)t_{seq}$ is the overhead caused by coherency, assuming t_{seq} is the ideal execution time in this problem.

We need to keep in mind that there are cases where there is not enough work for all the cores to execute, causing the mentioned overheads to be a factor of the cores that are actually performing the work and not just all the available cores. For this reason, we adjust Eq. (4) by changing the total number of cores (N) to the number of cores that are actually being utilized (M).

Assuming that we are running our application on N cores, with a grain size equal to g, n_t tasks are being created, and M cores are being utilized. If $n_t < N$, M would be equal to n_t, otherwise $M = N$.

Equation (3) is then converted into:

$$execution\_time = \alpha \left\lceil \frac{n_t}{N} \right\rceil + \sigma(M-1)t_{max} + \kappa M(M-1)t_{max} + t_{max}.$$
(5)

For a balanced parallel for-loop, when $N = 1$ all the work will be assigned to the only available core, resulting in $w_{max} = p_s$. When $N > 1$, in the general case at most $\left\lceil \frac{n_t}{N} \right\rceil$ tasks would be assigned to a core. Therefore, a grain size of g would result in a maximum amount of work of $g\left\lceil \frac{n_t}{N} \right\rceil$ being assigned to one core, causing $w_{max} = g\left\lceil \frac{n_t}{N} \right\rceil$.

Also t_{max}, the time to execute w_{max} amount of work, can be estimated as $t_{max} = t_{seq} \frac{w_{max}}{p_s}$, where t_{seq} is the time it takes to run the total amount of work, p_s, sequentially. Equation (5) is then simplified into Eq. (6).

$$execution\_time = \alpha \left\lceil \frac{n_t}{N} \right\rceil + t_{seq} \frac{w_{max}}{p_s}(1 + \sigma(M-1) + \kappa M(M-1))$$
(6)

We refer to (6) as our analytical model in the next sections.

3.1   Model Evaluation

In order to evaluate the model, we developed a simple parallel for-loop microbenchmark[1]. We refer to it as the for-loop microbenchmark. Each iteration consists of a while loop that makes sure the iteration lasts a certain amount of time (t_i). By setting $t_i = 1\mu sec$, and changing the number of iterations n, and chunk size c_s, we can see how the execution time changes when the microbenchmark is executed on different number of cores.

Having defined p_s as the total amount of work that has to be performed, for this microbenchmark, $p_s = t_i \times n$. Since $t_i = 1\mu sec$, then $p_s = n$. On the other hand, for this specific problem $w_{max} = t_{max}$, and $t_{seq} = p_s$.

The microbenchmark was then executed with different number of cores(N), number of iterations(n), and chunk sizes (c_s). For each n, c_s is changed from 1 to n in logarithmic scale. Each of these runs was executed on $1, 2, 3, ..., 8$ cores.

Using the collected data points for each problem size (p_s), the optimize.curve_fit package from *scipy* library in Python was used to fit our model to the collected data. Figure 1 shows the prediction results from the fitted model and the original data for $p_s = 100000$, on 8 cores.

The relative error of the prediction is calculated for each problem size based on Eq. (7), where p_k is the predicted value of the sample k, t_k is the true measured value, and K is the total number of samples.

$$Relative\_error = \frac{1}{K} \sum_{k=1}^{K} |1 - \frac{p_k}{t_k}|$$
(7)

---

[1] https://gist.github.com/shahrzad/b81e1eb252880aca48528d2de0bd1d10.

As discussed earlier, for a specific runtime system, the model parameters α and σ mostly depend on the system architecture and are expected to be constant for different problem sizes as long as they are executed on the same machine. Therefore, we suggest relying on the data collected from one problem size to find parameters α and σ. For this purpose, for problem sizes of 10000, 100000, 1000000, 10000000, 100000000, we used the parameters identified based on the data collected from one specific problem size, to estimate the execution time in terms of grain size and measure the relative error for the same problem size(Fig. 2a) and all other problem sizes(Fig. 2b).

Using the data collected for $p_s = 10000$ to estimate the model parameters generates higher prediction error on other problem sizes, but for other problem sizes we don't see a considerable change in prediction error. Since larger problem sizes require more data to be collected to cover the whole spectrum of grain sizes, $p_s = 100000$ was selected as a reasonable problem size to estimate the model parameters. Fitting our model to all the 512 data points collected for $p_s = 100000$, resulted in model parameters $\alpha = 2.42$ and $\sigma = 0.025$.

We suggest to run the for-loop microbenchmark on the desired system to run our parallel application on, for $p_s = 100000$, to estimate α and σ. Plugging the estimated parameters into Equation (6) would create the analytical model to be used for other balanced parallel for-loop applications executed on the same system.

Our experiments were run on a node consisting of two Intel(R) Xeon E5-2450 CPUs clocked at 2.1 GHZ amounting to a total of 16 cores and 48 GB RAM. Hyper-threading was turned off for the experiment. The versions of HPX used was 1.5.0.

3.2   Identifying the Optimal Range of Grain Size

The graph of execution time in terms of grain size in logarithmic scale, denoted as the *bathtub curve*, can be divided into three regions. We refer to these regions as the left side, the right side, and the flat regions of the graph. Figure 3 shows an example of the flat region of the execution time graph versus grain size in both linear and logarithmic scales. As it can be observed, the flat region contains a very small range of grain sizes.

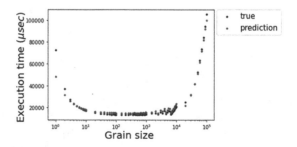

Fig. 1. The results of predicting the execution time based on the proposed model through curve fitting vs the real data for $p_s = 100000$, for 8 cores.

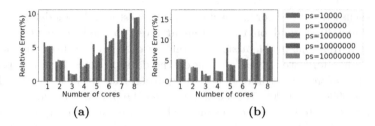

Fig. 2. The relative error of fitting the measured data for different problem sizes on (a) the same problem size and (b) other problem sizes, calculated for each number of cores.

3.2.1 Left Side of the Graph

In Equation (6), for small grain sizes the first term$(\alpha \lceil \frac{n_t}{N} \rceil)$ is the dominant factor while the second term$(t_{seq} \frac{w_{max}}{p_s} (1 + \sigma(M - 1)))$ roughly stays constant. Likewise, for large grain sizes the second factor is the dominant factor.

In order to find the lower-bound of the range for which the execution time stays constant, we can assume that the second factor is constant in that region. Also, we can change N to M, knowing that our concern is on the left side of the graph, where n_t is definitely greater than the number of cores. Taking the derivative of the function based on the grain size leads to:

$$\frac{\partial execution\_time}{\partial g} = \frac{\alpha}{N} \frac{\partial n_t}{\partial g} = \frac{\alpha}{N} \frac{\partial(\frac{p_s}{g})}{\partial g} = \frac{\alpha}{N} p_s \frac{-1}{g^2}. \tag{8}$$

From (8), it can be observed that for the left side of the graph, the rate of change is negative, and it decreases as the grain size increases. Here we are looking for the value of the grain size for which the rate of change becomes very small (we introduce a threshold λ_b, where $0 < \lambda_b \ll 1$, for this purpose).

$$\frac{\alpha}{N} p_s \frac{1}{g^2} \leq \lambda_b \Rightarrow g \geq \sqrt{\frac{\frac{\alpha}{N} p_s}{\lambda_b}} \tag{9}$$

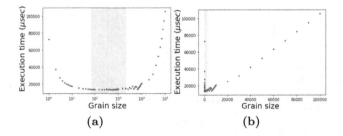

Fig. 3. The results of running the for-loop microbenchmark with $p_s = 100000$, on 8 cores in (a) logarithmic scale, and (b) linear scale.

Equation (9) can also be represented as shown in (10). This representation shows that when the ratio of the time it takes to execute one task to the total overhead of scheduling n_t tasks on N core, is greater than a threshold, we will end up in the flat region of the graph, close to the left side.

$$\frac{\alpha}{N}\frac{p_s}{g}\frac{1}{g} \leq \lambda_b \Rightarrow \frac{g}{\frac{\alpha}{N}n_t} \geq \frac{1}{\lambda_b} \tag{10}$$

3.2.2   Right Side of the Graph

At the right side of the graph, the overhead of creating the tasks is negligible, since only a few tasks are being created and the associated overhead is not significant compared to the execution time. On this side, w_{max} and consequently t_{max} are the dominant factors. In general we can estimate w_{max} with $g\lceil\frac{n_t}{N}\rceil$. There are grain sizes for which $\lceil\frac{n_t}{N}\rceil$ is the same, but w_{max} would be different. For all the values of g that create the same $\lceil\frac{n_t}{N}\rceil$, as g increases, the difference between w_{max} and $\frac{p_s}{N}$ increases. This means that for a range of grain sizes with the same value of $\lceil\frac{n_t}{N}\rceil$, as we get closer to the end of the range, we are observing that a much bigger amount of work is assigned to the core with the maximum amount of work, which would result in a higher execution time.

In the general case, if we denote $\lceil\frac{n_t}{N}\rceil$ as k, then:

$$k-1 < \frac{n_t}{N} = \frac{\left\lceil\frac{p_s}{g}\right\rceil}{N} \leq k \Rightarrow (k-1)N < \frac{p_s}{g} \leq kN. \tag{11}$$

If $k = 1$, then, $0 < \frac{p_s}{g} \leq N$ and therefore $\frac{p_s}{N} \leq g \leq p_s$. Otherwise, when $k > 1$ the following equation can be deduced.

$$\frac{p_s}{kN} \leq g < \frac{p_s}{(k-1)N} \tag{12}$$

Since $\lceil\frac{n_t}{N}\rceil = k$, and $w_{max} = g\lceil\frac{n_t}{N}\rceil = gk$, we can conclude for $k > 1$:

$$0 \leq w_{max} - \frac{p_s}{N} < \frac{1}{k-1}\frac{p_s}{N}. \tag{13}$$

And for $k = 1$, $w_{max} = g$, $n_t \leq N$, therefore $\frac{p_s}{N} \leq g \leq p_s$.

$$0 \leq w_{max} - \frac{p_s}{N} = g - \frac{p_s}{N} \leq (N-1)\frac{p_s}{N} \tag{14}$$

We define a new parameter $imbalance\_ratio$ as $(w_{max} - \frac{p_s}{N})/\frac{p_s}{N}$. Consequently,

$$\begin{cases} 0 \leq imbalance\_ratio \leq N-1 & \text{for } k=1 \\ 0 \leq imbalance\_ratio < \dfrac{1}{k-1} & \text{for } k>1 \end{cases} \tag{15}$$

Equation (15) shows that as the number of created tasks increases, while the number of tasks per core is the same, the imbalance factor decreases.

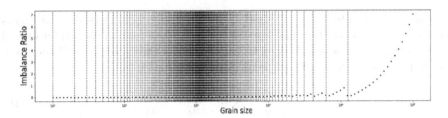

Fig. 4. The imbalance ratio calculated for different grain sizes for $p_s = 10000$, on 8 cores. At the area between each two green lines $k = \lceil \frac{n_t}{N} \rceil$ is constant.

Figure 4 shows how imbalance ratio changes for different grain sizes for $p_s = 10000$, on 8 cores. Each of the regions between two dashed green lines correspond to a specific value for $k = \lceil \frac{n_t}{N} \rceil$.

At each of the regions with $k > 1$, $\lceil \frac{n_t}{N} \rceil = k$, *imbalance_ratio* starts from 0 and approaches $\frac{1}{k-1}$ at the end of the region. When $k = 1$, *imbalance_ratio* increases linearly starting from 0 and reaching the maximum of $N - 1$ when $g = p_s$. As we move to larger grain sizes, $\lceil \frac{n_t}{N} \rceil$ decreases. We define a threshold, λ_s ($0 < \lambda_s < 1$), so that for *imbalance_ratios* smaller than this threshold, the imbalance effect is not considered significant. Our goal would then become finding the maximum grain size that would generate a reasonable imbalance (*imbalance_ratio* $\leq \lambda_s$), to make sure we should stay in the flat region of the bathtub curve of execution time against grain size.

Equation (14) states that for grain sizes greater than $\frac{p_s}{N}$, *imbalance_ratio* increases linearly with grain size from 0 to $N - 1$. While for grain sizes smaller than p_s, the maximum *imbalance_ratio* depends on $k = \lceil \frac{n_t}{N} \rceil$. To ensure *imbalance_ratio* is smaller than or equal to a threshold (λ_s), first we search the grain sizes smaller than $\frac{p_s}{N}$. Since $0 < \lambda_s < 1$, and $k \geq 2$ in this region, there exists a k such that $\frac{1}{k-1} \leq \lambda_s$.

If there exists a k_{min}, for which *imbalance_ratio* $< \frac{1}{k_{min}-1}$, where $\frac{1}{k_{min}-1} \leq \lambda_s$, then $\forall k < k_{min}$, maximum value of *imbalance_ratio* would be greater than λ_s. To find the grain size that creates maximum *imbalance_ratio* of λ_s:

$$imbalance\_ratio \leq \lambda_s \implies \frac{1}{k-1} \leq \lambda_s \implies k_{min} = \left\lceil 1 + \frac{1}{\lambda_s} \right\rceil + 1 \qquad (16)$$

Based on Equation (13), $g < \frac{p_s}{(k_{min}-1)N}$, and therefore:

$$g_{max} = \frac{p_s}{(k_{min}-1)N} - 1 = \frac{p_s}{(1 + \lceil \frac{1}{\lambda_s} \rceil)N} \qquad (17)$$

If $g < g_{max}$, we can ensure that *imbalance_ratio* never exceeds λ_s. Since we already found a match at grain sizes smaller than $\frac{p_s}{N}$, checking the rest of grain sizes would not be necessary.

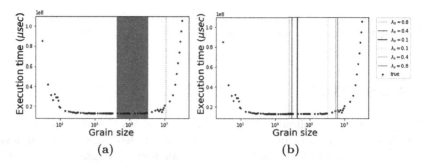

Fig. 5. (a)The identified range of grain sizes for $p_s = 100000000$ on 8 cores, with $\lambda_b = 0.01$ and $\lambda_s = 0.1$. The gray dashed line represents the grain size where work is equally divided among the cores, $\frac{p_s}{N}$. (b) The effect of λ_b and λ_s on the borders of the identified region for minimum execution time.

3.3 Identifying the Range of Grain Sizes for Minimum Execution Time

In the previous section, we introduced a method to identify the lower-bound and upper-bound of grain sizes for which we expect to observe the minimum execution time. Integrating Eq. (9) and Eq. (17) suggests the following range for minimum execution time, Where $0 \le \lambda_s \le 1$, and $\lambda_b, \lambda_s \ll 1$:

$$\sqrt{\frac{(\frac{\alpha}{N})p_s}{\lambda_b}} \le g \le \frac{p_s}{(1 + \lceil \frac{1}{\lambda_s} \rceil)N}. \tag{18}$$

Here λ_b indicates the slope of the graph at the left side of the graph where overhead of tasks is the dominant factor. Grain sizes smaller than $\sqrt{((\frac{\alpha}{N})p_s)/\lambda_b}$ would create a slope of more than λ_b. As for λ_s, a grain size greater than $\frac{p_s}{(1+\lceil \frac{1}{\lambda_s} \rceil)N}$ could generate an *imbalance_ratio* of greater than λ_s.

3.4 Locating the Flat Region of the Execution Time vs Grain Size Graph for the For-Loop Microbenchmark

In this section we used Eq. (18) to identify the flat region of the execution time vs grain size graph for the parallel for-loop microbenchmark. For this purpose, we set both λ_b and λ_s to 0.1.

In Fig. 5a the identified region for minimum execution time is shown in green, for $p_s = 10000000$, executed on 8 cores.

Selecting a greater value for λ_b would move the left border of the region to left, for a larger acceptable slope of change of execution time in terms of grain size. On the other hand, selecting a smaller value for λ_s would result in shifting the right border of the region to left, imposing a higher restriction on *imbalance_ratio*, as shown in Fig. 5b. λ_b and λ_s could be selected depending on how strict one wants to be in terms of slope of changes and imbalance ratio. In the meanwhile, based on our experiments we suggest $\lambda_b = 0.01$ and $\lambda_s = 0.1$ as reasonable values for

4   Related Work

Akhmetova et al. [1] utilized a system emulator to study the effect of task granularity in system performance. They also provide an algorithm to automatically aggregate tasks into larger tasks based on the calculated task granularity in order to improve the performance.

Grubel et al. also study the effect of the task size on performance of HPX applications[6]. They suggest using a number of performance metrics in order to identify the optimum grain size to improve the adaptivity at runtime.

In [13], the authors use thresholds to decide on whether to inline a task or not at runtime. The imposed threshold for task inlining on a specific architecture then converts into the problem to what portion of the execution time of the task should be spent for scheduling the task, so that it would be worth to be executed as a separate task. This is in compliance with our findings in this paper for λ_b, as shown in Eq. (10), where we suggest in order to land in the flat region of the execution time versus grain size graph, the ratio of the grain size over the scheduling overhead of one task on one core should be greater than the given threshold.

5   Conclusions and Future Work

In this paper we discussed the importance of task granularity on the achievable performance in AMTs. We offered an analytical model for execution time of a parallel application with a balanced for-loop, in terms of grain size and the number of cores. A for-loop microbenchmark was developed to validate this model and, a method has been provided to estimate the range of grain sizes to achieve the minimum execution time. At the next step, we suggested that we can use the developed for-loop microbenchmark with a fixed problem size to find the model parameters of a runtime system on a specific architecture. The identified parameters can then build the analytical model for arbitrary balanced parallel for-loop applications on the same machine.

For simplification and due to the nature of the for-loop microbenchmark we based our work on, we had ignored the κ parameter in USL model. For future work, we would like to study the effect of this parameter on both execution time and the upper-bound for the identified range.

Acknowledgment. The authors are grateful for the support of this work by the LSU Center for Computation & Technology and by the DTIC project: Phylanx Engine Enhancement and Visualizations Development (Contract Number: FA8075-14-D-0002/0007).

References

1. Akhmetova, D., Kestor, G., Gioiosa, R., Markidis, S., Laure, E.: On the application task granularity and the interplay with the scheduling overhead in many-core shared memory systems. In: 2015 IEEE International Conference on Cluster Computing, pp. 428–437. IEEE (2015)
2. Amdahl, G.M.: Validity of the single processor approach to achieving large scale computing capabilities. In: Proceedings of the Spring Joint Computer Conference, 18–20 April 1967, pp. 483–485. ACM (1967)
3. Bennett, J., et al.: Asynchronous many-task runtime system analysis and assessment for next generation platforms. US Department of Energy, Sandia National Laboratories Report, Rep. no. SAND2015-8312 (2015)
4. Gao, G.R., Sterling, T., Stevens, R., Hereld, M., Zhu, W.: Parallex: a study of a new parallel computation model. In: 2007 IEEE International Parallel and Distributed Processing Symposium, pp. 1–6. IEEE (2007)
5. Grama, A., Kumar, V., Gupta, A., Karypis, G.: Introduction to Parallel Computing. Pearson Education, Boston (2003)
6. Grubel, P., Kaiser, H., Cook, J., Serio, A.: The performance implication of task size for applications on the HPX runtime system. In: 2015 IEEE International Conference on Cluster Computing, pp. 682–689. IEEE (2015)
7. Grubel, P., Kaiser, H., Huck, K., Cook, J.: Using intrinsic performance counters to assess efficiency in task-based parallel applications. In: 2016 IEEE International Parallel and Distributed Processing Symposium Workshops (IPDPSW), pp. 1692–1701. IEEE (2016)
8. Gunther, N.J.: The practical performance analyst. iuniverse. com inc. Lincoln, Nebraska (2000)
9. Gunther, N.J.: What is Guerrilla Capacity Planning? Springer, Heidelberg (2007). https://doi.org/10.1007/978-3-540-31010-5_1
10. Kaiser, H., Brodowicz, M., Sterling, T.: Parallex an advanced parallel execution model for scaling-impaired applications. In: 2009 International Conference on Parallel Processing Workshops, pp. 394–401. IEEE (2009)
11. Kaiser, H., Heller, T., Adelstein-Lelbach, B., Serio, A., Fey, D.: HPX: a task based programming model in a global address space. In: Proceedings of the 8th International Conference on Partitioned Global Address Space Programming Models, p. 6. ACM (2014)
12. Kulkarni, A., Lumsdaine, A.: A comparative study of asynchronous many-tasking runtimes: Cilk, charm++, parallex and am++. arXiv preprint arXiv:1904.00518 (2019)
13. Wagle, B., Monil, M.A.H., Huck, K., Malony, A.D., Serio, A., Kaiser, H.: Runtime adaptive task inlining on asynchronous multitasking runtime systems. In: Proceedings of the 48th International Conference on Parallel Processing, pp. 1–10 (2019)

An Experimental Study of SYCL Task Graph Parallelism for Large-Scale Machine Learning Workloads

Cheng-Hsiang Chiu$^{(\boxtimes)}$, Dian-Lun Lin, and Tsung-Wei Huang

University of Utah, Salt Lake City, UT, USA
{cheng-hsiang.chiu,dian-lun.lin,tsung-wei.huang}@utah.edu

Abstract. Task graph parallelism has emerged as an important tool to efficiently execute large machine learning workloads on GPUs. Users describe a GPU workload in a *task dependency graph* rather than aggregated GPU operations and dependencies, allowing the runtime to run whole-graph scheduling optimization to significantly improve the performance. While the new *CUDA graph* execution model has demonstrated significant success on this front, the counterpart for SYCL, a general-purpose heterogeneous programming model using standard C++, remains nascent. Unlike CUDA graph, the SYCL runtime leverages out-of-order queues to implicitly create a task execution graph induced by data dependencies. For explicit task dependencies, users are responsible for creating SYCL events and synchronizing them at a non-negligible cost. Furthermore, there is no specialized graph execution model that allows users to offload a task graph directly onto a SYCL device in a similar way to CUDA graph. This paper conducts an experimental study of SYCL's default task graph parallelism by comparing it with CUDA graph on large-scale machine learning workloads in the recent HPEC Graph Challenge. Our result highlights the need for a new SYCL graph execution model in the standard.

Keywords: CUDA Graph · Task graph parallelism · High performance computing

1 Introduction

Modern GPUs are fast and, in many scenarios, the time taken by each GPU operation (e.g., kernel or memory copy) is now measured in microseconds. The overheads associated with the submission of each operation to the GPU, also at the microsecond scale, are becoming significant and can dominate the performance of a GPU algorithm. For instance, inferencing a large neural network launches many dependent kernels on partitioned data and models. If each of these operations is launched to the GPU separately and repetitively, the overheads can combine to form a significant overall degradation to performance.

© Springer Nature Switzerland AG 2022
R. Chaves et al. (Eds.): Euro-Par 2021, LNCS 13098, pp. 468–479, 2022.
https://doi.org/10.1007/978-3-031-06156-1_37

To overcome the overheads of kernel calls, CUDA has recently introduced a new graph programming model, namely *CUDA graph* [20], that allows users to describe a large GPU workload in a single task graph and offload the task graph directly onto a GPU using a single CPU call. This new execution model opens several exciting opportunities for further accelerating the performance of large-scale machine learning workloads that compose thousands of GPU operations (i.g., kernels and memory copies). For instance, the recent research at 2021 Nvidia GTC has shown over 3× performance improvement in TensorFlow by replacing stream-based execution with CUDA graph [23]. In the same line, our research of CUDA graph has achieved 2× speed-up over existing stream-based solutions in completing the inference workloads of large sparse deep neural networks (DNN) that compose more than 46K GPU operations and 69K dependencies [17].

In addition to CUDA, SYCL [16] has emerged as a promising alternative to GPU programming using completely standard C++. As more ML systems start leveraging SYCL to design their back-ends (e.g., Intel oneAPI [15]), enabling direct task graph parallelism on a SYCL device is a high priority for efficiently executing large-scale machine learning workloads that define thousands of GPU operations and dependencies. The default SYCL runtime counts on an *out-of-order* queue to dynamically construct a task execution graph for submitted kernels described in *command group function objects*. Task dependencies are implicitly inferred from data dependencies extracted from *accessor* objects. In a unified shared memory (USM) [7,22] environment where accessors are not required, users must explicitly construct dependencies between submitted tasks and synchronize their events. This organization adds burdens to developers and can be error-prone because of tedious event management.

Consequently, this paper introduces a high-level programming interface called *syclFlow* [21] to express task graph parallelism with SYCL. We leverage the out-of-order property of the SYCL queue to design a simple and efficient scheduling algorithm using topological sort. We compare the performance of syclFlow with CUDA graph on a large-scale machine learning workload from the HPEC Sparse DNN Inference Challenge [11]. The largest DNN model spans 1920 layers each of 65536 neurons and composes over 46K GPU operations to complete the inference loop. Under the same kernel algorithm, SYCL can be up to 5× slower than CUDA graph as a result of execution overheads (e.g., submission calls, event synchronizations). The experiment results highlight the need for a new SYCL graph execution model that allows explicit task graph parallelism on a SYCL device.

2   The Proposed SYCL Task Graph Programming Model

Our SYCL task graph programming model, *syclFlow*, enables users to describe workloads in a *task dependency graph*. Once a task graph is given, we schedule and submit dependent tasks to the SYCL runtime using out-of-order queue and event synchronization.

2.1   Task Graph Construction in SyclFlow

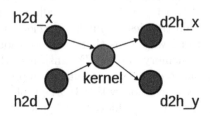

Fig. 1. An example of GPU task graph. There are one kernel, denoted in a red circle, and four memory copies, denoted in blue circles.

syclFlow allows users to construct a task dependency graph using standard C++17 and SYCL20 based on USM. Figure 1 illustrates a GPU task graph of five tasks (one kernel, **kernel**, two host-to-device memory copies, **h2d_x** and **h2d_y**, and two device-to-host memory copies, **d2h_x**, and **d2h_y**) and four dependencies. Listing 1.1 implements Fig. 1 using the proposed syclFlow programming model. We create a syclFlow object (**sf**), use **parallel_for** and **copy** to construct five task graph nodes, and relate the dependencies between nodes using **precede** and **succeed**. The code explains itself, inspired by our Taskflow project [12].

Listing 1.1. Example code of Figure 1 using syclFlow.

```
syclFlow sf;
syclTask h2d_x = sf.copy(dx, hx, size);
syclTask h2d_y = sf.copy(dy, hy, size);
syclTask kernel = sf.parallel_for(dx, dy);
syclTask d2h_x = sf.copy(hx, dx, size);
syclTask d2h_y = sf.copy(hy, dy, size);
kernel.succeed(h2d_x, h2d_y);
kernel.precede(d2h_x, d2h_y);
```

2.2   Task Graph Scheduling in SyclFlow

Since syclFlow uses SYCL's out-of-order queue in which the SYCL runtime may not schedule tasks in the same order of their submissions, we have to schedule a user's task dependency graph before submitting tasks to SYCL. Algorithm 1 presents our scheduler. In Line 1, we apply topological sort algorithm to sort a user's task dependency graph and get the sorted graph in T. In Lines 2–4, we submit each task to the queue and get an event back. In Line 5, we synchronize the whole execution by **queue.wait**. This scheduling is the notable overhead that syclFlow has on top of SYCL. Please refer to Sect. 3 for detailed runtime breakdown. Algorithm 2 briefs the **submit** function. In Line 1, we declare a command group function object for a task. In Lines 2–4, we use **depends_on** to specify the dependencies between the task and its dependents and encapsulate the dependencies together with the task in the command group function object. In Line 5, we return the command group function object as an event.

Algorithm 1: syclFlow's scheduler

Input: G: syclFlow task dependency graph defined by users
Input: $queue$: a SYCL queue associated with a SYCL device
1 $T \leftarrow$ topological_sort(G)
2 **for** $task \in T$ **do**
3 $\quad |\quad task.event = queue.submit(task)$
4 **end**
5 $queue.wait()$

Algorithm 2: queue.submit

Input: $task$: a user's task
1 $cgf \leftarrow$ create_command_group_function_object$(task)$
2 **for** $p \in task.dependents$ **do**
3 $\quad |\quad cgf.depends\_on(p.event)$
4 **end**
5 return_event(cgf)

Listing 1.2. Example code of syclFlow::on to directly create a SYCL task.

```
syclFlow sf;
syclTask task = sf.on(
  [=](sycl::handler& handler) {
    handler.require(accessor);
    handler.single_task([=](){
      data[0] = 1;
    });
  }
);
```

Figure 2 demonstrates how syclFlow offloads a task dependency graph to a SYCL device and interacts with the SYCL runtime using an out-of-order queue and the **depends_on** method to schedule dependent tasks. The SYCL runtime schedules the submitted command group function objects and implicitly constructs its task graph based on submitted events.

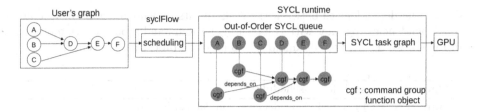

Fig. 2. syclFlow offloads a user-specified task dependency graph to a SYCL device. The SYCL runtime schedules command group function objects from out-of-order queue and constructs a task graph based on submitted events. Every arrow between two cgfs denotes a dependency using `depends_on` method.

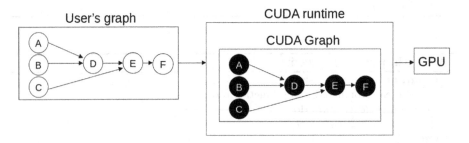

Fig. 3. Transformation of a user's task dependency graph to CUDA graph.

syclFlow also allows users to exploit the full functionality of SYCL using **on** method to directly create a SYCL task from a command group object. Listing 1.2 demonstrates the usage of **on** which takes a command group object to perform a task assigning a constant value, 1, to the element in a data array.

It is worth noting that the CUDA graph execution model is very different from the SYCL runtime, as shown in Fig. 3. The CUDA runtime directly transforms a given CUDA graph into an executable graph in no need of additional user-level scheduling. This organization also allows the CUDA runtime to perform whole-graph optimization to significantly improve the performance. The synchronization overhead is minimized because CUDA graph does not synchronize tasks but the whole graph at once. That is, the synchronization overhead is limited to the number of CUDA graph submissions rather than the size of the graph.

3   Experimental Results

We demonstrate the significance of GPU task graph parallelism on large-scale machine learning workloads. The goal of this experiment is to highlight the need for a new SYCL graph execution model that does not require additional scheduling at the user level. We base our experiment on IEEE HPEC Sparse Deep Neural Network Inference Challenge [11]. The challenge is to speed up the computation of inference on extremely large DNNs. Table 1 shows the statistics of the benchmarks. We leverage the award-winning algorithm [17] to design our SYCL kernels and task graph parallelism with syclFlow. Figure 4 shows a partial task graph of our algorithm. We run the experiments on a Ubuntu Linux 20.04.2 LTS (Focal Fossa) x86 64-bit machine with Intel(R) Core(TM) i7-9700K Processor at 3.6 GHz, one GeForce RTX 2080 GPU with 8 GB memory, and 32 GB RAM. All programs are compiled by using Nvidia CUDA nvcc 11.1 on a host compiler of DPC++ clang [6] with C++17 standards.

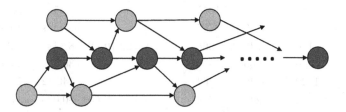

Fig. 4. Schematic view of a partial task graph in the inference workload based on our algorithm in [17]. A blue node represents a memory copy, and a red node denotes a kernel. The entire task graph on the largest DNN composes 3K tasks and 5K dependencies.

Performance Comparison. Table 1 compares the elapsed runtime (in seconds) between syclFlow and CUDA graph on executing 12 DNN models using one GPU. The execution time of syclFlow is longer than CUDA graph across all models. For example, in the DNN model of 4096 neurons and 1920 layers, it takes 26.32 s for syclFlow to complete, whereas CUDA graph can finish in 19.66 s. In addition, the gap between syclFlow and CUDA graph keeps increasing as we enlarge the size of the DNN models. For instance, in the largest model of 65536 neurons and 480 layers, syclFlow is more than 5× slower than CUDA graph. Figure 5 visualizes the trend.

Synchronization Overhead. Figure 6 lists the number of event synchronizations of syclFlow and CUDA graph on completing the inference of the DNN models with 1024 neurons. The default number of batch iterations in the inference loop is 12 [17]. Since CUDA graph constructs the graph only once when users submit a task dependency graph to the CUDA runtime, the number of event synchronizations is equal to the number of submissions. However, syclFlow requires frequent synchronizations between the user-level scheduler and the SYCL runtime. The number of synchronized events grows as we increase the number of layers in the DNN model, which in turn increases the size of the syclFlow graph. Figure 7 details the runtime breakdown of syclFlow and CUDA graph. We can easily see that in syclFlow event synchronizations consume 41%, which is as much as the kernel activities. While in CUDA graph, synchronization only costs 1.33%.

Table 1. Comparison of the total execution time between syclFlow and cudaGraph for completing 12 DNN models.

Model					syclFlow	cudaGraph
#Neurons	#Layers	#Tasks	#Dependencies	Size	Time	Time
1024	120	246	364	1.25 GB	0.55 s	0.47 s
	480	966	1444		1.86 s	1.53 s
	1920	3846	5764		6.98 s	5.79 s
4096	120	246	364	5.40 GB	1.96 s	1.48 s
	480	966	1444		6.85 s	5.11 s
	1920	3846	5764		26.32 s	19.66 s
16384	120	246	364	22.70 GB	8.94 s	4.36 s
	480	966	1444		30.51 s	14.82 s
	1920	3846	5764		146.82 s	57.23 s
65536	120	246	364	94.70 GB	80.08 s	17.29 s
	480	966	1444		273.29 s	51.92 s
	1920	3846	5764		> 600 s	162.20 s

Need for a New SYCL Graph Model. While we can devise a way to program and execute task graphs using the current SYCL standards (e.g., out-of-order queue, event synchronizations), this experiment highlights a critical need for a new SYCL graph execution model which allows us to *directly* offload task graph parallelism onto a SYCL device. This is especially important for accelerating large-scale machine learning workloads. Specifically, modern GPUs are very fast and the overhead of kernel calls and user-level scheduling have become very expensive in many machine learning task graphs that compose thousands of dependent GPU operators. These task graphs normally do not change once the neural network architecture is decided, and there is no need to repetitively offload the same task graph using expensive host function calls and scheduling methods.

4   Related Work

Task graph-based programming models have received much attention over the last few years. Taskflow [12] develops a simple and powerful task programming model, which enables efficient implementations of heterogeneous decomposition strategies and leverages both static and dynamic task graph constructions to incorporate computational patterns. PaRSEC [2] expresses applications as DAG of tasks with labeled edges designating data dependencies. It provides a generic framework for architecture-aware scheduling and management of micro-tasks on distributed many-core heterogeneous architectures. Kokkos's functional approaches [8] provide task graph constructions. It allows applications to achieve performance portability on diverse many-core architectures. Legion [1] describes a runtime system that dynamically extracts parallelism from Legion

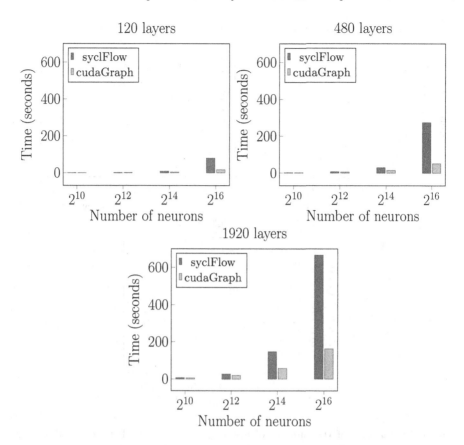

Fig. 5. Comparison of execution time between syclFlow and CUDA graph on different DNN models. The performance gap between syclFlow and CUDA graph increases as we enlarge the DNN model sizes.

programs, using a distributed, parallel scheduling algorithm that identifies both independent tasks and nested parallelism. While these frameworks offer means to describe heterogeneous workloads in different forms of task graphs, they do not target direct task graph parallelism on a GPU.

CUDA graph is one of the early programming models that allow users to program task graph directly on a GPU. There are two ways to program a CUDA graph, explicit graph construction and implicit stream capturing. Explicit CUDA graph construction is often the most efficient, but it requires all the parameters known upfront, which is impossible for many high-performance third-party libraries, such as cuSparse [5], cuBLAS [4], and cuDNN [19]. The second option is implicit graph construction, which captures a CUDA graph using existing stream-based application programming interfaces (APIs). Implicit CUDA graph construction is more flexible and general, allowing users to manually allocate and control streams. However, it requires users to wrangle with concurrency details

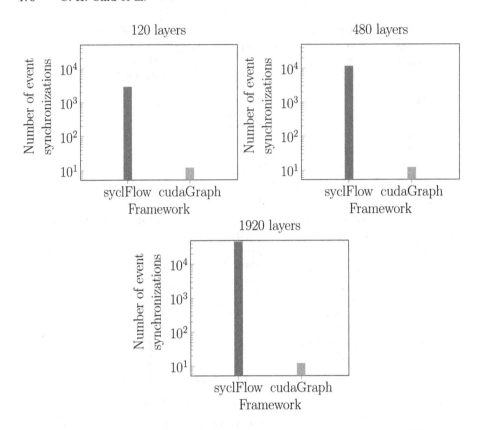

Fig. 6. Comparison of the number of event synchronizations between syclFlow and CUDA graph on DNN models with 1024 neurons. As the models increment, the synchronization overhead keeps the same for CUDA graph, whereas syclFlow suffers seriously from the overhead.

through events and streams that are known difficult to program correctly. To simplify CUDA graph programming, Lin and Huang propose a unified interface coupled with an optimization method to program CUDA graph in both explicit and implicit modes [18].

SYCL is a programming model that allows users to write C++ single-source heterogeneous code. Users submit tasks to an out-of-order queue that is associated with a SYCL device (e.g., CPU, GPU, FPGA). The SYCL runtime schedules tasks from the out-of-order queue and constructs their dependencies based on user-specified events and/or data dependencies from buffer accessor objects. This type of task parallelism is different from CUDA graph, which takes the whole graph to schedule and performs whole-graph optimization to reduce overheads of synchronization and kernel calls.

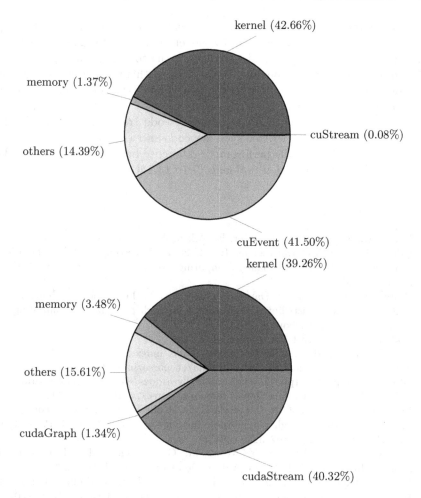

Fig. 7. Runtime breakdown of syclFlow (on the top, 1320.72 ms in total) and CUDA graph (on the bottom, 1097.44 ms in total) on a model with 120 layers and 1024 neurons. Kernel refers to the kernel activities, memory includes memory copy and memory set, cuEvent presents event-related APIs, cuStream contains stream-related APIs, cudaGraph denotes all of the APIs associated with cudaGraph, and cudaStream covers APIs about cudaStream.

5   Conclusion

In this paper, we have introduced syclFlow to enable efficient task graph programming using standard C++ and SYCL. We have compared the performance of syclFlow using the default task graph parallelism of the SYCL runtime with the new CUDA graph programming model on large-scale machine learning workloads. The experiments have shown that offloading task graph parallelism directly on a GPU can have a significant impact on the performance. For example, at the largest model of over 46K dependent GPU operations, CUDA graph can outperform syclFlow more than 5× faster. This paper signals a need for a new SYCL graph execution model that allows us to offload task graph parallelism directly on a SYCL device. At the time of this writing, we are actively collaborating with Codeplay [3] to design a new SYCL Graph standard through Khronos [16].

Our future work plans to design a source-code translation algorithm that automatically translates a written syclFlow code into a CUDA graph equivalent. We also plan to measure the performance difference between SYCL and CUDA graph in large-scale simulation problems [9,10,13,14].

References

1. Bauer, M., Treichler, S., Slaughter, E., Aiken, A.: Legion: expressing locality and independence with logical regions. In: SC 2012: Proceedings of the International Conference on High Performance Computing, Networking, Storage and Analysis, pp. 1–11. IEEE (2012)
2. Bosilca, G., Bouteiller, A., Danalis, A., Herault, T., Lemariner, P., Dongarra, J.: DAGuE: a generic distributed DAG engine for high performance computing, pp. 1151–1158. IEEE, Anchorage (2011)
3. Codeplay Software Ltd. https://codeplay.com
4. cuBLAS. https://docs.nvidia.com/cuda/cublas/index.html
5. cuSPARSE. https://docs.nvidia.com/cuda/cusparse/index.html
6. DPC++ Compiler. https://intel.github.io/llvm-docs/GetStartedGuide.html
7. DPC++ Reference: Unified Shared Memory. https://reurl.cc/5oYVOz
8. Edwards, H.C., Trott, C.R., Sunderland, D.: Kokkos: enabling manycore performance portability through polymorphic memory access patterns. J. Parallel Distrib. Comput. **74**(12), 3202–3216 (2014)
9. Guo, G., Huang, T.W., Lin, Y., Wong, M.: GPU-accelerated path-based timing analysis. In: ACM/IEEE Design Automation Conference (DAC) (2021)
10. Guo, Z., Huang, T.W., Lin, Y.: GPU-accelerated static timing analysis. In: IEEE/ACM International Conference on Computer-aided Design (ICCAD), pp. 1–8 (2020)
11. HPEC Sparse Deep Neural Network Inference Challenge. https://graphchallenge.mit.edu/challenges
12. Huang, T.W., Lin, C.X., Guo, G., Wong, M.: Cpp-taskflow: fast task-based parallel programming using modern c++. In: 2019 IEEE International Parallel and Distributed Processing Symposium (IPDPS), pp. 974–983. IEEE (2019)
13. Huang, T.W., Lin, C.X., Wong, M.D.F.: OpenTimer v2: a parallel incremental timing analysis engine. IEEE Trans. Comput.-Aided Des. Integr. Circ. Syst. (TCAD) **40**(4), 776–789 (2021)
14. Huang, T.W., Wong, M.: OpenTimer: a high-performance timing analysis tool. In: IEEE/ACM International Conference on Computer-aided Design (ICCAD), pp. 895–902 (2015)
15. Intel oneAPI. https://reurl.cc/2bpNzX
16. Khronos SYCL group. https://www.khronos.org/sycl/
17. Lin, D.L., Huang, T.W.: A novel inference algorithm for large sparse neural network using task graph parallelism. In: 2020 IEEE High Performance Extreme Computing Conference (HPEC), pp. 1–7. IEEE (2020)

18. Lin, D.L., Huang, T.W.: Efficient GPU computation using task graph parallelism. In: 2021 IEEE/ACM European Conference on Parallel and Distributed Computing. IEEE (2021)
19. NVIDIA cdDNN. https://developer.nvidia.com/cudnn
20. NVIDIA CUDA Graph. https://developer.nvidia.com/blog/cuda-graphs/
21. syclFlow. https://taskflow.github.io/taskflow/GPUTaskingsyclFlow.html
22. Unified Shared Memory. https://reurl.cc/WElyRx
23. Yao, J., Li, C.: CUDA graph in TensorFlow. In: Nvidia GPU Technology Conference (GTC) (2021)

FleCSI 2.0: The Flexible Computational Science Infrastructure Project

Ben Bergen[1]($\boxtimes$), Irina Demeshko[1]($\boxtimes$), Charles Ferenbaugh[1], Davis Herring[2]($\boxtimes$),
Li-Ta Lo[1], Julien Loiseau[1], Navamita Ray[1], and Andrew Reisner[1]

[1] Applied Computer Science Group (CCS-7), Los Alamos National Laboratory,
Los Alamos, NM 87545, USA
{bergen,irina,cferenbaugh,ollie,jloiseau,nray,areisner}@lanl.gov
[2] Lagrangian Codes Group (XCP-1), Los Alamos National Laboratory,
Los Alamos, NM 87545, USA
herring@lanl.gov

Abstract. The FleCSI 2.0 programming system supports multiphysics application development through a runtime abstraction layer, and by providing core topology types that can be customized for specific numerical methods. The abstraction layer provides a single-source programming interface for distributed and shared-memory data parallelism through *task* and *kernel* execution, and has been demonstrated to introduce virtually no runtime overhead. FleCSI's core topology types represent a rich set of basic data structures that can be specialized to create application-facing interfaces for a variety of different physics packages. Using the FleCSI control and data models, it is straightforward to compose multiple packages to create full multiphysics applications. When used with a task-based backend, FleCSI offers extended runtime analysis that can increase task concurrency, facilitate load balancing, and allow for portability across heterogeneous computing architectures.

Keywords: Multiphysics · Computational science · Applied mathematics · Task-based runtimes · Heterogeneity · Performance portability · Accelerators

1 Introduction

FleCSI is a C++ framework designed to support multiphysics application development through a runtime abstraction layer and a collection of useful topology and data types. Many of these capabilities take the form of class and function templates whose behavior is customized by application-specific functions and data and policy types. The abstraction layer insulates developers from underlying complexity, while providing a single-source, integrated programming model that is mapped on top of different low-level backends. FleCSI introduces a functional programming model with runtime, control, execution, and data abstractions that are consistent both with MPI [11] and with state-of-the-art, task-based backends

© Springer Nature Switzerland AG 2022
R. Chaves et al. (Eds.): Euro-Par 2021, LNCS 13098, pp. 480–495, 2022.
https://doi.org/10.1007/978-3-031-06156-1_38

such as Legion [3] and HPX [14]. When configured with one of the task-based backends, FleCSI provides dynamic scheduling of data and task placement for increased concurrency and application performance.

1.1 Structure

This paper describes the main features and goals of the FleCSI 2.0 programming system. It provides an overview and examples of the programming model and its components. These are explained in Sect. 2. Brief descriptions of the core topology types are given in Sect. 3. In Sect. 4, two sample applications that use FleCSI 2.0, *Model for Prediction Across Scales (MPAS)* and *FleCSPH* are discussed. Some performance results regarding runtime overhead of the abstraction layer are presented in Sect. 4.3, with concluding remarks and future work in Sect. 5.

1.2 Related Work

FleCSI is a *unified* runtime in the sense that it supports a single interface for programming both the distributed and shared-memory components of modern computing systems. Two similarly unified programming systems are *Uintah* [12] and the *Multi-Processor Computing runtime (MPC)* [17].

Like FleCSI, Uintah uses a task-based runtime for distributed-memory execution. However, Uintah's task concurrency must be explicitly scheduled by the user. MPC transparently enables shared-memory support with MPI through an *MPI+X* programming model. A significant feature of MPC is its ability to run MPI processes *inside* of threads. This approach can reduce message latency (*memcpy* of messages), and requires fewer communication endpoints. The primary advantage of FleCSI over these systems is that, under FleCSI, tasks and data can be dynamically mapped to compute resources (when using a task-based backend), while Uintah and MPC both employ a static mapping aligned with the runtime processes, i.e., ranks.

2 Programming Model

The FleCSI 2.0 programming model provides explicit runtime, control, data, and execution models that are designed to provide users with a rich environment for application development on state-of-the-art heterogeneous system architectures. These are described in the following sections.

2.1 Runtime Model

The runtime model is how you control the FleCSI runtime system itself. The basic interface includes the functions: `initialize`, `start`, and `finalize`. These are abstractions of the underlying runtime interfaces, e.g., Legion, MPI, HPX, and Kokkos [9], whereby the correct combination of start-up, execution, and shut-down processes will be invoked, depending on the configuration of FleCSI. The runtime model also provides support for creating command-line options, a logging utility called *flog*, and a timing and profiling interface to Caliper [6].

This model will be extended in a future feature release to provide a richer set of options to allow more precise placement of processes and memory allocations in order to address the performance challenges of running on modern, heterogeneous architectures that have deep, complex memory hierarchies, and which require exploitation of processor–memory affinities to achieve the best throughput.

2.2   Control Model

The FleCSI control model is how the overall execution structure of a FleCSI-based program is defined. FleCSI provides a core control type that can be customized with specialization-defined control points (the skeleton of the application structure). Application developers register actions under the control points, which may have dependencies on each other. FleCSI sorts the actions under a control point to create a runtime program order. Along with *tasks* and *kernels* (parts of the execution model), the control model forms an execution hierarchy with the following relationships:

- **Control Points:** Identify the high-level stages of the application. The execution order of the control points is statically defined. Cycles may be defined over any subset of the control points. The control points form a *control-flow graph (CFG)*.
- **Actions:** Registered under control points. Any two actions under a single control point may have a dependency defined between them. The actions under a single control point form a *directed acyclic graph (DAG)*. Actions allow composition of *contributed* packages. Actions are always executed in a sequential program order defined by: 1.) the order of the control points, and then 2.) the topologically sorted order of the DAG of actions under each control point.
- **Tasks:** Executed from inside of an action. Task launch may be *single* or *index*. Tasks operate on data that are logically distributed over a partitioned address space. Dependency analysis (Legion backend only) allows tasks to be executed concurrently by the runtime. A given *point task* may be executed on any runtime process on any address space (Legion backend only).
- **Kernels:** Executed from inside of a task. Kernels execute data-parallel operations over a local address space. Memory consistency of kernel execution is explicit (*relaxed-consistency*).

This model replaces the normal hard-coded execution structure of an application, instead providing a well-defined, extensible mechanism that can easily be verified and visualized. Figure 1 shows output from a FleCSI-based program using the command-line argument --control-model.

The primary advantage of this approach is that FleCSI-based applications can add new actions to any of the DAGs in the model, with associated dependencies, without requiring modification to the core application code. Because of FleCSI's data model (discussed in Sect. 2.3) these new actions will fold seamlessly into the existing control structure, allowing extensibility and experimentation.

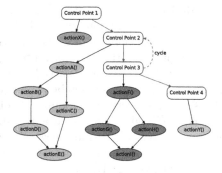

Fig. 1. Example FleCSI control model.

2.3   Data Model

Because FleCSI tasks may be executed on any memory space, all the application's data must be managed by the runtime so that a copy of it may be made available in that memory space and any changes propagated to the next task needing it. (Global variables may also be used, but only for information that is constant across and throughout the simulation, since which process executes which task is arbitrary.) The FleCSI data model closely follows the Legion model, but with some simplifications and elaborations described in the following subsections. Legion provides a data model based on associative arrays called *regions* whose multi-index keys are called *index points*. The domain of keys is called an *index space*, which may have an arbitrary shape but for performance reasons is often hyperrectangular.

A region is a collective object whose storage is typically distributed across multiple memory spaces. A *partition* is a collection of subsets of an index space (or a region based on it) that may be mapped separately; the collection is indexed with integer *colors*, and each subset is called a *subspace*. Multiple unrelated partitions of a single region may exist; it is often the case that the subsets in each are disjoint, that their union is the entire region, or both. In particular, tasks that operate on disjoint subsets can write to them in parallel; read-only access to subsets that overlap those from different partitions can be used to automatically transfer data between sequences of such tasks.

Each region has some number of *fields* defined on it of various types. Legion specifies a type only as a number of bytes and, optionally, a set of serialization functions to marshal heap allocations between memory spaces. Each field is available throughout the index space, but memory is allocated only for the field-subspace pairs that are actually used.

FleCSI organizes multiple related regions, e.g., the cells and vertices of a mesh, into *topologies*. Since FleCSI does not use the Legion feature of creating multiple regions from the same index space, the term "index space" is used in the user interface to describe a selector among the regions for a topology. Each topology type is defined as a *specialization* of one of the *core* topology types defined by FleCSI that specifies a number of properties like the dimensionality of a mesh or which kinds of connectivity information to store explicitly.

Extended Index Space. To allow most tasks to treat its local application data as a traditional, contiguous array, FleCSI stores application data on a particular sort of two-dimensional index space based on *rows*. Each such Extended Index Space is typically partitioned into subsets that are prefixes of each row, such that each color is the index of a (partial) row. The prefixes need not all be the same length, and the partitions can be recreated with different lengths: the underlying index space has a very large number of columns, most of which are never realized in memory. If Legion is in use, it automatically copies the contents of a row that has grown into a prefix of any new allocation. Otherwise, the restricted form of index spaces significantly simplifies the implementation of a backend based on another runtime, e.g., HPX.

For certain topologies, e.g., an unstructured mesh, each row comprises *exclusive, shared,* and *ghost* index points: the field values at each ghost point are copies of those at a particular shared point specified by a *copy plan* created by such a topology. Whenever ghost values are required by a task, FleCSI performs the copies specified in the plan if the shared values have been changed since the previous copy. This copying is explicit from the perspective of the runtime but implicit from the perspective of the author of the relevant tasks. Other topologies, e.g., a set of particles, have more dynamic communication patterns; temporarily copying data into a special *buffer* field implements these copies in terms of an ordinary copy plan for the buffers.

Accessors. Fields are registered by creating objects of a *field definition* type, parameterized on the data type as well as the type of the topology, prior to initializing FleCSI. Every instance of the nominated topology type is then equipped with that field, although since each has its own partitions memory is not in general allocated for all of them.

Since the runtime must in general move field data to make it available to a task, ordinary pointers to it are available only inside a task. These are wrapped into *accessors* which provide one of several interfaces for the field values and specify the privileges required by a task. Outside a task, an opaque *field reference* is used instead that nominates a field definition and a topology instance. When a field reference is passed as an argument to a task that declares a compatible accessor as a parameter, the runtime provides a pointer to the relevant array in the task's memory space to use for the parameter.

FleCSI's operation may be described as a distributed version of the C++ memory allocation expression `new T[n]`: `T` is specified by the field definition, `n` is specified by the topology, and the resulting pointer eventually appears as the task parameter.

Layouts. While FleCSI's model for index spaces is simpler and more restricted than the Legion model, its model for data types is more complicated. In addition to restricting accessors to using the type specified in a field definition, FleCSI provides several *layouts* for representing non-trivial objects. The element types used with a layout must themselves be bitwise-copyable; for efficiency, FleCSI does not use mechanisms like Legion's serialization interface for transfer between memory spaces.

The default layout is *dense*, which is simply a one-dimensional array of the specified type T. The special case of a *single* element, useful for metadata pertaining to one color of a topology, is provided for convenience. The *ragged* layout emulates a std::vector<T> at each index point. The *sparse* layout emulates a std::map<std::size_t,T> at each index point. The *particle* layout stores an unordered collection of T objects with efficient insertion, removal, and iteration; it is similar to the "bucket array" data structure, albeit with a single bucket.

All of these are implemented recursively in terms of one or more simpler accessors, with a *raw* accessor that manages uninitialized memory (rather than objects) as the base case. The field definitions follow the same structure, automatically registering fields necessary for storing metadata like the sizes of individual ragged arrays. Ragged and sparse fields require support from the topology for allocating memory for the array elements, which is provided centrally for all but the simplest topologies.

Topology Instances. Application developers create a topology instance with the assistance of a *topology slot*, which allows the specialization to contribute to the topology's initialization and allows the client to defer it (so that slots can be declared statically if desired). A topology instance is created from a *coloring* which describes the memory layout required and is constructed using its own slot that automatically utilizes an MPI task (Sect. 2.4), as is commonly required for initialization from external data sources. Listing 1.1 illustrates the typical process of initializing a topology with these types given a specialization Sect. 3.1.

Listing 1.1. Topology initialization

```
1   topology :: cslot  color ;
2   topology :: slot  topo ;
3
4   void  setup_color () {
5       // May be distributed  rather  than  duplicated :
6       auto  data  =  load (" file  name" );
7       color . allocate ( data . header () ,  data . body () );
8   }
9
10  void  setup_topology () {
11      topo . allocate ( color . get () );
12  }
```

A topology slot may also be passed to a task with a *topology accessor* as a parameter. Such an accessor uses internal fields established by the topology to interpret the contents of flat arrays in terms of its logical structure. Much like accessors for dynamic layouts like ragged, these are implemented in terms of accessors for those structural fields. Field indices are typically supplied by a topology accessor as "strong typedef" objects to reduce the chance of misconstruing them as pertaining to another index space. Flat arrays can be interpreted

as having multiple dimensions through the use of a limited implementation of
mdspan as proposed for C++23 [7].

2.4   Execution Model

FleCSI has two mechanisms for expressing work: tasks and kernels. Tasks operate
on data distributed to one or more address spaces, and use data privileges to
maintain memory consistency. Kernels operate on data in a single address space,
but require explicit barriers to ensure consistency. This is generally referred to
as a relaxed-consistency memory model.

Listing 1.2. Single-Source Execution

```
1   const  field<double>:: definition<topology ,
2     topology :: entities> values ;
3
4   void  init_field (topology :: accessor<ro> t ,
5       field<double>:: accessor<rw> f) {
6           forall(e, t.entities()) {
7               f(e) = 1.0;  // dummy initialization
8           };
9   }
10
11  void  setup_field () {
12      execute<init_field >(topo , values(topo ));
13  }
```

Listing 1.2 shows a continuation of Listing 1.1 that uses the execute method
to invoke a task (line 12). There are several things to observe about this code
example:

- Tasks are invoked using the execute function. FleCSI also provides the
  reduce, and test functions. Invocations of reduce capture the task return
  value in a future, which can be queried like f.get() to retrieve the reduced
  value (distributed-memory). The test function executes a task as a reduction and returns the sum of the point task returns, i.e., a value of zero means
  success.
- Privileges on accessors passed to the task, e.g., the rw in field<double>::
  accessor<rw> (line 5), determine the memory consistency operations that
  will be performed on the respective data upon the next task invocation. Valid
  privileges are na (no access), ro (read-only), wo (write-only), and rw (read-
  write). The privilege na can be used to defer consistency updates.
- The forall invocation (line 6) executes the loop body in shared-memory,
  data-parallel over the specified iterator, e.g., t.entities(), potentially handling any data motion that is required to move data to the correct address
  space. Depending on the backend runtimes used, this code example can seamlessly execute a task in distributed-memory, data parallel over a collection of

nodes, and in shared-memory, data parallel on attached GPU devices on each node.

3   Core Topologies

Each core topology type supports a number of numerical methods with similar data requirements. FleCSI itself implements these types in terms of internal facilities that are not themselves exposed to clients. In contrast, FleCSI defines only the few specializations used by those facilities; others may be defined by applications or by libraries of specializations that are themselves suitably generic.

For example, consider the data representations for the following methods: *particle-in-cell (PIC)*, *molecular dynamics (MD)*, *material point method (MPM)*, *smoothed-particle hydrodynamics (SPH)*, and *Monte Carlo*. These methods are all based on particles, but they vary as to whether interactions between the particles are direct or are mediated by fields stored on a mesh. Here, only MD and SPH feature direct interactions; such methods typically need ghost particles to calculate them, as well as efficient neighbor lookups. The `topo::ntree` topology (Sect. 3.4) supports these methods, organizing the particles into an octree for an $\mathcal{O}(logN)$ nearest-neighbor search.

For the non-interacting particle methods considered here, a primary concern in parallel implementations is to identify *active* particles in the local memory space, and to efficiently move particles between memory spaces. The `topo::set` topology (Sect. 3.5) supports these methods, organizing the particles using the particle layout (Sect. 2.3) for an $\mathcal{O}(1)$ step to the next active particle (using a *low-complexity jump-counting pattern skipfield* data structure) [4,5].

Other combinations are possible. For example, many MD codes reduce search complexity by imposing a *Cartesian* mesh on the domain with the mesh increments set to some *cutoff* metric. The particles for each cell in this approach can be stored in a ragged field (Sect. 2.3) defined on an `topo::narray` topology (Sect. 3.3).

In addition to allowing specialization of the core types, FleCSI's data model also allows easy composition of topologies into more complex types. Consider the design of a data structure to support *block-structured adaptive mesh refinement (AMR)*. The `topo::ntree` topology is well-suited for tracking refinement because of its fast neighbor lookup. This can be combined with a specialization of `topo::narray` to provide a structured mesh interface at each node of the tree. Field data registered at the nodes can be *viewed* using `util::mdspan`.

The primary take-away from this section should be that the FleCSI core topology types and layouts provide data structure support for a wide variety of applied methods, which can be composed to support complex, multi-physics applications development. Table 2 in Appendix A provides some suggested applications of the core types for common numerical methods.

3.1   Specialization Structure

The notion of a *specialization* is formalized in the FleCSI class structure with the `topo::specialization` type, as shown in Listing 1.3. The specialization serves both as a policy for the core topology and as an interface for the application; its general structure is the same for all of the FleCSI core topologies, although the specific details are different for each.

Listing 1.3. Specialization Structure

```
1   struct my_topo : topo::specialization<topo::topology, my_topo> {
2
3     enum index_space {vertices, integration};
4
5     template<class B>
6     struct interface : B {
7       // Iterator over an Index Space
8       template<index_space IndexSpace>
9       auto entities() {/* ... */}
10
11      // Iterator over entities at an entity
12      template<index_space To, index_space From>
13      auto entities(topo::id<From> from) const {/* ... */ }
14    };
15
16  }; // struct my_topo
```

All FleCSI topology types define iterators over the *entities* of the topology, with relational types, e.g., `topo::unstructured`, and `topo::ntree`, also defining *sub-entity* iterators.

3.2   topo::unstructured

The `topo::unstructured` topology provides a *graph-like* data structure, suitable for defining unstructured meshes. Specializations can define an arbitrary number of entity types and can control what connectivity information is *stored* (as opposed to what must be *computed*), allowing flexibility in memory vs compute complexity. Coloring utilities are provided with a *mesh definition* abstraction for scalable distribution of input meshes. In addition to the standard *entity*, and *sub-entity* iterators, `topo::unstructured` allows users to define custom iterators using *entity lists*, which are useful for tracking, e.g., domain boundary interfaces.

3.3   topo::narray

The `topo::narray` topology is an n-dimensional array data structure, with support for arbitrary *halo* and *boundary* depths, and optional periodicity in each axis. Halo dependencies optionally include diagonal connections. Listing 1.4 shows an example of a two-dimensional, *Cartesian* mesh interface created using `topo::narray`.

Listing 1.4. *Cartesian* Mesh Example using `topo::narray`

```
1   void poisson::task::smooth(mesh::accessor<ro> m,
2     field<double>::accessor<rw, ro> ua,
3     field<double>::accessor<ro, ro> fa) {
4     auto u = m.mdspan<mesh::vertices>(ua);
5     auto f = m.mdspan<mesh::vertices>(fa);
6     const auto dxdy = m.dxdy();
7     const auto dx_over_dy = m.xdelta() / m.ydelta();
8     const auto dy_over_dx = m.ydelta() / m.xdelta();
9     const auto factor = 1.0 / (2 * (dx_over_dy + dy_over_dx));
10
11    for(auto j : m.vertices<mesh::y_axis>()) {
12      for(auto i : m.vertices<mesh::x_axis>()) {
13        u[j][i] = factor *
14                  (dxdy * f[j][i] +
15                   dy_over_dx * (u[j][i + 1] + u[j][i - 1]) +
16                   dx_over_dy * (u[j + 1][i] + u[j - 1][i]));
17      }
18    }
19  }
```

3.4   topo::ntree

The `topo::ntree` topology provides special 1, 2, or 3 dimensional hashed tree support, e.g., $n \equiv 3 \Rightarrow$ a *hashed octree*, based on the *Barnes–Hut approximation* [2] with a hashing strategy derived from *Warren & Salmon* [22]. Particle distribution is supported using a naive coloring of a sorted *Morton (Z-Order)*, or *Hilbert* space-filling curve [1].

FleCSI provides several iterator patterns for accessing and modifying the tree. In particular, direct entity and node access, and both *Depth-First Search (DFS)* and *Breadth-First Search (BFS)* traversals are supported, with DFS support for *postorder, preorder, reverse postorder*, and *reverse preorder* variants. Users can also develop custom traversals using *sub-entity* or *sub-node* iterators. Listing 1.5 provides examples of DFS and BFS traversal iterators.

Listing 1.5. NTree Iterator Example

```
1   // Depth−First Traversal with reverse preorder
2   for(auto n : t.dfs<reverse_preorder>()) { /* ... */ }
3
4   // Breadth−First Traversal
5   for(auto n : t.bfs()) { /* ... */ }
```

As with other FleCSI topology types, `topo::ntree` supports field definition using the FleCSI data model (Sect. 2.3) and implicit dependency consistency through accessor permissions. Neighbor interactions are controlled by the user's specialization through rules that define *node-node, entity-entity*, and *node-entity* interactions. Using these rules, the runtime automatically retrieves dependencies from other colors as needed. The tree can be re-sorted and re-distributed as needed to track particle evolution.

3.5 topo::set

The `topo::set` topology is designed to support non-interacting particle methods, i.e., those that do not have direct particle-particle interactions, using the *particle* layout discussed in Sect. 2.3. The topology extends the basic iterators and distributed-memory support of the underlying layout with customizable interfaces for coloring and binning particles, and specialized accessors that can be used to track local particles as they evolve, potentially leaving their original color, with or without *path-dependent* trajectories. The `topo::set` topology is *dependent* in FleCSI's nomenclature because individual particles are *colored* according to their relationship to an *independent* topology, e.g., a distributed mesh.

4   Sample Applications

To demonstrate the use of FleCSI in implementing simulation codes, two applications are described representing disparate FleCSI topologies. In addition to covering multiple FleCSI topologies, these applications demonstrate the implementation of important numerical methods relevant to many simulation codes. A simple investigation of abstraction overhead in the context of these applications is used to verify its minimal impact on application performance.

4.1 MPAS-O-FleCSI

`MPAS-O-FleCSI` is an FleCSI-based implementation of models from MPAS (Model for Prediction Across Scales) [19]. It is part of the CANGA project, that aims at investigating task-based approaches for Earth System Models to achieve maximum performance and better manage architectural and scientific complexity. Currently, several simulation applications are developed on the `MPAS-O-FleCSI` framework, including the shallow water core. The shallow water core of `MPAS-O- FleCSI` implements the numerical scheme from [20] to solve the nonlinear shallow water equations using a C-grid finite-volume discretization on Variable-resolution Spherical Voronoi Tessellations (SCVTs) [13]. The unstructured topology is used to support SCVTs for `MPAS-O-FleCSI` with mesh files read using HDF5 (Fig. 5).

4.2 FleCSPH

FleCSPH [15] is a multiphysics Smoothed Particle Hydrodynamics (SPH) simulation code, using the FleCSI 2.0 `topo::ntree` topology, allowing efficient computation of bulk transport and long-range interactions (Fig. 6). FleCSPH is a capable simulation application, including initial data generators, particle relaxation with external potentials, *weighted Voronoi tessellations (WVT)* and *artificial pressure method (APM)*, flexible boundary conditions, and complexity reduction using *Fast Multipole Method (FMM)* (up to 4th order). Angular and linear momentum are conserved using a novel FMM algorithm.

With a primary focus on astrophysics, FleCSPH also includes support for gravitational waveform extraction and gravitational radiation reaction, and both analytic and tabulated *equation of state (EOS)* calculations. The application is easily extended to support new features and user-specific problem setups. Standard HDF5 formats based on H5part are used for input and output.

4.3 Abstraction Overhead

Through extensions of its underlying runtime models, FleCSI provides various usability and portability benefits. Leveraging Legion and Kokkos, FleCSI enables applications to be run on diverse hardware and in a heterogeneous environment. Additionally, FleCSI provides type checking and iterators for tasks facilitating increased usability. To be effective, however, the cost of such abstractions must not significantly impact the performance of applications.

The shallow water core from `MPAS-O-FleCSI` is used to investigate abstraction overheads of FleCSI execution and data structures. To this end, we first consider a vector triad from stream [16] (see Algorithm 1).

Algorithm 1. Vector Triad

1: **for** $i = 1, \ldots, N$ **do**
2:     $A[i] = B[i] + C[i] * D[i]$
3: **end for**

This provides a baseline for performance investigation as an expectation for performance is easily obtained on a computation relevant to the memory bound nature of second order finite-volume calculations.

Figure 2 shows performance of the vector triad computed over cells in an MPAS mesh on a Power 9 CPU. The FleCSI line shows the vector triad implemented in a FleCSI task using FleCSI fields, iterators (`forall` abstraction using Kokkos with the OpenMP [8] backend), and accessors on the MPAS specialization of `topo::unstructured`. The OpenMP line shows the vector triad implemented in OpenMP using sizes consistent with the number of cells in the given MPAS mesh. Figure 2 demonstrates relatively small overhead when compared to OpenMP.

Figure 3 shows performance of the vector triad on a Volta GPU. The FleCSI line shows the performance of the vector triad implemented in a FleCSI task using the `forall` abstraction with the MPAS unstructured topology specialization. The Kokkos line shows performance of the vector triad using Kokkos with sizes consistent to the number of cells in the corresponding MPAS mesh. Figure 3 shows the abstraction overhead is largest for small mesh sizes with the highest variability.

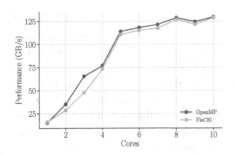

Fig. 2. Vector triad over 64 million cells in an MPAS mesh on Power 9 CPU.

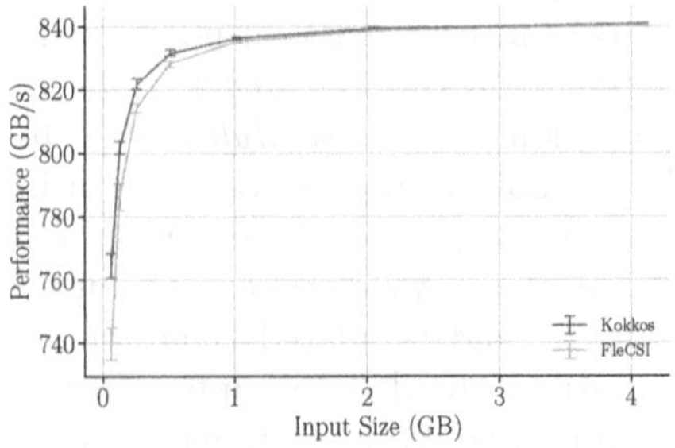

Fig. 3. Vector triad over cells in an MPAS mesh on Volta. Error bars show variation over ten runs

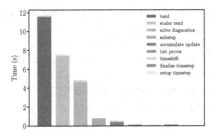

Fig. 4. Shallow water core task execution and runtime overhead.

Figure 4 shows the run time of tasks in the time integration loop of the shallow water core in `MPAS-O-FleCSI`. The FleCSI overhead associated with these tasks is shown above each bar.

Overall, the FleCSI overhead associated with these tasks is insignificant relative to the run time of the task.

5   Conclusions and Future Work

FleCSI 2.0 offers many improvements, and extended capabilities over the original FleCSI 1.4 release, including a completely C++17-compliant interface, new topology types, more flexible topology instance control, better support for scalable topology colorings, a composable internal interface for developing and implementing new topology types, full implementation of FleCSI's explicit programming model components, arbitrary launch domain support for *M-to-N color* to *process* mappings (execution model only), improved profiling utilities, and a fully serializable logging utility (FLOG) that can aid in code development and debugging.

A future minor release of FleCSI 2.0 will add support for arbitrary data mappings, using *color maps* to extend the capability provided by our current *M-to-N* execution model. This will enable straightforward implementations of complex mapping algorithms, e.g., parallel rendezvous [18]. Future work will also include refinement and integration of a previously-developed model for multi-material representations, additional topology support (In particular, support for *K-D Trees*.), a new interface for controlling *tuneables* in conjunction with several custom mappers targeting upcoming DOE supercomputers, e.g., Crossroads [10] and El Capitan [21], and improved scalability and performance.

Acknowledgments. FleCSI 2.0 is the culmination of several years of research and development, with many important contributors. We would like to acknowledge the following individuals for direct code contributions:

Table 1. Direct Code Contributors to FleCSI

Dani Barrack	Marc Charest	Scot Halverson
Christoph Junghans	Sumathi Lakshmiranganatha	Jonas Lippuner
Nick Moss	Robert Pavel	Jonathan Pieterila Graham
Galen Shipman	Lukas Spies	Martin Staley
Karen Tsai	John Wohlbier	Wei Wu

The initial design and development of FleCSI was funded under the Advanced Technology Development and Mitigation (ATDM) subprogram of LANL's ASC program (NNSA/DOE). This work would not have been possible without close collaborations with the Legion and HPX teams, and the Ristra Project (part of ATDM). We would also like to acknowledge the leadership of the Ristra project: Aimee Hungerford, and David Daniel. The FleCSI project and the Darwin compute cluster are both funded by the Computational Systems and Software Environments (CSSE) subprogram of LANL's ASC program (NNSA/DOE).

FleCSI website: https://flecsi.org.
Source code and issue tracking: https://github.com/flecsi/flecsi.
This work is approved for unlimited release: LA-UR-21-25604

A   Topology Applications

As mentioned in Sect. 3, this table gives some suggestions for the particular numerical methods that can be implemented with the various FleCSI core topology types. This list is meant only as an example, and is by no means exhaustive.

Table 2. Suggested FleCSI Topology Applications

Applied Method	Core Topologies
Lagrangian Hydrodynamics	topo::unstructured, topo::narray
Eulerian Hydrodynamics	topo::narray, topo::ntree
Smoothed-Particle Hydrodynamics	topo::ntree
Finite Element Method	topo::unstructured, topo::narray
Finite Volume Method	topo::unstructured, topo::narray
Discontinuous Galerkin	topo::unstructured, topo::narray
Material-Point Method	topo::set
Particle-In-Cell	topo::set
Monte Carlo (particle coloring)	topo::ntree
Monte Carlo (mesh coloring)	topo::set

B   Sample Figures

Fig. 5. Example of MPAS mesh used to setup a standard shallow water test case from [23].

Fig. 6. Simulation of a neutron star merger disk outflow using FleCSPH.

References

1. Bader, M.: Space-Filling Curves: An Introduction with Applications in Scientific Computing. Springer, Cham (2012)
2. Barnes, J.E., Hut, P.: A hierarchical O(n-log-n) force calculation algorithm. Nature **324**, 446 (1986)
3. Bauer, M., Treichler, S., Slaughter, E., Aiken, A.: Legion: expressing locality and independence with logical regions. In: Proceedings of the International Conference on High Performance Computing, Networking, Storage and Analysis, SC 2012, Washington, DC, USA. IEEE Computer Society Press (2012)
4. Bentley, M.: The high complexity jump-counting pattern (2019). https://www.plflib.org. Accessed 10 June 2021
5. Bentley, M.: The low complexity jump-counting pattern (2019). https://www.plflib.org. Accessed 10 June 2021
6. Boehme, D., et al.: Caliper: performance introspection for HPC software stacks. In: Proceedings of the International Conference for High Performance Computing, Networking, Storage and Analysis, SC 2016, pp. 550–560 (2016). https://doi.org/10.1109/SC.2016.46
7. Technical Committee in-progress C++23 (2021). https://isocpp.org/std/the-standard. Accessed 14 June 2021
8. Dagum, L., Menon, R.: OpenMP: an industry-standard API for shared-memory programming. IEEE Comput. Sci. Eng. **5**(1), 46–55 (1998). https://doi.org/10.1109/99.660313
9. Edwards, H.C., Trott, C.R., Sunderland, D.: Kokkos: enabling manycore performance portability through polymorphic memory access patterns. J. Parallel Distrib. Comput. **74**(12), 3202–3216 (2014). https://doi.org/10.1016/j.jpdc.2014.07.003. Domain-Specific Languages and High-Level Frameworks for High-Performance Computing

10. The Alliance for Computing at Extreme Scale (ACES): Crossroads: a critical element for improved predictive capability (2021). https://www.lanl.gov/projects/crossroads. Accessed 14 June 2021
11. Message Passing Interface Forum: MPI: a message-passing interface standard. Technical report, USA (1994)
12. Holmen, J.K., Sahasrabudhe, D., Berzins, M.: A heterogeneous MPI+ PPL task scheduling approach for asynchronous many-task runtime systems. In: Proceedings of the Practice and Experience in Advanced Research Computing 2021 on Sustainability, Success and Impact (PEARC21). ACM (2021)
13. Ju, L., Ringler, T., Gunzburger, M.: Voronoi tessellations and their application to climate and global modeling. In: Lauritzen, P., Jablonowski, C., Taylor, M., Nair, R. (eds.) Numerical Techniques for Global Atmospheric Models. LNCSE, vol. 80, pp. 313–342. Springer, Heidelberg (2011). https://doi.org/10.1007/978-3-642-11640-7_10
14. Kaiser, H., Brodowicz, M., Sterling, T.: Parallex an advanced parallel execution model for scaling-impaired applications. In: 2009 International Conference on Parallel Processing Workshops, pp. 394–401 (2009). https://doi.org/10.1109/ICPPW.2009.14
15. Loiseau, J., et al.: FleCSPH: the next generation fleCSIble parallel computational infrastructure for smoothed particle hydrodynamics. SoftwareX **12**, 100602 (2020)
16. McCalpin, J.D.: Memory bandwidth and machine balance in current high performance computers. In: IEEE Computer Society Technical Committee on Computer Architecture (TCCA) Newsletter, pp. 19–25, December 1995
17. Pérache, M., Carribault, P., Jourdren, H.: MPC-MPI: an MPI implementation reducing the overall memory consumption. In: Ropo, M., Westerholm, J., Dongarra, J. (eds.) EuroPVM/MPI 2009. LNCS, vol. 5759, pp. 94–103. Springer, Heidelberg (2009). https://doi.org/10.1007/978-3-642-03770-2_16
18. Plimpton, S.J., Hendrickson, B., Stewart, J.R.: A parallel rendezvous algorithm for interpolation between multiple grids. J. Parallel Distrib. Comput. **64**(2), 266–276 (2004). https://doi.org/10.1016/j.jpdc.2003.11.006
19. Ringler, T., Petersen, M., Higdon, R.L., Jacobsen, D., Jones, P.W., Maltrud, M.: A multi-resolution approach to global ocean modeling. Ocean Model. **69**, 211–232 (2013)
20. Ringler, T.D., Thuburn, J., Klemp, J.B., Skamarock, W.C.: A unified approach to energy conservation and potential vorticity dynamics for arbitrarily-structured c-grids. J. Comput. Phys. **229**(9), 3065–3090 (2010)
21. Thomas, J.: LINI and HPE to partner with AMD on El Capitan, projected as world's fastest supercomputer (2021). https://www.llnl.gov/news/llnl-and-hpe-partner-amd-el-capitan-projected-worlds-fastest-supercomputer. Accessed 06 June 2021
22. Warren, M.S., Salmon, J.K.: A parallel hashed oct-tree n-body algorithm. In: Proceedings of the 1993 ACM/IEEE Conference on Supercomputing, Supercomputing 1993, pp. 12–21. ACM, New York (1993). https://doi.org/10.1145/169627.169640
23. Williamson, D.L., Drake, J.B., Hack, J.J., Jakob, R., Swarztrauber, P.N.: A standard test set for numerical approximations to the shallow water equations in spherical geometry. J. Comput. Phys. **102**(1), 211–224 (1992)

Enabling Support for Zero Copy Semantics in an Asynchronous Task-Based Programming Model

Nitin Bhat[1]([✉]), Sam White[2], and Laxmikant V. Kale[1,2]

[1] Charmworks, Inc., Urbana, IL, USA
nitin@hpccharm.com
[2] Department of Computer Science, University of Illinois at Urbana-Champaign,
Urbana, IL, USA
{white67,kale}@illinois.edu

Abstract. Communication is critical to the scalable and efficient performance of scientific simulations on extreme scale computing systems. Part of the promise of task-based programming models is that they can naturally overlap communication with computation and exploit locality between tasks. Copy-based semantics using eager communication protocols easily enable such asynchrony by alleviating the responsibility of buffer management from the user, both on the sender and the receiver. However, these semantics increase memory allocations and copies and in turn affect application memory footprint and performance, especially with large message buffers.

In this work we describe how the so-called "zero copy" messaging semantics can be supported in Converse, the message-driven parallel programming framework that is used by Charm++, by implementing support for user-owned buffer transfers in its lower level runtime system, LRTS. These semantics work on user-provided buffers and do not semantically require copies by either the user or the runtime system. We motivate our work by reviewing the existing messaging model in Converse/Charm++, identify its semantic shortcomings, and define new LRTS and Converse APIs to support zero copy communication based on RDMA capabilities. We demonstrate the utility of our new communication interfaces with benchmarks written in Converse. The result is up to 91% of message latency improvement and improved memory usage. These advances will enable future work on user-facing APIs in Charm++.

Keywords: Charm++ · Converse · RDMA · Parallel programming · Asynchronous tasking · Communication optimizations

1 Introduction

With the advent of Exascale computing, the importance of efficient data movement is expected to increase greatly. In fact, the underlying technological factors

© Springer Nature Switzerland AG 2022
R. Chaves et al. (Eds.): Euro-Par 2021, LNCS 13098, pp. 496–505, 2022.
https://doi.org/10.1007/978-3-031-06156-1_39

that led to dramatic increase in within-node computational capacity, without a proportionate increase in communication capabilities entail that even on small clusters, communication issues present significant challenges. RDMA, which stands for Remote Direct Memory Access, is a network capability that allows a machine to read from or write to a remote machine's memory without the involvement of the Operating System or CPUs. One sided communication with the help of RDMA supported hardware is the natural choice for large messages as it has proven to reduce latencies and increase bandwidth for large payloads in High Performance Computing (HPC) networks. RDMA also benefits from so-called "zero copy" semantics, where the data being transferred is not copied between the layers of the network stack (zero copy means no intermediate copies). The bypassing of CPU along with the elimination of copies ensure lower latencies and higher throughput for RDMA enabled networks over regular networks.

Since memory-bound operations are much slower in comparison to the CPU, it has been observed that memory intensive operations act as the primary bottleneck in numerous applications and thus reduce application performance and increase energy consumption. For this reason, reducing memory pressure by saving the cost of allocations and copies helps in improving application performance significantly.

2   Background, Motivation and Contributions

Converse [6] is a complete but low level message-driven (i.e. task based) parallel programming system. It supports a scheduler that handles user-level threads as well as stackless tasks. The latter may be created locally or from remote processors, which is similar to active messages. Each such task has a handler reference and a data payload, and possibly other metadata such as priorities. In its current usage, on the source PE (processing element, typically used to denote a CPU core), the data payload has to be copied from the user data structure to a contiguous message that includes the message metadata. Similarly, on the destination PE, the payload has to be copied from the received message into the user data structure. It is this copying on both the source and destination that we wish to optimize.

Converse is designed to be used as a substrate for implementing parallel languages, but Charm++ is the most well-known system that uses it. Charm++ is an asynchronous parallel programming model and runtime system based on the idea of overdecomposition and migratable objects [1]. A Charm++ program is expressed in the form of interacting migratable C++ objects called *chares*, which interact via asynchronous method invocations. In such a method invocation, the passed parameters are copied ("marshaled") into a *Converse* message along with required metadata to encode information such as recipient object and handler references. This copying ensures that the user passed parameters are safe to be overwritten immediately on the source chare after the entry method invocation. On the destination chare, such copying from the received Converse message into the user data structures is again required to use the received data beyond the scope of the entry method since the runtime system frees the message for safe memory management. Thus the optimization we aim at is useful (necessary but not sufficient) to optimize Charm++ and its myriad applications.

Now consider a situation in which a user of Converse (either end programmer or the Charm++ runtime) needs to send multiple large data arrays, along with other scalar data. All the large arrays must be copied into a Converse message on the sending processor and on the receiving processor they typically have to be copied into application data structures. With large buffers, these copies come at the price of increased memory footprint, higher latency, and lower bandwidth. In this work, we aim to address the limitations of the current messaging semantics in Converse and propose a new zero copy messaging model that will allow communicating data "in-place". This will allow the user to avoid additional allocations and copies, and facilitate reuse of user buffers while still benefiting as much as possible from the asynchrony that underlies Converse (and Charm++) execution model.

3   Design and Implementation

The Charm++ software stack consists of three primary software layers: Charm++, Converse, and LRTS, with support for various networking layers beneath LRTS. Charm++ is the high level layer interfacing with the user code to support processor virtualization through the idea of coarse grained task and data objects called chares. Converse is a portability layer beneath Charm++ that supports message handling and uses a scheduler to enqueue received messages and invoke message handlers by using an appropriate dequeueing strategy. The networking layer which is below Converse is called the Low Level Runtime System (LRTS). The LRTS represents a set of APIs used by Converse to perform networking operations like sending and receiving messages. Each networking machine layer implements this set of APIs using provider-specific implementations, hiding their implementation details from the upper layers of the Charm++ software stack.

3.1   LRTS API

The basic functionality for performing a zero copy transfer of a buffer is dependent on the underlying network and its capabilities. HPC specific networks like UCX, OFI, GNI, and Verbs provide native support for RDMA operations, whereas network libraries like TCP and UDP used primarily over ethernet, do not natively support RDMA operations. Since each networking layer has its own implementation for supporting zero copy transfers, we define a unified LRTS API for zero copy transfers and implement the API for each networking layer. We provide the following LRTS methods for implementing zero copy functionality:

- void LrtsSetRdmaBufferInfo(void *info, const void *ptr, int size, int mode)
- void LrtsDeregisterMem(const void *ptr, void *info, int pe, int mode)
- void LrtsIssueRget(NcpyOperationInfo *ncpyOpInfo)
- void LrtsIssueRput(NcpyOperationInfo *ncpyOpInfo)

LrtsSetRdmaBufferInfo is used to set the network specific metadata information for a buffer or a memory region that is intended to be used for an RDMA operation. For most RDMA supported layers, this involves registration of the memory region and storing that information in the info object. LrtsDeregisterMem is used to deregister an already registered region of memory. LrtsIssueRget is used to perform an RDMA Get or Read operation from a remote buffer. Similarly, LrtsIssueRput is used to perform an RDMA Put or Write operation to a remote buffer. Since buffer information pertaining to both the local and the remote buffer is required to perform a Get or Put operation, the wrapper object NcpyOperationInfo is used to store the metadata information of both the buffers, including completion handling information which is used to call the registered higher level completion function on completion of a Get or Put. These low-level LRTS APIs described above will provide the infrastructure for higher-level abstractions in Converse and Charm++. In this section, we briefly describe the implementation of the LRTS APIs for different networking layers and for the special case of transfers within a physical node.

Networking Layers. Native networking layers provide explicit control to the user to design and tune the usage of the network library's API as intended. Such layers also typically require the user to explicitly manage pinned or registered memory. In our work, we have chosen to implement the basic functionality for performing zero copy operations on four popular native HPC networking layers that require explicit pinned memory management. These include Unified Communication X (UCX) [8], OpenFabrics Interfaces (OFI) [4], uGNI or GNI, and Verbs. For these networking layers, in our implementation, inside LrtsSetRdmaBufferInfo, we use the network library provided method to register the buffer and store the memory handle (or memory region) along with any additional information (like rkey) in the info object. Similarly, in LrtsDeregisterMem, we use the method to deregister the buffer using the memory handle available in the info object. Since all these networking layers natively supports RDMA operations, we directly use the Get and Put methods provided by each of the network libraries to perform RDMA Get and Put operations inside LrtsIssueRget and LrtsIssueRput respectively. Completion handling is performed by polling a completion queue and calling an appropriate higher level completion function using a heap object in the case of OFI, GNI, and Verbs. UCX supports a ucp_send_callback_t argument provided in the Get and Put calls, which can be set to a specific function, which is invoked on completion. Inside the ucp callback function, the common higher level completion function is invoked. In addition to native networking layers, Charm++ also provides an MPI networking layer to be used for interoperation with MPI or on new machines without reliable support yet for a native layer. Since MPI internally manages pinned memory, our implementation is simplified and simply uses matching MPI_Isend and MPI_Irecv calls to perform "zero copy" reads and writes. For networking layers that do not natively support RDMA, like TCP and UDP, we have also provided a copy based implementation in order to maintain API consistency.

Intra-node. Communication between endpoints that are on the same physical node is common on many-core nodes. We use Cross Memory Attach (CMA) [10] for performing reads and writes between processes within the same host. CMA is a mechanism that was introduced in Linux kernel version 3.2 to improve communication performance between processes of the same physical node. A `process_vm_readv` call is used in `LrtsIssueRget` and a `process_vm_writev` call is used in `LrtsIssueRput` to perform CMA read and write operations. These calls are synchronous and complete inline, allowing us to perform completion handling immediately upon returning from the CMA call. For transfers within the same process, we further optimize the communication with a user-space memcpy operation for optimal performance.

3.2   Converse API

The API for zero copy semantics in Converse is built on top of the basic functionality of the lower level, which is unified by the LRTS API. Since the metadata information of both the local and remote buffer is required to perform an RDMA operation, we support a 2-phase protocol: rely on the existing messaging API in Converse to transfer the metadata information, followed by the one-sided (say, `get`) API to execute the large data transfer. The metadata associated with a buffer includes information like the pointer, size, home PE, memory registration information (which is required for most RDMA networks), and any other data fields used for notifying the user on completion of the zero copy transfer. This metadata information in encapsulated into a class we provide called `CmiNcpyBuffer`. This class contains methods such as `get` and `put` to perform RDMA Get and Put operations respectively. Additionally, methods called `registerMem` and `deregisterMem` perform memory registration and deregistration. `registerMem` is called from the constructor of `CmiNcpyBuffer` to perform memory registration of the buffer during declaration of this object. The user is responsible for invoking `deregisterMem` after the completion of the RDMA transfer.

The above public methods of `CmiNcpyBuffer` constitute the zero copy API in Converse. The user is required to first construct and send the metadata object `CmiNcpyBuffer` of one PE to the other participating PE, using the existing messaging API in Converse. This is illustrated in Fig. 1 where `destMetadataHandler`

```
// Inside a converse method.. Declare a CmiNcpyBuffer object
CmiNcpyBuffer srcMeta(myBuffer, buffSize, srcDoneHandler);

// Invoke a remote method passing my CmiNcpyBuffer object
buffObjMsg *msg = (buffObjMsg *)CmiAlloc(sizeof(buffObjMsg));
CmiSetHandler(msg, destMetadataHandler);
msg->buffObj = srcMeta;
CmiSyncSendAndFree(remotePe, sizeof(buffObjMsg), msg);
```

Fig. 1. CmiNcpyBuffer object creation and handover

is the target handler for the message. This handler on the destination constructs a local `CmiNcpyBuffer` and calls the `get` method as shown in Fig. 2.

```
void destMetadataHandler(buffObjMsg *msg) {
  CmiNcpyBuffer *srcMeta = msg->buffObj;
  CmiNcpyBuffer destMeta(myBuffer, buffSize, destDoneHandler);
  destMeta.get(*srcMeta);
}
```

Fig. 2. Remote PE performing Get operation

On completion of zero copy transfers in Converse, the runtime system invokes the handlers passed by the user in the `CmiNcpyBuffer` object constructors. When the source handler **srcDoneHandler** is called, the buffer can be safely modified or freed as shown in Fig. 3. Similarly, inside **destDoneHandler**, the user is guaranteed that the data transfer into the destination buffer is complete and the user can begin operating on the newly available data as shown in Fig. 3. The runtime invocation of these handler functions on completion enables the user to be asynchronously notified about reuse of source buffer and arrival of data in the destination buffer. This is essential to integrate our protocol in a message-driven execution model and makes it more efficient in comparison to the MPI model, which requires the user to make a blocking `MPI_Wait` call or repeatedly call `MPI_Test` to determine completion. This scheme also allows one to wait modularly for multiple data transfers, even across library boundaries.

```
void srcDoneHandler(char *msg) {
  free(myBuffer);  // free the buffer
}
void destDoneHandler(char *msg) {
  // received data, begin computing
  computeValues();
}
```

Fig. 3. Source and Destination Handler function

The implementation of the Direct API is relatively straightforward. The user is responsible for explicitly sending over the remote metadata information using a `CmiNcpyBuffer` object as seen in Fig. 1. When the `get` method is called on `CmiNcpyBuffer` by passing the source object, the Converse implementation creates a `NcpyOperationInfo` object from the two `CmiNcpyBuffer` objects and simply makes a call to `LrtsIssueRget`. The converse completion function registered with LRTS initiates the invocation of both the source and destination handler functions passed by the user. PUT based one sided operations are supported in a similar manner.

4   Results

Table 1. Benchmarking machines and their configuration

Machine	Cores/Node	Memory/Node	Network	Charm build
iForge	40	192 GB	Infiniband	ucx, verbs
Stampede2	68	96 GB	Omni-Path	ofi
Cori	32	128 GB	Aries	gni, mpi
Linux workstation	4	8 GB	Ethernet	netlrts(udp)

We conducted our performance experiments on three HPC machines and one general purpose linux machine as summarized in Table 1. All our converse builds are configured to use the non-SMP version, which uses one CPU core as a single PE for one process. For benchmarking, we use 2 PEs on 1 node for intra-node messaging and 1 PE each on 2 nodes for inter-node messaging. In our experiments, we use a point-to-point ping-pong benchmark written in Converse. This measures the one-way messaging latency for different message sizes between two processes that exchange messages using their user buffers for a fixed number of iterations. Since our ping-pong benchmark requires exchange of data directly from the user buffers, in the Regular API we explicitly make a copy from the received message into the user owned buffer. This is not required in the zero copy API because the data transfer always happens directly from the sender owned buffer to the receiver owned buffer. Across iterations, since the same buffers are used for a particular message size, it is only required to register the buffer at the beginning of all the iterations corresponding to that size. This allows the zero copy API to perform the `get` operation persistently using the same buffer information objects.

Figures 4 and 5 illustrate the improvements in intra-node and inter-node latency with zero copy API on four different machines. As seen in all the latency plots, the regular messaging API performs better than the zero copy API for smaller messages. This is because of the time taken for the extra memory allocation and copy performed in the regular API being small in comparison to the additional latency incurred in sending the metadata information message for the zero copy API. Starting from medium to large messages, we see that the zero copy API begins to perform better than the regular API and the improvement increases with message size. This can be again explained by the cost of performing the additional allocation and copy, which begins to proportionally increase with message size, whereas the metadata message latency remains constant. The range of performance improvements in latency and the threshold message sizes above which the zero copy API begins to perform better than the regular API is summarized in Table 2 for intra-node transfers and Table 3 for inter-node transfers.

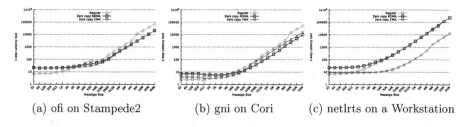

(a) ofi on Stampede2   (b) gni on Cori   (c) netlrts on a Workstation

Fig. 4. Comparison of intra-node latency between regular and zero copy API

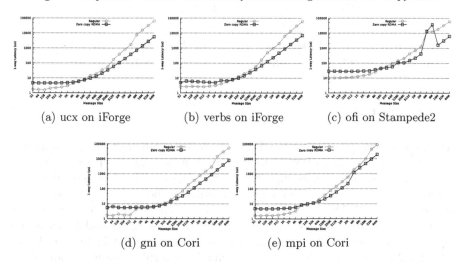

(a) ucx on iForge   (b) verbs on iForge   (c) ofi on Stampede2

(d) gni on Cori   (e) mpi on Cori

Fig. 5. Comparison of inter-node latency between regular and zero copy API

Cross Memory Attach (CMA) is supported on Stampede2, Cori and the commodity linux workstation. Figure 4 highlights the performance between the regular API and the zero copy API with both CMA and RDMA on intra-host transfers between 2 PEs. On Stampede2, CMA performs better than RDMA (using ofi) for most message sizes, esp in the medium message size range because of the expensive network operations in comparison to using shared memory. However, on Cori, CMA outperforms RDMA (using gni) only upto a threshold size. Beyond this, the advantage of bypassing the CPU as done in the case of RDMA outweighs the benefit of using shared memory, which still requires kernel intervention. On the linux workstation as seen in Fig. 4c, because of no support for RDMA, we use the copy based implementation underneath to maintain API consistency. The additional overhead of sending the metadata message incurred in the zero copy API, leads to the poorer performance as compared to the regular API for smaller message sizes. As the message size increases, this additional overhead becomes minuscule in comparison to the cost of allocations and copying, leading to similar performance between regular and the copy-based zero copy API, and much better performance for CMA based zero copy API.

Table 2. Improvement in intra-node latency with zero copy messaging API.

Metric	Stampede2		Cori		Workstation
	CMA	ofi	CMA	gni	CMA
SpeedUp	1.2x – 3.72x	1.4x – 3.7x	1.13x – 3.5x	1.2x – 5.8x	1.3x – 26x
Threshold size	8K	16K	1K	16K	512

Table 3. Improvement in inter-node latency with zero copy messaging API.

Metric	iForge		Stampede2	Cori	
	ucx	verbs	ofi	gni	mpi
SpeedUp	1.1x – 11.4x	1.2x – 8.4x	1.3x – 11.5x	1.2x – 7.8x	1.07x – 4.7x
Threshold size	16K	32K	32K	16K	32K

5   Related Work

RDMA has been well studied and applied to numerous parallel programming models over time. MPI's library model meant it has always operated on user-owned memory rather than explicit message objects. This has allowed library implementors to hide eager and rendezvous protocols behind two-sided send/recv operations [7]. PGAS models, such as UPC [9] and Chapel [3], aim to hide communication from users, so incorporating RDMA into those models has mostly been done in the lower levels of the runtime system and not in the user-facing API. GasNet serves as a lower level communication substrate for various task-based programming systems and has had RDMA incorporated into its design. Legion [2], which builds on top of GasNet, strives to hide communication from users and manage data movement automatically based on task dependencies. HPX [5] is another example of a tasking model that hides communication behind higher-level abstractions such as futures and executors.

6   Conclusion

With the growing complexity of exascale software applications and hardware architectures, task-based programming models appear promising. Asynchrony and the ability to migrate tasks and data around the system to balance computational load will be important for overall performance and scalability. In this work, we identified the shortcomings with the current messaging API in Charm++ for sending and receiving large buffers. We also added support for zero copy messaging in Converse and LRTS to enable the development of zero copy user APIs in Charm++.

Future work includes implementing Charm++ user-facing APIs on top of this work and improving the performance of our new APIs. We plan to implement two key optimizations. First, by adding a registration cache that will intelligently handle memory registrations and deregistrations. Second, by developing a generic memory pool for allocating all the small sized heap objects that we use in our implementation. We believe these optimizations will allow us to extract better performance from our new APIs.

References

1. Acun, B., et al.: Parallel Programming with Migratable Objects: Charm++ in Practice. SC (2014)
2. Bauer, M., Treichler, S., Slaughter, E., Aiken, A.: Legion: expressing locality and independence with logical regions. In: Proceedings of the International Conference on High Performance Computing, Networking, Storage and Analysis, p. 66. IEEE Computer Society Press (2012)
3. Chamberlain, B., Callahan, D., Zima, H.: Parallel programmability and the chapel language. Int. J. High Perform. Comput. Appl. 21, 291–312 (2007)
4. Grun, P., et al.: A brief introduction to the openfabrics interfaces - a new network API for maximizing high performance application efficiency. In: 2015 IEEE 23rd Annual Symposium on High-Performance Interconnects, pp. 34–39 (2015). https://doi.org/10.1109/HOTI.2015.19
5. Kaiser, H., Brodowicz, M., Sterling, T.: Parallex an advanced parallel execution model for scaling-impaired applications. In: ICPPW 2009: Proceedings of the 2009 International Conference on Parallel Processing Workshops, pp. 394–401. IEEE Computer Society, Washington (2009)
6. Kalé, L., Bhandarkar, M., Jagathesan, N., Krishnan, S., Yelon, J.: Converse: an interoperable framework for parallel programming. In: International Parallel Processing Symposium (1996)
7. Liu, J., Wu, J., Panda, D.K.: High performance RDMA-based MPI implementation over infiniband. Int. J. Parallel Program. 32, 167198 (2004)
8. Shamis, P., et al.: UCX: an open source framework for HPC network APIS and beyond. In: 2015 IEEE 23rd Annual Symposium on High-Performance Interconnects, pp. 40–43 (2015). https://doi.org/10.1109/HOTI.2015.13
9. El-Ghazawi, T., Carlson, W., Sterling, T., Yelick, K.: UPC: Distributed Shared Memory Programming. John Wiley & Sons Inc., Hoboken (2005). https://doi.org/10.1002/0471478369.app1
10. Vienne, J.: Benefits of cross memory attach for MPI libraries on HPC clusters. In: Proceedings of the 2014 Annual Conference on Extreme Science and Engineering Discovery Environment, XSEDE 2014. Association for Computing Machinery, New York (2014). https://doi.org/10.1145/2616498.2616532

Euro-Par PhD Symposium

Euro-Par PhD Symposium

PhD Symposium Description

Euro-Par PhD Symposium aims at gathering students working toward a Ph.D. in broadly defined areas related to parallel and distributed processing. This event provides a unique opportunity for the students to present and discuss their ongoing dissertation research with the large Euro-Par research community. The Euro-Par PhD Symposium strives at establishing itself as one of the premier European forums for Ph.D. students in parallel and distributed computing. For this reason, it focuses on providing a productive platform where the Ph.D. students can get feedback on their research from some of the key players in European scientific community, while also giving an opportunity for industry to get insights on the break-through academic work that is currently in progress.

The first Euro-Par PhD Symposium (2021) was held virtually in Lisbon, Portugal. The format of the PhD Symposium included 10 presentations of Ph.D. students and it received good attendance of around 30 people on average throughout the day. This year, the Euro-Par PhD Symposium received 12 submissions from 10 countries. The rigorous submission processes included an extended abstract and the endorsement letter from the official Ph.D. adviser(s). A thorough peer-reviewing process coupled with in depth discussions and agreement among reviewers (when applicable) resulted in 10 extended abstracts being accepted for presentation at the Euro-Par PhD Symposium 2021. The review process focused on the quality of the submissions, their innovation, and applicability to the topics covered by the Euro-Par conference.

The accepted extended abstracts represent an interesting mix of topics, addressing the efficient processing of machine learning workloads, impact of communication and computation in distributed and heterogeneous systems, parallel approaches and fault tolerance for linear algebra kernels, as well as profiling tools and tasking models for multi-cores. The chairs would like to thank all the Program Committee members, authors, presenters, attendees and the Euro-Par organizers for their help and support in making the first Euro-Par PhD Symposium a successful event.

Organization

Chairs

Didem Unat   Koç University, Turkey

Aleksandar Ilic   INESC-ID, IST, Universidade de Lisboa, Portugal

Program Committee

Mehmet Esat Belviranli   Colorado School of Mines, USA

Xing Cai   Simula Research Laboratory, Norway

Anshu Dubey   Argonne National Lab, USA

Francisco D. Igual   Universidad Complutense de Madrid, Spain

Sergio Santander-Jiménez   University of Extremadura, Spain

Lena Oden   FernUniversität Hagen, Germany

Interferences Between Communications and Computations in Distributed HPC Systems

Philippe Swartvagher[✉] [iD]

Inria Bordeaux – Sud-Ouest, 33405 Talence, France
philippe.swartvagher@inria.fr

Abstract. Overlapping communications with computations in distributed applications should increase their performances and allow to reach better scalability. This implies, by construction, communications are executed in parallel of computations. In this work, we explore the impact of computations on communication performances and *vice-versa*, with a focus on the role of memory contention. One main observation is that highly memory-bound computations can have a severe impact on network bandwidth.

Keywords: HPC · MPI · Memory contention

1 Introduction

Doing in parallel communications and computations (with non-blocking MPI calls or even more complex systems such as task-based runtime systems) is an increasing trend to get higher performances. It has been observed [2,3], that, sometimes, when computations and communications are executed side by side, communications are slower than nominal performances and computations can also be degraded.

Since possible interactions between communications and computations, and especially the impact on communication performances, are not well detailed in the literature (but only mentioned), we propose in this work to study the possible causes of these interferences and measure their impact on both communication and computing performances. Reported observations here deal with the impact of memory contention. Since we target HPC systems, we consider only fast networks (here, INFINIBAND) as well as inter-node communications.

We describe here our experimental protocol, provide first results and then discuss future work.

Advisers: Alexandre DENIS and Emmanuel JEANNOT
Inria Bordeaux – Sud-Ouest, 33405 Talence, France
{alexandre.denis,emmanuel.jeannot}@inria.fr

2   Methodology

Our goal is to measure performances of communications and computations when they are run side by side. To achieve this, we have designed a multithreaded and parallel benchmark using MPI+OpenMP. Per MPI process, one thread is dedicated to communications (it submits communication instructions and ensures MPI progression) and other threads (driven by OpenMP) do computations. This configuration mimics how some runtime systems work. The communication benchmark performs ping-pongs to measure network latency and bandwidth.

2.1   Benchmarking Protocol

We need to compare performances of communications and computations when they are executed alone and when they are executed together. Therefore we decomposed our benchmark into the following steps:

1. Computation without communication
2. Communication without computation
3. Computation with side by side communication

Computations and communications use different data and hence are completely independent. Plots to represent results compare performance of communications and computations when they are executed separately or simultaneously. The former are represented by plain curves and the later by dashed curves.

Regarding performances of communications, we use two metrics: *latency* by exchanging 4 bytes of data (one `float`), and *bandwidth* evaluated for 64 MB message size.

According to which effect we want to observe, instructions done by computing threads will be different. Computations have to be embarrassingly parallel to always get the maximum level of parallelism and avoid an overhead caused by scheduling and dependencies. Moreover we use weak scalability to easily change the number of computing cores (and thus change the level of parallelism).

To see the impact of memory contention caused by data used for computations and data used for communications, we generate memory contention by computing cores doing memory-bound kernels: `COPY` ($b[i] \leftarrow a[i]$) and `TRIAD` ($c[i] \leftarrow a[i] + C \times b[i]$) from the STREAM benchmark suite [4]. Moreover, to really produce memory contention, we allocate memory on a single NUMA node, to increase the traffic on the memory bus between cores belonging to different NUMA nodes. The performance of the computing benchmark is measured using the memory bandwidth *per core* (hence higher is better).

2.2   Experimental Environment

We ran our own benchmark suite[1] on several clusters with different characteristics: from small experimental clusters to large production ones. We present

---

[1] Available on https://gitlab.inria.fr/pswartva/memory-contention.

here the results obtained on **henri** nodes which are dual INTEL Xeon Gold 6140 at 2.3 GHz with 36 cores split across 4 NUMA nodes and 96 GB of RAM and equipped with INFINIBAND ConnectX-4 EDR. **henri** nodes run LINUX 5.7.7 with DEBIAN 10, GCC 9.3. We show results obtained with MADMPI, the MPI interface of NEWMADELEINE [1]; we observed similar results with other MPI implementations, such as OPENMPI 4.0.

3   First Observations

Our first hypothesis was that data accessed for computations and for communications may create contention on the memory bus, thus reducing performances. To test this hypothesis, we applied protocol described in previous section.

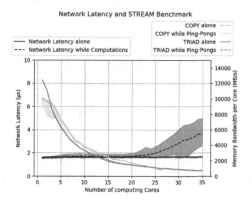

Fig. 1. Network latency (for 4 B) with memory-bound computations in parallel

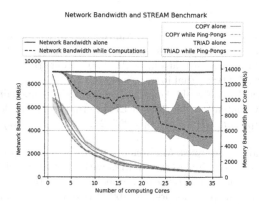

Fig. 2. Network bandwidth (for 64 MB) with memory-bound computations in parallel

Figure 1 shows that network latency is impacted by the STREAM operations when there are at least 22 computing cores and this impact can double the regular latency when all available cores are computing. However, STREAM operations are not impacted by the ping-pong benchmark. The network bandwidth is impacted sooner, from 3 computing cores (Fig. 2). When all available cores are computing, the network bandwidth is reduced by almost two third from the regular network bandwidth. Memory bandwidth measured by the STREAM benchmark is lower when network bandwidth is measured at the same time as when network latency is measured, which is expected because one bandwidth ping-pong transfers more data than a latency ping-pong (64 MB *vs* 4 B).

4   Conclusion

Overlapping communications with computations is a well-known technique to increase performance of applications. However, our first experiments report memory contention caused by data used for communications and for computations can reduce performances of communications and computations.

The rest of our study explores parameters impacting interferences between communications and computations such as the placement of data and threads, the size of the data transmitted through the network and the arithmetic intensity of instructions executed by computing threads. We also measure the effect of the variations of processor frequencies and the effect of using a task-based runtime system.

As future works, we would like to better understand origins of these interferences to predict and quantify them. We would also like to measure the impact of data movements between main memory and GPUs. This knowledge could then be used in runtime systems to better predict performances and thus better schedules tasks to minimize the impacts of the interferences between computations and communications.

References

1. Aumage, O., Brunet, E., Furmento, N., Namyst, R.: New Madeleine: a fast communication scheduling engine for high performance networks. In: Workshop on Communication Architecture for Clusters, CAC 2007, Long Beach, California, United States, March 2007. https://hal.inria.fr/inria-00127356
2. Groves, T., Grant, R.E., Arnold, D.: NiMC: characterizing and eliminating network-induced memory contention. In: 2016 IEEE International Parallel and Distributed Processing Symposium (IPDPS), pp. 253–262 (2016). https://doi.org/10.1109/IPDPS.2016.29
3. Langguth, J., Cai, X., Sourouri, M.: Memory bandwidth contention: communication vs computation tradeoffs in supercomputers with multicore architectures. In: 2018 IEEE 24th International Conference on Parallel and Distributed Systems (ICPADS), pp. 497–506 (2018). https://doi.org/10.1109/PADSW.2018.8644601
4. McCalpin, J.: Memory bandwidth and machine balance in high performance computers. IEEE Tech. Committee Comput. Architect. Newslett. 19–25 (1995)

Memory Efficient Deep Neural Network Training

Alena Shilova[1,2](✉) (iD)

[1] Inria Bordeaux – Sud-Ouest, Bordeaux, France
alena.shilova@inria.fr
[2] University of Bordeaux, Bordeaux, France

Abstract. Recently Artificial Intelligence (AI) has demonstrated a huge progress in solving complex problems such as image classification, text generation, translation... Its success is due to a development of hardware and algorithms making possible the emergence of Deep Neural Networks (DNNs). Such DNNs are composed of a number of operations from numerical linear algebra, whose order is defined with a Directed Acyclic Graph (DAG). These DNNs operate at the limit of the computational resources, and to go to deeper and more complex neural networks it is necessary either to design more powerful computational resources or optimize their usage. In our work, we address in particular the problem of lowering memory usage during the training of DNNs.

Keywords: Neural networks · Rematerialization · Offloading · Model parallelism

The functioning of DNNs in practice can be described in the following way: an input (e.g. a batch of images) is passed to the DAG of the neural network, processed further with all operations in the correct order and at the end the predictions (outputs of the DAG) are returned. Then the predictions can be applied for solving the problem of interest. The execution of the DNNs for obtaining the predictions is called inference. On the other hand, before the model can be used for the inference, this model should be trained. Training is performed within several iterations and during each iteration the weights (model parameters) are updated so that the prediction error was small.

Inference and training have different resource requirements. Inference is usually done on embedded devices like smartphones. In contrast, training is more memory and computationally expensive, usually done on clusters of machines and take hours or sometimes days to be finished. In our work we propose methods that help to limit the memory consumption of the training in two settings: training on a single machine and distributed training.

Advisors: Olivier Beaumont, Lionel Eyraud-Dubois, and Alexis Joly.

R. Chaves et al. (Eds.): Euro-Par 2021, LNCS 13098, pp. 515–519, 2022.
https://doi.org/10.1007/978-3-031-06156-1_41

1   Training on a Single Device

There are two major sources of memory consumption during the training phase. The first one comes from storing the model weights, while the second one comes from the activations (intermediate outputs of the DAG). To understand why it is important to keep activations, let us notice that one training iteration consists of two passes over the DAG: forward and backward propagations. During the forward propagation the inputs are propagated through the DAG to compute predictions, which is then followed by the evaluation of the loss function, showing how close the predictions are to the true target values. At the same time, updating weights requires the gradients of the loss with respect to the weights, which are computed during the backward propagation. The backward propagation first computes the gradient of the loss with respect to the predictions and then these values are propagated through the graph in the reverse order to evaluate the gradients of other weights using the chain rule. Gradient computation often requires the corresponding activation as an input: if $y = wg(x)$ and $\mathcal{L} = f(wg(x))$, while $a = g(x)$ is the activation of the operation g, $\mathcal{L}$ is loss and w is the weight, then $\frac{\partial \mathcal{L}}{\partial w} = \frac{\partial f}{\partial y}\frac{\partial y}{\partial w} = \frac{\partial f}{\partial y}a$. As a consequence, the combination of forward and backward propagation results in complex data dependencies depicted in Fig. 1. It shows an example of data dependencies of a simple DNN with L sequential layers (operations in DNNs), where the activations of forward operations F_i are the inputs of backward operations B_{i+1} and B_i.

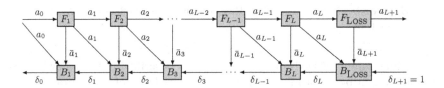

Fig. 1. Data dependencies induced the training phase of Sequential Deep Neural Networks.

Activations are not needed to be present in the memory all the time. Instead, they can be discarded and recomputed later (Rematerialization) or offloaded to the larger memory and prefetched later (Offloading). Solving the respective optimization problem can help significantly reduce the memory usage.

Rematerialization is the technique that allows to reduce memory consumption by discarding some activations, in particular the ones with a long lifetime, and recomputing them afterwards from the values that have been kept. This problem was well studied in Automatic Differentiation (AD) community in application to adjoint chains. Adjoint chains can be depicted as in Fig. 1, where all forward steps and backward steps have the same execution costs and each activation occupies only one unit of memory m (homogeneous chains). This problem is solved with a simple dynamic programming [4], whose complexity is $O(L^2m)$, where L is the number of layers (normally $L < 1000$). Due to the similarity between the computational graphs, the same solutions can be adapted for DNNs [3]. Still, the DNNs are more complex than adjoint chains because of their heterogeneity and more general DAG structure, hence the direct application of AD approaches results in the sub-optimal performance. Our work, despite not covering the DAG case, investigates the case of heterogeneous chains, which correspond to many practical DNNs. We found a dynamic programming algorithm that yields optimal rematerialization schedules in $O(L^6 m)$ and also proposed its relaxation which finds a solution in $O(L^3 m)$. In practice, this relaxed version proved to provide as good solutions as optimal ones under reasonable time (<1 min). The experiments confirmed the better performance of our algorithm with respect to the previous state-of-the-art. Based on it, we also designed a tool compatible with PyTorch[1]. The detailed results can be found in [5].

An alternative to the Rematerialization is Offloading. It exploits the two-level memory hierarchy that, for example, takes place between a GPU performing the training and a CPU. The modern GPUs have much smaller memory than CPUs, therefore when a GPU is running out of memory, the surplus can be sent to the CPU for a temporary storage. It is especially helpful when dealing with the first activations that may stay idle for a long time. As there are no additional recomputations, an overhead can be avoided by overlapping the communications with the computations. However, often the bandwidth being not very high prevents from hiding entirely the communications, leading to idle times when waiting for the end of transfers to release the memory. Thus, the careful selection and scheduling of the transfers is required. The naive approach [7] that offloads all activations and synchronizes after each operation may suffer from huge delays. We formulate the problem of finding the minimal overhead as an optimization problem which depends on the choice of activations to be offloaded and the schedule of the data transfers. In our paper [1] we proved that this problem is strongly NP-complete. In addition, we proposed two relaxations of this problem that can be solved optimally in polynomial and pseudo-polynomial times respectively. Their solutions can become heuristics for solving the general problem. We compared them with the previously known techniques through experiments, which showed that our heuristics overcome other known tools in most cases.

2   Training on Multiple Nodes

It is common to perform training on several machines to speed up the convergence. The most practiced in this regard is Data Parallelism, which replicates the model across all resources and in this way processes several images in parallel. The operations are performed independently, including the updates. Still, for the model to converge, it is important to do regular weight synchronizations, which are costly if weights are large. Furthermore, such an approach may suffer from memory issues as each worker has its own copy of weights and activations. In this case Data Parallelism should be combined with Rematerialization or Offloading.

---

[1] https://gitlab.inria.fr/hiepacs/rotor.

On the other hand, memory load can be significantly alleviated if both weights and activations are distributed across the available machines. Model Parallelism achieves it by assigning each processor to a part of a DNN. However, as the execution of the DNN is very sequential, there is no much opportunity to parallelize it and most of time the resources remain idle. Nevertheless, this method can be combined with pipelining: once a GPU executes forward operations on one batch, it can proceed to the next batch, without waiting for the backward operations to be available. When no processor is idle, then perfect scalability is reached. PipeDream [6] implements this idea and finds a load balancing with a dynamic programming. If the perfect load balancing is found, then in case of zero communication PipeDream can keep the resources constantly busy. Still, to ensure the validity of the training, it requires to store several copies of the weights and activations per processor, almost canceling the benefits of distributing them in the first place. In our work, we addressed the downsides of PipeDream and proposed improvements of the load balancing and scheduling (see [2]).

3   Future Works

We plan to continue working on improving memory saving methods. One promising direction is the combination of Offloading and Rematerialization, that can profit from the strong points of both methods. Moreover, we are going to test our tools on real use cases, one of which is training Pl@ntNet[2], an application for plant recognition. Because of memory limit, training deeper models with large images is not possible, hindering its further development. With our methods this obstacle can be overcome, creating new opportunities for further growth.

References

1. Beaumont, O., Eyraud-Dubois, L., Shilova, A.: Optimal GPU-CPU offloading strategies for deep neural network training. In: Malawski, M., Rzadca, K. (eds.) Euro-Par 2020. LNCS, vol. 12247, pp. 151–166. Springer, Cham (2020). https://doi.org/10.1007/978-3-030-57675-2_10
2. Beaumont, O., Eyraud-Dubois, L., Shilova, A.: Pipelined model parallelism: complexity results and memory considerations (2020)
3. Chen, T., Xu, B., Zhang, C., Guestrin, C.: Training deep nets with sublinear memory cost. arXiv preprint arXiv:1604.06174 (2016)
4. Griewank, A., Walther, A.: Algorithm 799: revolve: an implementation of checkpointing for the reverse or adjoint mode of computational differentiation. ACM Trans. Math. Softw. (TOMS) 26(1), 19–45 (2000)
5. Herrmann, J., Beaumont, O., Eyraud-Dubois, L., Hermann, J., Joly, A., Shilova, A.: Optimal checkpointing for heterogeneous chains: how to train deep neural networks with limited memory. arXiv preprint arXiv:1911.13214 (2019)

---

[2] https://plantnet.org/.

6. Narayanan, D., et al.: Pipedream: generalized pipeline parallelism for DNN training. In: Proceedings of the 27th ACM Symposium on Operating Systems Principles, pp. 1–15 (2019)
7. Rhu, M., Gimelshein, N., Clemons, J., Zulfiqar, A., Keckler, S.W.: vDNN: virtualized deep neural networks for scalable, memory-efficient neural network design. In: 2016 49th Annual IEEE/ACM International Symposium on Microarchitecture (MICRO), pp. 1–13. IEEE (2016)

A Low Overhead Tasking Model
for OpenMP

Chenle Yu[1,2](✉) ⓘ, Sara Royuela[1](✉) ⓘ, and Eduardo Quiñones[1](✉) ⓘ

[1] Barcelona Supercomputing Center, Barcelona, Spain
{chenle.yu,sara.royuela,eduardo.quinones}@bsc.es
[2] Universitat Politècnica de Catalunya, Barcelona, Spain

Abstract. OpenMP is a parallel programming model widely used on shared-memory systems. Over the years, the OpenMP community tries to extend the OpenMP Specification to adapt it to modern architectures and expand its usage to other domains such as Embedded Systems. Our work focuses on improving the OpenMP tasking model by reducing the task runtime overhead. To do so, we propose a new OpenMP framework, namely, taskgraph, based on the concept of task dependency graph, where nodes are OpenMP tasks and edges describe the dependencies among them. The new framework is shown to be particularly suitable for fine-grain parallelism. It can be extended to other programming models with ease, improving the interoperability of OpenMP with different programming models, such as CUDA.

Keywords: OpenMP · Fine-grain parallelism · GPU · CUDA

1 What Is Missing and What We Propose

With the increasing complexity of embedded applications (e.g., ADAS for Advanced Driver-Assistance Systems), there is a rising need in the Safety-Critical Embedded System industry to utilize modern multi-core or many-core processing units. Consequently, the existing serial code must be parallelized, and OpenMP is considered as a candidate to ease this process. However, originally introduced to be used in the HPC domain, OpenMP specification is not conforming with the Predictability and Determinism requirements for Safety-Critical Embedded Systems.

To cope with this limitation, the OpenMP tasking model has been extensively studied in the Embedded System domain by virtue of the similarities between OpenMP Task Dependency Graph (TDG) and DAG (Directed Acyclic Graph) representation of Real-Time tasks. M. Serrano et al. analyzed the timing aspect of OpenMP tasks [5]. S. Royuela et al. shared their insights into the OpenMP 4.5 specification and the modifications needed to make it functional-safe [4]. Roberto E. Vargas [6] and A. Munera [3] proposed different frameworks capable of reducing OpenMP tasking model's memory consumption for embedded systems by statically generating the TDG corresponding to the OpenMP program annotated with **task** directive.

© Springer Nature Switzerland AG 2022
R. Chaves et al. (Eds.): Euro-Par 2021, LNCS 13098, pp. 520–524, 2022.
https://doi.org/10.1007/978-3-031-06156-1_42

Inspired by their work, we propose a new OpenMP framework, namely `taskgraph`, targeting fine-grain parallelism [8]. The framework is based on generating the Task Dependency Graph corresponding to an OpenMP taskified region, that is, a block of user code solely composed of control-flow statements and OpenMP tasks, no sequential code is declared between them. The generation can be static at compile-time if all task data is known beforehand. Otherwise, the TDG will be recorded at runtime, when the `taskgraph` region is executed for the first time. In cases where the TDG is run multiple times after being generated, we name such an execution model as *define-once-run-repeatedly*. According to our experiments, the TDG execution reduces the runtime overhead related to the shared resource contention and the task management (such as task creation, dependency resolution, etc.). Consequently, this increases the performance of the OpenMP tasking model, an important aspect that the aforementioned work did not accomplish.

Fortunately, other parallel programming models also use TDG representation to express the workflow, as is the case for CUDA Graph[1] introduced by Nvidia. Although demonstrated to be more efficient, CUDA Graph demands considerable effort from application developers to build: on average, to set one graph node, 8 CUDA Runtime API function calls are needed[2]. This incites us to build a mechanism in OpenMP capable of transforming an OpenMP TDG into a CUDA Graph. By doing so, we enhance the interoperability of OpenMP with CUDA and improve the CUDA Graph programmability, alleviating the effort needed to run applications at scale on Nvidia GPUs.

We propose to add `taskgraph` as an OpenMP clause to `task` and `target` directives. Listing 1 shows an example of using this clause.

```
#pragma omp parallel
#pragma omp single
#pragma omp task/target taskgraph
for (i=0; i<M; i+=BS) {
  for (j=0; j<N; j+=BS) {
    if (i==0 && j==0)
      #pragma omp task depend (out: Mat[i+BS-1][j+BS-1])
      processing_block (i,j);
    ...
  }
}
```

List. 1. Excerpt of HOG (Histogram of Oriented Gradients) object detection algorithm

---

[1] https://developer.nvidia.com/blog/cuda-graphs/.

[2] https://github.com/NVIDIA/cuda-samples/tree/master/Samples/simpleCudaGraphs.

2   Implementation and Preliminary Results

The lowering of `taskgraph` is implemented on top of the Mercurium compiler[3], a modular and lightweight compiler developed by Barcelona Supercomputing Center. The runtime implementation of `taskgraph` is based on the GCC 7.3.0 GOMP library. Main runtime improvements comprise i) introducing a new set of lightweight data structures to manage tasks within a `taskgraph` region, ii) updating existing queueing mechanism to handle the new data structures, iii) a recording mechanism that captures all task data at runtime and creates a TDG from this information.

2.1   Performance of `taskgraph`

Taking Listing 1 as an example, if M, N and BS (Block Size), variables determining the control flow, are known at compile-time (referred to as *Dataless taskgraph* case), we will be able to create a TDG with the correct task dependencies before execution. This allows the resolution of task dependencies at compile-time, resulting in runtime overhead reductions. Moreover, if all data needed by tasks can be captured at compile-time (referred to as *taskgraph* case), it is possible to create task instances while compiling. Consequently, the runtime overhead can further be alleviated.

Both scenarios are presented in Fig. 1(a), where we show the speedup obtained by executing the HOG application with a fixed problem size. Hence, in the x-axis, by increasing the number of tasks, we reduce the task granularity. The experiment was realized on a node of Marenostrum 4 cluster [1], equipped with 2 Intel Xeon 8160 CPUs, having 24 physical cores each. As the figure depicts, our method provides similar performance for coarse-grain tasks, and it delivers better speedup when the task granularity is small.

Figure 1(b) shows the benefits of taskgraph in another scenario, where the same set of tasks needs to be executed multiple times. This often occurs in simulation applications, iterative problem solvers and applications used on embedded systems: e.g., N-body simulation, Gauss-Seidel iterative method, etc. In this experiment, the repetitive execution of the same taskgraph reduces task-related overhead (task creation and task dependency resolution) at every iteration, resulting in a better speedup.

2.2   `taskgraph` for Heterogeneous Computing

Although OpenMP already supports device tasks with its `target` directive, the performance of offloaded work is often worse than the manually written code. Our work tackles this problem by generating CUDA code from the `target taskgraph` directive [7]. In Fig. 2, we compare the performance of original OpenMP offloading using `target` directive and the `taskgraph` generated CUDA

---

[3] https://pm.bsc.es/mcxx.

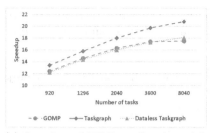
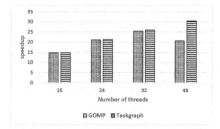

(a) Speedup of HOG application with different task granularities, 24 threads

(b) Speedup of HOG application after 128 iterations

Fig. 1. Speedup comparison with `taskgraph` and the original GOMP runtime

code. The experiment used an embedded Xavier GPU and a node of CTE-POWER cluster [2] of Barcelona Supercomputing Center, with 2 Power9 8335-GTH CPUs and 4 V100 as GPUs. The chart shows that the original OpenMP offloading performance is one order of magnitude slower than the generated CUDA code.

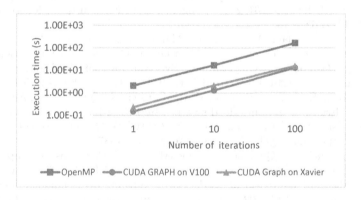

Fig. 2. Execution time (seconds) of Cholesky matrix decomposition

3   Conclusion and Future Perspectives

In this work, we present our new OpenMP framework `taskgraph` that reduces OpenMP tasking model's overhead by using Task Dependency Graph. The results show that this method provides better performance in different scenarios: i) when the TDG can be created at compile time, ii) and when the TDG is built at run time and is executed multiple times. In both cases, `taskgraph` allows us to define-once-run-repeatedly, delivering promising performance compared to the original GOMP runtime. As a future objective, we plan to implement `taskgraph` on LLVM, we expect a performance gain of the same magnitude as for GCC runtime, since both OpenMP implementations are impacted similarly by the task granularity.

Acknowledgements. This work has been supported by the EU H2020 project AMPERE under the grant agreement no. 871669.

References

1. BSC: MareNostrum IV User's Guide (2017). https://www.bsc.es/support/MareNostrum4-ug.pdf
2. BSC: CTE-POWER User's Guide (2020). https://www.bsc.es/user-support/power.php
3. Munera, A., Royuela, S., Quinones, E.: Towards a qualifiable OpenMP framework for embedded systems. In: Proceedings of the 2020 Design, Automation and Test in Europe Conference and Exhibition, DATE, vol. 2020, no. 2, pp. 903–908 (2020). https://doi.org/10.23919/DATE48585.2020.9116230
4. Royuela, S., Duran, A., Serrano, M.A., Quiñones, E., Martorell, X.: A functional safety OpenMP* for critical real-time embedded systems. In: de Supinski, B.R., Olivier, S.L., Terboven, C., Chapman, B.M., Müller, M.S. (eds.) IWOMP 2017. LNCS, vol. 10468, pp. 231–245. Springer, Cham (2017). https://doi.org/10.1007/978-3-319-65578-9_16
5. Serrano, M.A., Melani, A., Vargas, R., Marongiu, A., Bertogna, M., Quiñones, E.: Timing characterization of OpenMP4 tasking model. In: 2015 International Conference on Compilers, Architecture and Synthesis for Embedded Systems, CASES 2015, pp. 157–166 (2015). https://doi.org/10.1109/CASES.2015.7324556
6. Vargas, R.E., Royuela, S., Serrano, M.A., Martorell, X., Quinones, E.: A lightweight OpenMP4 run-time for embedded systems. In: Proceedings of the Asia and South Pacific Design Automation Conference, ASP-DAC, 25–28-January(line 1), pp. 43–49 (2016). https://doi.org/10.1109/ASPDAC.2016.7427987
7. Yu, C., Royuela, S., Quiñones, E.: OpenMP to CUDA graphs: a compiler-based transformation to enhance the programmability of NVIDIA devices. In: Proceedings of the 23rd International Workshop on Software and Compilers for Embedded Systems, SCOPES 2020, pp. 42–47 (2020). https://doi.org/10.1145/3378678.3391881
8. Yu, C., Royuela, S., Quiñones, E.: Enhancing OpenMP tasking model: performance and portability. In: Proceedings of the 17th International Workshop on OpenMP, IWOMP 2021, Bristol, UK (2021). https://doi.org/10.1007/978-3-030-85262-7_3

Parallelization and Auto-scheduling of Data Access Queries in ML Workloads

Pawel Bratek[1]([✉]), Lukasz Szustak[1], and Jaroslaw Zola[2]

[1] Czestochowa University of Technology, Dabrowskiego 69,
42-201 Czestochowa, Poland
{pawel.bratek,lukasz.szustak}@pcz.pl
[2] University at Buffalo, Buffalo, NY 14260, USA
jzola@buffalo.edu

Abstract. We propose an auto-scheduling mechanism to execute counting queries in machine learning applications. Our approach improves the runtime efficiency of query streams by selecting, in the on-line manner, the optimal execution strategy for each query. We also discuss how to scale up counting queries in multi-threaded applications.

Keywords: Data access queries · Auto-scheduling · Machine learning · SABNAtk

1 Introduction and Problem Formulation

Counting data records with instances that support some specific configuration of the selected variables is one of the basic operations used by machine learning algorithms. The problem manifests itself each time a probability distribution has to be estimated, and spans applications ranging from Bayesian networks learning through association rule mining and classification [2,4] all the way to deep learning [6] and information retrieval [5].

Counting is typically viewed as a black-box procedure, and implemented using simple and not necessarily efficient strategies, e.g., contingency tables. At the same time, in many applications it accounts for over 90% of the total execution time [1]. Consequently, improving performance of counting can directly translate into better performance of these applications. The current specialized approaches based on data indexing, such as ADtrees [3], have limited applicability due to the significant preprocessing and memory overheads. Recently, Karan et al. [1] proposed SABNAtk, a new strategy in which counting queries and their context of execution are abstracted such that the counts can be aggregated as a stream, irrespective of the user-defined downstream processing.

Consider a set of n categorical random variables $\mathcal{X} = \{X_1, X_2, \ldots, X_n\}$, where the domain of variable X_i is represented by r_i states $[x_{i1}, \ldots, x_{ir_i}]$. Let $D = [D_1, D_2, \ldots, D_n]$ be a complete database of instances of $\mathcal{X}$, where D_i, $|D_i| = m$, records observed states of X_i. Given the set of input variables

© Springer Nature Switzerland AG 2022
R. Chaves et al. (Eds.): Euro-Par 2021, LNCS 13098, pp. 525–529, 2022.
https://doi.org/10.1007/978-3-031-06156-1_43

$\{X_i, X_j, \ldots\} \subseteq \mathcal{X}$ represented by database D, the counting query $\text{COUNT}((X_i = x_i) \wedge (X_j = x_j) \wedge \ldots)$ returns the size of the support in D for the specific assignment $[x_i, x_j, \ldots]$ of variables $\{X_i, X_j, \ldots\}$. For example, the result of executing query $\text{COUNT}((X_1 = 3) \wedge (X_2 = 1) \wedge (X_3 = 2))$ over database D shown in Fig. 1 is 2, because there are two instances matching the query condition. Simple counting query generalizes to a set of queries over the same set of variables $\text{COUNT}(X_i, X_j, \ldots)$, in which we want to retrieve all non-zero answers to queries $\text{COUNT}((X_i = x_i) \wedge (X_j = x_j) \wedge \ldots)$ for all possible assignments of query variables. We will say that individual queries within COUNT query share context. For example, the answer to query $\text{COUNT}(X_1, X_3)$ would return the following list of counts: $[((1, 2), 2), ((2, 1), 2), ((3, 2), 3)]$, where each entry is in the form $((x_i, x_j), \text{COUNT}((X_1 = x_i) \wedge (X_3 = x_j)))$.

The starting point for our work are counting strategies proposed in [1], and implemented in the open-source C++17 library SABNAtk. In SABNAtk, the counting queries COUNT can be answered using one of three strategies: 1) simple contingency table (CT), in which contingency table over all possible states of query variables is constructed, 2) bitmap counter (BC) in which input data is represented via bitmaps and counting is reduced to bitmap intersecting and bit counting, and 3) radix counter (RC) in which counting is based on columnar data partitioning similar to radix sorting. Which of the strategies is the best depends on many factors (e.g., query variables, data complexity, etc.) and hence it is not possible to state *a-priori* that one strategy dominates the others (see Fig. 2). In this work, we focus on scaling up SABNAtk in multi-threaded applications. Specifically, we seek to introduce a new auto-scheduling mechanism that learns online strategy to select optimal query processing counter.

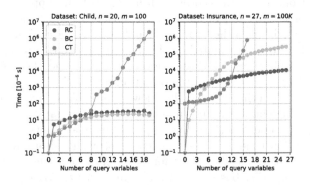

	D_1	D_2	D_3
1	2	2	1
2	3	1	2
3	1	3	2
4	1	2	2
5	2	1	1
6	1	1	2
7	3	1	2
8	3	2	2

Fig. 1. Toy example of database D with three variables.

Fig. 2. Execution time of counting queries by different query strategies depending on the number of query variables (shorter is better). Each point represents an average time of ten randomly generated queries

2   Proposed Approach and Preliminary Results

To enable multi-threaded execution, we focus on two main questions: 1) how to efficiently execute any individual query, and 2) how to deal with a batch of queries generated concurrently by multiple threads? The strategies implemented within SABNAtk are stateless. Consequently, the simplest approach is to execute a query within the thread that issued it. However, in the real-world applications, it is common that consecutive queries share some of the query variables (i.e., context). Hence we propose to introduce a queuing and query rewriting mechanism to mitigate redundant data accesses.

To address the first question, we first experimentally assess and then theoretically characterize performance of each of SABNAtk's counting strategies. Figure 2 shows one representative example of execution profile. From the figure, it follows that the choice of the optimal strategy is non-trivial. At the same time, choosing the right counter offers significant reduction in the query execution time.

Our key idea is to pose the problem of selecting the optimal query execution strategy as an online regression problem. To this end, we first analytically derive the asymptotic average complexity of each counter as a function of the query size and the query complexity. The regression function is fit on-the-fly concurrently with serving the queries. Initially, the choice of strategy is random to mitigate overfitting, and as the execution proceeds, it becomes guided by our trained regression function.

Consider a single query $COUNT(X_1, X_2, \ldots, X_N)$ of size N. Additionally, let $q = \prod_{i=1}^{N} r_i$ be the product of arity of query variables. The cost of the CT strategy is given by $N \cdot m + q$ in both worst and average case. The average complexity of BC depends directly on the input data and hence is difficult to characterize exactly. Therefore, we make a simplifying assumption that each variable $X_i \in \mathcal{X}$ is derived from a multinomial distribution with K equiprobable states $[x_{i1}, \ldots, x_{iK}]$. Then from the Bernoulli scheme and the properties of expectation we can derive the cost as $m \times \sum_{L=0}^{N} K^L \cdot (1 - (1 - \frac{1}{K^L})^m)$. Finally, the cost of RC is asymptotically linear and amounts to $N \cdot m$. The derived average complexities allow us to define the following functions as query execution cost predictors:

$$CT(N, K, m, \boldsymbol{\beta}) = \beta_1 \cdot N \cdot m + \beta_2 \cdot K^{\beta_3 \cdot N} + \beta_4$$

$$BC(N, K, m, \boldsymbol{\beta}) = \begin{cases} \beta_1 \cdot m \cdot \dfrac{(K^{\beta_2 \cdot N + 1} - 1)}{(K - 1)} & N \leq N_0 \\ BC(N_0, K, m, \beta_1, \beta_2) + \beta_3 \cdot (N - N_0) \cdot m + \beta_4 & N > N_0, \end{cases}$$

$$RC(N, m, \boldsymbol{\beta}) = \beta_1 \cdot N \cdot m + \beta_2,$$

where N_0 is a number satisfying the condition: $K^{N_0} < m \wedge K^{N_0+1} > m$. The parameter K follows from the assumption about input data, and in practice, can be replaced by the arithmetic mean of the arity of variables included in the query (or any other meaningful statistics, e.g., median, etc.).

We use defined functions to build online regression model $Y = f(\boldsymbol{X}, \boldsymbol{\beta}) + \epsilon$ for each counter. Our approach assumes a stream of incoming queries that initially are performed by randomly selected counters. We count cycles needed for their executions using Performance Application Programming Interface (PAPI) and apply them to the regression model as observations of the dependent variable Y. For a given query, we choose a counter with the smallest estimated cost of execution. We update the values of vector β after each query realization what results in better knowledge about the efficiency of counters depending on the query complexity.

In Table 1 we outline our preliminary results. Here the improvement factor shows how the auto-scheduling mechanism improves the overall performance. To obtain the baseline, we executed 1000 randomly generated queries for each of the presented configurations, and collected the total realization time of these queries using a randomly selected counter for each of them. Then we processed exactly the same query stream using our proposed auto-scheduling mechanism. The improvement factor is the ratio of the two runtimes. As shown in Table 1, our strategy offers improvement from $10.74\times$ to $778.21\times$ depending on the input data. These are very significant improvements considering that in real-world scenarios average ML application has to handle billions of queries.

Table 1. Improvement factor with respect to random strategy

Dataset	n	Improvement factor		
		$m = 1K$	$m = 10K$	$m = 100K$
Child	20	778.21	87.95	22.62
Insurance	27	533.30	63.15	16.64
Mildew	35	282.58	19.17	26.69
Alarm	37	311.74	18.24	10.74
Barley	48	145.81	15.22	17.04

Currently, we work on query queuing and rewriting mechanism for multi-threaded environments. The problem is challenging as it requires careful choice of on-line strategies to decide when sufficient number of queries are queued to improve average query processing speed while maintaining acceptable latency.

Acknowledgments. This research was supported by the National Science Centre (Poland) under grant no. UMO-2017/26/D/ST6/00687.

References

1. Karan, S., Eichhorn, M., Hurlburt, B., Iraci, G., Zola, J.: Fast counting in machine learning applications. In: Uncertainty in Artificial Intelligence (2018)
2. Kohavi, R.: Scaling up the accuracy of Naive-Bayes classifiers: a decision-tree hybrid. In: International Conference on Knowledge Discovery and Data Mining, pp. 202–207 (1996)

3. Moore, A., Lee, M.: Cached sufficient statistics for efficient machine learning with large datasets. J. Artif. Intell. Res. **8**, 67–91 (1998)
4. Quinlan, J.: Bagging, boosting, and c4.5. In: AAAI Innovative Applications of Artificial Intelligence Conferences, pp. 725–730 (1996)
5. Ramos, J.: Using TF-IDF to determine word relevance in document queries. In: Instructional Conference on Machine Learning, pp. 133–142 (2003)
6. Salakhutdinov, R., Hinton, G.: Deep Boltzmann machines. In: International Conference on Artificial Intelligence and Statistics, pp. 448–455 (2009)

Application-Based Fault Tolerance for Numerical Linear Algebra at Large Scale

Daniel Alberto Torres González$^{(\boxtimes)}$

LIPN, CNRS UMR 7030, Université Sorbonne Paris Nord, Villetaneuse, France
torres@lipn.univ-paris13.fr

Abstract. Large scale architectures provide us with high computing power, but as the size of the systems grows, computation units are more likely to fail. Fault-tolerant mechanisms have arisen in parallel computing to face the challenge of dealing with all possible errors that may occur at any moment during the execution of parallel programs. Algorithms used by fault-tolerant programs must scale and be resilient to software/hardware failures. Recent parallel algorithms have demonstrated properties that can be exploited to make them fault-tolerant. In my thesis, I design, implement and evaluate parallel and distributed fault-tolerant numerical computation kernels for dense linear algebra. I take advantage of intrinsic algebraic and algorithmic properties of communication-avoiding algorithms in order to make them fault-tolerant. I am focusing on dense matrix factorization kernels: I have results on LU and preliminary results on QR. Using performance evaluation and formal methods, I am showing that they can tolerate crash-type failures, either re-spawning new processes on-the-fly or ignoring the error.

Keywords: Fault tolerance · High Performance Computing · Linear algebra · Matrix factorizations · LU

1 Introduction

High Performance Computing (HPC) systems continue growing exponentially; the number of processors and nodes is increasing. *Top500* is a statistical list with ranks and details of the 500 world's most powerful supercomputers. The November 2020 Top500 ranking shows that 5 machines feature more than a million of cores and all 500 machines listed have more than 10 000 cores (not including accelerators). Meanwhile, as the number of hardware components increases, the overall system Mean Time Between Failures (MTBF) is reduced to only a few hours [12]. For instance, the supercomputer Blue Waters located at the National Center for Supercomputing Applications (NCSA) at the University of Illinois had an MTBF of approximately 4.8 h [11]. Therefore, fault tolerance is necessary for

C. Coti and L. Petrucci—Advisors.

© Springer Nature Switzerland AG 2022
R. Chaves et al. (Eds.): Euro-Par 2021, LNCS 13098, pp. 530–534, 2022.
https://doi.org/10.1007/978-3-031-06156-1_44

such large scale systems to ensure that computational intensive applications can survive failures with a small overhead.

The total number of hardware and software components, the complexity of these components and the system reliability, availability and scalability are factors to deal with in HPC systems, because hardware or software failures may occur anytime during the execution of high parallel applications [9].

I am working in the context of *fail-stop* failures. Several approaches exist to handle failures. System-level fault tolerance is transparent to the user: the distributed run-time environment implements mechanisms such as rollback recovery and the application does not need to be modified [5]. In my thesis, I am following an *application-based* approach: my goal is to provide computation kernels that can survive failures. I use the *User-Level Failure Mitigation* model [2]. Moreover, in order to make sure that the application can survive failures at any moment of the execution, I verify reliability properties of my algorithms with formal methods.

2   General Description

My work focuses on adding fault-tolerant mechanisms to dense linear algebra algorithms to make them able to survive in volatile environments in spite of failures. My work is based on communication-avoiding algorithms, in which I take advantage of properties that can be exploited to design new scalable and robust fault-tolerant algorithms, for instance introducing redundancy of intermediate results [3,7]. Fault-tolerant algorithms must be designed and evaluated considering how robust they are and how much computational overhead they introduce with respect to a non-fault-tolerant algorithm [4].

To model and validate the robustness and the resilience of my algorithms, I use formal methods (Coloured Petri Net model). A formal model developed in this thesis [6] can be seen in Fig. 1b. It helps proving reliability and correct functioning of a fault-tolerant tall and skinny algorithm.

To measure the cost of our fault-tolerant mechanisms on the performance, I first consider a failure-free execution with no fault-tolerance mechanism as the baseline; I measure the overhead of the fault-tolerance mechanism on a failure-free execution; last, I measure the cost of the recovery procedure by injecting a random failure during the execution. Results show that these fault-tolerant algorithms introduce very little computational overhead.

3   LU Factorization Algorithms and Experiments

Many applications in linear algebra rely on a LU factorization, either for a tall-and-skinny matrix or on a wider, potentially square, matrix. The TSLU algorithm was designed for a *tall and skinny* input matrix (i.e. a matrix with M rows and N columns, with $M \gg N$); the data is distributed between processes along a 1D distribution, allowing each of them holding complete lines.

The first phase consists of finding *pivot rows* to improve the numerical stability of the computation. In TSLU we are using a specific algorithm, called *tournament pivoting*, in order to find the best row-pivots to factor the entire matrix at low communication cost. The *Communication-Avoiding LU* (CALU) [10] algorithm also factors a matrix as $A = LU$, taking a potentially square matrix as input. It iterates over block-column sub-matrices called *panels*. A panel is the leftmost block-column sub-matrix. Since a panel is a tall and skinny matrix, CALU uses TSLU to compute the LU factorization of each panel. CALU uses a 2D grid of processes dividing the square matrix into smaller sub-blocks and assigning each sub-block to be calculated to one process on the grid [1]. At each iteration, it takes the leftmost non-processed panel and computes its LU factorization [8,13].

FT-TSLU and FT-CALU are the fault-tolerant versions of TSLU and CALU proposed in this research. They can recover from crash-type process failures at run-time and proceed with the computation beyond them. When an error is detected by the run-time environment, they re-spawn all the failed processes at once, repair the communicator used by the processes to exchange information and the current state on the calculation of a matrix. To achieve this last property, they keep track on the intermediate results obtained at each step backing them up on memory or on a storage device. Hence, all processes are able to share their previous known results with a process to be restored. The restoration procedure proposed in this work has been designed to allow any process in the global communicator to detect errors at any point of the algorithm, independently from the task a process is in charge of.

Figure 1a shows execution times for CALU/FT-CALU, showing that our algorithms scale satisfactorily as the number of processes increases. Also note that non-fault-tolerant and fault-tolerant failure-free executions are similar. Thus, added fault tolerance mechanisms generate a small overhead over non-fault-tolerant algorithms, but it is minimal compared to the total execution time.

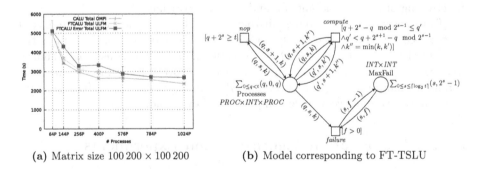

(a) Matrix size $100\,200 \times 100\,200$ (b) Model corresponding to FT-TSLU

Fig. 1. FT-CALU execution times and FT-TSLU Petri Net

I have designed algorithms for QR and Cholesky factorizations following a similar approach, and I am currently performing their performance evaluation.

4   Conclusions and Perspectives

My work aims at handling failures, which cannot be avoided at extreme scale, with the imminence of exascale. My goal is to design algorithms that can proceed with the computation in spite of failures. I have already designed and implemented algorithms that validate my approach, since they have shown good scalability and little overhead when failures occur. I am pursuing my efforts to design new fault-tolerant mechanisms for other dense and sparse linear algebra kernels: QR, Cholesky, and algorithms for sparse matrices. Compared with LU, the main difference resides on the trailing matrix update phase. Also, a general formal model for fault-tolerant communication-avoiding algorithms is still under development. Its design is thought to prove how failures can be represented and modeled using the abstraction provided by Coloured Petri Nets. It can also work on the design of proofs for future fault-tolerant algorithms.

References

1. Agullo, E., Coti, C., Dongarra, J., Hérault, T., Langem, J.: QR factorization of tall and skinny matrices in a grid computing environment. In: 2010 IEEE International Symposium on Parallel Distributed Processing (IPDPS), pp. 1–11 (2010)
2. Bland, W., Bouteiller, A., Herault, T., Hursey, J., Bosilca, G., Dongarra, J.J.: An evaluation of user-level failure mitigation support in MPI. In: Träff, J.L., Benkner, S., Dongarra, J.J. (eds.) EuroMPI 2012. LNCS, vol. 7490, pp. 193–203. Springer, Heidelberg (2012). https://doi.org/10.1007/978-3-642-33518-1_24
3. Coti, C.: Exploiting redundant computation in communication-avoiding algorithms for algorithm-based fault tolerance. In: 2016 IEEE Big Data Security, IEEE HPSC, and IEEE IDS, pp. 214–219 (2016)
4. Coti, C.: Scalable, robust, fault-tolerant parallel QR factorization. In: 2016 IEEE CSE and IEEE EUC and DCABES, pp. 626–633 (2016)
5. Coti, C., et al.: Blocking vs. non-blocking coordinated checkpointing for large-scale fault tolerant MPI. In: SC 2006, p. 18 (2006)
6. Coti, C., Petrucci, L., Torres González, D.A.: Fault-tolerant matrix factorisation: a formal model and proof. In: 6th International Workshop on Synthesis of Complex Parameters (SynCoP) (2019)
7. Demmel, J., Grigori, L., Hoemmen, M., Langou, J.: Communication-avoiding parallel and sequential QR factorizations. CoRR abs/0806.2159 (2008)
8. Demmel, J., Grigori, L., Hoemmen, M., Langou, J.: Communication-optimal parallel and sequential QR and LU factorizations. SIAM J. Sci. Comput. 34(1), 206–239 (2012)
9. Dongarra, J., et al.: The international exascale software project roadmap. Int. J. High Perform. Comput. Appl. 25, 3–60 (2011)
10. Grigori, L., Demmel, J.W., Xiang, H.: CALU: a communication optimal LU factorization algorithm. SIAM J. Matrix Anal. Appl. 32(4), 1317–1350 (2011)
11. Martino, C.D., Kalbarczyk, Z., Iyer, R.K., Baccanico, F., Fullop, J., Kramer, W.: Lessons learned from the analysis of system failures at petascale: the case of Blue Waters. In: IEEE/IFIP DSN 2014, pp. 610–621 (2014)

12. Reed, D., Lu, C., Mendes, C.: Reliability challenges in large systems. Future Gener. Comput. Syst. **22**(3), 293–302 (2006)

13. Solomonik, E., Demmel, J.: Communication-optimal parallel 2.5D matrix multiplication and LU factorization algorithms. In: Jeannot, E., Namyst, R., Roman, J. (eds.) Euro-Par 2011. LNCS, vol. 6853, pp. 90–109. Springer, Heidelberg (2011). https://doi.org/10.1007/978-3-642-23397-5_10

Communication Overlapping Pipelined Conjugate Gradients for Distributed Memory Systems and Heterogeneous Architectures

Manasi Tiwari[(✉)] and Sathish Vadhiyar

Department of Computational and Data Sciences, Indian Institute of Science,
Bangalore, India
{manasitiwari,vss}@iisc.ac.in

Abstract. Preconditioned Conjugate Gradient (PCG) method has been one of the widely used methods for solving linear systems of equations for sparse problems. Pipelined PCG (PIPECG) attempts to eliminate the dependencies in the computations in the PCG algorithm and overlap non-dependent computations by reorganizing the traditional PCG code and using non-blocking allreduces . We have developed a novel pipelined PCG algorithm called PIPECG-OATI (One Allreduce per Two Iterations) which reduces the number of non-blocking allreduces to one per two iterations and provides large overlap of global communication and computations at higher number of cores in distributed memory CPU systems. PIPECG-OATI gives up to 3× speedup over PCG and 1.73× speedup over PIPECG at large number of cores.

For GPU accelerated heterogeneous architectures, we have developed three methods for efficient execution of the PIPECG algorithm. These methods achieve task and data parallelism. Our methods give considerable performance improvements over PCG CPU and GPU implementations of Paralution and PETSc libraries.

Keywords: Preconditioned Conjugate Gradient · Overlapping communication and computations · Distributed memory systems · Heterogeneous architectures

1 PIPECG-OATI for Distributed Memory Systems

1.1 Problem Statement

The main computational kernels in Preconditioned Conjugate Gradient (PCG) [3] are Sparse Matrix Vector Product (SPMV), Preconditioner Application (PC), Vector-Multiply-Adds (VMAs) and Dot Products. For distributed memory systems, the bottleneck in PCG are the three dot products per iteration. They result in synchronization and waiting of the processors which cannot be overlapped with any independent computations. As the number of cores increase,

© Springer Nature Switzerland AG 2022
R. Chaves et al. (Eds.): Euro-Par 2021, LNCS 13098, pp. 535–539, 2022.
https://doi.org/10.1007/978-3-031-06156-1_45

the time taken for allreduce increases and the cores wait for a longer time. The pipelined PCG method (PIPECG) [2] was introduced for distributed memory systems. It reduces the number of allreduces in PCG to one per iteration and overlaps it with one PC and one SPMV. While this is a reasonable strategy for smaller number of cores, executions of the PIPECG code at larger number of cores show that the time taken by the allreduce can not be fully overlapped by the PC and SPMV.

As we are moving to the exascale era, in order to obtain good performance at larger number of cores, we must reduce the number of allreduces in the PCG method even more and remove dependencies between computations so that non blocking allreduce can be used to overlap global communication with more computations.

1.2   Methodology

In order to solve the aforementioned problem, we propose a novel algorithm, PIPECG-OATI (PIPECG-One Allreduce per Two Iterations) [5], which combines two iterations of PIPECG, reduces the number of non-blocking allreduces to one per two iterations and then overlaps them with two PCs and two SPMVs. This is done at the cost of introducing extra VMA operations.

The primary challenge in combining two iterations of PIPECG and pipelining it is that it has dependencies that require an extra PC and an extra SPMV for each combined-iteration. So, a total of three PCs and three SPMVs would be required in a combined-iteration as opposed to two PCs and two SPMVs in two uncombined iterations. Since the PC and SPMV are the most computationally intensive kernels in each iteration, an extra PC and SPMV would degrade the performance of PIPECG-OATI. To deal with this challenge, we introduced new non-recurrence computations in each iteration of PIPECG-OATI which brings down the number of PCs and SPMVs to two per combined-iteration.

For achieving PIPECG-OATI from PIPECG, we follow the below steps:

1. Collect the PCs and SPMVs of two iterations at one point in the combined-iteration by introducing recurrence relations.
2. Collect the dot products of two iterations at one point in the combined-iteration by expressing the vectors as recurrence relations.
3. As the new dot products will need results of PC and SPMV beforehand, introduce recurrence relations for these PC and SPMV.
4. To deal with extra PC and SPMV, introduce new non-recurrence computations.

An elaborate derivation can be found in [5].

1.3   Experiments and Results

We have implemented our PIPECG-OATI method along with optimizations like merged vector operations in the PETSc library [1][1]. We ran tests on our Insti-

---

[1] Available as KSPPIPECG2. URL: https://www.mcs.anl.gov/petsc/petsc-master/docs/manualpages/KSP/KSPPIPECG2.html.

tute's supercomputer cluster called SahasraT, a Cray-XC40 machine which has 1376 compute nodes. Each node has two CPU sockets with 12 cores each, 128 GB RAM and connected using Cray Aries interconnect. We use Jacobi precondi- tioner in all tests.

Figure 1 shows the strong scaling of different methods on a 125-pt 3D Poisson problem with 2M unknowns on up to 110 nodes (2640 processes). Our method, PIPECG-OATI, is compared with PCG, PIPECG and other pipelined variants like PIPECG3 method available in PETSc. We observe from Fig. 1 that PCG reaches 21× speedup and PIPECG reaches 26× speedup after which speedup degrades due to increased allreduce costs which are not overlapped with either any or enough computations. We see that PIPECG3 reaches 34× speedup. PIPECG-OATI reaches 36× speedup. It performs better than PCG and PIPECG because at higher number of cores, the overlap provided by PIPECG-OATI becomes more than the overlap provided by PIPECG. It performs better than PIPECG3 because of lesser number of FLOPS.

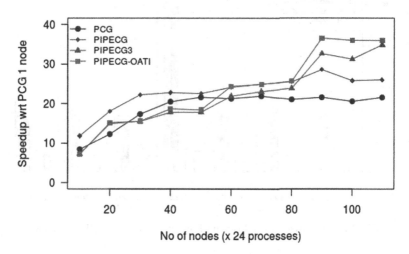

Fig. 1. Strong scaling of different methods on a 125-pt Poisson problem with 2M unknowns.

2 PIPECG Executions for GPU Accelerated Architectures

We have developed three methods for efficient execution of PIPECG method for GPU accelerated systems so that we can make use of all the resources available in the GPU node. The first two methods, Hybrid-PIPECG-1 and Hybrid-PIPECG-2, achieve task parallelism by executing dot products on the CPU while executing the PC and SPMV kernels on the GPU. The third method, Hybrid-PIPECG-3 achieves data parallelism by decomposing the workload between CPU and GPU based on a performance model. The performance model takes into account the relative performance of CPU and GPU using some initial executions and performs 2D data decomposition. Our methods give up to 8× speedup over PCG CPU implementation of Paralution [4] and PETSc libraries for different matrices as shown in Fig. 2. Our methods give up to 5× speedup speedup over PCG GPU implementation of Paralution and PETSc libraries. Hybrid-PIPECG-3 method also provides an efficient solution for solving problems that cannot be fit into the GPU memory and gives up to 2.5× speedup for such problems. Further details can be found in [6].

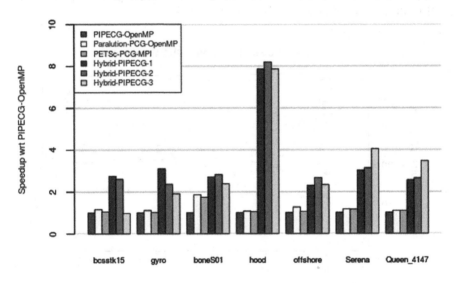

Fig. 2. Comparison of hybrid methods with various CPU versions.

3   Conclusion and Future Work

In this work, we have presented PIPECG-OATI, which reduces the number of allreduces to one per two iterations and overlaps the allreduce with two PCs and two SPMVs. We have also presented Hybrid PIPECG methods for GPU accelerated systems. We are working on developing further pipelined methods which will provide greater overlap than PIPECG-OATI. We are also developing multi-node multi-GPU version for efficient executions of pipelined CG methods on GPU accelerated architectures to explore very large problem sizes.

References

1. Balay, S., Gropp, W.D., McInnes, L.C., Smith, B.F.: Efficient management of parallelism in object oriented numerical software libraries. In: Modern Software Tools in Scientific Computing, pp. 163–202. Birkhäuser Press (1997)
2. Ghysels, P., Vanroose, W.: Hiding global synchronization latency in the preconditioned conjugate gradient algorithm. Parallel Comput. **40**(7), 224–238 (2014)
3. Hestenes, M.R., Stiefel, E.: Methods of conjugate gradients for solving linear systems. J. Res. Nat. Bur. Stan. **49**, 409–436 (1952)
4. Labs, P.: Paralution v1.1.0 (2020). http://www.paralution.com/
5. Tiwari, M., Vadhiyar, S.: Pipelined preconditioned conjugate gradient methods for distributed memory systems. In: 27th IEEE International Conference on High Performance Computing, Data, and Analytics 2020
6. Tiwari, M., Vadhiyar, S.: Efficient executions of pipelined conjugate gradient method on heterogeneous architectures (2021). arXiv.org

Scalable Hybrid Parallel ILU Preconditioner to Solve Sparse Linear Systems

Raju Ram[1,2(✉)], Daniel Grünewald[1], and Nicolas R. Gauger[2]

[1] Fraunhofer ITWM, Competence Center High Performance Computing,
Kaiserslautern, Germany
raju.ram@fraunhofer.de
[2] Chair for Scientific Computing, Technische Universität Kaiserslautern,
Kaiserslautern, Germany

Abstract. Incomplete LU (ILU) preconditioners are widely used to improve the convergence of general-purpose large sparse linear systems in computational simulations because of their robustness, accuracy, and usability as a black-box preconditioner. However, the ILU factorization and the subsequent triangular solve are sequential for sparse matrices in their original form. Multilevel nested dissection (MLND) ordering can resolve that issue and expose some parallelism. This work investigates the parallel efficiency of a hybrid parallel ILU preconditioner that combines a restricted additive Schwarz (RAS) method on the process level with a shared memory parallel MLND Crout ILU method on the core level. We employ the GASPI programming model to efficiently implement the data exchange on the process level. We show the scalability results of our approach for the convection-diffusion problem.

Keywords: Sparse linear systems · Parallel ILU preconditioner · Domain decomposition · GASPI · METIS · Task-level parallelism

1 Research Problem

Solution of the large sparse linear system $Ax = b$, arising after discretization of the partial differential equations (PDE), is one major computational task of chemistry, physics, and engineering-based simulations. Krylov subspace-based iterative methods are preferred over direct methods due to lesser time complexity and memory requirements. These solvers use preconditioners to accelerate their convergence. Incomplete LU (ILU) is widely used as a preconditioner because of its robustness, accuracy, and usability as a black-box preconditioner for general purpose (asymmetric, indefinite) linear systems. On the other hand, parallel Krylov solvers with good scalability features are required to fully exploit the increasing parallelism provided by modern hardware. Scalability measures the parallel efficiency of an implementation. Better scalability allows

© Springer Nature Switzerland AG 2022
R. Chaves et al. (Eds.): Euro-Par 2021, LNCS 13098, pp. 540–544, 2022.
https://doi.org/10.1007/978-3-031-06156-1_46

simulation of more detailed models, more precise parameter studies, and more cost-efficient resource utilization. The scalability of ILU-preconditioned Krylov solvers is restricted due to the sequential nature of preconditioner operations such as factorization and solution to the triangular systems. We combine the thread-level parallelism approach described in [1] with Schwarz preconditioners at the distributed level to address the scalability challenges in ILU preconditioner on modern hardware.

2   Methodology

We propose a two-level domain decomposition (DD) preconditioner following a hybrid execution model which fits the memory hierarchies of modern hardware architectures well. For distributed memory parallelism, we use the GASPI communication API [3] since it provides fine-grained communication across processes. The communication is single-sided, asynchronous, and is complemented by lightweight synchronization primitives. For shared-memory parallelism, we use data dependency-driven task-based parallelism using pthreads.

2.1   Distributed Memory Parallelism

We use the Additive Schwarz (AS) method at the first level of DD and associate one sub-domain with each GASPI process. Thereby, the vertex set V of the graph corresponding to the matrix A is decomposed into N non-overlapping sub-domains V_i^0 such that $V = \bigcup_{i=1}^{N} V_i^0$ and $V_i^0 \bigcap V_j^0 = \emptyset$ for $i \neq j$. This decomposition may be augmented by a so called δ-overlap to generate partitions V_i^δ ($\delta \geq 1$), where $V_i^\delta \supset V_i^0$ is obtained by including all the immediate neighboring vertices of the vertices in V_i^0 up to distance δ. Restriction operators $R_i^\delta \in \mathbf{R}^{|V_i^\delta| \times |V|}$ and scaling operators $D_i^\delta \in \mathbf{R}^{|V_i^\delta| \times |V_i^\delta|}$ associated with each V_i^δ and can be defined such that a partition of unity $\mathbb{1} = \sum_{i=0}^{N} (R_i^\delta)^T D_i^\delta R_i^\delta$ is formed. Here, the transpose $(R_i^\delta)^T$ corresponds to the expansion operator. Then, AS decomposes the global problem $Ax = b$ into sub-domain solve problems $A_i x_i = b_i$, which can be solved in parallel and whose solutions are patched together a posteriori. The sub-domain matrix A_i is defined as $A_i := (R_i^\delta A (R_i^\delta)^T)$. Depending on the sub-domain partitioning, different preconditioners can be implemented:

1) Non-overlapping AS preconditioner: $M_{AS}^{-1} = \sum_{i=1}^{N} (R_i^0)^T A_i^{-1} R_i^0$
2) Restricted AS (RAS) preconditioner: $M_{RAS}^{-1} = \sum_{i=1}^{N} (R_i^0)^T D_i^\delta A_i^{-1} R_i^\delta$.

We use $\delta = 1$ in RAS which is known to converge faster than AS method [2].

2.2   Shared Memory Parallelism

The global matrix A loses coupling information across sub-domains in the first level of the DD approach. This effect becomes more severe with the increasing number of sub-domains. To prevent this, we introduce the second level of

DD that partitions the distributed memory subdomain further using multilevel nested dissection (MLND) as described in [1]. MLND preserves the information of the matrix A_i and allows to obtain fine granular parallelism. We use the multi-threading version of METIS to generate the MLND permutation Π in our implementation. MLND reorders A_i into $A_{i,perm}$ such that $A_{i,perm} = \Pi^T A_i \Pi$. Independent local matrices are extracted from $A_{i,perm}$ which are then factorized in a task-parallel way. Similarly, we solve the triangular system using the same MLND task tree structure exploiting the local dependency in the tasks. We provide a custom data structure SPA to handle sparsity during the Crout ILU factorization. Our SPA based implementation is significantly faster than C++ STL based data structures such as std::map and std::unordered_map [4].

3   Preliminary Results

We discretize the following 3D convection-diffusion PDE using second order finite differences on a regular rectangular mesh in an unit cube $(x, y, z) \in \Omega = (0,1)^3$.

$$\Delta u + k^2 * x^2 \left(\frac{\partial u}{\partial x} + \frac{\partial u}{\partial y} + \frac{\partial u}{\partial z} \right) = f(x, y, z), \ k^2 = 100 \tag{1}$$

We set $f(x, y, z)$ such that the solution $u(x, y, z)$ of the above PDE is equal to $exp(xyz) * sin(\pi x) * sin(\pi y) * sin(\pi z)$ and use Dirichlet boundary conditions as $u(\partial \Omega) = f(\partial \Omega)$. We solve the linear system using GMRES(30) solver with termination criteria of relative residual as 10^{-9}. The performance is evaluated on a cluster of 2.4 GHz Intel(R) Xeon(R) Gold 6148 CPU dual socket nodes, each socket with 20 cores which are connected by EDR Infiniband interconnects. We start one GASPI process per socket in our experiments.

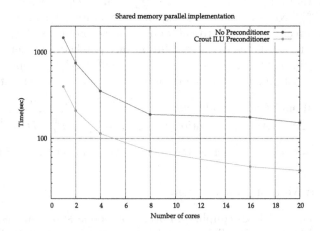

Fig. 1. GMRES runtime(s) for matrix size 8 million and MLND tree height as 5

First, we investigate the shared memory performance. On 1 GASPI process with 20 cores, MLND Crout ILU preconditioned GMRES achieves the parallel efficiency of **47.21**%. This allows to obtain **3.58**x gain in preconditioned GMRES run-time compared to plain GMRES on 20 cores (Fig. 1).

Second, we evaluate the performance of the hybrid implementation. On 64 GASPI processes each having 20 cores, RAS preconditioned GMRES(30) achieves a parallel efficiency of **83.61**%. This is superior to the AS preconditioned GMRES(30) parallel efficiency of **65.60**% and is because RAS has limited the increase of GMRES(30) iterations for the higher number of GASPI processes (Table 1). We obtain **3.88**x gain in GMRES(30) run-time using MLND Crout ILU based RAS preconditioner in comparison to no preconditioner on 64 processes each having 20 cores (Fig. 2).

Table 1. GMRES iterations with different Schwarz preconditioners

# GASPI processes	# Iterations using AS	# Iterations using RAS
1	326	326
8	390	333
16	452	348
32	539	378
64	724	425

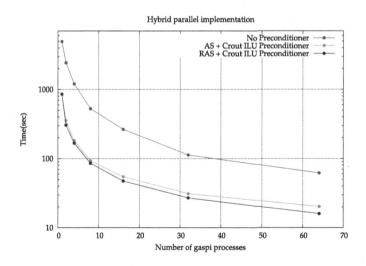

Fig. 2. GMRES runtime(s) for matrix size 64 million and 20 cores per process

4   Future Outlook

The parallel efficiency of the MLND Crout ILU-based RAS preconditioner is promising. To handle real-world large problems, we have introduced more robust features such as row and col-based permutation, inverse-based droppings, and MC64 matching and currently testing them on various real-world linear systems.

References

1. Aliaga, J.I., Bollhöfer, M., Martı, A.F., Quintana-Ortı, E.S., et al.: Exploiting thread-level parallelism in the iterative solution of sparse linear systems. Parallel Comput. **37**(3), 183–202 (2011)
2. Efstathiou, E., Gander, M.J.: Why restricted additive Schwarz converges faster than additive Schwarz. BIT Numer. Math. **43**(5), 945–959 (2003)
3. Grünewald, D., Simmendinger, C.: The GASPI API specification and its implementation GPI 2.0. In: Proceedings of the 7th International Conference on PGAS Programming Models, vol. 243 (2013)
4. Ram, R., Grünewald, D., Gauger, N.R.: Data structures to implement the Sparse Vector in Crout ILU preconditioner. Sparse Days 2019 (2019)

Collaborative, Distributed, Scalable and Low-Cost Platform Based on Microservices, Containers, Mobile Devices and Cloud Services to Solve Compute-Intensive Tasks

David Petrocelli[1,2]([✉]), Armando De Giusti[3,4], and Marcelo Naiouf[3]

[1] Computer Science School, La Plata National University, La Plata, Argentina
dmpetrocelli@gmail.com
[2] Lujan National University, Luján, Argentina
[3] Instituto de Investigación en Informática LIDI (III-LIDI), Computer Science, La Plata National University - CIC-PBA, La Plata, Argentina
{degiusti,mnaiouf}@lidi.info.unlp.edu.ar
[4] CONICET - National Council of Scientific and Technical Research, Buenos Aires, Argentina

Abstract. When solving compute-intensive tasks, CPU/GPU hardware resources and specialized Grid, Custer, Cloud infrastructure are commonly used to achieve high performance. However, this requires a high initial capital expense and ongoing maintenance costs. In contrast, ARM-based mobile devices regularly see improvement in their capacity, stability, and processing power daily while becoming ever more ubiquitous and requiring no massive capital or operating expenditures thanks to their reduced size and energy efficiency. Given this shifting computer paradigm, it is conceivable that a cost- and power-efficient solution for our world's HPC processing tasks would include ARM-based mobile devices, while they are idle during recharging periods. We proposed, developed, deployed and evaluated a distributed, collaborative, elastic and low-cost platform to solve HPC tasks recycling ARM mobile resources based on Cloud, microservices and containers, efficiently orchestrated via Kubernetes. To validate the system scalability, flexibility, and performance a lot of concurrent video transcoding scenarios were run. The results showed the system allows for improvements in terms of scalability, flexibility, stability, efficiency, and cost for HPC workloads.

Keywords: Kubernetes · Containers · Video transcoding · Microservices · Cloud computing · Mobile computing · Distributed and collaborative computing

1 Introduction

To build a high-quality, distributed, collaborative, and scalable platform that was able to process processing-intensive tasks requires the adoption of the newest techniques, technologies, tools, and infrastructure patterns that allow taking advantage of all the available benefits on today's computing resources (On-Premise, Cloud and Mobile). We

© Springer Nature Switzerland AG 2022
R. Chaves et al. (Eds.): Euro-Par 2021, LNCS 13098, pp. 545–548, 2022.
https://doi.org/10.1007/978-3-031-06156-1_47

implemented the following features: a) Lightweight and scalable services (Microservices), b) Auto-scalable infrastructure to guarantee a cost and power-efficient usage of resources (Container and Container Orchestration), and c) Reusage of processing cycles from idle, low-priced, cost-efficient and powerful mobile devices [1–3].

To accomplish the research goals, the following activities were carried out: 1) A bibliographical review from research papers, postgraduate thesis, articles, among others. 2) A review of distributed systems' current state and best practices to build distributed platforms (development tools, techniques and technologies). 3) Design, development and implementation of the HPC system modules. It covered: 3.a) Development of x86 and mobile Android ARM Worker. 3.b) Platform administration and management Dockerized microservices modules. 3.c) Dockerized queue (tasks) and database (statistics) services modules. Finally, 3.d) Kubernetes orchestrator integration to manage, implement and automate container deployments in a flexible, efficient and optimized way. 4) To define and analyze the relevant features to support the integration of video compression as the HPC task. For that aim, it was necessary to study digital video features, codecs, formats and qualities, likewise, to analyze distributed transcoding mechanisms and the open-source tools. In addition, determine representative audiovisual resources to perform transcoding tasks. 5) To define metrics and experimentation scenarios and choose x86 platforms and ARM devices to run the experimentation scenarios. Finally, 6) analyze the results and derive a conclusion from the data.

2   Collaborating Computing Network Architecture for HPC

Based on features we described earlier, the architecture developed and deployed is composed by: a) Dockerized administration and management microservice platform; b) Dockerized queue (tasks) and database (statistics) services; c) Kubernetes framework for orchestration, scaling, replication and container automation and d) x86 and Android ARM mobile workers (Fig. 1), as it is shown below.

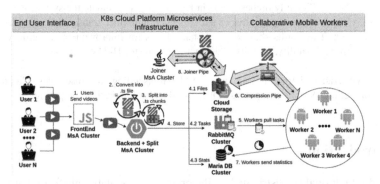

Fig. 1. Collaborating computing network architecture diagram.

We adopted SaaS Kubernetes (K8s) [4] on AWS (EKS) and Azure (AKS) to host, orchestrate, heal and monitor our distributed Dockerized services. We configured an auto-scalability mechanism based on CPU and memory container resources utilization thresholds, guaranteeing services (pods) high availability, efficient distribution and scaling across the cluster nodes. Lastly, we configured DNS to interconnect containers, expose public services (frontend) and provide traffic routing and load balancing.

The front-end service allows clients to upload video files and select the encoding parameters. It also allows users to visualize information about their ongoing and finished tasks. Once the source files are received in the backend microservices, they are converted into a Video Transport Stream File (ts) due to it being the recommended format for video streaming [5]. In testing, its usage impacts positively on latency, playback compatibility and viewing experience [6]. Once converted, files are split into smaller chunks [7] and stored in a low-cost blob cloud storage [8]. We used both Azure Storage and Amazon S3 to store data reliably and cheaply, upload and download stream files, and distribute files via Content Delivery Networks for lower latency and caching.

Using Bitnami RabbitMQ and MariaDB Kubernetes helm charts, we built an auto-scalable and fault-tolerant queue and database system where jobs and statistics are published respectively. RabbitMQ is used to securely and asynchronously store, publish and distribute backend service jobs to worker processing nodes. High Availability is guaranteed by RabbitMQ Policies and non-losing tasks are guaranteed by implementing a manual ACK mode model where should a server error, client-side issue, execution time-out happen, RabbitMQ thread moves the task back to queue. MariaDB is used to register job information (parameters, chunks, completed tasks and storage endpoint). Furthermore, it stores information about executed tasks (task, worker node and executed time). We use this data to evaluate the platform and worker efficiency in different scenarios. High Availability is configured via Galera active-active mode.

Meanwhile, workers are continuously pulling from the RabbitMQ queue to obtain tasks and compress using the FFmpeg library. When chunks are completely processed, the Joiner backend microservice gathers parts and uploads them to the cloud storage endpoint. Both worker and joiner, process tasks parallelly using Linux pipelines. While the source is stream downloaded via HTTP GET curl request, is also processed by FFmpeg and parallelly streamed to the cloud storage via HTTP PUT curl request. As a result, disk and memory operations are reduced, improving system performance.

3   Platform Test and Obtained Results

We defined two test scenarios to validate platform capabilities when solving HPC tasks. The first one verifies and compares the performance and power consumption for both x86 and ARM-based worker processing devices via Effectiveness Index (EI) metric. EI was based on power-usage metrics (watts) and processing time metrics (ms) for each transcoding job. As a result, its value can be higher, equal or lower than 1. When higher, it indicated that mobile devices have a better power-usage/performance index than their x86 counterparts. When EI is lower, x86 wins out. Equal values mean a similar result. The results obtained on [9], showed that the EI index was always higher than 5 (5–16 range, depending on the tasks performed) meaning ARM devices were able to process these tasks at a significant efficiency advantage compared to by their x86 counterparts.

The second test scenario was envisioned to be a validation of platform behavior, efficiency, performance, scalability and flexibility when executing heavy concurrent workloads [10]. Based on three load environments (E1, E2 and E3), the platform services were stressed by validating cluster and horizontal auto-scaling features and analyzing its impact in execution time. E1 defines a fixed workload and changes the worker nodes number and capacity. On the contrary, E2 sets a fixed configuration for worker nodes and varies the amount and size of source files. Finally, E3 proved the system flexibility, running concurrent curl requests using the same video source file.

For E1, the results showed time is reduced whenever node capacity is increased (31%–47%). When the number of nodes is doubled, the response time is nearly halved by about 40–45%. In E2, the total processing time increases according to $f(x) = a * x + c$. Despite this, it was verified that the platform remained stable. Lastly, in E3, job time for concurrent tasks was related to nodes capacity and networking.

4 Preliminary Conclusions

Based upon the aforementioned experiments, the platform could be considered an interesting alternative infrastructure for HPC tasks. Thanks to K8s integration, the results showed stability, scalability, good response time, efficiency, and cost-optimized results for a variety of scenarios. Regarding mobile workers, we tested ARM devices that are capable of encoding video with a competitive performance/cost advantage over traditional x86 workers. We have recently improved, via Linux pipeline implementation, worker stability, performance and efficiency.

References

1. Hirsch, M., et al.: Augmenting computing capabilities at the edge by jointly exploiting mobile devices: a survey. Future Gener. Comput. Syst. **88**, 644–662 (2018)
2. Vasile, C.V., Pattinson, C., Kor, A.-L.: Mobile phones and energy consumption. In: Kharchenko, V., Kondratenko, Y., Kacprzyk, J. (eds.) Green IT Engineering: Social, Business and Industrial Applications. SSDC, vol. 171, pp. 243–271. Springer, Cham (2019). https://doi.org/10.1007/978-3-030-00253-4_11
3. Andatech - Qualcomm Snapdragon 888 Performance Preview: Big Gains for Next-Gen Android Flagships. https://bit.ly/3y5U8up. Accessed 12 May 2021
4. Hausenblas, M., Schimanski, S.: Programming Kubernetes: Developing Cloud-Native Applications. O'Reilly Media, Sebastopol (2019)
5. ETSI - Specification for the use of Video and Audio Coding in Broadcasting Applications based on the MPEG-2 Transport Stream. https://bit.ly/36segJI. Accessed 12 May 2021
6. 2019 Global Media Format Report. https://bit.ly/2ZBmZIi. Accessed 12 May 2021
7. Dash Industry Forum - Guidelines for Implementation: DASH-IF Interoperability Points. https://bit.ly/3ghFxTT. Accessed 12 May 2021
8. Daher, Z., Hajjdiab, H.: Cloud storage comparative analysis Amazon Simple storage vs. Microsoft Azure Blob storage. Int. J. Mach. Learn. **8**(1), 85 (2018)
9. Petrocelli, D., De Giusti, A., Naiouf, M.: Hybrid elastic ARM&Cloud HPC collaborative platform for generic tasks. In: Naiouf, M., Chichizola, F., Rucci, E. (eds.) JCC&BD 2019. CCIS, vol. 1050, pp. 16–27. Springer, Cham (2019). https://doi.org/10.1007/978-3-030-27713-0_2
10. Petrocelli, D., De Giusti, A.E. Naiouf, M.: Plataforma colaborativa, elástica, de bajo costo y consumo basada en recursos de la Nube, contenedores y móviles para HPC. 7ª Conferencia Ibero Americana Computação Aplicada (2020)

Model-Based Loop Perforation

Daniel Maier$^{(\boxtimes)}$ and Ben Juurlink

Technische Universität Berlin, Berlin, Germany
daniel.maier@tu-berlin.de

Abstract. In many applications there is a gap between the accuracy
provided by the platform and the accuracy that is required by the application to produce good-enough results. Exploiting this gap specifically
is the concept of Approximate Computing, where a small reduction in
accuracy is traded for better performance or a reduction in energy consumption. We assess applications regarding their suitability to be approximated. We propose a novel approach for memory-aware perforation of
GPU kernels. The technique is further optimized, and we show its applicability on embedded GPUs. In order to fully utilize the opportunities
of our approach, we propose a novel framework for automatic loop nest
approximation based on polyhedral compilation. Our approach generalizes state-of-the-art perforation techniques and introduces new multi-
dimensional perforation schemes. Moreover, the approach is augmented
with a reconstruction technique that significantly improves the accuracy
of the results. As the transformation space is potentially large, we propose a pruning method to remove low-quality transformations.

Keywords: Approximate Computing · Compiler · GPU · Loop
optimization · Kernel perforation

1 Introduction

Applications often provide inherent resilience towards small errors [2]. We
observe a gap between the accuracy required by these applications on one
hand and the accuracy provided by a system on the other hand. Exploiting
this gap explicitly is known as Approximate Computing. Good candidates are
applications that already have to deal with inexact data such as signal processing algorithms, e.g., employed in image processing applications. Many different
approaches that leverage the aforementioned gap have been presented in the last
years, ranging from hardware-based techniques such as approximate storage [10],
lossy memory compression [3] to software and software-based techniques such as
loop perforation [4] and precision tuning [1].

We study the potential of general-purpose applications to be approximated
using loop perforation. We explore how loop perforation can be refined to exploit
local memory on GPUs in order to improve the accuracy. Then, we adapt these
techniques, so they can be also employed on embedded GPUs. Finally, we show
how the Polyhedral Model can be used to perforate loop nests using multidimensional perforation schemes.

© Springer Nature Switzerland AG 2022
R. Chaves et al. (Eds.): Euro-Par 2021, LNCS 13098, pp. 549–554, 2022.
https://doi.org/10.1007/978-3-031-06156-1_48

2   Potential Applications to be Approximated

We study the potential of a wide range of applications to be approximated using loop perforation. Loop perforation is a general-purpose technique where some iterations of compute-intense loops are skipped. In Fig. 1, we assess the suitability of applications from PolyBench/C [8] to be approximated using loop perforation. Each column corresponds to a specific error budget. A shadowed square represents one or more solutions for an error budget. The shading indicates the speedup that can be achieved, darker colors indicate a higher speedup. Groups of applications are indicated using horizontal lines, and they are labeled on the right side.

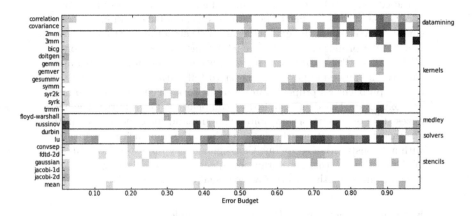

Fig. 1. Suitability of applications for approximation (Color figure online)

We observe that applications show different outcomes. Remarkably, for almost all applications, there is an approximation with low error. For datamining applications, the pattern of approximations is similar. Some approximations have low or medium error, and most have higher error.

For the group of kernel applications, we find heterogeneous results. Applications based on matrix multiplication like 2MM, 3MM, GEMM, GEMMVER show few approximations with low error. This outcome is likely due to the far-ranging influence of local errors due to the way row/column-based matrix multiplication.

The two solver applications show different pattern: DURBIN has few approximations with medium speedup; LU has many approximations, which are spread evenly across the error budget. Some approximations have a very high speedup.

For the stencil applications, there are fewer approximations in general, which can be attributed to a smaller number of loops in the applications. JACOBI-1D and JACOBI-2D have only a few approximations with low error.

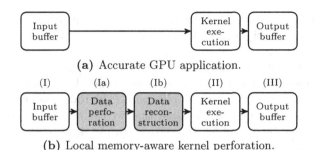

(a) Accurate GPU application.

(b) Local memory-aware kernel perforation.

Fig. 2. Local memory-aware kernel perforation.

3   Local Memory-Aware Kernel Perforation

We introduce a novel approximation technique that is specifically designed to approximate general-purpose GPU kernels [5]. Our approach extends state-of-the-art approximation techniques such as the row-/column-based schemes used in Paraprox [9] by exploiting the fast local memory to deliver more accurate solutions. A typical GPU application (Fig. 2a) first loads data from the input buffer (I) in the GPU global memory. Then it executes the kernel (II). Finally, the result is written to the output buffer in global memory (III).

On GPUs, the latency for accessing the global memory is very high. GPUs hide this latency by their massively parallel architecture and by using the scheduler. Performance can be improved by using the fast local memory to reduce the number of global memory accesses. Local memory has a significantly lower latency than global memory, however its size is limited. We exploit local memory to improve the accuracy of approximations. We introduce two additional steps (in Fig. 2b): data perforation (Ia) and data reconstruction (Ib). During the

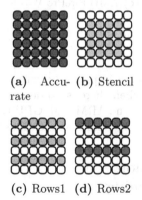

(a) Accurate   **(b)** Stencil

(c) Rows1   **(d)** Rows2

Fig. 3. 2D perforation schemes. (Color figure online)

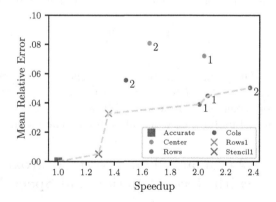

Fig. 4. Speedup/accuracy of the median application for different perforation schemes. (Color figure online)

data perforation phase, we partially load the input data. Which parts are loaded and which parts are skipped are determined by perforation schemes. In the data reconstruction phase, data elements that were not loaded are reconstructed by interpolation. We introduce three schemes shown in Fig. 3. Colored elements are loaded from memory and white elements are omitted. The stencil scheme (b) is designed specifically for stencil applications. The rows schemes (c and d) are universally applicable. Our results show that we can achieve speedups of 1.6×– 3× given an error budget of 6% on average. In Fig. 4, we show selected results for the MEDIAN application. We mark state-of-the-art Paraprox' results using a dot and our approach using x. The dashed line indicates the Pareto front.

4   Approximating Memory-Bound Applications on Embedded GPUs

We evaluate Kernel Perforation on embedded GPUs [7]. Embedded GPUs are a challenging platform for kernel perforation, as the computing capabilities are fundamentally different from desktop GPUs. Furthermore, some embedded GPUs are not equipped with local memory. We compare performance of approximated applications on two embedded GPUs (Qualcomm Adreno 506 and ARM Mali T860 MP2) with a desktop GPU (AMD FirePro W5100).

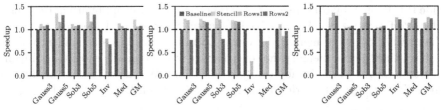

(a) Qualcomm Adreno 506 (b) ARM Mali T860 MP2 (c) AMD FirePro W5100

Fig. 5. Speedup on embedded and desktop GPUs.

Our results, depicted in Fig. 5, show that our technique improves performance on embedded GPUs (a and b) by up to 38%. Even when there is no dedicated local memory mapped in hardware, as it is the case for the ARM Mali GPU (b), kernel perforation can still be used to accelerate memory-bound applications.

5   Automatic Loop Nest Approximation with Reconstruction and Space Pruning

Polyhedral compilation has been proven to be an effective way to reason about loops. We explore how the polyhedral model can be effectively used for the implementation of automatic approximation techniques targeting loop nests [6].

The Polyhedral Model represents loops by points on a lattice that are bounded by affine inequalities. Loop transformations are expressed as operations that operate on the lattice. These transformations can be applied subsequently. Finally, the optimized loop code is synthesized in the code generation phase. Results are shown in Fig. 6.

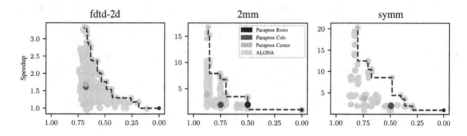

Fig. 6. Configurations generated by ALONA and state-of-the-art techniques.

We identify loop perforation as a loop transformation. Consequently, we use the Polyhedral Model to perforate loop nests. We implement loop perforation in two steps: First, we shrink the iteration domain. Then, we adjust memory accesses in order to achieve uniform perforations across the iteration domain. The number of possible perforated code versions grows with the number of loop nests and is potentially very large. In order to reduce the number of code versions required to be analyzed, we use our pruning method that allows for ordering the configurations by a Barvinok-based score. This score represents the ratio of perforated and accurate loop iterations.

As reconstruction has shown to have a big impact on accuracy [5], we augment the code generation phase with a reconstruction step. We perform a case-study and study the effects of reconstruction. The results are shown in Fig. 7. We evaluate the effects of reconstruction by comparing performance and accuracy of approximations *with* reconstruction and *without* reconstruction. We find that reconstruction is very effective: on average, we improve the error by 30% while retaining 60% of the speedup.

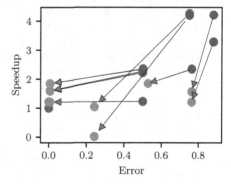

Fig. 7. Effects of reconstruction

6   Conclusion

We assess applications regarding their suitability to be approximated using a general-purpose approximation technique. The suitability of applications to be approximated varies when given different error budgets. We present kernel perforation, a novel approach for approximating applications specifically tailored to the memory architecture of GPUs. We demonstrate how the technique can be employed on embedded GPUs. Furthermore, we show how model-based loop perforation and reconstruction can be integrated in compilers and used in a way that is compatible to traditional loop optimizations. When compared to state-of-the-art solutions, our optimization space is much larger and contains many superior solutions both in terms of performance and accuracy. Finding good solutions in the large optimization space is a new challenge which we have started tackling using our optimization space pruning. Future work can explore how to intelligently pick promising configurations without testing many code versions. We show that reconstruction is very powerful in terms of improving the accuracy of the approximations. Further research in this direction is required in order to fully exploit the opportunities opened up by our work.

References

1. Cherubin, S., Cattaneo, D., Chiari, M., Di Bello, A., Agosta, G.: TAFFO: tuning assistant for floating to fixed point optimization. IEEE Embed. Syst. Lett. **12**(1), 5–8 (2019)
2. Chippa, V.K., Chakradhar, S.T., Roy, K., Raghunathan, A.: Analysis and characterization of inherent application resilience for approximate computing. In: Proceedings of the 50th Annual Design Automation Conference, pp. 1–9 (2013)
3. Lal, S., Lucas, J., Juurlink, B.: SLC: memory access granularity aware selective lossy compression for GPUs. In: 2019 Design, Automation & Test in Europe Conference & Exhibition (DATE), pp. 1184–1189. IEEE (2019)
4. Li, S., Park, S., Mahlke, S.: Sculptor: flexible approximation with selective dynamic loop perforation. In: Proceedings of the 2018 International Conference on Supercomputing, pp. 341–351 (2018)
5. Maier, D., Cosenza, B., Juurlink, B.: Local memory-aware kernel perforation. In: Proceedings of the 2018 International Symposium on Code Generation and Optimization, pp. 278–287 (2018)
6. Maier, D., Cosenza, B., Juurlink, B.: ALONA: automatic loop nest approximation with reconstruction and space pruning. In: Sousa, L., Roma, N., Tomás, P. (eds.) Euro-Par 2021. LNCS, vol. 12820, pp. 3–18. Springer, Cham (2021). https://doi.org/10.1007/978-3-030-85665-6_1
7. Maier, D., Mammeri, N., Cosenza, B., Juurlink, B.: Approximating memory-bound applications on mobile GPUs. In: 2019 International Conference on High Performance Computing & Simulation (HPCS), pp. 329–335. IEEE (2019)
8. Pouchet, L.N.: PolyBench/C. http://www.cse.ohio-state.edu/~pouchet/software/polybench/
9. Samadi, M., Jamshidi, D.A., Lee, J., Mahlke, S.: Paraprox: pattern-based approximation for data parallel applications. In: Proceedings of the 19th International Conference on Architectural Support for Programming Languages and Operating Systems, pp. 35–50 (2014)
10. Sampson, A., Nelson, J., Strauss, K., Ceze, L.: Approximate storage in solid-state memories. TOCS **32**, 1–23 (2014)

Low-Overhead Reuse Distance Profiling Tool for Multicore

Muhammad Aditya Sasongko[1]($\boxtimes$) (iD), Milind Chabbi[2] (iD), and Didem Unat[1] (iD)

[1] Koç University, Istanbul, Turkey
{msasongko17,dunat}@ku.edu.tr
[2] Scalable Machines Research, San Jose, CA, USA
milind@scalablemachines.org

Abstract. With the increase in core count in multicore systems, data movement is one of the main sources of performance slowdown in parallel applications and data locality has become a critical factor in application optimization. One of the important locality metrics is reuse distance, which shows the likelihood of a memory access to be a cache hit. In this work, we propose a low-overhead reuse distance profiling tool for multi-threaded applications. Our method relies on available hardware features in commodity CPUs, namely, Performance Monitoring Units (PMUs) and debug registers, to detect data reuse in private and shared caches by considering inter-thread cache line invalidations. Unlike prior approaches, our tool is fast, accurate, does not change the program behavior and can also handle shared cache accesses. Though it has low runtime ($2.9\times$) and memory overheads ($2.8\times$), our tool achieves 92% accuracy.

Keywords: Reuse distance · Hardware performance counters · Debug registers · Address sampling

1 Introduction

Data locality is a crucial performance indicator in shared-memory multicore machines, and it impacts energy consumption and performance more than computation [6]. One widely used locality metric is *reuse distance* – the number of unique memory locations that are accessed between the current access to a location (*reuse*) and the previous access to the same location (*use*). Reuse distance shows the prospect of a memory access to hit in a cache. If the reuse distance of an access is larger than the cache size, the access is likely to become a cache miss. Reuse is also affected by cache line invalidations in a multicore system as invalidated cache lines can no longer be accessed in local caches. Due to its ability to detect capacity and coherence misses in caches, reuse distance can be used to predict cache miss rates of certain applications running on machines with known cache configurations. Another possible use is to determine sizes of caches that can minimize costly memory accesses to DRAM for a given application. Because of these reasons, performance programmers and computer architects can benefit from tools or techniques that profile reuse distance.

© Springer Nature Switzerland AG 2022
R. Chaves et al. (Eds.): Euro-Par 2021, LNCS 13098, pp. 555–559, 2022.
https://doi.org/10.1007/978-3-031-06156-1_49

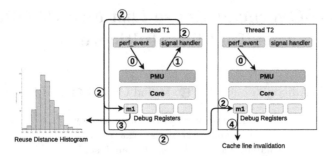

Fig. 1. One possible execution scenario when profiling reuse distances in L1 caches: (0) Every thread sets its PMUs to sample its memory accesses. (1) Thread T_1's PMU counter overflows on a load or a store that accesses address m_1. (2) T_1 arms its watchpoint and a watchpoint of the other threads (e.g. T_2) with address m_1 in debug registers. (3) T_1 accesses address m_1 again before any other threads, the watchpoint traps, reuse distance is computed. (4) Cache line invalidation occurs if T_2 stores to address m_1 before T_1 accesses m_1 again.

Even though there are several studies in the literature on reuse distance analysis [1,4,7,8], they have serious shortcomings and disadvantages. Hardware simulator and binary instrumentation-based solutions incur large overheads [1,4,8]. For example, Loca [8], a binary instrumentation-based reuse distance profiler, introduces 49× time and 40× memory overheads. Binary instrumentation-based solutions can also undesirably alter the parallel schedule thus the application behaviour of the monitored threads [2]. To our knowledge, there are only two publicly available open-source tools that measure reuse distances [7,8], both of which can detect reuse distances only for individual threads and cannot be used for multithreaded programs.

Due to the limitations of existing techniques in profiling multi-threaded applications, we need a fast and accurate tool to analyze reuse distance in multi-threaded codes. In this work, we develop a profiling tool that leverages commonly available hardware features in modern CPUs, i.e. PMUs and debug registers. Our tool incurs low overhead as it relies on existing hardware features without requiring any extra software layer. To profile multi-threaded codes, we propose two algorithms that measure reuse distances in private and shared caches. Our preliminary results are promising on Intel architectures and we plan to extend our tool to AMD and ARM-based multicore systems that support address sampling.

In the rest of this paper, we consider OS threads to be pinned to CPU cores and each core is not oversubscribed. Therefore, we use the words "threads" and "cores" interchangeably. Also, for simplicity, we assume threads do not share private caches (no simultaneous multi-threading [5]).

2 Profiling Algorithms and Preliminary Results

We propose an algorithm that measures reuse distances in L1 caches and shared L3 caches. The workflow of the algorithm is as follow. In the beginning, each

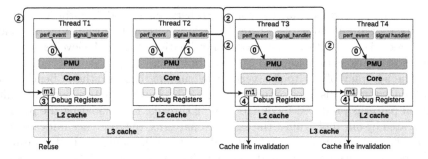

Fig. 2. One possible execution scenario when profiling reuse distances in L3 caches: (0) Each thread configures its PMUs to sample its memory accesses. (1) Thread T_2's PMU counter overflows on a load or a store to address m_1. (2) T_2 sets up watchpoints on other threads that share the same L3 cache with type WP_RW and on other threads that do not share the same L3 cache with type WP_WRITE. (3) T_1 accesses address m_1 before any other thread, its watchpoint traps, and time reuse distance in L3 is calculated. (4) Cache line invalidation at L3 level happens if T_3 or T_4 stores to m_1 before m_1 is accessed by T_1.

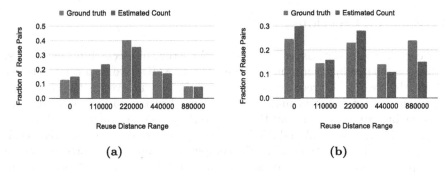

Fig. 3. Expected and estimated histograms of a bell-shaped and a multi-modal reuse distance patterns on 32 threads running on Intel Xeon Gold 6148 Skylake CPU.

thread configures its PMUs to sample load and store accesses. When a thread encounters a PMU counter overflow, the accessed effective address is collected as sampled data.

To profile reuse distances in L1 caches, the thread that faces a PMU counter overflow, say T_1, sets a watchpoint in all threads to monitor the sampled address. The reuse of that address is detected if the first trap after the watchpoint creation happens in T_1. If the first trap happens in another thread, say T_2, due to a store access, then a cache line invalidation is detected between T_1 and T_2, and any following trap in T_1 is no longer considered as a reuse. One possible execution scenario is shown in Fig. 1.

To profile reuse distances in a shared cache, the thread whose PMU encounters a counter overflow, say T_2, sets a watchpoint in a debug register in all of the other threads. When the first trap happens in any thread T_i that shares the same L3 cache, reuse distance is computed between T_2 and T_i. Otherwise, if the first trap occurs because of a store access in any thread T_j that does not share the same L3 cache with T_2, a cache line invalidation at L3 cache level is detected. One possible execution scenario is shown in Fig. 2.

The accuracy of our tool is verified by running it on synthetic benchmarks with known reuse distance patterns. Figure 3 displays the bell-shaped and multi-modal patterns produced by our tool on 32 threads. By comparing the patterns generated by our tool against the expected patterns, the tool's accuracy is shown to be 92% when running with 32 threads. Due to the sampling-based nature of our tool, the patterns generated by our tool do not exactly match the expected patterns, particularly the pattern in Fig. 3b. One way to improve the accuracy of our tool is by increasing sampling rate at the cost of performance degradation. The overhead numbers are obtained by running the tool on 10 PARSEC benchmarks.

We refer the readers to [3] for more details on our profiling algorithms, the accuracy verification experiment, and some use cases that demonstrate how our tool can be used for performance tuning on profiled applications.

3   Future Directions

Our current tool works using the PMU architecture of recent Intel processors. Other common architectures including ARM and AMD have somewhat different PMUs, the use of which requires further research. We will leverage the knowledge gained and target emerging multicore platforms, because no such tool exists for those architectures yet, and all the prior work focused on Intel x86. With the increased interest in ARM and AMD multicores, the outcomes of this thesis will be very valuable and impactful to the computing community. Moreover, one of the expected outcomes is to produce recommendations to the vendors on how to improve the cache coherency protocols, performance monitoring and instruction sampling capabilities of their chips. This provides invaluable information while assessing the functionalities of emerging multicore systems.

Acknowledgements. The work is supported by the Scientific and Technological Research Council of Turkey (TUBITAK), Grant no. 120E492. Dr. Didem Unat is supported by the Royal Society-Newton Advanced Fellowship.

References

1. Ling, M., Ge, J., Wang, G.: Fast modeling L2 cache reuse distance histograms using combined locality information from software traces. J. Syst. Architect. **108**, 101745 (2020). https://doi.org/10.1016/j.sysarc.2020.101745
2. Pericas, M., Taura, K., Matsuoka, S.: Scalable analysis of multicore data reuse and sharing. In: Proceedings of the 28th ACM International Conference on Supercomputing, ICS 2014, pp. 353–362. Association for Computing Machinery, New York, NY, USA (2014). https://doi.org/10.1145/2597652.2597674

3. Sasongko, M.A., Chabbi, M., Marzijarani, M.B., Unat, D.: ReuseTracker: fast yet accurate multicore reuse distance analyzer. ACM Trans. Architect. Code Optim. **19**, 1–25 (2021). https://doi.org/10.1145/3484199
4. Schuff, D.L., Kulkarni, M., Pai, V.S.: Accelerating multicore reuse distance analysis with sampling and parallelization. In: Proceedings of the 19th International Conference on Parallel Architectures and Compilation Techniques, PACT 2010, pp. 53–64. Association for Computing Machinery, New York, NY, USA (2010). https://doi.org/10.1145/1854273.1854286
5. Tullsen, D.M., Eggers, S.J., Levy, H.M.: Simultaneous multithreading: maximizing on-chip parallelism. In: Proceedings of the 22nd Annual International Symposium on Computer Architecture, ISCA 1995, pp. 392–403. Association for Computing Machinery, New York, NY, USA (1995). https://doi.org/10.1145/223982.224449
6. Unat, D., et al.: Trends in data locality abstractions for HPC systems. IEEE Trans. Parallel Distrib. Syst. **28**(10), 3007–3020 (2017). https://doi.org/10.1109/TPDS.2017.2703149
7. Wang, Q., Liu, X., Chabbi, M.: Featherlight reuse-distance measurement. In: 2019 IEEE International Symposium on High Performance Computer Architecture (HPCA), pp. 440–453. IEEE Computer Society, Los Alamitos, CA, USA (2019). https://doi.org/10.1109/HPCA.2019.00056
8. Xiang, X., Ding, C., Luo, H., Bao, B.: HOTL: a higher order theory of locality. SIGARCH Comput. Archit. News **41**(1), 343–356 (2013). https://doi.org/10.1145/2490301.2451153

Author Index